ROTHMANS GRAND PRIX MOTORCYCLE YEARBOOK 1988-89

Editor: Nick Harris

ROTHMANS
Queen Anne Press

A Queen Anne Press BOOK

First published in Great Britain in 1988 by
Queen Anne Press, a division of
Macdonald & Co (Publishers) Ltd
66–73 Shoe Lane
London EC4P 4AB

A member of Maxwell Pergamon Publishing Corporation plc

Jacket photographs *Front:* Wayne Gardner/Ray Daniel
Back: Steve Webster and Tony Hewitt/Ray Daniel

British Library Cataloguing in Publication Data

Rothmans Grand Prix motorcycle yearbook.——
1988–89.
1. Racing motorcycles. Racing. Races :
Grands Prix
796.7′5

ISBN 0–356–17186–8

Typeset by MS Filmsetting Limited, Frome, Somerset
Printed and bound in Great Britain by
Hazell Watson & Viney Limited,
Aylesbury, Bucks
Member of BPCC plc

Rothmans Grand Prix Motorcycle Yearbook 1988–89

CONTENTS

FOREWORD FROM ROTHMANS PUBLICATIONS LTD

The launch of the first *Rothmans Grand Prix Motorcycle Yearbook* was announced back in 1986, and at the time we expressed the hope that the book would become a welcome addition to Motorcycling literature.

We were delighted with the response from enthusiasts, a response which has quickly established the yearbook as the bible of the sport.

Much of the credit for that goes to Editor Nick Harris and his dedicated team of helpers, who produce an unparalleled and definitive work of reference.

Motorcycling continues to flourish and deserves to do so because it provides thrills and entertainment for a wide variety of people. Many of those thrills are reflected in the pages of this year's book, which again includes all the facts and figures of an exciting year.

We enjoy producing this publication. We hope that you enjoy reading it.

EDITORIAL PREFACE

It certainly doesn't seem like two years ago we were compiling the first edition of the *Rothmans Grand Prix Motorcycle Yearbook*. I hope since those pioneering days we have established the book as the bible of motorcycle racing. I've tried once again to combine all the statistics with bright and personal memories of the grands prix and major races, while calling upon the experts to help me.

Mick Woollett is probably known to readers as the man who compiles most of the statistics. This year he's blown his cover with a marvellous feature about his racing days as a sidecar passenger. Fellow grand prix traveller Michael Scott has done much to explain the technical intricacies of modern grand prix machines. Ray Daniel continues his nomadic lifestyle to bring us pictures from throughout Europe, while Phil Masters provides us with some superb shots, especially from thc TT races. The varied British championships get more complicated each year but Gary Pinchin's expertise and enthusiasm has unravelled their mysteries. The Irish love their racing and none more so than Ivan Davidson whose love of the sport is reflected in all his hard work, while Jim Reynolds is the acknowledged expert on the Classic scene. Combined with the publishing and design talents of Richard Beswick and Oscar Heini at Queen Anne Press, I feel we assembled a team worthy of such a great sport as motorcycle racing.

It's been another splendid year for the sport and especially in Britain, where 81,000 spectators spent the weekend watching the British Grand Prix at Donington. Steve Webster also retained his world sidecar title and wrote this year's foreword. There is no doubt the sport is flourishing abroad and is staging a massive comeback in Britain.

I'm proud to be involved with Rothmans and Queen Anne Press, because they have allowed me to show thousands of others just what a great sport and spectacle motorcycle racing is, particularly at a time when international sport in general is wracked with scandal and totally unacceptable financial gains. Grand Prix motorcycle racing has not been involved and long may that situation continue.

INTRODUCTION

STEVE WEBSTER

World Sidecar Champion

If you'd have told me before that final round of the world sidecar championship at Brno in Czechoslovakia that I'd be sitting down writing this foreword as World Champion, I would have laughed. Like most other people, I realised I had little chance of retaining the title. What then happened was a perfect example of getting out there and doing your very best. It worked perfectly for me and I'm so happy the world title has remained in Britain.

As World Champion I've campaigned very hard throughout the season to get sidecar racing a better deal in the grand prix world. Last year's *Rothmans Grand Prix Motorcycle Yearbook* gave the sidecars fantastic coverage. As you will see, it is the same this year and it's an example others should follow. On the track this year, the actual racing has been brilliant and you could not have got a better climax to the championship.

Earlier in the season, when we won the British Grand Prix at Donington Park millions of television viewers watched the superb BBC coverage. After the race we took half an hour to complete our lap of honour, accompanied by Colin Moynihan, the Minister for Sport, because so many people had swarmed onto the track to congratulate us. It was an afternoon neither myself nor my passenger Tony Hewitt will ever forget.

When Tony got injured, Gavin Simmons took over for that vital race in Czechoslovakia and without those two the championship would not have been retained for Britain. Sidecar racing is all about teamwork, as is life in general – you don't get far without a good team. My team will be working at full tilt throughout the winter to get everything prepared for next season. We are determined to win the championship for the third year in succession.

I know next year's *Rothmans Grand Prix Motorcycle Yearbook* will again include extensive coverage of the world championships. I also hope it will be reporting on a better deal for sidecar racing. I think we deserve it.

Ye of Little Faith

Nick Harris

I sat with my feet on a rather spartan Czechoslovakian desk, full of self-praise for what I thought had been a pretty good afternoon's work. After all, I'd just interviewed new World 500cc Champion Eddie Lawson live on BBC Radio and commentated on the race at Brno.

Outside the window, the 17-lap sidecar race, the final round of the world championship, had just started. The producer's voice from London crackled through my headphones asking if I wanted to complete my final voice piece for the sports news later that evening. I told him we'd better wait and leave around ten seconds for the result of the sidecar race; after all British World Champion Steve Webster had no chance of retaining his title. He was 18 points behind the Swiss pair of Rolf Biland and Kurt Waltisperg and was using a stand-in passenger, because of the injury to Tony Hewitt.

Stand-in passenger or not, Gavin Simmons was doing a pretty good job. I followed the progress of the British pair on the results monitor also stationed on the desk. They led the race but, with Biland quite happy to tootle along in fourth place, the championship seemed a foregone conclusion. My mind wandered on to the problems of getting back across the border into Austria that night, and how Oxford United would fare against Hull City the next afternoon. Even a glance out of the window at the end of every lap confirmed the positions. Then behind me, two cubicles back, my Dutch Radio colleague Hans van Loozenoord appeared to be having a heart attack and was banging on the window. I took my feet off the desk and turned round to see what the fuss was all about. His sign language indicated that something dramatic was happening out on the track. He could not have been nearer the truth.

Biland had suddenly dropped to ninth place and was obviously having mechanical problems. Those thoughts about borders and football vanished and new headlines flashed in front of my eyes. I told London what was happening and stood up and looked out of the window. Webster and Simmons raced into view over the brow of the hill and disappeared down the main straight chased by the Dutch pair of Egbert Streuer and Bernard Schnieders. I counted the next crews through to when Biland crested the hill on his bright yellow outfit, still in ninth place. That would have been enough to clinch the championship and so perhaps all our excitement had been a little premature. I sat down again but kept a very close eye on the monitor and also out of the window. Deep down, I believed Biland would hang on to ninth place and I still gave little chance to Webster retaining the title.

Directly below there was uproar in the pit lane and especially in Webster's pit, where his father Mick could not believe the sight that greeted the packed grandstands at the top of the hill. Biland and Waltisperg were coasting up to the line and came to a halt in front of the gentleman who would be waving the chequered flag. Unfortunately for them, that would be in four laps time. Their Krauser had stuck in third gear. They could only hope and pray that Streuer beat Webster if they were to win the title.

I was in complete panic by this time. I was shouting to London down the microphone, but they'd planned to cover other sports with the championship seemingly settled. They hastily rearranged their plans and on the last lap I went on-air. I was able to describe one of the most dramatic finishes both to a race and a championship, to the people back home,

Streuer had tried all he knew to pass the English pair but, somehow, they blocked every move and crossed the line first to keep the World title in Britain.

Suddenly, within the space of ten minutes everybody was interested. I rushed away to get both Steve and Gavin to the microphone and that ten seconds for the sports news was forgotten as the headlines were re-written. Typically, Steve fought his way through the crowds of well-wishers to speak to Stuart Hall back in the London studio. Gavin seemed totally bemused by the whole incredible situation. We then linked up with injured passenger Tony Hewitt, back home in Yorkshire, for a marvellous three-way conversation.

Forty-five minutes after I'd sat down with my feet on the desk I was outside standing proudly to attention. As the National Anthem boomed out over the massive 166,000 crowd, I not only felt a tear in my eye but a real pang of guilt for having doubted the true meaning of battling to the very end. The World title was to stay in England and we of little faith now salute Steve Webster, Tony Hewitt and Gavin Simmons.

1988 SEASON

WORLD 500cc CHAMPIONSHIP

Two years ago they said Eddie Lawson was lucky to win the 500cc championship because Freddie Spencer was injured. This year those same people said he was lucky because Wayne Gardner had so many problems with his Rothmans Honda. Yet the 29-year-old Californian has now won 26 500cc grands prix making him the third most successful 500cc rider of all time. The only people in front of him are his boss, Italian Giacomo Agostini and the late, great Mike Hailwood. You make your own luck in grand prix motorcycle racing. Lawson showed this season that he is one of the all-time greats.

Not only did he win seven grands prix in that smooth, precise style, but Lawson showed tremendous courage and determination when the odds were stacked against him. He rode to tenth place in Yugoslavia less than 24 hours after dislocating his shoulder. A week later he won the French Grand Prix at Paul Ricard. He will be the first to admit Gardner had his problems with the ill-handling Honda, but Lawson and Yamaha had done their homework during the winter; Honda and Gardner certainly had not. After Honda had put so much thought and preparation into building the perfect bike for Gardner to win the championship last year, it's difficult to believe that they assembled such an unwieldy brute for his defence. Last year Yamaha were accused of complacency after winning the title in 1986. The roles were firmly reversed this year with Yamaha coming up with the perfect machine for Lawson, while it was only Gardner's skill and courage that won him four grands prix and championship points on the ill-handling NSR.

The final championship outcome was always going to be between these two giants, although three riders in particular made quite clear their intentions of joining them next year. Many people, including myself, wondered at the wisdom of Kenny Roberts dropping Randy Mamola from his Lucky Strike Yamaha team and replacing him with Wayne Rainey. Despite his success in the American Superbike series he'd not enjoyed his only year of grand prix racing in the 1984 World 250cc Championship. The 27-year-old Californian put all that behind him to emerge as the latest American likely to grab world championship honours. He finished third in the championship, which included his first grand prix victory, and only failed to finish once, when he had a puncture in Brazil. His smooth and mature style had a Lawson look to it and he might well follow in the footsteps of his Yamaha rival.

The previous year in the States, Rainey had some great Superbike battles with Texan Kevin Schwantz. That rivalry spilled over into the grands prix, with Schwantz's impact just as great as that of his old adversary. Riding the Pepsi Suzuki, Schwantz won the opening round in Japan. It was Suzuki's first grand prix success for nearly six years and he followed it up with a second win in the pouring rain at the Nurburgring. Towards the end of the season he got involved in transfer talks with both Honda and Yamaha which affected his riding, although he bounced back with a third place in the final round. Injuries and mechanical problems conspired to keep the Texan down in eighth place in the final reckoning. Despite those talks he will stay with Suzuki and joins Rainey in a twin threat to the old firm.

Another rider to win his first grand prix, and also completing his first full championship season, was Australian Kevin Magee, team-mate to Rainey. He won at Jarama but never quite recaptured that form again. He was dogged by injuries and was also homesick for his native Australia, but his fifth place in the title race represented a marvellous debut season.

The two riders who finished either side of Magee in the championship did not win a grand prix. French veteran Christian Sarron was in pole position more than any other rider. Riding the Gauloises Yamaha, he tried not to crash as much as the previous year and finished fourth. He was involved in some tremendous races and did crash pretty frequently but, to his credit, not as much as before.

Behind Magee came Scotsman Niall Mackenzie, who'd promised so much early in the season. It's seven years since a British rider won a 500cc grand prix and Mackenzie knows better than anybody that our hopes are pinned firmly on his shoulders. He led the American Grand Prix to nearly half distance before falling prey to Lawson and Gardner. Then followed a real mixed bag of good and bad rides, a succession of engine seizures on his HB Honda, and injuries which eventually kept him down in sixth place. He's desperate to rewrite that record book, but really must win a grand prix race next season to confirm all that early promise.

Ron Haslam battled in typical fashion with the intricacies of the Honda-powered Elf 5. The hub-centre steering project was dropped by Elf at the end of the season. The British rider did a marvellous development job for the French team, but, without a special engine being constructed, the machine really had reached it's full potential. Sadly, Rob McElnea's return to the Suzuki camp was a disaster with the pleasant Humbersider crashing on far too many occasions. His neighbour Roger Burnett did little better. He replaced the injured Shunji Yatsushiro in the Rothmans Honda team at the last four grands prix, but, despite a good ride in Sweden, never did enough to convince Honda to retain his services in the team.

Unfortunately, despite the brave attempts by the likes of privateers Steve Manley and Eddie Laycock, there do not appear to be any new riders in Britain with the talent or experience to step into grand prix racing. While the Americans and Australians seem capable of plucking potential champions off trees, our future on the grand prix scene looks extremely bleak. Next year new team-mates Lawson and Gardner are sure to be slogging it out at the front with Rainey, Schwantz and Magee getting closer. Let's hope that Mackenzie re-writes Barry Sheene's seven-year-old record.

500cc

		J	USA	E	P	I	D	A	NL	B	Y	F	GB	S	CZ	Br	Total Points
1	Eddie Lawson, USA *(Yamaha)*	15	20	17	20	20	13	20	17	17	6	20	10	20	17	20	252
2	Wayne Gardner, Australia *(Honda)*	17	17	15	11	17	8	—	20	20	20	13	17	17	20	17	229
3	Wayne Rainey, USA *(Yamaha)*	10	13	10	17	15	17	15	9	11	15	11	20	11	15	—	189
4	Christian Sarron, France *(Yamaha)*	8	10	13	13	—	15	—	15	—	17	17	15	15	—	11	149
5	Kevin Magee, Australia *(Yamaha)*	9	—	20	15	11	11	10	13	—	11	7	11	10	—	10	138
6	Niall Mackenzie, GB *(Honda)*	13	15	11	9	5	7	—	11	5	—	—	13	13	10	13	125

7	Didier de Radigues, Belgium *(Yamaha)*	7	8	8	10	—	9	17	4	13	10	9	9	9	—	7	120
8	Kevin Schwantz, USA *(Suzuki)*	20	11	—	—	13	20	13	8	—	—	15	—	4	—	15	119
9	Pier-Francesco Chili, Italy *(Honda)*	2	—	9	—	10	10	11	10	8	5	8	8	7	13	9	110
10	Rob McElnea, GB *(Suzuki)*	—	7	4	8	4	5	7	6	10	8	5	—	3	8	8	83
11	Ron Haslam, GB *(Elf-Honda)*	4	9	6	—	—	—	8	3	9	7	6	2	5	9	—	68
12	Randy Mamola, USA *(Cagiva)*	—	—	—	—	9	—	—	—	15	13	10	5	6	—	—	58
13	Shunji Yatsushiro, Japan *(Honda)*	6	—	7	—	8	6	9	5	7	9	—	—	—	—	—	57
14	Patrick Igoa, France *(Yamaha)*	3	—	—	—	1	4	6	7	6	4	—	—	—	7	6	44
15	Tadahiko Taira, Japan *(Yamaha)*	11	—	—	—	6	—	—	—	—	—	—	6	2	11	—	36
16	Alessandro Valesi, Italy *(Honda)*	—	5	3	6	3	—	—	—	4	—	2	—	—	3	—	26

Eddie Lawson

17	Marco Papa, Italy *(Honda)*	—	—	—	7	—	2	—	2	2	—	—	—	—	4	—	17
18	Roger Burnett, GB *(Honda)*	—	—	—	—	—	—	—	—	—	—	—	7	8	—	—	15
19	Mike Baldwin, USA *(Honda)*	—	6	—	—	—	—	—	—	—	2	3	3	—	—	—	14
20	Raymond Roche, France *(Cagiva)*	—	—	5	—	7	—	—	—	—	—	—	—	1	—	—	13
21=	Fabio Barchitta, San Marino *(Honda)*	—	—	—	—	—	—	—	—	—	—	1	—	—	6	5	12
	Marco Gentile, Switzerland *(Fior)*	—	4	—	—	2	—	—	1	—	—	—	—	—	5	—	12
23=	Bruno Kneubuhler, Switzerland *(Honda)*	—	—	1	2	—	—	4	—	—	1	—	—	—	1	—	9
	Donnie McLeod, GB *(Honda)*	—	—	—	—	—	—	—	—	3	3	—	—	—	—	3	9
25	Daniel Amatriain, Spain *(Honda)*	—	—	2	5	—	—	—	—	—	—	—	—	—	—	—	7
26=	Gustav Reiner, W. Germany *(Honda)*	—	—	—	—	—	—	5	—	—	—	—	—	—	—	—	5
	Hikaru Miyagi, Japan *(Honda)*	5	—	—	—	—	—	—	—	—	—	—	—	—	—	—	5
28=	Fabio Biliotti, Italy *(Honda)*	—	—	—	—	—	—	3	—	—	—	—	1	—	—	—	4
	Bruce Campbell, Australia *(Elf-Honda)*	—	—	—	—	—	—	—	—	—	—	4	—	—	—	—	4
	Norihiko Fujiwara, Japan *(Yamaha)*	—	—	—	—	—	—	—	—	—	—	—	4	—	—	—	4
	Gonzalez de Nicolas, Spain *(Honda)*	—	—	—	—	—	—	—	—	—	—	—	—	—	—	4	4
	Steve Manley, GB *(Suzuki)*	—	—	—	4	—	—	—	—	—	—	—	—	—	—	—	4
33=	Peter Schleef, W. Germany *(Honda)*	—	—	—	—	—	3	—	—	—	—	—	—	—	—	—	3
	Rachel Nicotte, France, *(Honda)*	—	—	—	3	—	—	—	—	—	—	—	—	—	—	—	3
35=	Peter Linden Sweden, *(Honda)*	—	—	—	—	—	—	—	—	—	—	—	—	—	2	—	2
	Massimo Broccoli, Italy *(Honda)*	—	—	—	—	—	—	2	—	—	—	—	—	—	—	—	2
37=	Maarten Duyzers, Holland *(Honda)*	—	—	—	1	—	—	—	—	—	—	—	—	—	—	—	1
	Osamu Hiwatashi, Japan *(Honda)*	1	—	—	—	—	—	—	—	—	—	—	—	—	—	—	1
	Cees Doorakker, Holland *(Honda)*	—	—	—	—	—	—	—	—	1	—	—	—	—	—	—	1
	Michael Rudroff, W. Germany *(Honda)*	—	—	—	—	—	1	—	—	—	—	—	—	—	—	—	1
	Manfred Fischer, W. Germany *(Honda)*	—	—	—	—	—	—	1	—	—	—	—	—	—	—	—	1

WORLD 250cc CHAMPIONSHIP

There was little love lost between the two Spaniards Sito Pons and Juan Garriga, who fought a bitter battle to the end of the season. They wrestled tooth and nail in the 14 rounds leading up to a rather damp squib, at the final confrontation in Brazil. Pons grabbed the title for the Campsa Honda team in a typical hurly-burly 250cc championship that, as always, provided some marvellous racing, plenty of intrigue and moments of sadness.

Sito Pons

Virtually every round produced some great races. The final bend of the Dutch TT at Assen produced some real intrigue, when leaders Pons and Dominique Sarron collided in sight of the chequered flag. The unhappiest moment came when watching five-times World Champion Toni Mang walk away from his first-lap crash at the Yugoslavian Grand Prix. He'd broken his collarbone and, when it had not healed as quickly as he wanted, he retired from the sport. The 39-year-old West German was the most successful rider of all time in the 250cc class. He'd won 39 250cc grands prix in addition to eight in the 350cc class and one in the 125s. That makes him the sixth most successful rider in the 39-year-old history of grand prix racing.

Former architectural student Pons is hoping to plan his career along similar lines to that of Mang. The 27-year-old from Barcelona may have finished runner-up in 1986 and third last year, but he had to work very hard for his first world title. Sometimes he did not help himself. He crashed in the early laps at Jerez and then got involved in that pushing and shoving match with Sarron at Assen.

Twenty-five-year-old Garriga finished every race on his Ducados Yamaha. At the final reckoning, he failed by just ten points to catch Pons, after being knocked out of contention at the closing round in Brazil. He led the championship on a couple of occasions. While the other Yamaha-mounted contenders often struggled against the superior power of the Hondas, he combined hard riding and good technique to complete a marvellous season.

Another Yamaha rider to meet the Hondas head on was fiery Italian Luca Cadalora, riding in Giacomo Agostini's Marlboro team. The former 125cc World Champion won two grands prix in very different conditions, but crashed too often to be a serious championship contender. Swiss veteran Jacques Cornu also won twice. The 35-year-old had waited 14 years to win his first grand prix and the ovation he received from the crowd and his fellow competitors in Austria underlined his popularity. He went on to win a second grand prix, riding the Parisienne Honda, in France and eventually finished third in the championship. His determination was typified in Sweden when he broke his collarbone in a practice crash. He flew back home to have it strapped and returned for the race only to be brought down by Masahiro Shimizu.

Dominique Sarron also won two grands prix, riding the Rothmans Honda, to eventually finish joint fourth in the championship. Despite those wins, it was a disappointing final result for the popular Frenchman with crashes once again wrecking any chance of championship success. He leaves the 250cc class to join the 500s next season and could find the going tough, especially against his older brother Christian. He shared fourth place with West German Reinhold Roth, who missed the first round while recovering from a broken leg, sustained when he crashed in Japan the previous year. He finished in every one of the next 14 rounds on his HB Honda and will be a big threat next year, if he starts the season in full fitness.

Mang and Sarron are definitely leaving the 250 scene, while Garriga and Pons are being tempted to join the lucrative 500cc class. There are plenty of riders itching to take their place, including two Americans who have already shown the same talent and determination that brought the likes of Lawson, Spencer and Roberts so much success. Jim Filice made his one and only grand prix appearance at Laguna Seca and won the race riding the injured Shimizu's Honda. He hopes to return for a full season next year. Cocky John Kocinski had the cheek to tell Wayne Gardner he had no balls, because the Australian had thought the Laguna Seca circuit was dangerous. He combines that cheek with great talent and finished fourth and fifth in the opening two rounds, but crashed on his two other appearances. He returns for a full season in the Team Roberts Lucky Strike outfit to add excitement both on the track and in the paddock.

Frenchman Jean-Philippe Ruggia also has shown great promise on the Gauloises Yamaha, while Loris Reggiani's progress was halted by mechanical problems and crashes.

The king of the 250cc class, Toni Mang, may have retired, but others are already queuing up to take his place in a championship that retains it's reputation for close racing and excitement both on and off the track.

250cc		J	USA	E	P	I	D	A	NL	B	Y	F	GB	S	CZ	Br	Total Points
1	Sito Pons, Spain *(Honda)*	17	17	20	—	17	17	11	10	20	20	17	13	20	17	15	231
2	Juan Garriga, Spain *(Yamaha)*	10	6	17	20	15	15	15	20	10	17	13	15	17	20	11	221
3	Jacques Cornu, Switzerland *(Honda)*	13	9	13	15	8	—	20	17	17	10	20	9	—	9	6	166
4	Dominique Sarron, France *(Honda)*	—	15	13	—	20	7	13	—	—	15	15	17	15	8	20	158*
5	Reinhold Roth, W. Germany *(Honda)*	—	7	10	10	10	11	17	9	13	13	11	11	13	10	13	158
6	Luca Cadalora, Italy *(Yamaha)*	—	10	9	—	11	20	9	13	8	11	10	20	—	15	—	136
7	Jean-Philippe Ruggia, France *(Yamaha)*	9	3	15	11	7	3	3	5	7	—	9	10	9	5	8	104
8	Toni Mang, W. Germany *(Honda)*	20	8	—	9	6	8	6	15	15	—	—	—	—	—	—	87
9	Carlos Cardus, Spain *(Honda)*	7	—	—	—	—	—	—	4	9	8	8	4	11	11	9	71
10	Masahiro Shimizu, Japan *(Honda)*	—	—	11	17	13	—	10	—	—	—	—	7	—	3	7	68
11	Carlos Lavado, Venezuela *(Yamaha)*	3	—	—	—	9	—	—	—	11	—	—	8	—	7	17	55
12	Donnie McLeod, GB *(EMC)*	—	—	8	4	5	13	—	2	4	—	4	6	—	—	1	47
13	Loris Reggiani, Italy *(Aprilia)*	—	4	—	—	—	—	—	11	—	9	7	—	—	13	—	44
14	Martin Wimmer, W. Germany *(Yamaha)*	—	—	7	—	—	10	4	7	—	—	5	1	6	—	—	40
15	Manfred Herweh, W. Germany *(Honda)*	—	—	6	6	4	—	8	6	—	—	—	—	—	—	5	35
16	August Auinger, Austria *(Aprilia)*	—	2	5	—	1	—	—	—	3	2	6	—	8	—	4	31
17	Helmut Bradl, W. Germany *(Honda)*	—	—	—	—	—	6	—	—	2	—	—	—	5	4	10	27
18	Ivan Palazzese, Venezuela *(Yamaha)*	—	—	—	—	—	—	7	3	—	—	—	5	10	—	—	25
19	John Kocinski, USA, *(Yamaha)*	11	13	—	—	—	—	—	—	—	—	—	—	—	—	—	24
20	Harald Eckl, W. Germany *(Aprilia)*	—	—	1	2	3	—	2	—	—	7	—	3	—	1	3	22
21	Jim Filice, USA *(Honda)*	—	20	—	—	—	—	—	—	—	—	—	—	—	—	—	20*
22	Stefano Caracchi, Italy *(Honda)*	—	—	—	5	2	1	—	—	—	5	—	2	3	—	2	20
23	Bruno Casanova, Italy *(Aprilia)*	—	5	—	1	—	—	—	8	—	1	—	—	—	2	—	17
24	Masaru Kobayashi, Japan *(Honda)*	15	—	—	—	—	—	—	—	—	—	—	—	—	—	—	15

25=	Jean-Michel Mattioli, France *(Yamaha)*	—	—	4	7	—	—	—	—	—	—	—	—	1	—	—	12
	Maurizio Vitali, Italy *(Rotax)*	—	—	3	—	—	—	1	—	—	6	—	—	2	—	—	12
27=	Hans Becker, W. Germany *(Yamaha)*	—	—	—	—	—	5	—	—	6	—	—	—	—	—	—	11
	Bubba Shobert, USA *(Honda)*	—	11	—	—	—	—	—	—	—	—	—	—	—	—	—	11
29	Jean Foray, France *(Yamaha)*	—	—	—	—	—	9	—	—	—	—	1	—	—	—	—	10
	Jean-Francois Balde, France *(Rotax)*	—	—	—	—	—	—	—	—	—	3	—	—	7	—	—	10
	Alberto Puig, Spain *(Honda)*	—	—	2	8	—	—	—	—	—	—	—	—	—	—	—	10
32	Toshihiko Honma, Japan *(Yamaha)*	8	—	—	—	—	—	—	—	—	—	—	—	—	—	—	8
33=	Jochen Schmid, W. Germany *(Honda)*	—	—	—	—	—	—	—	—	—	—	—	—	—	6	—	6
	Masumitsu Taguchi, Japan *(Honda)*	6	—	—	—	—	—	—	—	—	—	—	—	—	—	—	6
35=	Seigo Kikuchi, Japan *(Honda)*	5	—	—	—	—	—	—	—	—	—	—	—	—	—	—	5
	Wilco Zeelenberg, Holland *(Yamaha)*	—	—	—	—	—	—	—	1	—	—	—	—	4	—	—	5
	Englebert Neumair, Austria *(Aprilia)*	—	—	—	—	—	—	5	—	—	—	—	—	—	—	—	5
	Guy Bertin, France *(Honda)*	—	—	—	—	—	—	—	5	—	—	—	—	—	—	—	5
39=	Kyoji Nanba, Japan *(Yamaha)*	4	—	—	—	—	—	—	—	—	—	—	—	—	—	—	4
	Urs Jucker, Switzerland *(Yamaha)*	—	—	—	—	—	—	—	—	—	4	—	—	—	—	—	4
	Herman Holder, W. Germany *(Rotax)*	—	—	—	—	—	4	—	—	—	—	—	—	—	—	—	4
42=	Urs Luzi, Switzerland *(Honda)*	—	—	—	3	—	—	—	—	—	—	—	—	—	—	—	3
	Paolo Casoli, Italy *(Garelli)*	—	—	—	—	—	2	—	—	1	—	—	—	—	—	—	3
	Gary Cowan, Ireland *(Yamaha)*	—	—	—	—	—	—	—	—	—	—	3	—	—	—	—	3
45=	Youichi Yamamoto, Japan *(Honda)*	2	—	—	—	—	—	—	—	—	—	—	—	—	—	—	2
	Massimo Matteoni, Italy *(Yamaha)*	—	—	—	—	—	—	—	—	—	—	2	—	—	—	—	2
47=	Keiji Tamura, Japan *(Yamaha)*	1	—	—	—	—	—	—	—	—	—	—	—	—	—	—	1
	Alan Carter, GB *(Yamaha)*	—	1	—	—	—	—	—	—	—	—	—	—	—	—	—	1

**Sarron and Filice took fifth and twenty-first places despite having the same points as Roth and Caracchi because both had scored wins.*

WORLD 125cc CHAMPIONSHIP

What a difference a year can make, certainly in the 11-round 125cc World Championship. Last year only a crash in the final round prevented Italian Fausto Gresini winning every grand prix. This year Gresini scored just 22 points as Spaniard Jorge Martinez and his all-red Derbi dominated the title race. The Spanish Derbi factory had done their homework, with only single-cylinder machines eligible in this year's championship. Garelli, who dominated last year's championship with their twin-cylinder machine, had not done theirs. It was left to another Italian Ezio Gianola, riding the RS Honda, to provide the real challenge to the Spanish might.

The result was some incredible races between Martinez and Gianola which thrilled crowds at every grand prix venue. The super-professional Martinez may have won the title, but the hard-riding Italian won thousands of new fans with some incredible displays of sheer determination. Time after time, with his head never out from behind the screen of his tiny Honda, 28-year-old Gianola would ride up the inside, round the outside or outbrake the champion-elect. Martinez seemed quite happy to play along until the crunch; then he would open the throttle of the Derbi and usually pull away. There was nothing Gianola could do about it.

The introduction of the single-cylinder limit was a great success, with often as many as six riders battling for second place, usually riding Hondas. Hans Spaan, Julian Miralles and Adi Stadler, plus Gastone Grassetti, Gerhard Waibel and Domenico Brigaglia, conjured up some superb races, which produced easily the most competitive solo class of the season. Martinez, known as Aspar the cobbler to the millions of fans back in Spain, opened his camapaign by winning in front of his home crowd at Jarama to set himself and the team on the right track. Gianola had retired with gearbox problems and Miralles was second. However, Gianola gave both Martinez and his team-mate Manuel Herreros a tough time when they came to his homeland, at Imola in the second round. On the very last lap though, he ran off the track at one of the many chicanes to eventually finish third.

Martinez made a rare mistake at the third round, and crashed in appalling conditions at the German Grand Prix at the Nurburgring. Gianola won and British riders were in the points for the first time this season. Ian McConnachie had a dreadful time with the works Cagiva, but secured his first finish of the year in tenth, with Kris Galatowicz 12th and Robin Appleyard 13th on their Hondas. Martinez bounced back after his tumble to win the next five rounds. Although Gianola always made him work very hard, he'd used his power advantage to score maximum points. At the fourth round in Austria, Dutchman Stefan Prein gave Gianola a taste of his own medicine, only just failing to knock him back to third by a wheel length. Two weeks later at Assen in Holland, Martinez gave Derbi their 60th grand prix victory, while Robin Milton scored his first points of the season in 14th place.

The closest race was at Spa in Belgium where heavy rain caused the race to be run in two legs. Martinez won by the skin of his teeth from Gianola to set up the chance of the 80/125cc double. Scottish-born American Richard Scott, who had typified the spirit of the class by travelling round Europe in a van with no sponsorship, was rewarded for his dedication with sixth place in the Spa drizzle. Coventry-based Kris Galatowicz is very much in the same boat and his 11th place in the next round in Yugoslavia was just reward.

Poor McConnachie looked set for a good place in that race, but his unreliable Cagiva seized while he was lying fourth.

Gianola beat Martinez fair and square at the British Grand Prix at Donington, but the Spaniard stayed on course for the title. He finished second after local hero Alex Bedford retired with a loose rear sprocket although Galatowicz's Sixth place kept the patriotic crowd happy.

Martinez finally clinched the title at Anderstorp in Sweden. He won the race, but Gianola tried everything to stop him in one of the most exciting rides of the season. The Spaniard completed the year as he started, by winning. Next year Honda have promised something special for Gianola. If the machine materialises it could turn out to be an even more exciting championship than this year, although that would be difficult.

125cc	E	I	D	A	NL	B	Y	F	GB	S	CZ	Total Points
1 Jorge Martinez, Spain *(Derbi)*	20	20	—	20	20	20	20	20	17	20	20	197
2 Ezio Gianola, Italy *(Honda)*	—	15	20	17	17	17	17	17	20	17	11	168
3 Hans Spaan, Holland *(Honda)*	6	11	15	10	15	13	2	4	6	13	15	110
4 Julian Miralles, Spain *(Honda)*	17	1	17	4	—	15	—	5	13	15	17	104
5 Domenico Brigaglia, Italy *(Rotax)*	—	—	8	—	13	5	13	13	15	2	—	69
6 Gastone Grassetti, Italy *(Honda)*	15	9	9	7	—	11	—	10	—	—	5	66
7 Adi Stadler, W. Germany *(Honda)*	11	8	—	5	6	3	9	7	—	11	3	63
8 Stefan Prein, W. Germany *(Honda)*	3	5	—	15	10	—	11	—	—	6	9	59
9 Lucio Pietroniro, Belgium *(Honda)*	8	—	—	—	—	9	15	8	1	8	7	56
10 Gerhard Waibel, W. Germany *(Honda)*	10	—	5	9	11	6	—	11	—	—	—	52
11 Hisashi Unemoto, Japan *(Honda)*	9	7	10	—	—	7	3	—	4	3	—	43
12 Alan Scott, USA *(Honda)*	—	3	—	—	—	10	7	—	11	1	6	38
13 Corrado Catalano, Italy *(Aprilia)*	—	—	—	—	8	—	—	15	—	—	13	36
14 Luis Reyes, Spain *(Garelli)*	—	10	7	—	—	—	8	9	—	—	—	34
15= Manuel Herreros, Spain *(Derbi)*	—	17	13	—	—	—	—	—	—	—	—	30
Heinz Luthi, Switzerland *(Honda)*	5	4	—	—	5	—	6	—	3	5	2	30
17 Koji Takada, Japan *(Honda)*	7	—	—	—	—	8	10	—	—	4	—	29
18 Johnny Wickstrom, Finland *(Honda)*	—	6	—	2	—	—	—	—	8	9	—	25
19= Alfred Waibel, W. Germany *(Honda)*	—	—	11	8	—	—	—	—	5	—	—	24
Pier-Paolo Bianchi, Italy *(Cagiva)*	—	13	—	—	7	4	—	—	—	—	—	24
21 Fausto Gresini, Italy *(Garelli)*	13	—	—	—	—	—	—	—	9	—	—	22
22= Kris Galatowicz, GB *(Honda)*	—	—	4	—	—	—	5	—	10	—	—	19
Josef Fischer, Austria *(Rotax)*	—	—	1	13	1	—	4	—	—	—	—	19
24 Hubert Abold, W. Germany *(Honda)*	—	—	—	6	9	—	—	3	—	—	—	18
25 Bady Hassaine, France *(Honda)*	—	—	2	—	—	—	—	—	2	10	—	14
26 Rob Milton, GB *(Rotax)*	—	—	—	—	2	—	1	—	—	—	10	13
27 Mike Leitner, Austria *(LCR-EMCO)*	—	—	—	11	—	—	—	—	—	—	—	11
28 Ian McConnachie, GB *(Cagiva)*	—	—	6	—	—	—	—	—	—	—	4	10
29= Jussi Hautaniemi, Finland *(Honda)*	—	2	—	—	4	1	—	—	—	—	1	8
Alex Bedford, GB *(Honda)*	—	—	—	—	—	—	—	—	—	—	8	8
31= Flemming Kistrup, Denmark *(Hummel)*	—	—	—	—	—	—	—	—	—	7	—	7
Alejandro Criville, Spain *(Derbi)*	—	—	—	—	—	—	—	—	7	—	—	7

33 = Ian Appleyard, GB *(Honda)*	—	—	3	1	—	2	—	—	—	—	—	6
Esa Kytola, Finland *(Honda)*	—	—	—	—	—	—	—	6	—	—	—	6
Thierry Feuz, Switzerland *(Rotax)*	—	—	—	3	3	—	—	—	—	—	—	6
36 Manuel Hernandez, Spain *(Honda)*	4	—	—	—	—	—	—	—	—	—	—	4
37 = Stefan Dorflinger, Switzerland *(Honda)*	2	—	—	—	—	—	—	—	—	—	—	2
Taru Rinne, Finland *(Honda)*	—	—	—	—	—	—	—	2	—	—	—	2
39 Paul Bordes, France *(Honda)*	1	—	—	—	—	—	—	—	—	—	—	1
40 Emilio Cuppini, Italy *(Honda)*	—	—	—	—	—	—	—	1	—	—	—	1

WORLD 80cc CHAMPIONSHIP

It was all rather predicable with Jorge Martinez easily retaining his title in a lack-lustre championship dominated by the Spanish Derbi factory. In fact, Martinez only got beaten once in the seven-round championship and that was in front of his home fans at the first round in Jarama. From that moment he was never headed again and clinched the title at the penultimate round in Yugoslavia. Team-mate Alex Criville was second, just three points in front of former 50cc and 80cc World Champion Stefan Dorflinger. The Swiss ace Dorflinger, riding the Marlboro Krauser, beat Martinez in that first round and looked capable of giving the 26-year-old Spanish World Champion a hard time. However, bad starts and crashes kept him out of the reckoning. Only in the last round, at Brno in Czechoslovakia, did he again show his true potential producing the race of the season. He failed by less than a quarter of a second to beat his great rival.

Martinez is not only a national hero back home in motor-cycle racing-mad Spain but also a millionaire. While the smaller classes attract little attention in Britain, they are big business in Spain and stars don't come bigger than Martinez. He's nicknamed 'Aspar', the cobbler, because of his father's occupation. He's following in the tradition of Spanish smallbike riders with Angel Nieto still a legend in his homeland after winning 13 world titles. Already there appears a wealth of young talent behind him to carry on those traditions in a country that encourages racing on smaller machines.

Another breeding ground for small bike riders has appeared in an unexpected place: the Eastern bloc countries. Bulgarian Bodgan Nikolov and Hungarian Karly Juhasz rode their Krausers into fourth and fifth places, respectively, in the championship, to provide some much needed success for those countries. Obviously the 80cc class in which it's comparatively cheap to run a team, is ideal for these riders who have shown great skill and technique.

Sadly, the class has attracted little interest in Britain, with Donington dropping it's round of the championship this year. Just two years ago we were celebrating Ian McConnachie's marvellous win at Silverstone. Since that triumph McConnachie's fortunes have stumped in the class. He signed to ride for the Spanish Autisa team at the beginning of the season, but after a series of breakdowns decided to concentrate his efforts in the 125cc class.

The success of the single-cylinder 125cc class has brought about the demise of the 80s and next year will be their last season. It does make sense to combine the two. Martinez and Derbi are sure to want to go out in a blaze of glory and it would take a brave punter to bet against them.

80cc

		E	P	I	WG	NL	Y	CZ	Total Points
1	Jorge Martinez, Spain *(Derbi)*	17	20	20	20	20	20	20	137
2	Alex Criville, Spain *(Derbi)*	15	15	13	17	—	15	15	90
3	Stefan Dorflinger, Switzerland *(Krauser)*	20	13	17	—	—	10	17	77
4	Manuel Herreros, Spain *(Derbi)*	13	17	15	15	—	9	—	69
5	Peter Ottl, W. Germany *(Krauser)*	11	11	9	—	17	17	—	65
6	Bodgan Nikolov, Bulgaria *(Krauser)*	8	8	10	—	8	11	10	55
7	Karoly Juhasz, Hungary *(Krauser)*	9	7	11	1	7	6	13	54
8	Jos van Dongen, Holland *(Casal)*	5	6	5	10	13	8	—	47
9	Giuseppe Ascareggi, Italy *(BBFT)*	—	10	8	11	6	—	11	46
10	Gabriele Gnani, Italy *(Gnani)*	—	9	3	13	2	—	9	36
11	Henri Torrontegui, Spain *(Autisa)*	10	—	—	—	11	7	—	28
12=	Gunter Schirnhofer, W. Germany *(Krauser)*	4	3	—	5	5	3	7	27
	Adrie Nijenhuis, Holland *(Casal)*	—	—	—	9	9	4	5	27
	Jorg Seel, W. Germany *(Seel)*	—	—	4	—	10	13	—	27
15	Bert Smit, Holland *(Minarelli)*	—	—	2	—	15	—	8	25
16	Rene Dunki, Switzerland *(Krauser)*	—	5	6	4	1	—	6	22
17	Reiner Koster, Switzerland *(LCR-Kroko)*	—	—	7	—	4	—	—	11
18=	Heinz Paschen, W. Germany *(Kiefer)*	—	—	—	8	—	—	2	10
	Hans Koopman, Holland *(Ziegler)*	—	—	—	7	3	—	—	10
20=	Serge Julin, Belgium *(Casal)*	7	—	1	—	—	—	—	8
	Jacques Bernard, Belgium *(Fantic)*	3	4	—	—	—	—	1	8
22=	Ian McConnachie, GB *(Autisa)*	6	—	—	—	—	—	—	6
	Paolo Priori, Italy *(Krauser)*	—	—	—	6	—	—	—	6
24=	Rainer Kunz, W. Germany *(Ziegler)*	—	—	—	—	—	5	—	5
	Josef Szabo, Hungary *(Kreidler)*	—	—	—	—	—	2	3	5
26	Janos Pintar, Yugoslavia *(Eberhardt)*	—	—	—	—	—	—	4	4
27=	Xavier Arumi, Spain *(Kreidler)*	1	2	—	—	—	—	—	3
	Stefan Braegger, Switzerland *(Casal)*	—	—	—	3	—	—	—	3
29=	Hubert Abold, W. Germany *(Krauser)*	2	—	—	—	—	—	—	2
	Hagen Klein, W. Germany *(Honda)*	—	—	—	2	—	—	—	2
31=	Jaime Mariano, Spain *(Cobas)*	—	1	—	—	—	—	—	1
	Alojz Pavlic, Yugoslavia *(Seel)*	—	—	—	—	—	1	—	1

Jorge Martinez

WORLD SIDECAR CHAMPIONSHIP

Sidecar racing continued to silence its critics with a dramatic finish to a magnificent world championship that could not be matched by the solo counterparts.

The final round in front of 166,000 fans at Brno in Czechoslovakia produced one of the biggest upsets of the last decade. It also kept that world championship crown on British shores in the very capable hands of Steve Webster, Tony Hewitt and a certain Gavin Simmons.

Going into that last round Webster trailed the Swiss pair Rolf Biland and Kurt Waltisperg by 18 points and was without his regular passenger Tony Hewitt. He'd been injured in a crash the previous week and so Gavin Simmons arrived at Brno for only his second ride with Webster and his second grand prix appearance.

Just three weeks earlier Biland was looking to making it a clean sweep of grands prix victories after winning the opening six rounds on his Krauser-powered LCR, beautifully prepared by Harald Bartol. Webster fought back, finding more power from his own Krauser engine to win in England and Sweden. However, with Biland finishing second on both occasions, he was still odds-on favourite to clinch his fifth world sidecar title.

Webster led the race with Biland quite happy in fourth place when suddenly the Swiss rider slowed with gearbox trouble. Four laps later he was out of the race. Despite the determined challenge of former World Champion Egbert Streuer, Webster and Simmons not only won the race but held onto the championship by a slender two points.

It was a bitter blow for Biland who looked to be running away with it until those final three rounds, but it was the type of finish that typified the season. Even when Biland was victorious in all those early races there were some amazing dices, often watched by millions of television viewers. From the very first round at Jerez in Spain Webster realised that he was in for a tough time against Biland. The Swiss ace has always been liable to push his luck by trying mechanical innovations that have often let him down at vital moments. Last year he watched Austrian tuning wizard Bartol help Webster towards that title and Biland decided he was the man for him.

He signed him on an exclusive contract paying out far more money than the cups of tea that were all Bartol sought from Webster last season The Austrian brought instant reliability to Biland's Krauser engine and mid-range power that the British pair could not match.

It was not until that memorable afternoon in the Donington sunshine that Webster got the better of his great rival in the seventh round. Once again the race was televised and had millions of patriotic armchair viewers on their feet as they slogged it out.

There was a repeat performance a week later at Anderstorp in Sweden but nobody could have forecast that final chapter – and that included Gavin Simmons. He only started racing this year and was regular passenger to Paul Atkinson in the European Championship. His performance at Brno was quite brilliant in a race in which Webster said he'd ridden the hardest he'd ever done in his life. Simmons' only problem after the race was rushing back home to York, with a hangover, to start work on Tuesday.

If they'd not been beset with mechanical problems the Dutch pair of Egbert Streuer and Bernard Schnieders would have probably made it a three-horse race for the championship. They had to settle for third but will be back next year. Alain Michel and Jean-Marc

Fresc fought off the challenge of the Swiss brothers Markus and Urs Egloff to grab fourth spot, although the Egloffs look the most promising of the new talent.

At the other end of the age scale British veteran Derek Jones completed a marvellous season with his passenger Australian Peter Brown. They kept just enough money in the kitty to keep racing and were rewarded with sixth place in the championship. Their pride on being on the rostrum at Spa, after finishing third, was one of the highlights of the season.

Prospects look good for next year with the sidecar crews determined to get enough money together to race at the American Grand Prix at Laguna Seca. Webster, as a true World Champion, has led the crusade for sidecar crews to clean up their act and treat the sport in the professional way it deserves.

Many solo teams treat sidecars very much as the poor relations of motorcycling but you only have to look at the quality of racing provided by chairs this year to realise what an important part of the grand prix scene they are. Just ask those television viewers in Britain.

Steve Webster and Tony Hewitt

Sidecar

		P	D	A	NL	B	F	GB	S	Cz	Total Points
1	Steve Webster, GB *(LCR-Krauser)* Tony Hewitt, GB and Gavin Simmons, GB	15	17	15	15	17	17	20	20	20	156
2	Rolf Biland, Switzerland *(LCR-Krauser)* Kurt Waltisperg, Switzerland	20	20	20	20	20	20	17	17	—	154
3	Egbert Streuer, Holland *(LCR-Yamaha)* Bernie Schnieders, Holland	17	2	11	17	—	7	11	15	17	97

The championship style of Steve Webster and Tony Hewitt.

4	Alain Michel, France *(LCR-Krauser)*	11	—	17	—	13	13	15	13	11	93
	Jean-Marc Fresc, France										
5	Marcus Egloff, Switzerland *(LCR-Yamaha)*	—	7	—	13	5	15	13	11	15	79
	Urs Egloff, Switzerland										
6	Derek Jones, GB *(LCR-Yamaha)*	8	3	8	11	15	—	9	7	8	69
	Peter Brown, GB										
7	Alfred Zurbrugg, Switzerland *(LCR-Yamaha)*	6	15	13	4	—	10	7	9	—	64
	Martin Zurbrugg, Switzerland										
8	Masato Kumano, Japan *(LCR-TEC)*	5	—	—	10	2	11	10	10	13	61
	Marcus Fahrni, Switzerland										
9	Bernd Scherer, W. Germany *(BSR-Krauser)*	4	11	7	—	7	3	6	6	10	54
	Thomas Shroder, W. Germany										
10	Steve Abbott, GB *(Windle-Yamaha)*	10	6	10	8	6	8	—	5	—	53
	Shaun Smith, GB										
11	Barry Brindley, GB *(Krauser-Yamaha)*	13	5	6	9	11	2	—	—	4	50
	Graham Rose, GB										
12	Fritz Stolzle, W. Germany *(LCR-Krauser)*	1	13	—	7	—	4	8	3	9	45
	Hubert Stolzle, W. Germany										
13	Yoshida Kumagaya, Japan *(LCR-Yamaha)*	—	4	—	6	10	9	5	8	—	42
	Brian Barlow, GB and Peter Linden, Sweden										
14	Wolfgang Stropek, Austria *(LCR-Krauser)*	7	10	3	2	8	—	—	—	5	35
	Hans-Peter Demling, Austria and Wilhelm Bock, Austria										
15	Theo van Kempen, Holland *(LCR-Krauser)*	9	9	4	—	4	6	—	—	2	34
	Simon Birchall, GB and Geral de Haas, Holland										
16	Pascal Larratte, France *(LCR-Yamaha)*	—	8	9	5	—	—	—	4	—	26
	Jacques Corbier, France										
17	Ivan Nigrowsky, France *(Seymaz-Yamaha)*	2	—	—	—	1	5	—	2	7	17
	Marcial Charpentier, France										
18	Andre Bosman, Australia *(LCR-Yamaha)*	—	—	5	—	3	—	2	—	—	10
	Dave Kellett, Australia										
19	Rolf Steinhaussen, W. Germany *(ADM)*	—	—	—	—	9	—	—	—	—	9
	Bruno Hiller, W. Germany										
20=	Gary Thomas, GB *(LCR-IMI)*	—	—	2	—	—	—	4	—	—	6
	Geral de Haas, Holland and Eckorst Rosinger, W. Germany										
	Wilhelm Kraus, W. Germany *(Busch)*	—	—	—	—	—	—	—	—	6	6
	Dieter Schuster, W. Germany										
22=	Dennis Bingham, GB *(LCR-Yamaha)*	3	—	1	—	—	—	—	—	—	4
	Gary Irlam, GB										
	Jean-Louis Millet, France *(GDF-Elf)*	—	—	—	—	—	—	3	—	1	4
	Claude Debroux, France										
	Clive Stirrat, GB *(LCR-Yamaha)*	—	—	—	—	—	—	1	—	3	4
	Simon Prior, GB										
25	Jan van Stekelenburg, Holland *(Windle-Yamaha)*	—	—	—	3	—	—	—	—	—	3
	R. Bettgens, Holland										
26=	Rene Progin, Switzerland *(Seymaz-Yamaha)*	—	—	—	—	—	1	—	—	—	1
	Yvan Hunziker, Switzerland										
	Doug Chivas, New Zealand *(LCR-Yamaha)*	—	—	—	—	—	—	—	1	—	1
	H. Olsson, Sweden										

JAPANESE GRAND PRIX, 27 March, Suzuka 3.641m/5.859k

A superb start to a long season. A long-awaited victory for Suzuki in the 500cc race and a classic old versus new encounter in the 20-lap 250cc event.

Kevin Schwantz's first grand prix victory, riding the Pepsi-sponsored RGV 500 Suzuki, was welcomed by everybody apart from his nearest rivals. It gave Suzuki their first 500cc grand prix victory for over five years and gave Honda and Yamaha something more to think about than just themselves. World Champion Wayne Gardner, riding the Rothmans NSR Honda, met the Schwantz challenge head-on but at the end was very lucky to finish intact.

Throughout the 22-lap encounter round the very difficult 3.64-mile Suzuka circuit he'd contested the lead with the young Texan. On the last lap he went off the track at over 130mph. He was desperately lucky to ride across the empty helicopter pad, the grass and back on the track to finish second. His great rival, former World Champion Eddie Lawson, made a slow start but fought through to third just in front of Scotsman Niall Mackenzie. Neither of them finished in the first round last year and so they were not too disappointed with their respective results.

Five-times World Champion Toni Mang was delighted with his win in a classic 250cc encounter. Not only did he have to fight off the usual predators but explosive newcomer John Kocinski. The 23-year-old American qualified third fastest, riding for his great mentor Kenny Roberts in the Lucky Strike Yamaha team. Despite ignition problems he finished fifth in his first grand prix appearance and if confidence in his own ability is any indication we are going to be hearing a great deal of him during the next few seasons.

Last year it poured with rain on race day at Suzuka. To make life more interesting it rained throughout the two days of official practice but was dry on the day itself this time round.

The four wet 500cc sessions gave the teams little chance to size up the opposition after the winter lay off although it was very obvious Randy Mamola, who won the Japanese Grand Prix last year, was having big problems. He'd switched to the Italian Cagiva factory after being sacked by Kenny Roberts. He only qualified in 16th place complaining of major carburation problems and little adhesion from the new Pirelli tyres. Local hero Tadahiko Taira qualified in pole position on the works Yamaha with Lawson, Schwantz, Gardner and Frenchman Christian Sarron making up the front row.

American Superbike Champion Wayne Rainey, who'd replaced Mamola in the Lucky Strike team, made a flying start from the second row on his first appearance at Suzuka. At the infamous Spoon corner Schwantz grabbed the lead. Gardner followed suit during that hectic first lap and we sat back waiting for him to push Schwantz back. The Suzuki man had different ideas and got his head down and started to pull away from his pursuers headed by Gardner followed by Japanese Honda rider Shinicho Ito, Sarron, Rainey and Marlboro Yamaha-mounted Lawson.

The Champion slowly clawed back the leader's advantage and as they started their fifth lap the extra power of the Honda propelled him into the lead. Within half a lap he realised just what a fight he had on his hands when Schwantz knocked him back to second.

Again he had to get his head down just to stay in contention with Schwantz. He was not helped by a carburation problem which made the power rush in when he opened the throttle. The Suzuki in front of him suffered no such problems although being down on top speed to the Honda. On the bends Schwantz was able to feed in the power to pull away while on the straights Gardner could pull back his advantage. On the eighth lap Gardner blasted back into the lead down the 170-mph back straight but Schwantz hung onto his back wheel like a leech. It was magnificent entertainment for the 80,000 crowd as Schwantz constantly moved alongside the Champion. On the 13th lap he raced round the outside to re-take the lead. It was Gardner's turn to hang on and wait his moment especially when they started to lap the backmarkers. His moment came halfway through the last lap but it was definitely not what he wanted. Schwantz had taken good advantage of those backmarkers to open up a 10-yard gap as they raced into that last lap. He closed, braking for the hairpin, but on the next bend, a 130-mph right hander, the back end of his Honda went sideways. He managed to straighten it and race off the track. Anywhere else on the circuit the consequences could have been far more serious. Schwantz had not looked behind for over a lap and was unaware of the goings on behind him. He knew for certain he'd won when he took the chequered flag and celebrated his magnificent win by riding most of his victory lap standing on the footrests with arms above his head. His joy at winning his first grand prix was understandable. For the Europeans it was further proof that America has a seemingly endless production line of prospective world champions.

Gardner was relieved to hang onto second place nearly nine seconds behind the winner. Unfortunately for him and the Rothmans team the race did not show up the handling problems that were to beset him later on.

With all the excitement at the front it was easy to overshadow some close racing behind. Lawson grabbed third place but only after a spirited fight by Mackenzie, riding the HB Honda. The Scotsman acutally raced into third spot two laps from the finish but Lawson relegated him to fourth on the same lap. Fastest qualifier Taira made an appalling start but was impressive in the dry to finish a creditable fifth in front of a private Lucky Strike battle between Rainey and his team-mate Australian Magee. Rainey held a one-tenth of a second advantage at the finish. We were going to see a great deal more of those two riders as the season progressed. Sarron eventually dropped to eighth in front of Belgian Didier de Radigues, making his debut on the Marlboro Yamaha. Japanese Rothmans Honda rider Shunji Yatsushiro made his customary bad start and could only finish 10th with Ron Haslam 12th on the Honda-powered Elf 5, despite very little pre-season practice.

Not so happy were the new Cagiva pairing of Mamola and Frenchman Raymond Roche. Both retired with carburation problems before half distance. Humbersider Rob McElnea crashed twice in practice and went out of the race on the 10th lap with a holed piston on his Pepsi Suzuki. Honda-mounted Ito crashed out of contention after a promising start.

Japanese riders know all about their weather. There was the shortest break in the clouds during the first 250cc practice session, Toshihiko Honma and Keiji Tamura took full advantage to qualify first and second respectively before the rain returned for the next three sessions. The two Yamaha men shared that front row with Kocinski and Honda-mounted Jacques Cornu and West German Herweh. Unfortunately Herweh did not take his place at the start of the race after breaking his collarbone crashing in a later session. Also missing was Italian Loris Reggiani who broke a bone in his right wrist when he crashed the Aprilia on Friday. Last year's championship runner-up Reinhold Roth, Japanese ace Masahiro Shimizu and West German Martin Wimmer were all absent still recovering from pre-season injuries.

Thirty-eight year old Mang hated the rain and was back on the fourth row of the grid. With the sun shining he rocketed from the start, riding the NSR Rothmans Honda, when the lights changed to commence an exhibition of pure class and style. The experienced Cornu, riding the Parisienne Honda, led from the line but cheeky Kocinski paid scant regard to age or reputations. He grabbed the lead on the first lap and was more than a little surprised when Mang pushed him back to second on lap two. The young Californian was desperate to show the World Champion that he'd arrived on the grand prix scene. Mang needed no reminding as Kocinski constantly dived inside him at the chicane in some desperate overtaking manoeuvres. The battle reached epic proportions with Spaniards Sito Pons, Carlos Cardus, Cornu and Japanese Yamaha ace Toshihiko Honma closing up to make a six-rider battle for the lead. It needed a cool head to not only stay on the machine but to work out a winning strategy. Five times World Champion Mang had just that. At half distance Pons snatched the lead and last year's winner Masuru Kobayashi caught the leading pack after a poor start. The pace never slackened with Mang back in front a lap later only for Kocinski to relegate him to second. Mang was back at the front at Kocinski's beloved chicane and the Californian dropped to fourth after some desperate braking. Mang got his head down to try and pull away from the bumping and boring that looked certain to end in tears. Kocinski followed but started to slow with ignition problems. He dropped to fifth with Pons, Kobayashi and Cornu setting after Mang. They caught him with three laps remaining to provide a superb finale to an already cracking race. Pons and Kobayashi constantly pulled alongside the leader but could not get their noses in front. On the last lap Mang left his braking just a little later and opened up a one-second advantage in typical style. Pons held off Kobayashi by a whisker with Cornu fourth in a blanket finish with Kocinski and Spaniard Juan Garriga.

Results

	500cc (22 laps, 80.10m/128.91k)	**m s**	**mph**	**kmh**
1	K. Schwantz, USA *(Suzuki)*	50 03.75	96.00	154.496
2	W. Gardner, Australia *(Honda)*	50 12.13	95.73	154.066
3	E. Lawson, USA *(Yamaha)*	50 16.47	95.60	153.844
4	N. Mackenzie, GB *(Honda)*	50 19.53	95.50	153.688
5	T. Taira, Japan *(Yamaha)*	50 40.13	94.85	152.647
6	W. Rainey, USA *(Yamaha)*	50 45.82	94.68	152.362
7	K. Magee, Australia *(Yamaha)*	50 45.93	94.67	152.356
8	C. Sarron, France *(Yamaha)*	50 48.94	94.58	152.206
9	D. de Radigues, Belgium *(Yamaha)*	51 04.96	94.08	151.410
10	S. Yatsurhiro, Japan *(Honda)*	51 14.04	93.81	150.963

11 H. Miyagi, Japan *(Honda)*; 12 R. Haslam, GB *(Elf-Honda)*; 13 P. Igoa, France *(Yamaha)*; 14 P. Chili, Italy *(Honda)*; 15 O. Hiwatashi, Japan *(Suzuki)*; 16 S. Katayama, Japan *(Yamaha)*; 17 M. Mizutani, Japan *(Suzuki)*. *21 laps:* 18 K. Kinoshita, Japan *(Honda)*; 19 A. Valesi, Italy *(Honda)*.

Gardner leads Schwantz, but the positions were reversed before the chequered flag.

Record lap: K. Schwantz, USA *(Suzuki)*, 2m 15.22s, 96.93mph/155.991kmh.
Modified circuit in use for first time so fastest lap establishes record.

World Championship positions: 1 K. Schwantz, 20 points; 2 W. Gardner, 17; 3 E. Lawson, 15; 4 N. Mackenzie, 13; 5 T. Taira, 11; 6 W. Rainey, 10; 7 K. Magee, 9; 8 C. Sarron, 8; 9 D. de Radigues, 7; 10 S. Yatsushiro, 6; 11 M. Miyagi, 5; 12 R. Haslam, 4; 13 P. Igoa, 3; 14 P. Chili, 2; 15 O. Hiwatashi, 1.

Practice leaderboard: 1 T. Taira, Japan *(Yamaha)*, 2m 32.01s; 2 E. Lawson, USA *(Yamaha)*, 2m 32.52s; 3 K. Schwantz, USA *(Suzuki)*, 2m 32.54s; 4 W. Gardner, Australia *(Honda)*, 2m 33.17s; 5 C. Sarron, France *(Yamaha)*, 2m 33.17s; 6 W. Rainey, USA *(Yamaha)*, 2m 33.33s; 7 K. Magee, Australia *(Yamaha)*, 2m 33.66s; 8 R. McElnea, GB

Vital points for Pons in Japan as he fights off Shimizu and Cornu.

(Suzuki), 2m 34.16s; 9 S. Ito, Japan *(Honda)*, 2m 34.64s; 10 R. Haslam, GB *(Elf-Honda)*, 2m 34.71s; 11 M. Mizutani, Japan *(Suzuki)*, 2m, 34.81s; 12 P. Chili, Italy *(Honda)*, 2m 34.98s; 13 D. de Radigues, Belgium *(Yamaha)*, 2m 35.00s; 14 S. Katayama, Japan *(Yamaha)*, 2m 35.10s; 15 H. Miyagi, Japan *(Honda)*, 2m 35.25s; 16 R. Mamola, USA *(Cagiva)*, 2m 36.17s; 17 N. Fujiwara, Japan *(Yamaha)*, 2m 36.45s; 18 N. Mackenzie, GB *(Honda)*, 2m 36.72s; 19 S. Yatsushiro, Japan *(Honda)*, 2m 36.74s; 20 R. Roche, France *(Cagiva)*, 2m 38.71s.

250cc (20 laps, 72.82m/117.19k)		**m**	**s**	**mph**	**kmh**
1	A. Mang, W. Germany *(Honda)*	47	14.26	92.49	148.850
2	S. Pons, Spain *(Honda)*	47	14.88	92.47	148.817
3	M. Kobayashi, Japan *(Honda)*	47	15.42	92.45	148.788
4	J. Cornu, Switzerland *(Honda)*	47	19.24	92.33	148.589
5	J. Kocinski, USA *(Yamaha)*	47	19.84	92.31	148.557
6	J. Garriga, Spain *(Yamaha)*	47	20.57	92.29	148.519
7	J. Ruggia, France *(Yamaha)*	47	21.60	92.25	148.465
8	T. Honma, Japan *(Yamaha)*	47	23.83	92.18	148·349
9	C. Cardus, Spain *(Honda)*	47	29.69	91.99	148.044
10	M. Taguchi, Japan *(Honda)*	47	33.44	91.87	147.849

11 S. Kikuchi, Japan *(Honda)*; 12 K. Nanba, Japan *(Yamaha)*; 13 C. Lavado, Venezuela *(Yamaha)*; 14 Y. Yamamoto, Japan *(Honda)*; 15 K. Tamura, Japan *(Yamaha)*; 16 Y. Hori, Japan *(Honda)*; 17 D. McLeod, GB *(EMC)*; 18 H. Tomita, Japan *(Honda)*; 19 J. Mattioli, France *(Yamaha)*; 20 U. Luzi, Switzerland *(Honda)*; 22 J. Balde, France *(Rotax)*; 22 K. Kozono, Japan *(Honda)*; 23 Y. Hasegawa, Japan *(Yamaha)*; 24 K. Mitchell, GB *(Yamaha)*; 25 A. Puig, Spain *(Honda)*; 26 A. Auinger, Austria *(Aprilia)*; 27 R. Delaby, Luxembourg *(Yamaha)*.

Record lap: S. Pons, Spain *(Honda)*, 2m 19.63s, 93.87mph/151.069kmh.
Modified circuit in use for first time so fastest lap establishes record.

World Championship positions: 1 A. Mang, 20 points; 2 S. Pons, 17; 3 M. Kobayashi, 15; 4 J. Cornu, 13; 5 J. Kocinski, 11; 6 J. Garriga, 10; 7 J. Ruggia, 9; 8 T. Honma, 8; 9 C. Cardus, 7; 10 M. Taguchi, 6; S. Kikuchi, 5; 12 K. Nanba, 4; 13 C. Lavado, 3; 14 Y. Yamamoto, 2; 15 K. Tamura, 1.

Practice leaderboard: 1 T. Honma, Japan *(Yamaha)*, 2m 19.79s; 2 K. Tamura, Japan *(Yamaha)*, 2m 20.59s; 3 J. Kocinski, USA *(Yamaha)*, 2m 21.30s; 4 J. Cornu, Switzerland *(Honda)*, 2m 21.36s; 5 J. Balde, France *(Rotax)*, 2m 21.90s; 6 M. Taguchi, Japan *(Honda)*, 2m 22.05s; 7 T. Yamamoto, Japan *(Yamaha)*, 2m 22.11s; 8 C. Cardus, Spain *(Honda)*, 2m 22.35s; 9 C. Lavado, Venezuela *(Yamaha)*, 2m 22.42s; 10 J. Ruggia, France *(Yamaha)*, 2m 22.54s; 11 Y. Hori, Japan *(Honda)*, 2m 22.70s; 12 H. Tomita, Japan *(Honda)*, 2m 22.90s; 13 L. Cadalora, Italy *(Yamaha)*, 2m 22.99s; 14 P. Casoli, Italy *(Garelli)*, 2m 23.10s; 15 A. Mang, W. Germany *(Honda)*, 2m 23.29s; 16 Y. Yamamoto, Japan *(Honda)*, 2m 23.31s; 17 J. Arai, Japan *(Yamaha)*, 2m 23.32s; 18 S. Pons, Spain *(Honda)*, 2m 23.48s; 19 L. Reggiani, Italy *(Aprilia)*, 2m 23.54s; 20 M. Kobayashi, Japan *(Honda)*, 2m 23.60s.

USA GRAND PRIX, 10 April, Laguna Seca, 2.196m/3.534k

Grand prix racing returned to the United States after a 23-year gap amid a storm of controversy about safety and facilities at the Californian Laguna Seca circuit. It was a shame that such vital issues should overshadow two brilliant home victories by Eddie Lawson and Jim Filice in front of a record 80,000 crowd.

For over a decade American riders and, especially three-times World Champion, Kenny Roberts, have moaned about safety and facilities at grands prix tracks in Europe. When the Europeans arrived in their own back garden they expected these things to be right – but sadly they were not. The circuit, beautifully situated in the hills above Monterey, was just not up to grand prix standards. The old part of the track, which contained the infamous corkscrew corner, was very bumpy and some corners did not have enough run off areas. Indeed the riders forced the organisers to knock down a wall, on the exit of the left hander into the start-and-finish straight, after unofficial practice. The teams used tents as pits garages with the paddock resembling a scene from *Ivanhoe* rather than a grand prix venue. Typically the sun shone the whole time which did much to cool tempers, but the fact that the grand prix went ahead did little to help the riders in their constant fight for safety and better facilities. The organisers at Laguna did everything in their powers to help the riders once they arrived. It appears they had been misled by some American grand prix stars who told them the circuit was safe and by the FIM who amazingly ratified the track even with that offending wall.

Those American riders also had the last laugh. Eddie Lawson rode at his elegant best to win the 40-lap 500cc race while Jim Filice made a sensational grand prix debut, winning the 250cc race in front of all the European stars.

It was another local man Wayne Rainey, riding the Lucky Strike Yamaha, that took pole position with Lawson alongside. Niall Mackenzie confirmed his recent good form by qualifying third. He felt his good time was due to the fact that the track was more like his local club circuit at Knockhill in Scotland. The two Kevins, Schwantz and Magee completed the front row with Gardner on the second row after qualifying sixth. Randy Mamola, a great campaigner for the Laguna Grand Prix, missed the big day. He crashed from his Cagiva in Friday's practice and was not fit enough to race.

Mackenzie raced from the line to lead up the rise and into the first left hander. Charging after him were Gardner, Schwantz, Rainey and quick-starting Ron Haslam riding the hub-centre steering Elf 5. Lawson made a bad start but surged up the inside of the first bend although he was only sixth at the end of the first lap. By the second lap he was past Haslam and became involved in a real dog fight with Schwantz and Rainey. Schwantz dropped back with carburation problems on his Pepsi Suzuki but Rainey would not let Lawson go without a fight. On the ninth lap the Marlboro Yamaha man finally got in front and set after the two leading Hondas.

Mackenzie ploughed a lonely and unfamiliar path at the front with Gardner just happy to stay aboard his ill-handling machine. Lawson, with tyres and machinery working perfectly, looked smoother than ever. It was only a matter of time before he caught the man who'd stolen his world title last year. It took him just six laps and on lap 15 he sent the screeching crowd wild. He dived underneath the bucking NSR Rothmans Honda at the first left hander and Mackenzie's new-found position of leader was immediately under threat. Three laps later the crowd screeched even louder as he repeated his overtaking technique at the same corner and Mackenzie was second.

He led by two seconds two laps after grabbing the lead and Mackenzie turned his attention to holding off Gardner. Despite his obvious problems the Australian closed and seven laps from the finish outbraked the Scotsman going into the corkscrew. Mackenzie fought back but was hampered by brake problems and at the finish was happy to be on the rostrum, despite leading for so long.

Lawson is usually shy and reserved even in victory but a win at his home grand prix changed all that. After crossing the line nearly eight seconds in front of Gardner he stopped and threw his crash helmet into the wildly cheering crowd.

Rainey and Schwantz continued their battles from their American Superbike Championship days in a superb duel for fourth spot. They scrapped away until Schwantz slowed and Rainey, despite tyre problems, grabbed fourth place with Christian Sarron sixth on the Gauloises Yamaha.

Haslam had a marvellous ride into seventh place despite almost colliding with Italian Pier-Francesco Chili and Japanese Shunji Yatsushiro when they fell in front of him. He was involved in a race-long battle with Lawson's Marlboro team-mate, Didier de Radigues with Pepsi Suzuki-mounted Rob McElnea ninth. American Mike Baldwin made a welcome return to grand prix racing finishing 10th on his privately entered Honda.

When Japanese star Masahiro Shimuzu declared himself unfit for the 250cc race his works Honda was surprisingly given to Californian Jim Filice for his grand prix debut. Surprising that is to European observers but to team manager Erv Kanemoto it was the correct decision. Filice went out and won the race comfortably with nearly 10 seconds to spare.

An American victory always looked on the cards with local favourite John Kocinski, riding the Lucky Strike Yamaha, grabbing pole position from Filice. Frenchman Dominique Sarron led the European challenge, riding the Rothmans Honda, qualifying third with Sito Pons and former World Champion Carlos Lavado completing the front row of the grid.

It was another American, dirt-track ace Bubba Shobert, riding the Camel-sponsored 1987 NSR Honda, who led from the off with Filice snapping at his heels. There had already been a false start with inexperienced American officials holding the riders too long on the line. Filice grabbed the lead on the second lap and that was the last the rest of the field saw of him.

Kocinski gave chase but soon slowed with a slippery rear tyre and got involved in a typical 250cc scrap with Sarron, Shobert and Spanish Honda stars Sito Pons and Carlos Cardus. He held up Pons and Sarron for nine laps before they both pounced. Pons then pulled away from Sarron, still having problems with the right hand he injured in a pre-season skiing accident.

Pons reduced Filice's lead to seven seconds at three-quarter distance but soon gave up the chase. He realised he had no chance of catching the leader and was happy in the knowledge that second place would give him the lead in the championship. Sarron was equally happy to score his first points of the season in third place while Kocinski fought off the late challenge of Shobert. The American dirt tracker was almost caught in a frantic last lap dash by former 125cc World Champion Luca Cadalora riding the Marlboro Yamaha.

The Italian had been battling throughout the 32 laps with Swiss ace Jacques Cornu and World Champion Toni Mang. He pulled away towards the finish but could not catch Shobert. Mang hated Laguna and was just happy to return home to Germany in one piece even though he dropped to second place in the championship. Reinhold Roth could not have chosen a tougher venue to test his injured leg. It stood up to the battering well and he finished ninth on the HB Honda in front of Spanish Yamaha rider Juan Garriga.

Expatriate Alan Carter was 15th on his Yamaha in his only grand prix appearance of the year. He planned to stay, however, to contest the US Championships. The sun kept shining throughout and the crowd was larger than that which greeted the Pope at the same venue last year. Hopefully the grand prix circus will return but there will have to be some major improvements. One thing that never seems to change is that American riders keep winning grand prix races.

Results

500cc (40 laps, 87.84m/141.361k)	**m**	**s**	**mph**	**kmh**
1 E. Lawson, USA *(Yamaha)*	60	48.07	86.68	139.497
2 W. Gardner, Australia *(Honda)*	60	55.61	86.50	139.210
3 N. Mackenzie, GB *(Honda)*	60	56.12	86.49	139.191
4 W. Rainey, USA *(Yamaha)*	61	02.71	86.35	138.970
5 K. Schwantz, USA *(Suzuki)*	61	15.53	86.03	138.456
6 C. Sarron, France *(Yamaha)*	62	07.28	84.84	136.534
7 R. Haslam, GB *(Elf-Honda)*	62	18.30	84.59	136.131

39 laps: 8 D. de Radigues, Belgium *(Yamaha)*; 9 R. McElnea, GB *(Suzuki)*; 10 M. Baldwin, USA *(Honda)*. *38 laps:* 11 A. Valesi, Italy *(Honda)*; 12 M. Gentile, Switzerland *(Honda)*. No other finishers.

Record lap: E. Lawson, USA *(Yamaha)*, 1m 29.96s, 87.87mph/141.407kmh.
Modified circuit in use for first time so fastest lap establishes record.

World Championship positions: 1 E. Lawson, 35 points; 2 W. Gardner, 34; 3 K. Schwantz, 31; 4 N. Mackenzie, 28; 5 W. Rainey, 23; 6 C. Sarron, 18; 7 D. de Radigues, 15; 8 R. Haslam, 13; 9 T. Taira, 11; 10 K. Magee, 9.

Practice leaderboard: 1 W. Rainey, USA *(Yamaha)*, 1m 29.21s; 2 E. Lawson, USA *(Yamaha)*, 1m 29.46s; 3 N. Mackenzie, GB *(Honda)*, 1m 29.47s; 4 K. Schwantz, USA *(Suzuki)*, 1m 29.49s; 5 K. Magee, Australia *(Yamaha)*, 1m 29.65s; 6 W. Gardner, Australia *(Honda)*, 1m 29.76s; 7 C. Sarron, France *(Yamaha)*, 1m 30.36s; 8 S. Yatsushiro, Japan *(Honda)*, 1m 31.44s; 9 D. de Radigues, Belgium *(Yamaha)*, 1m 31.69s; 10 P. Chili, Italy *(Honda)*, 1m 31.71s; 11 R. McElnea, GB *(Suzuki)*, 1m 31.77s; 12 R. Haslam, GB *(Elf-Honda)*, 1m 31.79s; 13 P. Igoa, France *(Yamaha)*, 1m 32.46s; 14 R. Roche, France *(Cagiva)*, 1m 32.47s; 15 M. Baldwin, USA *(Honda)*, 1m 32.84s; 16 R. Mamola, USA

(Cagiva), 1m 33.46s; 17 A. Valesi, Italy *(Honda)*, 1m 34.29s; 18 M. Gentile, Switzerland *(Honda)*, 1m 34.64s; 19 J. Long, USA *(Yamaha)*, 1m 40.65s; 20 E. Brown, USA *(Suzuki)*, 1m 41.49s.

250cc (31 laps, 68.07m/109.555k)		**m s**	**mph**	**kmh**
1	J. Filice, USA *(Honda)*	48 22.54	84.43	135.879
2	S. Pons, Spain *(Honda)*	48 32.39	84.41	135.420
3	D. Sarron, France *(Honda)*	48 44.32	83.81	134.872
4	J. Kocinski, USA *(Yamaha)*	48 47.88	83.70	134.704
5	B. Shobert, USA *(Honda)*	48 53.11	83.55	134.463
6	L. Cadalora, Italy *(Yamaha)*	48 55.77	83.48	134.342
7	J. Cornu, Switzerland *(Honda)*	49 00.26	83.35	134.135
8	A. Mang, W. Germany *(Honda)*	49 00.57	83.34	134.122
9	R. Roth, W. Germany *(Honda)*	49 14.34	82.95	133.495
10	J. Garriga, Spain *(Yamaha)*	49 17.55	82.86	133.352

11 B. Casanova, Italy *(Aprilia)*; 12 L. Reggiani, Italy *(Aprilia)*; 13 J. Ruggia, France *(Yamaha)*; 14 A. Auinger, Austria *(Aprilia)*; 15 A. Carter, GB *(Yamaha)*; 16 R. Renfrew, USA *(Honda)*; 17 M. Wimmer, W. Germany *(Yamaha)*; 18 D. McLeod, GB *(EMC)*. *30 laps:* 19 D. Greene, USA *(Honda)*; 20 J. Mattioli, France *(Yamaha)*; 21 H. Bradl, W. Germany *(Honda)*; 22 T. Stevens, USA *(Yamaha)*; 23 R. Oliver, USA *(Yamaha)*; 24 R. Delaby, Luxembourg *(Yamaha)*; 25 D. Brauneck, USA *(Yamaha)*; 26 J. Cornwell, USA *(Rotax)*. *25 laps:* 27 C. Lavado, Venezuela *(Yamaha)*.

Record lap: B. Casanova, Italy *(Aprilia)*, 1m 32.32s, 85.63mph/137.806kmh.
Modified circuit in use for first time so fastest lap establishes record.

World Championship positions: 1 S. Pons, 34 points; 2 A. Mang, 28; 3 J. Kocinski, 24; 4 J. Cornu, 22; 5 J. Filice, 20; 6 J. Garriga, 16; 7 M. Kobayshi and D. Sarron both 15; 9 J. Ruggia, 12; 10 B. Shobert, 11.

Practice leaderboard: 1 J. Kocinski, USA *(Yamaha)*, 1m 32.95s; 2 J. Filice, USA *(Honda)*, 1m 32.96s; 3 D. Sarron, France *(Honda)*, 1m 33.12s; 4 S. Pons, Spain *(Honda)*, 1m 33.18s; 5 C. Lavado, Venezuela *(Yamaha)*, 1m 33.37s; 6 C. Cardus, Spain *(Honda)*, 1m 33.43s; 7 J. Cornu, Switzerland *(Honda)*, 1m 33.49s; 8. J. Garriga, Spain *(Yamaha)*, 1m 33.55s; 9 B. Casanova, Italy *(Aprilia)*, 1m 33.74s; 10 A. Mang, W. Germany *(Honda)*, 1m 33.76s; 11 L. Cadalora, Italy *(Yamaha)*, 1m 33.78s; 12 R. Roth, W. Germany *(Honda)*, 1m 33.79s; 13 B. Shobert, USA *(Honda)*, 1m 33.97s; 14 M. Wimmer, W. Germany *(Yamaha)*, 1m 34.39s; 15 L. Reggiani, Italy *(Aprilia)*, 1m 34.39s; 16 D. McLeod, GB *(EMC)*, 1m 34.41s; 17 A. Auinger, Austria *(Aprilia)*, 1m 34.56s; 18 J. Ruggia, France *(Yamaha)*, 1m 34.63s; 19 J. Balde, France *(Rotax)*, 1m 34.64s; 20 A. Carter, GB *(Yamaha)*, 1m 34.79s.

Jim Filice celebrated his Grand Prix debut with a superb win in front of his home crowd.

Magee fights off the determined challenge of Lawson to secure his first grand prix victory.

SPANISH GRAND PRIX, 24 April, Jarama 2.058m/3.312k

The Australian flag flew proudly over Jarama once again. Two years ago Wayne Gardner won his first ever grand prix at the track in the hot, dusty northern outskirts of Madrid. This time his compatriot Kevin Magee broke his grand prix duck with an equally impressive victory, riding the Team Roberts Lucky Strike Yamaha. It was also another triumph for the sport as a whole: a crowd of over 100,000 watched the third winner of the three opening 500cc rounds, celebrating with the usual firecrackers when Spaniard Sito Pons opened up a 19-point lead in the 250cc championship with a start-to-finish victory. Jorge Martinez opened his and Derbi's account with a popular win in the new single-cylinder 125cc class. To the disappointment of his vast following he could not repeat his success in the 80cc race. However, his great rival, former world champion Stefan Dorflinger, secured a real morale-boosting victory for the Krauser team.

The pressure really told on the top 500cc men during practice, with Gardner heading an impressive list of fallers. Some blamed the cold weather, others the surface after a recent car race. The fact that it was the first European grand prix of the season, and that there were more works bikes on the grid than ever before, had more to do with it. Gardner crashed on the Saturday in a hectic two days of official practice rounds on the demanding 2.05-mile circuit. Christian Sarron crashed twice, while Niall Mackenzie, Rob McElnea, Ron Haslam, Kevin Schwantz and Tadahiko Taira all tested the strength of the Jarama tarmac. When the dust settled Taira was the only rider to miss the race and Magee was in pole on the front row.

Just half a second covered that front row, which consisted of Magee, Eddie Lawson, Sarron, Gardner and Wayne Rainey. The start of the 37-lap race was a shambles with Lawson, riding the Marlboro Yamaha, getting a flyer; but, despite an official protest from Honda after the race, he was not penalised. By the end of the first lap he had built up a 100-yard lead, with Pier-Francesco Chili, Sarron and Gardner giving chase. Magee had been caught out when the lights changed but was up in fourth place, with Mackenzie down in tenth after being boxed in on the first bend. Sarron, racing on form, was second a lap later, holding the Rothmans Honda of Gardner at bay for seven laps. Once past the Frenchman, Gardner was able to set his sights on Lawson.

Magee looked threatening and pushed Sarron back into fourth position. The champion managed to close on Lawson but then dramatically dropped back, suffering from a brake problem. Within a couple of laps Magee had passed him and Gardner dug in to hang onto third place and 15 championship points. Three laps later Magee, who had finished third at Jarama last year, closed onto Lawson's back wheel. For the next 13 laps he tried to pass but the experienced Lawson held him at bay. With 12 laps remaining he finally managed to squeeze the Lucky Strike Yamaha in front, round the back end of the circuit. Lawson was far from finished, however, and within two laps he was back in front after diving inside Magee at the end of the start-and-finish straight. Battle lines were drawn, with the lead changing three times in the next two corners.

Lapped backmarkers were beginning to get in the way. Six laps from the finish Magee took advantage of a backmarker to grab the lead and Lawson was having to work very hard to stay with the Australian. They were almost side by side as they started the dramatic last lap in which those dreaded backmarkers again played their part. Magee, capitalising on the situation, managed to squeeze past Shunji Yatsushiro and Ron Haslam while Lawson was held up – his chance had gone. Despite finishing second he increased his championship lead to three points over Gardner, who held onto third place. Sarron pushed him back to fourth for one lap but the Frenchman could not sustain the pressure. He finished fourth and Mackenzie fifth, which enabled him to hang onto third place in the championship. Rainey continued with great determination, despite problems with his Yamaha, and limped home a lonely sixth. The early pacesetter, Chili, was seventh and Didier de Radigues eighth. Haslam looked set for ninth until an ignition problem on the last lap pushed him back into tenth position behind Yatsushiro. It was a bad day for the Pepsi Suzuki team, with Schwantz retiring early on in the race with carburation problems and McElnea limping home 12th.

The first bend of the 31-lap 250cc race provided contrasting fortunes for two of Spain's top riders. Carlos Cardus was seriously injured when he fell from his Ducados Honda and lost his crash helmet. He was rushed to hospital with a fractured skull but happily recovered to return to grand prix racing later in the year. In the confusion Sito Pons, riding the Campsa NSR Honda, opened up a massive gap over the rest of field. By the second lap he was five seconds in front of world champion Toni Mang, Jacques Cornu, Reinhold Roth and Japanese ace, Masahiro Shimizu, who was making a welcome first appearance of the season. They were soon joined by Spaniard Juan Garriga, riding the Ducados Yamaha. But on the eighth lap another crash caused problems. Mang was highsided from his Rothmans Honda as he accelerated from the right-hander after the start-and-finish straight. He was unhurt and, while the others hesitated, Garriga closed the gap in dramatic fashion. Within a lap he had passed the Hondas of Cornu and Shimizu, and two laps later he swooped past Roth into second place.

Garriga soon realised he had little chance of catching Pons, and had to ride very hard to hang onto second place from the impressive young Frenchman Jean-Phillipe Ruggia, who was cutting through the field after a bad start on his Gauloises Yamaha. He displayed no signs of being overawed by the likes of Cornu, Roth or Shimizu as he charged into third place and closed on Garriga; he also showed that he has a sensible head on his young shoulders when his rear tyre started to slide. He settled down and slowed up to grab his first, but surely not last, place on a grand prix rostrum after finishing third behind the jubilant Spanish duo at the front. Not so happy were Frenchman Dominique Sarron, who crashed the Rothmans Honda, and Italian Loris Reggiani, who was flying on the Aprilia when it stopped with a holed piston. Cornu fought off fellow Honda men Shimizu and Roth for fourth spot. Luca Cadalora on his Marlboro Yamaha was seventh, ahead of a tremendous battle for eighth place. In a dash for the line Scotsman Donnie McLeod, riding Dr Joe Ehrlich's 7-Up EMC, got his first points of the season after fighting off the challenges of Martin Wimmer and Manfred Herweh.

Martinez has always been the darling of the Jarama crowd and they certainly celebrated his victory in the 28-lap 125cc race, especially since he was riding the all-red Spanish-built Derbi machine. He fought off the early challenge of hard-riding Italian Ezio Gianola and his RS Honda. Although his silencer fell apart he finished with nearly 18 seconds to spare. Behind him it was a very different story. Despite slowing because of gearbox problems, Gianola held onto second ahead of a superb six-rider battle for third. However, with three-quarters of the distance covered, his gear pedal broke off, leaving the tiny Honda stuck in fourth gear. He kept slipping the clutch in a desperate bid to stay in contention but on the last lap the Honda gave up the ghost. Spaniard Julian Miralles broke clear of the chasing group to clinch second place on his Honda, with Italian Gaston Grassetti pushing world champion Fausto Gresini to an unaccustomed fourth place on the single-cylinder Garelli.

The celebrating fans expected, or even demanded, a repeat performance by Martinez in the 22-lap 80cc race. However, their party was spoilt by former world champion Stefan Dorflinger of Switzerland. He made a slow start on the works Krauser but when Martinez slowed with carburation problems he started to fly. He grabbed the lead halfway through the race only to see Martinez fight back and go in front. Dorflinger put an end to the premature celebrations by taking the lead again a lap later. He pulled away to win by nearly five seconds from Martinez, with the Derbis of Alex Crivelle and Manuel Herreros third and fourth respectively.

Results

500cc (37 laps, 76.15m/122.54k)	**m**	**s**	**mph**	**kmh**
1 K. Magee, Australia *(Yamaha)*	54	52.47	83.26	133.991
2 E. Lawson, USA *(Yamaha)*	54	53.00	83.25	133.970
3 W. Gardner, Australia *(Honda)*	55	04.10	82.97	133.520
4 C. Sarron, France *(Yamaha)*	55	09.92	82.82	133.285
5 N. Mackenzie, GB *(Honda)*	55	19.46	82.58	132.902
6 W. Rainey, USA *(Yamaha)*	55	32.91	82.26	132.393
7 P. Chili, Italy *(Honda)*	56	04.55	81.48	131.121
8 D. de Radigues, Belgium *(Yamaha)*	56	05.37	81.45	131.089

36 laps: 9 S. Yatsushiro, Japan *(Honda)*; 10 R. Haslam, GB *(Elf-Honda)*; 11 R. Roche, France *(Cagiva)*; 12 R. McElnea, GB *(Suzuki)*; 13 A. Valesi, Italy *(Honda)*; 14 D. Amatriain, Spain *(Honda)*; 15 B. Kneubuhler, Switzerland *(Honda)*. *35 laps:* 16 S. Manley, GB *(Suzuki)*; 17 R. Nicotte, France *(Honda)*; 18 F. Barchitta, San Marino *(Honda)*; 19 N. Schmassman, Switzerland *(Honda)*; 20 J. Demierre, Switzerland *(Suzuki)*. *34 laps:* 21 M. Duyzers, Holland *(Honda)*; 22 C. Burki, Switzerland *(Honda)*.

Fastest lap: K. Magee, Australia *(Yamaha)*, 1m 28.09s, 84.11mph/135.351kmh.

Record lap: W. Gardner, Australia *(Honda)*, 1m 27.99s, 84.20mph/135.50kmh (1987).

World Championship positions: 1 E. Lawson, 52 points; 2 W. Gardner, 49; 3 N. Mackenzie, 39; 4 W. Rainey, 33; 5 K. Schwantz and C. Sarron both 31; 7 K. Magee, 29; 8 D. de Radigues, 23; 9 R. Haslam, 19; 10 S. Yatsushiro, 13.

Practice leaderboard: 1 K. Magee, Australia *(Yamaha)*, 1m 27.14s; 2 E. Lawson, USA *(Yamaha)*, 1m 27.35s; 3 C. Sarron, France *(Yamaha)*, 1m 27.62s; 4 W. Gardner, Australia *(Honda)*, 1m 27.69s; 5 W. Rainey, USA *(Yamaha)*, 1m 27.75s; 6 K. Schwantz, USA *(Suzuki)*; 1m 28.08s; 7 N. Mackenzie, GB *(Honda)*, 1m 28.12s; 8 D. de Radigues, Belgium *(Yamaha)*, 1m 28.57s; 9 T. Taira, Japan *(Yamaha)*, 1m 28.65s; 10 P. Chili, Italy *(Honda)*, 1m 28.83s; 11 M. Baldwin, USA *(Honda)*, 1m 29.27s; 12 S. Yatsushiro, Japan *(Yamaha)*, 1m 29.64s; 13 R. Haslam, GB *(Elf-Honda)*, 1m 29.81s; 14 R. McElnea,

GB *(Suzuki)*, 1m 29.84s; 15 G. Reiner, W. Germany *(Honda)*, 1m 30.43s; 16 D. Amatriain, Spain *(Honda)*, 1m 30.69s; 17 A. Valesi, Italy *(Honda)*, 1m 30.94s; 18 R. Roche, France *(Cagiva)*, 1m 31.10s; 19 W. von Muralt, Switzerland *(Suzuki)*, 1m 31.14s; 20 B. Kneubuhler, Switzerland *(Honda)*, 1m 31.68s.

The family man – Magee relaxes with son Jake.

250cc (31 laps, 63.80m/102.673k)		**m**	**s**	**mph**	**kmh**
1	S. Pons, Spain *(Honda)*	46	59.80	81.45	131.081
2	J. Garriga, Spain *(Yamaha)*	47	07.24	81.23	130.736
3	J. Ruggia, France *(Yamaha)*	47	09.11	81.18	130.650
4	J. Cornu, Switzerland *(Honda)*	47	18.65	80.91	130.211
5	M. Shimizu, Japan *(Honda)*	47	26.33	80.69	129.860
6	R. Roth, W. Germany *(Honda)*	47	28.94	80.61	129.741
7	L. Cadalora, Italy *(Yamaha)*	47	36.48	80.40	129.398
8	D. McLeod, GB *(EMC)*	47	42.07	80.24	129.146
9	M. Wimmer, W. Germany *(Yamaha)*	47	42.59	80.23	129.122
10	M. Herweh, W. Germany *(Yamaha)*	47	43.37	80.21	129.087

11 A. Auinger, Austria *(Aprilia)*; 12 J. Mattioli, France *(Yamaha)*; 13 M. Vitali, Italy *(Yamaha)*; 14 A. Puig, Spain *(Honda)*; 15 H. Eckl, W. Germany *(Honda)*; 16 S. Caracchi,
San Marino *(Honda)*; 17 T. Rapicault, France *(Fior)*; 18 X. Cardelus, Andorra *(Yamaha)*; 19 K. Mitchell, GB *(Yamaha)*; 20 A. Bronec, France *(Honda)*; 21 G. Bertin, France *(Yamaha)*. *30 laps*: 22 P. van den Goorbergh, Holland *(Honda)*; 23 G. Cowan, Ireland *(Yamaha)*.

Record lap: S. Pons, Spain *(Honda)*, 1m 30.12s, 82.20mph/132.293kmh.
Old record: J. Garriga, Spain *(Yamaha)*, 1m 30.41s, 81.94mph/131.874kmh (1987).

World Championship positions: 1 S. Pons, 54 points; 2 J. Cornu, 35; J. Garriga, 33; 4. A. Mang, 28; 5 J. Ruggia, 27; 6 J. Kocinski, 24; 7 J. Filice, 20; 8 L. Cadalora, 19; 9 M. Kobayashi and D. Sarron both 15.

Practice leaderboard: 1 C. Cardus, Spain *(Honda)*, 1m 29.50s; 2 S. Pons, Spain *(Honda)*, 1m 29.62s; 3 J. Cornu, Switzerland *(Honda)*, 1m 29.77s; 4 J. Garriga, Spain *(Yamaha)*, 1m 29.77s; 5 A. Mang, W. Germany *(Honda)*, 1m 29.79s; 6 C. Lavado, Venezuela *(Yamaha)*, 1m 29.95s; 7 R. Roth, W. Germany *(Honda)*, 1m 29.95s; 8 D. Sarron, France *(Honda)*, 1m 30.13s; 9 L. Reggiani, Italy *(Aprilia)*, 1m 30.17s; 10 J. Balde, France *(Rotax)*, 1m 30.19s; 11 J. Ruggia, France *(Yamaha)*, 1m 30.57s; 12 L. Cadalora, Italy *(Yamaha)*, 1m 30.61s; 13 M. Herweh, W. Germany *(Yamaha)*, 1m 30.68s; 14 D. McLeod, GB *(EMC)*, 1m 30.73s; 15 J. Mattioli, France *(Diamont)*, 1m 30.92s; 16 M. Wimmer, W. Germany *(Yamaha)*, 1m 31.04s; 17 M. Shimizu, Japan *(Honda)*, 1m 31.28s; 18 B. Casanova, Italy *(Aprilia)*, 1m 31.29s; 19 I. Palazzese, Venezuela *(Yamaha)*, 1m 31.36s; 20 X. Cardelus, Andorra *(Yamaha)*, 1m 31.52s.

125cc (28 laps, 57.62m/92.736k)		**m**	**s**	**mph**	**kmh**
1	J. Martinez, Spain *(Derbi)*	45	20.86	76.24	122.701
2	J. Miralles, Spain *(Honda)*	45	38.26	75.76	121.922
3	G. Grassetti, Italy *(Honda)*	45	40.75	75.69	121.811
4	F. Gresini, Italy *(Garelli)*	45	40.98	75.68	121.800
5	A. Stadler, W. Germany *(Honda)*	45	42.90	75.63	121.715
6	G. Waibel, W. Germany *(Honda)*	45	56.66	75.26	121.108
7	H. Unemoto, Japan *(Honda)*	45	56.80	75.25	121.101
8	L. Pietroniro, Belgium *(Honda)*	45	59.66	75.17	120.976
9	T. Koji, Japan *(Honda)*	45	59.84	75.16	120.968
10	H. Spaan, Holland *(Honda)*	46	00.46	74.85	120.464

11 H. Luthi, Switzerland *(Honda)*; 12 M. Hernandez, Spain *(Honda)*; 13 S. Prein, W. Germany *(Honda)*; 14 S. Dorflinger, Switzerland *(Honda)*; 15 P. Bordes, France *(Honda)*; 16 J. Bolart, Spain *(Cobas)*; 17 J. Fischer, Austria *(Rotax)*; 18 C. Galatowicz, GB *(Honda)*. *27 laps*: 19 C. Macciotta, Italy *(Honda)*; 20 B. Hassaine, Tunisia *(Honda)*; 21 T. Feuz, Switzerland *(Rotax)*; 22 R. Appleyard, GB *(Honda)*; 23 S. Bianchi, Italy *(Cordati)*; 24 P. Serra, France *(Honda)*; 25 K. Kindle, W. Germany *(Honda)*.

Fastest lap: J. Martinez, Spain *(Derbi)*, 1m 35.67s, 77.44mph/124.630kmh.

Record lap: A Auinger *(MBA)*, 1m 33.26s, 79.44mph/127.853kmh (1987).

World Championship positions: 1 J. Martinez, 20 points; 2 J. Miralles, 17; 3 G. Grassetti, 15; 4 F. Gresini, 13; 5 A. Stadler, 11; 6 G. Waibel, 10; 7 H. Unemoto, 9; 8 L. Pietroniro, 8; 9 T. Koji, 7; 10 H. Spaan, 6.

Practice leaderboard: 1 J. Martinez, Spain *(Derbi)*, 1m 35.55s; 2 E. Gianola, Italy *(Honda)*, 1m 36.12s; 3 J. Wickstrom, Finland *(Honda)*, 1m 36.68s; 4 F. Gresini, Italy

(Garelli), 1m 36.70s; 5 J. Miralles, Spain *(Derbi)*, 1m 36.97s; 6 G. Grassetti, Italy *(Honda)*, 1m 37.13s; 7 L. Reyes, Spain *(Garelli)*, 1m 37.51s; 8 H. Spaan, Holland *(Honda)*, 1m 37.54s; 9 L. Pietroniro, Belgium *(Honda)*, 1m 37.57s; 10 S. Dorflinger, Switzerland *(Honda)*, 1m 37.67s; 11 A. Stadler, W. Germany *(Honda)*, 1m 37.70s; 12 T. Koji, Japan *(Honda)*, 1m 37.73s; 13 G. Waibel, W. Germany *(Honda)*, 1m 37.85s; 14 R. Roses, Spain *(Metrakit)*, 1m 37.94s; 15 S. Prein, W. Germany *(Honda)*, 1m 38.01s; 16 M. Leitner, Austria *(Honda)*, 1m 38.03s; 17 H. Unemoto, Japan *(Honda)*, 1m 38.11s; 18 E. Kytola, Finland *(Honda)*, 1m 38.26s; 19 M. Herreros, Spain *(Derbi)*, 1m 38.48s; 20 J. Selini, France *(Honda)*, 1m 38.54s.

80cc (22 laps, 45.28m/72.864k)		**m**	**s**	**mph**	**kmh**
1	S. Dorflinger, Switzerland *(Krauser)*	36	58.81	73.46	118.223
2	J. Martinez, Spain *(Derbi)*	37	03.93	73.29	117.950
3	A. Criville, Spain *(Derbi)*	37	05.85	73.22	117.849
4	M. Herreros, Spain *(Derbi)*	37	20.34	72.75	117.086
5	P. Ottl, W. Germany *(Krauser)*	37	44.01	71.99	115.862
6	H. Torrontegui, Spain *(Autisa)*	37	44.39	71.98	115.843
7	K. Juhasz, Hungary *(Krauser)*	37	50.42	71.79	115.535
8	B. Nikolov, Bulgaria *(Krauser)*	38	20.15	70.86	114.042
9	S. Julin, Belgium *(Casal)*	38	33.25	70.46	113.396
10	I. McConnachie, GB *(Autisa)*	38	33.52	70.45	113.382

21 laps: 11 J. van Dongen, Holland *(Casal)*; 12 G. Schirnhofer, W. Germany *(Krauser)*; 13 J. Bernard, Belgium *(Fantic)*; 14 H. Abold, W. Germany *(Krauser)*; 15 X. Arumi, Spain *(Krauser)*; 16 R. Koster, Switzerland *(LCR)*; 17 A. Nijenhuis, Holland *(Casal)*; 18 A. Sanchez, Spain *(Cobas)*; 19 J. Cabanes, Spain *(Autisa)*; 20 J. Saez, Spain *(Autisa)*. *20 laps:* 21 J. Esteve, Spain *(Autisa)*; 22 P. Desmet, France *(Huvo)*; 23 D. Batchelor, GB *(Krauser)*.

Fastest lap: A. Criville, Spain *(Derbi)*, 1m 38.66s, 75.09mph/120.843kmh.

Record lap: J. Martinez, Spain *(Derbi)*, 1m 37.52s, 75.97mph/122.256kmh (1987).

World Championship positions: 1 S. Dorflinger, 20 points; 2 J. Martinez, 17; 3 A. Criville, 15; 4 M. Herreros, 13; 5 P. Ottl, 11; 6 H. Torrontegui, 10; 7 K. Juhasz, 9; 8 B. Nikolov, 8; 9 S. Julin, 7; 10 I. McConnachie, 6.

Practice leaderboard: 1 J. Martinez, Spain *(Derbi)*, 1m 38.32s; 2 S. Dorflinger, Switzerland *(Krauser)*, 1m 39.23s; 3 K. Juhasz, Hungary *(Krauser)*, 1m 40.56s; 4 A. Criville, Spain *(Derbi)*, 1m 40.83s; 5 H. Torrontegui, Spain *(Autisa)*, 1m 40.83s; 6 M. Herreros, Spain *(Derbi)*, 1m 41.05s; 7 P. Ottl, W. Germany *(Krauser)*, 1m 42.05s; 8 H. Abold, W. Germany *(Krauser)*, 1m 43.41s; 9 G. Ascareggi, Italy *(BBFT)*, 1m 43.46s; 10 I. McConnachie, GB *(Autisa)*, 1m 43.96s; 11 B. Nikolov, Bulgaria *(Krauser)*, 1m 44.14s; 12 G. Gnani, Italy *(Gnani)*, 1m 44.31s; 13 G. Schirnhofer, W. Germany *(Krauser)*, 1m 44.70s; 14 S. Julin, Belgium *(Casal)*, 1m 44.88s; 15 J. van Dongen, Holland *(Casal)*, 1m 44.91s; 16 R. Dunki, Switzerland *(Krauser)*, 1m 45.02s; 17 J. Mariano, Spain *(Cobas)*, 1m 45.80s; 18 R. Koster, Switzerland *(LCR)*, 1m 45.81s; 19 P. Priori, Italy *(Krauser)*, 1m 46.12s; 20 J. Bernard, Belgium *(Fantic)*, 1m 46.17s.

PORTUGUESE GRAND PRIX, 1 May, Jerez 2.621m/4.218k

Former world champions Eddie Lawson and Rolf Biland reaped a healthy harvest in the sherry-producing capital of Jerez at the grand prix nobody knew what to call. Originally it was going to be the Portuguese Grand Prix at Estoril, but the circuit was not up to the required safety standards. It was then switched to Jerez in southern Spain, but the Portuguese Government were not happy about the adverse publicity they had received. They banned their federation putting their name to the race. In the end it was sold to the highest bidder and was officially tagged the Gran Premio Expo 92. Happily, events on the tight 2.62-mile circuit were less confusing. The 40,000 crowd enthused over the performances of Spanish heroes Juan Garriga in the crash-littered 250cc race and Jorge Martinez in a superb 80cc event.

Last year the 500cc race at Jerez proved a significant pointer to the remainder of the season, with Wayne Gardner a convincing winner over Lawson. Twelve months on it provided an equally important pointer, with the roles very firmly reversed in favour of the Marlboro Yamaha rider. He rode a superb race to secure his second grand prix victory of the season, while Gardner realised something that he had suspected at Jarama and Laguna Seca – that Honda had made a dreadful mistake. He limped home in fifth place after a frightening ride on the ill-handling NSR Rothmans Honda and dropped 12 points behind Lawson in the championship table.

The writing was on the wall for the world champion after practice. He scraped on to the front row of the grid in fifth place behind the daunting Yamaha foursome of Lawson, Lucky Strike team-mates Wayne Rainey and Kevin Magee, and Frenchman Christian Sarron. Fresh from their success the previous week the Lucky Strike Yamaha team and manager Kenny Roberts were really fired up. Rainey barged fellow Californian Lawson out of the way at the first bend to snatch the lead. Chased by Pepsi Suzuki-mounted Kevin Schwantz, Lawson, Sarron, Magee, Didier de Radigues and Gardner, he fought his way clear of the pack. Schwantz looked very impressive but retired on the sixth lap with flooded carburettors. Magee moved into second place, with Lawson having problems shaking off a very determined Sarron. A long way back, and right out of contention, Gardner was having to use all the track to stay in front of de Radigues in a private battle for fifth.

With half of the 29-lap race completed Rainey had opened up a three-second lead over Magee and was seriously considering how to celebrate his first grand prix victory. Sarron pushed Lawson, who was having front tyre problems, down to fourth and the pattern looked set for Team Roberts. Lawson had different ideas and raced past Sarron. With less petrol in his tank and the tyre really warm he was getting the grip his speed demanded. The storm cones were flying for the two at the front.

That storm turned into a hurricane when their tyres started to go off. After a couple of bad slides Rainey knew he would have to slow the pace and Lawson, for the first time, got the scent of victory in his nostrils. He relegated the sliding Magee to third with nine laps remaining and set after his prey.

The former champion slashed Rainey's lead by three seconds in just four laps and then waited for his moment. Rainey blocked him all the way, but with just under two laps remaining he picked his spot. There was nothing Rainey could do but watch him disappear and reflect on how close he had come to victory. His time will come.

At the flag Lawson, with nearly a two-second margin, collected 20 points, a new lap record and a real psychological advantage over Gardner. Behind Rainey, Magee grabbed third place from Sarron on the last corner after the Frenchman had led him for the last two laps. Over 20 seconds behind him came a totally detuned Gardner. He finally got the better of the spirited de Radigues but realised, with wheel spin and sliding making life intolerable, that even at this early stage his championship chances were slim. Niall Mackenzie and Rob McElnea finished in seventh and eighth places respectively, with Steve Manley in 13th place gaining his first world championship points on his ageing Suzuki. Ron Haslam made a good start on the Elf 5 but retired, while lying in third place on the first lap, when the rear brake locked solid.

You would have thought a good shower of rain would have suited Yorkshiremen Steven Webster and Tony Hewitt at the first defence of their world sidecar title. Unfortunately nothing could have been further from the truth. Former world champions Rolf Biland and Kurth Waltisperg had set the paddock buzzing by lapping faster than the solos during practice on their Krauser-powered LCR outfit. Webster qualified second but two seconds behind. However, he knew Biland would not be able to produce that sort of pace on his race tyres. As soon as the race started the drizzle began to fall, and when Biland spun off on the second lap prospects looked good for the champions. The drizzle then turned into a torrential downpour. Webster was leading through the spray after four laps but then stuck up his hand to halt the proceedings. It was too dangerous and safety won the day. Biland got back on the track. He was 9.4 seconds down on time to the Yorkshire pair as they lined up for the 19-lap second leg, with the overall winner coming from the combined times of both races. Webster, looking at the clearing clouds, gambled on a hard rear tyre on his Krauser/LCR, hoping the track would dry quickly. It proved a big mistake, with the track drying only in the last few laps. Until then he could only slip and slide his way round as Biland, using soft wet tyres, decimated that 9.4-second advantage in just five laps. He was chased hard by former champions, the Dutch pair Egbert Streuer and Bernard Schnieders, who were also using soft wet tyres on their Yamaha LCR. He held firm to become the overall winner by over two seconds from Streuer, with Webster a relieved third. He had actually dropped to fourth in the early stages of the second leg behind Markus and Urs Egloff and Barry Brindley and Graeme Rose. The Egloffs retired with a water-logged engine and Brindley slowed with a misfire to push him back to fourth. Despite a spin on the last lap Brindley finished a superb fourth ahead of the French pair of Alain Michel and Jean-Marc Fresc. Steve Abbott and Shaun Smith were sixth, with veteran Derek Jones and passenger Peter Brown a bored eighth.

Juan Garriga took full advantage of others' misfortunes to score his first grand prix victory in the dramatic 25-lap encounter that was a total disaster for many of the top men.

The crashes did not even wait for the race to start. Former world champion Carlos Lavado crashed his HB Yamaha on the warm-up lap after qualifying in pole position. On the first lap of the race proper, championship leader Sito Pons had a rush of blood to his head and crashed his Campsa NS Honda. He tried to ride up the inside of countryman Alberto Puig after just half a lap. He didn't make it and saw his 19-point championship lead slashed to a single point. On the second lap on the fast right-hander behind the pits there was a fearful collision between Italians Loris Reggiani and Luca Cadalora. Both men and their respective Aprilia and Marlboro Yamaha machines were flung up the track but they were not seriously injured.

Garriga, riding the Ducados Yamaha, had been ahead of the crashes although he was given a tough time at the front by the impressive Japanese debutant Masahiro Shimizu. Riding the NS Honda he chased hard for the opening five laps but then settled into a safe second place ahead of a tremendous scrap for third place. 34-year-old Jacques Cornu, riding the Parisienne Honda, eventually fought off the combined French challenge of Dominique Sarron and Jean-Phillipe Ruggia in the best battle of the race. They constantly swapped positions, with Ruggia doing well to stick with the two Hondas. At the finish he had to settle for fifth, with Sarron almost catching Cornu on the line. World champion Toni Mang was a disappointing seventh behind his great rival Reinhold Roth, while Puig jumped back on his Honda after his clash with Pons to finish a brave eighth. Scotsman Donnie McLeod, riding his 7-Up EMC, picked up four hard-earned points in 12th place.

World champion Martinez was given a torrid time in a superb 18-lap 80cc race by his fellow countryman and teammates. The antics of the Derbi trio – Martinez, Manuel Herreros and Alex Criville – kept the home crowd on their feet. Just half a second separated them in a breathtaking finish, with Martinez grabbing the lead in the championship after his morale-boosting win. Former champion Stefan Dorflinger, his conqueror at Jarama, made another appalling start and, despite setting the fastest lap, had to settle for fourth place behind the Derbi trio.

Results

500cc (29 laps, 76.01m/122.321k)	**m**	**s**	**mph**	**kmh**
1 E. Lawson, USA *(Yamaha)*	53	47.99	84.77	136.419
2 W. Rainey, USA *(Yamaha)*	53	49.63	84.72	136.350
3 K. Magee, Australia *(Yamaha)*	53	55.66	84.57	136.096
4 C. Sarron, France *(Yamaha)*	53	55.78	84.56	136.091
5 W. Gardner, Australia *(Honda)*	54	16.62	84.02	135.220
6 D. de Radigues, Belgium *(Yamaha)*	54	18.51	83.97	135.141
7 N. Mackenzie, GB *(Honda)*	55	00.02	82.92	133.441
8 R. McElnea, GB *(Suzuki)*	55	25.41	82.28	132.423

28 laps: 9 M. Papa, Italy *(Honda)*; 10 A. Valesi, Italy *(Honda)*; 11 D. Amatriain, Spain *(Honda)*; 12 S. Manley, GB *(Suzuki)*; 13 R. Nicotte, France *(Honda)*; *27 laps:* 14 B. Kneubuhler, Switzerland *(Honda)*; 15 M. Duyzers, Holland *(Honda)*; 16 N. Schmassmann, Switzerland *(Honda)*; 17 J. Doppler, Austria *(Honda)*; 18 I. Pratt, GB *(Suzuki)*.

Record lap: E. Lawson, USA *(Yamaha)*, 1m 49.29s, 86.33mph/138.940kmh.
Old record: W. Gardner, Australia *(Honda)*, 1m 51.08s, 84.94mph/136.703kmh (1987).

World Championship positions: 1 E. Lawson, 72 points; 2 W. Gardner, 60; 3 W. Rainey, 50; 4 N. Mackenzie, 48; 5 C. Sarron and K. Magee both 44; 7 D. de Radigues, 33; 8 K. Schwantz, 31; 9 R. Haslam and R. McElnea both 19.

Lawson storms past Sarron on his way to his late victory.

Practice leaderboard: 1 E. Lawson, USA *(Yamaha)*, 1m 50.12s; 2 W. Rainey, USA *(Yamaha)*, 1m 50.23s; 3 K. Magee, Australia *(Yamaha)*, 1m 50.29s; 4 C. Sarron, France *(Yamaha)*, 1m 50.52s; 5 W. Gardner, Australia *(Honda)*, 1m 50.58s; 6 K. Schwantz, USA *(Suzuki)*, 1m 50.95s; 7 N. Mackenzie, GB *(Honda)*, 1m 51.25s; 8 D. de Radigues, Belgium *(Yamaha)*, 1m 51.56s; 9 R. Haslam, GB *(Elf-Honda)*, 1m 51.86s; 10 P. Chili, Italy *(Honda)*, 1m 52.11s; 11 R. McElnea, GB *(Suzuki)*, 1m 52.29s; 12 S. Yatsushiro, Japan *(Honda)*, 1m 52.64s; 13 M. Papa, Italy *(Honda)*, 1m 53.69s; 14 A. Valesi, Italy *(Honda)*, 1m 55.35s; 15 F. Barchitta, San Marino *(Honda)*; 1m 55.40s; 16 D. Amatriain, Spain *(Honda)*, 1m 55.62s; 17 M. Gentile, Switzerland *(Fior)*, 1m 55.67s; 18 R. Roche, France *(Cagiva)*, 1m 55.68s; 19 R. Nicotte, France *(Honda)*, 1m 55.94s; 20 E. Laycock, Ireland *(Honda)*, 1m 56.32s.

250cc (25 laps, 65.52m/105.449k)	**m s**	**mph**	**kmh**
1 J. Garriga, Spain *(Yamaha)*	47 22.77	82.98	133.534
2 H. Shimizu, Japan *(Honda)*	47 28.38	82.82	133.276
3 J. Cornu, Switzerland *(Honda)*	47 31.51	82.72	133.129
4 D. Sarron, France *(Honda)*	47 31.96	82.71	133.108
5 J. Ruggia, France *(Yamaha)*	47 33.17	82.67	133.052
6 R. Roth, W. Germany *(Honda)*	47 46.95	82.28	132.412
7 A. Mang, W. Germany *(Honda)*	47 48.49	82.23	132.341
8 A. Puig, Spain *(Honda)*	48 01.06	81.87	131.764
9 J. Mattioli, France *(Yamaha)*	48 02.11	81.84	131.716
10 M. Herweh, W. Germany *(Yamaha)*	48 06.76	81.71	131.504

11 S. Caracchi, San Marino *(Honda)*; 12 D. McLeod, GB *(EMC)*; 13 U. Luzi, Switzerland *(Honda)*; 14 H. Eckl, W. Germany *(Aprilia)*; 15 B. Casanova, Italy *(Aprilia)*; 16 T. Rapicault, France *(Rotax)*; 17 M. Vitali, Italy *(Aprilia)*; 18 G. Cowan, Ireland *(Yamaha)*; 19 B. Bonhuil, France *(Honda)*; 20 E. Neumair, Austria *(Rotax)*; 21 I. Palazzese, Venezuela *(Yamaha)*; 22 B. Haenggeli, Switzerland *(Honda)*; 23 J. Schmid, W. Germany *(Honda)*; 24 R. Delaby, Luxembourg *(Yamaha)*; 25 J. Lopez, Spain *(Honda)*.

Record lap: J. Garriga, Spain *(Yamaha)*, 1m 51.65s, 84.51mph/136.00kmh.
Old record: M. Wimmer, W. Germany *(Yamaha)*, 1m 53.08s, 83.44mph/132.284kmh (1987).

World Championship positions: 1 S. Pons, 54 points; 2 J. Garriga, 53; 3 J. Cornu, 50; 4 J. Ruggia, 38; 5 A. Mang, 31; 6 D. Sarron and H. Shimizu both 28; 8 R. Roth, 27; 9 J. Kocinski, 24; 10 J. Filice, 20.

Practice leaderboard: 1 C. Lavado, Venezuela *(Yamaha)*, 1m 51.57s; 2 L. Cadalora, Italy *(Yamaha)*, 1m 51.74s; 3 S. Pons, Spain *(Honda)*, 1m 51.77s; 4 J. Garriga, Spain *(Yamaha)*, 1m 51.93s; 5 D. Sarron, France *(Honda)*, 1m 52.35s; 6 J. Ruggia, France *(Yamaha)*, 1m 52.77s; 7 J. Cornu, Switzerland *(Honda)*, 1m 52.86s; 8 L. Reggiani, Italy *(Aprilia)*, 1m 52.90s; 9 M. Shimizu, Japan *(Honda)*, 1m 53.20s; 10 M. Herweh, W. Germany *(Yamaha)*, 1m 53.38s; 11 A. Puig, Spain *(Honda)*, 1m 53.52s; 12 R. Roth, W. Germany *(Honda)*, 1m 53.53s; 13 A. Mang, W. Germany *(Honda)*, 1m 53.60s; 14 J. Mattioli, France *(Yamaha)*, 1m 53.62s; 15 H. Eckl, W. Germany *(Aprilia)*, 1m 53.69s; 16 U. Luzi, Switzerland *(Honda)*, 1m 53.76s; 17 M. Vitali, Italy *(Aprilia)*, 1m 53.80s; 18 J. Balde, France *(Rotax)*, 1m 53.85s; 19 M. Wimmer, W. Germany *(Yamaha)*, 1m 54.01s; 20 D. McLeod, GB *(EMC)*, 1m 54.02s.

80cc (18 laps, 47.18m/79.92k)	**m s**	**mph**	**kmh**
1 J. Martinez, Spain *(Derbi)*	37 36.39	75.27	121.134
2 M. Herreros, Spain *(Derbi)*	37 36.64	75.26	121.120
3 A. Criville, Spain *(Derbi)*	37 36.92	75.25	121.105
4 S. Dorflinger, Switzerland *(Krauser)*	37 57.62	74.56	120.005
5 P. Ottl, W. Germany *(Krauser)*	38 10.99	74.13	119.304

6	G. Ascareggi, Italy *(BGFT)*	38 18.49	73.89	118.915
7	G. Gnani, Italy *(Krauser)*	38 22.70	73.75	118.698
8	B. Nikolov, Bulgaria *(Krauser)*	38 23.07	73.74	118.679
9	K. Juhasz, Hungary *(Krauser)*	38 43.70	73.09	117.625
10	J. van Dongen, Holland *(Casal)*	38 47.40	72.97	117.438

11 R. Dunki, Switzerland *(Krauser)*; 12 J. Bernard, Belgium *(Fantic)*; 13 G. Schirnhofer, W. Germany *(Krauser)*; 14 J. Arumi, Spain *(Krauser)*; 15 J. Mariano, Spain *(Cobas)*; 16 I. McConnachie, GB *(Autisa)*. *17 laps:* 17 R. Koster, Switzerland *(Casal)*; 18 E. Palencia, Spain *(Arbizu)*; 19 J. Debon, Spain *(Huvo)*; 20 P. Desmet, France *(Huvo)*; 21 J. Gali, Spain *(Krauser)*; 22 A. Nijenhuis, Holland *(Casal)*; 23 H. Paschen, W. Germany *(Casal)*; 24 T. Engl, W. Germany *(Krauser)*.

Fastest lap: S. Dorflinger, Switzerland *(Krauser)*, 2m 03.41s, 76.46mph/123.043kmh.

Record lap: J. Martinez, Spain *(Derbi)* 2m 02.50s, 77.03mph/123.958kmh (1987).

World Championship positions: 1 J. Martinez, 37 points; 2 S. Dorflinger, 33; 3 A. Criville and M. Herreros both 30; 5 P. Ottl, 22; 6 K. Juhasz and B. Nikolov both 16; 8 J. van Dongen, 11, 9 H. Torrontegui and G. Ascareggi both 10.

Practice leaderboard: 1 J. Martinez, Spain *(Derbi)*, 2m 01.96s; 2 A. Criville, Spain *(Derbi)*, 2m 03.01s; 3 S. Dorflinger, Switzerland *(Krauser)*, 2m 03.51s; 4 M. Herreros, Spain *(Derbi)*, 2m 04.10s; 5 N. Bogdan, Bulgaria *(Krauser)*, 2m 05.64s; 6 P. Ottl, W. Germany *(Krauser)*, 2m 06.15s; 7 F. Torrentegui, Spain *(Autisa)*, 2m 06.24s; 8 J. Mariano, Spain *(Cobas)*, 2m 06.36s; 9 R. Dunki, Switzerland *(Krauser)*, 2m 06.49s; 10 I. McConnachie, GB *(Autisa)*, 2m 07.22s; 11 G. Ascareggi, Italy *(BGFT)*, 2m 08.00s; 12 K. Juhasz, Hungary *(Krauser)*, 2m 08.29s; 13 G. Gnani, Italy *(Krauser)*, 2m 08.47s; 14 J. Saez, Spain *(Autisa)*, 2m 08.59s; 15 J. Bernard, Belgium *(Fantic)*, 2m 08.77s; 16 S. Julin, Belgium *(Casal)*, 2m 08.86s; 17 G. Schirnhofer, W. Germany *(Krauser)*, 2m 09.03s; 18 X. Arumi, Spain *(Krauser)*, 2m 09.15s; 19 J. van Dongen, Holland *(Casal)*, 2m 09.27s; 20 S. Edwards, GB *(Casal)*, 2m 10.04s.

Sidecar (22 laps, 57.66m/92.796k)		**m s**	**mph**	**kmh**
1	R. Biland, Switzerland K. Waltisperg, Switzerland *(LCR-Krauser)*	49 05.45	70.47	113.418
2	E. Streuer, Holland B. Schnieders, Holland *(LCR-Yamaha)*	49 07.38	70.43	113.343
3	S. Webster, GB T. Hewitt, GB *(LCR-Krauser)*	49 38.50	69.69	112.159
4	B. Brindley, GB G. Rose, GB *(Yamaha)*	50 27.06	68.57	110.360

5	A. Michel, France J. Fresc, France *(LCR-Krauser)*	50 33.14	68.44	110.139
6	S. Abbott, GB S. Smith, GB *(Windle-Yamaha)*	50 52.18	68.01	109.451
7	T. van Kempen, Holland S. Birchall, Holland *(LCR-Yamaha)*	51 14.20	67.52	108.667
8	D. Jones, GB P. Brown, GB *(LCR-Yamaha)*	51 18.52	67.42	108.515
9	W. Stropek, Austria H. Demling, Austria *(LCR-Krauser)*	51 35.18	67.06	107.931

21 laps: 10 A. Zurbrugg/M. Zurbrugg, Switzerland *(LCR-Yamaha)*; 11 M. Kumano/M. Fahrni, Japan/Switzerland *(LCR-TEC)*; 12 B. Scherer/T. Schroder, W. Germany *(BSR-Krauser)*; 13 D. Bingham/G. Irlam, GB *(LCR-Yamaha)*; 14 I. Nigrowsky/M. Charpentier, France *(Seymaz-Yamaha)*; 15 F. Stolzle/H. Stolzle, W. Germany *(LCR-Krauser)*.

Fastest lap: S. Webster/T. Hewitt, GB *(LCR-Krauser)*, 1m 56.87s, 80.68mph/129.838kmh.

Record lap: R. Biland/K. Waltisperg, Switzerland *(LCR-Krauser)*, 1m 53.58s, 83.07mph/133.693kmh (1987).

World Championship positions: 1 Biland/Waltisperg, 20 points; 2 Streuer/Schnieders, 17; 3 Webster/Hewitt, 15; 4 Brindley/Rose, 13; 5 Michel/Fresc, 11; 6 Abbott/Smith, 10; 7 van Kempen/Birchall, 9; 8 Jones/Brown, 8; 9 Stropek/Demling, 7; 10 Zurbrugg/Zurbrugg, 6.

Practice leaderboard: 1 R. Biland/K. Waltisperg, Switzerland *(LCR-Krauser)*, 1m 49.37s; 2 S. Webster/T. Hewitt, GB *(LCR-Krauser)*, 1m 51.57s; 3 A. Michel/J. Fresc, France *(LCR-Krauser)*, 1m 52.84s; 4 E. Streuer/B. Schnieders, Holland *(LCR-Yamaha)*, 1m 53.01s; 5 M. Kumano/H. Fahrni, Japan/Switzerland *(LCR-TEC)*, 1m 53.39s; 6 A. Zurbrugg/M. Zurbrugg, Switzerland *(LCR-Yamaha)*, 1m 54.17s; 7 R. Steinhausen/B. Hiller, W. Germany *(Busch)*, 1m 54.93s; 8 Y. Kumagaya/B. Barlow, Japan/GB *(Windle-Yamaha)*, 1m 55.47s; 9 M. Egloff/U. Egloff, Switzerland *(LCR-ADM)*, 1m 55.55s; 10 S. Abbott/S. Smith, GB *(Windle-Yamaha)*, 1m 55.86s; 11 A. Bosman/D. Kellett, Australia *(LCR-Yamaha)*, 1m 55.98s; 12 P. Larratte/J. Corbier, France *(LCR-Yamaha)*, 1m 56.29s; 13 D. Jones/P. Brown, GB *(LCR-Yamaha)*, 1m 56.30s; 14 B. Brindley/G. Rose, GB *(Yamaha)*, 1m 56.39s; 15 T. van Kempen/S. Birchall, Holland/GB *(LCR-Yamaha)*, 1m 56.84s; 16 F. Stolzle/H. Stolzle, W. Germany *(LCR-Krauser)*, 1m 57.05s; 17 W. Stropek/H. Demling, Austria *(LCR-Krauser)*, 1m 57.36s; 18 B. Scherer/T. Schroder, W. Germany *(BSR-Krauser)*, 1m 57.70s; 19 I. Nigrowsky/M. Charpentier, France *(Seymaz-Yamaha)*, 1m 57.75s; 20 D. Bingham/G. Irlam, GB *(Yamaha)*, 1m 58.58s.

ITALIAN GRAND PRIX, 22 May, Imola 3.14m/5.059k

Grand prix racing made a dramatic return to the chicane-infested Dino Ferrari circuit at Imola. Events more than made up for the five-year absence: Eddie Lawson remained cool, after an early scare, to record his third 500cc win of the season and Dominique Sarron opened his account in an equally crash-littered 250cc race. Meanwhile, Spaniard Jorge Martinez continued on his merry way in both the 80 and 125cc races.

The opening official practice sessions on Friday, round the 3.14-mile circuit on the outskirts of Imola, gave every indication of what was to follow. On the wet track – covered in rubber from the recent Formula One car race – Lawson, Didier de Radigues, Niall Mackenzie, Pier-Francesco Chili and Ron Haslam all fell without injury. Wayne Gardner did not even practise, fuelling rumours that he had hurt himself in a crash during testing in Yugoslavia. Gardner did go out when the track dried and was in fact in pole position for the race. What he did not tell the press or his opponents was that he had broken five bones in that crash and was wearing a special plaster cast to cover the injury to his left foot. Honda had also quickly built a new frame for the Rothmans NSR machine which went some way to alleviating the wheelspin that had dogged him in the previous three races. Lawson qualified in only seventh place on the Marlboro Yamaha but raced from the second row at the start of the 25-lap event to lead into the first chicane. He led at the end of the first lap from team-mate de Radigues, Pepsi Suzuki star Kevin Schwantz and Gardner. The champion moved into second place on the third lap with de Radigues, who had crashed twice in practice, hanging on to his back wheel. On the tenth lap de Radigues crashed into the straw bales and pushed Wayne Rainey, riding the Lucky Strike Yamaha, into third place. Both the Californian and Schwantz, behind him, slowed with brake problems brought on by the combination of chicanes and fast straights.

As always, Lawson was super cool at the front although a desperate Gardner almost managed to pull alongside him on a couple of occasions. At half distance Gardner got into a big slide and caught his broken foot under the footrest; he realised he had no chance of catching his great rival. Others behind were not so sensible about their chances. Sarron led a cut-and-thrust battle for sixth place, heading Kevin Magee and Niall Mackenzie, when he crashed on the infamous tenth lap. The Frenchman lay unconscious on the track and his two pursuers had to take rapid evasive action. Mackenzie had just outbraked Magee going into the chicane and ran across the grass into the Armco barrier to miss Sarron. He managed to remount and, despite a big hole in his fairing and bent handlebars, he soldiered on to finish a brave 11th. Magee was luckier. He ran on to the grass but managed to stay on the Lucky Strike Yamaha with only Chili getting past. He then engaged in battle with the Italian and they swapped positions until Magee cleared off four laps from the finish to grab fifth place. Rainey and Schwantz took frequent excursions over, rather than through, the chicanes on their way to third and fourth places respectively.

A confident Lawson had no such worries and finished with over 15 seconds to spare and a championship lead of 15 points after a superb, trouble-free, ride. To the delight of the partisan 80,000 crowd Randy Mamola, using all his skill and nerve, slid the Pirelli-shod Cagiva into seventh after a tremendous battle with Shunji Yatsushiro, team-mate Raymond Roche and Japanese Yamaha star Tadahiko Taira. The second half of that battle between Roche and Taira ended in disaster. Roche crossed the line in ninth place and immediately ran out of petrol. Taira was going flat out over the line and rammed the Frenchman from behind, sending them both and their machines spinning down the track. Roche broke his foot and Taira his arm. Haslam finished just out of the points with severe brake problems on his Elf 5 while Rob McElnea had a lonely ride into 12th.

The 22-lap 250cc race followed and the crashes continued. They started at the very first chicane when Spaniard Alberto Puig, deputising for the injured Carlos Cardus, crashed and brought down a pack of riders. These included American John Kocinski, riding the new carbon-fibre-framed Lucky Strike Yamaha, and Scotsman Donnie McLeod. Kocinski could not restart but McLeod remounted for a heroic ride on his 7UP EMC. Sarron, with Spaniards Sito Pons and Juan Garriga in his slipstream, was ahead of all the mayhem. Behind them the sparks really flew in a wild run-in for fourth place between Jacques Cornu, Loris Reggiani, Luca Cadalora and Masahiro Shimizu. The grass was used and fairings bashed. It was obvious it could not last. It came to a predictable end on the sixth lap. Three laps earlier Reggiani had somehow managed to squeeze his Aprilia past the Honda of Cornu. He was followed by the Honda of Shimizu and when the Japanese rider dived in front to grab fourth he sent Reggiani cartwheeling down the track.

Despite Pons showing Sarron the front wheel of his Campsa Honda a couple of times it was less hectic at the front. Pons, after his crash at Jerez, settled for a safe second place and 17 championship points, while Sarron, riding the NS250 Rothmans Honda, cruised to his first victory of the season. At the chequered flag he held almost a nine-second advantage, while Pons increased his championship lead over Garriga to three points.

Garriga, riding the Ducados Yamaha, did not have the speed to match the Hondas and had to work hard to keep the determined Shimizu down in fourth. An excursion on to the grass slowed Shimizu's charge, while Italian Luca Cadalora rode well on the Marlboro Yamaha to finish fifth. He beat West German Reinhold Roth in a desperate last-lap dash, with former world champion Carlos Lavado just behind on his HB Yamaha.

Cornu dropped back to eighth with world champion Toni Mang, continuing his disastrous season, down in tenth. He missed the warm-up lap with a power valve problem on his Rothmans Honda and never got going in the race because of more dreaded brake problems. Behind him came the battling McLeod who was down in 30th place after his first-lap tumble. As he carved his way back through the field he was lapping 3.5 seconds quicker than his practice times. Five championship points were scant reward for such a fine ride.

There was another first-lap pile-up in the superb 18-lap 125cc race on Saturday afternoon. It did not affect the major participants led by world 80cc champion Jorge Martinez riding the works Derbi. For the second race running he played with his team-mates and Honda-mounted Italian, Ezio Gianola, before clearing off for a comfortable victory that had not looked possible in the early laps. Gianola even led at one stage before Martinez, using the superior power of the Derbi, pulled away. His team-mate Manuel Herreros continued the battle with the determined Italian. Both riders had their moments on the grass with Herreros getting the better of the final encounter to hang on to second place. Former champion Pier-Paolo Bianchi headed a fabulous battle for fourth in which half a second covered four riders.

Martinez completed his obligatory double by winning the 14-lap 80cc race, although it might have been a different story had former champion Stefan Dorflinger not made his usual bad start. After an early skirmish with team-mates Herreros and Alex Criville and Hungarian Karoly Juhasz, Martinez was cruising to a comfortable victory when he got the hurry-up signals. Dorflinger, riding the works Krauser, was flying through the field and had pushed aside Herreros and Criville in one lap. Martinez got the message, set the fastest lap, and won with nearly six seconds to spare with Dorflinger second.

Six broken bones and now it's raining! Tension in the faces of Gardner, girlfriend Donna and mechanic Mick Roberts.

Results

500cc (25 laps, 78.60m/126.499k)	**m**	**s**	**mph**	**kmh**
1 E. Lawson, USA *(Yamaha)*	48	17.16	97.67	157.188
2 W. Gardner, Australia *(Honda)*	48	32.67	97.15	156.350
3 W. Rainey, USA *(Yamaha)*	48	43.90	96.78	155.749

4	K. Schwantz, USA *(Suzuki)*	48 50.02	96.34	155.055
5	K. Magee, Australia *(Yamaha)*	49 05.65	96.06	154.599
6	P. Chili, Italy *(Honda)*	49 10.28	95.91	154.357
7	R. Mamola, USA *(Cagiva)*	49 32.27	95.20	153.215
8	S. Yatsushiro, Japan *(Honda)*	49 33.93	95.15	153.129
9	R. Roche, France *(Cagiva)*	49 34.37	95.13	153.106
10	T. Taira, Japan *(Yamaha)*	49 35.17	95.11	153.065

11 N. Mackenzie, GB *(Honda)*; 12 R. McElnea, GB *(Suzuki)*. *24 laps:* 13 A. Valesi, Italy *(Honda)*; 14 M. Gentile, Switzerland *(Honda)*; 15 P. Igoa, France *(Yamaha)*; 16 R. Haslam, GB *(Elf-Honda)*; 17 A. Rota, Italy *(Honda)*; 18 F. Barchitta, San Marino *(Honda)*; 19 B. Kneubuhler, Switzerland *(Honda)*; 20 R. Balbi, Italy *(Honda)*; 21 R. Ari, Finland *(Honda)*; 22 P. Skold, Sweden *(Honda)*. *23 laps:* 23 R. Nicotte, France *(Honda)*; 24 M. Papa, Italy *(Honda)*; 25 M. Duyzers, Holland *(Honda)*; 26 N. Schmassmann, Switzerland *(Honda)*.

Record lap: E. Lawson, USA *(Yamaha)*, 1m 54.41s, 98.935mph/159.217kmh.

World Championship positions: 1 E. Lawson, 92 points; 2 W. Gardner, 77; 3 W. Rainey, 65; 4 K. Magee, 55; 5 N. Mackenzie, 53; 6 K. Schwantz and C. Sarron both 44; 8 D. de Radigues, 33; 9 R. McElnea, 23; 10 S. Yatsushiro and P. Chili both 21.

Practice leaderboard: 1 W. Gardner, Australia *(Honda)*, 1m 55.03s; 2 D. de Radigues, Belgium *(Yamaha)*, 1m 55.23s; 3 C. Sarron, France *(Yamaha)*, 1m 55.24s; 4 W. Rainey, USA *(Yamaha)*, 1m 55.36s; 5 K. Schwantz, USA *(Suzuki)*, 1m 55.46s; 6 K. Magee, Australia *(Yamaha)*, 1m 55.57s; 7 E. Lawson, USA *(Yamaha)*, 1m 55.74s; 8 R. Mamola, USA *(Cagiva)*, 1m 56.19s; 9 P. Chili, Italy *(Honda)*, 1m 56.33s; 10 N. Mackenzie, GB *(Honda)*, 1m 56.53s; 11 R. Roche, France *(Cagiva)*, 1m 57.17s; 12 T. Taira, Japan *(Yamaha)*, 1m 57.25s; 13 R. McElnea, GB *(Suzuki)*, 1m 57.89s; 14 P. Igoa, France *(Yamaha)*, 1m 57.97s; 15 R. Haslam, GB *(Elf-Honda)*, 1m 57.98s; 16 S. Yatsushiro, Japan *(Honda)*, 1m 58.37s; 17 M. Broccoli, Italy *(Cagiva)*, 2m 00.35s; 18 R. Burnett, GB *(Honda)*, 2m 00.36s; 19 M. Papa, Italy *(Honda)*, 2m 00.51s; 20 A. Valesi, Italy *(Honda)*, 2m 00.62s.

250cc (22 laps, 69.17m/111.319k)		**m s**	**mph**	**kmh**
1	D. Sarron, France *(Honda)*	43 57.53	94.41	151.492
2	S. Pons, Spain *(Honda)*	44 06.17	94.10	151.444
3	J. Garriga, Spain *(Yamaha)*	44 13.41	93.85	151.031
4	M. Shimizu, Japan *(Honda)*	44 17.80	93.69	150.782
5	L. Cadalora, Italy *(Yamaha)*	44 25.57	93.42	150.342
6	R. Roth, W. Germany *(Honda)*	44 29.43	93.28	150.125
7	C. Lavado, Venezuela *(Yamaha)*	44 32.42	93.18	149.957
8	J. Cornu, Switzerland *(Honda)*	44 35.57	93.07	149.780
9	J. Ruggia, France *(Yamaha)*	44 37.66	92.99	149.663
10	A. Mang, W. Germany *(Honda)*	44 45.64	92.72	149.221

11 D. McLeod, GB *(EMC)*; 12 M. Herweh, W. Germany *(Yamaha)*; 13 H. Eckl, W. Germany *(Aprilia)*; 14 S. Caracchi, San Marino *(Honda)*; 15 A. Auinger, Austria *(Aprilia)* ; 16 M. Matteoni, Italy *(Yamaha)*; 17 P. Casoli, Italy *(Garelli)*; 18 S. Minich, Austria *(Yamaha)*; 19 X. Cardelus, Andorra *(Aprilia)*; 20 J. Foray, France *(Yamaha)*; 21 U. Luzi, Switzerland *(Honda)*. *21 laps:* 22 J. Mattioli, France *(Yamaha)*; 23 U. Jucker, Switzerland *(Yamaha)*.

Record lap: D. Sarron, France *(Honda)*, 1m 58.69s, 95.36mph/153.475kmh

World Championship positions: 1 S. Pons, 71 points; 2 J. Garriga, 68; 3 J. Cornu, 58; 4 D. Sarron, 48; 5 J. Ruggia, 45; 6 A. Mang, 43; 7 M. Shimizu, 41; 8 R. Roth, 37; 9 L. Cadalora, 30; 10 D. McLeod, 17.

Practice leaderboard: 1 D. Sarron, France *(Honda)*; 1m 59.99s; 2 C. Lavado, Venezuela *(Yamaha)*, 2m 00.13s; 3 J. Garriga, Spain *(Yamaha)*, 2m 00.17s; 4 S. Pons, Spain *(Honda)*, 2m 00.46s; 5 L. Cadalora, Italy *(Yamaha)*, 2m 00.67s; 6 R. Roth, W. Germany *(Honda)*; 2m 01.01s; 7 M. Shimizu, Japan *(Honda)*, 2m 01.07s; 8 A. Puig, Spain *(Honda)*, 2m 01.10s; 9 J. Cornu, Switzerland *(Honda)*, 2m 01.63s; 10 M. Wimmer, W. Germany *(Yamaha)*, 2m 02.05s; 11 L. Reggiani, Italy *(Aprilia)*, 2m 02.19s; 12 B. Casanova, Italy *(Aprilia)* 2m 02.22s; 13 J. Kocinski, USA *(Yamaha)*, 2m 02.38s; 14 A. Mang, W. Germany *(Honda)*, 2m 02.55s; 15 M. Herweh, W. Germany *(Yamaha)*, 2m 02.84s; 16 M. Vitali, Italy *(Yamaha)*, 2m 02.97s; 17 A. Preining, Austria *(Aprilia)*, 2m 03.18s; 18 D. McLeod, GB *(EMC)*, 2m 03.29s; 19 A. Auinger, Austria *(Aprilia)*, 2m 03.35s; 20 J. Ruggia, France *(Yamaha)*, 2m 03.36s.

125cc (18 laps, 56.64m/91.157k)		**m**	**s**	**mph**	**kmh**
1	J. Martinez, Spain *(Derbi)*	39	16.43	86.46	139.146
2	M. Herreros, Spain *(Derbi)*	39	25.13	86.21	138.751
3	E. Gianola, Italy *(Honda)*	39	29.29	86.06	138.507
4	P. Bianchi, Italy *(Cagiva)*	39	30.10	86.04	138.460
5	H. Spaan, Holland *(Honda)*	39	30.25	86.03	138.452
6	L. Reyes, Spain *(Garelli)*	39	30.43	86.02	138.441
7	G. Grassetti, Italy *(Honda)*	39	30.66	86.01	138.430
8	A. Stadler, W. Germany *(Honda)*	39	31.57	85.98	138.374
9	H. Unemoto, Japan *(Honda)*	39	51.58	85.26	137.217
10	J. Wickstrom, Finland *(Honda)*	39	52.47	85.22	137.160

11 S. Prein, W. Germany *(Honda)*; 12 H. Luthi, Switzerland *(Honda)*; 13 A. Scott, USA *(Honda)*; 14 J. Hautaniemi, Finland *(Honda)*; 15 J. Miralles, Spain *(Honda)*; 16 E. Kytola, Finland *(Honda)*; 17 J. Fischer, Austria *(Rotax)*; 18 A. Waibel, W. Germany *(Honda)*; 19 K. Galatowicz, GB *(Honda)*; 20 D. Brigaglia, Italy *(Gazzaniga)*; 21 C. Macciotta, Italy *(Honda)*; 22 K. Takada, Japan *(Honda)*; 23 H. Abold, W. Germany *(Honda)*; 24 J. Selini, France *(Honda)*; 25 T. Feuz, Switzerland *(Ferac)*. *17 laps*: 26 S. Bianchi *(Cordati)*.

Record lap: J. Martinez, Spain *(Derbi)*, 2m 08.39s, 88.16mph/141.880kmh.

World Championship positions: 1 J. Martinez, 40 points; 2 G. Grassetti, 24; 3 A. Stadler, 19; 4 J. Miralles, 18; 5 H. Spaan and M. Herreros both 17; 7 H. Unemoto, 16; 8 E. Gianola, 15; 9 P. Bianchi, 13; 10 L. Reyes, 10.

Practice leaderboard: 1 J. Martinez, Spain *(Derbi)*, 2m 08.14s; 2 E. Gianola, Italy *(Honda)*, 2m 08.72s; 3 F. Gresini, Italy *(Garelli)*, 2m 10.04s; 4 P. Bianchi, Italy *(Cagiva)*, 2m 10.21s; 5 C. Catalano, Italy *(Aprilia)*, 2m 10.27s; 6 G. Grassetti, Italy *(Honda)*, 2m 10.33s; 7 H. Spaan, Holland *(Honda)*, 2m 11.01s; 8 A. Brasini, Italy *(MBA)*, 2m 11.36s; 9 M. Herreros, Spain *(Derbi)*, 2m 11.40s; 10 L. Pietroniro, Belgium *(Honda)*, 2m 11.43s; 11 A. Stadler, W. Germany *(Honda)*, 2m 11.54s; 12 J. Miralles, Spain *(Honda)*, 2m 11.60s; 13 S. Dorflinger, Switzerland *(Honda)*, 2m 11.66s; 14 I. McConnachie, GB *(Cagiva)*, 2m 11.66s; 15 H. Luthi, Switzerland *(Honda)*, 2m 11.84s; 16 J. Fischer, Austria *(Rotax)*, 2m 12.18s; 17 J. Hautaniemi, Finland *(Honda)*, 2m 12.19s; 18 M. Leitner, Austria *(Emco)*, 2m 12.21s; 19 L. Reyes, Spain *(Garelli)*, 2m 12.26s; 20 J. Wickstrom, Finland *(Honda)*, 2m 12.56s.

80cc (14 laps, 44.01m/70.840k)		**m**	**s**	**mph**	**kmh**
1	J. Martinez, Spain *(Derbi)*	31	49.85	82.97	133.531
2	S. Dorflinger, Switzerland *(Krauser)*	31	55.20	82.74	133.157
3	M. Herreros, Spain *(Derbi)*	31	58.29	82.61	132.943
4	A. Criville, Spain *(Derbi)*	31	59.65	82.55	132.850
5	K. Juhasz, Hungary *(Krauser)*	32	10.19	82.10	132.123
6	B. Nikolov, Bulgaria *(Krauser)*	32	35.77	81.02	130.395
7	P. Ottl, W. Germany *(Krauser)*	32	44.75	80.65	129.799
8	G. Ascareggi, Italy *(BBFT)*	32	59.61	80.05	128.825
9	R. Koster, Switzerland *(LCR)*	33	01.27	79.99	128.729
10	R. Dunki, Switzerland *(Krauser)*	33	01.55	79.97	128.706

11 J. van Dongen, Holland *(Casal)*; 12 J. Seel, W. Germany *(Seel)*; 13 G. Gnani, Italy *(Gnani)*; 14 B. Smit, Holland *(Casal)*; 15 S. Julin, Belgium *(Casal)*; 16 M. Ehinger, W. Germany *(Krauser)*; 17 P. Bordes, France *(RB)*; 18 R. Kunz, W. Germany *(Ziegler)*; 19 L. Robert, France *(Casal)*; 20 H. Koopman, Holland *(Casal)*; 21 S. Braegger, Switzerland *(Casal)*. *13 laps:* 22 R. Hobl, W. Germany *(Krauser)*; 23 S. Milano, Italy *(Krauser)*; 24 K. Besseling, Holland *(Casal)*; 25 P. Desnet, France *(Huvo)*; 26 S. Edwards, GB *(Casal)*; 27 A. Pavlic, Yugoslavia *(Seel)*; 28 C. Baert, Belgium *(Casal)*.

Record lap: J. Martinez, Spain *(Derbi)*, 2m 12.75s, 85.26mph/137.220kmh.

World Championship positions: 1 J. Martinez, 57 points; 2 S. Dorflinger, 50; 3 M. Herreros, 45; 4 A. Criville, 43; 5 P. Ottl, 31; 6 K. Juhasz, 27; 7 B. Nikolov, 26; 8 G. Ascareggi, 18; 9 J. van Dongen, 16; 10 G. Gnani, 12.

Practice leaderboard: 1 J. Martinez, Spain *(Derbi)*, 2m 12.00s; 2 S. Dorflinger, Switzerland *(Krauser)*, 2m 13.81s; 3 A. Criville, Spain *(Derbi)*, 2m 16.75s; 4 M. Herreros, Spain *(Derbi)*, 2m 17.14s; 5 N. Bogdan, Bulgaria *(Krauser)*, 2m 18.21s; 6 G. Ascareggi, Italy *(BBFT)*, 2m 19.75s; 7 H. Torrontegui, Spain *(Autisa)*, 2m 19.91s; 8 J. Seel, W. Germany *(Seel)*, 2m 20.44s; 9 K. Juhasz, Hungary *(Krauser)*, 2m 20.57s; 10 R. Koster, Switzerland *(LCR)*, 2m 20.81s; 11 G. Gnani, Italy *(Gnani)*, 2m 21.17s; 12 S. Julin, Belgium *(Casal)*, 2m 21.42s; 13 J. van Dongen, Holland *(Casal)*, 2m 21.53s; 14 B. Smit, Holland *(Casal)*, 2m 21.63s; 15 P. Ottl, W. Germany *(Krauser)*, 2m 21.73s; 16 G. Schirnhofer, W. Germany *(Krauser)*, 2m 22.09s; 17 P. Bordes, France *(RB)*, 2m 22.48s; 18 A. Nijenhuis, Holland *(Casal)*, 2m 22.78s; 19 J. Torrens, Spain *(Cobas)*, 2m 23.20s; 20 X. Arumi, Spain *(Krauser)*, 2m 23.59s.

WEST GERMAN GRAND PRIX, 28/29 May, Nurburgring 2.822m/4.542k

Thick mist and heavy rain ruined the weekend for most people at the Nurburgring – with a few notable exceptions.Texan Kevin Schwantz won his second grand prix of the season with a brilliant demonstration of wet-weather riding in the 30-lap 500cc race. Italian Luca Cadalora scored his first-ever victory in the 250cc class, riding the Marlboro Yamaha on the drying track. Honda won their first 125cc grand prix for 20 years thanks to another fine wet-ride by Ezio Gianola. The sidecar crews protested about having to race on Saturday but they actually got the best of the weather. In perfect conditions Rolf Biland and Kurt Waltisperg inflicted another defeat on battling world champions Steve Webster and Tony Hewitt.

The weather conditions meant there were only two 500cc practice sessions round the purpose-built 2.82-mile circuit in the heart of the Eifel mountains. On the very last lap Wayne Gardner grabbed pole from Wayne Rainey with Sarron, Lawson and Magee completing the front row. His joy was short-lived when he woke the next morning to find the rain pouring down. He knew the fiery power characteristics of the NSR Rothmans Honda would not suit the conditions and he was right. He got the machine sideways off the line and was down in ninth place as the pack, headed by Rainey and followed by a great wall of spray, raced into the first chicane. By the end of the first lap, rain expert Christian Sarron led, riding the Sonauto Gauloises Yamaha, followed by Lawson and Schwantz. Both Sarron and Schwantz got into big slides, but as Lawson sensibly dropped back the Pepsi Suzuki star grabbed the lead and held on to it from the second lap. Lawson's lap boards told him Gardner was down in ninth. The experienced former world champion settled down to a steady ride in fourth place and out of trouble on the Marlboro Yamaha.

Things were not so steady behind Schwantz, with Sarron and Magee contesting second as if the whole championship depended on it. They were caught by Magee's Lucky Strike team-mate, Rainey, who sensibly got used to the conditions before mounting his very effective charge through the spray. By the eighth lap he was up into second and started to close on Schwantz, his great rival from his American Superbike Championship days. Schwantz countered with the fastest lap of the day and when Rainey took to the grass in the Esses the battle at the front was over. The race for third between Sarron and Magee was very different. The Australian waited patiently for his chance but it never came. On the 20th lap he slid off on to the grass. He quickly remounted having dropped only one place to fifth behind Lawson, who was still watching Gardner's progress via his lap board.

It all became rather predictable at the front with nobody wanting to take risks even when it stopped raining at three-quarter distance. Gardner started to move up when the rain stopped and progressed into seventh place in front of Pier-Francesco Chili. Then the heavens opened and Chili started to fly. He pushed Gardner back to eighth after the champion had taken to the grass. Three laps from the finish he overtook Didier de Radigues, riding the second Marlboro Yamaha, and set after Magee. He failed to catch him by less than one-fifth of a second after a tremendous late burst.

At the finish Schwantz celebrated his second grand prix win with some typical standing-on-the-footrests and hands-in-the-air-riding. He had 25 seconds to spare over Rainey. Lawson increased his championship lead to 20 points over Gardner who was eighth, one

Schwantz's reflection clearly seen on the rain-sodden Nurburgring track.

The flat-out style of Ezio Gianola was rewarded with the 125cc victory.

place in front of an equally disappointed Niall Mackenzie who was lapped by the leader.

The sun broke through the clouds at the start of the 25-lap 250cc race. The track was still streaming wet and the riders stuck to wet tyres, which did not help their progress when the track dried dramatically towards the finish. Cadalora raced away from the start, chased by the Hondas of Toni Mang and Sito Pons and Donnie McLeod riding the 7UP EMC. Mang, with the home crowd behind him, snatched the lead on the fourth lap; Pons and Cadalora battled for second place as McLeod dropped back. American John Kocinski, riding the carbon-framed Lucky Strike Yamaha, overtook him but then crashed for the second week running. He joined Japanese ace Masahiro Shimizu and Frenchman Thierry Rapicault, who were early fallers.

As the track dried everyone's tyres started to overheat. Cadalora got back to the front and began to pull away, and McLeod, riding brilliantly, started to haul in Mang and Pons. With six laps remaining he dumped world champion Mang back to fourth and set after Pons. The Spaniard increased the pace with 17 precious points at stake and McLeod settled back to what he thought was a safe third place. Unfortunately for the Scotsman, Juan Garriga was fully charged on the Ducados Yamaha and chasing hard. He caught McLeod completely cold on the very last lap and pushed him off the winner's rostrum into fourth place. Mang was in even bigger trouble on his Rothmans Honda which was shedding rubber with gay abandon. He slipped to eighth with Reinhold Roth, Martin Wimmer and Frenchman Jean Foray overtaking him during the last couple of laps. Team-mate Dominique Sarron fared even worse and finished ninth.

Honda-mounted Gianola blew the 125cc championship wide apart with a superb display of wet-weather riding in the 23-lap race. He led from start to finish while others, including his great rival Jorge Martinez, fell by the wayside. The Spanish Derbi supremo blotted his copybook when he crashed on the third lap while chasing the leader. In a frantic race through the spray for second place Spanish Honda rider Julian Miralles pipped Dutchman Hans Spaan, riding a similar RS Honda. Spaan actually crashed but remounted to hold on to third, one second ahead of Derbi number two Manuel Herreros. It was a good day for Britain's unsung heroes in the class. Ian McConnachie was tenth on the Cagiva with Honda-mounted Chris Galatowicz and Robin Appleyard 12th and 13th respectively.

Martinez made no such mistakes in the equally wet 18-lap 80cc event which started the day's proceedings. The world champion cleared off from the start and was never seen again. His Derbi team-mates 18-year-old Alex Criville and Manuel Herreros, were given an early fright by yet another Spaniard Herri Torrontegui. Riding the Autisa, the Barcelona rider pushed the Derbis out of second place but then crashed on the tenth lap to make it plain sailing for a Derbi one/two/three. Former champion Stefan Dorflinger was another faller: he came to grief on the seventh lap while lying fourth.

The superb sidecar race had a familiar ring to it by the end of the season, Biland toying with the opposition before racing away on the last lap. In perfect conditions and in front of millions of television viewers the sidecar lads put on a show to be proud of in a fabulous 25-lap race that did much to dispel the gloom of the weather. Webster and Hewitt led from the line on their Krauser LCR. Former champions Egbert Streuer and Bernard Schnieders were stranded with a broken gear linkage bolt, but despite losing three laps they soon joined in the fun. Biland and Waltisperg grabbed the lead on the second lap but dramatically dropped to fifth when their Bartol-tuned Krauser engine died. It picked up almost immediately and they rejoined the fray, which was turning into a five-way battle although Streuer was three laps down. The impressive Swiss brothers Alfred and Martin Zurbrugg and the French pair Alain Michel and Jean-Marc Fresc were soon involved in the superb battle for the lead. Webster and Biland continually swapped the lead but the Zurbruggs shocked them both with a brief visit to the front on the seventh lap. Streuer may have been three laps down but he was determined to grab his share of the televised action. He 'led' briefly to prove his point before letting the real race continue. Michel dropped out with a broken gearbox shaft. The Zurbruggs faded and it was left to the Yorkshire pair to try to stem the Biland tide. They held firm until the last lap when the former champion stormed past. He pulled away to secure almost a three-second advantage and decimate Streuer's old lap record. The Zurbrugg brothers were a worthy third, with passenger Martin sporting a bleeding toe where his boot had been worn away at the height of the battle.

Results

500cc (30 laps, 84.67m/136.260k)	**m**	**s**	**mph**	**kmh**
1 K. Schwantz, USA *(Suzuki)*	61	52.27	82.11	132.139
2 W. Rainey, USA *(Yamaha)*	62	17.30	81.55	131.254
3 C. Sarron, France *(Yamaha)*	62	43.82	80.98	130.329
4 E. Lawson, USA *(Yamaha)*	63	01.01	80.61	129.736
5 K. Magee, Australia *(Yamaha)*	63	04.44	80.54	129.619
6 P. Chili, Italy *(Honda)*	63	04.82	80.53	129.606
7 D. de Radigues, Belgium *(Yamaha)*	63	12.56	80.37	129.341
8 W. Gardner, Australia *(Honda)*	63	36.15	79.87	128.542

29 laps: 9 N. Mackenzie, GB *(Honda)*; 10 S. Yatsushiro, Japan *(Honda)*; 11 R. McElnea, GB *(Suzuki)*; 12 P. Igoa, France *(Yamaha)*. *28 laps:* 13 P. Schleef, W. Germany *(Honda)*; 14 M. Papa, Italy *(Honda)*; 15 M. Rudroff, W. Germany *(Honda)*; 16 A. Valesi, Italy *(Honda)*; 17 M. Gentile, Switzerland *(Honda)*; 18 W. Von Muralt, Switzerland *(Suzuki)*; 19 M. Duyzers, Holland *(Honda)*. *27 laps:* 20 J. Doppler, Austria *(Honda)*; 21 H. Schuetz, W. Germany *(Honda)*; 22 A. Ramo, Finland *(Honda)*; 23 P. Skold, Sweden *(Honda)*; 24 N. Schmassmann, Switzerland *(Honda)*. *26 laps:* 25 B. Knuebuhler, Switzerland *(Honda)*.

Fastest lap: K. Schwantz, USA *(Suzuki)*, 1m 59.08s, 85.32mph/137.312kmh.

Record lap: E. Lawson, USA *(Yamaha)*, 1m 43.24s, 98.91mph/158.380kmh (1986).

World Championship positions: 1 E. Lawson, 105 points; 2 W. Gardner, 85; 3 W. Rainey, 82; 4 K. Magee, 66; 5 K. Schwantz, 64; 6 N. Mackenzie, 60; 7 C. Sarron, 59; 8 D. de Radigues, 42; 9 P. Chili, 31; 10 R. McElnea, 28.

Practice leaderboard: 1 W. Gardner, Australia *(Honda)*, 1m 41.31s; 2 W. Rainey, USA *(Yamaha)*, 1m 41.75s; 3 C. Sarron, France *(Yamaha)*, 1m 42.13s; 4 E. Lawson, USA *(Yamaha)*, 1m 42.51s; 5 K. Magee, Australia *(Yamaha)*, 1m 42.61s; 6 N. Mackenzie, GB *(Honda)*, 1m 43.06s; 7 S. Yatsushiro, Japan *(Honda)*, 1m 43.20s; 8 R. Mamola, USA

(Cagiva), 1m 43.63s; 9 K. Schwantz, USA *(Suzuki)*, 1m 43.79s; 10 R. McElnea, GB *(Suzuki)*, 1m 43.88s; 11 D. de Radigues, Belgium *(Yamaha)*, 1m 43.89s; 12 R. Haslam, GB *(Elf-Honda)*, 1m 44.21s; 13 P. Chili, Italy *(Honda)*, 1m 44.72s; 14 P. Igoa, France *(Yamaha)*, 1m 44.79s; 15 M. Broccoli, Italy *(Cagiva)*, 1m 46.25s; 16 M. Papa, Italy *(Honda)*, 1m 46.74s; 17 M. Gentile, Switzerland *(Honda)*, 1m 46.96s; 18 P. Schleef, W. Germany *(Honda)*, 1m 46.98s; 19 M. Fischer, W. Germany *(Honda)*, 1m 47.76s; 20 M. Duyzers, Holland *(Honda)*, 1m 47.76s.

	250cc (25 laps, 70.55m/113.550k)	**m**	**s**	**mph**	**kmh**
1	L. Cadalora, Italy *(Yamaha)*	51	12.96	82.66	133.024
2	S. Pons, Spain *(Honda)*	51	27.29	82.27	132.407
3	J. Garriga, Spain *(Yamaha)*	51	31.52	82.16	132.226
4	D. McLeod, GB *(EMC)*	51	33.42	82.11	132.145
5	R. Roth, W. Germany *(Honda)*	51	35.83	82.05	132.042
6	M. Wimmer, W. Germany *(Yamaha)*	51	42.81	81.86	131.745
7	J. Foray, France *(Yamaha)*	51	50.86	81.65	131.404
8	A. Mang, W. Germany *(Honda)*	51	54.44	81.59	131.253
9	D. Sarron, France *(Honda)*	51	59.31	81.43	131.048
10	H. Bradl, W. Germany *(Honda)*	52	00.15	81.42	131.012

11 H. Becker, W. Germany *(Yamaha)*; 12 H. Holder, W. Germany *(Rotax)*; 13 J. Ruggia, France *(Yamaha)*; 14 P. Casoli, Italy *(Garelli)*; 15 S. Caracchi, San Marino *(Honda)*; 16 A. Preining, Austria *(Aprilia)*; 17 A. Puig, Spain *(Honda)*; 18 H. Duffard, France *(Honda)*; 19 H. Lindner, Austria *(Honda)*; 20 B. Schick, W. Germany *(Honda)*; 21 J. Cornu, Switzerland *(Honda)*; 22 L. Mella, Spain *(Honda)*; 23 B. Haenggeli, Switzerland *(Honda)*; 24 J. Schmid, W. Germany *(Honda)*; 25 B. Bonhuil, France *(Honda)*. *24 laps:* 26 I. Troisi, Venezuela *(Yamaha)*; 27 X. Cardelus, Andorra *(Honda)*; 28 G. Haeberle, W. Germany *(Rotax)*; 29 P. van der Goorbergh, Holland *(Honda)*.

Fastest lap: J. Garriga, Spain *(Yamaha)*, 1m 56.62s, 87.12mph/140.209kmh.

Record lap: A. Mang, W. Germany *(Honda)*, 1m 46.90s, 95.05mph/152.957kmh (1986).

World Championship positions: 1 S. Pons, 88 points; 2 J. Garriga, 83; 3 J. Cornu, 58; 4 D. Sarron, 55; 5 A. Mang, 51; 6 L. Cadalora, 50; 7 J. Ruggia and R. Roth both 48; 9 M. Shimizu, 41; 10 D. McLeod, 30.

Practice leaderboard: 1 T. Rapicault, France *(Fior)*, 2m 02.35s; 2 A. Mang, W. Germany *(Honda)*, 2m 02.46s; 3 R. Zanatta, Argentina *(Yamaha)*, 2m 02.62s; 4 M. Wimmer, W. Germany *(Yamaha)*, 2m 02.81s; 5 A. Auinger, Austria *(Aprilia)*, 2m 02.87s; 6 L. Cadalora, Italy *(Yamaha)*, 2m 02.89s; 7 A. Puig, Spain *(Honda)*, 2m 03.23s; 8 S. Caracchi, San Marino *(Honda)*, 2m 03.29s; 9 D. Sarron, France *(Honda)*, 2m 03.43s; 10 H. Lindner, Austria *(Honda)*, 2m 03.45s; 11 J. Kocinski, USA *(Yamaha)*, 2m 03.51s; 12 E. Neumair, Austria *(Aprilia)*, 2m 03.54s; 13 D. McLeod, GB *(EMC)*, 2m 03.65s; 14 S. Pons, Spain *(Honda)*, 2m 03.66s; 15 P. Casoli, Italy *(Garelli)*, 2m 03.84s; 16 R. Roth, W. Germany *(Honda)*, 2m 03.91s; 17 H. Holder, W. Germany *(Rotax)*, 2m 04.05s; 18 H. Duffard, France *(Honda)*, 2m 04.12s; 19 M. Shimizu, Japan *(Honda)*, 2m 04.15s; 20 J. Schmid, W. Germany *(Honda)*, 2m 04.17s.

125cc (23 laps, 64.91m/104.466k)	**m**	**s**	**mph**	**kmh**
1 E. Gianola, Italy *(Honda)*	51	18.77	75.90	122.151
2 J. Miralles, Spain *(Honda)*	51	26.81	75.70	121.833
3 H. Spaan, Holland *(Honda)*	51	27.70	75.68	121.798
4 M. Herreros, Spain *(Derbi)*	51	28.72	75.63	121.718
5 A. Waibel, W. Germany *(Waibel)*	52	00.42	74.89	120.521
6 H. Unemoto, Japan *(Honda)*	52	04.20	74.79	120.375
7 G. Grassetti, Italy *(Honda)*	52	22.95	74.35	119.657
8 D. Brigaglia, Italy *(Rotax)*	52	23.54	74.34	119.635
9 L. Reyes, Spain, *(Garelli)*	52	28.35	74.22	119.452
10 I. McConnachie, GB *(Cagiva)*	52	32.02	74.14	119.313

11 G. Waibel, W. Germany *(Honda)*; 12 K. Galatowicz, GB *(Honda)*; 13 R. Appleyard, GB *(Honda)*; 14 B. Hassaine, France *(Honda)*. *22 laps:* 15 J. Fischer, Austria *(Rotax)*; 16 R. Strack, W. Germany *(Honda)*; 17 P. Bordes, France *(Honda)*.

Fastest lap: A. Waibel, W. Germany *(Waibel)*, 2m 10.92s, 77.60mph/124.894kmh.

Record lap: L. Cadalora, Italy *(Garelli)*, 1m 51.73s, 90.94mph/146.354kmh (1986).

World Championship positions: 1 J. Martinez, 40 points; 2 J. Miralles and E. Gianola both 35; 4 G. Grassetti, 33; 5 H. Spaan, 32; 6 M. Herreros, 30; 7 H. Unemoto, 26; 8 A. Stadler, 19; 9 L. Reyes, 17; 10 G. Waibel, 15.

Practice leaderboard: 1 H. Spaan, Holland *(Honda)*, 1m 54.49s; 2 J. Martinez, Spain *(Derbi)*, 1m 54.61s; 3 L. Pietroniro, Belgium *(Honda)*, 1m 54.69s; 4 G. Grassetti, Italy *(Honda)*, 1m 54.73s; 5 E. Gianola, Italy *(Honda)*, 1m 54.82s; 6 M. Leitner, Austria *(Emco)*, 1m 55.25s; 7 A. Stadler, W. Germany *(Honda)*, 1m 55.75s; 8 H. Abold, W. Germany *(Honda)*, 1m 55.99s; 9 J. Fischer, Austria *(Rotax)*, 1m 56.00s; 10 D. Brigaglia, Italy *(Rotax)*, 1m 56.36s; 11 J. Miralles, Spain *(Honda)*, 1m 56.46s; 12 H. Unemoto, Japan *(Honda)*, 1m 56.58s; 13 A. Waibel, W. Germany *(Waibel)*, 1m 56.81s; 14 P. Bianchi, Italy *(Cagiva)*, 1m 57.01s; 15 G. Waibel, W. Germany *(Honda)*, 1m 57.20s; 16 M. Herreros, Spain *(Derbi)*, 1m 57.20s; 17 L. Reyes, Spain *(Garelli)*, 1m 57.22s; 18 S. Julin, Belgium *(Rotax)*, 1m 57.26s; 19 T. Koji, Japan *(Honda)*, 1m 57.27s; 20 S. Prein, W. Germany *(Honda)*, 1m 57.32s.

80cc (18 laps, 50.79m/81.756k)	**m**	**s**	**mph**	**kmh**
1 J. Martinez, Spain *(Derbi)*	41	44.45	73.02	117.519
2 A. Criville, Spain *(Derbi)*	42	09.40	72.26	116.360
3 M. Herreros, Spain *(Derbi)*	42	15.43	72.10	116.037
4 G. Gnani, Italy *(Gnani)*	42	44.13	71.32	114.784
5 G. Ascareggi, Italy *(BBFT)*	43	08.00	70.66	113.725
6 J. van Dongen, Holland *(Casal)*	43	18.17	70.39	113.280
7 A. Nijenhuis, Holland *(Casal)*	43	43.87	69.70	112.170
8 H. Paschen, W. Germany *(Kiefer)*	43	50.38	69.53	111.893
9 H. Koopman, Holland *(Ziegler)*	43	50.98	69.51	111.867
10 P. Priori, Italy *(Krauser)*	44	02.95	69.19	111.361

11 G. Schirnhofer, W. Germany *(Krauser)*; 12 R. Dunki, Switzerland *(Krauser)*; 13 S. Braegger, Switzerland *(Casal)*. *17 laps:* 14 H. Klein, W. Germany *(Honda)*; 15 K. Juhasz, Hungary *(Krauser)*; 16 B. Smit, Holland *(Minarelli)*; 17 R. Waldmann, W. Germany *(Seel)*; 18 M. Ehinger, W. Germany *(Krauser)*; 19 P. Bordes, France *(RB)*; 20 R. Hobl, W. Germany *(Krauser)*; 21 R. Scheidhauer, W. Germany *(Seel)*. *16 laps:* 22 J. Bernard, Belgium *(Fantic)*.

Fastest lap: J. Martinez, Spain *(Derbi)*, 2m 16.43s, 74.47mph/119.850kmh.

Record lap: I. McConnachie, GB *(Krauser)*, 1m 57.01s, 86.83mph/139.741kmh (1986).

World Championship positions: 1 J. Martinez, 77 points; 2 A. Criville and M. Herreros both 60; 4 S. Dorflinger, 50; 5 P. Ottl, 31; 6 G. Ascareggi, 29; 7 K. Juhasz, 28; 8 J. van Dongen and B. Nikolov both 26; 10 G. Gnani, 25.

Practice leaderboard: 1 J. Martinez, Spain *(Derbi)*, 1m 57.72s; 2 A. Criville, Spain *(Derbi)*, 1m 59.23s; 3 S. Dorflinger, Switzerland *(Krauser)*, 1m 59.40s; 4 M. Herreros, Spain *(Derbi)*, 2m 00.40s; 5 H. Torrontegui, Spain *(Autisa)*, 2m 00.53s; 6 P. Ottl, W. Germany *(Krauser)*, 2m 00.95s; 7 K. Juhasz, Hungary *(Krauser)*, 2m 02.33s; 8 S. Julin, Belgium *(Casal)*, 2m 02.62s; 9 J. Bernard, Belgium *(Fantic)*, 2m 03.65s; 10 J. van Dongen, Holland *(Casal)*, 2m 03.70s; 11 R. Scheidhauer, W. Germany *(Seel)*, 2m 03.75s; 12 B. Smit, Holland *(Minarelli)*, 2m 03.93s; 13 H. Koopman, Holland *(Ziegler)*, 2m 04.29s; 14 G. Ascareggi, Italy *(BBFT)*, 2m 04.35s; 15 G. Schirnhofer, W. Germany *(Krauser)*, 2m 04.58s; 16 H. Paschen, W. Germany *(Kiefer)*, 2m 04.65s; 17 J. Torrens, Spain *(Cobas)*, 2m 04.90s; 18 G. Gnani, Italy *(Gnani)*, 2m 04.95s; 19 J. Seel, W. Germany *(Seel)*, 2m 05.19s; 20 R. Kunz, W. Germany *(Ziegler)*, 2m 05.51s.

	Sidecar (25 laps, 70.55m/113.550k)	**m**	**s**	**mph**	**kmh**
1	R. Biland, Switzerland K. Waltisperg, Switzerland *(LCR-Krauser)*	45	28.87	93.07	149.798
2	S. Webster, GB T. Hewitt, GB *(LCR-Krauser)*	45	30.79	93.03	149.692
3	A. Zurbrugg, Switzerland M. Zurbrugg, Switzerland *(LCR-Yamaha)*	45	57.24	92.12	148.256
4	F. Stolzle, W. Germany H. Stolzle, W. Germany *(LCR-Krauser)*	46	09.54	91.71	147.598
5	B. Scherer, W. Germany D. Schroder, W. Germany *(BSR-Krauser)*	46	17.52	91.45	147.174
6	W. Stropek, Austria H. Demling, Austria *(LCR-Krauser)*	46	26.36	91.16	146.707
7	T. van Kempen, Holland S. Birchall, GB *(LCR-Yamaha)*	46	41.40	90.67	145.919
8	P. Larratte, France J. Corbier, France *(LCR-Yamaha)*	46	52.97	90.20	145.319
9	M. Egloff, Switzerland U. Egloff, Switzerland *(LCR-Yamaha)*	46	58.71	90.11	145.023
10	S. Abbott, GB S. Smith, GB *(Windle-Yamaha)*	47	01.97	90.01	144.856

Biland leads Webster and the traffic jam at the start of the magnificent sidecar race.

11 B. Brindley/G. Rose, GB *(Windle-Krauser)*; 12 H. Kumagaya/B. Barlow, Japan/GB *(Windle-Yamaha)*. *24 laps:* 13 D. Jones/P. Brown, GB *(LCR-Yamaha)*. *20 laps:* 14 E. Streuer/B. Schnieders, Holland *(LCR-Yamaha)*.

Record lap: R. Biland/K. Waltisperg, Switzerland *(LCR-Krauser)* 1m 45.55s, 96.26mph/154.914kmh.
Old record: E. Streuer/B. Schnieders, Holland *(LCR-Yamaha)*, 1m 47.60s, 94.43mph/151.962kmh (1986).

World Championship positions: 1 Biland/Waltisperg, 40 points; 2 Webster/Hewitt, 32; 3 Zurbrugg/Zurbrugg, 21; 4 Streuer/Schnieders, 19; 5 Brindley/Rose and van Kempen/Birchall both 18; 7 Stropek/Demling, 17; 8 Abbott/Smith, 16; 9 Scherer/Schroder, 15; 10 Stolzle/Stolzle, 14.

Practice leaderboard: 1 Biland/Waltisperg, Switzerland *(LCR-Krauser)*, 1m 45.73s; 2 Webster/Hewitt, GB *(LCR-Krauser)*, 1m 47.82s; 3 Zurbrugg/Zurbrugg, Switzerland *(LCR-Yamaha)*, 1m 48.46s; 4 Michel/Fresc, France *(LCR-Krauser)*, 1m 48.83s; 5 Kumano/Fahrni, Japan/Switzerland *(LCR-Yamaha)*, 1m 49.82s; 6 Streuer/Schnieders, Holland *(LCR-Yamaha)*, 1m 50.11s; 7 Stolzle/Stolzle, W. Germany *(LCR-Krauser)*, 1m 50.64s; 8 Abbott/Smith, GB *(Windle-Yamaha)*, 1m 50.68s; 9 Egloff/Egloff, Switzerland *(LCR-Yamaha)*, 1m 51.14s; 10 Scherer/Schroder, W. Germany *(BSR-Krauser)*, 1m 51.33s; 11 Brindley/Rose, GB *(Windle-Krauser)*, 1m 52.23s; 12 Stropek/Demling, Austria *(LCR-Krauser)*, 1m 52.29s; 13 Bosman/Kellett, Australia *(LCR-Yamaha)*, 1m 52.44s; 14 Steinhausen/Hiller, W. Germany *(ADM)*, 1m 52.66s; 15 Kumagaya/Barlow, GB *(Windle-Yamaha)*, 1m 52.75s; 16 Larratte/Corbier, France *(LCR-Yamaha)*, 1m 52.80s; 17 Jones/Brown, GB *(LCR-Yamaha)*, 1m 52.86s; 18 van Kempen/Birchall, Holland/GB *(LCR-Yamaha)*, 1m 53.55s; 19 Wyssen/Wyssen, Switzerland *(LCR-Yamaha)*, 1m 53.57s; 20 Progin/Hunziker, Switzerland *(Seymaz-Yamaha)*, 1m 53.75s.

AUSTRIAN GRAND PRIX, 12 June, Salzburgring 2.63m/4.241k

We were to look back at the end of the season and point to the day at the Salzburgring that decided the outcome of the 500cc championship. Any lingering hopes Wayne Gardner had of retaining his title disappeared in a cloud of dust on the 16th lap when his Rothmans NSR Honda seized and he crashed. Eddie Lawson won his fourth grand prix of the season in majestic style to lead Gardner by a massive 40 points. Rolf Biland and Jorge Martinez continued their domination of the sidecar and 125cc championships, but Jacques Cornu at last scored a grand prix victory in a superb 250cc race.

Many experts felt that the ultra-quick, and certainly dangerous, 2.63-mile Salzburgring would suit the power characteristics of the works Hondas and give them their first 500cc victory of the season. The four official practice sessions knocked that theory for six. Yamaha still dominated: Christian Sarron, riding the Gauloises Yamaha, and Lawson, riding the Marlboro Yamaha, were the two fastest qualifiers. Scotsman Niall Mackenzie, despite a number of seizures, kept the Honda flag flying in third with Pepsi Suzuki star Kevin Schwantz fourth and Gardner fifth.

Sadly, but so predictably, Sarron, after a bad start, crashed on the first lap and it was Gardner who led up the hill. Lawson clung to his rear wheel round the Armco-lined track, with Lucky Strike Yamaha-mounted Wayne Rainey third in front of Didier de Radigues, Australian Kevin Magee and fast-starting Ron Haslam. This was the race Gardner was determined to win and the race in which Lawson was equally determined to push him further down the points table. The result was a magnificent, no-holds-barred scrap round the fastest grand prix circuit in the world. The aggressive style of Gardner versus the super-cool Lawson kept the 90,000 crowd packed on the sides of the valley at fever pitch. They were often side by side at over 160mph, with Gardner leading for the first six laps until Lawson took his turn. De Radigues was riding brilliantly to stay with the leading pair until they hotted up the pace for what promised to be a magnificent climax. Then disaster struck Gardner and the Honda camp. Lawson had just snatched the lead on the 16th lap when Gardner felt the NSR tighten up coming down the hill. He whipped in the clutch. Hoping it might have been a brake problem he fed it back in approaching the chicane. The back wheel locked and he was highsided from the bike. He was unhurt but as he walked away he knew his chances of retaining his title had all but disappeared.

Two laps earlier Mackenzie had crashed at the same place while battling for sixth, and Lawson and de Radigues settled into a comfortable rhythm for a Marlboro Yamaha one/two that did not promise a bright remainder of the season for the others. De Radigues was understandably delighted with his second place comfortably ahead of Rainey. The Californian Lucky Strike rider took over second place in the championship from Gardner after a steady, impressive performance that was almost spoilt by Schwantz on the last lap. The Texan Suzuki rider was involved in a hectic battle with Italian Pier-Francesco Chili, riding the HB Honda, for fourth place. At one stage he cut across the chicane, showering Chili with gravel which broke the screen of the Italian's machine. Schwantz pulled away towards the finish and closed on Rainey. He failed by just over one second to catch him at the chequered flag after 29 laps. Magee, Rainey's Lucky Strike team-mate, had crashed heavily in practice and broken his finger. Despite the pain he battled bravely to finish sixth, with Japanese Rothmans Honda rider Shunji Yatsushiro seventh. Ron Haslam picked up some useful points in eighth, despite suffering from a stomach bug. He just pipped fellow Briton, Rob McElnea, riding the second Pepsi Suzuki which got slower and slower. Frenchman Patrick Igoa made a welcome return to the leaderboard in tenth place following his crash in America. There was no such joy for the unhappy Randy Mamola who retired, once again, when his Cagiva seized on the 12th lap.

35-year-old Swiss veteran Jacques Cornu had waited 14 years for his first grand prix victory. When it finally came, after a fabulous four-rider battle, he celebrated by riding round the track with a ten-foot high Swiss flag. He started like an express train on his Parisienne Honda and raced away from the battling trio of Reinhold Roth, Juan Garriga and Dominique Sarron. He had been in pole position and looked set for a comfortable victory. With six laps remaining he slowed when the tyres started to slide, and the trio behind pounced on him. They were soon locked together, each taking their turn at the front. The yellow-and-white fairing of Roth's HB Honda led most of the time. However, Cornu was not going to let his big chance slip and he plotted his move carefully on the all-important last lap. He slipstreamed Roth going up the hill and grabbed the lead at the top. He held firm until the finish with just over half a second to spare. It was the most popular win of the season for the rider who has contributed so much to grand prix racing. It was even tighter behind him with yet another old-timer, Roth, getting the better of 'young pretenders' Garriga and Sarron. He collided with Garriga's Ducados Yamaha a couple of bends from the finish, almost bringing down Sarron, riding the Rothmans Honda. Garriga stayed on and got on the winners' rostrum in third place, with a disappointed Sarron less than one-tenth of a second behind in fourth spot. Behind all the drama came Spaniard Sito Pons, riding the Campsa Honda, who was fifth. Despite lack of revs and having to fight off the determined challenge of Japanese Honda rider Masahiro Shimizu he held on to his championship lead by a single point from the in-form Garriga. Italian Luca Cadalora rode hard into seventh but never found the pace from the Marlboro Yamaha to chase the Hondas ahead of him. It was another very disappointing day for world champion Toni Mang. He made a bad start on the Rothmans Honda after choosing too high a first gear and could never pull back. He eventually finished tenth behind West German Honda privateer Manfred Herweh and Venezuelan Ivan Palazzese.

Martinez used the extra speed of his works Derbi to play games with the baying pack of Hondas in the 22-lap 125cc race. For over half the race his was the lone red machine in the pack of eight screaming Hondas that spread across the track like a swarm of brightly-coloured bees. It provided a magnificent sight and the Spaniard even had the confidence to allow three people, headed by Italian Ezio Gianola, to pass him just before half distance. With three-quarter distance approaching he decided that was enough and got his head down beneath the screen for the first time and left the Hondas to their own devices. Just two seconds covered the remaining seven places, with Gianola consolidating second place in the championship by pushing West German Stefan Prein down into third place.

The best race of the day was once again the sidecars with a frightening display of skill and aggression between the Armco. It was almost a shame that there had to be a winner but Rolf Biland and Kurt Waltisperg made it three grands prix wins in a row with yet another last-lap break. Until then they had been exchanging blows throughout 22 superb laps with Frenchmen Alain Michel and Jean-Marc Fresc and British world champions Steve Webster and Tony Hewitt. Often they were in a line across the track at over 120mph, jostling and pushing for the advantage.

Biland timed to perfection his run to the line on his Krauser-powered LCR and crossed with almost two seconds to spare. Michel held off Webster by less than half a second. Former world champions Egbert Streuer and Bernard Schnieders led the race after one lap but they had cooked their Yamaha's clutch on the line. They had to slow to let it cool off but fought back to finish fifth behind the Swiss brothers Alfred and Martin Zurbrugg.

Results

500cc (29 laps, 76.46m/123.047k)		**m**	**s**	**mph**	**kmh**
1	E. Lawson, USA *(Yamaha)*	39	40.63	115.62	186.072
2	D. de Radigues, Belgium *(Yamaha)*	39	46.42	115.34	185.621
3	W. Rainey, USA *(Yamaha)*	39	53.18	115.01	185.096
4	K. Schwantz, USA *(Suzuki)*	39	54.22	114.96	185.016
5	P. Chili, Italy *(Honda)*	39	59.94	114.69	184.575
6	K. Magee, Australia *(Yamaha)*	40	02.70	114.56	184.363
7	S. Yatsushiro, Japan *(Honda)*	40	07.46	114.33	183.999
8	R. Haslam, GB *(Elf-Honda)*	40	40.08	112.80	181.539
9	R. McElnea, GB *(Suzuki)*	40	41.00	112.76	181.470
10	P. Igoa, France *(Yamaha)*	40	48.29	112.42	180.930

28 laps: 11 G. Reiner, W. Germany *(Honda)*; 12 B. Kneubuhler, Switzerland *(Honda)*; 13 F. Biliotti, Italy *(Honda)*; 14 M. Broccoli, Italy *(Cagiva)*; 15 M. Fischer, W. Germany *(Honda)*; 16 A. Leuthe, Luxembourg *(Suzuki)*; 17 F. Holzmeier, W. Germany *(Honda)*; 18 J. Doppler, Austria *(Honda)*; 19 N. Schmassmann, Switzerland *(Honda)*; 20 G. Jung, W. Germany *(Honda)*. *27 laps:* 21 H. Schuetz, W. Germany *(Honda)*.

Record lap: D. de Radigues, Belgium *(Yamaha)*, 1m 20.61s, 117.74mph/189.490kmh.
Old record: W. Gardner, Australia *(Honda)*, 1m 21.77s; 116.07mph/186.802kmh (1987).

World Championship positions: 1 E. Lawson, 125 points; 2 W. Rainey, 97; 3 W. Gardner, 85; 4 K. Schwantz, 77; 5 K. Magee, 76; 6 N. Mackenzie, 76; 7 C. Sarron and D. de Radigues both 59; 9 P. Chili, 42; 10 S. Yatsushiro, 36.

Practice leaderboard: 1 C. Sarron, France *(Yamaha)*, 1m 20.18s; 2 E. Lawson, USA *(Yamaha)*, 1m 20.37s; 3 N. Mackenzie, GB *(Honda)*, 1m 20.71s; 4 K. Schwantz, USA *(Suzuki)*, 1m 20.97s; 5 W. Gardner, Australia *(Honda)*, 1m 21.04s; 6 D. de Radigues, Belgium *(Yamaha)*, 1m 21.15s; 7 P. Chili, Italy *(Honda)*, 1m 21.33s; 8 W. Rainey, USA *(Yamaha)*, 1m 21.54s; 9 S. Yatsushiro, Japan *(Honda)*, 1m 21.63s; 10 R. McElnea, GB *(Suzuki)*, 1m 21.93s; 11 K. Magee, Australia *(Yamaha)*, 1m 22.11s; 12 R. Haslam, GB *(Elf-Honda)*, 1m 22.41s; 13 P. Igoa, France *(Yamaha)*, 1m 22.63s; 14 R. Mamola, USA *(Cagiva)*, 1m 23.29s; 15 M. Papa, Italy *(Honda)*, 1m 23.80s; 16 A. Valesi, Italy *(Honda)*, 1m 24.17s; 17 G. Reiner, W. Germany *(Honda)*, 1m 24.25s; 18 F. Biliotti, Italy *(Honda)*, 1m 24.50s; 19 B. Kneubuhler, Switzerland *(Honda)*, 1m 24.51s; 20 M. Broccoli, Italy *(Cagiva)*, 1m 24.53s.

Every picture tells a story – Gardner seconds after his crash.

Gardner hits the Austrian ground and kisses goodbye to his championship

250cc (24 laps, 63.28m/101.832k)		**m**	**s**	**mph**	**kmh**
1	J. Cornu, Switzerland *(Honda)*	34	29.23	110.09	177.165
2	R. Roth, W. Germany *(Honda)*	34	29.85	110.05	177.112
3	J. Garriga, Spain *(Yamaha)*	34	30.21	110.03	177.081
4	D. Sarron, France *(Honda)*	34	30.50	110.02	177.056
5	S. Pons, Spain *(Honda)*	34	39.29	109.55	176.308
6	H. Shimizu, Japan *(Honda)*	34	39.54	109.54	176.287
7	L. Cadalora, Italy *(Yamaha)*	34	57.87	108.58	174.745
8	M. Herweh, W. Germany *(Yamaha)*	34	58.17	108.57	174.721
9	I. Palazzese, Venezuela *(Yamaha)*	34	58.50	108.54	174.671
10	A. Mang, W. Germany *(Honda)*	35	01.25	108.25	174.217

11 E. Neumair, Austria *(Aprilia)*; 12 M. Wimmer, W. Germany *(Yamaha)*; 13 J. Ruggia, France *(Yamaha)*; 14 H. Eckl, W. Germany *(Aprilia)*; 15 M. Vitali, Italy *(Rotax)*; 16 D. McLeod, GB *(EMC)*; 17 G. Bertin, France *(Yamaha)*; 18 A. Auinger, Austria *(Aprilia)*; 19 S. Klabacher, Austria *(Aprilia)*; 20 H. Becker, W. Germany *(Yamaha)*; 21 H. Bradl, W. Germany *(Honda)*; 22 S. Caracchi, San Marino *(Honda)*; 23 J. Balde, France *(Rotax)*; 24 K. Mitchell, GB *(Yamaha)*; 25 M. Matteoni, Italy *(Yamaha)*; 26 I. Troisi, Venezuela *(Yamaha)*; 27 J. Schmid, W. Germany *(Honda)*. *23 laps:* 28 G. Cowan, Ireland *(Yamaha)*.

Record lap: J. Cornu, Switzerland *(Honda)*, 1m 24.82s, 111.90mph/180.085kmh.
Old record: C. Cardus, Spain *(Honda)*, 1m 26.39s, 109.87mph/176.812kmh (1987).

World Championship positions: 1 S. Pons, 99 points; 2 J. Garriga, 98; 3 J. Cornu, 78; 4 D. Sarron, 68; 5 R. Roth, 65; 6 L. Cadalora, 59; 7 A. Mang, 57; 8 J. Ruggia, 51; 9 H. Shimizu, 51; 10 D. McLeod, 30.

Cornu celebrates his first grand prix victory by displaying the Swiss flag to the vast crowd.

Practice leaderboard: 1 J. Cornu, Switzerland *(Honda)*, 1m 25.19s; 2 R. Roth, W. Germany *(Honda)*, 1m 25.23s; 3 D. Sarron, France *(Honda)*, 1m 25.26s; 4 L. Cadalora, Italy *(Yamaha)*, 1m 25.29s; 5 S. Pons, Spain *(Honda)*, 1m 25.55s; 6 J. Garriga, Spain *(Yamaha)*, 1m 25.85s; 7 A. Mang, W. Germany *(Honda)*, 1m 25.96s; 8 C. Lavado, Venezuela *(Yamaha)*, 1m 26.02s; 9 I. Palazzese, Venezuela *(Yamaha)*, 1m 26.03s; 10 M. Herweh, W. Germany *(Yamaha)*, 1m 26.05s; 11 H. Shimizu, Japan *(Honda)*, 1m 26.24s; 12 C. Cardus, Spain *(Honda)*, 1m 26.41s; 13 B. Casanova, Italy *(Aprilia)*, 1m 26.53s; 14 E. Neumair, Austria *(Aprilia)*, 1m 26.55s; 15 J. Ruggia, France *(Yamaha)*, 1m 26.60s; 16 H. Eckl, W. Germany *(Aprilia)*, 1m 26.63s; 17 A. Auinger, Austria *(Aprilia)*, 1m 26.77s; 18 M. Wimmer, W. Germany *(Yamaha)*, 1m 26.93s; 19 H. Becker, W. Germany *(Yamaha)*, 1m 27.14s; 20 J. Balde, France *(Rotax)*, 1m 27.48s.

125cc (22 laps, 58.00m/93.346k)	**m**	**s**	**mph**	**kmh**
1 J. Martinez, Spain *(Derbi)*	35	03.59	99.26	159.749
2 E. Gianola, Italy *(Honda)*	35	07.91	99.06	159.421
3 S. Prein, W. Germany *(Honda)*	35	08.12	99.03	159.405
4 J. Fischer, Austria *(Rotax)*	35	08.86	99.01	159.349
5 M. Leitner, Austria *(LCR-Emco)*	35	09.08	99.00	159.333
6 H. Spaan, Holland *(Honda)*	35	09.16	98.98	159.301
7 G. Waibel, W. Germany *(Honda)*	35	09.67	98.97	159.288
8 A. Waibel, W. Germany *(Waibel)*	35	09.93	98.96	159.267
9 G. Grassetti, Italy *(Honda)*	35	13.04	98.82	159.034
10 H. Abold, W. Germany *(Honda)*	35	13.51	98.80	158.999

11 A. Stadler, W. Germany *(Honda)*; 12 J. Miralles, Spain *(Honda)*; 13 T. Feuz, Switzerland *(Rotax)*; 14 J. Wickstrom, Finland *(Honda)*; 15 R. Appleyard, GB *(Honda)*; 16 H. Unemoto, Japan *(Honda)*; 17 H. Luthi, Switzerland *(Honda)*; 18 A. Scott, USA *(Honda)*; 19 K. Takada, Japan *(Honda)*; 20 J. Seel, W. Germany *(Seel)*; 21 J. Selini, France *(Honda)*; 22 R. Milton, GB *(Rotax)*; 23 J. Hautaniemi, Finland *(Honda)*; 24 K. Galatowicz, GB *(Honda)*; 25 B. Hassaine, France *(Honda)*.

Fastest lap: H. Spaan, Holland *(Honda)*, 1m 33.51s, 101.50mph/163.349kmh.

Record lap: F. Gresini, Italy *(Garelli)*, 1m 30.58s, 104.79mph/168.633kmh (1987).

World Championship positions: 1 J. Martinez, 60 points; 2 E. Gianola, 52; 3 H. Spaan, 42; 4 G. Grassetti, 40; 5 J. Miralles, 39; 6 M. Herreros, 30; 7 H. Unemoto, 26; 8 A. Stadler and G. Waibel both 24; 10 S. Prein, 23.

Practice leaderboard: 1 J. Martinez, Spain *(Derbi)*, 1m 32.67s; 2 H. Spaan, Holland *(Honda)*, 1m 33.42s; 3 M. Herreros, Spain *(Derbi)*, 1m 33.91s; 4 S. Prein, W. Germany *(Honda)*, 1m 34.03s; 5 E. Gianola, Italy *(Honda)*, 1m 34.21s; 6 G. Waibel, W. Germany *(Honda)*, 1m 34.23s; 7 A. Stadler, W. Germany *(Honda)*, 1m 34.67s; 8 H. Abold, W. Germany *(Honda)*, 1m 34.69s; 9 M. Leitner, Austria *(LCR-Emco)*, 1m 34.89s; 10 G. Grassetti, Italy *(Honda)*, 1m 34.93s; 11 E. Kytola, Finland *(Honda)*, 1m 34.98s; 12 L. Pietroniro, Belgium *(Honda)*, 1m 35.03s; 13 A. Waibel, W. Germany *(Waibel)*, 1m 35.13s; 14 D. Brigaglia, Italy *(Rotax)*, 1m 35.19s; 15 J. Selini, France *(Honda)*, 1m 35.19s; 16 S. Dorflinger, Switzerland *(Honda)*, 1m 35.23s; 17 J. Fischer, Austria *(Rotax)*, 1m 35.30s; 18 J. Miralles, Spain *(Honda)*, 1m 35.30s; 19 J. Seel, W. Germany *(Seel)*, 1m 35.32s; 20 P. Bianchi, Italy *(Cagiva)*, 1m 35.37s.

Sidecar (22 laps, 58.00m/93.346k)	**m**	**s**	**mph**	**kmh**
1 R. Biland, Switzerland K. Waltisperg, Switzerland *(LCR-Krauser)*	32	11.52	108.11	173.980
2 A. Michel, France J. Fresc, France *(LCR-Krauser)*	32	13.42	108.00	173.809
3 S. Webster, GB T. Hewitt, GB *(LCR-Krauser)*	32	13.63	107.99	173.790

4	A. Zurbrugg, Switzerland M. Zurbrugg, Switzerland *(LCR-Yamaha)*	32 34.00	106.86	171.978
5	E. Streuer, Holland B. Schnieders, Holland *(LCR-Yamaha)*	32 47.41	106.14	170.806
6	S. Abbott, GB S. Smith, GB *(Windle-Yamaha)*	32 50.48	105.97	170.540
7	P. Larratte, France J. Corbier, France *(LCR-Yamaha)*	32 53.56	105.80	170.274
8	D. Jones, GB P. Brown, GB *(LCR-Yamaha)*	32 54.50	105.75	170.193
9	B. Scherer, W. Germany T. Schroder, W. Germany *(BSR-Krauser)*	33 10.06	104.93	168.862
10	B. Brindley, GB G. Rose, GB *(Krauser-Yamaha)*	33 10.56	104.90	168.820

11 A. Bosman/D. Kellett, Australia *(LCR-Yamaha)*; 12 T. van Kempen/S. Birchall, Holland/GB *(LCR-Yamaha)*; 13 W. Stropek/H. Demling, Austria *(LCR-Krauser)*. *21 laps:* 14 G. Thomas/G. de Haas, GB/Holland *(LCR-Krauser)*; 15 D. Bingham/G. Irlam, GB *(LCR-Yamaha)*. *17 laps:* 16 R. Progin/Y. Hunziker, Switzerland *(Seymaz-Yamaha)*.

Record lap: R. Biland/K. Waltisperg, Switzerland *(LCR-Krauser)*, 1m 25.87s; 110.53mph/177.883kmh.
Old record: A. Michel/J. Fresc, France *(LCR-Krauser)*, 1m 26.56s, 109.65mph/176.465kmh (1986).

World Championship positions: 1 Biland/Waltisperg, 60 points; 2 Webster/Hewitt, 47; 3 Zurbrugg/Zurbrugg, 34; 4 Streuer/Schnieders, 30; 5 Michel/Fresc, 28; 6 Abbott/Smith, 26; 7 Brindley/Rose, 24; 8 Scherer/Schroder, 22; 9 van Kempen/S. Birchall, 22; 10 Stropek/Demling, 20.

Practice leaderboard: 1 Biland/Waltisperg, Switzerland *(LCR-Krauser)*, 1m 23.82s; 2 Streuer/Schnieders, Holland *(LCR-Yamaha)*, 1m 26.22s; 3 Zurbrugg/Zurbrugg, Switzerland *(LCR-Yamaha)*, 1m 26.29s; 4 Webster/Hewitt, GB *(LCR-Krauser)*, 1m 26.30s; 5 Michel/Fresc, France *(LCR-Krauser)*, 1m 27.18s; 6 Egloff/Egloff, Switzerland *(LCR-Yamaha)*, 1m 27.23s; 7 Steinhausen/Hiller, W. Germany *(ADM-Krauser)*, 1m 27.74s; 8 Kumano/Fahrni, Japan/Switzerland *(LCR-Tec)*, 1m 27.81s; 9 Stropek/Demling, Austria *(LCR-Krauser)*, 1m 28.16s; 10 Larratte/Corbier, France *(LCR-Yamaha)*, 1m 28.70s; 11 Jones/Brown, GB *(LCR-Yamaha)*, 1m 28.76s; 12 Bosman/Kellett, Australia *(LCR-Yamaha)*, 1m 28.83s; 13 Kumagaya/Barlow, Japan/GB *(Windle-Yamaha)*, 1m 28.85s; 14 Abbott/Smith, GB *(Windle-Yamaha)*, 1m 28.96s; 15 Stolzle/Stolzle, W. Germany *(LCR-Krauser)*, 1m 29.21s; 16 Brindley/Rose, GB *(Krauser-Yamaha)*, 1m 29.43s; 17 van Kempen/Birchall, Holland/GB *(LCR-Yamaha)*, 1m 29.80s; 18 Nigrowsky/Charpentier, France *(Seymaz-Yamaha)*, 1m 29.82s; 19 Scherer/Schroder, W. Germany *(BSR-Krauser)*, 1m 30.09s; 20 D. Bingham/G. Irlam, GB *(LCR-Yamaha)*, 1m 30.67s.

DUTCH GRAND PRIX, 25 June, Assen 3.812m/6.134k

While the nation watched their soccer side win the European Nations Cup, 120,000 fans at Assen witnessed as much drama as any 90 minutes of football action could produce.

World Champion Wayne Gardner at last got back to winning, Pons and Sarron slogged it out into the very last chicane, and, about as predictable as England's demise in the football, Martinez won both the 80 and 125cc races and Rolf Biland the sidecars.

After seven grands prix without a victory Gardner's win in the 20-lap 500cc race was long overdue. It made little overall difference in the championship with Eddie Lawson finishing second, despite handling problems with his Marlboro Yamaha.

However the emphatic win gave Gardner and his Rothmans Honda team great heart, and just a chink of hope that the championship wasn't completely over, despite the massive 37-point deficit. Frenchman Christian Sarron qualified in pole position with Lawson, Magee, Gardner and de Radigues completing the front row. Dr Costa's mobile clinic was a busy place during practice. Kevin Schwantz was first to arrive with a broken toe that would not stay in place following a brush with the Assen tarmac. Close behind him came Scotsman Niall Mackenzie with three broken toes. Both rode in the race and collected valuable points.

Lawson blasted from the line on his Yamaha followed by Ron Haslam on the Elf 5. His challenge lasted just half a lap when his visor misted up and he dropped back to eventually finish a disappointing 13th. De Radigues protected his team leader's back for three laps until Gardner pushed him aside and set after Lawson. De Radigues tried to hang onto the champion's back wheel but slipped back and then crashed on the eighth lap. He remounted to finish 12th. Gardner was in a mean mood after so many disappointments and stalked the orange and white prey in front of him. On the 13th lap he dived into the lead and it was obvious that Lawson did not have the weapons to fight back. While Gardner poured on the coals at the front, Lawson, with the wrong tyre choice and rear end vibration, settled into a comfortable second and 17 vital championship points.

Once again the battle royal between the two best riders in the world just did not happen, although Gardner's three-day hangover after the race summed up his feelings better than any words.

Sarron made another messy start from pole position but took over third when de Radigues crashed. He rode sensibly for the remaining 12 laps to claim third place on the Gauloises Yamaha, despite some rear suspension problems towards the finish. Australian Kevin Magee chased him hard but never got near enough to mount a serious challenge, riding his spare Lucky Strike, Team Roberts Yamaha. His race bike broke a primary gear in the morning warm-up.

Mackenzie borrowed Gardner's special boot to protect his injured toes and had an eventful and successful time on the HB Honda. Fellow crock Schwantz hit him on the line and after recovering from the shock he was down in 15th place at the end of the first lap. He fought back with a real aggression that has not always been evident in his short grand prix career, carving his way through the field to finish a brilliant fifth, just five seconds behind Magee to renew hope of a British grand prix success in the not-too distant future.

Mackenzie's team-mate Pier-Francesco Chili made a good start but eventually dropped to sixth in front of a desperate dice for seventh. Californian Wayne Rainey and Texan

Schwantz had always been bitter rivals in their American Superbike days. Nothing has changed since they graduated to the grands prix. This time Rainey, despite front end vibration problems with his Lucky Strike Yamaha, held off the injured Pepsi Suzuki star by 0.67 seconds. His team-mate Rob McElnea was 10th but the ever-popular Randy Mamola dropped out of seventh when his Cagiva broke a crankcase seal.

Explosive tempers had to be restrained after a remarkable 18-lap 250cc race. It ended with the two leaders in the sand in sight of the chequered flag and a new leader in the championship. Spaniard Sito Pons and Frenchman Dominique Sarron had been scrapping it out at the front in a rare old battle that ended in disaster and scuffles for both. Pons, riding the Campsa Honda led as they approached the final chicane with the chequered flag being readied. Sarron pushed his Rothmans Honda up the inside, the brace of Hondas collided and went down like a couple of pheasants. Pons remounted and amid a sand storm, kicked up by his back wheel, screamed home in sixth place. Sarron was not so lucky and could not re-start. Words and some airy blows were thrown just after the race before the air cleared.

From the neutral umpire's chair it looked like a case of six of one and a half dozen of the other. While all the excitement continued in the sand pit, Spaniard Juan Garriga crossed the line a surprised – but very happy – winner, on his Ducados Yamaha. He was even happier when he learnt that Pons could only finish sixth, thus regaining his championship lead by nine points. He'd fought an equally tough duel with Swiss veteran Jacques Cornu, riding the Parisienne Honda, with an even better race for the unexpected third place.

World Champion Toni Mang, riding the Rothmans Honda, got back on the rostrum for the first time since Suzuka after a blanket finish in which he pipped Italians Luca Cadalora and Loris Reggiani. It was a great ride by Cadalora. He was last away on the Marlboro Yamaha. Pons limped home sixth in front of HB Honda star Reinhold Roth.

Grand prix crowds are getting used to the Spanish national anthem. The day started with those familiar tones rolling across the flat Dutch countryside after Martinez comfortably won the 12-lap 80cc race. He was in no mood for games and cleared off in the opening lap, never to be seen by the remainder of the field. Two of his pursuers crashed giving chase. Former World Champion Stefan Dorflinger fell from his Krauser pushing Derbi-mounted Alex Criville up into second. He fell at half distance with West German Peter Ottl grabbing second spot from local hero Bert Smit.

The following 16-lap 125cc race was a case of the same old story for the flying Spaniard and his bright red Derbi. He toyed with the opposition for three-quarters of the race before clearing off to give Derbi their 60th grand prix victory. As always hard riding Italian Ezio Gianola led the Honda charge together with Dutch veteran Hans Spaan, but when it mattered they could not match the pace of the Derbi and that national anthem boomed out once again.

Even the crowd's excitement on hearing of Holland's second goal in the soccer final could not alter the course of the 16-lap sidecar race. Rolf Biland and Kurt Waltisperg not only continued their clean sweep of this year's championship but also won the popular Swiss driver his 50th grand prix victory. Since taking on the experienced Harold Bartol to look after their Krauser engine those mechanical breakdowns, that always gave his rivals a chance, have been eliminated. The crowd's cheers also went out to former world champions – and local lads – Egbert Streuer and Bernard Schnieders. They pinched second place from British world champions Steve Webster and Tony Hewitt who had slowed to third with a jumping sprocket after leading in the early stages. They thus trailed Biland by 18 points in the championship and thought that a Biland breakdown was their only real chance of retaining their hard-won title.

Veteran Derek Jones and passenger Peter Brown were a brilliant fifth behind the impressive Egloff brothers. It earned them enough prize money to continue their unsponsored campaign. Barry Brindley and Steve Abbott were seventh and eighth respectively in a good race for British crews and an even better race for Biland.

Results

500cc (20 laps, 76.24m/122.68k)		**m**	**s**	**mph**	**kmh**
1	W. Gardner, Australia *(Honda)*	44	15.49	103.35	166.315
2	E. Lawson, USA *(Yamaha)*	44	26.80	102.91	165.610
3	C. Sarron, France *(Yamaha)*	44	35.22	102.58	165.088
4	K. Magee, Australia *(Yamaha)*	44	39.73	102.41	164.811
5	N. Mackenzie, GB *(Honda)*	44	44.92	102.21	164.492
6	P. Chili, Italy *(Honda)*	44	54.27	101.86	163.921
7	W. Rainey, USA *(Yamaha)*	44	57.13	101.75	163.747
8	K. Schwantz, USA *(Suzuki)*	44	57.80	101.73	163.707
9	P. Igoa, France *(Yamaha)*	45	04.48	101.47	163.302
10	R. McElnea, GB *(Suzuki)*	45	08.77	101.31	163.044

11 S. Yatsushiro, Japan *(Honda)*; 12 D. de Radigues, Belgium *(Yamaha)*; 13 R. Haslam, GB *(Elf-Honda)*; 14 M. Papa, Italy *(Honda)*. *19 laps:* 15 M. Gentile, Switzerland *(Fior)*; 16 F. Biliotti, Italy *(Honda)*; 17 B. Kneubuhler, Switzerland *(Honda)*; 18 D. Amatriain, Spain *(Honda)*; 19 M. Rudroff, W. Germany *(Honda)*; 20 E. Laycock, Ireland *(Honda)*; 21 J. Doppler, Austria *(Honda)*; 22 K. van der Endt, Holland *(Honda)*; 23 S. Habat, Yugoslavia *(Honda)*.

Record lap: W. Gardner, Australia *(Honda)*; 2m 11.28s, 104.52mph/168.208kmh.
Old record: W. Gardner, Australia *(Honda)*, 2m 14.28s, 102.18mph/164.450kmh (1986).

World Championship positions: 1 E. Lawson, 142 points; 2 W. Rainey, 106; 3 W. Gardner, 105; 4 K. Magee, 89; 5 K. Schwantz, 85; 6 C. Sarron, 74; 7 N. Mackenzie 71; 8 D. de Radigues, 63; 9 P. Chili, 52; 10 R. McElnea and S. Yatsushiro both 41.

Practice leaderboard: 1 C. Sarron, France *(Yamaha)*, 2m 10.94s; 2 E. Lawson, USA *(Yamaha)*, 2m 11.66s; 3 K. Magee, USA *(Yamaha)*, 2m 11.76s; 4 W. Gardner, Australia *(Honda)*, 2m 12.08s; 5 D. de Radigues, Belgium *(Yamaha)*, 2m 12.18s; 6 N. Mackenzie, GB *(Honda)*, 2m 12.95s; 7 W. Rainey, USA *(Yamaha)*, 2m 13.07s; 8 P. Chili, Italy *(Honda)*, 2m 13.38s; 9 R. Mamola, USA *(Cagiva)*, 2m 13.45s; 10 P. Igoa, France *(Yamaha)*, 2m 13.69s; 11 K. Schwantz, USA *(Suzuki)*, 2m 14.05s; 12 S. Yatsushiro, Japan *(Honda)*, 2m 14.15s; 13 R. McElnea, GB *(Suzuki)*, 2m 14.65s; 14 R. Haslam, GB *(Elf-Honda)*, 2m 15.05s; 15 F. Biliotti, Italy *(Honda)*, 2m 17.45s; 16 G. Reiner, W. Germany *(Honda)*, 2m 17.54s; 17 A. Valesi, Italy *(Honda)*, 2m 17.75s; 18 C. Doorakker, Holland *(Honda)*, 2m 17.75s; 19 F. Barchitta, San Marino *(Honda)*, 2m 17.77s; 20 M. Papa, Italy *(Honda)*, 2m 17.80s.

250cc (18 laps, 64.81m/104.28k)		**m**	**s**	**mph**	**kmh**
1	J. Garriga, Spain *(Yamaha)*	39	01.03	99.64	160.357
2	J. Cornu, Switzerland *(Honda)*	39	01.26	99.63	160.341
3	A. Mang, W. Germany *(Honda)*	39	11.01	99.22	159.676
4	L. Cadalora, Italy *(Yamaha)*	39	11.24	99.21	159.661
5	L. Reggiani, Italy *(Aprilia)*	39	11.56	99.19	159.639
6	S. Pons, Spain *(Honda)*	39	12.26	99.17	159.592
7	R. Roth, W. Germany *(Honda)*	39	19.84	98.84	159.079
8	B. Casanova, Italy *(Aprilia)*	39	38.22	98.08	157.849
9	M. Wimmer, W. Germany *(Yamaha)*	39	40.79	97.97	157.679
10	M. Herweh, W. Germany *(Yamaha)*	39	42.21	97.92	157.585

11 J. Ruggia, France *(Yamaha)*; 12 C. Cardus, Spain *(Honda)*; 13 I. Palazzese, Venezuela *(Yamaha)*; 14 D. McLeod, GB *(EMC)*; 15 W. Zeelenberg, Holland *(Yamaha)*; 16 J. Mattioli, France *(Yamaha)*; 17 A. Preining, Austria *(Aprilia)*; 18 U. Luzi, Switzerland *(Honda)*; 19 J. Balde, France *(Rotax)*; 20 H. Bradl, W. Germany *(Honda)*; 21 X. Cardelus, Andorra *(Aprilia)*; 22 J. Schmid, W. Germany *(Honda)*; 23 A. Auinger, Austria *(Aprilia)*; 24 J. Foray, France *(Yamaha)*; 25 P. van den Goorbergh, Holland *(Honda)*. *16 laps:* 26 G. Cowan, Ireland *(Yamaha)*.

Record lap: A Mang, W. Germany *(Honda)*, 2m 16.00s, 100.89mph/162.371kmh.
Old record: A. Mang, W. Germany *(Honda)*, 2m 17.75s, 99.61mph/160.308kmh (1987).

World Championship positions: 1 J. Garriga, 118 points; 2 S. Pons, 109; 3 J. Cornu, 95; 4 R. Roth, 74; 5 L. Cadalora and A. Mang both 72; 7 D. Sarron, 68; 8 J. Ruggia, 56; 9 M. Shimizu, 51; 10 D. McLeod, 32.

The moment of truth. Sarron (inside) and Pons about to fall out in a big way.

Practice leaderboard: 1 D. Sarron, France *(Honda)*, 2m 16.46s; 2 J. Garriga, Spain *(Yamaha)*, 2m 16.86s; 3 S. Pons, Spain *(Honda)*, 2m 16.97s; 4 J. Cornu, Switzerland *(Honda)*, 2m 17.15s; 5 R. Roth, W. Germany *(Honda)*, 2m 17.43s; 6 L. Cadalora, Italy *(Yamaha)*, 2m 17.46s; 7 C. Lavado, Venezuela *(Yamaha)*, 2m 18.03s; 8 L. Reggiani, Italy *(Aprilia)*, 2m 18.33s; 9 M. Wimmer, W. Germany *(Yamaha)*, 2m 18.38s; 10 A. Mang, W. Germany *(Honda)*, 2m 18.41s; 11 M. Shimizu, Japan *(Honda)*, 2m 18.53s; 12 B. Casanova, Italy *(Aprilia)*, 2m 18.56s; 13 J. Ruggia, France *(Yamaha)*, 2m 18.74s; 14 I. Palazzese, Venezuela *(Yamaha)*, 2m 19.00s; 15 C. Cardus, Spain *(Honda)*, 2m 19.04s; 16 D. McLeod, GB *(EMC)*, 2m 19.08s; 17 H. Eckl, W. Germany *(Aprilia)*, 2m 19.13s; 18 F. Ricci, Italy *(Aprilia)*, 2m 19.14s; 19 M. Vitali, Italy *(Rotax)*, 2m 19.18s; 20 J. Balde, France *(Rotax)*, 2m 19.40s.

125cc (16 laps, 60.99m/98.14k)		**m**	**s**	**mph**	**kmh**
1	J. Martinez, Spain *(Derbi)*	39	42.15	92.16	148.319
2	E. Gianola, Italy *(Honda)*	39	45.75	92.02	148.095
3	H. Spaan, Holland *(Honda)*	39	49.71	91.87	147.850
4	D. Brigaglia, Italy *(Rotax)*	40	00.41	91.46	147.191
5	G. Waibel, W. Germany *(Honda)*	40	01.57	91.42	147.120
6	S. Prein, W. Germany *(Honda)*	40	16.37	90.86	146.219
7	H. Abold, W. Germany *(Honda)*	40	24.81	90.54	145.710
8	C. Catalano, Italy *(Aprilia)*	40	29.49	90.36	145.429
9	P. Bianchi, Italy *(Cagiva)*	40	29.81	90.35	145.410
10	A. Stadler, W. Germany *(Honda)*	40	31.06	90.31	145.335

11 H. Luthi, Switzerland *(Honda)*; 12 J. Hautaniemi, Finland *(Honda)*; 13 T. Feuz, Switzerland *(Rotax)*; 14 R. Milton, GB *(Honda)*; 15 J. Fischer, Austria *(Rotax)*; 16 L. Reyes, Spain *(Garelli)*; 17 J. Wickstrom, Finland *(Honda)*; 18 K. Galatowicz, GB *(Honda)*; 19 J. Bolart, Spain *(Cobas)*; 20 A. Scott, USA *(Honda)*; 21 N. Peschke, W. Germany *(Rotax)*; 22 J. Seel, W. Germany *(Seel)*; 23 J. van Dongen, Holland *(Honda)*; 24 F. Kistrup, Denmark *(Honda)*. *14 laps:* 25 H. Unemoto, Japan *(Honda)*.

Fastest lap: J. Martinez, Spain *(Derbi)*, 2m 26.52s, 93.65mph/150.713kmh.
Record lap: F. Gresini, Italy *(Garelli)*, 2m 24.02s, 95.28mph/153.329kmh (1987).

World Championship positions: 1 J. Martinez, 80 points; 2 E. Gianola, 69; 3 H. Spaan, 57; 4 G. Grassetti, 40; 5 J. Miralles, 39; 6 G. Waibel, 35; 7 S. Prein, 33; 8 M. Herreros and A. Stadler both 30; 10 H. Unemoto, 26.

Practice leaderboard: 1 H. Spaan, Holland *(Honda)*, 2m 27.50s; 2 J. Martinez, Spain *(Derbi)*, 2m 27.57s; 3 P. Bianchi, Italy *(Cagiva)*, 2m 27.95s; 4 E. Gianola, Italy *(Honda)*, 2m 28.36s; 5 C. Catalano, Italy *(Aprilia)*, 2m 28.48s; 6 S. Dorflinger, Switzerland *(Honda)*, 2m 28.65s; 7 D. Brigaglia, Italy *(Rotax)*, 2m 28.67s; 8 H. Abold, W. Germany *(Honda)*, 2m 28.88s; 9 G. Grassetti, Italy *(Honda)*, 2m 29.02s; 10 S. Prein, W. Germany *(Honda)*, 2m 29.13s; 11 I. McConnachie, GB *(Cagiva)*, 2m 29.35s; 12 A. Stadler, W. Germany *(Honda)*, 2m 29.62s; 13 C. Miralles, Spain *(Honda)*, 2m 29.70s; 14 K. Takada, Japan *(Honda)*, 2m 29.83s; 15 G. Waibel, W. Germany *(Honda)*, 2m 29.89s; 16 M. Leitner, Austria *(Emco)*, 2m 29.93s; 17. A. Waibel, W. Germany *(Waibel)*, 2m 30.12s; 18

L. Reyes, Spain *(Garelli)* 2m 30.27s; 19 J. Hautaniemi, Finland *(Honda)*, 2m 30.32s; 20 F. Gresini, Italy *(Garelli)*, 2m 30.47s.

80cc (12 laps, 45.74m/73.61k)	**m**	**s**	**mph**	**kmh**
1 J. Martinez, Spain *(Derbi)*	31	22.38	87.47	140.773
2 P. Ottl, W. Germany *(Krauser)*	31	30.77	87.08	140.149
3 B. Smit, Holland *(Minarelli)*	31	52.43	86.10	138.560
4 J. van Dongen, Holland *(Casal)*	31	58.44	85.83	138.127
5 H. Torrontegui, Spain *(Autisa)*	32	02.72	85.66	137.820
6 J. Seel, W. Germany *(Seel)*	32	03.00	85.63	137.800
7 A. Nijenhuis, Holland *(Casal)*	32	04.07	85.58	137.723
8 B. Nikolov, Bulgaria *(Krauser)*	32	11.90	85.23	137.165
9 K. Juhasz, Hungary *(Krauser)*	32	21.63	84.80	136.477
10 G. Ascareggi, Italy *(BBFT)*	32	26.07	84.61	136.166

11 G. Schirnhofer, W. Germany *(Krauser)*; 12 R. Koster, Switzerland *(Casal)*; 13 H. Koopman, Holland *(Ziegler)*; 14 G. Gnani, Italy *(Gnani)*; 15 R. Dunki, Switzerland *(LCR)*; 16 X. Arumi, Spain *(Krauser)*; 17 J. Lutzenberger, W. Germany *(Eberhardt)*; 18 J. Saez, Spain *(Autisa)*; 19 S. Julin, Belgium *(Casal)*; 20 S. Braegger, Switzerland *(Casal)*; 21 T. Engl, W. Germany *(Esch)*; 22 R. Sassone, Italy *(BBFT)*; 23 L. Robert, France *(SPR)*; 24 P. Tibori, Hungary *(Casal)*; 25 A Pavlic, Yugoslavia *(Seel)*. *11 laps:* 26 J. Bernard, Belgium *(Fantic)*.

Fastest lap: P. Ottl, W. Germany *(Krauser)*, 2m 33.98s, 89.11mph/143.411kmh.
Record lap: I. McConnachie, GB *(Krauser)*, 2m 30.79s, 91.00mph/146.445kmh (1986).

World Championship positions: 1 J. Martinez, 97 points; 2 A. Criville and M. Herreros both 60; 4 S. Dorflinger, 50; 5 P. Ottl, 48; 6 J. van Dongen, 39; 7 G. Ascareggi and K. Juhasz both 35; 9 B. Nikolov, 34; 10 G. Gnani, 27.

Practice leaderboard: 1 J. Martinez, Spain *(Derbi)*, 2m 32.16s; 2 S. Dorflinger, Switzerland *(Krauser)*, 2m 34.44s; 3 P. Ottl, W. Germany *(Krauser)*, 2m 35.93s; 4. B. Smit, Holland *(Minarelli)*, 2m 37.58s; 5 A. Criville, Spain *(Derbi)*, 2m 38.54s; 6 J. van Dongen, Holland *(Casal)*, 2m 38.78s; 7 K. Juhasz, Hungary *(Krauser)*, 2m 39.17s; 8 R. Dunki, Switzerland *(LCR)*, 2m 39.63s; 9 M. Ehinder, W. Germany *(Krauser)*, 2m 39.71s; 10 J. Szabo, Hungary *(Krauser)*, 2m 39.97s; 11 A. Nijenhuis, Holland *(Casal)*, 2m 40.05s; 12 J. Seel, W. Germany *(Seel)*, 2m 40.13s; 13 B. Nikolov, Bulgaria *(Krauser)*, 2m 40.13s; 14 H. Torrontegui, Spain *(Autisa)*, 2m 40.54s; 15 H. Koopman, Holland *(Ziegler)*, 2m 41.09s; 16 C. Besseling, Holland *(CJB-BO)*, 2m 41.17s; 17 S. Julin, Belgium *(Casal)*, 2m 41.33s; 18 J. Bernard, Belgium *(Fantic)*, 2m 42.11s; 19 G. Ascareggi, Italy *(BBFT)*, 2m 42.14s; 20 G. Schirnhofer, W. Germany *(Krauser)*, 2m 42.42s.

Sidecar (16 laps, 60.99m/98.14k)	**m**	**s**	**mph**	**kmh**
1 R. Biland, Switzerland K. Waltisperg, Switzerland *(LCR-Krauser)*	37	10.68	98.42	158.390
2 E. Streuer, Holland B. Schnieders, Holland *(LCR-Yamaha)*	37	25.24	97.78	157.363

3	S. Webster, GB T. Hewitt, GB *(LCR-Krauser)*	37 45.77	96.89	155.937
4	M. Egloff, Switzerland U. Egloff, Switzerland *(LCR-Yamaha)*	37 56.71	96.43	155.188
5	D. Jones, GB P. Brown, GB *(LCR-Yamaha)*	38 06.62	96.01	154.516
6	M. Kumano, Japan M. Fahrni, Switzerland *(LCR-Yamaha)*	38 19.00	95.49	153.684
7	B. Brindley, GB G. Simmons, GB *(LCR-Yamaha)*	38 37.25	94.74	152.473
8	S. Abbot, GB S. Smith, GB *(Windle-Yamaha)*	38 48.62	94.28	151.729
9	F. Stolzle, W. Germany H. Stolzle, W. Germany *(LCR-Krauser)*	38 53.94	94.06	151.383
10	Y. Kumagaya, Japan B. Barlow, GB *(Windle-Yamaha)*	38 54.32	94.05	151.358

15 laps: 11 P. Larratte/E. Rosinger, France/W. Germany *(LCR-Yamaha)*; 12 A. Zurbrugg/M. Zurbrugg, Switzerland *(LCR-Yamaha)*; 13 J. van Stekelenburg/R. Bettgens, Holland *(Windle-Yamaha)*. *14 laps:* 14 W. Stropek/H. Demling, Austria *(Mibag Eigenbau)*.

Record lap: R. Biland/K. Waltisperg, Switzerland *(LCR-Krauser)*, 2m 17.35s, 99.90mph/160.775kmh.
Old record: R. Biland/K. Waltisperg, Switzerland *(LCR-Krauser)*, 2m 20.27s; 97.82mph/157.428kmh (1986).

World Championship positions: 1 Biland/Waltisperg, 80 points; 2 Webster/Hewitt, 62; 3 Streuer/Schnieders, 47; 4 Zurbrugg/Zurbrugg, 38; 5 Abbott/Smith, 34; 6 Brindley/ Rose, 33; 7 Jones/Brown, 30; 8 Michel/Fresc, 28; 9 Scherer/Schroder, Stropek/Demling, van Kempen/Birchall and Larratte/Corbier all 22.

Practice leaderboard: 1 Biland/Waltisperg, Switzerland *(LCR-Krauser)*, 2m 15.29s; 2 Streuer/Schnieders, Holland *(LCR-Yamaha)*, 2m 16.40s; 3 Webster/Hewitt, GB *(LCR-Krauser)*, 2m 17.18s; 4 Egloff/Egloff, Switzerland *(LCR-Yamaha)*, 2m 17.98s; 5 M. Kumano/M. Fahrni, Japan/Switzerland *(LCR-Yamaha)*, 2m 19.80s; 6 A. Michel/J. Fresc, France *(LCR-Krauser)*, 2m 20.59s; 7 Zurbrugg/Zurbrugg, Switzerland *(LCR-Yamaha)*, 2m 20.81s; 8 Brindley/Simmons, GB *(LCR-Yamaha)*, 2m 21.66s; 9 Kumagaya/Barlow, Japan/GB *(Windle-Yamaha)*, 2m 21.73s; 10 Jones/Brown, GB *(LCR-Yamaha)*, 2m 22.12s; 11 Abbott/Smith, GB *(Windle-Yamaha)*, 2m 22.62s; 12 Wyssen/Wyssen, Switzerland *(LCR-Yamaha)*, 2m 22.68s; 13 Stolzle/Stolzle, W. Germany *(LCR-Krauser)*, 2m 22.87s; 14 Nigrowsky/Charpentier, France *(Seymaz-Yamaha)*, 2m 23.23s; 15 Steinhausen/Hiller, W. Germany *(ADM)*, 2m 23.43s; 16 Larratte/Corbier, France *(LCR-Yamaha)*, 2m 23.55s; 17 Scherer/Schroder, W. Germany *(BSR-Krauser)*, 2m 23.86s; 18 Bosman/Kellett, Australia *(LCR-Yamaha)*, 2m 24.81s; 19 Stropek/Demling, Austria *(Mibag Eigenbau)*, 2m 24.89s; 20 van Stekelenburg/Bettgens, Holland *(Windle-Yamaha)*, 2m 24.93s.

BELGIAN GRAND PRIX, 3 July, Spa Francorchamps 4.312m/6.940k

A damp Spa is not a nice place for spectators. For riders it spells danger and once again the future of the famous venue, high in the Ardennes, as a grand prix motorcycle circuit is in doubt. Wayne Gardner's impressive victory in the 500cc race, Rolf Biland and Jorge Martinez's continued domination of their respective classes and an exciting victory by Sito Pons in the 250cc race may provide the memories for some people. However, for most, the horrendous accident involving Martin Wimmer and Loris Reggiani, that stopped the 250cc race, will be the most poignant memory of a miserable day. Incredibly neither rider was seriously injured but the way their machines bounced off the armco round the almost flat-out left-hand bend, just before the chicane, was a reminder of just how dangerous the 4.3 mile circuit can be.

Conditions could not have been worse for the 17-lap 500cc race. The famous Spa drizzle, that appears through the trees like smoke, made the track slippery and tyres were changed with gay abandon on the line. There had only been one dry period during the four practice sessions, and once again Christian Sarron led the way with Lawson, Rainey, Schwantz and Gardner making up the front row.

Gardner played games on the start line trying to psych out the opposition by changing tyres behind a protective sheet. All the time he'd picked a heavily cut intermediate on the front and lightly cut slick rear. He raced from the line on the Rothmans Honda pushing Schwantz, and the Pepsi Suzuki, aside at the left-hander at the bottom of the hill. Lawson was second at the end of the first lap, but Sarron, an acknowledged rain expert, was on the charge and relegated the championship leader to second and set after Gardner. He decimated the champion's three-second advantage and closed, through the spray, onto his back wheel. Gardner slowed the pace but still Sarron did not strike. He was waiting until the last lap to make his move – that last lap never came. Three laps from the finish his concentration wavered and the front wheel of his Gauloises Yamaha clipped a white line, and he went down, though thankfully without injury.

This gave Gardner the chance to cruise home for his second successive grand prix victory but, as at Assen, 'steady' Eddie had the championship situation well under control. Never taking any risks in the tricky conditions he successfully piloted the Marlboro Yamaha to another 17 championship points, and still had a 34-point lead at the end of the day.

The progress behind him of a certain Randy Mamola had the crowd on their feet and forgetting the rain. The Californian, who finished runner-up in the championship last year, is still the most popular rider on the grands prix scene despite a string of disastrous results on the Cagiva. With the Pirelli tyres working well in the damp, Mamola closed to within 10 seconds of Lawson but almost lost his place on the rostrum after some typical fooling. He pulled such a massive wheelie crossing the line he was almost caught by Lawson's team-mate, Didier de Radigues. He just held onto third place to face his standing ovation with tears of joy.

There were tears of a different sort from Schwantz who'd battled with de Radigues for most of the race before crashing two laps from the finish. He broke his right knee-cap and flew to Italy the next day for an operation.

Wayne Rainey kept the Lucky Strike Yamaha flag flying in fifth place with team-mate

Kevin Magee missing the race with concussion following a practice crash. Rob McElnea, riding the Pepsi Suzuki, produced his best result of the season in sixth place with Ron Haslam a very impressive seventh on the Elf 5. Niall Mackenzie never got to grips with the power of his NSR HB Honda in the damp and was a very disappointing 11th.

The opening race of the 250 was stopped after just four laps allowing the ambulances to reach the injured Wimmer and Reggiani. The paddock was silent as everybody feared the worst. Amazingly Wimmer got away with concussion, broken ribs and extensive bruising. Reggiani, who lay unconscious by the side of the track, escaped with a broken toe.

Wimmer's Yamaha had seized and hit the armco and bounced back into the track. Reggiani hit the wreckage flat out in top gear. Last year the riders refused to compete at Spa until a run-off area was built at the 130mph left-hander. A small but inadequate run off was built but there is still none at the bend where Wimmer seized.

Championship leader Juan Garriga was in front on the Ducados Yamaha when the race was stopped with Sito Pons, Jacques Cornu and Dominique Sarron in close attendance.

When the second leg was run over an hour later Garriga cursed his luck. An ignition problem made his Yamaha splutter off the line and there was no way he was going to hang onto overall victory from the two combined times.

There was a great melee at the front of the second race with Pons fighting it out with fellow Honda riders Mang, Sarron, Cornu, Reinhold Roth and Masahiro Shimizu. Something or somebody had to give and the unfortunate Sarron was the first. He lost the rear end of his Rothmans Honda on the fourth lap. Three laps later the pack was down to four when Shimizu slithered off into the mud.

At the front Pons and Mang swapped the lead with Cornu and Roth watching closely. It came down to a last lap confrontation and this time Pons made no mistake. He dived inside Mang at the bus stop chicane and the world champion messed up his counter attack at the hairpin. He allowed Cornu into second place with Roth fourth.

The unfortunate Garriga limped home in ninth place to claim sixth overall behind former world champion Carlos Lavado. He was even unhappier to lose his championship lead and trail by one point as the race for the title hotted up.

The 125cc riders held a long meeting after the 250cc contest to decide if they wanted to race following the fourth-lap crash, but after much discussion they came to the line.

The first part of the race lasted just three laps when the rain fell. Italian Ezio Gianola, using slick tyres on his Honda, led Martinez by just 0.24 seconds when the flag was shown. Gianola was determined to hang onto the lead when the second race got underway. He rode the Honda to the limit but Martinez just had to open the Derbi's throttle on the straights to claw back the advantage. However the finish was much closer than the champion wanted. He won the second race by just 0·68 seconds giving him overall victory by 0.44 seconds. It was a brave attempt by Gianola who trailed Martinez in the championship by 14 points.

Rolf Biland and Kurt Waltisperg usually make a race of the sidecar event before clearing off to win. In the 13-lap event they tried a different variation with the same end result. They led from the start, on their Krauser-powered LCR, but then spun at La Source. They'd built up such a big advantage they were able to straighten themselves out and retain the lead which they held to the finish.

World champions Steve Webster and Tony Hewitt were not so lucky when they spun their LCR at exactly the same spot. They dropped from second to third. Their luck changed when Egbert Streuer and Bernard Schnieders retired, from second, with a cracked cylinder head. The happiest pair on the rostrum were veteran Derek Jones and his Australian passenger Peter Brown. Jones grabbed his first place on the rostrum for six years when the French pair of Alain Michel and Jean-Marc Fresc spun, again at La Source, in sight of the chequered flag.

Randy Mamola is still the most popular rider with the fans and he shed tears of joy at Spa.

Results

500cc (17 laps, 73.31m/117.980k)		m	s	mph	kmh
1	W. Gardner, Australia *(Honda)*	46	55.21	93.74	150.869
2	E. Lawson, USA *(Yamaha)*	47	25.32	92.75	149.272
3	R. Mamola, USA *(Cagiva)*	47	35.99	92.41	148.715
4	D. de Radigues, Belgium *(Yamaha)*	47	36.82	92.38	148.672
5	W. Rainey, USA *(Yamaha)*	47	38.38	92.33	148.590
6	R. McElnea, GB *(Suzuki)*	48	12.54	91.24	146.836
7	R. Haslam, GB *(Elf-Honda)*	48	14.31	91.18	146.746
8	P. Chili, Italy *(Honda)*	48	39.44	90.40	145.483
9	S. Yatsushiro, Japan *(Honda)*	48	44.93	90.23	145.210
10	P. Igoa, France *(Yamaha)*	48	51.28	90.03	144.895

11 N. Mackenzie, GB *(Honda)*; 12 A. Valesi, Italy *(Honda)*. *16 laps:* 13 D. McLeod, GB *(Honda)*; 14 M. Papa, Italy *(Honda)*; 15 C. Doorakkers, Holland *(Honda)*; 16 F. Biliotti,

Italy *(Honda)*; 17 E. Laycock, Ireland *(Honda)*; 18 K. van der Endt, Holland *(Honda)*; 19 R. Nicotte, France *(Honda)*; 20 M. Baldwin, USA *(Honda)*; 21 J. Doppler, Austria *(Honda)*; 22 D. Amatriain, Spain *(Honda)*; 23 J. ten Napel, Holland *(Suzuki)*; 24 G. Jung, W. Germany *(Honda)*. *15 laps:* 25 B. Kneubuhler, Switzerland *(Honda)*; 26 A. Ramo, Finland *(Honda)*; 27 A. Leuthe, Luxembourg *(Suzuki)*; 28 N. Schmassmann, Switzerland *(Honda)*; 29 F. Barchitta, San Marino *(Honda)*; 30 M. Gentile, Switzerland *(Fior)*. *13 laps:* 31 K. Wulff, Denmark *(Honda)*.

Fastest lap: C. Sarron, France *(Yamaha)*, 2m 40.78s, 96.56mph/155.392kmh.

Sarron hangs onto Gardner's back wheel but tumbled late in the race.

Record lap: E. Lawson, USA *(Yamaha)*, 2m 28.35s, 104.647mph/168.412kmh (1985).

World Championship positions: 1 E. Lawson, 159 points; 2 W. Gardner, 125; 3 W. Rainey, 117; 4 K. Magee, 89; 5 K. Schwantz, 85; 6 D. de Radigues and N. Mackenzie both 76; 8 C. Sarron, 74; 9 P. Chili, 60; 10 R. McElnea, 51.

Practice leaderboard: 1 C. Sarron, France *(Yamaha)*, 2m 27.62s; 2 E. Lawson, USA *(Yamaha)*, 2m 29.64s; 3 W. Rainey, USA *(Yamaha)*, 2m 29.96s; 4 K. Schwantz, USA *(Suzuki)*, 2m 29.97s; 5 W. Gardner, Australia *(Honda)*, 2m 30.61s; 6 P. Chili, Italy *(Honda)*, 2m 30.68s; 7 D. de Radigues, Belgium *(Yamaha)*, 2m 31.06s; 8 R. McElnea, GB *(Suzuki)*, 2m 31.47s; 9 N. Mackenzie, GB *(Honda)*, 2m 31.52s; 10 R. Haslam, GB *(Elf-Honda)*, 2m 31.64s; 11 P. Igoa, France *(Yamaha)*, 2m 31.76s; 12 R. Mamola, USA *(Cagiva)*, 2m 32.33s; 13 M. Papa, Italy *(Honda)*, 2m 34.69s; 14 S. Yatsushiro, Japan *(Honda)*, 2m 34.94s; 15 A. Valesi, Italy *(Honda)*, 2m 35.48s; 16 F. Biliotti, Italy *(Honda)*, 2m 35.83s; 17 K. Magee, Australia *(Yamaha)*, 2m 36.38s; 18 M. Fischer, W. Germany *(Honda)*, 2m 37.12s; 19 C. Doorakkers, Holland *(Honda)*, 2m 37.13s; 20 D. McLeod, GB *(Honda)*, 2m 37.16s.

250cc (15 laps, 64.68m/104.100k)*	**m**	**s**	**mph**	**kmh**
1 S. Pons, Spain *(Honda)*	38	48.21	100.02	160.965
2 J. Cornu, Switzerland *(Honda)*	38	49.30	99.97	160.890
3 A. Mang, W. Germany *(Honda)*	38	49.94	99.95	160.848
4 R. Roth, W. Germany *(Honda)*	38	52.59	99.83	160.663
5 C. Lavado, Venezuela *(Yamaha)*	39	43.56	97.70	157.227
6 J. Garriga, Spain *(Yamaha)*	39	45.02	97.64	157.131
7 C. Cardus, Spain *(Honda)*	39	45.25	97.63	157.116
8 L. Cadalora, Italy *(Yamaha)*	39	46.93	97.56	157.005
9 J. Ruggia, France *(Yamaha)*	39	48.39	97.50	156.909
10 H. Becker, W. Germany *(Yamaha)*	40	07.97	96.71	155.633

11 G. Bertin, France *(Yamaha)*; 12 D. McLeod, GB *(EMC)*; 13 A. Auinger, Austria *(Aprilia)*; 14 H. Bradl, W. Germany *(Honda)*; 15 P. Casoli, Italy *(Garelli)*; 16 J. Cardelus, Andorra *(Aprilia)*; 17 S. Caracchi, Italy *(Honda)*; 18 J. Foray, France *(Yamaha)*; 19 J. Mattioli, France *(Yamaha)*; 20 J. Schmid, W. Germany *(Honda)*; 21 G. Cowan, Ireland *(Yamaha)*; 22 M. Matteoni, Italy *(Yamaha)*; 23 A. Bronec, France *(Honda)*. *14 laps:* 24 I. Troisi, Venezuela *(Yamaha)*; 25 E. Neumair, Austria *(Aprilia)*. *13 laps:* 26 W. Zeelenberg, Holland *(Yamaha)*.
**Because of an accident the race was run in two sections – one of three laps and one of 12. The times/speeds given are the aggregate of the two.*

Record lap: A. Mang, W. Germany *(Honda)*, 2m 32.06s, 102.096mph/164.304kmh.
Old record: F. Spencer, USA *(Honda)*, 2m 36.12s, 99.438mph/160.030kmh (1985).

World Championship positions: 1 S. Pons, 129 points; 2 J. Garriga, 128; 3 J. Cornu, 112; 4 A. Mang and R. Roth both 87; 6 L. Cadalora, 80; 7 D. Sarron, 68; 8 J. Ruggia, 63; 9 M. Shimizu, 51; 10 D. McLeod, 36.

Practice leaderboard: 1 J. Cornu, Switzerland *(Honda)*, 2m 33.09s; 2 D. Sarron, France *(Honda)*, 2m 34.16s; 3 J. Garriga, Spain *(Yamaha)*, 2m 34.30s; 4 R. Roth, W. Germany *(Honda)*, 2m 34.64s; 5 S. Pons, Spain *(Honda)*, 2m 34.64s; 6 M. Herweh, W. Germany *(Yamaha)*, 2m 34.97s; 7 C. Lavado, Venezuela *(Yamaha)*, 2m 35.34s; 8 A. Mang, W. Germany *(Honda)*, 2m 35.61s; 9 L. Reggiani, Italy *(Aprilia)*, 2m 36.28s; 10 C. Cardus, Spain *(Honda)*, 2m 36.48s; 11 I. Palazzese, Venezuela *(Yamaha)*, 2m 36.61s; 12 M. Wimmer, W. Germany *(Yamaha)*, 2m 37.03s; 13 D. McLeod, GB *(EMC)*, 2m 37.07s; 14 H. Eckl, W. Germany *(Aprilia)*, 2m 37.26s; 15 J. Ruggia, France *(Yamaha)*, 2m 37.29s; 16 L. Cadalora, Italy *(Yamaha)*, 2m 37.81s; 17 M. Shimizu, Japan *(Honda)* 2m 37.87s; 18 A. Auinger, Austria *(Aprilia)*, 2m 38.16s; 19 H. Becker, W. Germany *(Yamaha)*, 2m 38.51s; 20 G. Bertin, France *(Honda)*, 2m 38.65s.

125cc (13 laps, 56.06m/90.220k)*	**m**	**s**	**mph**	**kmh**
1 J. Martinez, Spain *(Derbi)*	38	36.01	87.14	140.238
2 E. Gianola, Italy *(Honda)*	38	36.45	87.12	140.211
3 J. Miralles, Spain *(Honda)*	38	48.09	86.69	139.510
4 H. Spaan, Holland *(Honda)*	38	53.24	86.50	139.202

5	G. Grassetti, Italy *(Honda)*	39 08.74	85.93	138.283
6	A. Scott, USA *(Honda)*	39 12.90	85.77	138.039
7	L. Pietroniro, Belgium *(Honda)*	39 13.41	85.76	138.009
8	K. Takada, Japan *(Honda)*	39 15.20	85.70	137.904
9	U. Hisashi, Japan *(Honda)*	39 22.46	85.43	137.480
10	G. Waibel, W. Germany *(Honda)*	39 32.54	85.06	136.896

11 D. Brigaglia, Italy *(Rotax)*; 12 P. Bianchi, Italy *(Cagiva)*; 13 A. Stadler, W. Germany *(Honda)*; 14 R. Appleyard, GB *(Honda)*; 15 J. Hautaniemi, Finland *(Honda)*; 16 H. Luthi, Switzerland *(Honda)*; 17 M. Hernandez, Spain *(Honda)*; 18 A. Waibel, W. Germany *(Honda)*; 19 K. Galatowicz, GB *(Honda)*; 20 B. Hassaine, France *(Honda)*; 21 R. Milton, GB *(Rotax)*; 22 H. Abold, W. Germany *(Honda)*; 23 T. Feuz, Switzerland *(Rotax)*; 24 M. Leitner, Austria *(Emco)*; 25 I. McConnachie, GB *(Cagiva)*; 26 J. van Dongen, Holland *(Honda)*; 27 J. Wickstrom, Finland *(Honda)*; 28 S. Julin, Belgium *(Rotax)*. *12 laps:* 29 E. Kytola, Finland *(Honda)*.
*Because of rain the race was run in two sections – one of three laps and one of 10. The times/speeds given are the aggregate of the two.

Fastest lap: G. Grassetti, Italy *(Honda)*, 2m 50.29s, 91.16mph/146.714kmh.

Record lap: A. Auinger, Austria *(MBA)*, 2m 45.36s, 93.88mph/151.088kmh (1985).

World championship positions: 1 J. Martinez, 100 points; 2 E. Gianola 86; 3 H. Spaan, 70; 4 J. Miralles, 54; 5 G. Grassetti, 51; 6 G. Waibel, 41; 7 S. Prein and A. Stadler both 33; 9 M. Herreros, 30; 10 H. Unemoto and D. Brigaglia both 26.

Practice leaderboard: 1 J. Martinez, Spain *(Derbi)*, 2m 46.28s; 2 H. Spaan, Holland *(Honda)*, 2m 47.00s; 3 D. Brigaglia, Italy *(Rotax)*, 2m 48.44s; 4 A. Criville, Spain *(Derbi)*, 2m 49.19s; 5 E. Gianola, Italy *(Honda)*, 2m 49.25s; 6 K. Takada, Japan *(Honda)*, 2m 49.54s; 7 H. Abold, W. Germany *(Honda)*, 2m 49.75s; 8 T. Feuz, Switzerland *(Rotax)*, 2m 50.06s; 9 E. Kytola, Finland *(Honda)*, 2m 50.11s; 10 H. Luthi, Switzerland *(Honda)*, 2m 50.22s; 11 A. Stadler, W. Germany *(Honda)*, 2m 50.33s; 12 G. Waibel, W. Germany *(Honda)*, 2m 50.42s; 13 I. McConnachie, GB *(Cagiva)*, 2m 50.46s; 14 G. Grassetti, Italy *(Honda)*, 2m 50.69s; 15 H. Unemoto, Japan *(Honda)*, 2m 50.76s; 16 A. Scott, USA *(Honda)*, 2m 50.86s; 17 L. Pietroniro, Belgium *(Honda)*, 2m 50.86s; 18 C. Catalano, Italy *(Aprilia)*, 2m 50.87s; 19 R. Bolart, Spain *(Cobas)*, 2m 51.88s; 20 J. Miralles, Spain *(Honda)*, 2m 51.91s.

Sidecar (13 laps, 56.06m/90.220k)		**m s**	**mph**	**kmh**
1	R. Biland, Switzerland K. Waltisperg, Switzerland *(LCR-Krauser)*	36 15.68	92.76	149.283
2	S. Webster, GB T. Hewitt, GB *(LCR-Krauser)*	36 29.63	92.17	148.332
3	D. Jones, GB P. Brown, GB *(LCR-Yamaha)*	37 24.40	89.92	144.712
4	A. Michel, France J. Fresc, France *(LCR-Krauser)*	37 25.12	89.89	144.666

5	B. Brindley, GB G. Rose, GB *(LCR-Yamaha)*	37 26.58	89.83	144.572
6	Y. Kumagaya, Japan B. Barlow, GB *(Windle-Yamaha)*	37 49.71	88.91	143.098
7	R. Steinhausen, W. Germany B. Hiller, W. Germany *(ADM)*	38 10.63	88.10	141.792
8	W. Stropek, Austria H. Demling, Austria *(Mibag Eigenbau)*	38 11.88	88.06	141.714
9	B. Scherer, W. Germany T. Schroder, W. Germany *(BSR-Krauser)*	38 12.60	88.02	141.657
10	S. Abbott, GB S. Smith, GB *(Windle-Yamaha)*	38 17.06	87.86	141.395

11 M. Egloff/U. Egloff, Switzerland *(ADM)*; 12 T. van Kempen/S. Birchall, Holland/GB *(LCR-Yamaha)*; 13 A. Bosman/D. Kellett, Australia *(LCR-Yamaha)*; 14 M. Kumano/M. Fahrni, Japan/Switzerland *(LCR-Tec)*; 15 I. Nigrowsky/M. Charpentier, France *(Seymaz-Yamaha)*; 16 C. Stirrat/S. Prior, GB *(LCR-Yamaha)*. *12 laps:* 17 F. Stolzle/H. Stolzle, W. Germany *(LCR-Krauser)*; 18 G. Thomas/J. Webb, GB *(LCR-Krauser)*; 19 A. Zurbrugg/M. Zurbrugg, Switzerland *(LCR-Yamaha)*. *11 laps:* 20 G. Knight/P. Coombes, GB *(Yamaha)*; 21 J. Millet/C. Debroux, France *(GDF)*.

Fastest lap: R. Biland/K. Waltisperg, Switzerland *(LCR-Krauser)*, 2m 38.51s, 97.94mph/157.618kmh.

Record lap: E. Streuer/B. Schnieders, Holland *(LCR-Yamaha)*, 2m 36.05s, 99.48mph/160.102kmh (1985).

World Championship positions: 1 Biland/Waltisperg, 100 points; 2 Webster/Hewitt, 79; 3 Streuer/Schnieders, 47; 4 Jones/Brown, 45; 5 Brindley/Rose, 44; 6 Michel/Fresc, 41; 7 Abbott/Smith, 40; 8 Zurbrugg/Zurbrugg, 38; 9 Stropek/Demling, 30; 10 Scherer/Schroder, 29.

Practice leaderboard: 1 Biland/Waltisperg, Switzerland *(LCR-Krauser)*, 2m 36.10s; 2 Streuer/Schnieders, Holland *(LCR-Yamaha)*, 2m 36.16s; 3 Webster/Hewitt, GB *(LCR-Krauser)*, 2m 36.67s; 4 Michel/Fresc, France *(LCR-Krauser)*, 2m 37.04s; 5 Egloff/Egloff, Switzerland *(LCR-Yamaha)*, 2m 37.18s; 6 Zurbrugg/Zurbrugg, Switzerland *(LCR-Yamaha)*, 2m 39.76s; 7 Kumano/Fahrni, Japan/Switzerland *(LCR-Tec)*, 2m 41.43s; 8 Stropek/Demling, Austria *(Mibag Eigenbau)*, 2m 41.71s; 9 Brindley/Rose, GB *(LCR-Yamaha)*, 2m 42.20s; 10 Steinhausen/Hiller, W. Germany *(ADM)*, 2m 42.74s; 11 Jones/Brown, GB *(LCR-Yamaha)*, 2m 43.24s; 12 Abbott/Smith, GB *(Windle-Yamaha)*, 2m 43.34s; 13 Nigrowsky/Charpentier, France *(Seymaz-Yamaha)*, 2m 43.36s; 14 van Kempen/Birchall, Holland/GB *(LCR-Yamaha)*, 2m 44.46s; 15 Kumagaya/Barlow, Japan/GB *(Windle-Yamaha)*, 2m 44.49s; 16 Scherer/Schroder, W. Germany *(BSR-Krauser)*, 2m 44.65s; 17 Stolzle/Stolzle, W. Germany *(LCR-Krauser)*, 2m 44.92s; 18 Bosman/Kellett, Australia *(LCR-Yamaha)*, 2m 45.90s; 19 Larratte/Corbier, France *(LCR-Yamaha)*, 2m 46.32s; 20 Progin/Hunziker, Switzerland *(Seymaz-Yamaha)*, 2m 46.83s.

YUGOSLAVIAN GRAND PRIX, 17 July, Rijeka-Grobnik 2.590m/4.168k

The Rijeka Autodromo lived up to its reputation of bringing the best down to earth. This time Eddie Lawson joined the likes of Wayne Gardner and Freddie Spencer, who've come to grief on the dusty, demanding circuit high in the hills above the Adriatic. News of the championship leader's tumble, in the final minutes of practice, spread like wildfire through the paddock. He'd tangled with Frenchman Patrick Igoa and fallen on his left shoulder.

Speculation about whether he'd be fit to ride in the 30-lap race round the twisty 2.59-mile circuit, raced through the paddock and especially in Wayne Gardner's Rothmans Honda camp. It was the luck the champion had been waiting for to close that massive 34-point gap.

Physio Dean Millar worked on Lawson's shoulder most of the night and the Californian declared himself fit to ride, but not to contest the lead, early the next morning. He'd qualified on the front row of the grid in fifth place, before his crash. Sarron made it four pole positions in a row and vowed not to fall off. Gardner was just behind him, Niall Mackenzie third quickest, after leading the way on his HB Honda with Wayne Rainey, as consistent as ever, fourth.

Rainey, riding the Lucky Strike Yamaha, led for the opening two laps before Gardner swooped past pursued by Sarron. Lawson was 10th at the end of the first lap but dropped to 11th on the second. Sarron locked onto Gardner's back wheel but did not try to pass for the next 13 laps. Then the Champion decided it was time to turn the screw. He rocketed away from Sarron for his third consecutive grand prix victory and immediately jumped off the bike to enquire where Lawson had finished. Tenth was the answer after an incredibly brave performance by the Marlboro Yamaha man, who just gritted his teeth and stuck to his task. He moved up a place on the last lap when Italian Pier-Francesco Chili crashed his HB Honda on the very last bend. Six points were scant reward for such a ride but it could make all the difference at the end of the year.

Randy Mamola was enjoying himself in the sunshine for the second grand prix running. At the end of last season he was sacked by the Kenny Roberts Lucky Strike Yamaha team to be replaced by Kevin Magee and Wayne Rainey. With his new mount, the Italian Cagiva, he was out to prove a point. From fifth place he stalked Magee for 24 laps before, at last, getting past the Australian who was still recovering from his Spa crash. Magee was in no mood to capitulate and relegated the crowd's hero back to fifth with just five laps remaining. Despite an overheated engine, Mamola came back for more and two bends from the finish stole fourth place, to the delight of the 80,000 crowd. Rainey was two seconds in front of him to consolidate his third place in the table. Mackenzie made a good start but retired on the fourth lap when his Honda seized. De Radigues was sixth, riding the Marlboro Yamaha, with Shunji Yatsushiro just pipping Rob McElnea for eighth place. His Pepsi Suzuki team-mate Kevin Schwantz missed the race because of his broken kneecap. Ron Haslam was ninth, despite brake and rear suspension problems, on his Elf 5 machine.

The two Spaniards chasing the 250cc championship, Sito Pons and Juan Garriga, fought a marvellous duel in the 26-lap 250 race. Pons, riding the Campsa Honda, knew Garriga's Ducados Yamaha would be a big threat round the Rijeka twists and turns. He was not mistaken. Pons led into the first bend. Not so lucky was World Champion Toni

Mang. His Rothmans Honda and Donnie McLeod's Seven-Up EMC touched. He fell and broke his collarbone. Garriga stuck to Pons like a leech but was ruining his tyres at the same time. Dominique Sarron battled with Garriga until he missed a gear on his Rothmans Honda and lost touch. After a couple of slides Garriga had to drop the pace and Sarron came back for a second chance. He got past the sliding Yamaha, but, on the last lap, got caught out by a backmarker. A grateful Garriga grabbed back second place from the disappointed Frenchman. At the front Pons just kept pushing up the pace. He had five seconds to spare at the finish to prise open a four-point lead in the championship.

The race for fourth was even tighter, with Honda-mounted Reinhold Roth and Jacques Cornu doing battle with the Marlboro Yamaha of fiery Italian Luca Cadalora. Cornu dropped back to watch the fun as Roth and Cadalora bashed it out to the line. Coming into the start-and-finish straight for the last time Roth pulled out of Cadalora's slipstream to claim fourth. The Italian was so upset he punched a hole through the screen of his fairing. Both Loris Reggiani and Carlos Cardus raced through the field after bad starts to finish seventh and eighth respectively.

To nobody's great surprise Jorge Martinez opened the day by winning the 17-lap 80cc race to clinch his third World title. The 25-year-old Spaniard let West German Peter Ottl do all the front running on his Krauser, before screaming by on the works Derbi to complete his total domination of the class this year. His young team-mate Alex Criville won a tremendous battle for third place pipping West German Jorg Seel and Bulgarian Bodgan Nikolov.

Martinez was going to have to wait a little longer to clinch the 125cc world crown although he took another step by winning the 22-lap 125cc event. In the early stages he played with the Honda of Ezio Gianola, the Cagiva of Britain's Ian McConnachie and the Rotax of Domenico Brigaglia. McConnachie was desperate for a good result, but his machine seized at the end of the ninth lap. Martinez and Gianola cleared off to fight their expected battle at the front with the usual outcome. Using the superior power of the Derbi, Martinez won by less than a second from the brave Italian who dropped to 17 points adrift in the championship table. Just over half a second covered the next four riders in an amazing finish. Belgian ace Lucio Pietroniro grabbed the final rostrum position on his Honda from Brigaglia and Honda men, West German Stefan Prein and Japanese Koji Takada.

Results

500cc (30 laps, 77.70m/125.04k)		**m**	**s**	**mph**	**kmh**
1	W. Gardner, Australia *(Honda)*	45	44.14	101.93	164.037
2	C. Sarron, France *(Yamaha)*	45	51.89	101.64	163.576
3	W. Rainey, USA *(Yamaha)*	46	05.48	101.14	162.772
4	R. Mamola, USA *(Cagiva)*	46	07.76	101.06	162.638
5	K. Magee, Australia *(Yamaha)*	46	07.99	101.05	162.627
6	D. de Radigues, Belgium *(Yamaha)*	46	42.43	99.81	160.626
7	S. Yatsushiro, Japan *(Honda)*	46	46.40	99.67	160.399
8	R. McElnea, GB *(Suzuki)*	46	46.57	99.66	160.389
9	R. Haslam, GB *(Elf-Honda)*	46	49.98	99.54	160.195
10	E. Lawson, USA *(Yamaha)*	47	03.89	99.05	159.405

11 P. Chili, Italy *(Honda)*. *29 laps:* 12 P. Igoa, France *(Yamaha)*; 13 D. McLeod, GB *(Honda)*; 14 M. Baldwin, USA *(Honda)*; 15 B. Kneubuhler, Switzerland *(Honda)*; 16 F. Barchitta, San Marino *(Honda)*; 17 F. Biliotti, Italy *(Honda)*; 18 K. Truchsess, Austria *(Honda)*; 19 D. Amatriain, Spain *(Honda)*; 20 E. Laycock, Ireland *(Honda)*; 21 A. Leuthe, Luxembourg *(Suzuki)*; 22 S. Habat, Yugoslavia *(Honda)*. *28 laps:* 23 W. von Muralt, Switzerland *(Suzuki)*; 24 J. Demierre, Switzerland *(Suzuki)*; 25 G. Jung, W. Germany *(Honda)*; 26 H. Schutz, W. Germany *(Honda)*.

Record lap: C. Sarron, France *(Yamaha)*, 1m 30.57s, 102.94mph/165.672kmh.
Old record: E. Lawson, USA *(Yamaha)*, 1m 31.78s, 101.58mph/163.487kmh (1985).

World Championship positions: 1 E. Lawson, 165 points; 2 W. Gardner, 145; 3 W. Rainey, 132; 4 K. Magee, 100; 5 C. Sarron, 91; 6 D. de Radigues, 86; 7 K. Schwantz, 85; 8 N. Mackenzie, 76; 9 P. Chili, 65; 10 R. McElnea, 59.

Practice leaderboard: 1 C. Sarron, France *(Yamaha)*, 1m 30.17s; 2 W. Gardner, Australia *(Honda)*, 1m 30.51s; 3 N. Mackenzie, GB *(Honda)*, 1m 30.60s; 4 W. Rainey, USA *(Yamaha)*, 1m 30.73s; 5 E. Lawson, USA *(Yamaha)*, 1m 30.95s; 6 R. Mamola, USA *(Cagiva)*, 1m 31.09s; 7 K. Magee, Australia *(Yamaha)*, 1m 31.16s; 8 D. de Radigues, Belgium *(Yamaha)*, 1m 31.40s; 9 P. Chili, Italy *(Honda)*, 1m 31.83s; 10 S. Yatsushiro, Japan *(Honda)*, 1m 32.06s; 11 R. McElnea, GB *(Suzuki)*, 1m 32.15s; 12 R. Haslam, GB *(Elf-Honda)*, 1m 32.49s; 13 P. Igoa, France *(Yamaha)*, 1m 33.40s; 14 R. Roche, France *(Cagiva)*, 1m 34.23s; 15 M. Gentile, Switzerland *(Fior)*, 1m 34.38s; 16 M. Papa, Italy *(Honda)*, 1m 34.42s; 17 A. Valesi, Italy *(Honda)*, 1m 34.43s; 18 M. Campbell, Australia *(Elf-Honda)*, 1m 34.59s; 19 D. McLeod, GB *(Honda)*, 1m 34.81s; 20 B. Kneubuhler, Switzerland *(Honda)*, 1m 34.85s.

250cc (26 laps, 67.34m/108.368k)		**m**	**s**	**mph**	**kmh**
1	S. Pons, Spain *(Honda)*	40	21.39	100.11	161.115
2	J. Garriga, Spain *(Yamaha)*	40	26.40	99.91	160.783
3	D. Sarron, France *(Honda)*	40	27.45	99.86	160.713
4	R. Roth, W. Germany *(Honda)*	40	45.59	99.12	159.521
5	L. Cadalora, Italy *(Yamaha)*	40	45.77	99.11	159.510
6	J. Cornu, Switzerland *(Honda)*	40	51.63	98.88	159.128
7	L. Reggiani, Italy *(Aprilia)*	41	22.45	97.65	157.152
8	C. Cardus, Spain *(Honda)*	41	32.95	97.24	156.491
9	H. Eckl, W. Germany *(Aprilia)*	41	36.22	97.11	156.286
10	M. Vitali, Italy *(Rotax)*	41	44.44	96.79	155.773

11 S. Carrachi, Italy *(Honda)*. *25 laps:* 12 U. Jucker, Switzerland *(Yamaha)*; 13 J. Balde, France *(Rotax)*; 14 A. Auinger, Austria *(Aprilia)*; 15 B. Casanova, Italy *(Aprilia)*; 16 G. Bertin, France *(Yamaha)*; 17 A. Preining, Austria *(Rotax)*; 18 M. Matteoni, Italy *(Yamaha)*; 19 B. Bonhuil, France *(Honda)*; 20 U. Luzi, Switzerland *(Honda)*; 21 R. Delaby, Luxembourg *(Yamaha)*; 22 J. Schmid, W. Germany *(Honda)*; 23 H. Lindner, Austria *(Honda)*; 24 B. Schick, W. Germany *(Honda)*.

Record lap: J. Garriga, Spain *(Yamaha)*, 1m 32.18s, 101.143mph/162.770kmh.
Old record: C. Lavado, Venezuela *(Yamaha)*, 1m 33.43s, 99.79mph/160.599kmh (1986).

World Championship positions: 1 S. Pons, 149 points; 2 J. Garriga, 145; 3 J. Cornu, 122; 4 R. Roth, 100; 5 L. Cadalora, 91; 6 A. Mang, 87; 7 D. Sarron, 83; 8 J. Ruggia, 63; 9 M. Shimizu, 51; 10 D. McLeod, 36.

Practice leaderboard: 1 S. Pons, Spain *(Honda)*, 1m 32.04s; 2 J. Garriga, Spain *(Yamaha)*, 1m 32.44s; 3 J. Cornu, Switzerland *(Honda)*, 1m 32.56s; 4 D. Sarron, France *(Honda)*, 1m 32.61s; 5 R. Roth, W. Germany *(Honda)*, 1m 32.88s; 6 C. Lavado, Venezuela *(Yamaha)*, 1m 32.89s; 7 L. Cadalora, Italy *(Yamaha)*, 1m 33.16s; 8 J. Ruggia, France *(Yamaha)*, 1m 33.39s; 9 M. Herweh, W. Germany *(Yamaha)*, 1m 33.64s; 10 A. Mang, W. Germany *(Honda)*, 1m 33.76s; 11 L. Reggiani, Italy *(Aprilia)*, 1m 33.99s; 12 C. Cardus, Spain *(Honda)*, 1m 34.01s; 13 H. Eckl, W. Germany *(Aprilia)*, 1m 34.03s; 14 M. Shimizu, Japan *(Honda)*, 1m 34.31s; 15 B. Casanova, Italy *(Aprilia)*, 1m 34.77s; 16 J. Mattioli, France *(Yamaha)*, 1m 34.87s; 17 J. Balde, France *(Rotax)*, 1m 35.03s; 18 H. Becker, W. Germany *(Yamaha)*, 1m 35.11s; 19 M. Vitali, Italy *(Rotax)*, 1m 35.19s; 20 D. McLeod, GB *(EMC)*, 1m 35.38s.

125cc (22 laps, 56.98m/91.696k)		**m**	**s**	**mph**	**kmh**
1	J. Martinez, Spain *(Derbi)*	37	01.64	92.33	148.586
2	E. Gianola, Italy *(Honda)*	37	02.55	92.29	148.525
3	L. Pietroniro, Belgium *(Honda)*	37	07.12	92.10	148.221
4	D. Brigaglia, Italy *(Rotax)*	37	07.26	92.09	148.211
5	S. Prein, W. Germany *(Honda)*	37	07.63	92.08	148.186
6	K. Takada, Japan *(Honda)*	37	07.76	92.07	148.177
7	A. Stadler, W. Germany *(Honda)*	37	16.75	91.70	147.582
8	L. Reyes, Spain *(Garelli)*	37	26.28	91.31	146.956
9	A. Scott, USA *(Honda)*	37	27.10	91.28	146.902
10	H. Luthi, Switzerland *(Honda)*	37	27.62	91.26	146.868

11 K. Galatowicz, GB *(Honda)*; 12 J. Fischer, Austria *(Rotax)*; 13 H. Unemoto, Japan *(Honda)*; 14 H. Spaan, Holland *(Honda)*; 15 R. Milton, GB *(Rotax)*; 16 J. Wickstrom, Finland *(Honda)*; 17 C. Macciotta, Italy *(Honda)*; 18 R. Appleyard, GB *(Honda)*; 19 T. Feuz, Switzerland *(Rotax)*. *21 laps:* 20 J. Seel, W. Germany *(Seel)*. *20 laps:* 21 B. Hassaine, France *(Honda)*.

Record lap: C. Catalano, Italy *(Aprilia)*, 1m 39.22s, 93.97mph/151.226kmh
Old record: E. Lazzarini, Italy *(Garelli)*, 1m 40.50s, 92.79mph/149.33kmh (1982).

World Championship positions: 1 J. Martinez, 120 points; 2 E. Gianola, 103; 3 H. Spaan, 72; 4 J. Miralles, 54; 5 G. Grassetti, 51; 6 S. Prein, 44; 7 A. Stadler, 42; 8 G. Waibel, 41; 9 D. Brigaglia, 39; 10 L. Pietroniro, 32.

Practice leaderboard: 1 J. Martinez, Spain *(Derbi)*, 1m 38.82s; 2 H. Spaan, Holland *(Honda)*, 1m 39.23s; 3 D. Brigaglia, Italy *(Rotax)*, 1m 39.34s; 4 H. Abold, W. Germany *(Honda)*, 1m 39.38s; 5 G. Grassetti, Italy *(Honda)*, 1m 39.48s; 6 C. Catalano, Italy *(Aprilia)*, 1m 39.57s; 7 K. Takada, Japan *(Honda)*, 1m 39.59s; 8 A. Stadler, W. Germany *(Honda)*, 1m 39.81s; 9 E. Gianola, Italy *(Honda)*, 1m 39.83s; 10 I. McConnachie, GB *(Cagiva)*, 1m 40.02s; 11 S. Prein, W. Germany *(Honda)*, 1m 40.09s; 12 M. Leitner, Austria *(Emco)*, 1m 40.25s; 13 L. Pietroniro, Belgium *(Honda)*, 1m 40.35s; 14 K.

Galatowicz, GB *(Honda)*, 1m 40.43s; 15 E. Kytola, Finland *(Honda)*, 1m 40.54s; 16 J. Fischer, Austria *(Rotax)*, 1m 40.57s; 17 L. Reyes, Spain *(Garelli)*, 1m 40.58s; 18 A. Scott, USA *(Honda)*, 1m 40.85s; 19 A. Waibel, W. Germany *(Honda)*, 1m 40.91s; 20 J. Wickstrom, Finland *(Honda)*, 1m 40.95s.

80cc (17 laps, 44.03m/70.856k)		m	s	mph	kmh
1	J. Martinez, Spain *(Derbi)*	29	32.75	89.41	143.890
2	P. Ottl, W. Germany *(Krauser)*	29	34.92	89.30	143.714
3	A. Criville, Spain *(Derbi)*	29	53.53	88.37	142.223
4	J. Seel, W. Germany *(Seel)*	29	54.88	88.31	142.115*
5	B. Nikolov, Bulgaria *(Krauser)*	29	54.88	88.31	142.115*
6	S. Dorflinger, Switzerland *(Krauser)*	30	03.06	87.90	141.470
7	M. Herreros, Spain *(Derbi)*	30	11.05	87.52	140.847
8	J. van Dongen, Holland *(Casal)*	30	11.20	87.51	140.835
9	H. Torrontegui, Spain *(Autisa)*	30	20.07	87.08	140.148
10	K. Juhasz, Hungary *(Krauser)*	30	21.15	87.03	140.065

11 R. Kunz, W. Germany *(Ziegler)*; 12 A. Nijenhuis, Holland *(Casal)*; 13 G. Schirnhofer, W. Germany *(Krauser)*; 14 J. Szabo, Hungary *(Krauser)*; 15 J. Pavlic, Yugoslavia *(Seel)*; 16 G. Gnani, Italy *(Gnani)*; 17 J. Mariano, Spain *(Krauser)*; 18 R. Koster, Switzerland *(Kroko)*; 19 X. Arumi, Spain *(Krauser)*; 20 S. Braegger, Switzerland *(Casal)*; 21 P. Priori, Italy *(Krauser)*; 22 H. Koopman, Holland *(Ziegler)*. *16 laps:* 23 J. Bernard, Belgium *(Fantic)*; 24 R. Dunki, Switzerland *(Krauser)*; 25 P. Tibori, Hungary *(Casal)*; 26 S. Julin, Belgium *(Casal)*; 27 T. Engl, W. Germany *(Esch)*; 28 P. Sovic, Yugoslavia *(Eberhardt)*; 29 L. Robert, France *(SPR)*; 30 B. Rokavec, Yugoslavia *(Seel)*; 31 C. Baert, Belgium *(Casal)*.
*Seel and Nikolov credited with same time/speed in official results but placed fourth and fifth.

Fastest lap: J. Martinez, Spain *(Derbi)*, 1m 42.55s, 90.91mph/146.304kmh.

Record lap: J. Martinez, Spain *(Derbi)*, 1m 40.16s, 93.09mph/149.808kmh (1986).

World championship positions: 1 J. Martinez, 117; 2 A. Criville, 75; 3 M. Herreros, 69; 4 P. Ottl, 65; S. Dorflinger, 60; 6 J. van Dongen, 47; 7 B. Nikolov, 45; 8 K. Juhasz, 41; 9 G. Ascareggi, 35; 10 G. Gnani and J. Seel both 27.
Practice leaderboard: 1 J. Martinez, Spain *(Derbi)*, 1m 42.83s; 2 S. Dorflinger, Switzerland *(Krauser)*, 1m 43.61s; 3 P. Ottl, W. Germany *(Krauser)*, 1m 43.93s; 4 B. Smit, Holland *(Krauser)*, 1m 44.59s; 5 G. Ascareggi, Italy *(BBFT)*, 1m 44.71s; 6 B. Nikolov, Bulgaria *(Krauser)*, 1m 45.02s; 7 J. Seel, W. Germany *(Seel)*, 1m 45.12s; 8 G. Schirnhofer, W. Germany *(Krauser)*, 1m 45.13s; 9 J. Szabo, Hungary *(Krauser)*, 1m 45.27s; 10 J. van Dongen, Holland *(Casal)*, 1m 45.27s; 11 R. Kunz, W. Germany *(Ziegler)*, 1m 45.56s; 12 A. Criville, Spain *(Derbi)*, 1m 45.68s; 13 K. Juhasz, Hungary *(Krauser)*, 1m 45.76s; 14 M. Herreros, Spain *(Derbi)*, 1m 45.93s; 15 R. Dunki, Switzerland *(Krauser)*, 1m 46.32s; 16 H. Torrontegui, Spain *(Autisa)*, 1m 46.38s; 17 G. Gnani, Italy *(Gnani)*, 1m 46.61s; 18 J. Pavlic, Yugoslavia *(Seel)*, 1m 46.64s; 19 S. Julin, Belgium *(Casal)*, 1m 46.79s; 20 A. Nijenhuis, Holland *(Casal)*, 1m 46.92s.

The moment Lawson almost lost the title. Top *Lawson falling from his Yamaha after colliding with Igoa.* Bottom *Igoa rushes to apologise as Lawson checks his dislocated shoulder.*

FRENCH GRAND PRIX, 24 July, Paul Ricard 3.61m/5.810k

It was the best 500cc grand prix race of the last decade. Twenty-one laps of breathtaking action in the sunshine that did so much to decide the outcome of this year's world title: Wayne Gardner's luck ran out and brave Eddie Lawson took full advantage.

Jacques Cornu waited 14 years for his first 250cc grand prix victory but it took him just seven weeks for his second after he outfoxed championship leader Sito Pons and – surprise, surprise – Jorge Martinez won the 125's and Rolf Biland and Kurt Waltisperg the sidecars.

Rarely has there been a better race than the 500 battle between Gardner, Lawson, Kevin Schwantz and local hero Christian Sarron during the 39-year history of the World Championship. Prospects looked promising at the start but the resulting scrap was better than anybody in the 60,000 sun-baked crowd could have imagined.

Sarron had once again qualified in pole position round the fast 3.61-mile circuit. Lawson, just a week after dislocating his shoulder, was third fastest behind the in-form Gardner, with Kevin Magee and Randy Mamola completing the front row. The question everybody was asking was, could Lawson's shoulder last 21 laps at that sort of pace? The Californian came up with the perfect answer.

Niall Mackenzie led from the lights on the HB Honda but his run of disasters continued. He retired with another seized engine after two heart-stopping laps. Schwantz on the Pepsi Suzuki led at the end of the first lap followed by Sarron, Rainey, Magee and Gardner. Lawson was down in eighth but was in no mood for any more lowly positions. By the sixth lap he joined Gardner, Sarron and Schwantz in a battle for the front that changed every few seconds. If you looked down to check your lap chart for a moment the lead had changed by the time you looked up again. They all had their turn at the front as they bounced off the kerbs – and each other – exchanging words and a few self-explanatory signals on the way. The leaders were never more than 15 yards apart and constantly slipstreamed each other down the 185mph, one-and-a-quarter mile Mistral straight before trying to outbrake each other, at the 100mph right-hander at the end: Lawson with a dislocated shoulder versus Schwantz with a wired-up right kneecap, versus Gardner, seeking his fourth grand prix victory in succession, versus local hero Sarron.

The battle continued until three laps from the finish when Gardner decided to break away on the NSR Rothmans Honda. He shattered the lap record and for the first time in the race a gap began to appear. Going into the last lap he led by three seconds and looked set for victory number four. We sat at the finish waiting for him to arrive when Lawson's orange and white Yamaha appeared to take the chequered flag from Sarron and Schwantz. Amid all the confusion Gardner limped across the line in fourth place, covered in oil. He punched a big dent in the tank through sheer frustration.

Going down the Mistral straight on the last lap a bolt in the primary drive had sheared or loosened, breaking into the water pump. Water pumped into the gearbox with the gearbox oil leaking out all over the bike and rider. With no water left, the engine seized less than a mile from the finish.

Gardner's disappointment must take nothing away from an amazing ride by Lawson. That 27-point championship lead more than made up for the pain as he rushed home to California for further treatment on his shoulder before the next encounter at Donington

Park. Schwantz was another brave man although it was difficult to name heroes and winners after such a race.

The race was a victory for grand prix motorcycle racing which must have gained millions more television fans, especially as it was shown with yet another boring Formula One car grand prix from Hockenheim.

With so much action it would be easy to forget the battle behind for leaderboard places. Wayne Rainey was a lonely fifth on his Lucky Strike Yamaha, despite tyre problems. Mamola, sporting a pair of natty bermuda shorts over his leathers, once again chased him hard but could never get the Cagiva near enough to challenge after making a bad start. Didier de Radigues, who almost joined me in the BBC commentary box, bike and all, at one stage, fought a frenzied duel with Pier-Francesco Chili. He grabbed seventh place by a quarter of a second with a sore Kevin Magee in front of Ron Haslam and Rob McElnea. Magee had crashed twice during practice, bruising his elbow.

The battle in the earlier 18-lap 250cc race was equally hot but with just two riders contesting every inch of the Paul Ricard tarmac for the front. Cornu and Pons constantly swapped the lead, although neither of them wanted to be ahead going down the Mistral on the last lap. Pons, riding the Campsa Honda, decided to try and make the break round the turns before the start of the infamous straight. He pushed the Honda to the limit and was 25 yards in front as they got their heads down for the 155mph one-and-a-quarter mile blast. Cornu, with a wealth of Endurance racing at Ricard, knew he'd got his man and there was nothing Pons could do. His Parisienne Honda was faster and Cornu closed the gap and then dived in front at the right-hander and the race was over. Pons was not going to take any risks in the final half mile with such a delicate championship lead. Once again the popular Cornu found a giant Swiss flag to parade on his victory lap. Pons was equally happy increasing his championship lead to eight points over Garriga who was fourth. Pons had been involved in a fabulous five-rider battle for third which, as always, threatened to explode. Dominique Sarron, Reinhold Roth, Masahiro Shimizu, Luca Cadalora and Garriga fought tooth and nail for that final rostrum place. The unfortunate Shimizu crashed coming into the start-and-finish straight. Cadalora dropped back with brake fluid on the rear tyre of his Marlboro Yamaha. Sarron pushed Garriga back to fourth in front of Roth and the ailing Cadalora. Garriga's only consolation was the fastest lap – but that did not earn him any extra championship points.

Martinez opened the proceedings with his seventh win in eight 125cc grands prix. As before he played with the opposition and kept the crowd happy before opening the throttle of his Derbi down the Mistral and that was that. Gianola, as always, rode his heart out on the outsped Honda but had to settle for second once again. The battle for third was not so clear-cut. American-based Scotsman, Allan Scott was third but crashed his Honda a few laps from the finish. Spaniard Julian Miralles came even closer but crashed his Honda coming into the start-and-finish area, in sight of the flag. He remounted to finish 11th with Italian Corrado Catalano grabbing a place on the rostrum after a good ride on the Aprilia.

Biland continued his total domination of the sidecar class making it six wins in a row. British World Champions Steve Webster and Tony Hewitt did everything in their powers to stop him but they just could not match his power out of the corners.

The winners played with the opposition before snatching the lead at half distance of the

16-lap race. Webster was second for the third time this season but trailed Biland by 24 points in the championship. The Swiss Egloff brothers, Markus and Urs, gained a well-deserved first appearance on the rostrum in third place with Frenchmen Alain Michel and Jean-Marc Fresc fourth. The tale of woe continued for former champions Egbert Streuer and Bernard Schnieders who dropped to ninth with a puncture. Derek Jones and Peter Brown came back down to earth, after their third place in Belgium, retiring with a broken gearbox. Steve Abbott and Shaun Smith kept the British flag flying in eighth, despite a bad start.

Results

500cc (21 laps, 75.81m/122.010k)		**m**	**s**	**mph**	**kmh**
1	E. Lawson, USA *(Yamaha)*	42	15.52	107.64	173.233
2	C. Sarron, France *(Yamaha)*	42	15.74	107.63	173.218
3	K. Schwantz, USA *(Suzuki)*	42	15.98	107.62	173.202
4	W. Gardner, Australia *(Honda)*	42	21.24	107.40	172.843
5	W. Rainey, USA *(Yamaha)*	42	33.15	106.90	172.037
6	R. Mamola, USA *(Cagiva)*	42	43.33	106.47	171.354
7	D. de Radigues, Belgium *(Yamaha)*	42	46.14	106.36	171.166
8	P. Chili, Italy *(Honda)*	42	46.39	106.34	171.149
9	K. Magee, USA *(Yamaha)*	42	50.63	106.17	170.867
10	R. Haslam, GB *(Elf-Honda)*	42	50.83	106.16	170.854

11 R. McElnea, GB *(Suzuki)*; 12 M. Campbell, Australia *(Elf-Honda)*; 13 M. Baldwin, USA *(Honda)*; 14 A. Valesi, Italy *(Honda)*; 15 F. Barchitta, San Marino *(Honda)*; 16 D. McLeod, GB *(Honda)*; 17 M. Gentile, Switzerland *(Fior)*. *20 laps*: 18 M. Papa, Italy *(Honda)*; 19 F. Biliotti, Italy *(Honda)*; 20 M. Fischer, W. Germany *(Honda)*; 21 E. Laycock, Ireland *(Honda)*; 22 C. Arciero, France *(Honda)*; 23 N. Schmassmann, Switzerland *(Honda)*; 24 M. Duyzers, Holland *(Honda)*.

Lawson, Gardner and Sarron fight out the race of the decade.

Record lap: W. Gardner, Australia *(Honda)*, 1m 59.27s, 108.97mph/175.367kmh.
Old record: E. Lawson, USA *(Yamaha)*, 2m 01.52s, 106.95mph/172.120kmh (1986).

World Championship positions: 1 E. Lawson, 185 points; 2 W. Gardner, 158; 3 W. Rainey, 143; 4 C. Sarron, 108; 5 K. Magee, 107; 6 K. Schwantz, 100; 7 D. de Radigues, 95; 8 N. Mackenzie, 76; 9 P. Chili, 73; 10 R. McElnea, 64.

Practice leaderboard: 1 C. Sarron, France *(Yamaha)*, 1m 58.81s; 2 W. Gardner, Australia *(Honda)*, 1m 59.68s; 3 E. Lawson, USA *(Yamaha)*, 2m 00.06s; 4 K. Magee, USA *(Yamaha)*, 2m 00.26s; 5 R. Mamola, USA *(Cagiva)*, 2m 00.28s; 6 P. Chili, Italy *(Honda)*, 2m 00.33s; 7 W. Rainey, USA *(Yamaha)*, 2m 00.44s; 8 N. Mackenzie, GB *(Honda)*, 2m 00.62s; 9 D. de Radigues, Belgium *(Yamaha)*, 2m 00.73s; 10 K. Schwantz, USA *(Suzuki)*, 2m 01.13s; 11 P. Igoa, France *(Yamaha)*, 2m 01.50s; 12 R. Haslam, GB *(Elf-Honda)*, 2m 01.57s; 13 R. McElnea, GB *(Suzuki)*, 2m 01.77s; 14 S. Yatsushiro, Japan *(Honda)*, 2m 02.90s; 15 B. Campbell, Australia *(Elf-Honda)*, 2m 03.95s; 16 M. Baldwin, USA *(Honda)*, 2m 04.14s; 17 R. Roche, France *(Cagiva)*, 2m 04.64s; 18 A. Valesi, Italy *(Honda)*, 2m 04.76s; 19 M. Papa, Italy *(Honda)*, 2m 04.96s; 20 M. Gentile, Switzerland *(Fior)*, 2m 05.08s.

250cc (18 laps, 64.98m/104.580k)		**m**	**s**	**mph**	**kmh**
1	J. Cornu, Switzerland *(Honda)*	37	23.94	104.25	167.780
2	S. Pons, Spain *(Honda)*	37	24.12	104.24	167.766
3	D. Sarron, France *(Honda)*	37	25.55	104.18	167.660
4	J. Garriga, Spain *(Yamaha)*	37	26.16	104.15	167.614
5	R. Roth, W. Germany *(Honda)*	37	26.36	104.14	167.599
6	L. Cadalora, Italy *(Yamaha)*	37	41.62	103.44	166.468
7	J. Ruggia, France *(Yamaha)*	37	47.79	103.15	166.015
8	C. Cardus, Spain *(Honda)*	38	09.87	102.78	164.415
9	L. Reggiani, Italy *(Aprilia)*	38	23.47	101.56	163.444
10	A. Auinger, Austria *(Aprilia)*	38	35.00	101.05	162.630

11 M. Wimmer, W. Germany *(Yamaha)*; 12 D. McLeod, GB *(EMC)*; 13 G. Cowan, Ireland *(Yamaha)*; 14 M. Matteoni, Italy *(Yamaha)*; 15 J. Foray, France *(Yamaha)*; 16 J. Mattioli, France *(Yamaha)*; 17 H. Bradl, W. Germany *(Honda)*; 18 U. Jucker, Switzerland *(Yamaha)*; 19 G. Bertin, France *(Yamaha)*; 20 J. Balde, France *(Rotax)*; 21 J. Cardelus, Andorra *(Aprilia)*; 22 K. Mitchell, GB *(Yamaha)*; 23 R. Delaby, Luxembourg *(Yamaha)*; 24 J. Schmid, W. Germany *(Honda)*; 25 C. Boudinot, France *(Fior-Rotax)*; 26 B. Bonhuil, France *(Honda)*. *17 laps:* 27 G. Riva, France *(Honda)*.

Record lap: J. Garriga, Spain *(Yamaha)*, 2m 03.37s, 105.35mph/169.539kmh.
Old record: C. Lavado, Venezuela *(Yamaha)*, 2m 06.95s, 102.38mph/164.758kmh (1986).

World Championship positions: 1 S. Pons, 166 points; 2 J. Garriga, 158; 3 J. Cornu, 142; 4 R. Roth, 111; 5 L. Cadalora, 101; 6 D. Sarron, 98; 7 A. Mang, 87; 8 J. Ruggia, 72; 9 M. Shimizu, 51; 10 D. McLeod, 40.

Cornu outfoxed Pons to snatch his second grand prix victory of the season.

Practice leaderboard: 1 D. Sarron, France *(Honda)*, 2m 04.03s; 2 S. Pons, Spain *(Honda)*, 2m 04.06s; 3 J. Cornu, Switzerland *(Honda)*, 2m 04.19s; 4 J. Garriga, Spain *(Yamaha)*, 2m 04.90s; 5 R. Roth, W. Germany *(Honda)* 2m 05.17s; 6 J. Ruggia, France *(Yamaha)*, 2m 05.20s; 7 L. Cadalora, Italy *(Yamaha)*, 2m 05.42s; 8 H. Eckl, W. Germany *(Aprilia)*, 2m 06.32s; 9 M. Shimizu, Japan *(Honda)*, 2m 06.43s; 10 M. Wimmer, W. Germany *(Yamaha)*, 2m 06.61s; 11 C. Cardus, Spain *(Honda)*, 2m 07.02s; 12 L. Reggiani, Italy *(Aprilia)*, 2m 07.36s; 13 D. McLeod, GB *(EMC)*, 2m 07.65s; 14 S. Caracchi, San Marino *(Honda)*, 2m 07.77s; 15 A. Auinger, Austria *(Aprilia)*, 2m 07.86s; 16 J. Balde, France *(Rotax)*, 2m 07.87s; 17 M. Vitali, Italy *(Rotax)* 2m 08.13s; 18 H. Becker, W. Germany *(Yamaha)*, 2m 08.13s; 19 J. Mattioli, France *(Yamaha)*, 2m 08.23s; 20 B. Casanova, Italy *(Aprilia)*, 2m 08.26s.

125cc (16 laps, 57.76m/92.95k)		**m**	**s**	**mph**	**kmh**
1	J. Martinez, Spain *(Derbi)*	36	19.91	95.39	153.518
2	E. Gianola, Italy *(Honda)*	36	21.67	95.31	153.394
3	C. Catalano, Italy *(Aprilia)*	36	32.52	94.84	152.635
4	D. Brigaglia, Italy *(Rotax)*	36	33.52	94.80	152.566
5	G. Waibel, W. Germany *(Honda)*	36	38.27	94.59	152.236
6	G. Grassetti, Italy *(Honda)*	36	38.46	94.58	152.223
7	L. Reyes, Spain *(Garelli)*	36	38.76	94.57	152.201
8	L. Pietroniro, Belgium *(Honda)*	36	39.15	94.56	152.175
9	A. Stadler, W. Germany *(Honda)*	36	39.33	94.55	152.163
10	E. Kytola, Finland *(Honda)*	36	40.18	94.51	152.104

11 J. Miralles, Spain *(Honda)*; 12 H. Spaan, Holland *(Honda)*; 13 H. Abold, W. Germany *(Honda)*; 14 T. Rinne, Finland *(Honda)*; 15 E. Cuppuni, Italy *(Honda)*; 16 I. McConnachie, GB *(Cagiva)*; 17 T. Feuz, Switzerland *(Rotax)*; 18 R. Milton, GB *(Rotax)*; 19 A. Waibel, W. Germany *(Waibel)*; 20 J. Selini, France *(Honda)*; 21 H. Unemoto, Japan *(Honda)*; 22 F. Kistrup, Denmark *(Hummel)*; 23 K. Galatowicz, GB *(Honda)*; 24 J. Hautaniemi, Finland *(Honda)*. *15 laps:* 25 D. Lanz, Switzerland *(Rotax)*.

Fastest lap: J. Martinez, Spain *(Derbi)*, 2m 14.70s, 96.48mph/155.176kmh.

Record lap: L. Cadalora, Italy *(Garelli)*, 2m 13.35s, 97.46mph/156.850kmh (1986).

World Championship positions: 1 J. Martinez, 140 points; 2 E. Gianola, 120; 3 H. Spaan, 76; 4 G. Grassetti, 61; 5 J. Miralles, 59; 6 G. Waibel and D. Brigaglia both 52; 8 A. Stadler, 49; 9 S. Prein, 44; 10 L. Pietroniro, 40.

Practice leaderboard: 1 E. Gianola, Italy *(Honda)*, 2m 14.78s; 2 J. Martinez, Spain *(Derbi)*, 2m 14.96s; 3 S. Prein, W. Germany *(Honda)*, 2m 15.86s; 4 I. McConnachie, GB *(Cagiva)*, 2m 16.47s; 5 H. Luthi, Switzerland *(Honda)*, 2m 16.56s; 6 A. Stadler, W. Germany *(Honda)*, 2m 16.59s; 7 C. Catalano, Italy *(Aprilia)*, 2m 16.61s; 8 A. Scott, USA *(Honda)*, 2m 16.80s; 9 L. Pietroniro, Belgium *(Honda)*, 2m 16.84s; 10 H. Spaan, Holland *(Honda)*, 2m 16.90s; 11 D. Brigaglia, Italy (Rotax), 2m 16.90s; 12 J. Miralles, Spain *(Honda)* 2m 17.05s; 13 A. Bedford, GB *(Honda)*, 2m 17.11s; 14 L. Reyes, Spain *(Garelli)*, 2m 17.18s; 15 E. Kytola, Finland *(Honda)*, 2m 17.36s; 16 K. Takada, Japan *(Honda)*, 2m 17.38s; 17 H. Abold, W. Germany *(Honda)*, 2m 17.43s; 18 J. Wickstrom, Finland *(Honda)*, 2m 17.56s; 19 G. Waibel, W. Germany *(Honda)*, 2m 17.60s; 20 G. Grassetti, Italy *(Honda)*, 2m 17.66s.

	Sidecar (16 laps, 57.76m/92.95k)	**m**	**s**	**mph**	**kmh**
1	R. Biland, Switzerland K. Waltisperg, Switzerland *(LCR-Krauser)*	33	47.80	102.55	165.034
2	S. Webster, GB T. Hewitt, GB *(LCR-Krauser)*	33	53.00	102.28	164.612
3	M. Egloff, Switzerland U. Egloff, Switzerland *(LCR-Yamaha)*	34	03.07	101.78	163.801
4	A. Michel, France J. Fresc, France *(LCR-Krauser)*	34	45.40	99.71	160.476
5	M. Kumano, Japan M. Fahrni, Switzerland *(LCR-Yamaha)*	34	53.77	99.31	159.834
6	A. Zurbrugg, Switzerland M. Zurbrugg, Switzerland *(LCR-Yamaha)*	34	57.31	99.15	159.564
7	Y. Kumagaya, Japan B. Barlow, GB *(Windle-Yamaha)*	35	03.26	98.87	159.113
8	S. Abbott, GB S. Smith, GB *(Windle-Yamaha)*	35	13.90	98.37	158.312
9	E. Streuer, Holland B. Schnieders, Holland *(LCR-Yamaha)*	35	14.85	98.32	158.241
10	T. van Kempen, Holland S. Birchall, GB *(LCR-Yamaha)*	35	21.51	98.02	157.744

11 Y. Nigrowsky/M. Charpentier, France *(Seymaz-Yamaha)*; 12 F. Stolzle/H. Stolzle, W. Germany *(Krauser-Yamaha)*; 13 B. Scherer/T. Schroder, W. Germany *(BSR-Krauser)*; 14 B. Brindley/G. Rose, GB *(Yamaha)*; 15 R. Progin/Y. Hunziker, Switzerland *(Seymaz-Yamaha)*. *15 laps:* 16 C. Stirrat/S. Prior, GB *(LCR-Yamaha)*; 17 A. Zini/C. Sonaglia, Italy *(LCR-Yamaha)*; 18 J. Millet/C. Debroux, France *(GDF)*; 19 E. Weber/E. Rosinger, W. Germany *(Sigwa)*; 20 P. Atkinson/G. Simmons, GB *(LCR-Yamaha)*; 21 T. Baker/J. Cochrane, GB *(Yamaha)*; 22 B. Smith/D. Smith, GB *(Windle-Yamaha)*.

Record lap: R. Biland/K. Waltisperg, Switzerland *(LCR-Krauser)*, 2m 05.23s, 103.78mph/167.021kmh.
Old record: S. Webster/T. Hewitt, GB *(LCR-Krauser)*, 2m 07.46s, 101.97mph/164.099kmh (1986).

World Championship positions: 1 Biland/Waltisperg, 120 points; 2 Webster/Hewitt, 96; 3 Michel/Fresc and Streuer/Schnieders both 54; 5 Abbott/Smith and Zurbrugg/Zurbrugg both 48; 7 Brindley/Rose, 46; 8 Jones/Brown, 45; 9 Egloff/Egloff, 40; 10 van Kempen/Birchall and Scherer/Schroder both 32.

Practice leaderboard: 1 Biland/Waltisperg, Switzerland *(LCR-Krauser)*, 2m 04.07s; 2 Webster/Hewitt, GB *(LCR-Krauser)*, 2m 05.04s; 3 Egloff/Egloff, Switzerland *(LCR-Yamaha)*, 2m 05.50s; 4 Streuer/Schnieders, Holland *(LCR-Yamaha)*, 2m 05.64s; 5 Michel/Fresc, France *(LCR-Krauser)*, 2m 07.21s; 6 Zurbrugg/Zurbrugg, Switzerland *(LCR-Yamaha)*, 2m 07.75s; 7 Kumano/Fahrni, Japan/Switzerland *(LCR-Yamaha)*, 2m 08.29s; 8 Steinhausen/Hiller, W. Germany *(ADM)*, 2m 08.84s; 9 Jones/Brown, GB *(LCR-Yamaha)*, 2m 09.92s; 10 Stropek/Haas, Austria *(Mibag-Krauser)*, 2m 10.24s; 11 Kumagaya/Barlow, Japan/GB *(Windle-Yamaha)*, 2m 10.32s; 12 Laratte/Corbier, France *(LCR-Yamaha)*, 2m 10.41s; 13 van Kempen/Birchall, Holland/GB *(LCR-Yamaha)*, 2m 10.74s; 14 Bosman/Kellett, Australia *(LCR-Yamaha)*, 2m 10.76s; 15 Abbott/Smith, GB *(Windle-Yamaha)*, 2m 11.19s; 16 Nigrowsky/Charpentier, France *(Seymaz-Yamaha)*, 2m 11.25s; 17 Stolzle/Stolzle, W. Germany *(LCR-Krauser)*, 2m 12.65s; 18 Scherer/Schroder, W. Germany *(BSR-Krauser)*, 2m 12.86s; 19 Zini/Sonaglia, Italy *(LCR-Yamaha)*, 2m 12.92s; 20 Progin/Hunziker, Switzerland *(Seymaz-Yamaha)*, 2m 13.23s.

BRITISH GRAND PRIX, 7 August, Donington Park 2.50m/4.023k

Grand prix racing continued its revival in Britain in 1988. Scorching hot weather enticed over 81,000 to Donington for the weekend of the British Grand Prix and the event matched the sunshine for enjoyment.

Californian Wayne Rainey revelled in the conditions to win his first 500cc grand prix, although Wayne Gardner, in second place, closed the gap on championship leader Eddie Lawson. Steve Webster inflicted the first defeat of the season on Rolf Biland in a fabulous sidecar race. Italian Luca Cadalora paid scant regard to the opposition in the 250cc contest while, everybody's favourite, Ezio Gianola beat his arch rival Jorge Martinez in the 125s.

It was billed as the great Gardner/Lawson showdown but the expected confrontation in the 30-lap 500cc race never materialised. Gardner had qualified in pole position, by putting in a fastest lap of one minute, 35.09 seconds in the first timed session on Friday morning – which was a good thing for him. On the Saturday morning he crashed while trying to pass some back markers and was lucky to escape with bruised ankles. Rainey, who'd had some great Transatlantic battles at Donington, was just on the front row. He'd qualified fifth fastest, riding Kenny Roberts's Lucky Strike Yamaha shod with Dunlop tyres constructed in nearby Birmingham.

Rainey screamed from the line and led into Redgate on the first lap. Both he and the crowd waited for the others to take him on but they didn't. The Dunlop tyres proved the perfect combination for the re-surfaced Donington and the hot weather, and the 27-year-old Californian kept pulling away.

Those early Transatlantic battles had been against his great rival, Texan Kevin Schwantz, but there was no repeat this time. Schwantz crashed his Pepsi Suzuki and cut his knee on the first lap trying to outbrake Ron Haslam at the chicane. Haslam, to the delight of his local fans, remounted the Honda-powered Elf 5 to eventually finish a brave 14th. Rainey's team-mate Kevin Magee also had to take evasive action but fought back to a brilliant fifth.

Gardner was second on the second lap but could make no impression on Rainey. On the fifth lap he went into the dirt at the dreaded chicane and dropped to fourth behind Christian Sarron and Niall Mackenzie. Lawson was faring even worse and was ninth at the end of the first lap, riding the Marlboro Yamaha. He had real problems getting past his own team-mate Didier de Radigues and Roger Burnett, replacing the injured Shunji Yatsushiro in the Rothmans Honda team.

Gardner was also having problems getting past Sarron and a very determined Mackenzie, riding the HB Honda. His front brake disc had buckled but, despite the problems, the hard-riding Australian was back into second on the 11th lap. From then the race settled into a steady pattern at the front with the crowd's attention focused on the fortunes of Lawson and the progress of Magee. At half distance Lawson, despite tyre and engine problems, was up into fifth place while Magee was flying after his first lap excursion. Eleven laps from the finish he pushed Lawson back to sixth to help his fellow Aussie Gardner in his battle to keep his championship crown.

At the finish Gardner had closed Lawson's lead to 20 points, although the day belonged to Rainey, who celebrated his first grand prix victory in style. Behind Lawson replacement

Burnett looked to be heading for a promising seventh place on his return to grand prix racing. However on the last lap he let de Radigues and Pier-Francesco Chili through to eventually finish ninth. His neighbour Rob McElnea was not so lucky, crashing out of 10th place at the same spot as team-mate Schwantz with just six laps remaining.

Randy Mamola had collected more than £12,000 for the Save the Children fund over the weekend but on the track could only finish 11th after suffering clutch problems on the Cagiva. Team-mate Raymond Roche was brought down by Japanese rider Norihiko Fujiwara.

Steve Webster and Tony Hewitt waited until the seventh round of the championship to inflict the first defeat of the season on Rolf Biland and Kurt Waltisperg in a magnificent 24-lap sidecar race in front of a patriotic home crowd. It also provided a magnificent spectacle for millions of television fans. At the finish it took the British pair nearly half an hour to complete their lap of honour, accompanied by Sports Minister Colin Moynihan. No wonder everybody wanted to shake their hands. The first 10 laps were an epic struggle between the Krauser-powered LCRs of Webster and Biland and the Yamaha LCR of former World Champions Egbert Streuer and Bernard Schnieders. They constantly swapped the lead until the unlucky Streuer slowed with a blistered rear tyre, leaving Webster and Biland to slog it out to the flag.

Webster led for three laps until lap 15 when Biland barged his way past. Webster was back in front a lap later but Biland grabbed back the advantage on the 18th lap and we waited for him to pull away, as he'd done on the six previous occasions. World Champion Webster was determined it was not going to happen and hung on grimly. Three laps from the finish he seized his chance at the Old Hairpin when he grabbed the lead. It was then a case of keeping his head down, apart from one sly look back at the Esses, and the throttle open. It worked, with the British pair opening up over a two-second advantage, although they still trailed Biland by 21 points in the championship with just two rounds remaining. The unfortunate Streuer limped home in fifth place behind Alain Michel and Jean-Marc Fresc, follwed by the Egloffs. Former British Grand Prix winner Derek Jones, with passenger Peter Brown was seventh behind Japanese star Masato Kumano.

Former 125cc World Champion Luca Cadalora was a comfortable winner of the 26-lap 250cc race on his Marlboro Yamaha while behind him the battles raged. After fighting off the early challenge of Dominique Sarron the Italian cruised away for his second 250cc grand prix victory. Sarron, riding the Rothmans Honda, rode a steady race to preserve his Michelin tyres. He watched from a safe distance the usual Spanish dogfight for the World title between Sito Pons and Juan Garriga. He then passed them both to finish a comfortable second. The battle for third was very different. Championship leader Pons, riding the Campsa Honda, and second placed Garriga, riding the Ducados Yamaha, went at it hammer and tongs.

There is little love lost between these two Spaniards chasing the world title, and it showed. They constantly outbraked each other and Garriga won this particular battle by passing his great rival at the Melbourne hairpin on the very last lap. The race for fifth was equally close with Reinhold Roth, riding the HB Honda, just holding off impressive French youngster Jean Phillipe Ruggia by less than one second. Swiss ace Jacques Cornu, who won the previous round in France, was a lonely seventh with Donnie McLeod the best British finisher in 10th place riding the 7 Up EMC.

Italian Gianola swamped the opposition in the 24-lap 125cc race to inflict only the second defeat of the year in the class on Jorge Martinez. Gianola's flat-out, head-down style and the power characteristics of his RS Honda were ideally suited to the Donington curves. He pulled away from the pack headed by British star Alex Bedford who had the cheek to head Martinez and that all-conquering Derbi. His glory lasted for 11 laps until he retired with a lose rear sprocket and Martinez, despite a collision with Hans Spaan in the early stages, moved into second.

The closest battle was for fourth with Spaniard Julian Miralles pipping Scottish-born American Allan Scott by 0.13 seconds. There was also a great ride by Coventry lad Chris Galatowicz who was sixth in front of World Champion Fausto Gresini. It was a marvellous weekend that did a great deal for grand prix motorcycle racing in Britain. An enormous crowd, perfect weather, millions of new television fans and not one arrest throughout the four glorious days.

Results

500cc (30 laps, 75.00m/120.69k)		m	s	mph	kmh
1	W. Rainey, USA *(Yamaha)*	48	33.67	92.66	149.13
2	W. Gardner, Australia *(Honda)*	48	40.64	92.44	148.77
3	C. Sarron, France *(Yamaha)*	48	42.45	92.38	148.68
4	N. Mackenzie, GB *(Honda)*	48	45.51	92.29	148.52
5	K. Magee, Australia *(Yamaha)*	49	10.42	91.51	147.27
6	E. Lawson, USA *(Yamaha)*	49	14.64	91.38	147.06
7	D. de Radigues, Belgium *(Yamaha)*	49	25.03	91.06	146.54
8	P. Chili, Italy *(Honda)*	49	25.48	91.04	146.52
9	R. Burnett, GB *(Honda)*	49	26.06	91.02	146.49
10	T. Taira, Japan *(Yamaha)*	49	55.51	90.13	145.05

11 R. Mamola, USA *(Cagiva)*; 12 N. Fujiwara, Japan *(Yamaha)*. *29 laps:* 13 M. Baldwin, USA *(Honda)*; 14 R. Haslam, GB *(Elf-Honda)*; 15 F. Biliotti, Italy *(Honda)*; 16 P. Igoa, France *(Yamaha)*; 17 E. Laycock, Ireland *(Honda)*; 18 F. Barchitta, San Marino *(Honda)*; 19 D. Amatriain, Spain *(Honda)*; 20 M. Gentile, Switzerland *(Fior)*. *28 laps:* 21 D. Leach, GB *(Suzuki)*; 22 M. Duyzers, Holland *(Honda)*; 23 S. Buckmaster, GB *(Honda)*; 24 K. van der Endt, Holland *(Honda)*; 25 N. Schmassmann, Switzerland *(Honda)*.

Record lap: C. Sarron, France *(Yamaha)*, 1m 36.21s, 93.54mph/150.54kmh.
Old record: T. Taira, Japan *(Yamaha)*, 1m 39.37s, 90.57mph/145.73kmh (1987).

World Championship positions: 1 E. Lawson, 195 points; 2 W. Gardner, 175; 3 W. Rainey, 163; 4 C. Sarron, 123; 5 K. Magee, 118; 6 D. de Radigues, 104; 7 K. Schwantz, 100; 8 N. Mackenzie, 89; 9 P. Chili, 81; 10 R. McElnea, 64.

Practice leaderboard: 1 W. Gardner, Australia *(Honda)*, 1m 35.09s; 2 E. Lawson, USA *(Yamaha)*, 1m 35.64s; 3 C. Sarron, France *(Yamaha)*, 1m 35.74s; 4 N. Mackenzie, GB *(Honda)*, 1m 36.04s; 5 W. Rainey, USA *(Yamaha)*, 1m 36.17s; 6 R. Mamola, USA *(Cagiva)*, 1m 36.33s; 7 D. de Radigues, Belgium *(Yamaha)*, 1m 36.52s; 8 T. Taira, Japan *(Yamaha)*, 1m 36.89s; 9 R. Burnett, GB *(Honda)*, 1m 37.01s; 10 R. Haslam, GB *(Elf-*

Honda), 1m 37.18s; 11 K. Magee, Australia *(Yamaha)*, 1m 37.34s; 12 K. Schwantz, USA *(Suzuki)*, 1m 37.40s; 13 R. McElnea, GB *(Suzuki)*, 1m 37.43s; 14 P. Chili, Italy *(Honda)*, 1m 37.56s; 15 R. Roche, France *(Cagiva)*, 1m 38.41s; 16 N. Fujiwara, Japan *(Yamaha)*, 1m 38.89s; 17 M. Baldwin, USA *(Honda)*, 1m 39.09s; 18 E. Laycock, Ireland *(Honda)*, 1m 39.11s; 19. M. Gentile, Switzerland *(Fior)*, 1m 39.53s; 20 F. Biliotti, Italy *(Honda)*, 1m 39.67s.

250cc (26 laps, 65.00m/104.60k)		**m**	**s**	**mph**	**kmh**
1	L. Cadalora, Italy *(Yamaha)*	43	16.38	90.12	145.04
2	D. Sarron, France *(Honda)*	43	19.84	90.00	144.84
3	J. Garriga, Spain *(Yamaha)*	43	21.55	89.94	144.75
4	S. Pons, Spain *(Honda)*	43	21.68	89.93	144.74
5	R. Roth, W. Germany *(Honda)*	43	31.99	89.58	144.17
6	J. Ruggia, France *(Yamaha)*	43	32.72	89.56	144.13
7	J. Cornu, Switzerland *(Honda)*	43	40.52	89.29	143.70
8	C. Lavado, Venezuela *(Yamaha)*	43	50.04	88.97	143.18
9	M. Shimizu, Japan *(Honda)*	43	58.34	88.69	142.73
10	D. McLeod, GB *(EMC)*	44	00.92	88.60	142.59

11 I. Palazzese, Venezuela *(Yamaha)*; 12 C. Cardus, Spain *(Honda)*; 13 H. Eckl, W. Germany *(Aprilia)*; 14 S. Caracchi, Italy *(Honda)*; 15 M. Wimmer, W. Germany *(Yamaha)*; 16 B. Casanova, Italy *(Aprilia)*; 17 A. Auinger, Austria *(Aprilia)*; 18 W. Zeelenberg, Holland *(Yamaha)*; 19 J. Schmid, W. Germany *(Honda)*; 20 U. Jucker, Switzerland *(Yamaha)*. *25 laps:* 21 A. Preining, Austria *(Aprilia)*; 22 C. Boudinet, France *(Fior-Rotax)*; 23 J. Balde, France *(Rotax)*; 24 N. Bosworth, GB *(Aprilia)*; 25 H. Lindner, Austria *(Honda)*.

Record lap: J. Garriga, Spain *(Yamaha)*, 1m 38.87s, 91.02mph/146.48kmh.
Old record: M. Wimmer, W. Germany *(Yamaha)*, 1m 42.28s, 87.99mph/141.58kmh (1987).

World championship positions: 1 S. Pons, 179 points; 2 J. Garriga, 173; 3 J. Cornu, 151; 4 R. Roth, 122; 5 L. Cadalora, 121; 6 D. Sarron, 115; 7 T. Mang, 87; 8 J. Ruggia, 82; 9 M. Shimizu, 58; 10 D. McLeod, 46.

Practice leaderboard: 1 J. Garriga, Spain *(Yamaha)*, 1m 38.22s; 2 L. Cadalora, Italy *(Yamaha)*, 1m 38.49s; 3 C. Lavado, Venezuela *(Yamaha)*, 1m 38.70s; 4 D. Sarron, France *(Honda)*, 1m 38.91s; 5 S. Pons, Spain *(Honda)*, 1m 39.26s; 6 J. Ruggia, France *(Yamaha)*, 1m 39.32s; 7 R. Roth, W. Germany *(Honda)*, 1m 39.40s; 8 J. Cornu, Switzerland *(Honda)*, 1m 39.44s; 9 I. Palazzese, Venezuela *(Yamaha)*, 1m 39.66s; 10 C. Cardus, Spain *(Honda)*, 1m 39.99s; 11. D. McLeod, GB *(EMC)*, 1m 40.08s; 12 M. Wimmer, W. Germany *(Yamaha)*, 1m 40.23s; 13 B. Casanova, Italy *(Aprilia)*, 1m 40.51s; 14 L. Reggiani, Italy *(Aprilia)*, 1m 40.54s; 15 P. Casoli, Italy *(Garelli)*, 1m 40.57s; 16 M. Shimizu, Japan *(Honda)*, 1m 40.63s; 17 H. Eckl, W. Germany *(Aprilia)*, 1m 40.68s; 18 M. Herweh, W. Germany *(Yamaha)*, 1m 40.93s; 19 G. Cowan, Ireland *(Yamaha)*, 1m 40.93s; 20 A. Auinger, Austria *(Aprilia)*, 1m 41.01s.

125cc (24 laps, 60.00m/96.56k)	**m**	**s**	**mph**	**kmh**
1 E. Gianola, Italy *(Honda)*	42	42.42	84.29	135.66
2 J. Martinez, Spain *(Derbi)*	43	14.39	83.25	133.98
3 D. Brigaglia, Italy *(Rotax)*	43	20.58	83.05	133.66
4 J. Miralles, Spain *(Honda)*	43	23.07	82.97	133.54
5 A. Scott, USA *(Honda)*	43	23.20	82.96	133.53
6 K. Galatowicz, GB *(Honda)*	43	30.28	82.74	133.17
7 F. Gresini, Italy *(Garelli)*	43	38.38	82.49	132.76
8 J. Wickstrom, Finland *(Honda)*	43	41.77	82.38	132.58
9 A. Criville, Spain *(Derbi)*	43	43.20	82.34	132.51
10 H. Spaan, Holland *(Honda)*	43	43.71	82.32	132.49

11 A. Waibel, W. Germany *(Honda)*; 12 H. Unemoto, Japan *(Honda)*; 13 H. Luthi, Switzerland *(Honda)*; 14 B. Hassaine, France *(Honda)*; 15 L. Pietroniro, Belgium *(Honda)*; 16 M. Herreros, Spain *(Derbi)*; 17 J. Bolart, Spain *(Cobas)*; 18 J. Hautaniemi, Finland *(Honda)*; 19 I. McConnachie, GB *(Cagiva)*; 20 G. Waibel, W. Germany *(Honda)*; 21 M. Hernandez, Spain *(Honda)*. *23 laps:* 22 M. Leitner, Austria *(Rotax)*; 23 H. Abold, W. Germany *(Honda)*; 24 K. Takada, Japan *(Honda)*; 25 A. Patterson, Ireland *(Honda)*.

Record lap: E. Gianola, Italy *(Honda)*, 1m 45.76s, 85.09mph/136.94kmh.
Old record: F. Gresini, Italy *(Garelli)*, 1m 48.24s, 83.14mph/133.77kmh (1987).

World Championship positions: 1 J. Martinez, 157 points; 2 E. Gianola, 140; 3 H. Spaan, 82; 4 J. Miralles, 72; 5 D. Brigaglia, 67; 6 G. Grassetti, 61; 7 G. Waibel, 52; 8 A. Stadler, 49; 9 S. Prein, 44; 10 L. Pietroniro, 41.

Practice leaderboard: 1 E. Gianola, Italy *(Honda)*, 1m 45.60s; 2 J. Martinez, Spain *(Derbi)*, 1m 46.17s; 3 A. Bedford, GB *(Honda)*, 1m 46.29s; 4 D. Brigaglia, Italy *(Rotax)*, 1m 46.71s; 5 H. Spaan, Holland *(Honda)*, 1m 46.79s; 6 C. Catalano, Italy *(Aprilia)*, 1m 47.11s; 7 J. Miralles, Spain *(Honda)*, 1m 47.34s; 8 A. Scott, USA *(Honda)*, 1m 47.35s; 9 L. Pietroniro, Belgium *(Honda)*, 1m 47.37s; 10 A. Stadler, W. Germany *(Honda)*, 1m 47.53s; 11 K. Galatowicz, GB *(Honda)*, 1m 47.64s; 12 G. Grassetti, Italy *(Honda)*, 1m 47.75s; 13 H. Unemoto, Japan *(Honda)*, 1m 47.81s; 14 K. Takada, Japan *(Honda)*, 1m 47.88s; 15 S. Prein, W. Germany *(Honda)*, 1m 47. 93; 16 I. McConnachie, GB *(Cagiva)*, 1m 47.97s; 17 M. Reyes, Spain *(Garelli)*, 1m 48.02s; 18 J. Wickstrom, Finland *(Honda)*, 1m 48.06s; 19 T. Feuz, Switzerland *(Rotax)*, 1m 48.11s; 20 G. Waibel, W. Germany *(Honda)*, 1m 48.18s.

Sidecar (24 laps, 60.00m/96.56k)	**m**	**s**	**mph**	**kmh**
1 S. Webster, GB T. Hewitt, GB *(LCR-Krauser)*	40	39.56	88.54	142.49
2 R. Biland, Switzerland K. Waltisperg, Switzerland *(LCR-Krauser)*	40	41.67	88.46	142.36
3 A. Michel, France J. Fresc, France *(LCR-Krauser)*	40	55.75	87.95	141.55

4	M. Egloff, Switzerland U. Egloff, Switzerland *(LCR-ADM)*	41 08.04	87.51	140.84
5	E. Streuer, Holland B. Schnieders, Holland *(LCR-Yamaha)*	41 09.81	87.45	140.74
6	M. Kumano, Japan M. Fahrni, Switzerland *(LCR-TEC)*	41 25.50	86.90	139.85
7	D. Jones, GB P. Brown, GB *(LCR-Yamaha)*	41 42.55	86.31	138.90
8	P. Stolzle, W. Germany H. Stolzle, W. Germany *(LCR-Krauser)*	41 56.24	85.84	138.14
9	A. Zurbrugg, Switzerland M. Zurbrugg, Switzerland *(LCR-Yamaha)*	41 59.02	85.74	137.99
10	B. Scherer, W. Germany T. Schroder, W. Germany *(BSR-Krauser)*	42 04.00	85.57	137.72

11 Y. Kumagaya/B. Barlow, Japan/GB *(Windle-Yamaha)*. *23 laps:* 12 G. Thomas/E. Rosinger, GB/W. Germany *(LCR-IMI)*; 13 J. Millet/C. Debroux, France *(GDF-ELF)*; 14 A. Bosman/D. Kellet, Australia *(LCR-Yamaha)*; 15 C. Stirrat/J. Prior, GB *(LCR-Yamaha)*; 16 R. Gardner/T. Strevens, GB *(Yamaha)*. *22 laps:* 17 R. Progin/Y. Hunziker, Switzerland *(Seymaz-Yamaha)*.

Record lap: R. Biland/K. Waltisperg, Switzerland *(LCR-Krauser)*, 1m 40.05s, 89.95mph/144.76kmh.
Old record: S. Webster/T. Hewitt, GB *(LCR-Krauser)*, 1m 41.71s, 88.48mph/142.36kmh (1987).

World championship positions: 1 Biland/Waltisperg, 137 points; 2 Webster/Hewitt, 116; 3 Michel/Fresc, 69; 4 Streuer/Schnieders, 65; 5 Zurbrugg/Zurbrugg, 55; 6 Jones/Brown, 54; 7 Egloff/Egloff, 53; 8 Abbott/Smith, 48; 9 Brindley/Rose, 46; 10 Kumano/Fahrni and Scherer/Schroder both 38.

Practice leaderboard: 1 Biland/Waltisperg, Switzerland *(LCR-Krauser)*, 1m 37.18s; 2 Webster/Hewitt, GB *(LCR-Krauser)*, 1m 39.05s; 3 Egloff/Egloff, Switzerland *(LCR-ADM)*, 1m 39.32s; 4 Streuer/Schnieders, Holland *(LCR-Yamaha)*, 1m 40.03s; 5 Michel/Fresc, France *(LCR-Krauser)*, 1m 40.25s; 6 Kumano/Fahrni, Japan/Switzerland *(LCR-TEC)*, 1m 40.69s; 7 Jones/Brown, GB *(LCR-Yamaha)*, 1m 41.28s; 8 Zurbrugg/Zurbrugg, Switzerland *(LCR-Yamaha)*, 1m 41.75s; 9 Kumagaya/Barlow, Japan/GB *(Windle-Yamaha)*, 1m 41.82s; 10 Steinhausen/Hiller, W. Germany *(ADM-Krauser)*, 1m 41.90s; 11 Abbott/Smith, GB *(Windle-Yamaha)*, 1m 42.17s; 12 Stropek/Campbell, Austria/GB *(Mibag-Krauser)*, 1m 42.36s; 13 Brindley/Rose, GB *(Krauser-Yamaha)*, 1m 42.37s; 14 Nigrowsky/Charpentier, France *(Seymaz-Yamaha)*, 1m 42.47s; 15 Larratte/Corbier, France *(LCR-Yamaha)*, 1m 42.48s; 16 Stolzle/Stolzle, W. Germany (LCR-Krauser), 1m 42.49s; 17 van Kempen/Birchall, Holland/GB *(LCR-Yamaha)*, 1m 42.79s; 18 Scherer/Schroder, W. Germany *(BSR-Krauser)*, 1m 43.07s; 19 Bosman/Kellet, Australia *(LCR-Yamaha)*, 1m 43.36s; 20 Thomas/Rosinger, GB/W. Germany *(IMI-LCR)*, 1m 43.63s.

Donington '88 – vast crowds, beautiful sunshine and magnificent racing.

Wayne Rainey led from start to finish to secure what will surely be the first of many grands prix victories.

SWEDISH GRAND PRIX, 14 August, Anderstorp 2.50m/4.031k

Eddie Lawson put one hand on Wayne Gardner's world crown in the Swedish Grand Prix with an emphatic victory over his bitter rival, while Steve Webster refused to let go of his world sidecar title. The British pair of Webster and Steve Hewitt inflicted the second defeat within seven days over Rolf Biland. Sito Pons won his grudge match with Juan Garriga in the 25-lap 250cc race while Jorge Martinez not only won the 125cc race, but clinched his second world title.

Anderstorp is pretty drab at the best of times but when it rains it's really miserable. It rained for most of practice and the only time it abated Lawson grabbed pole position and Gardner crashed once again. This time he bruised his back and took some skin off one hand. More worrying for him was the fact that he'd only qualified on the third row of the grid and had no time to set up the NSR Rothmans Honda for a dry race. It was dry when Wayne Rainey, fresh from his Donington success, led into the first bend of the 30-lap race. Gardner made a rocket start from the third row and was fourth at the end of the first lap with Lawson tucked in behind. The Californian was still very disappointed with his Donington performance and by the third lap grabbed the lead. Gardner relegated Rainey to third a lap later. Any thoughts he had of pushing the championship leader disappeared when he got into a big slide and then settled for a safe second place. At the front Lawson complained of lack of brakes on his Marlboro Yamaha but it made no difference to his progress. His lead – and chances of the championship – increased until he eased the pace to secure his most important victory of the season.

Christian Sarron and Niall Mackenzie continued their Donington battle with Rainey dropping back to fifth. Sarron, as he did the week before, eventually pulled away from Mackenzie, who had handling problems on his HB Honda. Lucky Strike Yamaha Australian Kevin Magee had engine problems on the first lap but once they'd cleared he started to fly. He was briefly engaged in a real old dog fight with Roger Burnett, Pier-Francesco Chili and Randy Mamola. He saw them off and then pushed Didier de Radigues back to seventh and the race became rather boring. The only real battle was for eighth with Burnett, desperate to prove himself in the Rothmans Honda team, constantly swapping places with Chili.

As always at Anderstorp it came to the crunch at the right-hander at the end of the main straight, which doubles up as the runway of the local airport. Burnett held the advantage and when Chili made a mess of it he crossed the line with a comfortable cushion. Despite some torrid slides Randy Mamola held onto 10th place, riding the Cagiva, with Ron Haslam 11th. It was a bad day for the Pepsi Suzuki team with Kevin Schwantz, not fully recovered from his Donington crash, 12th and a battered and bruised Rob McElnea 13th.

Lawson increased that championship lead to 23 points and Gardner flew back home to Monaco knowing that the championship was slipping rapidly from his grasp.

Rolf Biland's championship celebrations were put on ice once again with Webster and Hewitt ruining their party with a superb victory that was to have massive implications two weeks later in Czechoslovakia. Last year Webster clinched the world title at Anderstorp after finishing second to Biland, in a controversial race. This time there was no such controversy as he firmly reversed the roles. Markus and Urs Egloff led the way on their LCR Krauser, waiting for their countrymen Biland and Waltisperg to arrive. They turned up quickly enough and pushed second-placed Webster aside on the fourth lap and the Egloffs a lap later. Webster was determined not to let them pull away and stormed past Egloff on his Krauser/LCR and set after Biland. He surprised the Swiss ace by passing him down the main straight, a manoeuvre he could never have contemplated earlier in the year. The stage was set for a marvellous cat-and-mouse battle in which no quarter was asked or given. With two breathtaking laps remaining Biland led but Webster outbraked him going into the infamous right-hander and held firm until the chequered flag with just over one second to spare. It was a good job for the two leaders that Egbert Streuer and Bernard Schnieders only just qualified at the back of the grid after a series of mechanical catastrophes during practice. They raced through the field on their Yamaha-powered LCR to eventually finish third, only three seconds behind Biland.

Sito Pons increased his lead to nine points over his deadly rival Garriga after a superb 25-lap 250cc race. Once again the pair were constantly at each other's throats with Dominique Sarron and Reinhold Roth joining in a grandstand finish.

The Spanish civil war came to a head when Pons's Campsa Honda and Garriga's Ducados Yamaha clashed fairings on the last lap. Both riders stayed on with Pons holding off his deadly rival with just three tenths of a second to spare. Both riders expressed, pretty loudly, their separate views of the incident in a war of words after the race. As in most such cases it seemed six of one and half-a-dozen of the other. Honda men Sarron and Roth had closed on the two warring Spaniards during the closing stages and less than one second covered the four finishers.

Spare a thought for Swiss ace Jacques Cornu. He crashed and broke his collarbone in Friday's practice and then flew back to Zurich to have the injury strapped up. He returned late on Saturday night, determined to ride his Parisienne Honda the next day in order to preserve his third place in the championship. He was lying ninth in the race when he was brought down by Japanese Honda rider Masahiro Shimizu when he crashed. Luckily Cornu did not aggravate the injury and held onto that third spot.

Martinez has been given a rough ride all the way to the 125cc world title by hard-riding Ezio Gianola. His title-winning ride was no exception. Italian Gianola never lifted his head from behind the screen of his RS Honda for the complete 23 laps. He outbraked the champion elect and his works Derbi, riding round the outside and underneath of them. One thing he could not do was pass them on the straight and Martinez knew that. When it came to the crunch Martinez opened the throttle and just sneaked it at the flag to clinch the title. However most of the 40,000 crowd, perched high in the grandstands on the main straight, stood to salute Gianola after another fabulous display of flat out riding. Julian Miralles and Hans Spaan fought out just as close a battle for third on their tiny Hondas.

Anderstorp, because of its position in the calendar has often been the scene of world champions' triumphs. The facilities do not match the occasion. This year even the swimming pool had been drained and so new World Champion Martinez missed the traditional ducking.

Results

500cc (30 laps, 75.14m/120.03k)	**m**	**s**	**mph**	**kmh**
1 E. Lawson, USA *(Yamaha)*	47	59.28	93.95	151.200
2 W. Gardner, Australia *(Honda)*	48	12.32	93.53	150.519
3 C. Sarron, France *(Yamaha)*	48	18.62	93.32	150.191
4 N. Mackenzie, GB *(Honda)*	48	22.73	93.19	149.979
5 W. Rainey, USA *(Yamaha)*	48	29.36	92.98	149.637
6 K. Magee, Australia *(Yamaha)*	48	34.73	92.81	149.361
7 D. de Radigues, Belgium *(Yamaha)*	48	47.91	92.34	148.689
8 R. Burnett, GB *(Honda)*	48	50.44	92.31	148.561
9 P. Chili, Italy *(Honda)*	48	52.61	92.24	148.451
10 R. Mamola, USA *(Cagiva)*	48	58.80	92.05	148.138

11 R. Haslam, GB *(Elf-Honda)*; 12 K. Schwantz, USA *(Suzuki)*; 13 R. McElnea, GB *(Suzuki)*; 14 T. Taira, Japan *(Yamaha). 29 laps:* 15 R. Roche, France *(Cagiva)*; 16 F. Barchitta, San Marino *(Honda)*; 17 N. Fujiwara, Japan *(Yamaha)*; 18 P. Linden, Sweden *(Honda)*; 19 M. Gentile, Switzerland *(Fior)*; 20 B. Kneubuhler, Switzerland *(Honda)*; 21 P. Skold, Sweden *(Honda)*; 22 W. von Muralt, Switzerland *(Suzuki). 28 laps:* 23 S. Buckmaster, GB *(Honda)*; 24 C. Wulff, Denmark *(Honda)*; 25 A. Dahli, Sweden *(Suzuki)*; 26 C. Buerki, Switzerland *(Honda)*; 27 L. Johansson, Sweden *(Suzuki)*.

Record lap: E. Lawson, USA *(Yamaha)*, 1m 34.43s, 95.49mph/153.676s.
Old record: W. Gardner, Australia *(Honda)*, 1m 36.37s, 93.57mph/150.582kmh (1987).

World Championship positions: 1 E. Lawson, 215 points; 2 W. Gardner, 192; 3 W. Rainey, 174; 4 C. Sarron, 138; 5 K. Magee, 128; 6 D. de Radigues, 113; 7 K. Schwantz, 104; 8 N. Mackenzie, 102; 9 P. Chili, 88; 10 R. McElnea, 67.

Practice leaderboard: 1 E. Lawson, USA *(Yamaha)*, 1m 34.69s; 2 C. Sarron, France *(Yamaha)*, 1m 35.37s; 3 W. Rainey, USA *(Yamaha)*, 1m 35.70s; 4 N. Mackenzie, GB *(Honda)*, 1m 35.86s; 5 D. de Radigues, Belgium *(Yamaha)*, 1m 35.98s; 6 R. Mamola, USA *(Cagiva)*, 1m 35.98s; 7 R. Burnett, GB *(Honda)*, 1m 36.30s; 8 K. Magee, USA *(Yamaha)*, 1m 36.44s; 9 P. Chili, Italy *(Honda)*, 1m 36.68s; 10 R. Haslam, GB *(Elf-Honda)*, 1m 37.07s; 11 R. McElnea, GB *(Suzuki)*, 1m 37.49s; 12 K. Schwantz, USA *(Suzuki)*, 1m 37.93s; 13 W. Gardner, Australia *(Honda)*, 1m 38.15s; 14 P. Igoa, France *(Yamaha)*, 1m 38.89s; 15 M. Gentile, Switzerland *(Fior)*, 1m 39.07s; 16 P. Linden, Sweden *(Honda)*, 1m 39.11s; 17 T. Taira, Japan *(Yamaha)*, 1m 39.13s; 18 F. Barchitta, San Marino *(Honda)*, 1m 39.92s; 19 R. Roche, France *(Cagiva)*, 1m 40.66s; 20 A. Valesi, Italy *(Honda)*, 1m 40.71s.

250cc (25 laps, 62.62m/100.775k)	**m**	**s**	**mph**	**kmh**
1 S. Pons, Spain *(Honda)*	41	27.89	90.61	145.822
2 J. Garriga, Spain *(Yamaha)*	41	28.19	90.60	145.805
3 D. Sarron, France *(Honda)*	41	28.56	90.58	145.783
4 R. Roth, W. Germany *(Honda)*	41	28.80	90.57	145.769
5 C. Cardus, Spain *(Honda)*	41	45.73	89.96	144.784

6	I. Palazzese, Venezuela *(Yamaha)*	41 56.39	89.58	144.171
7	J. Ruggia, France *(Yamaha)*	41 58.17	89.52	144.069
8	A. Auinger, Austria *(Aprilia)*	42 01.11	89.41	143.901
9	J. Balde, France *(Rotax)*	42 01.35	89.40	143.887
10	M. Wimmer, W. Germany *(Yamaha)*	42 05.57	89.26	143.647

11 H. Bradl, W. Germany *(Honda)*; 12 W. Zeelenberg, Holland *(Yamaha)*; 13 S. Caracchi, Italy *(Honda)*; 14 M. Vitali, Italy *(Rotax)*; 15 J. Mattioli, France *(Yamaha)*; 16 U. Luzi, Switzerland *(Honda)*; 17 P. Casoli, Italy *(Garelli)*; 18 B. Casanova, Italy *(Aprilia)*; 19 A. Bronec, France *(Honda)*. *24 laps:* 20 B. Bonhuil, France *(Honda)*.

Record lap: R. Roth, W. Germany *(Honda)*, 1m 38.38s, 91.66mph/147.506kmh.
Old record: C. Lavado, Venezuela *(Yamaha)*, 1m 39.49s, 90.64mph/145.860kmh (1987).

Garriga leads Pons, Sarron and Roth in yet another tremendous 250cc encounter.

World Championship positions: 1 S. Pons, 199 points; 2 J. Garriga, 190; 3 J. Cornu, 151; 4 R. Roth, 135; 5 D. Sarron, 130; 6 L. Cadalora, 121; 7 J. Ruggia, 91; 8 A. Mang, 87; 9 M. Shimizu, 58; 10 C. Cardus, 51.

Practice leaderboard: 1 L. Cadalora, Italy *(Yamaha)*, 1m 38.24s; 2 J. Ruggia, France *(Yamaha)*, 1m 38.71s; 3 J. Garriga, Spain *(Yamaha)*, 1m 38.72s; 4 S. Pons Spain *(Honda)*, 1m 38.92s; 5 R. Roth, W. Germany *(Honda)*, 1m 39.18s; 6 C. Cardus, Spain *(Honda)*, 1m 39.34s; 7 H. Eckl, W. Germany *(Aprilia)*, 1m 39.38s; 8 J. Cornu, Switzerland *(Honda)*, 1m 39.38s; 9 D. Sarron, France *(Honda)*, 1m 39.43s; 10 M. Shimizu, Japan *(Honda)*, 1m 39.51s; 11 L. Reggiani, Italy *(Aprilia)*, 1m 39.53s; 12 C. Lavado, Venezuela *(Yamaha)*, 1m 39.57s; 13 J. Balde, France *(Rotax)*, 1m 39.71s; 14 I. Palazzese, Venezuela *(Yamaha)*, 1m 39.96s; 15 M. Wimmer, W. Germany *(Yamaha)*, 1m 40.20s; 16 D. McLeod, GB *(EMC)*, 1m 40.29s; 17 B. Casanova, Italy *(Aprilia)*, 1m 40.29s; 18 J. Mattioli, France *(Yamaha)*, 1m 40.31s; 19 A. Auinger, Austria *(Aprilia)*, 1m 40.38s; 20 S. Caracchi, Italy *(Honda)*, 1m 40.46s.

125cc (23 laps, 57.61m/92.71k)	**m s**	**mph**	**kmh**
1 J. Martinez, Spain *(Derbi)*	40 56.47	84.42	135.873
2 E. Gianola, Italy *(Honda)*	40 56.76	84.41	135.856
3 J. Miralles, Spain *(Honda)*	41 08.12	84.03	135.231
4 H. Spaan, Holland *(Honda)*	41 08.34	84.02	135.219
5 A. Stadler, W. Germany *(Honda)*	41 15.47	83.78	134.830
6 B. Hassaine, France *(Honda)*	41 20.79	83.60	134.541
7 J. Wickstrom, Finland *(Honda)*	41 21.35	83.58	134.510
8 L. Pietroniro, Belgium *(Honda)*	41 21.91	83.56	134.480
9 F. Kistrum, Denmark *(Hummel)*	41 24.19	83.48	134.356
10 S. Prein, W. Germany *(Honda)*	41 26.36	83.41	134.239

11 H. Luthi, Switzerland *(Honda)*; 12 K. Takada, Japan *(Honda)*; 13 H. Unemoto, Japan *(Honda)*; 14 D. Brigaglia, Italy *(Rotax)*; 15 A. Scott, USA *(Honda)*; 16 G. Waibel, W. Germany *(Honda)*; 17 S. Dorflinger, Switzerland *(Honda)*; 18 A. Waibel, W. Germany *(Honda)*; 19 R. Milton, GB *(Rotax)*; 20 J. Selini, France *(Honda)*; 21 A. Criville, Spain *(Derbi)*; 22 H. Abold, W. Germany *(Honda)*; 23 M. Hernandez, Spain *(Honda)*; 24 J. Hautaniemi, Finland *(Honda)*; 25 T. Rinne, Finland *(Honda)*. *22 laps:* 26 A. Sanches, Spain *(ADM)*; 27 T. Feuz, Switzerland *(Rotax)*.

Fastest lap: J. Martinez, Spain *(Derbi)*, 1m 45.36s, 85.58mph/137.733kmh.

Record lap: F. Gresini, Italy *(Garelli)*, 1m 43.79s, 86.88mph/139.817kmh (1987).

Old record: L. Cadalora, Italy *(Garelli)*, 1m 45.015s, 85.82mph/138.20kmh (1986).

World Championship positions: 1 J. Martinez, 177 points; 2 E. Gianola, 157; 3 H. Spaan, 95; 4 J. Miralles, 87; 5 D. Brigaglia, 69; 6 G. Grassetti, 61; 7 A. Stadler, 60; 8 G. Waibel, 52; 9 S. Prein, 50; 10 L. Pietroniro, 49.

Practice leaderboard: 1 J. Martinez, Spain *(Derbi)*, 1m 45.83s; 2 E. Gianola, Italy *(Honda)*, 1m 45.90s; 3 A. Stadler, W. Germany *(Honda)*, 1m 46.61s; 4 H. Spaan, Holland *(Honda)*, 1m 46.66s; 5 H. Luthi, Switzerland *(Honda)*, 1m 46.67s; 6 J. Miralles, Spain *(Honda)*, 1m 46.71s; 7 H. Abold, W. Germany *(Honda)*, 1m 46.87s; 8 F. Gresini, Italy *(Garelli)*, 1m 47.04s; 9 T. Rinne, Finland *(Honda)*, 1m 47.22s; 10 C. Catalano, Italy *(Aprilia)*, 1m 47.53s; 11 B. Hassaine, France *(Honda)*, 1m 47.63s; 12 G. Grassetti, Italy *(Honda)*, 1m 47.67s; 13 L. Pietroniro, Belgium *(Honda)*, 1m 47.69s; 14 F. Kistrup, Denmark *(Hummel)*, 1m 47.69s; 15 D. Brigaglia, Italy *(Rotax)*, 1m 47.72s; 16 K. Galatowicz, GB *(Honda)*, 1m 47.95s; 17 S. Dorflinger, Switzerland *(Honda)*, 1m 47.96s; 18 A. Scott, USA *(Honda)*, 1m 48.07s; 19 P. Bianchi, Italy *(Cagiva)*, 1m 48.09s; 20 S. Prein, W. Germany *(Honda)*, 1m 48.10s.

Sidecar (23 laps, 57.61m/92.71k)	**m s**	**mph**	**kmh**
1 S. Webster, GB	38 32.47	89.68	144.333
T. Hewitt, GB *(LCR-Krauser)*			
2 R. Biland, Switzerland	38 33.51	89.64	144.269
K. Waltisperg, Switzerland *(LCR-Krauser)*			

3	E. Streuer, Holland B. Schnieders, Holland *(LCR-Yamaha)*	38 36.30	89.53	144.095
4	A. Michel, France J. Fresc, France *(LCR-Krauser)*	38 52.65	88.91	143.085
5	M. Egloff, Switzerland U. Egloff, Switzerland *(LCR-ADM)*	39 20.32	87.86	141.407
6	M. Kumano, Japan M. Fahrni, Switzerland *(LCR-Yamaha)*	39 51.97	86.70	139.536
7	A. Zurbrugg, Switzerland M. Zurbrugg, Switzerland *(LCR-Yamaha)*	39 57.01	86.52	139.243
8	Y. Kumagaya, Japan P. Linden, Sweden *(Windle-Yamaha)*	40 09.50	86.07	138.521
9	D. Jones, GB P. Brown, GB *(LCR-Yamaha)*	40 24.00	85.51	137.693

22 laps: 10 B. Scherer/T. Schroder, W. Germany *(BSR-Krauser)*; 11 S. Abbott/S. Smith, GB *(Windle-Yamaha)*; 12 P. Larratte/J. Corbier, France *(LCR-Yamaha)*; 13 F. Stolzle/H. Stolzle, W. Germany *(LCR-Krauser)*; 14 I. Nigrowsky/M. Charpentier, France *(Seymaz-JPX)*; 15 D. Chivas/H. Olsson, New Zealand *(LCR-Yamaha)*. *21 laps:* 16 J. Millet/C. Debroux, France *(GDF-Elf)*; 17 B. Gallros/K. Andreasen, Sweden/Denmark *(Yamaha)*. *18 laps:* 18 R. Steinhausen/B. Hiller, W. Germany *(ADM-Krauser)*.

Record lap: R. Biland/K. Waltisperg, Switzerland *(LCR-Krauser)*, 1m 38.66s, 91.40mph/147.087kmh.
Old record: R. Biland/K. Waltisperg, Switzerland *(LCR-Krauser)*, 1m 39.59s, 90.54mph/145.713kmh (1987).

World Championship positions: 1 Biland/Waltisperg, 154 points; 2 Webster/Hewitt, 136; 3 Michel/Fresc, 82; 4 Streuer/Schnieders, 80; 5 Egloff/Egloff and Zurbrugg/Zurbrugg both 64; 7 Jones/Brown, 61; 8 Abbott/Smith, 53; 9 Kumano/Fahrni, 48; 10 Brindley/Rose, 46.

Practice leaderboard: 1 Webster/Hewitt, GB *(LCR-Krauser)*, 1m 39.68s; 2 Egloff/Egloff, Switzerland *(LCR-ADM)*, 1m 40.49s; 3 Michel/Fresc, France *(LCR-Krauser)*, 1m 40.83s; 4 Biland/Waltisperg, Switzerland *(LCR-Krauser)*, 1m 40.96s; 5 Kumano/Fahrni, Japan/Switzerland *(LCR-TEC)*, 1m 41.74s; 6 Zurbrugg/Zurbrugg, Switzerland *(LCR-Yamaha)*, 1m 43.09s; 7 Steinhausen/Hiller, W. Germany *(ADM-Krauser)*, 1m 43.61s; 8 Stropek/de Haas, Austria/Holland *(Mibag-Krauser)*, 1m 43.80s; 9 Scherer/Schroder, W. Germany *(BSR-Krauser)*, 1m 44.04s; 10 Larratte/Corbier, France *(LCR-Yamaha)*, 1m 44.09s; 11 Jones/Brown, GB *(LCR-Yamaha)*, 1m 44.29s; 12 Abbott/Smith, GB *(Windle-Yamaha)*, 1m 44.48s; 13 Kumagaya/Linden, Japan/Sweden *(Windle-Yamaha)*, 1m 44.73s; 14 Stolzle/Stolzle, W. Germany *(LCR-Krauser)*, 1m 44.94s; 15 Nigrowsky/Charpentier, France *(Seymaz-JPX)*, 1m 45.55s; 16 van Kempen/Birchall, Holland/GB *(LCR-Yamaha)*, 1m 45.56s; 17 Chivas/Olsson, New Zealand *(LCR-Yamaha)*, 1m 46.84s; 18 Millet/Debroux, France *(GDF-Elf)*, 1m 48.12s; 19 Gallros/Andreasen, Sweden/Denmark *(Yamaha)*, 1m 49.76s; 20 Streuer/Schnieders, Holland *(LCR-Yamaha)*, 1m 52.04s.

CZECHOSLOVAKIAN GRAND PRIX, 28 August, Brno 3.352m/5.39k

An amazing sequence of events at Brno produced World Champions in both the 500cc and sidecar championships. Eddie Lawson regained the 500cc crown, while Steve Webster and stand-in passenger Gavin Simmons caused the biggest upset for years by retaining a sidecar title that had seemed way beyond their reach before the dramatic race.

The 250cc Spanish civil war carried on into the final round with Juan Garriga just six points adrift of Sito Pons after winning a cracking 20-lap race. Double World Champion Jorge Martinez wrapped up his season by winning both the 80 and 125cc races, although he had to work very hard in both.

Lawson clinched his third world title after finishing second to Wayne Gardner in the 23-lap 500cc race, although much of the damage was done the previous day. A meeting of the riders confirmed they would not be going to the penultimate round in Argentina because the organisers had not carried out any of the work promised, following last year's fiasco. Now with just two rounds remaining, Lawson led Gardner by 23 points. With 20 points awarded for a win and 17 for second place, he only had to finish second behind Gardner in the race to steal the Australian's championship. The gap would be down to 20 points with one round remaining but Lawson would take the title even if he failed to score in the last round, because he'd won more grands prix than his rival, which is the deciding factor in the event of a tie.

The situation was made even more confusing because there was also doubt whether the final round of the championship could take place in Brazil because of financial problems. If the race had not gone ahead Lawson would have been Champion before the Czechoslovakian round. Happily the race in Brazil, thanks to a loan from the FIM, went ahead and the outcome of the championship was decided out on the track.

Gardner found the super-smooth 3.35 mile Brno circuit to be the perfect foil for his NSR Rothmans Honda. Those Donington and Anderstorp crashes were a distant memory as he qualified over one second quicker than Wayne Rainey to grab pole position. Lawson, riding the Marlboro Yamaha, was on the front row in fifth place. He knew exactly what he had to do although he was given a rough ride.

Gardner was determined to go out with a bang and grabbed the lead on the first lap and raced away for his most comfortable victory of the season. The eyes of the massive 166,000 crowd focused on the progress of Lawson and his orange and white Yamaha. For the first three laps he bided his time in seventh place before making his move, although his so-called partners gave him a tough time. He was soon involved in a titanic battle with the Lucky Strike Yamaha duo of Rainey and Kevin Magee, Frenchman Christian Sarron, riding the Gauloises Yamaha, and the lone Honda of Pier-Francesco Chili. Lawson was desperate to get past but had to ride with caution. At half distance Sarron, who was lying second, opened the door to let Lawson through. Unfortunately for the Frenchman everybody else followed him. He dropped to sixth and six laps later crashed out, without injury, trying to rectify the situation. Lawson tried desperately to pull away from the pack but they stuck to him, with Rainey leading the way. Team-mate Magee was recovering from a poor start but crashed out of fourth place with seven laps remaining.

At the front Gardner was fully aware of Lawson's progress. Towards the finish he slowed the pace trying to tempt Lawson into a mistake or give Rainey some time to pass him. The Champion elect has been around far too long to fall for the trick – he crossed the line nearly two seconds behind Gardner but with his championship title firmly in his grasp.

Rainey chased Lawson to the flag but had to settle for third, with Chili an impressive fourth. Japanese Yamaha rider Tadahiko Taira, who had led at the start, eventually dropped to fifth, in front of Scotsman Niall Mackenzie, who complained of problems with his front brake discs. Ron Haslam equalled the best ever grand prix position for the Elf 5 Honda finishing seventh on his penultimate ride on the bike, with Pepsi Suzuki-mounted Rob McElnea eighth. His team-mate Kevin Schwantz was not so lucky. He retired with a broken crankshaft four laps from the finish.

If the outcome of the 500cc race had been rather predictable, the following 17-lap sidecar race was pure theatre, resulting in one of the biggest upsets for years.

Just two rounds before this final race the Swiss pair of Rolf Biland and Kurt Waltisperg looked to be heading for a clean sweep of victories. They'd dominated the championship on their LCR Krauser and even when they were beaten into second place in the last two rounds by Webster, they led the Yorkshireman by 18 points. Even the current World Champion admitted his chances were slim, especially as his regular passenger Tony Hewitt had been injured in a crash the previous week. He was replaced by Gavin Simmons, who used to work with Webster at the Rowntrees chocolate factory in York, It was only his second ride with the World Champion and only his second grand prix.

The new pair raced from the start on their Krauser-powered LCR shadowed by the Egloff brothers, Streuer, and Biland who was quite happy to sit it out in fourth place. Former Champions Streuer and Bernard Schnieders, seeking their first grand prix victory of the season, moved into second place to harry Webster but the stage looked set for a nice comfortable finish to the season dominated by Biland. Suddenly the pit lane was awash with rumour – Biland was slowing. Could the impossible dream happen? Biland's bright yellow LCR outfit limped over the brow of the hill and through the start and finish. He was obviously in trouble but still holding ninth place – he'd have to drop to 15th to lose the championship even if Webster won the race.

Biland held on for three more nail-biting laps, but at the end of the 13th coasted up the hill with his Krauser engine stuck in third gear. He stopped on the finish line with both his and passenger Waltisperg's heads bowed in total despair. Webster and Simmons saw the yellow outfit by the side of the track but thought it was the Egloffs. They had no time to ponder because Streuer was chasing hard and had already shoved his front wheel alongside them on a couple of occasions. If he relegated the Yorkshiremen to second, Biland would win the title. The last four laps were the longest ever witnessed by a patriotic Brit. Streuer tried every trick in the book to pass Webster but he constantly slammed the door shut in the face of the Dutchman. They crossed the line with less than half a second to spare, passing the stranded Biland as they took the chequered flag.

As the National Anthem boomed out over the Czechoslovakian countryside Webster still could not believe the outcome. Regular passenger Hewitt celebrated with a glass of bitter back home in Yorkshire, while his brilliant stand-in, Gavin Simmons, was planning his route home to be back at work on Tuesday morning.

The only route Juan Garriga was planning after his 250cc victory was to that final confrontation in Brazil. He produced his ride of the season to keep his championship chances alive. He was tenth off the line in the 20-lap race but by the eighth lap had

Lawson's premature world championship victory even caught Marlboro by surprise – hence the tee-shirt.

Pons and Garriga continued their very private battle at Brno.

overhauled his deadly rival Pons to snatch the lead. Pons, riding the Campsa Honda, hung on grimly but after a few worrying moments gave up the chase. He was happy to secure 17 championship points and go into the final round with a six point advantage. While the Spaniards fought it out at the front the Italians clashed head-on battling for third. Luca Cadalora won the third place on the rostrum by just over half a second from Loris Reggiani, with Carlos Cardus and Reinhold Roth equally as close in their battle for fifth. Frenchman Dominique Sarron was the fastest qualifier on the Rothmans Honda but he crashed on the first lap. He remounted in last place but raced through the field to finish eighth, pipping former World Champion Carlos Lavado on the line.

Although he'd already clinched both 80 and 125cc World titles Jorge Martinez wanted to end the season on a winning note. The Hondas of Julian Miralles and Hans Spaan gave him, and the works Derbi, a tough time in the 17-lap 125cc race. Less than half a second covered the three at the finish. Former World Champion Stefan Dorflinger gave him an even harder time in the 13-lap 80cc race. Martinez had to use every ounce of power from the Derbi and his own skill to see off the challenge to end the year in which he has dominated the smaller classes.

Results

500cc (23 laps, 77.09m/124.062k)	**m**	**s**	**mph**	**kmh**
1 W. Gardner, Australia *(Honda)*	49	11.06	94.04	151.343
2 E. Lawson, USA *(Yamaha)*	49	12.97	93.98	151.245
3 W. Rainey, USA *(Yamaha)*	49	13.54	93.96	151.216
4 P. Chili, Italy *(Honda)*	49	26.74	93.54	150.543
5 T. Taira, Japan *(Yamaha)*	49	30.97	93.41	150.329
6 N. Mackenzie, GB *(Honda)*	49	40.50	93.11	149.848
7 R. Haslam, GB *(Elf-Honda)*	50	08.50	92.24	148.454
8 R. McElnea, GB *(Suzuki)*	50	09.30	92.22	148.414
9 P. Igoa, France *(Yamaha)*	50	10.42	92.18	148.359
10 F. Barchitta, San Marino *(Honda)*	50	57.02	90.78	146.098

11 M. Gentile, Switzerland *(Fior)*; 12 M. Papa, Italy *(Honda)*; 13 A. Valesi, Italy *(Honda)*. *22 laps:* 14 P. Linden, Sweden *(Honda)*; 15 B. Kneubuhler, Switzerland *(Honda)*; 16 F. Biliotti, Italy *(Honda)*; 17 W. von Muralt, Switzerland *(Suzuki)*; 18 S. Habat, Yugoslavia *(Honda)*; 19 M. Fischer, W. Germany *(Honda)*; 20 R. Nicotte, France *(Honda)*; 21 K. Truchsess, Austria *(Honda)*; 22 N. Schmassman, Switzerland *(Honda)*; 23 C. Wulff, Denmark *(Honda)*. *21 laps:* 24 C. Dekanek, Czechoslovakia *(Honda)*.

Record lap: W. Gardner, Australia *(Honda)*, 2m 06.24s, 95.58mph/153.821kmh.
Old record: W. Gardner, Australia *(Honda)*, 2m 08.20s, 94.12mph/151.470kmh (1987).

World Championship positions: 1 E. Lawson, 232 points; 2 W. Gardner, 212; 3 W. Rainey, 189; 4 C. Sarron, 138; 5 K. Magee, 128; 6 D. de Radigues, 113; 7 N. Mackenzie, 112; 8 K. Schwantz, 104; 9 P. Chili, 101; 10 R. McElnea, 75.

Practice leaderboard: 1 W. Gardner, Australia *(Honda)*, 2m 05.55s; 2 W. Rainey, USA *(Yamaha)*, 2m 06.80s; 3 C. Sarron, France *(Yamaha)*, 2m 06.86s; 4 N. Mackenzie, GB *(Honda)*, 2m 07.05s; 5 E. Lawson, USA *(Yamaha)*, 2m 07.20s; 6 K. Schwantz, USA *(Suzuki)*, 2m 07.39s; 7 P. Chili, Italy *(Honda)*, 2m 07.46s; 8 D. de Radigues, Belgium *(Yamaha)*, 2m 07.48s; 9 K. Magee, *Australia (Yamaha)*, 2m 07.55s; 10 R. Mamola, USA *(Cagiva)*, 2m 07.79s; 11 T. Taira, Japan *(Yamaha)*, 2m 07.94s; 12 R. Burnett, GB *(Honda)*, 2m 08.31s; 13 R. McElnea, GB *(Suzuki)*, 2m 08.34s; 14 P. Igoa, France *(Yamaha)*, 2m 08.63s; 15 R. Haslam, GB *(Elf-Honda)*, 2m 09.51s; 16 R. Roche, France *(Cagiva)*, 2m 10.68s; 17 F. Barchitta, San Marino *(Honda)*, 2m 11.34s; 18 M. Gentile, Switzerland *(Fior)*, 2m 11.93s; 19 K. Truchsess, Austria *(Honda)*, 2m 12.12s; 20 M. Papa, Italy *(Honda)*, 2m 12.17s.

250cc (20 laps, 67.04m/107.88k)		**m**	**s**	**mph**	**kmh**
1	J. Garriga, Spain *(Yamaha)*	43	54.72	91.59	147.404
2	S. Pons, Spain *(Honda)*	43	58.41	91.46	147.198
3	L. Cadalora, Italy *(Yamaha)*	44	05.20	91.23	146.820
4	L. Reggiani, Italy *(Aprilia)*	44	05.81	91.21	146.786
5	C. Cardus, Spain *(Honda)*	44	06.12	91.20	146.769
6	R. Roth, W. Germany *(Honda)*	44	06.42	91.18	146.752
7	J. Cornu, Switzerland *(Honda)*	44	10.03	91.06	146.552
8	D. Sarron, France *(Honda)*	44	24.81	90.56	145.739
9	C. Lavado, Venezuela *(Yamaha)*	44	24.91	90.55	145.734
10	J. Schmid, W. Germany *(Honda)*	44	25.77	90.52	145.687

11 J. Ruggia, France *(Yamaha)*; 12 H. Bradl, W. Germany *(Honda)*; 13 M. Shimizu, Japan *(Honda)*; 14 B. Casanova, Italy *(Aprilia)*; 15 H. Eckl, W. Germany *(Aprilia)*; 16 S. Caracchi, Italy *(Honda)*; 17 I. Palazzese, Venezuela *(Yamaha)*; 18 M. Wimmer, W. Germany *(Yamaha)*; 19 X. Cardelus, Andorra *(Aprilia)*; 20 G. Cowan, Ireland *(Yamaha)*; 21 J. Balde, France *(Rotax)*; 22 U. Luzi, Switzerland *(Honda)*; 23 J. Foray, France *(Yamaha)*; 24 M. Herweh, W. Germany *(Yamaha)*; 25 R. Delaby, Luxembourg, *(Yamaha)*; 26 P. Casoli, Italy *(Garelli)*; 27 J.Mattioli, France *(Yamaha)*; 28 M. Vitali, Italy *(Rotax)*; 29 M. Matteoni, Italy *(Yamaha)*; 30 H. Becker, W. Germany *(Yamaha)*; 31 A. Preining, Austria *(Aprilia)*; 32 K. Mitchell, GB *(Yamaha)*.

Record lap: J. Garriga, Spain *(Yamaha)*, 2m 09.79s, 92.96mph/149.614kmh.
Old record: C. Cardus, Spain *(Honda)*, 2m 12.25s, 91.24mph/146.831kmh (1987).

World Championship positions: 1 S. Pons, 216 points; 2 J. Garriga, 210; 3 J. Cornu, 160; 4 R. Roth, 145; 5 D. Sarron, 138, 6 L. Cadalora, 136; 7 J. Ruggia, 96; 8 A. Mang, 87; 9 C. Cardus, 62; 10 M. Shimizu, 61.

Practice leaderboard: 1 D. Sarron, France *(Honda)*, 2m 09.60s; 2 J. Garriga, Spain *(Yamaha)*, 2m 10.14s; 3 S. Pons, Spain *(Honda)*, 2m 10.19s; 4 C. Cardus, Spain *(Honda)*, 2m 10.46s; 5 R. Roth, W. Germany *(Honda)*, 2m 10.54s; 6 L. Cadalora, Italy *(Yamaha)*, 2m 10.60s; 7 J. Cornu, Switzerland *(Honda)*, 2m 10.86s; 8 C. Lavado, Venezuela *(Yamaha)*, 2m 11.41s; 9 J. Ruggia, France *(Yamaha)*, 2m 11.53s; 10 L. Reggiani, Italy *(Aprilia)*, 2m 11.54s; 11 M. Wimmer, W. Germany *(Yamaha)*, 2m 12.09s; 12 S. Caracchi,

Italy *(Honda)*, 2m 12.37s; 13 B. Casanova, Italy *(Aprilia)*, 2m 12.38s; 14 J. Schmid, W. Germany *(Honda)*, 2m 12.42s; 15 A. Auinger, Austria *(Aprilia)*, 2m 12.43s; 16 M. Shimizu, Japan *(Honda)*, 2m 12.52s; 17 I. Palazzese, Venezuela *(Yamaha)*, 2m 12.71s; 18 H. Bradl, W. Germany *(Honda)*, 2m 12.84s; 19 H. Eckl, W. Germany *(Aprilia)*, 2m 12.94s; 20 J. Mattioli, France *(Yamaha)*, 2m 12.95s.

125cc (17 laps, 56.98m/91.698k)		**m**	**s**	**mph**	**kmh**
1	J. Martinez, Spain *(Derbi)*	39	50.94	85.79	138.068
2	J. Miralles, Spain *(Honda)*	39	51.12	85.78	138.058
3	H. Spaan, Holland *(Honda)*	39	51.29	85.77	138.048
4	C. Catalano, Italy *(Aprilia)*	39	56.52	85.59	137.747
5	E. Gianola, Italy *(Honda)*	39	57.07	85.57	137.715
6	R. Milton, GB *(Rotax)*	40	05.76	85.26	137.218
7	S. Prein, W. Germany *(Honda)*	40	07.14	85.21	137.139
8	A. Bedford, GB *(Honda)*	40	14.33	84.96	136.731
9	L. Pietroniro, Belgium *(Honda)*	40	15.00	84.94	136.693
10	A. Scott, USA *(Honda)*	40	15.15	84.92	136.684

11 G. Grassetti, Italy *(Honda)*; 12 I. McConnachie, GB *(Cagiva)*; 13 A. Stadler, W. Germany *(Honda)*; 14 H. Luthi, Switzerland *(Honda)*; 15 J. Hautaniemi, Finland *(Honda)*; 16 A. Waibel, W. Germany *(Honda)*; 17 A. Criville, Spain *(Derbi)*; 18 B. Hassaine, France *(Honda)*; 19 J. Selini, France *(Honda)*; 20 G. Waibel, W. Germany *(Honda)*; 21 K. Takada, Japan *(Honda)*; 22 H. Unemoto, Japan *(Honda)*; 23 F. Kistrup, Denmark *(Hummel)*; 24 D. Brigaglia, Italy *(Rotax)*; 25 P. Bianchi, Italy *(Cagiva)*; 26 R. Bolart, Spain *(Rotax)*; 27 P. Scappini, Italy *(Honda)*; 28 J. Wickstrom, Finland *(Honda)*.

Fastest lap: J. Martinez, Spain *(Derbi)*, 2m 19.04s, 86.78mph/139.661kmh.

Record lap: B. Casanova, Italy *(Garelli)*, 2m 18.18s, 87.32mph/140.530kmh. (1987).

World Championship positions: 1 J. Martinez, 197 points; 2 E. Gianola, 168; 3 H. Spaan, 110; 4 J. Miralles, 104; 5 D. Brigaglia, 69; 6 G. Grassetti, 66; 7 A. Stadler, 63; 8 S. Prein, 59 9 G. Waibel, 52; 10 L. Pietroniro, 49.

Practice leaderboard: 1 H. Spaan, Holland *(Honda)*, 2m 19.15s; 2 J. Martinez, Spain *(Derbi)*, 2m 19.22s; 3 C. Catalano, Italy *(Aprilia)*, 2m 19.62s; 14 A. Waibel, W. Germany *(Honda)*, 2m 19.96s; 5 L. Pietroniro, Belgium *(Honda)*, 2m 20.00s; 6 E. Gianola, Italy *(Honda)*, 2m 20.03s; 7 S. Prein, W. Germany *(Honda)*, 2m 20.40s; 8 T. Rinne, Finland *(Honda)*, 2m 20.47s; 9 G. Grassetti, Italy *(Honda)*, 2m 20.53s; 10 H. Luthi, Switzerland *(Honda)*, 2m 20.59s; 11 E. Cuppini, Italy *(Honda)*, 2m 20.60s; 12 R. Milton, GB *(Rotax)*, 2m 20.62s; 13 J. Miralles, Spain *(Honda)*, 2m 20.66s; 14 P. Bianchi, Italy *(Cagiva)*, 2m 20.74s; 15 K. Takada, Japan *(Honda)*, 2m 20.82s; 16 I. McConnachie, GB *(Cagiva)*, 2m 21s; 17 D. Brigaglia, Italy *(Rotax)*, 2m 21.05s; 18 A. Bedford, GB *(Honda)*, 2m 21.19s; 19 J. Seel, W. Germany *(Seel)*, 2m 21.21s; 20 L. Reyes, Spain *(Garelli)*, 2m 21.22s.

Webster and Simmons produce the shock of the season.

Former work-mates in a chocolate factory, Steve Webster and Gavin Simmons combined to bring home the greatest prize.

80cc (13 laps, 43.57m/70.122k)	**m**	**s**	**mph**	**kmh**
1 J. Martinez, Spain *(Derbi)*	31	45.82	82.30	132.457
2 S. Dorflinger, Switzerland *(Krauser)*	31	46.06	82.27	132.440
3 A. Criville, Spain *(Derbi)*	32	07.22	81.39	130.986
4 K. Juhasz, Hungary *(Krauser)*	32	07.31	81.38	130.980
5 G. Ascareggi, Italy *(BBFT)*	32	07.78	81.36	130.948
6 B. Nikolov, Bulgaria *(Krauser)*	32	21.36	80.80	130.032
7 G. Gnani, Italy *(Gnani)*	32	21.60	80.79	130.016
8 B. Smit, Holland *(Krauser)*	32	30.22	80.43	129.441
9 G. Schirnhofer, W. Germany *(Krauser)*	32	30.51	80.42	129.422
10 R. Dunki, Switzerland *(LCR)*	32	44.21	79.86	128.519

11 A. Nijenhuis, Holland *(Casal)*; 12 J. Pintar, Yugoslavia *(Eberhardt)*; 13 J. Szabo, Hungary *(Krauser)*; 14 H. Paschen, W. Germany *(Keifer)*; 15 J. Bernard, Belgium *(Fantic)*; 16 R. Koster, Switzerland *(Casal)*; 17 C. Besseling, Holland *(CJB)*; 18 H. Torrontegui, Spain *(Autisa)*; 19 S. Edwards, GB *(Casal)*; 20 J. Torrens, Spain *(Cobas)*; 21 H. Klein, W. Germany *(Honda)*; 22 P. Priori, Italy *(Krauser)*; 23 A. Pavlic, Yugoslavia *(Seel)*; 24 T. Engel, W. Germany *(Krauser)*; 25 F. Arumi, Spain *(Krauser)*; 26 P. Tibor, Hungary *(Casal)*; 27 L. Robert, France *(SPR)*. *12 laps:* 28 S. Braegger, Switzerland *(Casal)*.

Fastest lap: J. Martinez, Spain *(Derbi)*, 2m 24.06s, 83.76mph/134.794kmh.

Record lap: S. Dorflinger, Switzerland *(Krauser)*, 2m 24.02s, 83. 78mph/134.831kmh (1987).

World Championship positions: 1 J. Martinez, 137 points; 2 A. Criville, 90; 3 S. Dorflinger, 77; 4 M. Herreros, 69; 5 P. Ottl, 65; 6 B. Nikolov, 55; 7 K. Juhasz, 54; 8 J. van Dongen, 47; 9 G. Ascareggi, 46; 10 G. Gnani, 36.

Practice leaderboard: 1 J. Martinez, Spain *(Derbi)*, 2m 24.38s; 2 S. Dorflinger, Switzerland *(Krauser)*, 2m 24.48s; 3 J. Seel, W. Germany *(Seel)*, 2m 26.60s; 4 B. Nikolov, Bulgaria *(Krauser)*, 2m 27.06s; 5 G. Schirnhofer, W. Germany *(Krauser)*, 2m 28.21s; 6 K. Juhasz, Hungary *(Krauser)*, 2m 28.34s; 7 J. van Dongen, Holland *(Casal)*, 2m 28.60s; 8 J. Szabo, Hungary *(Krauser)*, 2m 28.72s; 9 J. Torrens, Spain *(Cobas)*, 2m 28.77s; 10 M. Herreros, Spain *(Derbi)*, 2m 28.86s; 11 G. Gnani, Italy *(Gnani)*, 2m 28.91s; 12 G. Ascareggi, Italy *(BBFT)*, 2m 28.92s; 13 R. Dunki, Switzerland *(LCR)*, 2m 29.22s; 14 A. Criville, Spain *(Derbi)*, 2m 29.72s; 15 H. Torrontegui, Spain *(Autisa)*, 2m 29.89s; 16 B. Smit, Holland *(Krauser)*, 2m 30.21s; 17 H. Paschen, W. Germany *(Kiefer)*, 2m 30.23s; 18 C. Besseling, Holland *(CJB)*, 2m 30.30s; 19 R. Koster, Switzerland *(Casal)*, 2m 30.37s; 20 S. Braegger, Switzerland *(Casal)*, 2m 30.64s.

Sidecar (17 laps, 56.98m/91.698k)	**m**	**s**	**mph**	**kmh**
1 S. Webster, GB	37	14.88	91.78	147.709
G. Simmons, GB *(LCR-Krauser)*				
2 E. Streuer, Holland	37	15.33	91.76	147.680
B. Schnieders, Holland *(LCR-Yamaha)*				
3 M. Egloff, Switzerland	37	33.04	91.04	146.519
U. Egloff, Switzerland *(LCR-ADM)*				

4	M. Kumano, Japan M. Fahrni, Switzerland *(LCR-TEC)*	37 43.05	90.64	145.871
5	A. Michel, France J. Fresc, France *(LCR-Krauser)*	37 44.51	90.58	145.777
6	B. Scherer, W. Germany T. Schroder, W. Germany *(BSR-Krauser)*	38 19.01	89.22	143.589
7	F. Stolzle, W. Germany H. Stolzle, W. Germany *(LCR-Krauser)*	38 38.16	88.48	142.403
8	D. Jones, GB P. Brown, GB *(LCR-Yamaha)*	38 40.64	88.39	142.251
9	I. Nigrowsky, France M. Charpentier, France *(Seymaz-JPX)*	38 55.58	87.82	141.341
10	W. Kraus, W. Germany D. Schuster, W. Germany *(Busch)*	38 56.94	87.77	141.036

11 W. Stropek/W. Bock, Austria *(LCR-Krauser)*; 12 B. Brindley/G. Rose, GB *(Krauser-Yamaha)*; 13 C. Stirrat/S. Prior, GB *(LCR-Honda)*; 14 T. van Kempen/G. de Haas, Holland *(LCR-Yamaha)*; 15 J. Millet/C. Debroux, France *(GDF-Elf)*; 16 R. Progin/Y. Hunziker, Switzerland *(Seymaz)*; 17 R. Steinhausen/B. Hiller, W. Germany *(ADM)*; 18 J. Drew/B. Houghton, GB *(Yamaha)*. *16 laps:* 19 D. Bingham/G. Irlam, GB *(LCR-Yamaha)*; 20 G. Thomas/T. Derbi, GB *(Windle-Yamaha)*; 21 H. Hugli/A. Haenni, Switzerland *(Sigwa)*. *15 laps:* 22 E. Weber/E. Rosinger, W. Germany *(Sigwa)*.

Record lap: E. Streuer/B. Schnieders, Holland *(LCR-Yamaha)*, 2m 10.47s, 92.48mph/148.834kmh.
Old record: S. Webster/T. Hewitt, GB *(LCR-Krauser)*, 2m 11.44s, 91.80mph/147.736kmh (1987).

World Championship positions: 1 Webster/Hewitt/Simmons, 156 points; 2 Biland/Waltisperg, 154; 3 Streuer/Schnieders, 97; 4 Michel/Fresc, 93·5; 5 Egloff/Egloff, 79; 6 Jones/Brown, 69; 7 Zurbrugg/Zurbrugg, 64; 8 Kumano/Fahrni, 61; 9 Scherer/Schroder, 54; 10 Abbott/Smith, 53.

Practice leaderboard: 1 Biland/Waltisperg, Switzerland *(LCR-Krauser)*, 2m 08.28s; 2 Webster/Simmons, GB *(LCR-Krauser)*, 2m 09.49s; 3 Egloff/Egloff, Switzerland *(LCR-ADM)*, 2m 09.67s; 4 Streuer/Schnieders, Holland *(LCR-Yamaha)*, 2m 10.55s; 5 Kumano/Fahrni, Japan/Switzerland *(LCR-TEC)*, 2m 11.01s; 6 Michel/Fresc, France *(LCR-Krauser)*, 2m 11.39s; 7 Zurbrugg/Zurbrugg, Switzerland *(LCR-Yamaha)*, 2m 12.70s; 8 Kumagaya/Linden, Japan/Sweden *(Windle-Yamaha)*, 2m 13.12s; 9 Scherer/Schroder, W. Germany *(BSR-Krauser)*, 2m 13.17s; 10 Steinhausen/Hiller, W. Germany *(ADM)*, 2m 13.36s; 11 Jones/Brown, GB *(LCR-Yamaha)*, 2m 13.40s; 12 Kraus/Schuster, W. Germany *(Busch)*, 2m 13.83s; 13 Abbott/Smith, GB *(Windle-Yamaha)*, 2m 14.82s; 14 Stolzle/Stolzle, W. Germany *(LCR-Krauser)*, 2m 15.41s; 15 Brindley/Rose, GB *(Krauser-Yamaha)*, 2m 15.62s; 16 Weber/Rosinger, W. Germany *(Sigwa)*, 2m 16.26s; 17 van Kempen/de Haas, Holland *(LCR-Yamaha)*, 2m 16.50s 18 Stropek/Bock, Austria *(LCR-Krauser)*, 2m 16.56s; 19 Stirrat/Prior, GB *(LCR-Honda)*, 2m 16.75s; 20 Hugli/Haenni, Switzerland *(Sigwa)*, 2m 16.84s.

BRAZILIAN GRAND PRIX, 17 September, Goiania 2.38m/3.835k

This was the race Eddie Lawson really wanted to win. He did with a marvellous display of controlled riding in searing heat round a bumpy circuit. In the 250cc class the mighty Spanish showdown never materialised. Instead, Sito Pons clinched the world title from third place while Juan Garriga was knocked out of contention by fellow Yamaha riders. Once again, Goiania provided a marvellous atmosphere for the final round of the championship with the parties and Samba dancing probably remembered long after the memories of the two races fade away.

Tyres were always going to play an important part in the 32-lap 500cc race round the 2.38-mile circuit's uneven surface, and nobody's style was better suited than Lawson's. He'd qualified in second place, riding the Marlboro Yamaha, just four hundredths of a second slower than Wayne Gardner. The Australian was equally keen to end the season on a winning note after losing his much coveted world crown to Lawson three weeks earlier. Completing the front row were Kevin Schwantz, riding the Pepsi Suzuki, Ron Haslam and a battered Christian Sarron. He'd cracked a rib in a jet ski accident back home in France and had crashed in practice, damaging his ankle. It was to be the last appearance of the Honda powered centre-hub steering Elf 5 ridden by Haslam. It appeared the Brazilian timekeepers had given Haslam a little leaving present with that place on the front row.

Lawson made his intentions clear from the start and the orange and white Yamaha led half way round the first lap chased by Wayne Rainey and Schwantz. Gardner made a bad start on the NSR Rothmans Honda and was sixth at the end of the first lap. Rainey soon dropped off the pace with his Dunlop tyres giving his Lucky Strike Yamaha little grip. He then suffered a front tyre puncture and retired for the first time that season. The pace at the front matched the scorching 35-degree temperature with Schwantz contesting the lead with Lawson. At the end of the sixth lap the Texan outbraked Lawson at the end of the main straight and led for the next three laps.

Behind them, Gardner, despite handfuls of rear wheel spin, was fighting back. He grabbed third place from the ailing Rainey on the fifth lap and Lawson got the hurry-up signal from his pits. He passed Schwantz on the ninth lap and, in that smooth and precise style that is so forgiving to tyres, pulled away as Gardner set about Schwantz. The Suzuki man was having his own rear suspension problems and could only keep Gardner at bay for two more laps. Once in second place the deposed World Champion realised he had no chance of catching the man who'd stolen his world crown, and settled down to a lonely ride into second place. Lawson held a 13-second advantage at the finish to secure his seventh grand prix victory of the season and added a final insult by smashing Gardner's old lap record.

Schwantz was happy to be back on form, after having his mind on his possible transfer from Suzuki rather than on his riding. He finished third, in front of a spirited battle for fourth won by Scotsman Niall Mackenzie, riding the HB Honda. It's an important time for riders, with contracts being discussed, and Mackenzie was desperate to impress Honda to retain him next year. He went wide on the first bend and dropped to 12th place, but fought back. Riding as hard as he had all year he passed Sarron's Gauloises Yamaha. The wounded Frenchman retaliated and gave chase in the last few hectic laps, but failed to catch Mackenzie by just 1.2 seconds.

Australian Kevin Magee kept the Lucky Strike Yamaha flag flying by fighting off Italian Pier-Francesco Chili to finish sixth. In a mad dash to the line Magee just saw off the HB Honda rider despite an excursion onto the grass. Rob McElnea was having probably his last ride for the Pepsi Suzuki team after a disastrous season. He stormed past Didier de Radigues, riding the second Marlboro Yamaha, with five laps remaining to grab a hard-earned eighth place.

Both Haslam and Cagiva-mounted Randy Mamola were also battling with Magee, Chili, McElnea and de Radigues when they struck separate problems. Mamola was still the most popular rider with the disappointing crowd of just 10,000, but he crashed without injury. When adjusting the front brake he ran into a bend too fast, turned in hard to correct the mistake and was highsided off. Haslam so wanted a happy ending to the Elf saga but he retired just a couple of laps from the finish when his Honda engine seized for the second time after front brake problems. Roger Burnett's brief re-membership of the Rothmans Honda team came to an unhappy end when he crashed, breaking his toe, on the fourth lap after stalling on the line.

The situation before the start of the vital final round of the 250cc championship was simple. It brought an even larger group than normal of noisy but charming Spanish journalists. Ducados Yamaha-mounted Garriga had to win the race, with Campsa Honda-mounted Pons finishing fourth or below, for Garriga to clinch the title. Prospects looked good at the end of the first lap with Garriga sat in behind Pons. We waited for the fireworks to explode, but they came from a totally unexpected source on the second lap of the 27-lap race.

Former World Champion Carlos Lavado always rides hard but once back home in South America he rides even harder. He raced up the inside of Garriga with his HB Yamaha skipping wildly. West German Martin Wimmer had to take avoiding action and hit Garriga up the backside, knocking him onto the grass. Wimmer crashed but Garriga stayed on, though so far down the field that his championship chances had disappeared in a great plume of Goiania red dust. He fought back brilliantly to eventually finish fifth, but

While Pons clinched the title, Dominique Sarron ended his Rothmans Honda career on a winning note.

the experienced Pons knew the championship was his as long as he kept out of trouble. Despite the close attentions of Italian Loris Reggiani and HB Honda-mounted Reinhold Roth, he finished third in the race won by frenchman Dominique Sarron.

Making his last appearance in the Rothmans Honda team Pons kept cool amid all the goings-on around him. He'd qualified in pole position but it was Luca Cadalora who screamed from the line on his Marlboro Yamaha. The fiery Italian looked a likely winner but Sarron, who won the race last year had different ideas. He started to haul in his advantage and put the Italian under real pressure. At half distance Cadalora cracked when he braked too late going into a bend. The front end tucked under and down he went, leaving the way clear for Sarron's farewell party.

Despite his antics on the second lap, former World Champion Carlos Lavado had his best ride of the season into second place, finishing just five seconds behind the winner. Pons was looking for that easy ride into third but Reggiani and Roth did not give him an easy time. Reggiani retired when the ignition trigger broke on his Rotax-powered Aprilia, while Roth felt he would be none too popular with his Honda bosses, if he'd given the champion-elect a hard time.

West German Helmut Bradl rode the NSR Rothmans Honda into a brilliant sixth place on only his second appearance on the machine. His team-mate Jochen Schmid had also been going well but crashed, without injury, on the ninth lap. Swiss veteran Jacques Cornu completed a marvellous season that saw him clinch third place in the championship after finishing tenth. The party to bring down the curtain on the 1988 season went on long into the night. Eddie Lawson and Sito Pons had good reason to celebrate.

Results

500cc (32 laps, 76.25m/122.72k)		**m**	**s**	**mph**	**kmh**
1	E. Lawson, USA *(Yamaha)*	47	06.32	97.13	156.313
2	W. Gardner, Australia *(Honda)*	47	19.68	96.67	155.578
3	K. Schwantz, USA *(Suzuki)*	47	27.67	96.40	155.141
4	N. Mackenzie, GB *(Honda)*	47	30.44	96.31	154.990
5	C Sarron, France *(Yamaha)*	47	30.56	96.30	154.984
6	K. Magee, Australia *(Yamaha)*	48	18.60	94.70	152.415
7	P. Chili, Italy *(Honda)*	48	19.42	94.68	152.372
8	R. McElnea, GB *(Suzuki)*	48	21.17	94.62	152.280
9	D. de Radigues, Belgium *(Yamaha)*	48	29.62	94.35	151.838

31 laps: 10 P. Igoa, France *(Yamaha)*; 11 F. Barchitta, San Marino *(Honda)*; 12 G. de Nicolas, Spain *(Honda)*; 13 D. McLeod, GB *(Honda)*.

Record lap: E. Lawson, USA *(Yamaha)*; 1m 27.81s, 97.71mph/157.243kmh.
Old record: W. Gardner, Australia *(Honda)*, 1m 28.79s, 96.68mph/155.590kmh (1987).

World Championship positions: 1 E. Lawson, 252 points; 2 W. Gardner, 229; 3 W. Rainey, 189; 4 C. Sarron, 149; 5 K. Magee, 138; 6 N. Mackenzie, 125; 7 D. de Radigues, 120; 8 K. Schwantz, 119; 9 P. Chili, 110; 10 R. McElnea, 83.

Practice leaderboard: 1 W. Gardner, Australia *(Honda)*, 1m 26.93s; 2 E. Lawson, USA *(Yamaha)*, 1m 26.97s; 3 K. Schwantz, USA *(Suzuki)*, 1m 27.19s; 4 R. Haslam, GB *(Elf-*

Honda), 1m 27.44s; 5 C. Sarron, France *(Yamaha)*, 1m 27.81s; 6 P. Chili, Italy *(Honda)*, 1m 27.89s; 7 W. Rainey, USA *(Yamaha)*, 1m 27.93s; 8 K. Magee, Australia *(Yamaha)*, 1m 27.99s; 9 R. Mamola, USA *(Cagiva)*, 1m 28.02s; 10 D. de Radigues, Belgium *(Yamaha)*, 1m 28.05s; 11 N. Mackenzie, GB *(Honda)*, 1m 28.30s; 12 R. McElnea, GB *(Suzuki)*, 1m 28.76s; 13 R. Burnett, GB *(Honda)*, 1m 28.97s; 14 P. Igoa, France *(Yamaha)*, 1m 29.08s; 15 F. Barchitta, San Marino *(Honda)*, 1m 30.31s: 16 M. Gentile, Switzerland *(Fior)*, 1m 30.95s; 17 A. Valesi, Italy *(Honda)*, 1m 31.15s; 18 B. Kneubuhler, Switzerland *(Honda)*, 1m 31.16s; 19 D. McLeod, GB *(Honda)*, 1m 31.93s; 20 G. de Nicolas, Spain *(Honda)* 1m 36.53s.

250cc (27 laps, 64.34m/103.545k)		**m**	**s**	**mph**	**kmh**
1	D. Sarron, France *(Honda)*	41	04.39	93.99	151.259
2	C. Lavado, Venezuela *(Yamaha)*	41	09.71	93.78	150.933
3	S. Pons, Spain *(Honda)*	41	15.77	93.55	150.564
4	R. Roth, W. Germany *(Honda)*	41	16.03	93.54	150.548
5	J. Garriga, Spain *(Yamaha)*	41	21.07	93.35	150.242
6	H. Bradl, W. Germany *(Honda)*	41	22.73	93.29	150.141
7	C. Cardus, Spain *(Honda)*	41	24.43	93.23	150.039
8	J. Ruggia, France *(Yamaha)*	41	25.05	93.20	150.001
9	M. Shimizu, Japan *(Honda)*	41	34.85	92.84	149.412
10	J. Cornu, Switzerland *(Honda)*	41	43.25	92.53	148.911

11 M. Herweh, W. Germany *(Yamaha)*; 12 A. Auinger, Austria *(Aprilia)*; 13 H. Eckl, W. Germany *(Aprilia)*; 14 S. Caracchi, Italy *(Honda)*; 15 D. McLeod, GB *(EMC)*; 16 U. Luzi, Switzerland *(Honda)*; 17 L. Lavado, Venezuela *(Yamaha)*; 18 H. Becker, W. Germany *(Yamaha)*. 26 laps: 19 G. Bertin, France *(Yamaha)*; 20 J. Foray, France *(Yamaha)*; 21 A. Puig, Spain *(Honda)*; 22 J. Balde, France *(Rotax)*; 23 E. Aleman, Venezuela *(Yamaha)*.

Record lap: L. Cadalora, Italy *(Yamaha)*, 1m 30.09s, 95.23mph/153.263kmh.
Old record: S. Pons, Spain *(Honda)*, 1m 31.25s, 94.01mph/151.298kmh (1987).

World Championship positions: 1 S. Pons, 231 points; 2 J. Garriga, 221; 3 J. Cornu, 166; 4 D. Sarron, 158; 5 R. Roth, 158; 6 L. Cadalora, 136; 7 J. Ruggia, 104; 8 A. Mang, 87; 9 C. Cardus, 71; 10 M. Shimizu, 68.

Practice leaderboard: 1 D. Sarron, France *(Honda)*, 1m 29.20s; 2 S. Pons, Spain *(Honda)*, 1m 29.30s; 3 C. Lavado, Venezuela *(Yamaha)*, 1m 30.03s; 4 L. Cadalora, Italy *(Yamaha)*, 1m 30.10s; 5 J. Garriga, Spain *(Yamaha)*, 1m 30.10s; 6 C. Cardus, Spain *(Honda)*, 1m 30.30s; 7 J. Schmid, W. Germany *(Honda)*, 1m 30.35s; 8 J. Ruggia, France *(Yamaha)*, 1m 30.45s; 9 R. Roth, W. Germany *(Honda)*, 1m 30.55s; 10 L. Reggiani, Italy *(Aprilia)*, 1m 30.84s; 11 M. Wimmer, W. Germany *(Yamaha)*, 1m 30.86s; 12 J. Cornu, Switzerland *(Honda)*, 1m 30.88s; 13 H. Bradl, W. Germany *(Honda)*, 1m 31.04s; M. Shimizu, Japan *(Honda)*, 1m 31.05s; 15 H. Eckl, W. Germany *(Aprilia)*, 1m 31.05s; 16 M. Herweh, W. Germany *(Yamaha)*, 1m 31.35s; 17 A. Auinger, Austria *(Aprilia)*, 1m 31.54s; 18 J. Foray, France *(Yamaha)*, 1m 31.57s; 19 L. Lavado, Venezuela *(Yamaha)*, 1m 31.60s; 20 B. Casanova, Italy *(Aprilia)*, 1m 31.62s.

THE MACHINES
Michael Scott

Detail innovation within a pattern of general refinement was the technical message of 1988 – in other words, change in small matters, with the overall pattern remaining the same.

In the process, we saw Yamaha vault ahead after Honda stumbled earlier in the season. By the end of the year, after HRC (Honda Racing Corporation) had tidied up some of the details, the two giants of the 500 class were more or less equal again. Among the 250s it was more of the same, but the boot was on the other foot. While Yamaha's works bikes made a half-hearted attempt to catch up with the dominant Hondas, the Yamaha TZ production bike showed that a carefully thought-out but basically simple design could still reap big dividends.

The greatest basic change came in the 125cc class, where new rules saw the twin-cylinder machines of 1987 consigned to the scrap heap, and a new order of single-cylinder tiddlers take over. This shift of technical focus left the doomed 80cc machines to suffer from stagnation.

Among the solos, the technical initiative was in the hands of the factory-backed teams. Only the sidecars gave room for individual initiative, exemplified by Rolf Biland's powerful engine developments. But on three wheels, as on two, any technical adventures required generous funding. Racing is never cheap if you want to succeed at the highest level.

500cc – Plenty of user-friendly power

It goes without saying that the largest racing bikes produce massive amounts of horsepower. The trick in 1988 was to make that horsepower easily usable, and this was Honda's problem in the early part of the year. It was clear from Wayne Gardner's whooping wheelspin and lurid slides out of the corners that the 1988 version of the V4 Honda NSR had no shortage of urge. It took a major revision of the frame geometry, however, before he could harness the power to beat Eddie Lawson's Yamaha . . . by which time his rival already had a huge World Championship lead.

The top 500s are now producing approximately 160 horsepower, with a working rev range from approximately 9,000 to more than 12,000rpm. However, the best of them (in 1988 this meant the Yamahas) can provide pulling power from as low as 6,500rpm, and the swelling power curve rises smoothly, without peaks or troughs. To the rider this translates as more usable power – the bike is less fussy about gearing and more even-tempered in acceleration. Of course, a 160-horsepower machine can easily spin its rear wheel in the lower four of six gears. The important thing is that it should do so under the rider's precise control.

Ostensibly, the Honda NSR, the Yamaha YZR, the Cagiva and the Suzuki RGV are similar machines, and their configuration fits under the catch-all tag of V4. All use crankcase reed-valve induction, with the bank of carburettors between the vee, facing forward; all use some form of exhaust power valve. On paper, they appear much the same, although Honda use almost-square 54 × 54.5mm dimensions and a 112-degree vee; while Yamaha stick with their time-honoured 56 × 50.6mm dimensions, and a 70-degree vee (widened from 1987's 60 degrees to make more room for the carburettors, which had performed erratically in their restricted heat-prone position).

In reality, the engines have several major disparities, with the Honda's being the most different of all. While the others are twin-crankshaft machines – a pair of parallel twins geared together – the Honda is a single-crankshaft design. Honda's designers have taken the opportunity to phase the firing strokes equally, 90 degrees apart. This makes the engine easier to start and allows a lighter crankshaft (less flywheel effect is required). More importantly, the smoother running allows the use of narrower main bearings, which in turn produce less engine friction.

Another benefit of the single crankshaft is that it allows a more compact engine – in every dimension except width. Although the 1988 NSR engine was outwardly similar to the 1987 version, it was in fact completely redesigned and made smaller still. The previous major change had come in 1987, when the direction of engine rotation was inverted, to reverse the torque reaction that was tending to lift the front wheel at high engine speeds, causing unpredictable roadholding in fast corners. However, the major advantage lies in the reduced internal friction – the Honda engine requires only five main bearings, whereas a twin-crankshaft design requires six and also imposes extra drag from the gears which link the two crankshafts.

There are two drawbacks, though. The first is the greater gyroscopic effect of a single crankshaft. This tends to stabilise the bike at high rpm, making it less willing to change direction, minimised by making the crankshaft as short as possible. The second is the torque reaction. The Honda engine's equally spaced firing may also be something of a liability, in that the smoother and more continuous flow of power engenders more wheelspin.

The Yamaha (and the very similar Cagiva) have minimised drag by gearing the crankshafts directly together and to the clutch. The pair of crankshafts therefore rotate in opposite directions. Thus, though they have more internal friction than the Honda, they have the advantage in that torque reaction is self-cancelling. The shorter crankshafts also

The winning combination – Eddie Lawson's triumphant 500cc Yamaha stripped to its bones.

have a reduced gyroscopic effect. Such a design requires that two cylinders also fire together. It is theoretically possible to space the firing strokes at any interval you wish, but practical problems intervene, since the crankshaft gears fight one another unless the firing strokes on each are simultaneous. This 'big bang' timing appears to work in the rider's favour, making the engines effectively more torquey, and reducing the tendency towards runaway wheelspin.

The Suzuki engine is broadly similar to those of the Cagiva and the Yamaha, but echoes their earlier designs by interposing an 'idler' gear between the crankshafts, which spin in the same direction.

Apart from the private V3 Hondas, highly effective survivors from an earlier Honda design philosophy where simplicity ruled, and the handful of old square four Suzukis in private hands (effectively these are twin-crank V-twins, with a zero included angle), the only engine heresy came from Claude Fior. His eponymous machine borrowed technology discarded by the Japanese in the late Seventies (although preserved in the sidecar class), of an in-line four two-stroke. This configuration suffers all the torque reaction and gyroscopic problems of the Honda, and adds even greater crankshaft length – but the French designer has other ideas of centralising the machine's major masses, and thus did not mind the necessity of mounting the wide engine high up in the frame.

Things remained much as before in thermal matters: induction being from slide-type carburettors (round-slide for Honda, flat for the rest) through crankcase-mounted reed valves, with detail development centred on the reeds themselves.

Tuning work on the inlet, transfer and exhaust ports is an endless process, and the same applies to the resonant exhaust expansion chambers, which form the vital last link in turning a racing two-stroke from humble heat engine into a harmonically resonating musical instrument. All racing engines used some or another form of 'power valve' to vary the exhaust timing, thus broadening the effective rev range: the most notable detail change came from Yamaha, who switched from the flat guillotine valve to the rotating barrel type.

Another area of attention, especially in Yamaha's case, was engine cooling. Two-strokes run best below 70 degrees centigrade and, in an effort to keep temperatures below this level throughout a GP race, Yamaha teams tried a variety of radiator variations. The Marlboro and Gauloises squads eventually settled on a large supplementary radiator mounted horizontally in the seat behind the rider, used in races in hot weather. The Lucky Strike team mounted a small radiator behind the front number-plate in the fairing nose, taking the opportunity to reduce the size of the main radiator to improve aerodynamic penetration.

Frame, suspension and cycle parts

Fior (along with the French Elf) also chose heresy in frame and suspension design, eschewing the universal front forks in favour of a twin wishbone design using a single suspension unit.

All the rest stuck with hydraulically damped front forks, in Honda's case with hydraulic 'anti-dive', which slowed down the rate of fork compression under braking, and various designs of linkage imparting a rising rate from rear fork movement to monoshock suspension units. But there was a major change in the design of some of the front forks, with several Yamaha teams and Cagiva switching halfway through the season to 'inverted' forks supplied by the Scandinavian manufacturers Ohlins.

Quite simply, these are upside-down forks: with the damping fluids and mechanism mounted at the top (sprung) portion, with the unsprung slider at the wheel end now the inner part of the telescope. The main advantage lies in reducing unsprung weight, while the outer element of the telescope can also be more robust, bringing further advantages in front fork stiffness.

Rear suspension was universally the same, with detail variations, using a pivoted fork operating one or another kind of bell crank to impart a rising rate to the rear single monoshock unit. The major change at the rear was the appearance of arced pivoted forks. The left-hand leg was straight, as it must be to remain within the run of the drive chain; but the right-hand leg was – in the case of Yamaha, Cagiva and later Suzuki – arced upwards to make more room for the lower pair of exhaust expansion chambers, which now both exit on the same side. The extra space allows more freedom in the shaping of these resonant chambers, improving power without prejudicing cornering ground clearance.

The Elf 5 was the only GP bike to use the single trailing arm suspension method now increasingly favoured in endurance racing, and also adopted by Honda's RC30 ready-to-race production machine. This was among a number of unorthodoxies perpetuated by the idiosyncratic French team during their last year of GP competition – the other major heresy being the front suspension, achieved by an adapted lower link and McPherson strut, where the steering shaft is also a telescopic strut.

For 1988, the Elf was closer than ever to being competitive, with 1987's steel and aluminium frame members largely replaced with cast magnesium, now that matters of basic geometry were settled, and the great range of adjustment no longer required. This saved a lot of weight, but the Elf was condemned to using a 1987 NSR Honda engine, since dimensions of the new one were available too late to modify the frame castings.

With the more conventional frames, construction would appear to be a simple matter, since the principles have long been established. Current fashion dictates a beefy variation of the spine frame, with a substantial forked girder (fabricated in the case of the Yamaha, constructed from extruded complex-section tube by Honda) running from the steering head to the rear fork pivot, the engine suspended beneath.

The difficulties of Gardner's Rothmans Honda illustrate that frame design remains a sensitive area, where it is still quite easy for some of the world's most advanced engineers to get it wrong. The works Honda started the year as a more or less unmanageable beast, prone to uncontrollable wheelspin and very erratic handling under acceleration. Throughout the season HRC supplied a string of revised frames, with geometric changes including different steering head angles to slow the steering, while the rear fork pivot point was moved upwards. This increased the fork's 'droop', and meant that under power the rear wheel was pulled downwards by the taut drive chain.

One other significant component development appeared towards year-end. Carbon-fibre brakes discs have been seen before, but Wayne Rainey's British GP-winning Team Roberts Lucky Strike Yamaha was fitted with a new type of non-fibrous sintered material called 'carbon-carbon'. The AP-Lockheed brakes were tested for the first time only four days before the race, and obviously worked. Their advantage is not in braking power, but that they are smaller and lighter than steel discs, reducing the gyroscopic effect of the brakes and making the bike easier to turn, while also reducing unsprung weight.

250s and the rest

Honda's NSR V-twin – a single-crank engine that is fundamentally half of the 500cc V4 – continued to dominate the 250 class, with minimal changes compared with last year's successful machine.

Yamaha also made few revisions, and their twin-crank V-twin (also half of the 500) remained inferior in all aspects of performance except steering and roadholding. At all but a few circuits, the Honda's greater power was enough to prevail, although the machine was said to be harder to ride than Yamaha's YZR.

One of the best new machines of the season was Yamaha's production TZ, the bike available to privateers. Detailed refinement had revitalised the stalwart machine, the most important changes being moving the twin carburettors from the rear of the cylinders to the front. They faced forward, drawing cool clean air from an airbox under the radiator, while the exhausts gained a clean, almost straight run rearwards through the seat.

Aprilia, the top non-Japanese factory, joined the trend to V-twin engines with their own twin-crank design; while their production models used the ever-green tandem twin Rotax engine.

The inverted fork was even more popular among the 250s than the 500s; while the Italian Gazzaniga-Rotax showed another interesting variation on the theme. Their front suspension is basically a re-arranged telescopic fork, with the lower sliders linked by a substantial bridge, which operates a single 'mono-shock' suspension unit. As well as enhanced rigidity, this system offers simpler and quicker changes to spring rate and damping – it is the work of a moment to remove one suspension unit and replace it with another.

Major frame innovation again came from Kenny Roberts's team, when he picked up the composite-material carbon-fibre honeycomb sandwich frame technology discarded by Suzuki when they switched to the V4 500cc engine in 1987. Roberts's new bike duplicated TZ frame geometry, but substituted the carbon-fibre material for the aluminium of the delta-box frame, saving weight and enhancing stiffness.

The 125 class was the only one with a complete crop of new machinery, built to comply with the new single-cylinder rule. The capacity increase was too great a stretch to allow existing 80cc machines to be simply bored and stroked; but the dominant Derbi was in all respects very like their 80cc machine, suitably stretched in every dimension.

This beautifully handcrafted machine, with its horizontal cylinder and choice of slender straight-tube space-frame or carbon-fibre monocoque frame (the latter not actually used in 1988) was ranged up against a variety of machinery, the most numerous being the simple Honda production-racers, built in large numbers for a domestic Japanese championship. There was also a Rotax engine available, as well as a Cagiva; while the previously dominant Garelli built a single-cylinder engine, but suffered throughout the year mainly from handling problems that ruled them out of the front positions. The fashion was as for the 80cc machines: outward simplicity of a water-cooled single cylinder; inner sophistication of porting, tuning and exhaust shaping, to make the absolute most of a meagre ration of horsepower.

Derbi is the most experienced of competitors in the smaller class, but it was no accident that their domination came from the most expensively developed machine on the track. No matter what the engine size, racing success never comes cheaply.

WORLD SUPERBIKE CHAMPIONSHIP

Gary Pinchin

World Superbike finally became a reality in 1988 and immediately lived up to all the pre-season ballyhoo. The racing was always closely fought, there was healthy inter-manufacturer rivalry, it got world-wide television coverage and crowd figures were generally way up at circuits which had previously run F1 races. The championship was fought right to the final race in New Zealand and likeable American Fred Merkel clinched the crown with his Italian-entered Oscar Rumi Honda by just 5.5 points from Italian Yamaha privateer Fabrizio Pirovano. In the final analysis, eight different riders from six different nations won races during the 17-race series and all six of the marques competing won at least one race, Bimota the most with seven.

The opening round at Donington, which resulted in a win for Marco Lucchinelli on a factory Ducati 851 Superbike, probably grabbed more publicity for the series than all the pre-season promotion put together. The former World 500cc Champion clinched overall victory after fellow Italian Davide Tardozzi crashed his factory Bimota on the last lap of the second leg. He had been under pressure from Lucchinelli in the race, but, having already won the first leg, was virtually assured the overall, provided he shadowed Lucchinelli's every move.

Runner up overall was Fred Merkel, despite finishing both races with his from-the-crate Hondas on the verge of seizing. Engine problems plagued the considerable Honda RC30 line up. Many of the riders like Merkel had received their bikes late and just didn't have time to prepare for the Easter meeting. World F1 Champion, Virginio Ferrari didn't even qualify due to his late arrival and subsequent carburation problems which prevented him posting a qualifying time. Problems also hit the Bimota camp; together with the two works riders, Tardozzi and Belgian Stephane Mertens, the privateer ranks suffered fuel injection maladies which caused intermittent misfires and cut outs.

Race one saw Tardozzi take the flag by over a second from Lucchinelli with Irishman Joey Dunlop nearly half a minute adrift. Merkel was fourth, after scrapping with the private FZ750 Yamaha of Fabrizio Pirovano until the Italian ran off the track while lapping a backmarker. Mertens went out with a failure in the fuel injection department. With Lucchinelli wrapping up the second leg, and overall, Merkel finished second with a spare motor to assure the second place points quota. Roger Burnett finished third after a collision with a backmarker in race one had ruined hopes of a good start to the series.

After Donington, where both legs counted towards overall classification, it was decided by the FIM, under pressure from the series-organising Sports Marketing Company, to alter the points scoring so every leg counted, which meant that even if a rider retired from one race he could still possibly score in the other. Instead of the new-style FIM points, 20 for a win, 17 for second, etc., the FIM split the points, awarding 10 for a win, 8.5 for second down to 0.5 for 15th place in each race.

Over 45,000 people witnessed the thrilling races at the Hungaroring – round two in the championship – and they saw Fred Merkel snatch the points lead on the tortuous circuit. Merkel won the first race from Bimota twins Tardozzi and Mertens with Superbike 'rookie' Adrien Morillas fourth on the Kawasaki France GPX750. But in the second race it was Morillas who scored an upset victory, coming from behind. His win meant four different manufacturers had posted wins in four races. Mertens this time got the better of his teammate Tardozzi but Merkel's fifth-place finish behind Burnett was enough to give him a nine-point lead over Luchinelli, who could only finish ninth in race one and retired in the second leg with ignition failure.

At Hockenheim for the third round the story was so different. Merkel, short on parts for his Hondas, was way down the field and a double win for Tardozzi saw the Italian snatch the points lead by a 4.5 margin at the end of the day. Over 35,000 fans, more than ever had bothered to attend an F1 World round at the venue, saw Tardozzi in superb form. In the first lap he was challenged by Mertens until the Bimota's injection misfire again reared its head. That left Christophe Bouheben and Alex Vieira second and third on their Honda France machines – their first, but very effective appearance on the World Superbike circuit. Also coming into the action was Swiss Edwin Weibel on the Muhlenbach Honda. He surprised the establishment by qualifying on the front row and running with the leaders for the entire race. Burnett took fifth and Lucchinelli sixth. Morillas never featured in the frame after a heavy crash in training while the best Suzuki was that of local favourite Ernst Gschwender down in 18th place, a position reflecting the uncompetitive nature of the 1988 Suzuki in this competition.

In the second leg Mertens again showed he could match Tardozzi's pace, until the dreaded misfires struck his Bimota. Despite almost pulling in to retire on two occasions, the Belgian overcame the obvious frustrations to fight back into an eventual second place behind his runaway winning teammate. Vieira finished a lone third after challenging Tardozzi and Mertens in the opening laps along with his Honda France partner Bouheben, who retired with a blown motor while in second place. An eight-bike freight train fought out the eventual fourth place with Burnett grabbing the position from Dunlop coming into the stadium on the final lap. There was a big sort-out in the Sachscurve, two corners from home which saw Lucchinelli taking to the grass after a coming together with Ferrari and Dunlop. The Irishman held onto fifth followed by Kawasaki rider Eric Delcamp, Kenny Irons and Pirovano. But Ferrari dropped to ninth and Lucchinelli trailed in 11th after recovering from his high speed excursion into the sand trap.

Round four took a bumper entry of 96 to the Austrian Alps where a 10,000 crowd turned out at the ultra-fast Oesterreichring to see Lucchinelli prove once again the competitive nature of his big vee-twin Ducati taking the first race with relative ease. There was drama in the first turn, however, as Tardozzi ran into the back of Merkel's Honda and sent the American crashing out of the action. Tardozzi regained his composure to stage a fight back which saw him finish fifth among a seven-bike battle for second. Burnett had inherited the second place after Bouheben crashed at the chicane, but on the final lap he lost the front end in the very fast Tiroch Curve and was lucky to escape with only concussion after hitting the barrier at high speed. At the flag, Pirovano took second, from Aussie Mal Campbell (making his first appearance in the series), Vieira, and then Tardozzi.

Lucchinelli took the initial advantage in the second leg but was slowed and eventually retired with a broken spark plug. Tardozzi took the lead and was never headed despite a strong challenge from Bouheben in the early stages. Once again, there was a tremendous battle further back as Vieira, Pirovano, Morillas, Weibel, Campbell and Merkel constantly swapped positions until Merkel broke clear. Just as the American was looking good for third, his bike – fitted with an 18-litre tank, instead of his usual 24 litre version which had been damaged in the first-race crash – ran short of fuel. He dropped to eighth while Vieira took second from Weibel, Morillas, Campbell and Pirovano.

As they headed for Japan and round five at Sugo, Tardozzi held a slightly more comfortable 10.5 point lead over Lucchinelli and Pirovano. American Merkel sat behind the three Italians, 15 points adrift of the leader.

In Japan it was Canadian-based Kiwi Gary Goodfellow grabbing the headlines to give Suzuki their first Superbike win. Despite pain from an injured foot he won the first leg, changing his rear tyre mid-race after a wet track dried unexpectedly fast. Although on a charge and likely to grab victory anyway, the win was handed to Goodfellow on the last lap when leader Kunio Macchi on a Yamaha ran off the course under pressure from the flying Yoshimura team rider. Merkel pulled back valuable points by finishing second after Tardozzi had retired after 19 laps, while Pirovano was eliminated by a crash with Weibel.

Emergent Aussie star 23-year-old Mick Doohan won the second race, which was run in dry conditions. He had crashed out on the first lap of the previous race along with several others. The second leg had to be red-flagged due to oil on the course, which had brought down leading duo Lucchinelli and Michael Dowson. Merkel also went down a lap later in the same spot but remounted, though his crash brought the red flag.

From the restart Pirovano pulled his usual lightning getaway, but soon dropped off the pace set initially by Phillis and then by Doohan on the Marlboro Yamaha, the first win for the FZR in Superbike. Japanese Kenichiro Iwahashi was second on a Honda with Goodfellow third. Tardozzi was a grace saving fourth while Pirovano finished tenth one place ahead of the battered Merkel.

Back into Europe, the French organisers decided to run the Le Mans round as a straight race, which was duly won in the wet by Pirovano after a hectic ride which saw him off onto the grass several times. French Kawasaki teamster Eric Delcamp took second with Mertens third, but points-leader Tardozzi was struggling down in 12th. Merkel, still sore from his Sugo crash and another in an Italian national event, was sixth. The race put privateer Pirovano into the ever-changing points lead with 64, ahead of Tardozzi in second on 62 and Merkel in third on 57.5.

At Estoril, Portugal the Bimotas were back in control. Tardozzi won the first leg, but only after his teammate Mertens pulled over for him. Lucchinelli was third on the Ducati. Merkel fought long and hard to win fourth from British sensation Terry Rymer on the Sterns Disco Honda and Pirovano.

Tardozzi moved back into a slender six-point lead following a runner-up place in the second race. This time Mertens did not give up his lead. Merkel was fifth behind the exciting Rymer, who had besoted a dice with Lucchinelli and Pirovano.

In Australia, which suprisingly was boycotted by the Lucchinelli/Ducati effort, the Marlboro Yamaha pair of Doohan and Dowson dominated. Doohan won both races in fine style, smashing his own lap record in the first leg. The tight, twisty track did not favour Tardozzi who languished in 11th and 10th places in the respective races. Merkel, however, was in his element, finishing fourth in the first and a superb third in the second behind the home track stars. With Pirovano down in sixth and seventh the points chase suddenly looked so close: Tardozzi 86, Merkel and Pirovano both 83.5 and the final round at Manfeild, New Zealand was another scratchers' circuit.

In a wet opening leg Merkel was superb, winning the race after gambling on full wets despite a drying track. Pirovano took second with Goodfellow and Phillis keeping Tardozzi down in fifth. But it was two glaring Italian mistakes in the second leg, won by Mertens, which ultimately gave Merkel the title. First, Tardozzi crashed on the warm up lap, then Pirovano's crew messed up a tyre change which dropped him to 13th. Merkel meantime took a safe fifth, enough to clinch the title by 5.5 points from Pirovano. Tardozzi finished the series a further two points adrift.

Merkel – the first World Superbike Champion.

Results

Round 1 3 April, Donington Park, England (60 laps, 117.60 miles/189.25kms)

1 M. Lucchinelli, Italy *(Ducati)*, 1h 16m 7.72s, 92.54mph/148.924kmh
2 F. Merkel, USA *(Honda)*; 3 J. Dunlop, Ireland *(Honda)*; 4 R. Marshall, GB *(Suzuki)*; 5 F. Pirovano, Italy *(Yamaha)*; 6 K. Irons, GB *(Honda)*; 7 J. Suhonen, Finland *(Yamaha)*; 8 A. McGladdery, GB *(Suzuki)*; 9 S. Williams, GB *(Yamaha)*; 10 M. Farmer, Ireland *(Suzuki)*; 11 D. Leach, GB *(Yamaha)*; 12 T. Douglas, Canada *(Yamaha)*; 13 J. Lofthouse, GB *(Suzuki)*; 14 A. Moyce, GB *(Kawasaki)*; 15 E. Kuparinen, Finland *(Kawasaki)*.
Fastest lap: B. Shobert, USA *(Honda)*, 1m 14.10s, 95.07mph/152.99kmh

1st leg: 1 D. Tardozzi, Italy *(Bimota)*; 2 Lucchinelli; 3 Dunlop; 4 Merkel; 5 Marshall; 6 Irons.
2nd leg: 1 Lucchinelli; 2 Merkel; 3 R. Burnett, GB *(Honda)*; 4 Pirovano; 5 Dunlop; 6 Marshall.

Points for Donington round based on overall result from two legs. FIM altered system for subsequent rounds to count both legs as individual point scoring races.

Round 2 30 April, Hungaroring, Hungary (Both legs 25 laps, 62.369 miles/100.37kms)
1st leg
1 F. Merkel, USA *(Honda)*, 49m 39.78s, 75.29mph/121.164kmh
2 D. Tardozzi, Italy *(Bimota)*; 3 S. Mertens, Belgium *(Bimota)*; 4 A. Morillas, France *(Kawasaki)*; 5 F. Pirovano, Italy *(Yamaha)*; 6 J. Dunlop, Ireland *(Honda)*; 7 R. Rasmussen, Denmark *(Suzuki)*; 8 R. Burnett, GB *(Honda)*; 9 M. Lucchinelli, Italy *(Ducati)*; 10 E. Gschwender, W. Germany *(Suzuki)*; 11 E. Delcamp, France *(Kawasaki)*; 12 P. Iddon, GB *(Bimota)*; 13 M. Galinski, W. Germany *(Bimota)*; 14 J. Suhonen, Finland *(Yamaha)*; 15 A. McGladdery, GB *(Suzuki)*.
Fastest lap: R. Rasmussen, Denmark *(Suzuki)*, 1m 57.7s, 76.3mph/122.79kmh

2nd leg
1 A. Morillas, France *(Kawasaki)*, 49m 38.66s, 75.31mph/121.196kmh
2 S. Mertens, Belgium *(Bimota)*; 3 D. Tardozzi, Italy *(Bimota)*; 4 R. Burnett, GB *(Honda)*; 5 F. Merkel, USA *(Honda)*; 6 F. Pirovano, Italy *(Yamaha)*; 7 R. Rasmussen, Denmark *(Suzuki)*; 8 P. Iddon, GB *(Bimota)*; 9 E. Gschwender, W. Germany *(Suzuki)*; 10 J. Suhonen, Finland *(Yamaha)*; 11 V. Ferrari, Italy *(Honda)*; 12 A. Andersson, Sweden *(Suzuki)*; 13 E. Delcamp, France *(Kawasaki)*; 14 P. Rubatto, W. Germany *(Bimota)*; 15 J.-L. Guignabodet, France *(Honda)*.
Fastest lap: M. Lucchinelli, Italy *(Ducati)*, 1m 57.28s, 76.51mph/123.13kmh

Round 3 8 May, Hockenheim, West Germany (Both legs 15 laps, 63.28 miles/101. 829kms)

1st leg
1 D. Tardozzi, Italy *(Bimota)*, 33m 16.86s, 114.07mph/183.580kmh
2 C. Bouheben, France *(Honda)*; 3 A. Vieira, France *(Honda)*; 4 E. Weibel, Switzerland *(Honda)*; 5 R. Burnett, GB *(Honda)*; 6 M. Lucchinelli, Italy *(Ducati)*; 7 J. Dunlop, Ireland *(Honda)*; 8 A. Hoffman, W. Germany *(Honda)*; 9 E. Delcamp, France

(Kawasaki); 10 V. Ferrari, Italy *(Honda)*; 11 F. Pirovano, Italy *(Yamaha)*; 12 P. Iddon, GB *(Bimota)*; 13 S. Mertens, Belgium *(Bimota)*; 14 K. Irons, GB *(Honda)*; 15 P. Rubatto, W. Germany *(Bimota)*.
Fastest lap: C. Bouheben, France *(Honda)* 2m 11.98s, 115.063mph/185.171kmh

2nd leg
1 D. Tardozzi, Italy *(Bimota)*, 33m 23.05s, 113.72mph/183.013kmh
2 S. Mertens, Belgium *(Bimota)*; 3 A. Vieira, France *(Honda)*; 4 R. Burnett, GB *(Honda)*; 5 J. Dunlop, Ireland *(Honda)*; 6 E. Delcamp, France *(Kawasaki)*; 7 K. Irons, GB *(Honda)*; 8 F. Pirovano, Italy *(Yamaha)*; 9 V. Ferrari, Italy *(Honda)*; 10 A. Hoffman, W. Germany *(Honda)*; 11 M. Lucchinelli, Italy *(Ducati)*; 12 B. Schmidt, W. Germany *(Bimota)*; 13 P. Iddon, GB *(Bimota)*; 14 P. Rubatto, W. Germany *(Bimota)*; 15 M. Galinski, W. Germany *(Bimota)*.
Fastest lap: V. Ferrari, Italy *(Honda)* 2m 11.79s, 115.23mph/185.438kmh

Round 4 3 July, Zeltweg, Austria (Both legs 20 laps, 74 miles/119.088kms)

1st leg
1 M. Lucchinelli, Italy *(Ducati)*, 39m 19.045s, 111.004mph/178.638kmh
2 F. Pirovano, Italy *(Yamaha)*; 3 M. Campbell, Australia *(Honda)*; 4 A. Vieira, France *(Honda)*; 5 D. Tardozzi, Italy *(Bimota)*; 6 E. Weibel, Switzerland *(Honda)*; 7 A. Morillas, France *(Kawasaki)*; 8 R. Phillis, Australia *(Kawasaki)*; 9 A. Andersson, Sweden *(Suzuki)*; 10 E. Gschwender, W. Germany *(Suzuki)*; 11 K. H. Riegl, Austria *(Bimota)*; 12 D. Kempter, Austria *(Honda)*; 13 M. Udo, W. Germany *(Bimota)*; 14 D. Heinen, Belgium *(Honda)*; 15 M. Ricci, Italy *(Ducati)*.
Fastest lap: D. Tardozzi, Italy *(Bimota)*, 1m 54.07s, 114.78mph/182.72kmh

2nd leg
1 D. Tardozzi, Italy *(Bimota)*, 39m 15.668s, 111.163mph/178.894kmh
2 C. Bouheben, France *(Honda)*; 3 A. Vieira, France *(Honda)*; 4 E. Weibel, Switzerland *(Honda)*; 5 A. Morillas, France *(Kawasaki)*; 6 M. Campbell, Australia *(Honda)*; 7 F. Pirovano, Italy *(Yamaha)*; 8 F. Merkel, USA *(Honda)*; 9 M. Faberi, Italy *(Bimota)*; 10 E. Gschwender, W. Germany *(Suzuki)*; 11 P. Ramon, Belgium *(Honda)*; 12 A. Andersson, Sweden *(Suzuki)*; 13 J. Suhonen, Finland *(Yamaha)*; 14 M. Udo, W. Germany *(Bimota)*; 15 D. Kempter, W. Germany *(Honda)*.
Fastest lap: C. Bouheben, France *(Honda)*, 1m 56.69s, 112.19mph/180.56kmh

Round 5 28 August, Sugo, Japan (Both legs 25 laps, 58 miles/93.34kms)

1st leg
1 G. Goodfellow, Canada *(Suzuki)*, 45m 50.98s, 75.98mph/122.275kph
2 F. Merkel, USA *(Honda)*; 3 Y. Oshima, Japan *(Suzuki)*; 4 S. Mertens, Belgium *(Bimota)*; 5 M. Wantanabe, Japan *(Yamaha)*; 6 R. Phillis, Australia *(Kawasaki)*; 7 A. Slight, New Zealand *(Bimota)*; 8 T. Hanamura, Japan *(Yamaha)*; 9 K. Kobayashi, Japan *(Honda)*; 10 V. Ferrari, Italy *(Honda)*; 11 T. Kaneko, Japan *(Yamaha)*; 12 M. Lucchinelli, Italy *(Duçati)*; 13 H. Nakamura, Japan *(Suzuki)*; 14 S. Endo, Japan *(Honda)*; 15 A. Andersson, Sweden *(Suzuki)*.
Fastest lap: G. Goodfellow, Canada *(Suzuki)*, 1m 44.27s, 80.19mph/129.039kph

2nd leg
1 M. Doohan, Australia *(Yamaha)*, 41m 41.57s, 83.55mph/134.465 kph
2 K. Iwahashi, Japan *(Honda)*; 3 G. Goodfellow, Canada *(Suzuki)*; 4 D. Tardozzi, Italy *(Bimota)*; 5 E. Weibel, Switzerland *(Honda)*; 6 R. Phillis, Australia *(Kawasaki)*; 7 B. Morrison, GB *(Honda)*; 8 V. Ferrari, Italy *(Honda)*; 9 T. Hanamura, Japan *(Honda)*; 10 F. Pirovano, Italy *(Yamaha)*; 11 F. Merkel, USA *(Honda)*; 12 K. Kobayashi, Japan *(Honda)*; 13 Y. Oshima, Japan *(Suzuki)*; 14 A. Slight, New Zealand *(Bimota)*; 15 M. Campbell, Australia *(Honda)*.
Fastest lap: E. Weibel, Switzerland *(Honda)*, 1m 36.73s, 86.43mph/139.098kph

Round 6 4 September, Le Mans, France (24 laps, 63.12 miles/101.81kms)

1 F. Pirovano, Italy *(Yamaha)*, 49m 01.77s, 77.9mph/125.36kph
2 E. Delcamp, France *(Kawasaki)*; 3 S. Mertens, Belgium *(Bimota)*; 4 A. Vieira, France *(Honda)*; 5 C. Bouheben, France *(Honda)*; 6 F. Merkel, USA *(Honda)*; 7 R. Burnett, GB *(Honda)*; 8 T. Rymer, GB *(Honda)*; 9 M. Fabbri, Italy *(Bimota)*; 10 M. Lucchinelli, Italy *(Ducati)*; 11 J. Suhonen, Finland *(Yamaha)*; 12 D. Tardozzi, Italy *(Bimota)*; 13 A. Andersson, Sweden *(Suzuki)*; 14 J. Y. Mounier, France *(Yamaha)*; 15 M. Linscott, GB *(Honda)*.
Fastest lap: F. Pirovano, Italy *(Yamaha)*, 1m 56.79s, 81.73mph/131.528kph

Round 7 11 September, Estoril, Portugal (Both legs 22 laps, 59.47 miles/95.69kms)

1st leg
1 D. Tardozzi, Italy *(Bimota)*, 40m 22.45s, 88.37mph/142.219kph
2 S. Mertens, Belgium *(Bimota)*; 3 M. Lucchinelli, Italy *(Ducati)*; 4 F. Merkel, USA *(Honda)*; 5 T. Rymer, GB *(Honda)*; 6 F. Pirovano, Italy *(Yamaha)*; 7 P. Rubatto, West Germany *(Bimota)*; 8 A. Andersson, Sweden *(Suzuki)*; 9 P. Iddon, GB *(Bimota)*; 10 R. Dunlop, Ireland *(Honda)*; 11 M. Ricci, Italy *(Ducati)*; 12 E. Gschwender, West Germany *(Suzuki)*; 13. A. Gruschka, West Germany *(Honda)*; 14 J. L. Guignabodet, France *(Honda)*; 15 A. McGladdery, GB *(Honda)*.
Fastest lap: D. Tardozzi, Italy *(Bimota)*, 1m 48.65s, 89.56mph/144.132kph

2nd leg
1 S. Mertens, Belgium *(Bimota)*, 40m 08.79s, 88.87mph/143.026kph
2 D. Tardozzi, Italy *(Bimota)*; 3 T. Rymer, GB *(Honda)*; 4 M. Lucchinelli, Italy *(Ducati)*; 5 F. Merkel, USA *(Honda)*; 6 F. Pirovano, Italy *(Yamaha)*; 7 R. Dunlop, Ireland *(Honda)*; 8 P. Iddon, GB *(Bimota)*; 9 A. Andersson, Sweden *(Suzuki)*; 10 M. Ricci, Italy *(Ducati)*; 11 M. Fabbri, Italy *(Bimota)*; 12 A. McGladdery, GB *(Honda)*; 13 J. Suhonen, Finland *(Yamaha)*; 14 A. Gruschka, West Germany *(Honda)*; 15 J. L. Guignabodet, France *(Honda)*.
Fastest lap: R. Roche, France *(Ducati)*, 1m 48.33, 89.84mph/144.588kph

Round 8 25 September, Oran Park, Australia (Both legs 39 laps, 63.49 miles/102.18kms)

1st leg
1 M. Doohan, Australia *(Yamaha)*, 48m 10.58s
2 M. Dowson, Australia *(Yamaha)*; 3 R. Phillis, Australia *(Kawasaki)*; 4 F. Merkel, USA

(Honda); 5 M. Campbell, Australia *(Honda)*; 6 F. Pirovano, Italy *(Yamaha)*; 7 S. Mertens, Belgium *(Bimota)*; 8 G. Goodfellow, Canada *(Honda)*; 9 R. Scolyer, Australia *(Honda)*; 10 S. Gallagher, Australia *(Honda)*; 11 D. Tardozzi, Italy *(Bimota)*; 12 A. McGladdery, GB *(Honda)*; 13 J. Dunlop, Ireland *(Honda)*; 14 T. Rymer, GB *(Honda)*; 15 I. Pero, NZ *(Suzuki)*.
Fastest lap: M. Doohan, Australia *(Yamaha)*, 1m 12.82s, 80.49mph/129.53kmh

2nd leg
1 M. Doohan, Australia *(Yamaha)*, 48m 04.93s
2 M. Dowson, Australia *(Yamaha)*; 3 F. Merkel, USA *(Honda)*; 4 R. Phillis, Australia *(Kawasaki)*; 5 G. Goodfellow, Canada *(Honda)*; 6 S. Mertens, Belgium *(Bimota)*; 7 F. Pirovano, Italy *(Yamaha)*; 8 M. Campbell, Australia *(Honda)*; 9 R. Scolyer, Australia *(Honda)*; 10 D. Tardozzi, Italy *(Bimota)*; 11 T. Rymer, GB *(Honda)*; 12 S. Gallagher, Australia *(Honda)*; 13 A. McGladdery, GB *(Honda)*; 14 J. Dunlop, Ireland *(Honda)*; 15 L. Willing, Australia *(Yamaha)*.
Fastest lap: F. Merkel, USA *(Honda)*, 1m 12.69s, 80.63mph/129.75kmh

Round 9 2 October, Manfeild, New Zealand (Both legs 34 laps, 69.72 miles/112.2kms)

1st leg
1 F. Merkel, USA *(Honda)*, 44m 16.58s
2 F. Pirovano, Italy *(Yamaha)*; 3 G. Goddfellow, Canada *(Honda)*; 4 R. Phillis, Australia *(Kawasaki)*; 5 D. Tardozzi, Italy *(Bimota)*; 6 S. Mertens, Belgium *(Bimota)*; 7 T. Douglas, Canada *(Yamaha)*; 8 R. Scolyer, Australia *(Honda)*; 9 T. Rymer, GB *(Honda)*; 10 G. Williams, NZ *(Ducati)*; 11 M. Campbell, Australia *(Honda)*; 12 M. King, NZ *(Ducati)*; 13 A. Stroud, NZ *(Bimota)*; 14 A. McGladdery, GB *(Honda)*; 15 J. Dunlop, Ireland *(Honda)*.
Fastest lap: F. Merkel, USA *(Honda)*, 1m 16.12s, 89.13mph/143.441kmh

2nd leg
1 S. Mertens, Belgium (Bimota), 42m 30.86s
2 M. Campbell, Australia *(Honda)*; 3 R. Phillis, Australia *(Kawasaki)*; 4 R. Scolyer, Australia *(Honda)*; 5 F. Merkel, USA *(Honda)*; 6 G. Goodfellow, Canada *(Honda)*; 7 T. Rymer, GB *(Honda)*; 8 G. Williams, NZ *(Ducati)*; 9 A. Stroud, NZ *(Bimota)*; 10 A. McGladdery, GB *(Honda)*; 11 T. Douglas, Canada *(Yamaha)*; 12 J. Dunlop, Ireland *(Honda)*; 13 F. Pirovano, Italy *(Yamaha)*; 14 D. Warren, NZ *(Honda)*; 15 M. King, NZ *(Ducati)*.
Fastest lap: S. Mertens, Belgium *(Bimota)*, 1m 11.26s, 95.21mph/153.224kmh (record)

Final Championship Positions
1 F. Merkel, USA *(Honda)*, 99 points
2 F. Pirovano, Italy *(Yamaha)*, 93.5; 3 D. Tardozzi, Italy *(Bimota)*, 91.5; 4 S. Mertens, Belgium *(Bimota)*, 90.5; 5 M. Lucchinelli, Italy *(Ducati)*, 64; =6 R. Phillis, Australia *(Kawasaki)*, 42/A. Vieira, France *(Honda)*, 42; 8 G. Goodfellow, Canada *(Honda* and *Suzuki)*, 41.5; 9 M. Campbell, Australia *(Honda)*, 36; 10 T. Rymer, GB *(Honda)*, 32.5.

WORLD ENDURANCE CHAMPIONSHIP

Gary Pinchin

With no world championship planned for 1989, Herve Moineau and Thierry Crine became the the last World Endurance title holders. This year they retained the crown for Suzuki after winning the final round at Spa, but it was an abbreviated three-round series, the original calender decimated by promoters unwilling to gamble running unprofitable races. The three races which remained were of course the classics, the Le Mans 24-hours in April, the Suzuka Eight-hours and the Spa 24-hours, while for this year the Autumn Bol D'Or, the most popular of the European long distance events was not a championship race, alternating championship status, as it has for several years, with the Le Mans event.

Reigning champions Moineau and Bruno Le Bihan, teamed with Crine could do little about Honda superiority in the opening round at Le Mans. The race was dominated by the Honda RVF with Alex Vieira, Christophe Bouheben and Jean-Michel Mattioli winning by ten laps from the Kawasaki France ZXR7 of Jean-Louis Battistini, Pierre Bolle and Eric Delcamp. The Suzuki was third, a further seven laps adrift.

The next race on the schedule was the Suzuka eight-hour but this time Honda were humbled on their own test track by the Lucky Strike Grand Prix pairing of Kevin Magee – last year's winner – and Californian Wayne Rainey. With 150,000 fans looking on in the intense heat the Lucky Strike pair, on a special factory YZF750 Genesis, won by a lap from the GSX-R Suzuki of Kevin Schwantz and Doug Polen. Pierre Ettiene Samin and World Superbike star Adrien Morillas on the ZXR Kawasaki were third, followed by Moineau and Crine. The Suzuki pair closed to within two points of leaders Vieira and Bouheben, who could only finish tenth after Vieira had crashed whilst sixth. The meeting was an all-round disaster for the factory RVF Hondas. Wayne Gardner and Niall MacKenzie went out with a blown motor and the American pair Bubba Shobert and Jim Filice broke a gearbox. Japanese Misumitsu Taguchi and Shinichi Ito were the first Honda-mounted riders home in seventh place on an RVF.

With everything riding on the last round at Spa, it was an epic clash as the lead changed hands between the Vieira/Bouheben/Guignabodet Honda and the Suzuki of Moineau/Crine/le Bihan throughout the race. First Vieira tumbled on oil spilt by another competitor, then the Suzuki was forced to pit with a broken engine bolt. The race, and ultimately the title, was finally resolved in the Suzuki camp's favour when Bouheben fell at the chicane. English fans had plenty to cheer, with journalist Mat Oxley finishing fourth at Spa, teamed with Steve Manley and Eric McFarlane on the Team MCN Yamaha, to clinch sixth overall in the championship behind the French-based factory riders.

Results

France, Le Mans, 2–3 April **24 hours**

1 A. Vieira/C. Bouheben/J-M. Mattioli, France *(Honda)*, 747 laps, 83.75mph/134.01kmh; 2 J-L. Battistini/P. Bolle/E. Delcamp, France *(Kawasaki)*; 3 H. Moineau/B. Le Bihan/T. Crine, France *(Suzuki)*; 4 G. Furling/P. Rolland/V. Parisot,

France *(Kawasaki)*; 5 P. Lewis/M. Oxley/V. Kultalahti, Australia/GB/Sweden *(Yamaha)*; 6 A. Lussiani/M. Graziano/M. Simeon, France/Belgium*(Suzuki)*; 7 C. Berger/J-R. Garnier/P. Ronfort, France/Switzerland *(Honda)*; 8 M. Galbit/R. Nicotte/B. Gritton, France *(Suzuki)*; 9 C. Boudinot/O. Roullet/P. Salles, France *(Suzuki)*; 10 M. Sato/K. Coburn/T. Sharpless, Japan/Canada *(Yamaha)*; 11 E. Sergent/N. Diani/D. Hamdi, France *(Suzuki)*; 12 D. Railton/K. Nicholls/T. Thompson, GB *(Kawasaki)*; 13 A. Cottard/J. Guynon/J. Guynon, France *(Suzuki)*; 14 I. Green/A. Green/J. Zebedee, GB *(Honda)*; 15 P. Guittet/F. Brosse/E. Wurtz, France *(Honda)*.
Fastest lap: A. Vieira/C. Bouheben/J-M. Mattioli *(Honda)*, 1m 46.16s, 90.40mph/ 144.699kmh.

Japan, Suzuka, 31 July **Eight hours**
1 K. Magee/W. Rainey, Australia/America *(Yamaha)*, 202 laps, 91.48mph/147.22kmh; 2 K. Schwantz/D. Polen, America *(Suzuki)*; 3 P. Samin/A. Morillas, France *(Kawasaki)*; 4 H. Moineau/T. Crine, France *(Suzuki)*; 5 T. Sohwa/K. Tada, Japan *(Kawasaki)*; 6 K. Ballington/R. Phillis, South Africa/Australia *(Kawasaki)*; 7 M. Taguchi/S. Ito, Japan *(Honda)*; 8 M. Dowson/K. Macchi, Australia/Japan *(Yamaha)*; 9 M. Saitoh/M. Wantanabe, Japan *(Yamaha)*; 10 A. Vieira/C. Bouheben, France *(Honda)*; 11 R. Hubin/M. Simul, Belgium *(Kawasaki)*; 12 M. Abe/T. Ohshima, Japan *(Honda)*; 13 A. Kozono/S. Hagiwara, Japan *(Honda)*; 14 T. Yokoi/Y. Inoue, Japan *(Honda)*; 15 F. Merkel/V. Ferrari, Italy *(Honda)*.
Fastest lap: W. Gardner, Australia *(Honda)*, 2m 17.398s, 95.39mph/153.523kmh.

Belgium, Spa, 13–14 August **24 hours**

1 H. Moineau/T. Crine/B. Le Bihan, France *(Suzuki)* 509 laps, 92.10mph, 148.22kmh; 2 A. Vieira/J. L. Guignabodet/C. Bouheben, France *(Honda)*; 3 R. Hubin/M. Simul/M. Steven, Belgium *(Kawasaki)*; 4 M. Oxley/E. McFarlane/S. Manley, GB *(Yamaha)*; 5 J. Verkennse/E. Bragard/H. Sonnet, Belgium *(Honda)*; 6 P. Schuetz/H. Lehmann/F. Beck, Switzerland *(Kawasaki)*; 7 P. Mouchet/M. Masnada/B. Chateau, France *(Suzuki)*; 8 P. Lagamme/B. Lacrosse/A. Servais, Belgium *(Suzuki)*; 9 J. Lacrosse/A. Diaz/P. Orban, Belgium *(Suzuki)*; 10 U. Meier/U. Kallen/C. Monsch, Switzerland *(Honda)*; 11 J–P. Lecointe/M. Gargi/P–V. Deschamps, France *(Suzuki)*; 12 G. Jolivet/G. Furling/P. Rolland, France *(Suzuki)*; 13 T. Rymer/A. Green/I. Green, GB *(Honda)*; 14 M. Phillips/D. Bates/M. Bowen, GB *(Yamaha)*; 15 A. Heiler/G. Hever/M. Crnojevic, West Germany *(Suzuki)*.
No fastest lap available

Final World Championship points: 1 = H. Moineau, France *(Suzuki)* and T. Crine, France *(Suzuki)*, both 83 points; 3 = A. Vieira, France *(Honda)* and C. Bouheben, France *(Honda)*, both 80; 5 B. Le Bihan, France *(Suzuki)*, 70; 6 M. Oxley, GB *(Yamaha)*, 48; 7 J–M. Mattioli, France *(Honda)*, 40; 8 = R. Hubin, Belgium *(Kawasaki)*, M. Simul, Belgium *(Kawasaki)* and M. Steven, Belgium *(Kawasaki)* all 35.

TT FORMULA ONE WORLD CHAMPIONSHIP

Gary Pinchin

The World TT Formula One championship was bound to suffer once World Superbike took off. With many of the European F1 regulars voicing concern over racing on the public roads which made up part of the F1 series, it was no surprise many of them defected to the all permanent circuit schedule of Superbike. It meant very few riders took in the full TTF1 programme, but commitment to the series paid off for 23-year-old Carl Fogarty. The young lad from Blackburn won two races, and in the races contested only failed to score in Vila Real – through mechanical woes. He proved he could race on any type of circuit, which is really what the series is all about.

Not surprisingly, the championship got off to a shaky start in Japan when the only European to enter was Swede Anders Andersson, and he failed to score. In fact the only non-Japanese in the top fifteen were Canadian Gary Goodfellow, seventh with his Don Knit Sugano Yoshimura Suzuki, and young Kiwi prospect Aaron Slight, with a Super

Following in his father's footsteps . . . Carl Fogarty en route *to the TT Formula One World title.*

Angel Racing Team Bimota. The race was won by Noboru Muira on a Honda. Round two on the Isle of Man Mountain course was predictably won by Joey Dunlop with his privately entered Gemini Oils Honda. It was an impressive result for the new RC30 with the Ulsterman, Nick Jeffries, Roger Burnett, and Carl Fogarty filling out the top four places in this demanding 226.4 mile race.

The entry for Assen improved with the race taking place during the annual 'Speedweek'. Superbiker Burnett won and promptly announced he had no plans to contend the full series. West Germans Andreas Hoffman on a Honda and Bimota-mounted Peter Rubatto filled the rostrum places with Paul Iddon fourth, following up his previous best ever TT ride of fifth place. Swiss Edwin Weibel and another West German, Michael Galinski, completed the top six – all of them Superbike regulars. The likely F1 candidates Dunlop and Fogarty took eighth and ninth respectively.

The Vila Real round, so often held in burning heat, was interrupted by rain. The race was halted during a shower but by the restart the track was awash following a storm and eventually red flagged early. Welshman Steve Williams took the overall win with the conventionally carburated Fowlers Bimota but the finishers were only awarded half points for the shortened race. Dunlop was fourth behind Portuguese Manuel Joao and Britain's Dave Leach on the Padgett Bimota. Fogarty retired with a misfire, allowing Dunlop to build a 14.5 point cushion. Dunlop moved further ahead when he grabbed third at Kouvola, Finland, with Fogarty a close fourth. Frustrated Superbikers, Andersson and Rubatto, scored a one-two. They had found that the stringent rulebook had left their machines uncompetitive at Superbike level, but the more relaxed carburettor rules of F1 gave their bikes race-winning horsepower.

The entry for Dundrod was lacking any such European interlopers, but it produced a shock win for Fogarty as Dunlop hit trouble. The local hero chose the wrong tyre, a slick, in the damp conditions which allowed Fogarty the edge in the early running. But the young charger did not have an easy passage, having to beat fellow roads specialists Steve Hislop, Robert Dunlop and Nick Jeffries. Dunlop was seventh – a shattering blow to his morale as Fogarty closed to within 5.5 points in the points chase.

For Dunlop things got even worse in Pergusa, Sicily. He really needed a result there and even arrived early to acclimatise himself to the heat. However, things went sadly wrong when he crashed in the Friday practice and ended up in hospital with arm injuries and concussion. Rising from his sick bed he joined the race day grid only for his machine to break a valve spring in the warm up. With no Dunlop in the race Fogarty took maximum points, but again had to fight for his win. Gianluca Galasso, a 22-year-old Bimota factory recruit gave chase and at one stage looked to have the race won. As Fogarty settled for second, Galasso ran short of gas. He refueled but spilt petrol all over the bike caused him to crash at the next turn after the pits. Fogarty was home and dry, almost literally, as his bike also ran short of fuel on the penultimate lap. Luckily, he had a minute cushion over second placeman, Bodo Schmidt of West Germany, and was able to take on fuel without losing his hard-won position.

Arguably the best entry all year fronted for the final race at Donington with Grand Prix men Niall MacKenzie and Ron Halsam in the line-up on Hondas. Despite several engine failures in the Honda camp, they dominated the racing with MacKenzie heading a 1-2-3 for the RC30s, Burnett and Brian Morrison, on his Superstocker, completing the rostrum places. Haslam could only finish eighth with a slow machine, but the day really belonged to Fogarty who rode a faultless race in fifth behind Swedish Suzuki rider Andersson. Dunlop was way back in 11th place so the title fell to Fogarty by a huge 19.5 point margin.

Results

Round 1 15 May, Sugo, Japan (50 laps, 116.12 miles/186.87km)

1 N. Miura, Japan *(Honda)*
2 T. Sohwa, Japan *(Kawasaki)*; 3 S. Miyazaki, Japan *(Honda)*; 4 M. Saitoh, Japan *(Yamaha)*; 5 S. Katoh, Japan *(Yamaha)*; 6 T. Arata, Japan *(Yamaha)*; 7 G. Goodfellow, Canada *(Suzuki)*; 8 A. Sakaguchi, Japan *(Honda)*; 9 K. Iwahashi, Japan *(Honda)*; 10 M. Satoh, Japan *(Yamaha)*; 11 A. Slight, New Zealand *(Bimota)*; 12 M. Mori, Japan *(Yamaha)*; 13 T. Hanamura, Japan *(Honda)*; 14 K. Kobyashi, Japan *(Honda)*; 15 K. Morimitsu, Japan *(Honda)*.

Round 2 6 June, Isle of Man, Great Britain (6 laps, 226.4 miles/364.35km)

1 J. Dunlop, Ireland *(Honda)*, 1h 56m 50.2s, 116.25mph/187.08kmh
2 N. Jeffries, GB *(Honda)*; 3 R. Burnett, GB *(Honda)*; 4 C. Fogarty, GB *(Honda)*; 5 P. Iddon, GB *(Bimota)*; 6 M. Farmer, Ireland *(Suzuki)*; 7 B. Morrison, GB *(Honda)*; 8 S. Ward, GB *(Suzuki)*; 9 D. Leach, GB *(Bimota)*; 10 B. Reid, Ireland *(Kawasaki)*; 11 B. Woodland, GB *(Bimota)*; 12 G. Linder, GB *(Yamaha)*; 13 R. Dunlop, Ireland *(Honda)*; 14 P. Nicholls, GB *(Yamaha)*; 15 K. Wilson, Canada *(Suzuki)*.
Fastest lap: J. Dunlop, Ireland *(Honda)* 19m 5.8s, 118.54mph/190.77kmh (record)

Round 3 23 June, Assen, Holland (25 laps, 153.3 miles/246.71km)

1 R. Burnett, GB *(Honda)*, 58m 51.07s, 97.15mph/156.34kmh
2 A. Hoffman, W. Germany *(Honda)*; 3 P. Rubatto, West Germany *(Bimota)*; 4 P. Iddon, GB *(Bimota)*; 5 E. Weibel, Switzerland *(Honda)*; 6 M. Galinski, West Germany *(Bimota)*; 7 B. Schmidt, West Germany *(Bimota)*; 8 J. Dunlop, Ireland *(Honda)*; 9 C. Fogarty, GB *(Honda)*; 10 H. van der Mark, Netherlands *(Bimota)*; 11 S. Williams, GB *(Bimota)*; 12 P. Ramon, Belgium *(Honda)*; 13 J. de Vries, Netherlands *(Yamaha)*; 14 A. McGladdery, GB *(Suzuki)*; 15 C. Monsch, Switzerland *(Honda)*.
Fastest lap: R. Burnett, GB *(Honda)* 2m 18.47s, 99.09mph/159.47kmh (record)

Round 4 3 July, Vila Real, Portugal (16 laps, 68.75 miles/110.64km)

1 S. Williams, GB *(Bimota)* 51m 21.4s, 80.38mph/129.36kmh
2 M. Joao, Portugal *(Suzuki)*; 3 D. Leach, GB *(Bimota)*; 4 J. Dunlop, Ireland *(Honda)*; 5 P. Abnace, Belgium *(Yamaha)*; 6 W. Mitchell, GB *(Ducati)*; 7 P. Batista, Portugal *(Suzuki)*; 8 R. Dunlop, Ireland *(Honda)*; 9 P. Armes, GB *(Suzuki)*; 10 R. Sherry, Ireland *(Suzuki)*; 11 F. Jardin, Portugal *(Yamaha)*; 12 J. Caffrey, GB *(Yamaha)*; 13 E. Mascarenhas, Portugal *(Suzuki)*; 14 M. Granie, France *(Ducati)*; 15 R. Hutchinson, GB *(Suzuki)*.
Fastest lap: J. Dunlop, Ireland *(Honda)*, 2m 44.4s, 94.15mph/151.52kmh
Race run in two parts due to bad weather

Round 5 10 July, Kouvola, Finland (48 laps, 153.6m/247.188km)

1 A. Andersson, Sweden *(Suzuki)*, 1h 16m 04.88s; 2 P. Rubatto, West Germany *(Bimota)*; 3 J. Dunlop, Ireland *(Honda)*; 4 C. Fogarty, GB *(Honda)*; 5 R. Dunlop, Ireland *(Honda)*; R. Vartiainen, Finland *(Suzuki)*; 7 E. Rosman, Finland *(Suzuki)*; 8 E. Kuparinen, Finland *(Kawasaki)*; 9 J. Willemsen, Holland *(Suzuki)*; 10 R. Hutchinson, GB *(Suzuki)*; 11 P. Tolonen, Finland *(Suzuki)*; 12 C. Kit Choong, Malaysia *(Kawasaki)*; 13 J. Kivila, Finland *(Suzuki)*; 14 M. Granie, France *(Suzuki)*; 15 J. Suur-Inkeroin, Finland *(Yamaha)*.
Fastest lap: J. Dunlop, Ireland *(Honda)*, 1m 33.13s, 79.39mph/127.76kph

Round 6 30 July, Dundrod, Northern Ireland (13 laps, 97m)

1 C. Fogarty, GB *(Honda)*, 52m 2.0s, 111.01mph; 2 S. Hislop, GB *(Honda)*; 3 R. Dunlop, Ireland *(Honda)*; 4 N. Jeffries, GB *(Honda)*; 5 S. Williams, GB *(Bimota)*; 6 T. Moran, GB *(Yamaha)*; 7.J. Dunlop, Ireland *(Honda)*; 8 A. McGladdery, GB *(Honda)*; 9 B. Reid, Ireland *(Kawasaki)*; 10 D. Griffith, GB *(Honda)*; 11 A. Moyce, GB *(Kawasaki)*; 12 D. Leach, GB *(Suzuki)*; 13 S. Ward, GB *(Suzuki)*; 14 P. Cranston, Ireland *(Honda)*; 15 E. Laycock, Ireland *(Yamaha)*.
Fastest lap: C. Fogarty, GB *(Honda)* 15m 33.6s, 116.10mph.

Round 7 4 September, Pergusa, Sicily (32 laps, 100 miles)

1 C. Fogarty, GB *(Honda)*, 61m 32.919s, 95.89mph/154.32kph
2 B. Schmidt, West Germany *(Bimota)*; O. La Ferla, Italy *(Honda)*; 4 S. Williams, GB *(Bimota)*; 5 A. Prescuitti, Italy *(Yamaha)*; 6 R. Hutchinson, GB *(Suzuki)*; 7 C. Kit Choong, Malaysia *(Kawasaki)*; 8 R. Biagioli, Italy *(Honda)*; 9 R. Chiavaro, Italy *(Honda)*; 10 D. Woolams, GB *(Suzuki)*; 11 M. Pajic, Netherlands *(Kawasaki)*; 12 A. Mancuso, Italy *(Suzuki)*; 13 E. Fugardi, Italy *(Suzuki)*; 14 M. Grein, West Germany *(Suzuki)*; 15 J. Caffrey, GB *(Yamaha)*.
Fastest lap: G. Galasso, Italy *(Bimota)* 1m 52.729s, 98.23mph/158.078kph

Round 8 25 September, Donington Park, Great Britain, (40 laps, 100m/160.93k)

1 N. MacKenzie, GB *(Honda)*, 1h 7m 49.75s, 88.45mph/142.34kmh; 2 R. Burnett, GB *(Honda)*; 3 B. Morrison, GB *(Honda)*; 4 A. Andersson, Sweden *(Suzuki)*; 5 C. Fogarty, GB *(Honda)*; 6 S. Hislop, GB *(Honda)*; 7 K. Huewen, GB *(Bimota)*; 8 R. Haslam, GB *(Honda)*; 9 D. Dixon, GB *(Suzuki RG500)*; 10 P. Iddon, GB *(Bimota)*; 11 J. Dunlop, Ireland *(Honda)*; 12 G. Johnson, GB *(Bimota)*; 13 R. Stringer, GB *(Suzuki)*; 14 M. Linscott, GB *(Honda)*; 15 A. Moyce, GB *(Kawasaki)*.
Fastest lap: N. MacKenzie, GB *(Honda)*, 1m 39.74s, 90.23mph/145.21kmh (record).

Final Championship positions: 1 C. Fogarty, GB *(Honda)*, 84 points; 2 J. Dunlop, Ireland *(Honda)*; 63.5; 3 R. Burnett, GB *(Honda)*, 56; 4 S. Williams, GB *(Bimota)*, 39; 5 A. Andersson, Sweden *(Suzuki)*, 33 and R. Dunlop, Ireland *(Honda)*, 33; 7 P. Rubatto, West Germany *(Bimota)*, 32; 8= P. Iddon, GB *(Bimota)*, and N. Jeffries, GB *(Honda)*, both 30; 10 S. Hislop, GB *(Honda)*, 27.

Italian riders dominated the European Championships. Alberto Rota clinched the 500cc title before the final round.

Grand Prix star Niall Mackenzie returned home to win the final round of the TT Formula One world championship.

EUROPEAN CHAMPIONSHIP

GARY PINCHIN

It was a season to remember for the heavily-financed Team Italia squad in the European Championship as their riders, Emilio Cuppini, Fausto Ricci and Alberto Rota claimed the 125, 250 and 500 titles respectively. Communist bloc countries are not renowned for their road racing prowess, but the 80cc title went, in the final round, to Bulgarian Bodgan Nikolov claiming the crown by eight points from Hungarian Janos Szabo, both riders opting for Krauser machinery. The Sidecar series, only contested over five races, was dominated by the likeable Dutch brothers, Toni and Kilian Wyssen with their LCR, but once again British talent massed the ranks of the chair brigade with seven UK crews in the top ten of the final point standings.

The ten-round 250 series was fiercely competitive, but former grand prix rider (and winner of the 1984 Italian Grand Prix) Ricci was the only rider to have won more than two races. His title challenge came late with four wins on the Aprilia in the second half of the year. The early running was made by Italian Aprilia privateer Andrea Borgonovo and Austrian Andreas Preining on the Rotax-backed Aprilia, with sponsorship from Austrian erotic magazine publishers, OKM. Borgonovo's challenge faded with a poor finishing record in the second half of the year, culminating in a training crash at Donington, while 27-year-old Preining also had a couple of crashes to blunt his challenge.

Going into final round, Donington, only one rider stood between Ricci and the title; Renzo Colleoni, yet another Italian. Problems in the opening two rounds had left him playing a catch-up role all year. The 27-year-old, backed by Italian cosmetic company Dibi, did not win a single race but consistent finishing from round three, Hockenheim, onwards had him within 14 points of Ricci. But in the final race Colleoni scored only seventh place, his worst finish of the year, and Ricci took the crown with a ninth place following a rear-of-the-grid start. Donington was won by Dutchman Wilco Zeelenberg who showed superb mastery of the damp conditions late in the race to oust the early leader, Irishman Gary Cowan. The result for Zeelenberg was especially gratifying for him, riding a privately entered Yamaha. He had split from his sponsors Doc Shop Racing after the Dutch round where he finished second and missed the following three rounds.

By finishing every one of the nine races, and never lower than fourth, 25-year-old Rota was able to sew up the 500 class at the penultimate round at Jarama, where he scored his second victory of the year.

The series produced six different winners; Austrian Karl Truchsess on a Honda won in Germany and Czechoslovakia; sometime grand prix rider Fabio Barchitta from Italy took the Spanish and Dutch races; another Italian, Vittorio Scatola, struck gold for the Avia Paton team on home soil at Misano in April; Frenchman Rachel Nicotte, on a Honda, did likewise at Le Mans and Darren Dixon won the final Donington round on the Padgetts Suzuki, after an intriguing race which started in the wet and finished on a dry track. Suzuki privateer Steve Spray cursed his tyre choice, a wet front with an inter rear, having lost a good lead as the surface dried to Dixon, who opted for inters both front and rear.

With Rota confirmed champion and Austrian Michael Rudroff having secured the championship runner-up place in the penultimate round, British interest at Donington lay with Steve Manley, to see if he could clinch third place in the series. It was not to be. The exciting prospect from Essex suffered a derailed chain in the race when well placed. It summed up his season. Often brilliant rides for the unsponsored privateer were thwarted by mechanical faults caused primarily by running on a shoestring budget. He finished sixth in the series, as the best Suzuki rider, which says a lot about his hard riding in a championship dominated by the fast, reliable and expensive Honda triples.

Cuppini was without equal in the 125 class, or should that be his ex-works Garelli was? After a shaky start in Spain when he finished a poor ninth on the tight and twisty Jerez track, he was never beaten, recording seven straight wins. The winner of that first round, Alessandro Gramigni, took the runner-up slot in the series with the MBA and the consistent Swiss, Othmar Schuler, was third on another of the MBA twins which proliferated on the result sheets. Coventry's Kris Galatowicz finished a respectable ninth overall with his single-cylinder Honda. He didn't contest all the rounds but was particularly impressive with a third at the Jerez opener, where riding ability is paramount, and again late in the year in Misano and Jarama, where he netted fourth and sixth places respectively.

Bodgan Nikolov timed his 80cc championship run to perfection by winning the final round, his only victory in the seven races. Until the Jarama finale he had been hard pressed by double race-winner Szabo and Dutchman Andrie Nijenhuis, both on 54 points, 8 adrift of Nikolov. When his rivals could only muster fourth and eighth between them, the Bulgarian ran out an easy title holder.

Other race winners included Dutchman Bert Smit and West Germans Rolf Waldman, Peter Ottl and Reiner Scheidhauer.

Dutch crew Toni and Kilian Wyssen won four of the five Sidecar rounds and had clinched the title in France, although their 100 per cent winning record was spoilt by Frenchmen Ivan Nigrowski and Michel Charpentier. But there was still cause for celebration at final round Donington for the Dutch. Their race win came on the same day as passenger Kilian's 28th birthday. Toni is 30.

The Brits were out in force in the series, with Weston-super-Mare Kawasaki bike dealer George Hardwick and passenger Steve Parker taking second in the final reckoning after finishing fourth at Donington. They were expected to sew up the place at Le Mans, but flipped the outfit after colliding with a backmarker. Tony Baker lost out to Hardwick in the final race after gearbox problems forced him out at Donington. The Cumbrian-based sidecar manufacturer wound up third in the table ahead of Paul Atkinson and Gavin Simmons who lost any chance of claiming third place after gear shifting maladies slowed their progress at Donington.

Results

80cc

Round 1 12/13 March, Jerez, Spain (12 laps, 31.44 miles/50.59 kms)

1 R. Waldman, W. Germany *(Rotax)*, 25m 56.05s, 72.76mph/117.102 kph
2 J. Debon, Spain *(Arbizu)*; 3 M. Gschwander, W. Germany *(Seel)*; 4 P. Bordes, France

(RB); 5 R. Sassone, Italy *(BBFT)*; 6 J. Esteve, Spain *(Autisa)*; 7 J. Armu, Spain *(Krauser)*; 8 A. Sanchez, Spain *(JJ Cobas)*; 9 E. Palencia, Spain *(Arbizu)*; 10 J. Machado, Spain *(Arbizu)*; 11 B. Nikolov, Bulgaria *(Krauser)*; 12 P. Gschwander, W. Germany *(Seel)*; 13 P. Desmet, France *(Huvo)*; 14 P. Buzzi, Italy *(Unimoto)*; 15 C. Romero, Spain *(Honda)*.
Fastest lap: R. Waldman, W. Germany *(Rotax)*, 2m 08.05s, 73.69mph/118.584kph

Round 2 10 April, Misano, Italy (16 laps, 34.72 miles/55.874kms)

1 P. Ottl, W. Germany *(Krauser)*, 25m 01.056s, 83.17mph/133.844kph
2 R. Waldmann, W. Germany *(Seel)*; 3 G. Gnani, Italy *(Gnani)*; 4 B. Nikolov, Bulgaria *(Krauser)*; 5 R. Koster, Switzerland *(LCR)*; 6 J. Debon, Spain *(Arbizu)*; 7 P. Bordes, France *(RB)*; 8 J. Pintar, Yugoslavia *(Eberhardt)*; 9 J. Szabo, Hungary *(Krauser)*; 10 M. Torrens, Spain *(Arbizu)*; 11 S. Braegger, Switzerland *(Casal)*; 12 A. Nijenhuis, Netherlands *(Casal)*; 13 M. Gschwander, W. Germany *(Seel)*; 14 P. Tibori, Hungary *(Huvo Casal)*; 15 A. Pavlic, Yugoslavia *(Seel)*.
Fastest lap: P. Ottl, W. Germany *(Krauser)*, 1m 31.997s, 84.81mph/136.491kph

Round 3 7 May, Hockenheim, W. Germany (8 laps, 33.75 miles/54.308kms)

1 R. Scheidhauer, W. Germany *(Seel)*, 21m 31.23s, 94.09 mph/151.415kph
2 B. Smit, Netherlands *(Minarelli)*; 3 A. Nijenhuis, Netherlands *(Casal)*; 4 J. Lutzenberger, W. Germany *(Erberhardt)*; 5 P. Ottl, W. Germany *(Krauser)*; 6 J. Pintar, Yugoslavia *(Erberhardt)*; 7 H. Koopman, Netherlands *(Gibben-Ziegler)*; 8 A. Pavlic, Yugoslavia *(Seel)*; 9 M. Gschwander, W. Germany *(Seel)*; 10 S. Kurfiss, W. Germany *(Ziegler)*; 11 H. Klein, W. Germany *(Honda)*; 12 P. Gschwander, W. Germany *(Seel)*; 13 P. Bordes, France *(RB Moto)*; 14 P. Tibori, Hungary *(Casal)*; 15 JC Machado, Spain *(Arbizu)*.
Fastest lap: P. Ottl, W. Germany *(Krauser)*, 2m 35.51s, 97.65 miles/157.153kph

Round 4 15 May, Salzburgring, Austria (12 laps, 31.63 miles/50.916kms)

1 J. Szabo, Hungary *(Krauser)*, 20m 26.38s, 92.87mph/149.46kph
2 B. Nikolov, Bulgaria *(Krauser)*; 3 J. van Dongen, Netherlands *(Casal)*; 4 J. Lutzberger, W. Germany *(Erberhardt)*; 5 A. Nijenhuis, Netherlands *(Casal)*; 6 R. Kunz, W. Germany *(Ziegler)*; 7 S. Braegger, Switzerland *(Casal)*; 8 H. Koopman, Netherlands *(Ziegler)*; 9 M. Ehinger, W. Germany *(Krauser)*; 10 S. Kurfiss, W. Germany *(Ziegler)*; 11 J. Pintar, Yugoslavia *(Erberhardt)*; 12 P. Bordes, France *(RB Moto)*; 13 J. Esteve, Spain *(Autisa)*; 14 P. Gschwander, W. Germany *(Seel)*; 15 A. Pavlic, Spain *(Seel)*.
Fastest lap: R. Kunz, W. Germany *(Ziegler)*, 1m 38.85s, 96.02mph/154.53kph

Round 5 12 June, Most, Czechoslovakia (16 laps, 41.248 miles/66.38kms)

1 J. Szabo, Hungary *(Krauser)*, 30m 3.45s, 82.32mph/132.482kph
2 B. Nikolov, Bulgaria *(Krauser)*; 3 H. Koopman, Netherlands *(Ziegler)*; 4 P. Bordes, France *(RB Moto)*; 5 J. Pintar, Yugoslavia *(Eberhardt)*; 6 S. Braegger, Switzerland *(Casal)*; 7 R. Koster, Switzerland *(LCR Casal)*; 8 M. Gschwander, W. Germany *(Seel)*; 9 A. Nijenhuis, Netherlands *(Casal)*; 10 R. Kunz, W. Germany *(Ziegler)*; 11 R. Sassone, Italy *(BBFT)*; 12 P. Gschwander, W. Germany *(Seel)*; 13 J. Venacek, Czechoslovakia

(Krauser); 14 C. Baert, Belgium *(Casal)*; 15 K. Samak, Czechoslovakia *(Huvo Casal)*.
Fastest lap: J. Szabo, Hungary *(Krauser)*, 1m 51.37s, 83.32mph/134.08kph

Round 6 21 June, Assen, Netherlands (9 laps, 34.29 miles/55.182kms)

1 B. Smit, Netherlands *(Krauser)*, 24m 12.29s, 85.04mph/136.847kph
2 A. Nijenhuis, Netherlands *(Krauser)*; 3 R. Dunki, Switzerland *(Krauser)*; 4 J. Lutzenberger, W. Germany *(Eberhardt)*; 5 J. van Dongen, Netherlands *(Casal)*; 6 B. Nikolov, Bulgaria *(Krauser)*; 7 J. Bernard, Belgium *(Fantic)*; 8 M. Ehinger, W. Germany *(LCR Krauser)*; 9 J. Szabo, Hungary *(Krauser)*; 10 R. Koster, Switzerland *(LCR Casal)*; 11 J. Pintar, Yugoslavia *(Eberhardt)*; 12 K. Besseling, Netherlands *(CJB)*; 13 A. Pavlic, Yugoslavia *(Seel)*; 14 S. Braegger, Switzerland *(Casal)*; 15 T. Engl, W. Germany *(Krauser)*.
Fastest lap: P. Ottl, W. Germany *(Krauser)*, 2m 39.14s, 86.22mph/138.761kph

Round 7 11 September, Jarama, Spain (16 laps, 33.93 miles/52.99 kms)

1 B. Nikolov, Bulgaria *(Krauser)*, 27m 47.628s, 71.08mph/114.398kph
2 H. Koopman, Netherlands *(Ziegler)*; 3 J. Saez, Spain *(Autisa)*; 4 J. Szabo, Hungary *(Krauser)*; 5 M. Piazza, Italy *(Unimoto)*; 6. X. Arumi, Spain *(Krauser)*; 7. J. Bernard, Belgium *(Fantic)*; 8. A. Hijenhuis, Netherlands *(Casal)*; 9 J. Palencia, Spain *(Huvo)*; 10 J. Gali, Spain *(Motul)*; 11 R. Sassone, Italy *(Huvo)*; 12 P. Gschwander, West Germany *(Seel)*; 13 S. Kurfiss, West Germany *(Ziegler)*; 14 R. Gali, Spain *(Krauser)* 15 C. Baert, Belgium *(Casal)*.
Fastest lap: B. Nikolov, Bulgaria *(Krauser)*, 1m 42.723s, 72.13mph/116.073kph

125cc

Round 1 12/13 March, Jerez, Spain (17 laps, 44.54 miles/71.67kms)

1 A. Gramigni, Italy *(MBA)*, 35m 14.48s, 75.86mph/122.080kph
2 G. Debbia, Italy *(MBA)*; 3 K. Galatowicz, GB *(Honda)*; 4 J. Debon, Spain *(Arbizu)*; 5 A. Kempener, Belgium *(Rotax)*; 6 S. Penneses, Italy *(MBA)*; 7 M. Hernandez, Spain *(Beneti)*; 8 R. Dova, Italy *(AGV)*; 9 E. Cuppini, Italy *(Garelli)*; 10 J. C. Morillas, Spain *(JJ Cobas)*; 11 P. Bordes, France *(MBA)*; 12 F. G. de Nicolas, Spain *(JJ Cobas)*; 13 P. Micciarelli, Switzerland *(Honda)*; 14 T. Rinne, Finland *(MBA)*; 15 R. Murphy, Ireland *(Honda)*.
Fastest lap: A. Kempener, Belgium *(Rotax)*, 2m 00.03s, 78.24mph/125.915kph

Round 2 10 April, Misano, Italy (21 laps, 45.57 miles/73.338kms)

1 E. Cuppini, Italy *(Garelli)*, 31m 12.369s, 87.51mph/140.833kph
2 D. Romboni, Italy *(MBA)*; 3 A. Gramigni, Italy *(MBA)*; 4 G. Debbia, Italy *(MBA)*; 5 N. Pesche, W. Germany *(MBA)*; 6 R. Dovo, Italy *(AGV)*; 7 P. Bordes, France *(MBA)*; 8 P. Paolucci, Italy *(AGV)*; 9 A. Kempener, Belgium *(MBA)*; 10 A. Waibel, W. Germany *(Waibel)*; 11 R. Bucci, Italy *(AGV)*; 12 K. D. Kindle, Luxembourg *(Honda)*; 13 K. Galatowicz, GB *(Honda)*; 14 C. Jensen, Denmark *(MBA)*; 15 GP Rolland, France *(Honda)*.
Fastest lap: E. Cuppini, Italy *(Garelli)*, 1m 27.888s, 88.78mph/142.872kph

Round 3 8 May, Hockenheim, W. Germany (12 laps, 50.62 miles/81.463kms)

1 E. Cuppini, Italy *(Garelli)*, 29m 57.93s, 101.36mph/163.113kph
2 D. Hafeneger, W. Germany *(Moto-Wuelframix)* 3 O. Schuler, Switzerland *(MBA)*; 4 R. Dova, Italy *(AGV)*; 5 N. Peschke, W. Germany *(LCR)*; 6 A. Kempener, Belgium *(MBA)*; 7 A. Waibel, W. Germany *(Waibel)*; 8 T. Rinne, Finland *(MBA)*; 9 P. Bordes, France *(MBA)*; 10 J. Piepponen, Finland *(Garelli)*; 11 K. D. Kindle, Luxembourg *(Honda)*; 12 J. Pintar, Yugoslavia *(MBA)*; 13 D. Raudies, W. Germany *(MBA)*; 14 N. Hernandes, Spain *(Honda)*; 15 J. Vainio, Finland *(MBA)*.
Fastest lap: E. Cuppini, Italy *(Garelli)*, 2m 27.20s, 103.17mph/166.025kph

Round 4 15 May, Salzburgring, Austria (17 laps, 44.71 miles/71.951kms)

1 E. Cuppini, Italy *(Garelli)*, 27m 17.50s, 98.55mph/158.6kph
2 A. Gramigni, Italy *(MBA)*; 3 M. Baumann, Austria *(MBA)*; 4 A. Kempener, Belgium *(MBA)*; 5 O. Schuler, Switzerland *(MBA)*; 6 D. Hafeneger, W. Germany *(Moto Wuelframix)*; 7 P. Paolucci, Italy *(AGV)*; 8 T. Rinne, Finland *(MBA)*; 9 A. Gangelberger, Austria *(MBA)*; 10 R. Dova, Italy *(AGV)*; 11 J. Piepponen, Finland *(Garelli)*; 12 P. Bordes, France *(MBA)*; 13 K. D. Kindle, Luxembourg *(Honda)*;14 M. Hernandez, Spain *(Honda)*; 15 M. Nikolay, Belgium *(MBA)*.

Round 5 12 June, Most, Czechoslovakia (20 laps, 51.56 miles/82.98kms)

1 E. Cuppini, Italy *(Garelli)*, 35m 33.26s, 86.99mph/140.00kph
2 O. Schuler, Switzerland *(MBA)*; 3 A. Gramigni, Italy *(MBA)*; 4 T. Rinne, Finland *(MBA)*; 5 A. Kempener, Belgium *(MBA)*; 6 R. Rosnell, Finland *(MBA)*; 7 D. Raudies, W. Germany *(Honda)*; 8 B. Strack, W. Germany *(Honda)*; 9 C. Jensen, Denmark *(MBA)*; 10 U. Heider, W. Germany *(MBA)*; 11 P. Bordes, France *(MBA)*; 12 M. Baumann, Austria *(MBA)*; 13 R. Kunz, W. Germany *(Siku Rotax)*; 14 J. Amstutz, Switzerland *(Honda)*; 15 F. Gangelberger, Austria *(LCR)*.
Fastest lap: E. Cuppini, Italy *(Garelli)*, 1m46.13s, 87.43mph/140.70kph

Round 6 21 June, Assen, Netherlands (12 laps, 45.72 miles/73.577kms)

1 E. Cuppini, Italy *(Garelli)*, 30m 12.43s, 90.86mph/146.214kph
2 S. Prein, W. Germany *(Honda)*; 3 A. Gramigni, Italy *(MBA)*; 4 T. Rinne, Finland *(MBA)*; 5 A. Waibel, W. Germany *(Honda)*; 6 O. Schuler, Switzerland *(MBA)*; 7 N. Peschke, W. Germany *(Rotax)*; 8 R. Strack, W. Germany *(Honda)*; 9 A. Gangelberger, Austria *(MBA)*; 10 D. Raudies, W. Germany *(Honda)*; 11 R. Dova, Italy *(MBA)*; 12 K. D. Kindle, Luxembourg *(Honda)*; 13 M. Baumann, Austria *(MBA)*; 14 F. Kistrup, Denmark *(MBA)*; 15 A. Patterson, GB *(Honda)*.
Fastest lap: E. Cuppini, Italy *(Garelli)*, 2m 28.92s, 92.14mph/148.284kph

Round 7 10 July, Misano, San Marino, 2.17m/3.49km (21 laps, 45.50m/73.22km)

1 E. Cuppini, Italy *(Garelli)*, 30m 52.66s, 88.44mph/142.332kph; 2 A. Gramigni, Italy *(MBA)*; 3 D. Romboni, Italy *(AGV)*; 4 K. Galatowicz, GB *(Honda)*; 5 O. Schuler, Switzerland *(MBA)*; 6 G. Debbia, Italy *(MBA)*; 7 R. Dova, Italy *(AGV)*; 8 P. Scappini, Italy *(Faccioli)*; 9 H. Litz, West Germany *(MBA)*; 10 D. Raudies, West Germany *(Honda)*.
Fastest lap: D. Romboni, Italy *(AGV)*, 1m 26.53s, 90.06mph/144.947kph

Round 8 11 September, Jarama, Spain (22 laps, 42.28 miles/72.86kms)

1 E. Cuppini, Italy *(Garelli)*, 35m 38.889s, 76.21mph/122.640kph
2 G. Debbia, Italy *(MBA)*; 3 R. Strack, West Germany *(Honda)*; 4 T. Rinne, Finland *(Honda)*; 5 D. Romboni, Italy *(MBA)*; 6 K. Galatowicz, GB *(Honda)*; 7 R. Dova, Italy *(AGV)*; 8 J. Morillas, Spain *(JJ Cobas)*; 9 P. Bordes, France *(Honda)*; 10 A. Kempener, Belgium *(MBA)*; 11 A. Gramigni, Italy *(MBA)*; 12 D. Raudies, West Germany *(Honda)*; 13 L. D'Antin, Spain *(Honda)*; 14 M. Thurmayer, West Germany *(Honda)*; 15 A. Lasaosa, Spain *(Honda)*.
Fastest lap: E. Cuppini, Italy *(Garelli)*, 1m 35.256s, 77.78mph/125.172kph

250cc

Round 1 12/13 March, Jerez, Spain (20 laps, 52.40 miles/84.33kms)

1 A. Preining, Austria *(Aprilia Rotax)*, 39m 01.56s, 80.59mph/129.690kph
2 P. van den Goorbergh, Netherlands *(Honda)*; 3 C. Boudinot, France *(Fior Rotax)*; 4 U. Jucker, Switzerland *(Yamaha)*; 5 N. Crotta, Switzerland *(Aprilia)*; 6 R. Busch, W. Germany *(Aprilia)*; 7 W. Zeelenberg, Netherlands *(Yamaha)*; 8 B. Schick, W. Germany *(Honda)*; 9 J. M. Lopez, Spain *(Honda)*; 10 R. Orme, GB *(Yamaha)*; 11 Renato Colleoni, Italy *(Aprilia)*; 12 N. Kellemberger, Switzerland *(Yamaha)*; 13 H. Vontobel, Switzerland *(Yamaha)*; 14 A. Borgonovo, Italy *(Aprilia)*; 15 G. Singer, Italy *(Rotax)*.
Fastest lap: A. Preining, Austria *(Aprilia Rotax)*, 1m 54.66s, 81.97mph/131.917kph

Round 2 10 April, Misano, Italy (22 laps, 47.74 miles/76.827kms)

1 A. Borgonovo, Italy *(Aprilia)*, 31m 00.529s, 92.26mph/148.479kph
2 F. Ricci, Italy *(Yamaha)*; 3 B. Haenggeli, Switzerland *(Honda)*; 4 P. van den Goorbergh, Netherlands *(Honda)*; 5 H. Holder, W. Germany *(Seufert)*; 6 M. Iannetta, Italy *(Zamago)*; 7 B. Schick, W. Germany *(Honda)*; 8 C. Boudinot, France *(Fior Rotax)*; 9 W. Zeelenberg, Netherlands *(Yamaha)*; 10 Renato Colleoni, Italy *(Aprilia)*; 11 R. Busch, W. Germany *(Aprilia)*; 12 N. Crotta, Switzerland *(Aprilia)*; 13 T. Bacher, Austria *(Rotax)*; 14 R. Gauthier, France *(Yamaha)*; 15 G. Gambelli, Italy *(Honda)*.
Fastest lap: C. Boudinot, France *(Fior Rotax)*, 1m 23.517s, 93.43mph/150.350kph

Round 3 8 May, Hockenheim, W. Germany (12 laps, 50.62 miles/81.463kms)

1 E. Neumair, Austria *(Aprilia)*, 27m 35.19s, 110.10mph/177.180kph
2 A. Borgonovo, Italy *(Aprilia)*; 3 Renzo Colleoni, Italy *(Aprilia)*; 4 A. Preining, Austria *(Aprilia Rotax)*; 5 W. Zeelenberg, Netherlands *(Yamaha)*; 6 U. Jucker, Switzerland *(Yamaha)*; 7 S. Klabacher, Austria *(Aprilia)*; 8 N. Crotta, Switzerland *(Aprilia)*; 9 R. Busch, W. Germany *(Aprilia)*; 10 R. Orme, GB *(Spondon Rotax)*; 11 M. Fueg, W. Germany *(Rotax)*; 12 H. Holder, W. Germany *(Seufert)*; 13 J. Hutter, Austria *(Honda)*; 14 Renato Colleoni, Italy *(Aprilia)*; 15 H. Becker, W. Germany *(Yamaha)*.
Fastest lap: A. Borgonovo, Italy *(Aprilia)*, 2m 16.26s; 111.45mph/179.355kph

Round 4 17 May, Salzburgring, Austria (18 laps, 47.34 miles/76.18kms)

1 A. Borgonovo, Italy *(Aprilia)*, 26m 35.39s, 107.25mph/172.59kph

2 S. Klabacher, Austria *(Aprilia)*; 3 F. Ricci, Italy *(Aprilia)*; 4 A. Preining, Austria *(Aprilia)*; 5 Renzo Colleoni, Italy *(Aprilia)*; 6 P. van den Goorbergh, Netherlands *(Honda)*; 7 J. Hutter, Austria *(Honda)*; 8 N. Crotta, Italy *(Aprilia)*; 9 M. Houssin, Belgium *(Yamaha)*; 10 B. Schick, W. Germany *(Bischof)*; 11 H. Becker, W. Germany *(Yamaha)*; 12 H. Holder, W. Germany *(Siefert)*; 13 C. Doorakkers, Netherlands *(Honda)*; 14 B. Haenggeli, Switzerland *(Honda)*; 15 W. Horhager, Austria *(Honda)*.

Round 5 12 June, Most, Czechoslovakia (22 laps, 56.72 miles/91.28kms)

1 F. Ricci, Italy *(Aprilia)*, 36m 32.86s, 93.09mph/149.814kph
2 A. Borgonovo, Italy *(Aprilia)*; 3 Renzo Colleoni, Italy *(Aprilia)*; 4 K. Doorakkers, Netherlands *(Honda)*; 5 R. Busch, W. Germany *(Aprilia)*; 6 U. Jucker, Switzerland *(Yamaha)*; 7 W. Zeelenberg, Netherlands *(Yamaha)*; 8 R. Orme, GB *(Yamaha)*; 9 Renato Colleoni, Italy *(Aprilia)*; 10 F. Protat, France *(Pelosi)*; 11 N. Bosworth, GB *(Aprilia)*; 12 B. Haenggeli, Switzerland *(Honda)*; 13 F. Girod-Roux, France *(Yamaha)*; 14 S. Hutter, Austria *(Honda)*; 15 C. Boudinot, France *(Fior Rotax)*.
Fastest lap: F. Ricci, Italy *(Aprilia)*, 1m 39.22s, 93.52mph/150.50kph

Round 6 21 June, Assen, Netherlands (14 laps, 53.34 miles/85.840kms)

1 F. Ricci, Italy *(Aprilia)*, 33m 05.55s, 96.75mph/155.702kph
2 W. Zeelenberg, Netherlands *(Yamaha)*; 3 N. Bosworth, GB *(Aprilia)*; 4 E. Neumair, Austria *(Aprilia)*; 5 R. Busch, W. Germany *(Aprilia)*; 6 Renzo Colleoni, Italy *(Aprilia)*; 7 H. Backer, W. Germany *(Yamaha)*; 8 J. Hutter, Austria *(Honda)*; 9 H. Holder, W. Germany *(Yamaha)*; 10 Renato Colleoni, Italy *(Aprilia)*; 11 C. Boudinet, France *(Fior Rotax)*; 12 B. Schick, W. Germany *(Honda)*; 13 P. van den Goorbergh, Netherlands *(Honda)*; 14 B. Haenggeli, Switzerland *(Honda)*; 15 N. Crotta, Switzerland *(Aprilia)*.
Fastest lap: F. Ricci, Italy *(Aprilia)*, 2m 20.14s, 97.91mph/157.574kph

Round 7 10 July, Misano, San Marino 2.17m/3.49km (22 laps, 47.68m/76.736km)

1 A. Preining, Austria *(Aprilia)*, 30m 36.67s, 93.46mph/150.408kph; 2 Renzo Colleoni, Italy *(Aprilia)*; 3 E. Neumair, Austria *(Aprilia)*; 4 A. Borgonovo, Austria *(Aprilia)*; 5 Renato Colleoni, Italy *(Aprilia)*; 6 C. Boudinot, France *(Fior)*; 7 U. Jucker, Switzerland *(Yamaha)*; 8 R. Antonellini, Italy *(Yamaha)*; 9 B. Haenggeli, Switzerland *(Honda)*; 10 B. Schick, West Germany *(Honda)*.
Fastest lap: Renzo Colleoni, Italy *(Aprilia)*, 1m 22.34s, 94.76mph/152.499kph

Round 8 4 September, Le Mans, France (18 laps, 47.34 miles/76.18kms)

1 F. Ricci, Italy *(Aprilia)*, 38m 34.15s, 74.245mph/119.483kph
2 Renzo Colleoni, Italy *(Aprilia)*; 3 B. Haenggeli, Switzerland *(Honda)*; 4 B. Bonhuil, France *(Honda)*; 5 H. Duffard, France *(Honda)*; 6 B. Kassner, West Germany *(Yamaha)*; 7 S. Minich, Belgium *(Yamaha)*; 8 A. Borgonovo, Italy *(Aprilia)*; 9 U. Jucker, Switzerland *(Yamaha)*; 10 M. Houssin, Belgium *(Yamaha)*; 11 A. Preining, Austria *(Aprilia)*; 12 G. Gambelli, Italy *(Honda)*; 13 A. Bronec, France *(Honda)*; 14 M. Biegert, West Germany *(Honda)*; 15 L. Naveau, Belgium *(Honda)*.
Fastest lap: S. Minich, Austria *(Yamaha)*; 2m 06.7s, 74.728mph/120.253kph

Round 9 11 September, Jarama, Spain (23 laps, 47.33miles/76.17kms)

1 F. Ricci, Italy *(Aprilia)*, 35m 33.880s, 79.86mph/128.516kph
2 A. Preining, Austria *(Aprilia)*; 3 U. Jucker, Switzerland *(Yamaha)*; 4 Renzo Colleoni, Italy *(Aprilia)*; 5 E. Neumair, Austria *(Rotax)*; 6 B. Bonhuil, France *(Honda)*; 7 C. Munoz, Spain *(JJ Cobas)*; 8 P. van den Goorbegh, Netherlands *(Honda)*; 9 J. Hutter, Austria *(Honda)*; 10 A. Bronec, France *(Honda)*; 11 K. Doorakkers, Netherlands *(Honda)*; 12 B. Issazadhe, Sweden *(Honda)*; 13 R. Busch, West Germany *(Aprilia)*; 14 C. Boudinot, France *(Fior)*; 15 G. Gambelli, Italy *(Honda)*.
Fastest lap: U. Jucker, Switzerland *(Yamaha)*, 1m 31.563s, 80.92mph/130.220kph

Round 10 25 September, Donington Park (20 laps, 50m/80.465k)

1 W. Zeelenberg, Netherlands *(Yamaha)*, 34m 50.82s, 86.09mph/138.546kmh; 2 G. Cowan, Ireland *(Yamaha)*; 3 W. Coulter, Ireland *(Honda)*; 4 U. Jucker, Switzerland *(Yamaha)*; 5 A. Carter, GB *(Yamaha)*; 6 A. Preining, Austria *(Aprilia)*; 7 Renzo Colleoni, Italy *(Aprilia)*; 8 C. Boudinot, France *(Fior)*; 9 F. Ricci, Italy *(Aprilia)*; 10 S. Patrickson, GB *(Rotax)*; 11 Renato Colleoni, Italy *(Aprilia)*; 12 F. Furlan, Italy *(Honda)*; 13 J. Hutter, Austria *(Honda)*; 14 A. Kempener, Belgium *(Aprilia)*; 15 R. Antonellini, Italy *(Yamaha)*.
Fastest lap: G. Cowan, Ireland *(Yamaha)*, 1m 41.21s, 88.92mph/143.10kmh

500cc

Round 1 12/13 March, Jerez, Spain (23 laps, 60.26 miles/96.98kms)

1 F. Barchitta, San Marino *(Honda)*, 45m 09.67s, 80.09mph/128.890kph
2 A. Rota, Italy *(Honda)*; 3 V. Scatola, Italy *(Paton)*; 4 S. Manley, GB *(Suzuki)*; 5 K. Truchsess, Austria *(Honda)*; 6 M. Valdo, Italy *(Paton)*; 7 P. Schleef, W. Germany *(Honda)*; 8 M. Duyzer, Netherlands *(Honda)*; 9 N. Schmasmann, Switzerland *(Honda)*; 10 M. Rudroff, W. Germany *(Honda)*; 11 D. Leach, GB *(Suzuki)*; 12 I. Pratt, GB *(Suzuki)*; 13 R. Zeller, Austria *(Honda)*; 14 J. Doppler, Austria *(Honda)*; 15 T. Zasiansen, Norway *(Suzuki)*.
Fastest lap: V. Scatola, Italy *(Paton)*, 1m 55.76s, 81.51mph/131.174kph

Round 2 10 April, Misano, Italy (26 laps, 56.42 miles/90.796kms)

1 V. Scatola, Italy *(Paton)*, 36m 27.405s, 92.74mph/149.253kph
2 A. Rota, Italy *(Honda)*; 3 R. Balbi, Italy *(Honda)*; 4 S. Manley GB *(Suzuki)*; 5 K. Truchsess, Austria *(Honda)*; 6 M. Rudroff, W. Germany *(Honda)*; 7 R. Boggiani, Italy *(Suzuki)*; 8 D. Dixon, GB *(Suzuki)*; 9 L. Becheroni, Italy *(Suzuki)*; 10 A. Ramo, Finland *(Honda)*; 11 B. Scatola, Italy *(Honda)*; 12 M. Maestri, Italy *(Suzuki)*; 13 S. Habat, Yugoslavia *(Honda)*; 14 J. L. Demierre, Switzerland *(Suzuki)*; 15 A. Leuthe, Luxembourg *(Suzuki)*.
Fastest lap: V. Scatola, Italy *(Paton)*, 1m 22.939s, 94.08mph/151.398kph

Round 3 8 May, Hockenheim, W. Germany (14 laps, 59.06 miles/95.040kms)

1 K. Truchsess, Austria *(Honda)*, 31m 18.01s, 113.21mph/182.185kph
2 M. Rudroff, W. Germany *(Honda)*; 3 G. Jung, W. Germany *(Honda)*; 4 A. Rota, Italy

(Honda); 5 J. Doppler, Austria *(Honda)*; 6 P. Skoeld, Sweden *(Honda)*; 7 S. Manley, GB *(Suzuki)*; 8 A. Ramo, Finland *(Honda)*; 9 M. Duyzers, Netherlands *(Honda)*; 10 D. Dixon, GB *(Suzuki)*; 11 S. Pennese, Italy *(Honda)*; 12 J. L. Demierre, Switzerland *(Suzuki)*; 13 H. Klingebiel, W. Germany *(Suzuki)*; 14 A. Meyer, W. Germany *(Honda)*; 15 L. Johansson, Sweden *(Suzuki)*.
Fastest lap: K. Truchsess, Austria *(Honda)*, 2m 13.08s, 114.11mph/183.641kph

Round 4 12 June, Most, Czechoslovakia (24 laps, 61.87 miles/99.57kms)

1 K. Truchsess, Austria *(Honda)*, 40m 14.07s, 92.25mph/148.458kph
2 A. Rota, Italy *(Honda)*; 3 M. Duyzers, Netherlands *(Honda)*; 4 M. Rudroff, W. Germany *(Honda)*; 5 S. Pennese, Italy *(Honda)*; 6 M. Valdo, Italy *(Paton)*; 7 M. Maestri, Italy *(Suzuki)*; 8 A. Ramo, Finland *(Honda)*; 9 H. Butz, W. Germany *(Honda)*; 10 I. Pratt, GB *(Suzuki)*; 11 R. Gachter, Switzerland *(Yamaha)*; 12 H. Klingebiel, W. Germany *(Suzuki)*; 13 R. Zeller, Austria *(Honda)*; 14 M. Kaplan, Austria *(Honda)*; 15 M. Morselli, Italy *(Honda)*.
Fastest lap: A. Rota, Italy *(Honda)*, 1m 39.96s, 92.83mph/149.39kph

Round 5 21 June, Assen, Netherlands (15 laps, 57.15 miles/91.971kms)

1 F. Barchitta, San Marino *(Honda)*, 35m 23.95s, 96.91mph/155.953kph
2 M. Duyzers, Netherlands *(Honda)*; 3 A. Rota, Italy *(Honda)*; 4 S. Manley, GB *(Suzuki)*; 5 H. de Vries, Netherlands *(Honda)*; 6 S. Pennese, Italy *(Honda)*; 7 M. Rudroff, W. Germany *(Honda)*; 8 S. Habat, Yugoslavia *(Honda)*; 9 K. van der Endt, Netherlands *(Honda)*; 10 J. Doppler, Austria *(Honda)*; 11 H. Butz, W. Germany *(Honda)*; 12 T. Louwes, Netherlands *(Suzuki)*; 13 B. Scatola, Italy *(Suzuki)*; 14 H. Schutz, W. Germany *(Honda)*; 15 J. L. Demierre, Switzerland *(Suzuki)*.
Fastest lap: F. Barchitta, San Marino *(Honda)*, 2m 20.37s, 97.75mph/157.316kph

Round 6 10 July, Misano, San Marino 2.17m/3.49km (27 laps, 58.52m/94.176km)

1 A. Rota, Italy *(Honda)*, 37m 27.69s, 93.73mph/150.836kph; 2 M. Broccoli, Italy *(Cagiva)*; 3 F. Barchitta, San Marino *(Honda)*; 4 M. Massimo, Italy *(Suzuki)*; 5 R. Balbi, Italy *(Honda)*; 6 A. Leuthe, Luxembourg *(Suzuki)*; 7 M. Rudroff, West Germany *(Honda)*; 8 S. Pennese, Italy *(Honda)*; 9 V. Scatola, Italy *(Paton)*; 10 M. Duyzers, Netherlands *(Honda)*.
Fastest lap: A. Rota, Italy *(Honda)*, 1m 22.32s, 94.78mph/152.536kph

Round 7 4 September, Le Mans, France (22 laps, 57.86 miles/93.11kms)

1 R. Nicotte, France *(Honda)*, 44m 39.42s, 78.37mph/126.127kph
2 D. Leach, GB *(Suzuki)*; 3 A. Rota, Italy *(Honda)*; 4 M. Rudroff, West Germany *(Honda)*; 5 M. Trosch, West Germany *(Honda)*; 6 A. Meyer, West Germany *(Honda)*; 7 H. Klingebeil, West Germany *(Suzuki)*; 8 B. Andrault, France *(Suzuki)*; 9 D. Pauget, France *(Honda)*; 10 T. Paavilainen, Finland *(Suzuki)*; 11 V. Scatola, Italy *(Paton)*; 12 M. Phillips, GB *(Suzuki)*; 13 N. Schmassann, Switzerland *(Honda)*; 14 C. Burki, Switzerland *(Honda)*; 15 J. L. Demierre, Switzerland *(Suzuki)*.
Fastest lap: D. Leach, GB *(Suzuki)* & A. Rota, Italy *(Honda)*, 1m 55.5s, 81.974mph/131.913kph.

Round 8 11 September, Jarama, Spain (28 laps, 57.62 miles/92.73kms)

1 A. Rota, Italy *(Honda)*, 43m 51.798s, 78.83mph/126.854kph
2 A. Leuthe, Luxembourg *(Suzuki)*; 3. V. Scatola, Italy *(Paton)*; 4 M. Duyzers, Netherlands *(Honda)*; 5 S. Pennese, Italy *(Honda)*; 6 S. Manley, GB *(Suzuki)*; 7 H. Schmassmann, Switzerland *(Honda)*; 8 M. Rudroff, West Germany *(Honda)*; 9 J. L. Demierre, Switzerland *(Suzuki)*; 10 M. Phillips, GB *(Suzuki)*; 11 C. Burki, Switzerland *(Suzuki)*; 12 H. Klingebiel, West Germany *(Suzuki)*; 13 I. Lovasi, Hungary *(Yamaha)*; 14 K. Steinberger, Austria *(Suzuki)*; 15 L. Bori, Hungary *(Yamaha)*.
Fastest lap: A. Rota, Italy *(Honda)*, 1m 32.762, 79.87mph/128.537kph

Round 9 25 September, Donington Park (25 laps, 62.5m/100.58k)

1 D. Dixon, GB *(Suzuki)*, 45m 24.65s, 82.57mph/132.89kmh; 2 S. Spray, GB *(Suzuki)*; 3 K. Doorakkers, Netherlands *(Honda)*; 4 T. Bastiansen, Norway *(Suzuki)*; 5 M. Valdo, Italy *(Paton)*; 6 A. Rota, Italy *(Honda)*; 7 V. Scatola, Italy *(Paton)*; 8 M. Phillips, GB *(Suzuki)*; 9 D. Hedegard, Sweden *(Suzuki)*; 10 H. Klingebiel, Switzerland *(Suzuki)*; 11 S. Pennese, Italy *(Honda)*; 12 G. Bruhn, Sweden *(Honda)*; 13 L. Johansson, Sweden *(Suzuki)*; 14 M. Grein, West Germany *(Suzuki)*.
Only 14 finishers
Fastest lap: D. Dixon, GB *(Suzuki)*, 1m 44.07, 86.48mph/139.18kmh

Sidecar

Round 1 8 May, Hockenheim, W. Germany (12 laps, 50.62 miles/81.463kms)
1 T. Wyssen/K. Wyssen, Switzerland *(LCR Yamaha)*, 28m 39.87s, 105.96mph/170.517kph
2 R. Gardner/T. Strevens, GB *(Yamaha)*; 3 G. Knight/P. Coombes, GB *(Yamaha)*; 4 T. Baker/J. Cochrane, GB *(Baker Yamaha)*; 5 M. Burcombe/J. Gibbard, GB *(Krauser)*; 6 A. Heck/K. Sturm, W. Germany *(Schwarzel LCR)*; 7 E. Lauer/N. Wild, W. Germany *(Honda Busch)*; 8 H. Golemba/R. Barrillon, France *(Yamaha)*; 9 L. Hurst/G. Hurst, GB *(Yamaha)*; 10 R. Clerc/C. Goudard, Switzerland *(Seymaz Yamaha)*; 11 P. Atkinson/G. Simmons, GB *(LCR)*; 12 Lorielle/Lorielle, France *(Elf Seymaz)*; 13 P. Lemstrap/E. Nap, Netherlands *(Yamaha)*; 14 G. Thomas/K. Morgan, GB *(Yamaha)*; 15 K. Howles/S. Pointer, GB *(LCR)*.
Fastest lap: T. Wyssen/K. Wyssen, Switzerland *(LCR Yamaha)*, 2m 21.54s, 107.29mph/172.664kph

Round 2 12 June, Most, Czechoslovakia (21 laps, 54.14 miles/87.12kms)

1 T. Wyssen/K. Wyssen, Switzerland *(LCR Yamaha)*, 36m 06.99s, 89.92mph/144.712kph
2 J. Evans/I. Gaunt, GB *(Yamaha)*; 3 G. Hardwick/Day, GB *(LCR)*; 4 B. Smith/D. Smith, GB *(Windle Yamaha)*; 5 P. Atkinson/G. Simmons, GB *(LCR Yamaha)*; 6 J. Stekelenberg/R. Bettgens, Netherlands *(Windle Yamaha)*; 7 H. Golemba/R. Barrillon, France *(LCR Yamaha)*; 8 A. Heck/A. Racke, W. Germany *(Schwarzel Yamaha)*; 9 J. Heriot/J. L. Heriot, France *(Yamaha)*; 10 K. Howels/S. Pointer, GB *(LCR Yamaha)*; 11 P. Lemstrap/E. Nap, Netherlands *(LCR Yamaha)*; 12 M. Burcombe/J. Gibbard, GB *(LCR Krauser)*; 13 E. Lauer/N. Wild, W. Germany *(Busch Honda)*; 14 R. Gardner/T.

Strevens, GB *(LCR Yamaha)*; 15 R. Clerc/C. Gaudard, Switzerland *(Yamaha)*.
Fastest lap: T. Wyssen/K. Wyssen, Netherlands *(LCR Yamaha)*, 1m41.18s, 91.71mph/147.59kph

Round 3 21 June, Assen, Netherlands (12 laps, 45.72 miles/73.577kms)

1 T. Wyssen/K. Wyssen, Netherlands *(LCR Yamaha)*, 30m 00.51s, 91.452mph/ 147.174kph
2 G. Hardwick/S. Parker, GB *(LCR)*; 3 T. Baker/J. Cochrane, GB *(Baker Yamaha)*; 4 P. Atkinson/G. Simmons, GB *(LCR Yamaha)*; 5 J. Evans/I. Gaunt, GB *(Yamaha)*; 6 J. van Stekelenberg/R. Bettgens, Netherlands *(Windle Yamaha)*; 7 R. Clerc/C. Gaudard, Switzerland *(Seymaz JPX)*; 8 K. Howles/S. Pointer, GB *(LCR Yamaha)*; 9 A. Gieseman/G. Gieseman, W. Germany *(LCR Yamaha)*; 10 G. Arlati/V. Montanelli, Italy *(LCR Yamaha)*; 11 G. Thomas/K. Morgan, GB *(Yamaha)*; 12 B. Gallros/K. Andreasen, Sweden *(LCR Yamaha)*; 13 P. Lemstrap/G. de Haas, Netherlands *(Yamaha)*; only 13 classified as finishers.
Fastest lap: T. Wyssen/K. Wyssen, Switzerland *(LCR Yamaha)*, 2m 27.14s, 93.26mph/150.077kph

Round 4 4 September, Le Mans, France (17 laps, 45.05 miles/72.50kms)

1 I. Nigrowsky/M. Charpentier, France *(Semaz JPX)*, 32m 30.93s, 93.66mph/150.72kph
2 T. Wyssen/K. Wyssen, Netherlands *(LCR Yamaha)*; 3 W. Kraus/U. Schuster, West Germany *(Busch)*; 4 T. Baker/A. Wadworth, GB *(Baker Yamaha)*; 5 C. Stirrat/S. Prior, GB *(GPX LCR)*; 6 J. van Stekelenburg/R. Bettgens, Netherlands *(Windle Yamaha)*; 7 D. Lacour/P. Marais, France *(Busch Suzuki)*; 8 B. Smith/D. Smith, GB *(Windle Yamaha)*; 9 E. Weber/E. Rosinger, West Germany *(Sigma)*; 10 R. Clerc/C. Gaudard, Switzerland *(Seymaz)*; 11 P. Atkinson/G. Simmons, GB *(LCR Yamaha)*; 12 J. Drew/B. Houghton, GB *(Windle Yamaha)*; 13 P. Lemstra/G. de Hass, Netherlands *(LCR Yamaha)*; 14 K. Howles/S. Parker, GB *(LCR Yamaha)*; 15 G. Thomas/K. Morgan, GB *(Yamaha)*.
Fastest lap: W. Kraus/U. Schuster, West Germany *(Busch)* 1m 52.91s; 87.34mph/ 136.0218kph

Round 5 25 September, Donington Park (20 laps, 50m/80.465k)

1 T. Wyssen/K. Wyssen, Netherlands *(LCR Yamaha)*, 35m 15.43s, 85.08mph, 136.93kmh; 2 R. Gardner/T. Strevens, GB *(LCR Yamaha)*; 3 C. Stirrat/S. Prior, GB *(LCR)*; 4 G. Thomas/E. Rosinger, GB *(LCR)*; 5 G. Hardwick/S. Parker, GB *(LCR)*; 6 B. Smith/D. Smith, GB *(Windle Yamaha)*; 7 R. Clerc/F. Luond, France *(Seymaz JPX)*; 8 J. Evans/I. Gaunt, GB *(LCR)*; 9 M. Burcombe/J. Gibbard, GB *(LCR Krauser)*; 10 J. van Stekelenberg/R. Bettgens, Netherlands *(Windle)*; 11 H. Golemba/A. Barillon, France *(Yamaha)*; 12 P. Atkinson/G. Simmons, GB *(LCR Yamaha)*; 13 K. Howles/S. Pointer, GB *(LCR)*; 14 L. Hurst/P. Coombes, GB *(Honda)*; 15 G. Knight/P. Jackson, GB *(Yamaha)*.
Fastest lap: R. Gardner/T. Strevens, GB *(LCR Yamaha)*, 1m 44.21s, 86.36mph/ 138.98kmh.

Final European Championship positions

500cc
1 A. Rota, Italy *(Honda)*, 144 points; 2 M. Rudroff, West Germany *(Honda)*, 85; 3 V. Scatola, Italy *(Paton)*, 69; 4 M. Duyzers, Netherlands *(Honda)*, 66; 5 K. Truchsess, Austria *(Honda)*, 62; 6 S. Manley, GB *(Suzuki)*, 61; 7 F. Barchitta, Italy *(Honda)*, 55; 8 S. Pennese, Italy *(Honda)*, 50; 9 M. Valdo, Italy *(Paton)*, 33; 10 D. Dixon, GB *(Suzuki)*, 29.

250cc
1 F. Ricci, Italy *(Aprilia)*, 119 points; 2 Renzo Colleoni, Italy *(Aprilia)*, 107; 3 A. Preining, Austria *(Aprilia)*, 98; 4 A. Borgonovo, Italy *(Aprilia)*, 97; 5 U. Jucker, Switzerland *(Yamaha)*, 77; 6 W. Zeelenberg, Netherlands *(Yamaha)*, 73; 7 E. Neumair, Austria *(Aprilia)*, 59; 8 C. Boudinot, France *(Fior)*, 49; 9 R. Busch, West Germany *(Aprilia)*, 47; 10 B. Haenggeli, Switzerland *(Honda)*, 45.

125cc
1 E. Cuppini, Italy *(Garelli)*, 147 points; 2 A. Gramigni, Italy *(MBA)*, 104; 3 O. Schuler, Switzerland *(MBA)*, 64; 4 R. Dova, Italy *(AGV)*, 60; 5 A. Kempener, Belgium *(MBA)*, 58; 6=G. Debbia, Italy *(MBA)*, and T. Rinne, Finland *(Honda)*, both 57; 8 D. Romboni, Italy *(MBA)*, 43; 9 K. Galatowicz, GB *(Honda)*, 41; 10 P. Bordes, France *(MBA)*, 37.

80cc
1 B. Nikolov, Bulgaria *(Krauser)*, 82 points; 2 J. Szabo, Hungary *(Krauser)*, 67; 3 A. Nijenhuis, Netherlands *(Casal)*, 62; 4 H. Koopman, Netherlands *(Ziegler)*, 49; 5 P. Bordes, France *(RB Moto)*, 42; 6=J. Lutzenberger, West Germany *(Eberhardt)* and J. Pintar, Yugoslavia *(Eberhardt)*, both 39; 8 B. Smit, Netherlands *(Krauser)*, 37; 9 R. Waldman, West Germany *(Rotax)*, 37; 10 M. Gschwander, West Germany *(Seel)*, 33.

Sidecar
1 T. Wyssen/K. Wyssen, Netherlands *(LCR Yamaha)*, 97 points; 2 G. Hardwick/S. Parker, GB *(LCR)*, 43; 3 T. Baker/J. Cochrane/A. Wadworth, GB *(Baker Yamaha)*, 41; 4 P. Atkinson/G. Simmons, GB *(LCR Yamaha)*, 38; 5=J. Evans/I. Gaunt, GB *(LCR)*, R. Gardner/T. Strevens, GB *(LCR Yamaha)* and J. van Stekelenberg/R. Bettgens, Netherlands *(Windle)*, all 36; 8 B. Smith/D. Smith, GB *(Windle Yamaha)*, 31; 9 R. Clerc/C. Goudard/F. Luond, France *(Seymaz JPX)*, 30; 10 C. Stirrat/S. Prior, GB *(LCR)*, 26.

1988 ISLE OF MAN TT RACES, 3 June – 8 June, Mountain Circuit 37.73m/60.719k

It was a great TT in 1988 – but one that had that familiar dark cloud hanging ominously over the proceedings, following three fatal accidents. Of course the TT is always going to be dangerous and there will always be riders wanting to compete on the $37\frac{3}{4}$ mile mountain circuit, the most demanding in the world.

What must be done is to make both practice and racing as safe as the nature of the course will allow. This has not always been the case – especially with the already limited practice sessions, often curtailed or cancelled because of the unpredictable Manx weather.

The eight-race programme was always far too large to fit into two weeks of practice and racing, particularly with one session ruled out because of rain. The fatal crash of over-age Brian Warburton, in the Production C race, also brought the races a great deal of bad publicity, although it would be difficult for the ACU to check everybody's birth certificate. The race programme is now going to be streamlined and qualification times tightened up, which surely will help. There will always be accidents but everybody must be working, as one, to minimise them and their severity.

In a successful effort to lure the manufacturers and dealers back to the Island the present day TT races are very much Production based. This does not always please the TT purist, but the racing has never been better with lap records tumbling. The TT has to live with the times and this year it proved it's still the greatest motorcycle event, or perhaps festival, in the world. 50,000 visitors enjoyed all the traditional delights plus one not so traditional, some decent weather.

Ulsterman Joey Dunlop can be relied upon to make most of the headlines during TT fortnight and this year was no exception. Not an ill-fated trip in a fishing boat this time but his second TT hat trick and a driving ban, following a drink driving charge. When the roads were closed and he'd not had a drink his performances were stunning and left nobody in any doubt that he's the greatest rider of road circuits in the world today. In the six-lap TT Formula One race on Monday morning he rewrote the record books riding the race-kitted RC 30 Honda after he'd not received the RVF racing machine from Honda. He led from start to finish, breaking his own outright lap record on the second lap and decimating the four-year-old race record. His second lap in perfect conditions was sensational, averaging 118.54mph in 19 minutes 5.8 seconds, although that record lasted just four days.

He was constantly chased hard by impressive Scotsman Steve Hislop on a similar machine. Fresh from his victory in the Production B event on Saturday he put in a superb second lap of 118.44mph but retired with a seized engine at Ballaugh with just one-and-a-half laps to go. His one hair-raising moment came at Dorans bend when he gouged a piece out of his helmet thinking the wall was an ivy hedge. His departure promoted a great battle on the roads between TT stalwarts Nick Jefferies and Geoff Johnson. The two fought out a short circuit duel round the mountain track until Johnson retired on the last lap at Ballacraine with oil pouring from his Bimota Yamaha. Honda-mounted Jefferies continued to clinch second place from a similarly mounted Roger Burnett. The former Senior TT winner fought back bravely after riding 30 miles of the first lap with a flat rear tyre. Lancashire lad Carl Fogarty made it a Honda foursome with Paul Iddon breaking their domination, finishing fifth on the Bimota Yamaha. It was a disaster for Suzuki with Roger Marshall, Phil Mellor, Jamie Whitham and Trevor Nation all failing to finish.

Kawasaki's return to the Island came to grief on the third lap when Roger Hurst crashed out of fifth place at Brandish. Dunlop's victory in the six-lap Senior on Friday was not so clear cut in an epic race that produced two heroes. The first was Dunlop, with another superb display of riding the RC30 Honda between the kerbs. The second was his countryman Steve Cull. He established a new lap record before seeing his RS Honda destroyed by fire less than five miles from the finish of the 226.4-mile race.

For the opening three laps the two Irishmen swapped the lead with Cull bringing the crowd to their feet with a new lap record of 119.08mph in 19 minutes 41.2 seconds. Cull started to drop back with a holed expansion chamber and was down to fourth place, but still determined to finish when the bike burst into flames just past Creg-ny-Baa on the last lap. He was left with that absolute lap record – and a bill for £25,000.

Hislop was second once again with Johnson third. Roger Marshall at last finished on the Suzuki. After changing plugs he really flew on the last lap, averaging 118.19mph, and pushed his great mate Roger Burnett down to fifth.

Despite a fuel stop problem Dunlop, riding the RS 250 Honda, fought off the challenge of the brave Brian Reid to win the three-lap Junior race on Wednesday morning. Reid gave his great rival a hard time, despite riding with a broken toe on his EMC. When Dunlop messed up the pit stop and dropped the fuel cap into the fairing he closed right up, but Dunlop eventually pulled away to win by 20 seconds. Former winner Eddie Laycock was third, on another EMC, while Brian Morrison won the Formula Two Class on his CBR 600 Honda. Steve Hislop may have finished a lowly 24th after having to replace broken exhaust pipes in lengthy pit stops, but he still set a new lap record on his Yamaha of 113.41mph.

Anti-production race protesters were very thin on the ground after the superb four-lap Production A race on Wednesday afternoon which produced one of the closest TT finishes of all time. Just 0·8 seconds separated Yorkshire Yamaha riders Dave Leach and Geoff Johnson. Despite a jumping chain Leach just held Johnson at bay to average a staggering 114.32mph on his FZR road-going Yamaha. Johnson had front disc problems with his Yamaha, but still put in a record lap of 116.55mph, over three mph quicker than Trevor Nation's 1986 record. Once-a-year racer Kevin Wilson was third on his GSX Suzuki with Phil Mellor fourth on a similar machine.

The four-lap Production B race on Saturday afternoon was not as close, but just as interesting, with Hislop and Morrison slogging it out on their RC 30 Hondas. They had had to stop three times to take on fuel but were still in a class of their own with Hislop coming out on top by 12 seconds. Yamaha-mounted Geoff Johnson and Suzuki star Jamie Whitham chased hard but their machinery just did not have the legs to catch the Hondas. In a dramatic last lap Morrison closed the gap to three seconds at Ballaugh but slowed coming down the mountain when his Honda ran short of fuel. Johnson led briefly at the start of the second lap, after the two Hondas had stopped for fuel, but they soon raced past and extended their lead when he also had to pit for petrol.

The evening before Morrison won the Class C Production race after a superb clash with Kawasaki-mounted Roger Hurst. For most of the four-lap race Hurst looked likely to give Kawasaki a memorable return to the Island but Morrison had different ideas. Hurst led for the opening three laps but Morrison, who led on the roads throughout riding his CBR 600 Honda, slowly pulled back the advantage and snatched the lead at Ballaugh on the last lap. Just one-fifth of a second separated Hislop and Leach in a marvellous battle for third, with the Scotsman snatching it on the line.

Barry Woodland won the Production D class for the third year in succession. On the last lap he was lucky to stay on his FZR 400R Yamaha when Brian Warburton's Honda cannoned into him at Greeba Bridge. Until then he was cruising to victory but in the incident he lost his brakes. He limped home just 16 seconds in front of Australian Graeme McGregor, riding the 250 Suzuki he took over the morning of the race. Brian Reid was third in front of journalist Mat Oxley.

Veteran Mick Boddice achieved a lifelong ambition with a double sidecar victory. Former passenger Chas Birks returned to the chair of their 700 Yamaha outfit two years after their crash at Greeba Castle. In the first race on Saturday the old combination completed a perfect non-stop race after fitting a special 16-gallon fuel tank to avoid a fuel stop. Tony Baker looked set for second place until he ran out of petrol at Creg-ny-Baa on the last lap. Kenny Howles and Steve Pointer moved into that second spot on their 700 Yamaha outfit with former winners, 50-year-old Lowry Burton and Pat Cushnahan third.

Mick Hamblin and Bob Smith won the hotly contested Formula Two class. The experienced Dave Saville and Dave Hall led by over a minute at Ramsey on the last lap but dropped to second with fuel starvation.

Boddice's second victory two days later was much harder. The clutch broke on his Yamaha on the first lap. From that moment it was a tough ride for the driver and passenger Birks. Going into the last lap Howles led by two seconds but, with his great moment of triumph looming, he slowed when the chain started jumping the rear sprocket. Boddice grabbed his chance to win his sixth TT with the unfortunate Howles dropping to third behind Burton.

Saville made up for disappointments in the first Formula Two race by winning the second and clinching overall victory. He really had to get his head down on the last lap to beat Hamblin's 26-second advantage from the first race.

A great TT indeed. Next year 13-times winner Dunlop returns to try and break the late Mike Hailwood's 14-win record. Let's hope he can do it – and that dark cloud starts to drift away.

Fifty-seven year old Brian Warburton was killed when he crashed his CBR 600 Honda at Appledene on the third lap of the Production C and D race. Warburton was a well known rider on Northern circuits in the early 70s but had not raced for 12 years. He had been to the Isle of Man before practice week to familiarise himself with the circuit.

Sidecar passenger Ricky Dumble died when he and Scott Renwick crashed their Yamaha into a garden wall at Bray Hill during sidecar practice. The 30-year-old passenger was a market trader from Oakley, near Fife in Scotland.

Electrician Kenny Harmer was killed instantly when he crashed his Honda at the Waterworks during practice. The 37-year-old from Charnock Richard, Lancashire hit a road sign going into the bend.

Results

Friday, 3 June
Production Machines Class C (400cc two-strokes/600cc four-strokes – 3 laps, 113.19m/182.157k)

		h	m	s	mph	kmh
1	B. Morrison, GB *(600 Honda)*	1	23	30.8	108.42	174.480
2	R. Hurst, GB *(600 Kawasaki)*	1	23	33.8	108.36	174.383
3	S. Hislop, GB *(600 Honda)*	1	23	55.6	107.89	173.627
4	D. Leach, GB *(600 Honda)*	1	23	55.8	107.88	173.611
5	S. Ward, GB *(600 Honda)*	1	24	13.4	107.51	173.015
6	A. Batson, GB *(600 Honda)*	1	24	44.0	106.86	171.969
7	K. Mawdsley, GB *(600 Honda)*	1	24	53.8	106.66	171.647
8	R. Swann, GB *(600 Kawasaki)*	1	25	04.6	106.43	171.277
9	M. Seward, GB *(600 Honda)*	1	25	17.0	106.17	170.859
10	N. Jefferies, GB *(600 Honda)*	1	25	17.2	106.17	170.859

11 J. Dunlop, Ireland *(600 Honda)*; 12 C. Fogarty, GB *(600 Honda)*; 13 P. Mellor, GB *(Suzuki)*; 14 R. Jackson, GB *(600 Honda)*; 15 P. Nicholls, GB *(600 Honda)*; 16 R. Dunlop, Ireland *(600 Honda)*; 17 M. Wheeler, GB *(600 Kawasaki)*; 18 D. Dean, GB *(600 Honda)*; 19 H. Selby, GB *(600 Kawasaki)*; 20 D. Glass, GB *(600 Honda)*; 21 D. Griffith, GB *(600 Honda)*; 22 J. Whitham, GB *(600 Suzuki)*; 23 P. Armes, GB *(600 Honda)*; 24 P. Boast GB *(600 Honda)*; 25 R. Knight, GB *(600 Honda)*; 26 R. Talton, GB *(600 Honda)*; 27 R. Burnett, GB *(600 Honda)*; 28 S. Linsdell, GB *(600 Yamaha)*; 29 S. Dowey, GB *(600 Kawasaki)*; 30 M. Birkinshaw, GB *(600 Honda)*; 31 C. Corner, GB *(600 Honda)*; 32 M. Robinson, GB *(600 Honda)*; 33 P. Cranston, Ireland *(600 Honda)*; 34 P. Davis, GB *(600 Honda)*; 35 K. Fox, GB *(600 Honda)*; 36 R. Price, GB *(600 Kawasaki)*; 37 J. Woodie, GB *(Honda)*; 38 M. Casey, GB *(600 Honda)*; 39 J. Hodson, GB *(600 Honda)*; 40 D. Ashton, GB *(600 Honda)*; 41 R. Holden, GB *(600 Suzuki)*; 42 N. Verity, GB *(600 Honda)*; 43 C. Petty, GB *(600 Honda)*; 44 M. Granie, France *(600 Honda)*; 45 T. Rutter, GB *(600 Honda)*; 46 D. O'Leary, GB *(600 Honda)*; 47 M. Farmer, Ireland *(600 Suzuki)*; 48 K. Nicholls, GB *(600 Honda)*; 49 A. Ross, GB *(Honda)*; 50 I. Waine, GB *(600 Honda)*; 51 J. Dewar, GB *(600 Honda)*; 52 P. Wakefield, GB *(Honda)*; 53 D. Bates *(400 Honda)*; 54 P. Martin, GB *(600 Honda)*; 55 G. Morscher, Austria *(600 Honda)*; 56 C. Jeffs, GB *(600 Kawasaki)*; 57 P. Hunt, GB *(500 Gilera)*; 58 S. Graham, GB *(400 Honda)*; 59 J. Nightingale, GB *(600 Honda)*; 60 G. Dickinson, GB *(600 Honda)*.

Record lap: S. Hislop, GB *(600 Honda)*, 20m 36.6s, 109.83mph/176.749kmh.
Old record: G. Padgett, GB *(400 Suzuki)*, 21.40.6s, 104.43mph/168.059kmh (1986).

Practice leaderboard: 1 R. Hurst, GB *(600 Kawasaki)*, 21m 11.6s; 2 B. Jackson, GB *(600 Honda)*, 21m 12.4s; 3 S. Hislop, GB *(600 Honda)*, 21m 22.4s; 4 S. Ward, GB *(600 Honda)*, 21m 36.8s; 5 K. Mawdsley, GB *(600 Honda)*, 21m 37.8s; 6 P. Mellor, GB *(600 Suzuki)*, 21m 45.8s; 7 D. Leach, GB *(600 Honda)*, 21m 49.6s; 8 R. Swann, GB *(600 Kawasaki)*, 21m 59.0s; 9 N. Jefferies, GB *(600 Honda)*, 21m 59.8s; 10 T. Nation, GB *(600 Suzuki)*, 22m 00.2s; 11 J. Dunlop, Ireland *(600 Honda)*, 22m 00.8s; 12 A. Batson, GB *(600 Honda)*, 22m 00.8s; 13 M. Wheeler, GB *(600 Kawasaki)*, 22m 01.0s; 14 J. Whitham,

GB *(600 Suzuki)*, 22m 01.6s; 15 P. Boast, GB *(600 Honda)*, 22m 03.0s; 16 B. Morrison, GB *(600 Honda)*, 22m 05.0s; 17 R. Haynes, GB *(600 Kawasaki)*, 22m 10.0s; 18 M. Robinson, GB *(600 Honda)*, 22m 15.4s; 19 M. Birkinshaw, GB *(600 Honda)*, 22m 15.4s; 20 D. Griffith, GB *(600 Honda)*, 22m 16.6s.

Production Machines Class D (250cc two-strokes/400cc four-strokes, 3 laps, 113.19m/182.157k)

		h	m	s	mph	kmh
1	B. Woodland, GB *(400 Yamaha)*	1	28	35.2	102.21	164.486
2	G. McGregor, Australia *(250 Suzuki)*	1	28	51.2	101.91	164.003
3	B. Reid, Ireland *(400 Yamaha)*	1	28	55.8	101.82	163.858
4	M. Oxley, GB *(400 Yamaha)*	1	29	05.8	101.63	163.553
5	E. Laycock, Ireland *(400 Yamaha)*	1	29	15.6	101.44	163.247
6	I. Duffus, GB *(400 Yamaha)*	1	29	46.8	100.85	162.297
7	C. Bevan, GB *(400 Yamaha)*	1	30	16.0	100.31	161.428
8	S. Cull, Ireland *(250 Suzuki)*	1	31	05.2	99.41	159.980
9	N. Tuxworth, GB *(400 Yamaha)*	1	32	04.8	98.34	158.258
10	C. Faulkner, GB *(250 Yamaha)*	1	32	13.4	98.18	158.001

11 A. Bassett, GB *(250 Yamaha)*; 12 I. McMillan, GB *(250 Yamaha)*; 13 M. Chatterton, GB *(250 Yamaha)*; 14 G. Lee, GB *(250 Yamaha)*; 15 D. Eaves, GB *(250 Yamaha)*; 16 J. Rae, GB *(250 Yamaha)*; 17 S. Murray, GB *(250 Yamaha)*; 18 D. Grigson, GB *(250 Yamaha)*; 19 I. Jones, GB *(250 Honda)*; 20 R. Steele, GB *(250 Yamaha)*; 21 A. Brew, GB *(250 Yamaha)*; 22 G. Broughton, GB *(250 Yamaha)*; 23 D. Trollope, GB *(400 Yamaha)*; 24 R. Allan, GB *(250 Yamaha)*; 25 R. Simmons, GB *(250 Yamaha)*; 26 D. Smith, GB *(250 Yamaha)*; 27 T. Hughes, GB *(250 Honda)*; 28 M. Cain, GB *(250 Suzuki)*; 29 L. Skinner, GB *(250 Yamaha)*; 30 A. Perkins, New Zealand *(250 Yamaha)*; 31 G. Jones, GB *(250 Yamaha)*.

Record lap: B. Woodland, GB *(400 Yamaha)*, 21m 48.6s, 103.79mph/167.029kmh.
Old record: B. Woodland, GB *(400 Yamaha)*, 21m 54.0s, 103.36mph/166.337kmh (1987).
Australia *(250 Suzuki)*, 22m 48.8s; 5 C. Bevan, GB *(400 Yamaha)*; 22m 48.8s; 6 I. Duffus, GB *(400 Yamaha)*, 22m 49.0s; 7 S. Cull, Ireland *(250 Suzuki)*, 22m 55.2s; 8 E. Laycock, Ireland *(400 Yamaha)*, 23m 15.0s; 9 B. Reid, Ireland *(400 Yamaha)*, 23m 18.6s; 10 G. Broughton, GB *(250 Yamaha)*, 23m 22.2s; 11 C. Faulkner, GB *(250 Yamaha)*, 23m 25.2s; 12 G. Lee, GB *(250 Yamaha)*, 23m 46.0s; 13 M. Chatterton, GB *(250 Yamaha)*, 24m 01.2s; 14 A. Bassett, GB *(250 Yamaha)*, 24m 05.6s; 15 N. Tuxworth, GB *(400 Yamaha)*, 24m 16.0s; 16 J. Rae, GB *(250 Yamaha)*, 24m 20.6s; 17 J. Kiddie, GB *(250 Yamaha)*, 24m 26.2s; 18 D. Grigson, GB *(250 Yamaha)*, 24m 42.2s; 19 I. McMillan, GB *(250 Yamaha)*, 24m 42.6s; 20 A. Brew, GB *(250 Yamaha)*, 24m 56.6s.

Saturday, 4 June

Production Machines Class B (500cc two-strokes/750cc four-strokes, 4 laps, 150.92m/242.875k)

		h	m	s	mph	kmh
1	S. Hislop, GB *(750 Honda)*	1	20	38.2	112.29	180.708
2	B. Morrison, GB *(750 Honda)*	1	20	50.6	112.00	180.241
3	G. Johnson, GB *(750 Bimota-Yamaha)*	1	21	19.0	111.35	179.195
4	J. Whitham, GB *(750 Suzuki)*	1	21	40.0	110.88	178.439
5	J. Dunlop, Ireland *(750 Honda)*	1	21	49.4	110.66	178.085
6	N. Jefferies, GB *(750 Honda)*	1	21	59.8	110.43	177.714
7	K. Wilson, Canada *(750 Suzuki)*	1	22	05.8	110.29	177.489
8	D. Leach, GB *(750 Yamaha)*	1	23	10.2	108.87	175.204
9	A. Batson, GB *(750 Suzuki)*	1	23	14.8	108.77	175.043
10	S. Ward, GB *(750 Suzuki)*	1	23	16.0	108.74	174.995

11 I. Young, GB *(750 Suzuki)*; 12 S. Linsdell, GB *(750 Yamaha)*; 13 B. Heath, GB *(750 Honda)*; 14 R. Haynes, GB *(750 Kawasaki)*; 15 I. Duffus, GB *(750 Honda)*; 16 M. Farmer, Ireland *(750 Suzuki)*; 17 R. Marshall, GB *(750 Suzuki)*; 18 H. Selby, GB *(750 Suzuki)*; 19 R. Rose, GB *(750 Suzuki)*; 20 M. Wheeler, GB *(750 Suzuki)*; 21 C. Fargher, GB *(750 Suzuki)*; 22 P. Iddon, GB *(750 Suzuki)*; 23 P. Hogg, GB *(750 Suzuki)*; 24 B. Craine, GB *(750 Suzuki)*; 25 D. Coates, GB *(750 Suzuki)*; 26 R. Holden, GB *(750 Suzuki)*; 27 I. Martin, GB *(750 Yamaha)*; 28 N. Barton, GB *(750 Honda)*; 29 A. Jackson, GB *(750 Suzuki)*; 30 B. Woodland, GB *(750 Yamaha)*; 31 G. Tunstall, GB *(750 Yamaha)*; 32 D. Chatterton, GB *(750 Suzuki)*; 33 H-O. Butenuth, W. Germany *(750 Honda)*; 34 K. Buckley, GB *(750 Yamaha)*; 35 G. Rondelli, GB *(750 Suzuki)*; 36 J. Byrne, Ireland *(750 Suzuki)*; 37 J. Lofthouse, GB *(750 Suzuki)*; 38 A. Dugdale, GB *(750 Yamaha)*; 39 S. Richardson, GB *(750 Suzuki)*; 40 D. Eaves, GB *(750 Suzuki)*; 41 S. Noon, GB *(Suzuki)*; 42 S. Berwick, GB *(750 Suzuki)*; 43 M. Hunt, GB *(750 Yamaha)*; 44 J. Raybould, GB *(750 Suzuki)*; 45 M. Linscott, GB *(750 Suzuki)*; 46 R. Sutcliffe, GB *(750 Suzuki)*; 47 B. Smith, GB *(750 Honda)*; 48 D. Madsen-Mygdal, GB *(750 Honda)*; 49 M. Nofer, GB *(750 Suzuki)*; 50 C. Petty, GB *(750 Suzuki)*; 51 D. Gallagher, GB *(750 Suzuki)*; 52 T. Rutter, GB *(750 Suzuki)*; 53 I. Gibson, Ireland *(750 Kawasaki)*; 54 C. O'Neill, Ireland *(750 Suzuki)*; 55 N. Verity, GB *(750 Kawasaki)*; 56 F. Finch, GB *(750 Suzuki)*; 57 A. Brew, GB *(750 Suzuki)*; 58 N. Rigg, GB *(750 Suzuki)*; 59 P. Lunney, Ireland *(750 Yamaha)*; 60 N. Crawford, GB *(750 Suzuki)*; 61 R. Steele, GB *(750 Suzuki)*; 62 H. Chittka, W. Germany *(750 Suzuki)*; 63 H. Hart, GB *(750 Kawasaki)*; 64 R. Evans, GB *(750 Suzuki)*; 65 P. Catterall, GB *(750 Suzuki)*; 66 R. Sanders, Australia *(750 Suzuki)*; 67 A. Evans, GB *(750 Ducati)*; 68 G. Bilger, W. Germany *(750 Suzuki)*; 69 D. Lloyd, Canada *(750 Suzuki)*.

Record lap: G. Johnson, GB *(Bimota-Yamaha)*, 20m 02.2s, 112.98mph/181.817kmh.
Old record: T. Nation, GB *(Yamaha)*, 20m 16.6s, 111.64mph/179.662kmh (1987).

Practice leaderboard: 1 S. Hislop, GB *(750 Honda)*, 19m 58.0s; 2 B. Morrison, GB *(750 Honda)*, 20m 23.4s; 3 N. Jefferies, GB *(750 Honda)*, 20m 43.6s; 4 G. Johnson, GB *(750 Bimota-Yamaha)*, 20m 45.4s; 5 J. Whitham, GB *(750 Suzuki)*, 20m 45.6s; 6 P. Mellor, GB *(750 Suzuki)*, 20m 48.0s; 7 N. Barton, GB *(750 Honda)*, 20m 49.4s; 8 S. Ward, GB *(750*

Steve Hislop flat out between the banks on his way to victory in the Production B TT.
Mick Boddice and Chas Birks and Tony Baker and James Cochrane avoid a lamp-post in Parliament Square, Ramsey.

Suzuki), 21m 00.4s; 9 B. Heath, GB *(750 Honda)*, 21m 03.8s; 10 S. Linsdell, GB *(750 Yamaha)*, 21m 05.4s; 11 M. Nelson, GB *(750 Suzuki)*, 21m 07.8s; 12 D. Eaves, GB *(750 Suzuki)*, 21m 08.4s; 13 P. Bateson, GB *(750 Suzuki)*, 21m 08.8s; 14 T. Nation, GB *(750 Suzuki)*, 21m 11.8s; 15 I. Young, GB *(750 Suzuki)*, 21m 13.4s; 16 R. Haynes, GB *(750 Kawasaki)*, 21m 14.0s; 17 B. Craine, GB *(750 Suzuki)*, 21m 17.6s; 18 R. Rose, GB *(750 Suzuki)*, 21m 21.0s; 19 R. Marshall, GB *(750 Suzuki)*, 21m 21.4s; 20 I. Duffus, GB *(750 Honda)*, 21m 23.4s.

First Sidecar Race (3 laps, 113.19m/182.157k)

		h m s	mph	kmh
1	M. Boddice, GB C. Birks, GB *(700 Yamaha)*	1 03 54.4	106.27	171.028
2	K. Howles, GB S. Pointer, GB *(700 Yamaha)*	1 04 15.4	105.69	170.086
3	L. Burton, Ireland P. Cushnahan, Ireland *(700 Yamaha)*	1 04 21.4	105.52	169.813
4	D. Plummer, GB S. Parker, GB *(700 Yamaha)*	1 05 16.4	104.04	167.431
5	D. Hallam, GB S. Parker, GB *(700 Yamaha)*	1 05 24.2	103.83	167.093
6	D. Molyneux, GB A. Langton, GB *(700 Yamaha)*	1 05 37.6	103.48	166.530
7	M. Burcombe, GB C. Hardman, GB *(700 Yamaha)*	1 05 41.8	103.37	166.353
8	D. Brown, GB B. Nelson, GB *(750 Yamaha)*	1 05 46.0	103.26	166.176
9	A. Oates, GB J. Bibbard, GB *(700 Yamaha)*	1 07 17.6	100.92	162.410
10	E. Cornes, GB G. Wellington, GB *(750 Yamaha)*	1 08 14.4	99.52	160.157

11 A. May/I. Finch, GB *(750 Yamaha)*; 12 H. Lunemann/M. Cain, W. Germany/GB *(750 Yamaha)*; 13 R. Bellas/G. Knight, GB *(1135 Suzuki)*; 14 S. Pullan/T. Darby, GB *(700 Yamaha)*; 15 I. Pugh/D. Samuel, GB *(700 Yamaha)*; 16 G. Shand/J. Shedden, GB *(998 Suzuki)*; 17 M. Hamblin/R. Smith, GB *(350 F2 Yamaha)*; 18 G. Davies/P. Chappell, GB *(700 Yamaha)*; 19 D. Saville/D. Hall, GB *(350 F2 Yamaha)*; 20 D. Hawes/E. Kiff, GB *(350 F2 Yamaha)*; 21 M. Staiano/A. Fisher, GB *(700 Yamaha)*; 22 J. Holden/D. Burgess, GB *(350 F2 Yamaha)*; 23 D. Founds/G. Irlam, GB *(350 F2 Yamaha)*; 24 K. Brown/S. Langham, GB *(700 Yamaha)*; 25 D. Rumble Snr/S. Wilson, GB *(998 Suzuki)*; 26 T. Eade/F. McDermott, GB *(750 Yamaha)*; 27 J. Phillips/M. Hollis, GB *(750 Yamaha)*; 28 P. Gallagher/D. Gent, GB *(350 F2 Yamaha)*; 29 S. Applegate/R. Appleton, GB *(750 Yamaha)*; 30 B. Cubbon/G. Manon, GB *(750 Yamaha)*; 31 C. Jacobs/K. Waller, GB *(750 Yamaha)*; 32 A. Lewis/W. Annandale, GB *(350 F2 Yamaha)*; 33 D. Casson/M. Ellis, GB *(350 F2 Yamaha)*; 34 B. Davie/G. Morrison, GB *(750 Yamaha)*; 35 G. Roberts/G. Roberts, GB *(997 Kawasaki)*; 36 D. Carnell/A. Peach, GB *(750 Yamaha)*; 37 C. Pritchard/C. Price, GB *(997 Kawasaki)*; 38 R. Munro/S. Christie, GB *(998 Suzuki)*; 39 C.

Andrews/M. Andrews, GB *(750 Yamaha)*; 40 A. Shand/N. Miller, GB *(350 F2 Yamaha)*; 41 M. Dwyer/D. Statham, GB *(350 F2 Yamaha)*; 42 S. Worthington/G. Scott, GB *(350 F2 Yamaha)*; 43 J. Mulchay/F. McGettigan, GB *(998 Suzuki)*.
Fastest lap: M. Boddice/C. Birks, GB *(700 Yamaha)*, 21m 07.6s, 107.15mph/172.436kmh.

Practice leaderboard: 1 M. Boddice/C. Birks, GB *(700 Yamaha)*, 21m 39.4s; 2 D. Molyneux/A. Langton, GB *(700 Yamaha)*, 22m 08.0s; 3 L. Burton/P. Cushnahan, Ireland *(700 Yamaha)*, 22m 15.8s; 4 T. Baker/J. Cochrane, GB *(700 Yamaha)*, 22m 19.2s; 5 G. Rushbrook/G. Leitch, GB *(700 Yamaha)*, 22m 19.2s; 6 D. Brown/B. Nelson, GB *(700 Yamaha)*, 22m 19.2s; 7 N. Smith/D. Wells, GB *(700 Yamaha)*, 22m 33.0s; 8 K. Howles/S. Pointer, GB *(700 Yamaha)*, 22m 34.6s; 9 D. Hall/S. Parker, GB *(700 Yamaha)*, 22m 40.4s; 10 L. Schwartz/L. Gustavsson, Sweden *(750 Yamaha)*, 22m 41.4s; 11 M. Burcombe/C. Hardman, GB *(700 Yamaha)*, 22m 42.2s; 12 E. Cornes/G. Wellington, GB *(750 Yamaha)*, 22m 48.4s; 13 D. Plummer/B. Marris, GB *(700 Yamaha)*, 23m 05.0s; 14 M. Murphy/J. Cushnahan, Ireland *(700 Yamaha)*, 23m 05.4s; 15 B. Davie/G. Morrison, GB *(750 Yamaha)*, 23m 17.8s; 16 R. Corkhill/P. Magee, GB *(700 Yamaha)*, 23m 19.2s; 17 D. Rumble Jnr/G. Keep, GB *(998 Suzuki)*, 23m 20.0s; 18 L. Pallister/I. Marriner, GB *(750 Yamaha)*, 23m 24.0s; 19 A. Oates/H. Oates, GB *(700 Yamaha)*, 23m 36.6s; 20 G. Shand/J. Shedden, GB *(998 Suzuki)*, 23m 47.2s.

Monday, 6 June

TT Formula One 750cc (6 laps, 226.38m/364.313k)

		h m s	mph	kmh
1	J. Dunlop, Ireland *(Honda)*	1 56 50.2	116.25	187.081
2	N. Jefferies, GB *(Honda)*	1 57 58.2	115.13	185.278
3	R. Burnett, GB *(Honda)*	2 00 05.2	113.09	181.995
4	C. Fogarty, GB *(Honda)*	2 00 19.0	112.89	181.673
5	P. Iddon, GB *(Bimota-Yamaha)*	2 00 28.2	112.74	181.432
6	M. Farmer, Ireland *(Suzuki)*	2 00 45.4	112.48	181.014
7	B. Morrison, GB *(Honda)*	2 01 51.6	111.46	179.372
8	S. Ward, GB *(Suzuki)*	2 02 05.2	111.25	179.034
9	D. Leach, GB *(Bimota-Yamaha)*	2 02 40.4	110.72	178.213
10	B. Reid, Ireland *(Kawasaki)*	2 02 50.2	110.57	177.940

11 B. Woodland, GB *(Bimota-Yamaha)*; 12 G. Linder, GB *(Yamaha)*; 13 R. Dunlop, Ireland *(Honda)*; 14 P. Nicholls, GB *(500 Yamaha)*; 15 K. Wilson, Canada *(Suzuki)*; 16 B. Heath, GB *(350 Yamaha)*; 17 I. Young, GB *(Suzuki)*; 18 R. Jackson, GB *(Suzuki)*; 19 R. Haynes, GB *(Kawasaki)*; 20 M. Wheeler, GB *(Suzuki)*; 21 D. Chatterton, GB *(Suzuki)*; 22 R. Rose, GB *(Suzuki)*; 23 G. Radcliffe, GB *(Honda)*; 24 C. Gable, GB *(Honda)*; 25 E. Galbraith, GB *(Suzuki)*; 26 J. Lofthouse, GB *(Suzuki)*; 27 P. Boast, GB *(Yamaha)*; 28 D. Coates, GB *(Suzuki)*; 29 K. Buckley, GB *(750 Yamaha)*; 30 C. Fargher, GB *(750 Suzuki)*; 31 P. Davies, GB *(Suzuki)*; 32 S. Johnson, GB *(Suzuki)*; 33 R. Sutcliffe, GB *(Suzuki)*; 34 D. Bates, GB *(Suzuki)*; 35 S. Richardson, GB *(Suzuki)*; 36 M. Westmorland, GB *(Yamaha)*; 37 G. Tunstall, GB *(Yamaha)*; 38 J. Caffrey, GB *(Yamaha)*; 39 S. Berwick, GB *(Suzuki)*; 40 A. Ross, GB *(Suzuki)*; 41 D. Madsen-

Mygdal, GB *(Honda)*; 42 S. Noon, GB *(Suzuki)*; 43 M. Williams, GB *(Honda)*; 44 M. Stengl, Austria *(Suzuki)*; 45 S. Taylor, GB *(Suzuki)*; 46 M. Bowen, GB *(Suzuki)*; 47 M. Guymer, GB *(Honda)*; 48 A. Jackson, GB *(Suzuki)*; 49 G. Higginson, GB *(Suzuki)*; 50 J. Raybould, GB *(Suzuki)*; 51 R. Sherry, GB *(Suzuki)*; 52 M. Brookes, GB *(Ducati)*; 53 I. Martin, GB *(Yamaha)*; 54 B. Richards, GB *(Suzuki)*; 55 N. Stothert, GB *(Suzuki)*; 56 A. Moll, W. Germany *(Suzuki)*; 57 H. Bolliger, Switzerland *(Suzuki)*; 58 D. Woolams, GB *(Suzuki)*; 59 D. Kerby, GB *(Kawasaki)*; 60 N. Crawford, GB *(Suzuki)*; 61 R. Jeffreys, GB *(Yamaha)*; 62 C. Choong, Malaysia *(Kawasaki)*; 63 M. Grein, W. Germany *(Suzuki)*.

Record lap: J. Dunlop, Ireland *(Honda)*, 19m 05.8s, 118.54mph/190.766kmh.
Old record: J. Dunlop, Ireland *(Honda)*, 19m 15.4s, 117.55mph/189.173kmh (1987).

Practice leaderboard: 1 R. Marshall, GB *(Suzuki)*, 19m 44.2s; 2 G. Johnson, GB *(Bimota-Yamaha)*, 19m 45.6s; 3 J. Dunlop, Ireland *(Honda)*, 19m 48.0s; 4 N. Jefferies, GB *(Honda)*, 19m 55.4s; 5 S. Hislop, GB *(Honda)*, 20 m 10.2s; 6 P. Mellor, GB *(Suzuki)*, 20m 23.0s; 7 C. Fogarty, GB *(Honda)*, 20m 31.8s; 8 R. Burnett, GB *(Honda)*, 20m 32.2s; 9 B. Morrison, GB *(Honda)*, 20m 34.4s; 10 P. Iddon, GB *(Bimota-Yamaha)*, 20m 35.6s; 11 B. Woodland, GB *(Bimota-Yamaha)*, 20m 36.6s; 12 D. Ireland, New Zealand *(Yamaha)*, 20m 39.8s; 13 R. Hurst, GB *(Kawasaki)*, 20m 41.8s; 14 M. Farmer, Ireland *(Suzuki)*, 20m 44.8s; 15 G. McGregor, Australia *(Yamaha)*, 20m 47.4s; 16 J. Whitham, GB *(Suzuki)*, 20m 47.6s; 17 H. Selby, GB *(Yamaha)*, 20m 52.8s; 18 M. Phillips, GB *(Bimota-Yamaha)*, 21m 01.6s; 19 T. Moran, GB *(Yamaha)*, 21m 05.0s; 20 K. Wilson, Canada *(Suzuki)*, 21m 06.8s.

Second Sidecar Race (3 laps, 113.19m/182.157k)

		h m s	mph	kmh
1	M. Boddice, GB C. Birks, GB *(700 Yamaha)*	1 03 47.4	106.46	171.326
2	L. Burton, Ireland P. Cushnahan, Ireland *(700 Yamaha)*	1 04 06.4	105.93	170.473
3	K. Howles, GB S. Pointer, GB *(700 Yamaha)*	1 04 35.8	105.13	169.185
4	D. Hallam, GB S. Parker, GB *(700 Yamaha)*	1 05 06.6	104.30	167.849
5	M. Burcombe, GB C. Hardman, GB *(700 Yamaha)*	1 05 16.4	104.04	167.431
6	D. Plummer, GB B. Marris, GB *(700 Yamaha)*	1 05 18.8	103.98	167.335
7	M. Murphy, Ireland J. Cushnahan, Ireland *(700 Yamaha)*	1 07 32.0	100.56	161.831
8	A. Oates, GB J. Gibbard, GB *(700 Yamaha)*	1 07 44.0	100.26	161.348
9	E. Cornes, GB G. Wellington, GB *(750 Yamaha)*	1 07 59.0	99.89	160.752
10	S. Pullan, GB T. Darby, GB *(700 Yamaha)*	1 08 41.4	98.87	159.111

11 R. Bellas/G. Knight, GB *(1135 Suzuki)*; 12 G. Shand/J. Shedden, GB *(998 Suzuki)*; 13 H. Lunemann/M. Cain, W. Germany/GB *(750 Yamaha)*; 14 N. Smith/D. Wells, GB *(700 Yamaha)*; 15 D. Saville/D. Hall, GB *(350 F2 Yamaha)*; 16 D. Keen/R. Parker, GB *(350 F2 Yamaha)*; 17 G. Davies/P. Chappell, GB *(700 Yamaha)*; 18 M. Hamblin/R. Smith, GB *(350 F2 Yamaha)*; 19 D. Rumble Snr/S. Wilson, GB *(998 Suzuki)*; 20 G. Flynn/R. Burgess, GB *(700 Yamaha)*; 21 T. Eade/F. McDermott, GB *(750 Yamaha)*; 22 L. Pallister/I. Marriner, GB *(750 Yamaha)*; 23 J. Heys/C. Hefti, GB *(350 F2 Yamaha)*; 24 D. Founds/G. Irlam, GB *(350 F2 Yamaha)*; 25 C. Pritchard/C. Price, GB *(997 Kawasaki)*; 26 W. Scarth/L. Scarth, GB *(750 Yamaha)*; 27 B. Copson/B. Campbell, GB *(750 Yamaha)*; 28 B. Cubbon/G. Mahon, GB *(750 Yamaha)*; 29 R. Suess/W. Villiger, Switzerland *(500 Yamaha)*; 30 J. Booth/K. Robert, GB *(350 F2 Yamaha)*; 31 G. Roberts/G. Roberts, GB *(997 Kawasaki)*; 32 A. Shand/N. Miller, GB *(350 F2 Yamaha)*; 33 J. Muldoon/W. Castello, GB *(750 Yamaha)*; 34 J. Coles/G. Mapletoft, GB *(700 Yamaha)*; 35 P. Kneale/B. Kneale, GB *(350 F2 Yamaha)*; 36 D. French/S. Lavender, GB *(350 F2 Yamaha)*; 37 D. Matthewman/D. Snape, GB *(350 F2 Yamaha)*; 38 M. Dwyer/D. Statham, GB *(350 F2 Yamaha)*; 39 S. Judkins/N. Moore, GB *(350 F2 Yamaha)*.

Fastest lap: L. Burton/P. Cushnahan, Ireland *(700 Yamaha)*, 21m 01.6s, 107.66mph/ 173.257kmh.

Practice leaderboard: Both sidecar races were contested by the same teams. See First Sidecar race for top 20 in combined practice sessions.

Wednesday, 8 June

Junior TT (250cc grand prix machines plus Formula Two machines – 350cc two-strokes/600cc four-strokes – 4 laps, 150.92m/242.875k)

		h	m	s	mph	kmh
1	J. Dunlop, Ireland *(250 Honda)*	1	20	56.6	111.87	180.032
2	B. Reid, Ireland *(250 EMC)*	1	21	16.0	111.42	179.308
3	E. Laycock, Ireland *(250 EMC)*	1	21	58.4	110.46	177.763
4	B. Morrison, GB *(600 Honda)*	1	22	16.8	110.05	177.103
5	J. Rea, Ireland *(350 Yamaha)*	1	23	08.4	108.91	175.574
6	S. Cull, Ireland *(250 Honda)*	1	23	11.2	108.85	175.172
7	B. Heath, GB *(350 Yamaha)*	1	23	13.8	108.79	175.075
8	M. Seward, GB *(600 Honda)*	1	23	31.4	108.41	174.464
9	S. Williams, GB *(350 Yamaha)*	1	23	32.0	108.40	174.448
10	I. Young, GB *(600 Honda)*	1	24	04.4	107.70	173.321

11 K. Mawdsley, GB *(600 Honda)*; 12 C. Ryding, GB *(350 Yamaha)*; 13 D. Leach, GB *(350 Yamaha)*; 14 B. Jackson, GB (*600 Honda)*; 15 R. Talton, GB *(600 Honda)*; 16 P. Boast, GB *(600 Honda)*; 17 C. Faulkner, GB *(350 Yamaha)*; 18 D. Glass, GB *(600 Honda)*; 19 D. Coates, GB *(350 Yamaha)*; 20 S. Henshaw, GB *(600 Honda)*; 21 R. Haynes, GB *(600 Kawasaki)*; 22 A. Jackson, GB *(310 Yamaha)*; 23 R. Swallow, GB *(350 Yamaha)*; 24 S. Hislop, GB *(350 Yamaha)*; 25 D. Griffith, GB *(600 Honda)*; 26 R. Hanna, GB *(350 Yamaha)*; 27 R. Knight, GB *(600 Honda)*; 28 M. Booys, GB *(350 Yamaha)*; 29 P. Davies, GB *(600 Honda)*; 30 R. Boland, GB *(250 EMC)*; 31 A. Ross, GB *(600 Honda)*; 32 G. Higginson, GB *(250 Honda)*; 33 C. Petty, GB *(600 Honda)*; 34 M. Nelson, GB *(250 Yamaha)*; 35 K. Nicholls, GB *(600 Honda)*; 36 T. Sanders, GB *(350 Yamaha)*;

Two Irish World Champions, Joey Dunlop and Brian Reid, slog it out on the shorter circuit at Ginger Hall.

Trevor Nation gave the Norton team and the whole of Britain something to cheer about with some winning performances at the end of the season.

37 T. Rutter, GB *(600 Honda)*; 38 J. Dewar, GB *(600 Honda)*; 39 M. Williams, GB *(350 Yamaha)*; 40 F. Morrison, GB *(250 Yamaha)*; 41 M. Brookes, GB *(600 Ducati)*; 42 N. Rigg, GB *(350 Yamaha)*; 43 T. Hutchinson, GB *(350 Yamaha)*; 44 D. Smith, GB *(350 Yamaha)*; 45 J. Hogg, GB *(250 Rotax)*; 46 P. Evans, GB *(600 Ducati)*; 47 J. Nightingale, GB *(600 Yamaha)*; 48 M. Kirwan, GB *(310 Yamaha)*; 49 T. Hughes, GB *(250 Honda)*; 50 G. Morss, GB *(350 Yamaha)*.

Record lap: S. Hislop, GB *(350 Yamaha)*, 19m 57.6s, 113.41mph/182.510kmh.
Old record: B. Reid, Ireland *(250 EMC)*, 20m 11.8s, 112.08mph/180.370kmh (1985).

Practice leaderboard: 1 B. Morrison, GB *(600 Honda)*, 20m 40.6s; 2 B. Heath, GB *(350 Yamaha)*, 20m 48.0s; 3 B. Reid, Ireland *(250 EMC)*, 21m 18.0s; 4 C. Fogarty, GB *(250 Honda)*, 21m 19.4s; 5 J. Rea, Ireland *(350 Yamaha)*, 21m 27.2s; 6 P. Nicholls, GB *(250 Honda)*, 21m 27.6s; 7 J. Weeden, GB *(350 Yamaha)*, 21m 28.6s; 8 D. Leach, GB *(250 Yamaha)*, 21m 28.8s; 9 K. Mawdsley, GB *(600 Honda)*, 21m 30.4s; 10 R. Haynes, GB *(600 Kawasaki)*, 21m 33.0s; 11 J. Dunlop, Ireland *(250 Honda)*, 21m 37.4s; 12 M. Nelson, GB *(250 Yamaha)*; 21m 38.4s; 13 I. Jones, GB *(250 Yamaha)*, 21m 45.6s; 14 D. Chatterton, GB *(350 Yamaha)*, 21m 47.6s; 15 E. Laycock, Ireland *(250 EMC)*, 21m 52.4s; 16 D. Glass, GB *(600 Honda)*, 21m 52.6s; 17 S. Ward, GB *(600 Honda)*, 22m 01.0s; 18 R. Swann, GB *(600 Kawasaki)*, 22m 01.6s; 19 R. Talton, GB *(600 Honda)*, 22m 09.8s; 20 S. Henshaw, GB *(600 Honda)*, 22m 09.8s.

Production Machines Class A (1,300cc four-strokes – 4 laps, 150.92m/242.875k)

		h	m	s	mph	kmh
1	D. Leach, GB *(1000 Yamaha)*	1	19	12.2	114.32	183.975
2	G. Johnson, GB *(1000 Yamaha)*	1	19	13.0	114.30	183.942
3	K. Wilson, Canada *(1100 Suzuki)*	1	19	33.8	113.81	183.154
4	P. Mellor, GB *(1100 Suzuki)*	1	20	22.6	112.65	181.287
5	R. Haynes, GB *(1000 Kawasaki)*	1	20	55.0	111.90	180.080
6	M. Jefferies, GB *(1000 Honda)*	1	21	00.8	111.77	179.871
7	R. Hurst, GB *(1000 Kawasaki)*	1	21	30.8	111.08	178.761
8	M. Seward, GB *(1000 Yamaha)*	1	21	44.8	110.77	178.262
9	H. Selby, GB *(1100 Suzuki)*	1	21	49.0	110.67	178.101
10	R. Marshall, GB *(1100 Suzuki)*	1	21	49.6	110.66	178.085

11 P. Hunt, GB *(1000 Kawasaki)*; 12 I. Duffus, GB *(1000 Yamaha)*; 13 B. Morrison, GB *(1000 Honda)*; 14 S. Henshaw, GB *(1000 Yamaha)*; 15 G. Thrush, GB *(1000 Yamaha)*; 16 M. Wheeler, GB *(1000 Yamaha)*; 17 K. Mawdsley, GB *(1000 Yamaha)*; 18 B. Woodland, GB *(1000 Yamaha)*; 19 P. Hogg, GB *(1000 Yamaha)*; 20 C. Corner, GB *(1000 Yamaha)*; 21 S. Dowey, GB *(1000 Yamaha)*; 22 M. Phillips, GB *(1000 Yamaha)*; 23 M. Birkinshaw, GB *(1000 Yamaha)*; 24 G. Tate, GB *(1000 Yamaha)*; 25 R. Swann, GB *(1000 Kawasaki)*; 26 R. Knight, GB *(1100 Suzuki)*; 27 B. Raynor, GB *(1000 Yamaha)*; 28 J. Toner, GB *(1100 Suzuki)*; 29 E. Roberts, GB *(1000 Yamaha)*; 30 R. Wright, GB *(1000 Yamaha)*; 31 J. Crellin, GB *(1000 Yamaha)*; 32 C. Petty, GB *(1100 Suzuki)*; 33 P. Beale, GB *(1000 Yamaha)*; 34 N. Munro, GB *(1000 Yamaha)*; 35 N. Tuxworth, GB *(1000 Yamaha)*; 36 G. Martin, GB *(1100 Suzuki)*; 37 D. Ashton, GB *(1100 Suzuki)*; 38 R. Thomson, GB *(1000 Yamaha)*; 39 I. Waine, GB *(1000 Honda)*; 40 N. Kneen, GB *(1000*

Yamaha); 41 P. Armes, GB *(1000 Kawasaki)*; 42 S. Bevington, GB *(1000 Yamaha)*; 43 M. McDiarmid, GB *(1000 Yamaha)*; 44 R. Evans, GB *(1000 Yamaha)*; 45 A. Moll, W. Germany *(1100 Suzuki)*.

Record lap: G. Johnson, GB *(1000 Yamaha)*, 19m 25.4s, 116.55mph/187.563kmh. *Old record:* T. Nation, GB *(1100 Suzuki)*, 19m 59.2s; 113.26mph/182.269kmh (1986).

Practice leaderboard: 1 D. Leach, GB *(1000 Yamaha)*, 20m 18.6s; 2 G. Johnson, GB *(1000 Yamaha)*, 20m 19.6s; 3 P. Mellor, GB *(1100 Suzuki)*, 20m 24.4s; 4 R. Marshall, GB *(1100 Suzuki)*, 20m 28.0s; 5 A. Batson, GB *(1000 Yamaha)*, 20m 40.6s; 6 R. Haynes, GB *(1000 Kawasaki)*, 20m 48.8s; 7 P. Hunt, GB *(1000 Kawasaki)*, 20m 49.4s; 8 B. Woodland, GB *(1000 Yamaha)*, 20m 55.6s; 9 M. Seward, GB *(1000 Yamaha)*, 20m 55.6s; 10 S. Dowey, GB *(1000 Yamaha)*, 20m 56.2s; 11 P. Hogg, GB *(1000 Yamaha)*, 20m 56.6s; 12 H. Selby, GB *(1100 Suzuki)*, 20m 57.0s; 13 B. Morrison, GB *(1000 Honda)*, 21m 01.0s; 14 K. Wilson, Canada *(1100 Suzuki)*, 21m 01.4s; 15 I. Duffus, GB *(1000 Yamaha)*, 21m 05.8s; 16 R. Swann, GB *(1000 Kawasaki)*, 21m 06.4s; 17 R. Knight, GB *(1100 Suzuki)*, 21m 08.0s; 18 T. Nation, GB *(1100 Suzuki)*, 21m 12.4s; 19 M. Wheeler, GB *(1000 Yamaha)*, 21m 17.0s; 20 P. Armes, GB *(1000 Kawasaki)*, 21m 18.6s.

Friday, 10 June

Senior TT (1,200cc open class machines, 6 laps, 226.38m/364.313k)

		h m s	mph	kmh
1	J. Dunlop, Ireland *(750 Honda)*	1 55 42.6	117.38	188.899
2	S. Hislop, GB *(750 Honda)*	1 56 33.2	116.53	187.531
3	G. Johnson, GB *(750 Bimota-Yamaha)*	1 57 12.8	115.84	186.421
4	R. Marshall, GB *(1100 Suzuki)*	1 58 12.0	114.91	184.924
5	R. Burnett, GB *(750 Honda)*	1 58 25.8	114.69	184.570
6	B. Morrison, GB *(750 Honda)*	1 59 01.6	114.11	183.637
7	C. Fogarty, GB *(750 Honda)*	1 59 13.8	113.92	183.331
8	E. Laycock, Ireland *(500 Honda)*	1 59 26.2	113.72	183.009
9	S. Ward, GB *(1100 Suzuki)*	2 00 09.6	113.03	181.899
10	S. McClements, Ireland *(750 Suzuki)*	2 01 03.4	112.20	180.563

11 M. Farmer, Ireland *(1100 Suzuki)*; 12 R. Dunlop, Ireland *(750 Honda)*; 13 R. Haynes, GB *(1000 Kawasaki)*; 14 K. Wilson, Canada *(1100 Suzuki)*; 15 M. Phillips, GB *(750 Bimota-Yamaha)*; 16 P. Mellor, GB *(750 Suzuki)*; 17 T. Moran, GB *(750 Yamaha)*; 18 B. Reid, Ireland *(750 Kawasaki)*; 19 G. Tate, GB *(1000 Yamaha)*; 20 M. Wheeler, GB *(1000 Yamaha)*; 21 S. Dowey, GB *(1000 Yamaha)*; 22 B. Jackson, GB *(750 Suzuki)*; 23 R. Holden, GB *(750 Suzuki)*; 24 E. Galbraith, GB *(750 Suzuki)*; 25 I. Lougher, GB *(500 Suzuki)*; 26 K. Mawdsley, GB *(600 Honda)*; 27 P. Boast, GB *(750 Yamaha)*; 28 M. Linscott, GB *(750 Suzuki)*; 29 S. Johnson, GB *(750 Suzuki)*; 30 R. Knight, GB *(1100 Suzuki)*; 31 B. Raynor, GB *(1000 Yamaha)*; 32 G. Radcliffe, GB *(750 Honda)*; 33 S. Buckmaster, GB *(600 Norton)*; 34 R. Rose, GB *(750 Suzuki)*; 35 D. Dean, GB *(750 Honda)*; 36 R. Sutcliffe, GB *(750 Suzuki)*; 37 D. Chatterton, GB *(750 Suzuki)*; 38 P. Davies, GB *(1000 Yamaha)*; 39 D. Coates, GB *(750 Suzuki)*; 40 M. Lucas, GB *(1100*

Kawasaki); 41 D. Bates, GB *(750 Suzuki)*; 42 M. Swann, Ireland *(500 Suzuki)*; 43 R. Talton, GB *(750 Suzuki)*; 44 T. Nation, GB *(600 Norton)*; 45 R. Crossley, GB *(1100 Suzuki)*; 46 S. Taylor, GB *(750 Suzuki)*; 47 S. Richardson, GB *(750 Suzuki)*; 48 A. Dugdale, GB *(750 Suzuki)*; 49 A. Jackson, GB *(750 Suzuki)*; 50 A. Moll, W. Germany *(1000 Yamaha)*; 51 I. Martin, GB *(750 Yamaha)*; 52 D. Ashton, GB *(1100 Suzuki)*; 53 M. Stengl, Austria *(750 Suzuki)*; 54 R. Thomson, GB *(1000 Yamaha)*; 55 J. Hodson, GB *(600 Honda)*; 56 M. Bowen, GB *(750 Suzuki)*; 57 M. Hunt, GB *(750 Yamaha)*; 58 J. Crellin, GB *(1000 Yamaha)*; 59 S. Moore, Ireland *(750 Yamaha)*; 60 B. Richards, GB *(750 Suzuki)*; 61 N. Stothert, GB *(750 Suzuki)*; 62 H. Bolliger, Switzerland *(750 Suzuki)*; 63 T. Rutter, GB *(750 Suzuki)*; 64 M. Guymer, GB *(750 Honda)*; 65 M. Grein, W. Germany *(750 Suzuki)*; 66 D. Kerby, GB *(1100 Kawasaki)*; 67 H-O. Butenuth, W. Germany *(900 BMW)*; 68 D. Leach, GB *(500 Suzuki)*.
Record lap: S. Cull, Ireland *(500 Honda)*, 19m 00.6s, 119.08mph/191.635kmh.
Old record: J. Dunlop, Ireland *(500 Honda)*, 19m 06. 4s, 118.47mph/190.653kmh (1984).

Practice leaderboard: 1 S. Henshaw, GB *(500 Suzuki)*, 19m 49.4s; 2 P. Mellor, GB *(750 Suzuki)*, 19m 50.8s; 3 S. Cull, Ireland *(500 Honda)*, 20m 15.0s; 4 J. Rea, Ireland *(500 Suzuki)*, 20m 19.4s; 5 E. Laycock, Ireland *(500 Honda)*, 20m 22.8s; 6 T. Nation, GB *(600 Norton)*, 20m 25.0s; 7 S. McClements, Ireland *(750 Honda)*, 20m 32.8s; 8 B. Heath, GB *(500 Suzuki)*, 20m 36.6s; 9 S. Ward, GB *(1100 Suzuki)*, 20m 38.6s; 10 K. Mawdsley, GB *(1000 Yamaha)*, 20m 50.2s; 11 D. Ireland, New Zealand *(750 Yamaha)*, 20m 54.4s; 12 D. Griffith, GB *(750 Yamaha)*, 20m 55.2s; 13 R. Haynes, GB *(1000 Kawasaki)*, 20m 57.2s; 14 G. Linder, GB *(750 Yamaha)*, 20m 58.8s; 15 P. Davies, GB *(1000 Yamaha)*, 21m 07.6s; 16 C. Fargher, GB *(500 Suzuki)*, 21m 12.6s; 17 M. Lucas, GB *(1100 Kawasaki)*, 21m 14.8s; 18 G. Radcliffe, GB *(750 Honda)*, 21m 17.6s; 19 D. Leach, GB *(500 Suzuki)*, 21m 18.2s; 20 G. Tate, GB *(1000 Kawasaki)* 21m 24.0s.

The king of the roads – Joey Dunlop races through the Gooseneck on his way to his third win of the week.

Steve Cull delights the shirtsleeved crowd on his way to that new ultimate lap record at the TT.

Bubba Schobert was not only the star of the Eurolantic Challenge but also won the AMA Superbike Championship.

AMA SUPERBIKE CHAMPIONSHIP

The AMA Superbike championship was an exciting confrontation between the American Honda VFR750 Interceptor of Bubba Shobert and the Yoshimura Suzuki GSX-R750 of Doug Polen. Both Texans, they took the fight right to the final race at Sears Point where Shobert, enjoying an eight-point lead going into the race, shadowed Polen through the entire race to clinch his first ever road racing title.

With their 1987-spec factory bikes, the two matched each other through the series but it was a Polen crash at the penultimate round at Mid Ohio which effectively settled the final outcome. As Shobert took that race, Polen remounted to trail in sixth. They traded three wins apiece with Kevin Schwantz the only other winner in the series. He took the Daytona 200 on a Yoshimura Suzuki before jetting off to join the grand prix trial.

The superiority of the expensive factory machines overshadowed the series. Back-up riders, Doug Chandler for Honda and Scott Gray for Yoshimura Suzuki, finished third and fourth respectively in the points, leaving the privateers to scrabble around for the middle-order placings. The situation has led the AMA to investigate an alternative, more stringently controlled production-based class to replace the current costly formula.

The Castrol-sponsored 250GP class was a John Kocinski benefit for the second successive season. Kenny Roberts' protege won six of seven races with the Team Nordica Roberts Yamaha and his teammate, Thomas Stevens from Florida, placed second in the series. Californian Richard Oliver was the championship's only other race winner. The Lassak Yamaha rider took the Elkhart Lake event from Stevens. Oliver was fourth in the final standings behind the John Hasty Racing Yamaha of Doug Brauneck. Britain's Alan Carter was fifth overall, his best results on the other Lassak Racing Yamaha coming at Daytona and the final Sears Point round, finishing second to Kocinski both times.

Maryland's Dale Quarterley sped his booming Fast By Ferracci Ducati 851S to the Pro Twins title, winning four races including the final one at Sears Point.

Ducati enjoyed superiority in this class with former match race team member John Long second overall, former multi-times Twins champion Jimmy Adamo third and Kevin Erion fourth. Defending champion Doug Brauneck could only finish fifth in the points with the Dr John Wittner Guzzi. Although Ducati posted five wins – four to Quarterly and one to Long – Roger Marshall gave the Quantel Cosworth its first AMA victory at Daytona in March and Honda factory rider Doug Chandler came out on top at Mid Ohio with the Commonwealth Honda, a machine which featured a re-worked flat-track racing vee-twin motor.

Results

Round 1 6 March, Daytona, Florida (57 laps, 200 miles)

1 K. Schwantz *(Suzuki)*; 1h 52m 56.479s, 107.801mph
2 D. Polen *(Suzuki)*; 3 B. Shobert *(Honda)*; 4 S. Gray *(Suzuki)*; 5 R. McMurter *(Yamaha)*; 6 M. Harth *(Suzuki)*; 7 D. Quarterley *(Suzuki)*; 8 R. Renfrow *(Honda)*; 9 S. Russell *(Suzuki)*; 10 J. Farmer *(Suzuki)*.

Round 2 15 May, Road, Atlanta, Georgia (24 laps, 60 miles)

1 B. Shobert *(Honda)*, 35m 54.309s, 101.066mph
2 D. Polen *(Suzuki)*; 3 D. Chandler *(Honda)*; 4 M. Baldwin *(Suzuki)*; 5 J. Ashmead *(Honda)*; 6 R. Renfrow *(Suzuki)*; 7 R. McMurter *(Yamaha)*; 8 D. Quarterley *(Suzuki)*; 9 R. Shaw *(Yamaha)*; 10 D. Sadowski *(Suzuki)*.

Round 3 19 June, Louden, New Hampshire (38 laps, 60 miles)

1 D. Polen *(Suzuki)*, 43m 43.250s, 83.438mph
2 B. Shobert *(Honda)*; 3 D. Chandler *(Honda)*; 4 R. Renfrow *(Suzuki)*; 5 D. Sadowski *(Suzuki)*; 6 R. McMurter *(Honda)*; 7 S. Russell *(Suzuki)*; 8 M. Bougas *(Suzuki)*; 9 J. Ashmead *(Honda)*; 10 T. Kipp *(Yamaha)*.

Round 4 26 June, Elkhart Lake, Wisconsin (15 laps, 60 miles)

1 D. Polen *(Suzuki)*, 35m 24.159s, 101.687mph
2 B. Shobert *(Honda)*; 3 R. Renfrow *(Suzuki)*; 4 S. Gray *(Suzuki)*; 5 J. Ashmead *(Honda)*; 6 M. Chin *(Yamaha)*; 7 S. Russell *(Suzuki)*; 8 D. Sadowski *(Suzuki)*; 9 M. Harth *(Suzuki)* 10 W. Cooley *(Honda)*.

Round 5 10 July, Laguna Seca, California, (2 × 28 laps, 60 miles)

1 B. Shobert *(Honda)*, 1h 28m 9s, 83.691mph
2 D. Polen *(Suzuki)*; 3 D. Chandler *(Honda)*; 4 G. Goodfellow *(Honda)*; 5 S. Gray *(Suzuki)*; 6 R. Arnaiz *(Yamaha)*; 7 P. Bray *(Suzuki)*; 8 S. Dick *(Suzuki)*; 9 S. MacDonald *(Yamaha)*; 10 T. Kipp *(Yamaha)*.

Round 6 7 August, Mid Ohio, Ohio (25 laps, 60 miles)

1 B. Shobert *(Honda)*, 40m 14.509s, 89.459mph
2 S. Gray *(Suzuki)*; 3 D. Chandler *(Honda)*; 4 D. Quarterley *(Suzuki)*; 5 J. Ashmead *(Honda)*; 6 D. Polen *(Suzuki)*; 7 M. Chin *(Yamaha)*; 8 R. Renfrow *(Suzuki)*; 9 D. Chivington *(Suzuki)*; 10 W. Cooley *(Honda)*.

Round 7 2 October, Sears Point, California (24 laps, 60 miles)

1 D. Polen *(Suzuki)*, 42m 28.309s, 84.762mph
2 B. Shobert *(Honda)*; 3 D. Chandler *(Honda)*; 4 D. Quarterley *(Suzuki)*; 5 D. Sadowski *(Suzuki)*; 6 R. Arnaiz *(Yamaha)*; 7. J. Domay *(Suzuki)*; 8 J. Pittman *(Suzuki)*; 9 K. Pinkstaff *(Suzuki)*. 10 C. Rayborn *(Suzuki)*.

Final Championship Positions
1 B. Shobert *(Honda)*, 121 points
2 D. Polen *(Suzuki)*, 117; 3 D. Chandler *(Honda)*, 65; 4 S. Gray *(Suzuki)*, 48; 5 R. Renfrow *(Suzuki)*, 47; 6 J. Ashmead *(Honda)*, 38; 7 D. Quarterley *(Suzuki)*, 37; 8 D. Sadowski *(Suzuki)*, 32; 9 R. McMurter *(Honda(*, 27; 10 S. Russell *(Suzuki)*, 22.

AMA 250

Results

Round 1 6 March, Daytona, Florida (18 laps, 64.08 miles)

1 J. Kocinski *(Yamaha)*, 36m 48.799s, 104.393mph
2 A. Carter *(Yamaha)*; 3 D. Coe *(Rotax)*; 4 K. Ballington *(Honda)*; 5 B. Shobert *(Honda)*; 6 T. Stevens *(Yamaha)*; 7 R. Moore *(Yamaha)*; 8 R. Petersen *(Honda)*; 9 D. Brauneck *(Yamaha)*; 10 A. Leisner *(Aprilia)*.

Round 2 15 May, Road, Atlanta, Georgia (20 laps, 50 miles)

1 J. Kocinski *(Yamaha)*, 30m 21.599s, 99.605mph
2 T. Stevens *(Yamaha)*; 3 R. Oliver *(Yamaha)*; 4 A. Carter *(Yamaha)*; 5 J. Filice *(Honda)*; 6 K. Ballington *(Honda)*; 7 J. Cornwell *(Rotax)*; 8 J. Stephens *(Aprilia)*; 9 D. Busby *(Yamaha)*; 10 R. Moore *(Yamaha)*.

Round 3 19 June, Louden, New Hampshire (32 laps, 50 miles)

1 J. Kocinski *(Yamaha)*, 37m 12.769s, 82.552mph
2 D. Greene *(Yamaha)*; 3 T. Stevens *(Yamaha)*; 4 R. Oliver *(Yamaha)*; 5 A. Leisner *(Aprilia)*; 6 D. Brauneck *(Yamaha)*; 7 S. Crevier *(Yamaha)*; 8 J. Stevens *(Aprilia)*; 9 C. D'Aluisio *(Honda)*; 10 R. Moore *(Yamaha)*.

Round 4 26 June, Elkhart Lake, Wisconsin (13 laps, 52 miles)

1 R. Oliver *(Yamaha)*, 31m 45.879s; 98.222mph
2 T. Stevens *(Yamaha)*; 3 D. Brauneck *(Yamaha)*; 4 A. Leisner *(Aprilia)*; 5 R. Petersen *(Honda)*; 6 A. Carter *(Yamaha)*; 7 S. Crevier *(Yamaha)*; 8 R. Moore *(Yamaha)*; 9 D. Greene *(Yamaha)*; 10 M. de Guidice *(Yamaha)*.

Round 5 10 July, Laguna Seca, California, (23 laps, 50.6 miles)

1 J. Kocinski *(Yamaha)*, 36m 41.619s, 82.589mph
2 T. Stevens *(Yamaha)*; 3 D. Brauneck *(Yamaha)*; 4 R. Moore *(Yamaha)*; 5 R. Oliver *(Yamaha)*; 6 S. Crevier *(Yamaha)*; 7 E. Kondo *(Spondon)*; 8 J. Stephens *(Aprilia)*; 9 D. Coe *(Rotax)*; 10 C. D'Aluisio *(Honda)*.

Round 6 7 August, Mid Ohio, Ohio (21 laps, 50 miles)

1 J. Kocinski *(Yamaha)*, 33m 59.469s, 88.964mph
2 T. Stevens *(Yamaha)*; 3 D. Brauneck *(Yamaha)*; 4 J. Filice *(Honda)*; 5 A. Leisner *(Aprilia)*; 6 D. Greene *(Honda)*; 7 K. Ballington *(Honda)*; 8 S. Crevier *(Yamaha)*; 9 C. D'Alusio *(Honda)*; 10 R. Moore *(Yamaha)*.

Round 7 2 October, Sears Point, California (20 laps, 50 miles)
1 J. Kocinski *(Yamaha)*, 35m 42.109s, 84.029mph
2 A. Carter *(Yamaha)*; 3 D. Greene *(Yamaha)*; 4 D. Brauneck *(Yamaha)*; 5 S. Crevier *(Yamaha)*; 6 R. Moore *(Yamaha)*; 7 T. Stevens *(Yamaha)*; 8 J. Filice *(Honda)*; 9 E. Knodo *(Yamaha)*; 10 D. Busby *(Yamaha)*.

Final Championship Positions
1 J. Kocinski *(Yamaha)*, 120 points
2 T. Stevens *(Yamaha)*, 94; 3 D. Brauneck *(Yamaha)*, 65; 4 R. Oliver *(Yamaha)*, 56; 5 A. Carter *(Yamaha)*, 52; 6. R. Moore *(Yamaha)*, 50; 7 D. Greene *(Yamaha)*, 48; 8 S. Crevier *(Yamaha)*, 45; 9 A. Leisner *(Aprilia)*, 36; =10 K. Ballington *(Honda)*, 28/J. Filice *(Honda)*, 28.

AMA PRO TWINS

Results

Round 1 6 March, Daytona, Florida (10 laps, 35.6 miles)

1 R. Marshall *(Quantel-Cosworth)*; 2 S. Caracchi *(Ducati)*; 3 D. Brauneck *(Moto Guzzi)*; 4 C. Oldfield *(Bimota)*; 5 J. Long *(Ducati)*; 6 D. Quarterley *(Ducati)*; 7 A. Cathcart *(Ducati)*; 8 R. Reiman *(Harley Davidson)*; 9 K. Erion *(Ducati)*; 10 K. Leibman *(Ducati)*.

Round 2 15 May, Road, Atlanta, Georgia (16 laps, 40 miles)

1 J. Long *(Cagiva)*; 2 D. Quarterley *(Cagiva)*; 3 J. Adamo *(Ducati)*; 4 D. Keiffer *(Ducati)*; 5 K. Erion *(Ducati)*; 6 D. Summers *(Ducati)*; 7 R. Kirnec *(Harley Davidson)*; 8 K. Stansy *(Ducati)*; 9 H. van Staden *(Ducati)*; 10 E. Phillippe *(Ducati)*.

Round 3 19 June, Louden, New Hampshire (25 laps, 40 miles)

1 D. Quarterley *(Ducati)*; 2 K. Erion *(Ducati)*; 3 P. Real *(Ducati)*; 4 W. Elliott *(Ducati)*; 5 E. Abdo *(Honda)*; 6 K. Leibmann *(Ducati)*; 7 P. Johnson *(Cagiva)*; 8 M. Robinson *(Ducati)*; 9 D. Brauneck *(Moto Guzzi)*; 10 J. Adamo *(Ducati)*.

Round 4 26 June, Elkhart Lake, Wisconsin (10 laps, 40 miles)

1 D. Quarterley *(Ducati)*; 2 D. Brauneck *(Moto Guzzi)*; 3 J. Long *(Ducati)*; 4 R. Shemwell *(Ducati)*; 5 K. Blais *(Ducati)*; 6 P. Johnson *(Ducati)*; 7 K. Erion *(Ducati)*; 8 F. Mzarek *(Ducati)*; 9 R. Sears *(Ducati)*; 10 K. Leibmann *(Ducati)*.

Round 5 10 July, Laguna Seca, California, (14 laps, 31 miles)

1 D. Quarterley *(Ducati)*
2 P. Lewis *(Honda)*; 3 J. Long *(Ducati)*; 4 J. Adamo *(Ducati)*; 5 R. Shemwell *(Ducati)*; 6 K. Erion *(Ducati)*; 7 P. Johnson *(Ducati)*; 8 D. Summers *(Ducati)*; 9 R. Baker *(Yamaha)*; 10 E. Schless *(Cagiva)*.

Round 6 7 August, Mid Ohio, Ohio (17 laps, 40 miles)

1 D. Chandler *(Honda)*, 28m 17.209s, 86.542mph
2 D. Quarterley *(Ducati)*; 3 J. Adamo *(Ducati)*; 4 J. Long *(Ducati)*; 5 M. Tunstall *(Ducati)*; 6 K. Erion *(Ducati)*; 7 R. Shemwell *(Ducati)* 8 G. Stas *(Ducati)*; 9 R. Kirnec *(Harley Davidson)*; 10 R. Griffiths *(Moto Guzzi)*.

Round 7 2 October, Sears Point, California (16 laps, 40 miles)
1 D. Quarterley *(Ducati)*, 29m 16.479s, 81.982mph
2 D. Brauneck *(Moto Guzzi)*; 3 J. Adamo *(Ducati)*; 4 R. Shemwell *(Ducati)*; 5 D. Summers *(Ducati)*; 6 M. Yarrow *(Yamaha)*; 7 G. Seim *(Ducati)*; 8 E. Schless *(Cagiva)*; 9 W. Rodgers *(BMW)*; 10 A. Chambers *(Ducati)*.

Final Championship Positions
1 D. Quarterley *(Ducati)*, 121 points
2 J. Long *(Ducati)*, 70; 3 J. Adamo *(Ducati)*, 59; 4 K. Erion *(Ducati)*, 58; 5 D. Brauneck *(Moto Guzzi)*, 51; 6 R. Shemwell *(Ducati)*, 40; 7 P. Johnson *(Ducati)*, 27; 8 D. Summers *(Ducati)*, 26; 9 K. Leibman *(Ducati)*, 23; 10 D. Chandler *(Honda)*, 20.

BRITISH FORMULA ONE

Whether the ACU realised it at the time, they pulled off a coup by reintroducing the British Formula One championship. With interest in Superstock waning due to the dominant nature of the RC30 Hondas, and Brian Morrison in particular, F1 was a refreshing diversion with all four Japanese importer teams participating. What made the series even more interesting was the ACU's relaxation of the rulebook which allowed 500cc two-strokes, the rotary Nortons and the Quantel Cosworth into the competition.

It was the RG500 and Norton which helped produce a series full of fairy-tale success. Darren Dixon, on the verge of retirement at the end of 1987 due to lack of finance, was hired by Padgett's of Batley and promptly won the championship on their RG500 Suzuki. After overcoming handling problems early on, the Norton became unbeatable in the second half of the season. Trevor Nation won two races and Dixon's RG500 sparring partner Steve Spray, a total privateer, was given a ride on the Norton in the final race at Brands and scored a third win for the rotary.

The series received a big boost when it was announced that several of the races would benefit from television coverage by the BBC. The first such coverage was at the opening race which drew a healthy 5,000 spectators at the featureless Carnaby airfield circuit in addition to the countless TV viewers. They were all treated to an intriguing race as Darren Dixon brought the Padgett's of Batley 500 Suzuki stroker through the field to win from the Honda RC30 of Brian Morrison.

Mark Phillips led the early running on his Loctite Bimota after disposing of fast-starting Mark Farmer, but was unable to prevent Dixon from charging through. Morrison was fortunate to be in the race at all having suffered two falls during the weekend but salvaged a runner-up placing. Roger Hurst was fourth on the very special Kawasaki ZXR750 direct from Japan for a revitalised UK Team Green effort. Adding to the variety of machinery in the frame, young Heron Suzuki rider Jamie Whitham took fifth on a GSX-R fourstroke with privateer Steve Spray completing the top six with his RG500. The Norton team failed to turn up after a problematical Saturday at the North West 200, while reigning British Champion Roger Marshall was never in the hunt with the Cosworth after an excursion to avoid the usual first-turn mêlée.

The second round of the championship was run in conjunction with the King of Donington and featured Ron Haslam and Roger Burnett in the line up. Burnett fronted on his World Superbike Honda while Haslam rode the same Ron Grant-fettled RC30 he had used in the Easter Eurolantic competition.

On his favourite circuit Haslam was the victor from Burnett, but it was Steve Spray who caused the real upset by taking third on his Suzuki after earlier dicing with Haslam for the lead. Nation took fourth from Fogarty, with Phil Mellor sixth on the Suzuki ahead of Morrison. Dixon fell at the Old Hairpin whilst challenging Spray for the lead, Irons dumped his Honda at the chicane and Whitham hit neutral around Coppice and went down.

Third round Cadwell was overshadowed by the death of Kenny Irons. He crashed into the back of Keith Huewen's Bimota during the warm-up lap and was pronounced dead on arrival at hospital.

The race, in front of TV cameras again, was won by Dixon after a superb scrap with Morrison, both setting a new lap record. Fogarty, the early leader, confirmed his prowess on the big four-strokes by taking third place.

For the fourth round in succession, the F1 combatants were treated to fine weather as they lined up for the Knockhill race. In front of his home supporters Morrison was in a dominant mood and set a new outright lap record on his way to victory. Fogarty was again an early leader but was overtaken by Whitham and Dixon, who were the eventual second and third place men, ahead of Hislop, Phillips and the fading Fogarty. Rymer on his Superstocker was seventh in front of the expensive Kawasaki of Hurst.

Going into the fifth round at Mallory Morrison led the points chase with 43 from Dixon's 40, but this was another TV race and the Padgett's runner had by now developed a taste for screen glory.

This time his win was fortuitous rather than planned as the two front runners, Morrison and Whitham both crashed heavily at the Devil's Elbow when Morrison lost the front end. Both riders were uninjured, save for minor abrasions and bruises, but Dixon's third TV win elevated him to points leader status over Morrison. Hurst grabbed Kawasaki's best result with the ZXR, finishing second after being shadowed through much of the race by 'Mez' Mellor. Spray took fourth from Fogarty and Hislop, the lower order being well strung out.

Television coverage at Thruxton meant another win for Dixon, but the race was marred by a serious accident which left Roger Hurst fighting for his life in hospital with serious head injuries. Thankfully he is now recovering, but he missed the remainder of the season.

The Hurst crash caused the race to be stopped and Dixon ran the three-lap re-run without a steering damper to take the race by 0.30 of a second from Jamie Whitham. Now showing all his old form, Phil Mellor continued the Suzuki run of success, which had hit top gear since reverting to the '87-spec F1 chassis at the Knockhill round, with a third place. Morrison pulled out with handling problems on the Honda while the ever-improving Norton took fourth in the hands of Trevor Nation with a new lap record into the bargain.

There was much jubilation for Brit bike fans at Mallory for the seventh round when Nation finally got the big win Norton had been waiting for, although stand-in Andy McGladdery had won the previous weekend at an ACU Star Cadwell race on the rotary.

Kenny Irons will be missed by everybody.

British racing lost a great friend when Kenny Irons was killed in a freak accident at Cadwell Park at the end of June. His considerable talent and impish sense of fun will be tragically missed at paddocks throughout the country. The 27-year-old from Luton crashed into the back of Keith Huewen's Yamaha during the warming-up lap for the British Formula One Championship race. He was hit by another crashed machine as he lay at the side of the track.

Irons looked destined for grand prix stardom, despite a tough time with the works Suzuki team last year. He came up through the very competitive Yamaha Pro-Am series which he won in 1984. He subsequently switched to the MCN Superstock series, which he won for the Loctite Yamaha team in 1986.

Irons was signed for Suzuki and competed in the World 500cc Championship on their new RGV 500 machine. It was a frustrating year but, typically, Irons always kept smiling. He finished sixth at the soaking French Grand Prix at Le Mans but, surprisingly, was not retained.

Kenny didn't moan or bitch in public but got on with the job of setting up his own team to compete in Britain and in the World Superbike Championship. Most experts agreed it would not be long before he was back in grand prix racing, where his talent and skill deserved to be.

But it was no easy ride for Nation. Throughout the race Whitham had been pressuring the Norton rider, but Nation was still showing the tremendous power of the 588cc motor, pulling wheelies on almost every lap as he powered out of the Devil's Elbow and onto the front straight. Dixon took third to keep his title chances alive but Morrison's hopes were fading fast as he could only finish sixth.

At Scarborough Whitham moved into second place in the points after a superb win. It was a second bonus for the Suzuki camp, with Mellor, having recorded his best result of the year in the runner-up slot. Gary Thrush was third in only his second outing on Andy McGladdery's Tillston's RC30. Steve Spray scored his first result for three rounds in fourth, veteran Steve Henshaw took fifth and Dixon was sixth.

Norton had decided not to race at Scarborough, but came back with a bang at Cadwell with Nation winning from Whitham. It was a double celebration for the Norton team as Nation had already been crowned King of Cadwell in the previous day's feature race. In the championship event he was pushed a little harder by the Suzuki rider. Dixon took third to clinch the title, while newly-crowned World TTF1 champion Carl Fogarty was fourth.

In the final race of the series at Brands in October, Norton called up Steve Spray to take over the ride vacated by Buckmaster, who had decided to take up the offer of a ride on Chas Mortimer's RS500 Honda. Twenty-five-year old Spray immediately took to the potent rotary and, despite having only ridden the bike for the first time in Friday's unofficial practice, sped to a memorable double. Not only did he dominate the TTF1 point-paying race, he also took the Powerbike International event.

Spray led the F1 race from the first turn with teammate Nation, Suzuki pair Whitham and Mellor plus Dixon close behind. Nation pulled out at Druids mid-way through the race when a detached oil feed to the rotors sent the engine temperature soaring to danger level. Despite not having Nation there to fight a rearguard action, Spray held on magnificently to win, actually increasing his lead in the final laps, while Dixon got the better of the official Heron Suzuki pair. Steve Chambers took an excellent fifth with his Superstock spec Honda, just besting a tight battle involving Buckmaster and McGladdery, who lost his Francis Neill Honda at Clearways on the final lap but escaped a huge shunt with minor abrasions.

Round 1 22 May, Carnaby (18 laps, 21.6 miles)

1 D. Dixon *(500 Suzuki)*, 16m 27.1s, 79.43mph
2 B. Morrison *(750 Honda)*; 3 M. Phillips *(750 Bimota)*; 4 R. Hurst *(750 Kawasaki)*; 5 J. Whitham *(750 Suzuki)*; 6 S. Spray *(500 Suzuki)*; 7 P. Iddon *(750 Bimota)*; 8 M. Farmer *(750 Suzuki)*; 9 C. Fogarty *(750 Honda)*; 10 R. Stringer *(750 Suzuki)*.
Record lap: D. Dixon *(500 Suzuki)*, 53.5s, 81.42mph

Round 2 26 June, Cadwell Park (10 laps, 21.74 miles)

1 D. Dixon *(500 Suzuki)*, 16m 2s, 81.5mph
2 B. Morrison *(750 Honda)*; 3 C. Fogarty *(750 Honda)*; 4 J. Whitham *(750 Suzuki)*; 5 S. Spray *(500 Suzuki)*; 6 M. Phillips *(750 Bimota)*; 7 T. Rymer *(750 Honda)*; 8 A. McGladdery *(750 Suzuki)*; 9 R. Knapp *(750 Kawasaki)*; 10 G. Weston *(750 Suzuki)*.
Record lap: D. Dixon *(500 Suzuki)* and B. Morrison *(750 Honda)*, 1m 34.3s, 82.99mph

Round 3 19 June, Donington Park (12 laps, 23.48 miles)

1 R. Haslam *(750 Honda)*, 15m 12.9s, 93.11mph
2 R. Burnett *(750 Honda)*; 3 S. Spray *(500 Suzuki)*; 4 T. Nation *(588 Norton)*; 5 C. Fogarty *(750 Honda)*; 6 P. Mellor *(750 Suzuki)*; 7 B. Morrison *(750 Honda)*; 8 P. Iddon *(750 Bimota)*; 9 M. Farmer *(750 Suzuki)*; 10 S. Williams *(750 Bimota)*.
Record lap: R. Burnett *(750 Honda)*, 1m 14.2s, 94.94mph

Round 4 10 July, Knockhill (15 laps, 19.335 miles)

1 B. Morrison *(750 Honda)*, 13m 59.9s, 82.87mph
2 J. Whitham *(750 Suzuki)*; 3 D. Dixon *(500 Suzuki)*; 4 S. Hislop *(750 Honda)*; 5 M. Phillips *(750 Bimota)*; 6 C. Fogarty *(750 Honda)*; 7 T. Rymer *(750 Honda)*; 8 R. Hurst *(750 Kawasaki)*; 9 P. Mellor *(750 Suzuki)*; 10 S. Spray *(500 Suzuki)*.
Record lap: B. Morrison *(750 Honda)*, 54.9s, 84.52mph

Round 5 24 July, Mallory Park (12 laps, 16.44 miles)

1 D. Dixon *(500 Suzuki)*, 14m 5.4s, 93.34mph
2 R. Hurst *(750 Kawasaki)*; 3 P. Mellor *(750 Suzuki)*; 4 S. Spray *(500 Suzuki)*; 5 C. Fogarty *(750 Honda)*; 6 S. Hislop *(750 Honda)*; 7 T. Nation *(588 Norton)*; 8 K. Huewen *(750 Bimota)*; 9 S. Buckmaster *(588 Norton)*; 10 R. Stringer *(750 Suzuki)*.
Fastest lap: J. Whitham *(750 Suzuki)*, 51.4s, 95.95mph

Round 6 20 August, Thruxton (10 laps, 23.56 miles)

1 D. Dixon *(500 Suzuki)*, 14m 00.70s, 100.89mph
2 J. Whitham *(750 Suzuki)*; 3 P. Mellor *(750 Suzuki)*; 4 T. Nation *(588 Norton)*; 5 S. Chambers *(750 Honda)*; 6 S. Williams *(750 Bimota)*; 7 A. McGladdery *(750 Honda)*; 8 M. Linscott *(750 Honda)*; 9 D. Ireland *(750 Honda)*; 10 C. Corner *(750 Honda)*.
Fastest lap: T. Nation, 1m 22.30s, 103.06mph

Round 7 3 September, Mallory Park (15 laps, 20.55 miles)

1 T. Nation *(588 Norton)*, 12m 57.2s, 95.18mph
2 J. Whitham *(750 Suzuki)*; 3 D. Dixon *(500 Suzuki)*; 4 P. Mellor *(750 Suzuki)*; 5 S. Hislop *(750 Honda)*; 6 B. Morrison *(750 Honda)*; 7 K. Huewen *(750 Bimota)*; 8 S. Chambers *(750 Honda)*; 9 S. Buckmaster *(588 Norton)*; 10 M. Seward *(750 Honda)*.
Fastest lap: T. Nation *(588 Norton)*, 50.9s, 96.89mph (outright lap record)

Round 8 10 September, Scarborough (12 laps, 28.92 miles)

1 J. Whitham *(750 Suzuki)*, 21m 24.2s, 82.43mph
2 P. Mellor *(750 Suzuki)*; 3 G. Thrush *(750 Honda)*; 4 S. Spray *(500 Suzuki)*; 5 S. Henshaw *(750 Honda)*; 6 D. Dixon *(500 Suzuki)*; 7 R. Hutchinson *(750 Suzuki)*; 8 D. Leach *(500 Suzuki)*; 9 S. Berwick *(750 Suzuki)*; 10 R. Sherry *(750 Suzuki)*.
Fastest lap: J. Whitham *(750 Suzuki)*, 1m 45.4s, 82.43mph

Round 9 2 October, Cadwell Park (10 laps, 21.74 miles)

1 T. Nation *(588 Norton)*, 15m 49.6s, 82.41mph
2 J. Whitham *(750 Suzuki)*; 3 D. Dixon *(500 Suzuki)*; 4 C. Fogarty *(750 Honda)*; 5 P. Mellor *(750 Suzuki)*; 6 B. Morrison *(750 Honda)*; 7 S. Chambers *(750 Honda)*; 8 D. Leach *(500 Suzuki)*; 9 S. Buckmaster *(588 Norton)*; 10 S. Hislop, *(750 Honda)*.
Fastest lap: T. Nation *(588 Norton)*, 1m 33.7s, 83.52mph (record)

Round 10 23 October, Brands Hatch (14 laps, 16.85 miles)

1 S. Spray *(588 Norton)*, 11m 28.1s, 88.15mph
2 D. Dixon *(500 Suzuki)*; 3 P. Mellor *(750 Suzuki)*; 4 J. Whitham *(750 Suzuki)*; 5 S. Buckmaster *(500 Honda)*; 6 S. Chambers *(750 Honda)*; 7 K. Huewen *(750 Bimota)*; 8 P. Iddon *(750 Bimota)*; 9 M. Farmer *(750 Kawasaki)*; 10 D. Leach *(750 Honda)*.
Fastest lap: J. Whitham *(750 Suzuki)* & D. Dixon *(500 Suzuki)* 48.3s, 89.70mph

Final Championship Positions (10 rounds, best eight scores count)
1 D. Dixon, 102 (107) points
2 J. Whitham, 85; 3 P. Mellor, 63; =4 B. Morrison and S. Spray, 53; 6 T. Nation, 50; 7 C. Fogarty, 37; 8 R. Hurst, 23; 9 M. Phillips, 21; 10 S. Hislop, 20.

MCN/EBC BRAKES SUPERSTOCK CHAMPIONSHIP

Gary Pinchin

After the thrilling 1987 Superstock series with Yamaha, Suzuki and Honda all fielding competitive bikes and packs of up to ten riders battling for the lead at the majority of races, this year's series was something of an anticlimax. With the introduction of the Honda VFR750R, better known as the RC30, the 1988 version of the series effectively became a one-make challenge and one rider, Brian Morrison on a Ron Grant-built, Jim Hendy-wrenched, Honda RC30, stood head and shoulders above the rest as he dominated the racing from the green light.

The series was further hit by pre-season controversy after the organisers introduced a control tyre ruling, which gave Dunlop and their cross-plys a monopoly. The rule meant that many riders involved in the '87 series who had kept their bikes and had run radials would have to buy complete sets of new wheels to accommodate the narrower tyres. It also meant owners of the new Hondas early in the season were forced to import special wheels or cut down and re-weld their existing standard wheels.

Another disappointing element of the championship was the boycott by the official Heron Suzuki squad from the racing. They argued the control tyre rule mean the new GSX-R 750J swing arm would require modifications before the tyre would fit, so they withdrew. The re-emergent Team Green Kawasaki outfit also declined to take part in the series, so for 1988 only two works squads were competing: Honda and Loctite Yamaha.

The first round at Brands Hatch was marred by several crashes and the death of a track marshal who was hit by wreckage resulting from a terrible crash involving Kiwi Des Barry and Chris Slack. Both riders were also badly injured and, although Barry was to resume racing in July, Slack had to sit out the season in preparation for a 1989 comeback.

It had taken three attempts to run the race but after the fatal crash the results were declared and half points awarded. Morrison won on aggregate time by 2/10ths of a second from Kenny Irons' privately entered Bridge Garage of Exeter RC30. Darren Dixon on a Padgett's Suzuki took third, after leading the final portion before the red flag, from another Suzuki exponent, Terry Rymer, the local Brands hotshoe who had shook the establishment the previous year when he won the same event.

The series then moved across the Irish Sea to Mondello, a bumpy but exacting 1.24 mile circuit near Dublin. This time Irons beat Morrison with Northern Ireland's Mark Farmer third on a Suzuki. All three survived a protest for jumping the start. Morrison, repeating his Brands performance, grabbed fastest lap – a new track record by over four mph. Mark Phillips, a crasher on oil at Brands, was fourth on the Loctite Yamaha from Andy McGladdery's Suzuki and Rymer completed the top six.

At Mallory, Morrison returned to the winner's circle and moved into a 14.5 point lead over Irons who could only finish seventh with a rear shock absorber problem. Although the RC30's were winning, Phillips again rode his heart out for second, but still finished seven seconds behind the Honda. This round marked a new development in the series. With nothing remotely competitive between the Hondas, several riders had been airing ideas of swapping to the vee-fours. Trevor Nation fronted at Mallory with one and promptly took fourth behind Dixon's Suzuki but in front of Rymer.

At Donington Rymer also had a Honda and sure enough the leaderboard read Honda 1-2-3-4. Morrison again won, setting fastest lap, from Irons, Nation and Rymer. The feature of the race was Nation clinching third on the line from Rymer after an epic race-long battle. Phillips was again best of the rest in fifth but only after Farmer had dumped his Suzuki at Craner Curves. Scot Steve Hislop brought his RC30 into sixth ahead of Ray Stringer's Suzuki.

When the Superstock regulars reached Knockhill, they were still reeling from the news of Kenny Irons death at Cadwell the week before. Morrison continued his relentless pace winning again and Steve Hislop, getting to grips with short circuit racing on his RC30, took second, making it a joyful occasion for the Scots on home soil. Stringer had actually led in the opening stages, but Rymer took over only for his shock to go off. He held onto third from Phillips, Nation and then Stringer.

At Snetterton Morrison won, once more setting a record lap. Hislop again finished second from Steve Chambers, his best result of the year, and he too had now gone the RC30 route. Phillips was fourth with Nation beating Rymer, who was carrying a hand injury from Saturday's training crash, for fifth.

Round seven at Cadwell Park on the Woodlands circuit produced some of the closest racing up-front the series had seen – at least in the early laps. Morrison had crashed the previous weekend at Mallory in an F1 race and was carrying a badly bruised and very sore leg injury. He opted to ride but came under fire from Trevor Nation. Nation pushed Morrison very hard and looked like he might get by until his motor overheated and lost power. That left the way clear for Morrison to collect the winner's spoils yet again and the

Jamie Whitham, Ray Swann and Darren Dixon fought many fine battles throughout the year.

Scotsman Brian Morrison dominated the British season on his Honda.

fastest lap. Nation kept a lone second from an equally lone Mark Phillips. Chambers was fourth from a hard-charging Stringer. Then came Hislop from a very disappointed Keith Huewen. He had clinched the '87 championship in this very race last year but his Yamaha was clearly no match for the Hondas. Rymer, a non-starter at Cadwell due to bent valves in his Honda motor, was to take no further part in the series. Instead, he preferred to gain valuable experience in the World Superbike competition in preparation for a full World assault in '89.

Morrison wrapped up the title at Thruxton with another virtuoso performance which left the field nearly half a lap adrift. Chambers grabbed his best result of the year, finishing second despite crashing during practice at the chicane. Local favourite Nation was third, but Gary Weston turned in a splendid ride on his Suzuki for fourth – by far his best ride in the series.

It had to happen sooner or later and at Mallory Steve Hislop actually took the chequered flag in front of Morrison, although the two Scots shared the fastest lap. But it was another lacklustre race with Nation third in front of Chambers, Phillips, and Stringer.

For the final three rounds at Cadwell, Kirkistown and Brands it was all Morrison. He also set fastest lap at each event, a feat he managed to complete in every single race. Morrison deserves every praise for his achievements. Rarely has one man dominated a championship in such a way, but in truth the series was simply a shadow of its former exciting self.

Results

Round 1 2 May, Brands Hatch (9 laps, 10.8 miles)

1 B. Morrison *(Honda)*, 7m 49s, 83.14mph
2 K. Irons *(Honda)*; 3 D. Dixon *(Suzuki)*; 4 T. Rymer *(Suzuki)*; 5 G. Weston *(Suzuki)*; 6 A. McGladdery *(Suzuki)*; 7 S. Chambers *(Yamaha)*; 8 D. Barry *(Yamaha)*; 9 T. Nation *(Suzuki)*; 10 D. Crampton *(Suzuki)*.
Half points awarded
Fastest lap: B. Morrison *(Honda)*, 50.3s, 86.14mph

Round 2 15 May, Mondello Park (15 laps, 18.6 miles)

1 K. Irons *(Honda)*, 15m 23.1s, 72.54mph
2 B. Morrison *(Honda)*; 3 M. Farmer *(Suzuki)*; 4 M. Phillips *(Yamaha)*; 5 A. McGladdery *(Suzuki)*; 6 T. Rymer *(Suzuki)*; 7 G. Fowler *(Yamaha)*; 8 R. Stringer *(Suzuki)*; 9 P. Borley *(Yamaha)*; 10 J. Lofthouse *(Suzuki)*.
Fastest lap: B. Morrison *(Honda)*, 1m 0.51s, 73.77mph (record)

Round 3 12 June, Mallory Park (15 laps, 20.55 miles)

1 B. Morrison *(Honda)*, 13m 21.8s; 92.26mph
2 M. Phillips *(Yamaha)*; 3 D. Dixon *(Suzuki)*; 4 T. Nation *(Honda)*; 5 T. Rymer *(Suzuki)*; 6 R. Stringer *(Suzuki)*; 7 K. Irons *(Honda)*; 8 M. Farmer *(Suzuki)*; 9 K. Mawdsley *(Suzuki)*; 10 S. Chambers *(Yamaha)*.
Fastest lap: B. Morrison *(Honda)*, 52.7s, 93.58mph

Round 4 19 June, Donington Park (15 laps, 29.36 miles)

1 B. Morrison *(Honda)*, 19m 90s, 92.62mph
2 K. Irons *(Honda)*; 3 T. Nation *(Honda)*; 4 T. Rymer *(Honda)*; 5 M. Phillips *(Yamaha)*; 6 S. Hislop *(Honda)*; 7 R. Stringer *(Suzuki)*; 8 K. Huewen *(Yamaha)*; 9 S. Chambers *(Yamaha)*; 10 D. Crampton *(Suzuki)*.
Fastest lap: B. Morrison *(Honda)*, 1m 14.8s, 94.18mph (record)

Round 5 10 July, Knockhill (15 laps, 19.335m)

1 B. Morrison *(Honda)*, 14m 44.4s, 82.43mph
2 S. Hislop *(Honda)*; 3 T. Rymer *(Honda)*; 4 M. Phillips *(Yamaha)*; 5 T. Nation *(Honda)*; 6 R. Stringer *(Suzuki)*; 7 G. Weston *(Suzuki)*; 8 D. Dixon *(Suzuki)*; 9 K. Huewen *(Yamaha)*; 10 D. Heal *(Honda)*.
Fastest lap: B. Morrison *(Honda)*, 55.1s, 84.22mph

Round 6 17 July, Snetterton (12 laps, 23.004m)

1 B. Morrison *(Honda)*, 13m 56.6s, 98.98mph
2 S. Hislop *(Honda)*; 3 S. Chambers *(Honda)*; 4 T. Nation *(Honda)*; 5 T. Rymer *(Honda)*; 6 D. Dixon *(Suzuki)*; 7 M. Jupp *(Yamaha)*; 8 M. Phillips *(Yamaha)*; 9 D. Crampton *(Suzuki)*; 10 C. Corner, *(Honda)*.
Record lap: B. Morrison *(Honda)*, 1m 8.7s, 100.45mph

Round 7 31 July, Cadwell Park (25 laps, 21.225m)

1 B. Morrison *(Honda)*, 18m 56.8s, 67.21mph
2 T. Nation *(Honda)*; 3 M. Phillips *(Yamaha)*; 4 S. Chambers *(Honda)*; 5 R. Stringer *(Suzuki)*; 6 S. Hislop *(Honda)*; 7 K. Huewen *(Yamaha)*; 8 P. Brookes *(Suzuki)*; 9 D. Dixon *(Honda)*; 10 C. Breeze *(Yamaha)*.
Fastest lap: B. Morrison *(Honda)*, 44.6s, 68.53mph

Round 8 20 August, Thruxton (10 laps 23.56m)

1 B. Morrison *(Honda)*, 14m 15.80s, 99.11mph
2 S. Chambers *(Honda)*; 3 T. Nation *(Honda)*; 4 G. Weston *(Suzuki)*; 5 D. Ireland *(Honda)*; 6 A. McGladdery *(Honda)*; 7 D. Crampton *(Suzuki)*; 8 R. Stringer *(Suzuki)*; 9 M. Jupp *(Yamaha)*; 10 M. Phillips *(Yamaha)*.
Fastest lap: B. Morrison *(Honda)*, 1m 23.60s 101.45mph

Round 9 3 September, Mallory Park (15 laps, 20.55 miles)

1 S. Hislop *(Honda)*, 13m 08.8s, 93.78mph
2 B. Morrison *(Honda)*; 3 T. Nation *(Honda)*; 4 S. Chambers *(Honda)*; 5 M. Phillips *(Yamaha)*; 6 R. Stringer *(Suzuki)*; 7 K. Huewen *(Yamaha)*; 8 C. Corner *(Honda)*; 9 G. Weston *(Suzuki)*; 10 D. Barry *(Yamaha)*.
Fastest lap: S. Hislop *(Honda)* and B. Morrison *(Honda)*, 51.7s, 95.39mph

Round 10 2 October, Cadwell Park (10 laps, 21.74 miles)

1 B. Morrison *(Honda)*, 16m 2.8s, 81.25mph
2 S. Chambers *(Honda)*; 3 T. Nation *(Honda)*; 4 S. Hislop *(Honda)*; 5 G. Thrush *(Honda)*; 6 G. Weston *(Suzuki)*; 7 D. Crompton *(Suzuki)*; 8 K. Heuwen *(Yamaha)*; 9 D. Griffith *(Honda)*; 10 D. Ireland *(Honda)*.
Fastest lap: B. Morrison *(Honda)*, 1m 34.1s, 83.17mph (record)

Round 11 8 October, Kirkistown (12 laps, 17.952 miles)

1 B. Morrison *(Honda)*, 15m 36.02s, 80.55mph
2 S. Hislop *(Honda)*; 3 T. Nation *(Honda)*; 4 D. Griffith *(Honda)*; 5 K. Heuwen *(Yamaha)*; 6 G. Weston *(Suzuki)*; 7 G. Farlow *(Suzuki)*; 8 D. Barry *(Yamaha)*; 9 E. Galbraith *(Suzuki)*; 10 D. Ireland *(Honda)*.
Fastest lap: B. Morrison *(Honda)*, 1m 5.16s, 82.65mph

Round 12 23 October, Brands Hatch (15 laps, 18.05 miles)

1 B. Morrison *(Honda)*; 12m 27.2s, 86.98mph
2 S. Chambers *(Honda)*; 3 T. Nation *(Honda)*; 4 G. Weston *(Suzuki)*; 5 K. Huewen *(Yamaha)*; 6 D. Dixon *(Suzuki)*; 7 D. Ireland *(Honda)*; 8 D. Griffith *(Honda)*; 9 G. Thrush *(Honda)*; 10 G. Baldock *(Yamaha)*.
Fastest lap: B. Morrison *(Honda)*, 49.0s, 88.42mph

Final Championship Positions

1 B. Morrison 188.5 points
2 T. Nation, 95; 3 S. Hislop, 70; 4 S. Chambers, 67; 5 M. Phillips, 54; 6 T. Rymer, 39; 7 K. Irons, 37; 8 G. Weston, 35; 9 R. Stringer, 31; 10 D. Dixon, 30.

BRITISH JUNIOR

Steve Patrickson again dominated the major domestic championship for pure-bred racing 250cc/350cc machinery, this year called the 'Junior' class – surely the most underrated, underpublicised class in the entire British championship schedule?

With the Derek Clarke/Raydel Racing Rotax, Patrickson built a healthy lead by scoring heavily in the first eight races, including four wins, of the rather drawn-out fifteen-round series, but then suffered reliability problems with the temperamental Rotax motor, which took the edge off his fine season. He nevertheless scored his fifth win with a quite superb effort at Thruxton, but was confirmed Champion whilst sidelined with a seizure at Mallory with three more rounds of the championship remaining.

Irishman Woolsey Coulter clinched second place overall by winning the final round at Brands and in doing so prevented Rob Orme from completing a unique 1–2 for sponsor Derek Clarke. Orme wound up third in the series, five points ahead of the luckless Peter Hubbard. The most consistent finisher in the series, Hubbard was second going into the final round but crashed his Keppel Yamaha in practice and badly broke his leg.

The season for the 'Juniors' began at Donington during the Easter Eurolantic meeting and Kevin Mitchell did the business on his Grand Prix Yamaha TZ250U. Steve Williams was an impressive runner-up on an old 350 Yamaha in the Fowlers of Bristol colours. Making Williams' efforts even more noteworthy was the fact that the Welsh veteran had also completed two lengthy World Superbike races the same day! Irishman Woolsey Coulter was third on Francis Neill's Honda, with reigning British Champion Steve Patrickson fourth on a Nico Bakker-framed Rotax, as his new Hejira was not yet ready for action. Steve Hislop made it a good day for the 350s, finishing fifth.

At Brands in early May Nigel Bosworth showed why he was embarking on a full season of European Championship racing. He stole the show with his Keppel Racing Aprilia. Patrickson edged Mitchell for second but the GP regular continued to hold the points advantage. All three shared a new lap record.

At televised Carnaby, Patrickson, still on the Bakker Rotax, was firmly in control after despatching pacesetter Mark Westmorland to a distant second place and snatched the points lead from the absent Mitchell. Rising star John Reynolds, a former motocrosser, was third on his eight-year-old 350 Yamaha from Coulter's year-old 250 Honda.

Patrickson repeated the win at Mallory to open a 25-point lead, but Reynolds this time took second on that old 350 with Keppel Racing's other runner, Peter Hubbard, third.

On to Donington and Rob Orme won from a chasing Patrickson. Bosworth had been challenging Orme's scant lead but crashed at the chicane. Williams, back on the trail, took third from Ian Newton, his best result with the carbon fibre Rotax he was developing. At Cadwell it was business as usual for Patrickson, who by now had given up waiting for the Hejira and resigned himself to continuing with the four-year-old Bakker chassis which was, after all, proving its worth. He beat Orme by 5.3 seconds on this occasion with Alan Jeffrey continuing his promising transition from the 500s in third. At Knockhill Orme won his second race of the year with Fogarty second, Scot Greig Ramsey third on his 'U' spec Yamaha, Coulter fourth and Patrickson only fifth. Further back were Terry Sanders on a 350 and Chris Martin scoring his best result of the series in a comeback year with an Aprilia.

Snetterton was a straight shootout between Euro jockeys Bosworth and Orme, the former running out the winner after Orme got off at the high speed Corams. Patrickson was second to extend his point lead to 51 over the crashing Orme. Steve Hislop was fifth and Ian Newton eighth; significant results for Honda Britain-supplied NSRs, neither having made the results in their debuts at Knockhill.

At Mallory Bosworth repeated the dose but only after the best race of the series. He fought long and hard with Orme, Hislop and Reynolds. Hislop went off at a good pace from the start but was eventually reeled in by the pursuing trio. Patrickson sat on the sidelines watching the action after his Rotax crank had broken.

The Cadwell Woodland circuit claimed its usual crop of runners at the hairpin. Bosworth never even made it to the final after being centrepunched by Paul Grubb in a qualifying heat. In the final Terry Saunders looped a brakie when he locked up the front end and brought several riders to grief including Mitchell. Others taking evasive action in the incident included Orme, Hislop and Patrickson, but they all fought their way back into the point-scoring positions. Woolsey Coulter, after an overnight drive from a successful outing at the Ulster Grand Prix, was a runaway winner, with Patrickson a closing second after the first turn mêlée. Hislop fought back to third but Orme lost it at Hall Bends with four laps left. Hubbard was fourth, Mark Barker on a Honda fifth and Andy Muggleton, celebrating a return to open class racing with an ex-Grieg Ramsey Yamaha, sixth.

Although the BBC TV cameras were at Thruxton, they failed to capture the Junior final which was the best race of the day, with Patrickson winning a typically close scrap from Pete Hubbard, Coulter and Mitchell. Patrickson's late braking into the final chicane was the breathtaking show stealer of the race during his dice with Bosworth, who eventually crashed at the fast village curve, injuring his foot.

Back to Mallory and Patrickson hit trouble again, retiring early on, but he wrapped up the title whilst watching the race from the hairpin. It was another epic as Mitchell just got the verdict from the ever-improving Newton, who was at last getting to grips with the Honda after the mid-season swap. Orme was third with Hubbard fourth. Again the TV cameras were not rolling for this exciter!

Mitchell made it two in a row when he won at Scarborough the following weekend from Hubbard. Mark Barker took third, his best result in the series on the Honda, and talented young Irish hope, Leslie McMaster, was fourth.

Hislop took his first win in the championship in the penultimate round at Cadwell with a runaway effort. Behind him, the action was as hectic as usual with Orme getting the verdict in a blanket finish runner-up battle which also included Mitchell, Hubbard and Coulter. Bosworth took a chasing fifth and the fastest lap, after being forced onto the grass along with Ian Newton when Terry Sanders fell.

The final round at Brands Hatch went Coulter's way in a race which any one of seven looked likely to win. At middle distance in the 14-lapper Gary Cowan looked the favourite having broken clear of the pack but he slid his East West Transport Yamaha to earth at Druids leaving Coulter to lead them home. But his advantage was never certain. Newton, Orme, who had crashed in practice the previous day, Williams, again impressing on the 350, and Patrickson kept up the pressure with a mere 0.9 of a second separating them at the flag.

Coulter may have clinched the runner-up place in the series and Honda, thanks to another fine Ian Newton ride, may have scored an impressive 1–2 in the race, but Patrickson and Rotax ran out the emphatic champions of what is likely to be the last ever combined 250/350 British championship. Next year the 250s will run alone and the 350s will be consigned to the ACU Star series. The days of competing in a major British championship with a £1,500 350 Yamaha against the £10,000+250s are over.

Round 1 3 April, Donington Park (10 laps, 19.57 miles)

1 K. Mitchell *(250 Yamaha)*, 15m 3.87s, 77.94mph
2 S. Williams *(350 Yamaha)*; 3 W. Coulter *(250 Honda)*; 4 S. Patrickson *(250 Rotax)*; 5 S. Hislop *(350 Yamaha)*; 6 D. Higgins *(350 Yamaha)*; 7 A. Godber *(250 Yamaha)*; 8 S. Sawford *(250 Yamaha)*; 9 P. Hubbard *(250 Yamaha)*; 10 D. Redgate *(250 Yamaha)*.
Fastest lap: K. Mitchell *(Yamaha)*, 1m 28.43s, 79.66mph

Round 2 2 May, Brands Hatch (14 laps, 16.8 miles)

1 N. Bosworth *(250 Aprilia)*, 11m 51.5s, 82.25mph
2 S. Patrickson *(250 Rotax)*; 3 K. Mitchell *(250 Yamaha)*; 4 P. Hubbard *(250 Yamaha)*; 5 A. Godber *(250 Yamaha)*; 6 S. Hislop *(350 Yamaha)*; 7 C. Fogarty *(250 Honda)*; 8 A. Jeffrey *(250 Yamaha)*; 9 M. Barker *(250 Honda)*; 10 J. Reynolds *(350 Yamaha)*.
Fastest lap: N. Bosworth *(250 Aprilia)*, K. Mitchell *(250 Yamaha)* and S. Patrickson *(250 Rotax)*, 49.9s, 86.83mph

Round 3 22 May, Carnaby (14 laps, 16.8 miles)

1 S. Patrickson *(250 Rotax)*, 13m 7.9s, 77.4mph
2 M. Westmorland *(250 Honda)*; 3 J. Reynolds *(350 Yamaha)*; 4 W. Coulter *(250 Honda)*; 5 D. Butler *(250 Yamaha)*; 6 M. Barker *(250 Honda)*; 7 A. Godber *(250 Yamaha)*; 8 T. Hutton *(250 Yamaha)*; 9 T. Sanders *(350 Yamaha)*; 10 P. Weston *(350 Yamaha)*.
Fastest lap: S. Patrickson *(250 Rotax)*, 55.2s, 78.91mph.

Round 4 12 June, Mallory Park (12 laps, 16.44 miles)
1 S. Patrickson *(250 Rotax)*, 10m 51.5s, 90.84mph
2 J. Reynolds *(350 Yamaha)*; 3 P. Hubbard *(250 Yamaha)*; 4 A. Godber *(250 Yamaha)*; 5 D. Butler *(250 Yamaha)*; 6 D. Higgins *(350 Yamaha)*; 7 M. Nelson *(350 Yamaha)*; 8 S. Bevington *(350 Yamaha)*; 9 A. Jeffrey *(250 Yamaha)*; 10 M. Barker *(250 Honda)*.
Fastest lap: S. Patrickson *(Rotax)*, 52.9s, 93.23mph

Round 5 19 June, Donington Park (10 laps, 19.57 miles)

1 R. Orme *(250 Yamaha)*, 12m 56.5s, 90.73mph
2 S. Patrickson *(250 Rotax)*; 3 S. Williams *(350 Yamaha)*; 4 I. Newton *(250 Rotax)*; 5 P. Hubbard *(250 Yamaha)*; 6 A. Jeffrey *(250 Yamaha)*; 7 B. Stanley *(350 Yamaha)*; 8 G. Ramsey *(250 Yamaha)*; 9 T. Sanders *(350 Yamaha)*; 10 S. Tomes *(350 Yamaha)*.
Fastest lap: S. Patrickson *(Rotax)*, 1m 16.0s, 92.07mph (record)

Round 6 26 June, Cadwell Park (8 laps, 17.39 miles)

1 S. Patrickson *(250 Rotax)* 13m 4.2s, 79.84mph
2 R. Orme *(250 Yamaha)*; 3 A. Jeffrey *(250 Yamaha)*; 4 I. Newton *(250 Rotax)*; 5 T. Sanders *(350 Yamaha)*; 6 M. Westmorland *(250 Honda)*; 7 D. Butler *(250 Yamaha)*; 8 P. Hubbard *(250 Yamaha)*; 9 J. Reynolds *(350 Yamaha)*; 10 T. Couzens *(250 Rotax)*.
Fastest lap: S. Patrickson *(Rotax)*, 1m 36.0s, 81.52mph (record)

Round 7 10 July, Knockhill (12 laps, 15.46m)

1 R. Orme *(250 Rotax)*, 11m 43.3s, 79.18mph
2 C. Fogarty *(250 Honda)*; 3 G. Ramsey *(250 Yamaha)*; 4 W. Coulter *(250 Honda)*; 5 S. Patrickson *(250 Rotax)*; 6 T. Sanders *(350 Yamaha)*; 7 C. Martin *(250 Aprilia)*; 8 J. Reynolds *(350 Yamaha)*; 9 I. Newton *(250 Honda)*; 10 P. Hubbard *(250 Yamaha)*.
Record lap: C. Fogarty *(250 Honda)* and S. Patrickson *(250 Rotax)*, 57.5s, 80.7mph

Round 8 17 July, Snetterton (10 laps, 19.17m)

1 N. Bosworth *(250 Aprilia)*, 11m 58.8s, 96.01mph
2 S. Patrickson *(250 Rotax)*; 3 T. Sanders *(350 Yamaha)*; 4 W. Coulter *(250 Honda)*; 5 S. Hislop *(250 Honda)*; 6 P. Hubbard *(250 Yamaha)*; 7 S. Moss *(350 Yamaha)*; 8 I. Newton *(250 Honda)*; 9 R. Orme *(250 Rotax)*; 10 M. Nelson *(250 Yamaha)*.
Fastest lap: N. Bosworth *(250 Aprilia)*, 1m 10.6s, 97.75mph

Round 9 24 July, Mallory Park (12 laps, 16.44m)

1 N. Bosworth *(250 Aprilia)*, 10m 52.3s, 90.73mph
2 S. Hislop *(250 Honda)*; 3 R. Orme *(250 Rotax)*; 4 J. Reynolds *(350 Yamaha)*; 5 W. Coulter *(250 Honda)*; 6 I. Newton *(250 Honda)*; 7 P. Hubbard *(250 Yamaha)*; 8 T. Sanders *(350 Yamaha)*; 9 A. Godber *(250 Yamaha)*; 10 S. Sawford *(250 Yamaha)*.
Fastest lap: N. Bosworth *(250 Aprilia)*, 52.7s, 93.58mph

Round 10 31 July, Cadwell Park (25 laps, 21.225m)

1 W. Coulter *(250 Honda)*, 19m 28s, 65.42mph
2 S. Patrickson *(250 Rotax)*; 3 S. Hislop *(250 Honda)*; 4 P. Hubbard *(250 Yamaha)*; 5 M. Barker *(250 Honda)*; 6 A. Muggleton *(250 Yamaha)*; 7 M. Llewelyn *(350 Yamaha)*; 8 A. Lewis *(350 Yamaha)*; 9 T. Couzens *(250 Rotax)*; 10 A. Garner *(250 Yamaha)*.
Fastest lap: S. Hislop *(250 Honda)*, 45.5s, 67.17mph.

Round 11 20 August, Thruxton (10 laps 23.56m)

1 S. Patrickson *(250 Rotax)*, 14m 12.4s, 99.50mph
2 P. Hubbard *(250 Yamaha)*; 3 W. Coulter *(250 Yamaha)*; 4 K. Mitchell *(250 Yamaha)*; 5 R. Orme *(250 Rotax)*; 6 S. Hislop *(250 Honda)*; 7 S. Williams *(350 Yamaha)*; 8 A. Jeffrey *(250 Yamaha)*; 9 S. Coker *(350 Exactweld)*; 10 S. Sawford *(250 Yamaha)*.
Fastest lap: P. Hubbard *(250 Yamaha)*, 1m 23.50s, 101.58mph.

Round 12 3 September, Mallory Park, (15 laps, 20.55 miles)

1 K. Mitchell *(250 Yamaha)*, 13m 18.3s, 92.67mph
2 I. Newton *(250 Honda)*; 3 R. Orme *(250 Rotax)*; 4 P. Hubbard *(250 Yamaha)*; 5 A. Muggleton *(250 Yamaha)*; 6 T. Sanders *(350 Yamaha)*; 7 G. Ramsey *(250 Yamaha)*; 8 W. Coulter *(250 Honda)*; 9. J. Reynolds *(250 Yamaha)*; 10 M. Barker *(250 Honda)*.
Fastest lap: K. Mitchell *(250 Yamaha)*, 52.1s, 94.66mph

Round 13 10 September, Scarborough (12 laps, 28.92 miles)

1 K. Mitchell *(250 Yamaha)*, 22m 07.7s, 78.53mph
2 P. Hubbard *(250 Yamaha)*; 3 M. Barker *(250 Honda)*; 4 L. McMaster *(250 Yamaha)*; 5 W. Coulter *(250 Honda)*; 6 S. Dowey *(250 Rotax)*; 7 S. Patrickson *(250 Rotax)*; 8 P. Wakefield *(250 Rotax)*; 9 B. Parrish *(350 Yamaha)*; 10 D. Wallis *(250 Yamaha)*.
Fastest lap: S. Hislop *(Honda)*, 1m 48.3s, 80.23mph

Round 14 2 October, Cadwell Park (10 laps, 21.74 miles)

1 S. Hislop *(250 Honda)*, 13m 4.7s, 79.78mph

2 R. Orme *(250 Rotax)*; 3 K. Mitchell *(250 Yamaha)*; 4 P. Hubbard *(250 Yamaha)*; 5 W. Coulter *(250 Honda)*; 6 N. Bosworth *(250 Aprilia)*; 7 A. Jeffrey *(250 Yamaha)*; 8 I. Newton *(250 Honda)*; 9 M. Barker *(250 Honda)*; 10 A. Godber *(250 EMC)*.
Fastest lap: N. Bosworth *(250 Aprilia)*, 1m 35.4s, 82.03mph (record)

Round 15 23 October, Brands Hatch (14 laps, 16.85 miles)

1 W. Coulter *(250 Honda)*, 11m 50.1s, 85.42mph
2 I. Newton *(250 Honda)*; 3 R. Orme *(250 Rotax)*; 4 S. Williams *(350 Yamaha)*; 5 S. Patrickson *(250 Rotax)*; 6 M. Barker *(250 Honda)*; 7 E. Laycock *(250 EMC)*; 8 T. Hutton *(250 Yamaha)*; 9 C. Brennan *(250 Honda)*; 10 P. McCallen *(250 Honda)*.
Fastest lap: G. Cowan *(250 Yamaha)*; 49.6s, 87.35mph

Final Championship positions (15 rounds, best 13 scores count)

1 S. Patrickson, 132 points
2 W. Coulter, 95; 3 R. Orme, 92; 4 P. Hubbard, 87; 5 K. Mitchell, 73; 6 S. Hislop, 59; 7 I. Newton, 53; 8 N. Bosworth, 50; 9 J. Reynolds, 38; 10 S. Williams, 34.

BRITISH PRODUCTION

Against all odds Heron Suzuki rider James Whitham won the British Production title. At the start of the season it looked like the new GSX-R750J would be hopelessly outclassed by the GSX1100 Suzukis and FZR1000 Yamahas.

Geoff Johnson on Avon tyres scored a win and a second in the first two races with a Yamaha and Ian Wilson won round two at Brands on an 1100 GSX-R with Metzeler rubber but the controversial arrival of Michelin TX tyres transformed Whitham's efforts and he won the third round at Carnaby. He took the next one at Mallory but a new name was also emerging, that of 18-year-old Ian Simpson with the Scotspeed 1100 Suzuki. He had ridden a 750 in the opening race at Donington, pronounced it uncompetitive and bought the 1100. He then started figuring in the top three and then won at Donington.

Other riders had a shot at the front, although both Johnson and Wilson were injured in separate crashes at Knockhill which ruled them out for much of the season. Brian Morrison won at Cadwell with the Metzeler-backed Honda RC30, Iain Duffus took a popular local win at Knockhill, Mark Phillips won twice with a Dunlop-shod Loctite Yamaha, rejuvenated Scot Howard Selby took Mallory with his Suzuki 110 on Metzelers and Trevor Nation won twice at Cadwell, once on a Yamaha and once on a Suzuki, both bikes on Pirelli tyres.

All the time, however, it was Whitham and Simpson racking up the big scores on a regular basis. Both won again, Whitham at Mallory and Simpson at Thruxton, where Whitham raced an 1100. Simpson ran out of luck in the later stages with three crashes in four races but he had done enough to impress and earned a full Heron Suzuki team ride for 1989.

Whitham sewed up the title at Scarborough which was just as well because he never scored another point in the last two races. He fell at Cadwell when the exhaust dug in and pitched him off. Then he was a non-starter in the final at Brands, won by Simpson, after he had collided with a backmarker in an earlier race. Although he had not crashed in the incident he was too sore to take to the grid.

Round 1 4 April, Donington Park (10 laps, 19.57 miles)

1 G. Johnson *(1000 Yamaha)*, 13m 19.56s, 88.11mph
2 A. Cummings *(1000 Yamaha)*; 3 R. Hurst *(1000 Kawasaki)*; 4 C. Corner *(1000 Yamaha)*; 5 I. Wilson *(1100 Suzuki)*; 6 R. Swann *(1000 Kawasaki)*; 7 J. Whitham *(750 Suzuki)*; 8 J. Lofthouse *(750 Suzuki)*; 9 B. Morrison *(750 Honda)*; 10 H. Selby *(1100 Suzuki)*.
Fastest lap: I. Wilson *(1100 Suzuki)*, 1m 18.65s, 89.57mph

Round 2 2 May, Brands Hatch (14 laps, 16.8 miles)

1 I. Wilson *(1100 Suzuki)*, 12m 11.9s, 82.88mph
2 G. Johnson *(1000 Yamaha)*; 3 I. Simpson *(1100 Suzuki)*; 4 M. Phillips *(1100 Yamaha)*; 5 R. Haynes *(1000 Kawasaki)*; 6 B. Morrison *(750 Honda)*; 7 E. McFarlane *(1000 Yamaha)*; 8 G. Read *(1100 Suzuki)*; 9 J. Whitham *(750 Suzuki)*; 10 H. Selby *(1100 Suzuki)*.
Fastest lap: I. Wilson *(1100 Suzuki)* & G. Read *(1100 Suzuki)*, 51.2s, 84.63mph

Round 3 22 May, Carnaby (14 laps, 16.8 miles)

1 J. Whitham *(750 Suzuki)*, 13m 20.1s, 76.42mph
2 I. Simpson *(1100 Suzuki)*; 3 I. Wilson *(1100 Suzuki)*; 4 R. Hurst *(1000 Kawasaki)*; 5 A. Cummings *(1000 Yamaha)*; 6 C. Corner *(1000 Yamaha)*; 7 R. Swann *(1000 Kawasaki)*; 8 P. Mellor *(750 Suzuki)*; 9 G. Thrush *(1000 Yamaha)*; 10 A. McDonald *(1100 Suzuki)*.
Fastest lap: J. Whitham *(750 Suzuki)* 56.1s, 77.65mph (record)

Round 4 12 June, Mallory Park (12 laps, 16.44 miles)

1 J. Whitham *(750 Suzuki)*, 11m 0.8s, 89.56mph
2 G. Read *(1100 Suzuki)*; 3 I. Simpson *(1100 Suzuki)*; 4 B. Morrison *(750 Honda)*; 5 G. Johnson *(1000 Yamaha)*; 6 C. White *(1100 Suzuki)*; 7 H. Selby *(1100 Suzuki)*; 8 G. Thrush *(1000 Yamaha)*; 9 M. Phillips *(1000 Yamaha)*; 10 P. Mellor *(750 Suzuki)*.
Fastest lap: B. Morrison *(750 Honda)*, 53.9s, 91.5mph (record)

Round 5 19 June, Donington Park (10 laps, 19.57 miles)

1 I. Simpson *(1100 Suzuki)*, 13m 9.3s, 89.25mph
2 B. Morrison *(750 Honda)*; 3 G. Johnson *(1000 Yamaha)*; 4 J. Whitham *(750 Suzuki)*; 5 G. Thrush *(1000 Yamaha)*; 6 H. Selby *(1100 Suzuki)*; 7 A. McDonald *(1100 Suzuki)*; 8 I. Wilson *(1100 Suzuki)*; 9 E. McFarlane *(1000 Yamaha)*; 10 D. Ashton *(1100 Suzuki)*.
Fastest lap: B. Morrison *(750 Honda)*, 1m 16.9s, 91.61mph (record)

Round 6 26 June, Cadwell Park (8 laps, 17.39 miles)

1 B. Morrison *(750 Honda)*, 13m 21.4s, 78.12mph
2 J. Whitham *(750 Suzuki)*; 3 I Simpson *(1100 Suzuki)*; 4 E. McFarlane *(1000 Yamaha)*;

5 G. Thrush *(1000 Yamaha)*; 6 H. Selby *(1100 Suzuki)*; 7 G. Johnson *(1000 Yamaha)*; 8 D. Ashton *(1100 Suzuki)*; 9 C. White *(1100 Suzuki)*; 10 A. McDonald *(1100 Suzuki)*.
Fastest lap: B. Morrison *(750 Honda)*, 1m 38.3s, 79.61mph (record)

Round 7 10 June, Knockhill (12 laps, 15.46m)

1 I. Duffus *(1100 Suzuki)*, 11m 45.2s, 78.96mph
2 H. Selby *(1100 Suzuki)*; 3 B. Morrison *(750 Honda)*; 4 R. Bennett *(1100 Suzuki)*; 5 E. McFarlane *(1000 Yamaha)*; 6 I. Simpson *(1100 Suzuki)*; 7 J. Whitham *(750 Suzuki)*; 8 A. McDonald *(1100 Suzuki)*; 9 T. Nation *(750 Honda)*; 10 G. Thrush *(1000 Yamaha)*.
Fastest lap: H. Selby *(1100 Suzuki)*, 56.6s, 81.99mph

Round 8 17 July, Snetterton (10 laps, 19.17m)

1 M. Phillips *(1000 Yamaha)*, 12m 2.2s, 95.55mph
2 J. Whitham *(1100 Suzuki)*; 3 B. Morrison *(750 Honda)*; 4 G. Thrush *(1000 Yamaha)*; 5 I. Duffus (*1100 Suzuki)*; 6 I. Simpson (*1100 Suzuki)*; 7 D. Ashton *(1100 Suzuki)*; 8 R. Swann *(1000 Kawasaki)*; 9 T. Nation *(750 Honda)*; 10 R. Hurst *(1000 Kawasaki)*.
Fastest lap: J. Whitham *(750 Suzuki)* and B. Morrison *(750 Honda)*, 1m 11.2s, 96.92mph

Round 9 24 July, Mallory Park (12 laps, 16.44m)

1 J. Whitham *(750 Suzuki)*, 10m 50s, 91.05mph
2 I. Simpson *(1100 Suzuki)*; 3 I. Duffus *(1100 Suzuki)*; 4 M. Phillips *(1000 Yamaha)*; 5 H. Selby *(1100 Suzuki)*; 6 C. White (*1100 Suzuki)*; 7 A. McDonald *(1100 Suzuki)*; 8 R. Stringer *(750 Suzuki)*; 9 C. Gable *(750 Honda)*; 10 D. Ashton *(1100 Suzuki)*.
Fastest lap: J. Whitham *(750 Suzuki)*, 53.6s, 92.01mph

Round 10 31 July, Cadwell Park (20 laps, 16.98m)

1 T. Nation *(1000 Yamaha)*, 15m 49s, 64.41mph
2 R. Stringer *(750 Suzuki)*; 3 G. Thrush *(1000 Yamaha)*; 4 B. Morrison *(750 Honda)*; 5 J. Whitham *(750 Suzuki)*; 6 P. Mellor *(750 Suzuki)*; 7 A. Cummings *(1000 Yamaha)*; 8 H. Selby *(1100 Suzuki)*; 9 B. Doyle *(1100 Suzuki)*; 10 A. Batson (*1100 Suzuki)*.
Fastest lap: T. Nation *(1000 Yamaha)*, 46.6s, 65.59mph

Round 11 20 August, Thruxton (10 laps, 23.56m)

1 I. Simpson *(1100 Suzuki)*, 15m 08.80s, 93.33mph
2 J. Whitham *(1100 Suzuki)*; 3 D. Ashton *(1100 Suzuki)*; 4 M. Phillips *(1000 Yamaha)*; 5 C. White *(1100 Suzuki)*; 6 H. Selby *(1100 Suzuki)*; 7 G. Thrush (*1000 Yamaha)*; 8 A. Cummings *(1000 Yamaha)*; 9 E. McFarlane *(1000 Yamaha)*; 10 R. Stringer *(750 Suzuki)*.
Fastest lap: J. Whitham *(1100 Suzuki)*, 1m 26.20, 98.39mph

Round 12 3 September, Mallory Park (12 laps, 16.44 miles)

1 H. Selby *(1100 Suzuki)*, 10m 53.1s, 90.62mph
2 J. Whitham *(750 Suzuki)*; 3 R. Stringer *(750 Suzuki)*; 4 M. Phillips *(1000 Yamaha)*; 5 D. Ashton *(1100 Suzuki)*; 6 B. Morrison *(750 Honda)*; 7 C. White *(1100 Suzuki)*; 8 J. Gainey *(750 Honda)*; 9 P. Mellor *(750 Suzuki)*; 10 I. Wilson *(1100 Suzuki)*.
Fastest lap: J. Whitham *(750 Suzuki)*, 53.5s, 92.18mph

Round 13 10 September, Scarborough (12 laps, 28.92 miles)

1 M. Phillips *(1000 Yamaha)*, 22m 18.5s, 79.57mph
2 G. Johnson *(1000 Yamaha)*; 3 J. Whitham *(750 Suzuki)*; 4 P. Mellor *(750 Suzuki)*; 5 H. Selby *(1100 Suzuki)*; 6 A. McDonald *(1100 Suzuki)*; 7 M. Searle *(1000 Yamaha)*; 8 L. Carter *(750 Suzuki)*; 9 D. Holmes *(1000 Yamaha)*.
Fastest lap: J. Whitham *(750 Suzuki)*, 1m 49.2s, 79.57mph

Round 14 2 October, Cadwell Park (10 laps, 21.74 miles)

1 T. Nation *(1100 Suzuki)*, 13m 20s, 78.26mph
2 H. Selby *(1100 Suzuki)*; 3 I. Simpson *(1100 Suzuki)*; 4 B. Morrison *(750 Honda)*; 5 E. McFarlane *(1100 Suzuki)*; 6 A. McDonald *(1100 Suzuki)*; 7 G. Johnson *(1000 Yamaha)*; 8 A. Cummings *(1000 Yamaha)*; 9 G. Baldock *(1000 Yamaha)*; 10 P. Mellor *(750 Suzuki)*.
Fastest lap: T. Nation *(1100 Suzuki)* and G. Thrush *(1000 Yamaha)*, 1m 38.4s, 79.53mph.

Round 15 23 October, Brands Hatch (14 laps, 16.85 miles)

1 I. Simpson *(1100 Suzuki)*, 11m 59.6s, 84.29mph
2 E. McFarlane *(1100 Suzuki)*; 3 T. Nation *(1100 Suzuki)*; 4 B. Morrison *(750 Honda)*; 5 P. Mellor *(750 Suzuki)*; 6 G. Read *(1100 Suzuki)*; 7 G. Thrush *(1000 Yamaha)*; 8 C. Gable *(750 Honda)*; 9 A. Cummings *(1000 Yamaha)*; 10 H. Mason *(1100 Suzuki)*.
Fastest lap: I. Simpson *(1100 Suzuki)*, 50.8s, 85.29mph

Final Championship Positions (15 rounds, best 13 scores count)

1 J. Whitham, 128 points
2 I. Simpson, 119; 3 B. Morrison, 92; 4 H. Selby, 76; 5 M. Phillips, 64; 6 G. Johnson, 63; =7 G. Thrush and T. Nation, 44; 9 E. McFarlane, 40; 10 I. Wilson, 37.

BRITISH SENIORSTOCK

The new Seniorstock class turned out to be one of the best production-based formulae of the year. The championship went to the wire and was a grudge match between Honda-mounted Brian Morrison and Ray Swann of Team Green Kawasaki.

Morrison on his Bike Studio entered CBR600 had won eight times going into the final round and Swann four. They were on equal points, 150 each, but with riders having to drop their worst two scores, Swann was actually eight points adrift.

The two had a coming together at Scarborough which resulted in a crash for Morrison which he claimed was caused by Swann's reckless riding, but the officials did not uphold the Scot's claim.

Unfortunately the Brands race was something of an anticlimax. It was stopped twice through serious crashes, the second time when Swann slid off and injured his leg. That handed the title to Morrison who finished third on the day. The race was won by local Gary Weston, who had been showing great improvement as the season progressed on the

Cat Motorcycles CBR. The only other non-factory-entered winner was Kiwi Rodney Knapp who took the honours at Cadwell on Colin Aldridge's CBR.

Suzuki took a long time getting their GSX600F competitive but James Whitham's hard riding brought them a string of top-three finishes which were good enough for third in the championship. Whitham and teammate Phil Mellor scored a 1–2 in the controversial Scarborough race, scene of the Morrison/Swann tussle!

Round 1 April 4, Donington Park (10 laps, 19.57 miles)

1 B. Morrison *(Honda)*, 13m 17.68s, 88.32mph
2 G. Johnson *(Honda)*; 3 E. McFarlane *(Honda)*; 4 A. Cummings *(Honda)*; 5 R. Hurst *(Kawasaki)*; 6 I. Waine *(Honda)*; 7 B. Nicholson *(Honda)*; 8 C. Brenneck *(Honda)*; 9 A. McDonald *(Honda)*; 10 S. Hislop *(Honda)*.
Fastest lap: B. Morrison *(Honda)*, 1m 18.62s, 89.61mph (lap record)

Round 2 2 May, Brands Hatch (14 laps, 16.8 miles)

1 B. Morrison *(Honda)*, 12m 20.3s, 82.16mph
2 C. Brenneck *(Honda)*; 3 G. Johnson *(Honda)*; 4 R. Swann *(Kawasaki)*; 5 R. Hurst *(Kawasaki)*; 6 E. McFarlane *(Honda)*; 7 J. Moodie *(Honda)*; 8 M. Heath *(Honda)*; 9 I. Waine *(Honda)*; 10 P. Mellor *(Suzuki)*.
Fastest lap: C. Brenneck *(Honda)*, 51.4s, 84.30mph

Round 3 21 May, Carnaby (14 laps, 16.8 miles)

1 R. Knapp *(Honda)*, 13m 21s, 76.13mph
2 R. Hurst *(Kawasaki)*; 3 R. Swann *(Kawasaki)*; 4 I. Waine *(Honda)*; 5 J. Whitham *(Suzuki)*; 6 G. Johnson *(Honda)*; 7 E. McFarlane *(Honda)*; 8 M. Seward *(Honda)*; 9 J. Moodie *(Honda)*; 10 A. Cummings *(Honda)*.
Fastest lap: B. Morrison *(Honda)*, 55.8s, 78.06mph

Round 4 12 June, Mallory Park (9 laps, 12.33 miles)

1 R. Swann *(Kawasaki)*, 8m 23.9s, 88.08mph
2 B. Morrison *(Honda)*; 3 R. Hurst *(Kawasaki)*; 4 G. Johnson *(Honda)*; 5 P. Mellor *(Suzuki)*; 6 J. Reynolds *(Honda)*; 7 M. Heath *(Honda)*; 8 E. McFarlane *(Honda)*; 9 C. Brenneck *(Honda)*.
Fastest lap: B. Morrison *(Honda)*, 54.6s, 90.32mph

Round 5 19 June, Donington Park (10 laps, 19.57 miles)

1 B. Morrison *(Honda)*, 13m 16.7s, 88.42mph
2 R. Swann *(Kawasaki)*; 3 R. Hurst *(Kawasaki)*; 4 I. Waine *(Honda)*; 5 E. McFarlane *(Honda)*; 6 G. Johnson *(Honda)*; 7 R. Knapp *(Honda)*; 8 J. Moodie *(Honda)*; 9 M. Seward *(Honda)*; 10 A. Abbott *(Honda)*.
Fastest lap: B. Morrison *(Honda)*, R. Swann *(Kawasaki)* & R. Hurst *(Kawasaki)*, 1m 18.3s, 98.97mph (record)

Round 6 26 June, Cadwell Park (8 laps, 17.39 miles)

1 B. Morrison *(Honda)*, 13m 20.4s, 78.22mph
2 J. Whitham *(Suzuki)*; 3 R. Swann *(Kawasaki)*; 4 E. McFarlane *(Honda)*; 5 J. Reynolds *(Kawasaki)*; 6 G. Johnson *(Honda)*; 7 I. Waine *(Honda)*; 8 S. Abbott *(Honda)*; 9 I. Simpson *(Honda)*; 10 B. Nicholson *(Honda)*.
Fastest lap: B. Morrison *(Honda)* & J. Whitham *(Suzuki)*, 1m 38.9s, 79.13mph (record)

Round 7 10 July, Knockhill (12 laps, 15.46m)

1 B. Morrison *(Honda)*, 11m 52.s, 78.19mph
2 J. Whitham *(Suzuki)*; 3 R. Swann *(Kawasaki)*; 4 E. McFarlane *(Honda)*; 5 R. Knapp *(Honda)*; 6 J. Reynolds *(Honda)*; 7 S. Hislop *(Honda)*; 8 I. Duffus *(Honda)*; 9 G. Goodings *(Honda)*; 10 S. Abbott *(Honda)*.
Fastest lap: B. Morrison *(Honda)*, 57s, 81.41mph

Round 8 17 July, Snetterton (10 laps, 19.17m)

1 R. Swann *(Kawasaki)*, 12m 17.6s, 93.56mph
2 G. Weston *(Honda)*; 3 J. Whitham *(Suzuki)*; 4 P. Mellor *(Suzuki)*; 5 R. Haynes *(Kawasaki)*; 6 R. Knapp *(Honda)*; 7 K. Mawdsley *(Honda)*; 8 R. Hurst *(Kawasaki)*; 9 B. Nicholson *(Honda)*; 10 G. Goodings *(Honda)*.
Fastest lap: R. Swann *(Kawasaki)* and Roger Hurst *(Kawasaki)*, 1m 12.8s, 94.79mph

Round 9 24 July, Mallory Park (12 laps, 16.44m)

1 B. Morrison *(Honda)*, 10m 58.2s, 89.91mph
2 J. Whitham *(Suzuki)*; 3 R. Swann *(Kawasaki)*; 4 R. Hurst *(Kawasaki)*; 5 G. Weston *(Honda)*; 6 P. Mellor *(Suzuki)*; 7 M. Seward *(Honda)*; 8 I. Young *(Honda)*; 9 I. Simpson *(Suzuki)*; 10 T. Cummings *(Honda)*.
Fastest lap: B. Morrison *(Honda)*, J. Whitham *(Suzuki)* and G. Weston *(Honda)*, 54.1s, 91.16mph

Round 10 31 July, Cadwell Park (18 laps, 15.282m)

1 R. Swann *(Kawasaki)*, 14m 6.6s, 64.98mph
2 B. Morrison *(Honda)*; 3 J. Whitham *(Suzuki)*; 4 J. Reynolds *(Kawasaki)*; 5 R. Knapp *(Honda)*; 6 I. Waite *(Honda)*; 7 G. Weston *(Honda)*; 8 E. McFarlane *(Honda)*; 9 S. Abbott *(Honda)*; 10 R. Haynes *(Kawasaki)*.
Fastest lap: R. Swann *(Kawasaki)*, 46.10s, 66.30mph

Round 11 20 August, Thruxton (8 laps, 18.848m)

1 R. Swann *(Kawasaki)*, 11m 42.50s, 96.59mph
2 J. Reynolds *(Kawasaki)*; 3 R. Knapp *(Honda)*; 4 R. Hurst *(Kawasaki)*; 5 B. Morrison *(Honda)*; 6 G. Weston *(Honda)*; 7 J. Whitham *(Suzuki)*; 8 G. Johnson *(Honda)*; 9 G. Goodings *(Honda)*; 10 P. Mellor *(Suzuki)*.
Fastest lap: J. Reynolds *(Kawasaki)*, 1m 26.00s, 98.63mph

Round 12 3 September, Mallory Park (12 laps, 16.44 miles)

1 B. Morrison *(Honda)*, 10m 51.3s, 90.87mph
2 J. Whitham *(Suzuki)*; 3 G. Weston *(Honda)*; 4 R. Swann *(Kawasaki)*; 5. J. Reynolds *(Kawasaki)*; 6 P. Mellor *(Suzuki)*; 7 C. Brenneck *(Honda)*; 8 E. McFarlane *(Honda)*; 9 I. Scott *(Honda)*; 10 J. Moodie *(Honda)*.
Fastest lap: B. Morrison *(Honda)*, 53.6s, 92.01mph

Round 13 10 September, Scarborough (12 laps, 28.92 miles)

1 J. Whitham *(Suzuki)*; 22m 17.7s, 77.94mph
2 P. Mellor *(Suzuki)*; 3 R. Swann *(Kawasaki)*; 4 G. Johnson *(Honda)*; 5 E. McFarlane *(Honda)*; 6 S. Abbot *(Honda)*; 7 I. Waine *(Honda)*; 8 M. Seward *(Honda)*; 9 A. Cummings *(Honda)*; 10 D. Woolams *(Kawasaki)*.
Fastest lap: J. Whitham *(Suzuki)* and P. Mellor *(Suzuki)*, 1m 50.5s, 78.63mph

Round 14 2 October, Cadwell Park (10 laps, 21.74 miles)

1 B. Morrison *(Honda)*; 13m 13.0s, 78.95mph
2 R. Swann *(Kawasaki)*; 3 J. Whitham *(Suzuki)*; 4 J. Moodie *(Honda)*; 5 E. McFarlane *(Honda)*; 6 P. Mellor *(Suzuki)*; 7 C. Brenneck *(Honda)*; 8 G. Weston *(Honda)*; 9 I. Scott *(Honda)*; 10 B. Nicholson *(Honda)*.
Fastest lap: B. Morrison *(Honda)*, 1m 37.6s, 80.18mph (record)

Round 15 23 October, Brands Hatch (12 laps, 14.44 miles)

1 G. Weston *(Honda)*, 10m 27.1s, 82.91mph
2 J. Whitham *(Suzuki)*; 3 B. Morrison *(Honda)*; 4 J. Moodie *(Honda)*; 5 J. Reynolds *(Kawasaki)*; 6 B. Nicholson *(Honda)*; 7 P. Mellor *(Suzuki)*; 8 C. Brenneck *(Honda)*; 9 M. Farmer *(Kawasaki)*; 10 E. McFarlane *(Honda)*.
Fastest lap: G. Weston *(Honda)*, 50.9s, 85.12mph

Final Championship Positions (15 rounds, best 13 scores count)

1 B. Morrison, 160 points
2 R. Swann, 150; 3 J. Whitham, 115; =4 R. Hurst and E. McFarlane, 63; 6 G. Johnson, 56; 7 G. Weston, 55; 8 P. Mellor, 49; 9 J. Reynolds, 48; 10 R. Knapp, 46.

BRITISH JUNIORSTOCK

Juniorstock was the domain of Mike Edwards and his Charlie Williams Everything But Bikes-entered TZR250 Yamaha. The 26-year-old bike shop salesman won nine of the 14 races and only twice failed to finish outside the top three with his Tony Scott-tuned TZR. He missed the Saturday Thruxton event through work commitments and took a very uncharacteristic tumble in the final race at Brands.

Twenty-three-year-old Francis Williamson was overall runner-up with a Bob Farnham-tuned bike. His only win came at Snetterton but, like Edwards, is destined for a bright future. He was being nurtured through the season by Dave Hook of Haslemere

Motorcycles, the same enthusiast who helped the late Kenny Irons to Superstock glory in 1986 and then backed Roger Hurst last year.

Four other riders took wins: Jason Lodge, Brian Nicholson, Steve Ives and Mark Heath. The latter, a 20-year-old welder, won at Brands, but it was only his fourth TZR race since breaking his pelvis in a CBR crash at Donington earlier in the year.

Round 1 3 April, Donington Park (10 laps, 19.57 miles)

1 M. Edwards *(Yamaha)*, 14m 14.10s, 83.48mph
2 M. Heath *(Yamaha)*; 3 J. Lodge *(Yamaha)*; 4 S. Ives *(Yamaha)*; 5 P. Booler *(Yamaha)*; 6 C. Broughton *(Yamaha)*; 7 S. Worth *(Yamaha)*; 8 A. Cooper *(Yamaha)*; 9 J. MacDonald *(Yamaha)*; 10 A. Richards *(Yamaha)*.
Fastest lap: M. Heath *(Yamaha)*, 1m 23.64s, 84.23mph (lap record)

second round scheduled for Brands Hatch cancelled

Round 2 21 May, Carnaby (14 laps, 16.8 miles)

1 M. Edwards *(Yamaha)*, 13m 55.6s, 72.98mph
2 J. Lodge *(Yamaha)*; 3 M. Heath *(Yamaha)*; 4 S. Ives *(Yamaha)*; 5 S. Worth *(Yamaha)*; 6 J. Gittins *(Yamaha)*; 7 R. Goodall *(Yamaha)*; 8 C. Broughton *(Yamaha)*; 9 A. Cooper *(Yamaha)*; 10 D. Hobson *(Yamaha)*.
Fastest lap: M. Edwards *(Yamaha)*, 58.1s, 74.97mph

Round 3 12 June, Mallory Park (12 laps, 16.44 miles)

1 M. Edwards *(Yamaha)*, 11m 35.1s, 85.14mph
2 S. Ives *(Yamaha)*; 3 J. Lodge *(Yamaha)*; 4 J. MacDonald *(Yamaha)*; 5 P. Booler *(Yamaha)*; 6 D. Hobson *(Yamaha)*; 7 S. Tomes *(Yamaha)*; 8 N. Bagley *(Yamaha)*; 9 K. Ashurst *(Yamaha)*; 10 A. Cooper *(Yamaha)*.
Fastest lap: M. Edwards *(Yamaha)*, 56.9s, 86.67mph

Round 4 19 June, Donington Park (8 laps, 15.66 miles)

1 M. Edwards *(Yamaha)*, 11m 11.7s, 83.90mph
2 F. Williamson *(Yamaha)*; 3 T. Clow *(Yamaha)*; 4 A. Cooper *(Yamaha)*; 5 S. Worth *(Yamaha)*; 6 J. MacDonald *(Yamaha)*; 7 S. Ives *(Yamaha)*; 8 D. Perry *(Yamaha)*; 9 P. Booler *(Yamaha)*; 10 N. Bagley *(Yamaha)*.
Fastest lap: F. Williamson *(Yamaha)*, 1m 22.6s, 85.29mph (record)

Round 5 26 June, Cadwell Park (8 laps, 17.39 miles)

1 J. Lodge *(Yamaha)*, 14m 8.5s, 73.79mph
2 P. Booler *(Yamaha)*; 3 M. Edwards *(Yamaha)*; 4 A. Cooper *(Yamaha)*; 5 F. Williamson *(Yamaha)*; 6 D. Hobson *(Yamaha)*; 7 S. Tomes *(Yamaha)*; 8 J. MacDonald *(Yamaha)*; 9 S. Worth *(Yamaha)*; 10 A. Milton *(Yamaha)*.
Fastest lap: P. Booler *(Yamaha)*, 1m 43.6s, 75.54mph (record)

Round 6 9 July, Knockhill (12 laps, 15.46m)

1 M. Edwards *(Yamaha)*, 12m 33.2s, 73.93mph
2 F. Williamson *(Yamaha)*; 3 G. Lyell *(Yamaha)*; 4 S. Ives *(Yamaha)*; 5 P. Booler *(Yamaha)*; 6 R. Bennett *(Yamaha)*; 7 D. Hobson *(Yamaha)*; 8 S. Worth *(Yamaha)*; 9 T. Clow *(Yamaha)*; 10 D. Wallace *(Yamaha)*.
Fastest lap: F. Williamson *(Yamaha)*, 1m 17s, 75.21mph

Round 7 17 July, Snetterton (10 laps, 19.17m)

1 F. Williamson *(Yamaha)*, 12m 56.6s, 88.86mph)
2 M. Edwards *(Yamaha)*; 3 J. Lodge *(Yamaha)*; 4 B. Nicholson *(Yamaha)*; 5 P. Booler (Yamaha); 6 G. Holland *(Yamaha)*; 7 M. Langton *(Yamaha)*; 8 S. Ives *(Yamaha)*; 9 T. Clow *(Yamaha)*; 10 A. Cooper *(Yamaha)*.
Fastest lap: F. Williamson *(Yamaha)*, 1m 16.4s, 90.32mph

Round 8 24 July, Mallory Park (12 laps, 16.44m)

1 B. Nicholson *(Yamaha)*, 11m 31.7s, 85.56mph
2 F. Williamson *(Yamaha)*; 3 M. Edwards *(Yamaha)*; 4 P. Booler *(Yamaha)*; 5 M. Langton *(Yamaha)*; 6 S. Ives *(Yamaha)*; 7 G. Holland *(Yamaha)*; 8 S. Tomes *(Yamaha)*; 9 D. Hobson *(Yamaha)*; 10 T. Clow *(Yamaha)*.
Fastest lap: B. Nicholson *(Yamaha)*, 56.6s, 87.13mph

Round 9 31 July, Cadwell Park (18 laps, 15.282m)

1 M. Edwards *(Yamaha)*, 14m 45.6s, 62.12mph
2 P. Booler *(Yamaha)*; 3 S. Tomes *(Yamaha)*; 4 M. Langton *(Yamaha)*; 5 S. Worth *(Yamaha)*; 6 A. Cooper *(Yamaha)*; 7 M. Llewelyn *(Yamaha)*; 8 J. Clow *(Yamaha)*; 9 G. Holland *(Yamaha)*; 10 D. Wallis *(Yamaha)*.
Fastest lap: S. Tomes *(Yamaha)*, 46.8s, 63.94mph.

Round 10 20 August, Thruxton (8 laps, 18.848m)

1 S. Ives *(Yamaha)*, 12m 17.00s, 92.07mph
2 F. Williamson *(Yamaha)*; 3 J. Clow *(Yamaha)*; 4 S. Worth *(Yamaha)*; 5 A. Cooper *(Yamaha)*; 6 P. Booler *(Yamaha)*; 7 G. Lee *(Yamaha)*; 8 S. Tomes *(Yamaha)*; 9 K. Mallin *(Yamaha)*; 10 D. Wallis *(Yamaha)*.
Fastest lap: S. Ives *(Yamaha)*, 1m 30.10s, 94.14mph.

Round 11 3 September, Mallory Park (12 laps, 16.44 miles)

1 M. Edwards *(Yamaha)*, 11m 21.6s, 86.83mph
2 F. Williamson *(Yamaha)*; 3 P. Booler *(Yamaha)*; 4 M. Heath *(Yamaha)*; 5 S. Carter *(Yamaha)*; 6 A. Cooper *(Yamaha)*; 7 M. Llewellyn *(Yamaha)*; 8 K. Mallin *(Yamaha)*; 9 I. Wareham *(Yamaha)*; 10 G. Wolfe *(Yamaha)*.
Fastest lap: M. Edwards *(Yamaha)*, 55.9s, 88.22mph

Round 12 10 September, Scarborough (12 laps, 28.92 miles)
1 M. Edwards *(Yamaha)*, 17m 44.3s, 65.31 mph

2 R. Goodall *(Yamaha)*; 3 S. Ives *(Yamaha)*; 4 M. Langton *(Yamaha)*; 5 N. Barker *(Yamaha)*; 6 F. Williamson *(Yamaha)*; 7 S. Moss *(Yamaha)*; 8 S. Tomes *(Yamaha)*; 9 D. Wallis *(Yamaha)*; 10 D. Holmes *(Yamaha)*.
Fastest lap: M. Edwards *(Yamaha)*, 2m 10.6s, 66.53mph

Round 13 1 October, Cadwell Park (8 laps, 17.39 miles)

1 M. Edwards *(Yamaha)*, 13m 46.3s, 75.77mph
2 P. Booler *(Yamaha)*; 3 M. Heath *(Yamaha)*; 4 S. Ives *(Yamaha)*; 5 S. Carter *(Yamaha)*; 6 S. Tomes *(Yamaha)*; 7 K. Mallin *(Yamaha)*; 8 D. Wallis *(Yamaha)*; 9 R. Boyd *(Yamaha)*; 10 G. Wolfe *(Yamaha)*.
Fastest lap: M. Heath *(Yamaha)*, 1m 41.1s, 77.81mph

Round 14 22 October, Brands Hatch (14 laps. 16.85 miles)

1 M. Heath *(Yamaha)*, 12m 30.9s, 80.78mph
2 F. Williamson *(Yamaha)*; 3 S. Carter *(Yamaha)*; 4 S. Ives *(Yamaha)*; 5 R. Boyd *(Yamaha)*; 6 P. Booler *(Yamaha)*; 7 R. Wood *(Yamaha)*; 8 G. Woolfe *(Yamaha)*; 9 D. Wallace *(Yamaha)*; 10 D. Hobson *(Yamaha)*.
Fastest lap: M. Heath *(Yamaha)*; 52.2s, 83.00mph

Final Championship Positions (14 rounds, best 12 scores to count)
1 M. Edwards, 167 points
2 F. Williamson, 98; 3 P. Booler, 90; 4 S. Ives, 89; 5 J. Lodge, 57; 6 M. Heath, 55; 7 A. Cooper, 37; 8 S. Worth, 35; 9 S. Tomes, 32; 10 J. Clow, 28.

BRITISH CHAMPIONSHIP

Gary Pinchin

Back after a three-year lay-off, Burton-on-Trent's Alex Bedford cleaned up in the British 125cc Championship. He won seven of the eleven races in such a style that lap records around the country were left in tatters. He also won at Knockhill, but officials there saw fit to exclude him from the results after he had celebrated by standing on the saddle during his lap of honour!

While Bedford grabbed all the plaudits, Ireland's David Lemon sneaked up from fourth to second in the final standings with a strong second place in the final race at Brands. His season-long rival Steve Lawton could only finish seventh and Rob Orme was a non-starter.

Orme had only joined the 125 class mid season, riding Mike Pomfret's Rotax, but he soon became a leading figure, winning at Scarborough (admittedly after Bedford had punctured) and consistently finishing in the first three.

125cc

Round 1 3 April, Donington Park (10 laps, 19.57 miles)

1 M. Carkeek *(Scitsu)*, 15m 37.9s, 75.11mph
2 A. Bedford *(Honda)*; 3 D. Collinson *(Honda)*; 4 G. Dickinson *(MBA)*; 5 S. Lawton *(Honda)*; 6 P. Corrigan *(Honda)*; 7 R. Appleyard *(Honda)*; 8 C. Morgan *(EMC)*; 9 T. Flinton *(MBA)*; 10 C. Palmer *(MBA)*.
Fastest lap: M. Carkeek *(Scitsu)*, 1m 29.68s, 78.55mph

Round 2 2 May, Brands Hatch (14 laps, 16.8 miles)

1 A. Bedford *(Honda)*, 13m 04.3s, 77.34mph
2 D. Collinson *(Honda)*; 3 P. Baldock *(Honda)*; 4 S. Lawton *(Honda)*; 5 G. Buckle *(MBA)*; 6 C. Palmer *(MBA)*; 7 A. Cooper *(MBA)*; 8 M. Harrison *(Honda)*; 9 P. Corrigan *(Honda)*; 10 R. Blow *(Honda)*.
Fastest lap: A. Bedford *(Honda)*, 53.7s, 80.69mph

Round 3 21 May, Carnaby (12 laps, 14.4 miles)

1 A. Bedford *(Honda)*, 11m 49.7s, 73.70mph
2 K. Beckett *(Barton)*; 3 D. Lemon *(Honda)*; 4 S. Lawton *(Honda)*; 5 D. Collinson *(Honda)*; 6 C. Palmer *(MBA)*; 7 A. Caughey *(Honda)*; 8 P. Corrigan *(Honda)*; 9 C. Morgan *(Honda)*; 10 A. Cooper *(MBA)*.
Fastest lap: A. Bedford *(Honda)*, 57.7s, 75.49mph

Round 4 19 June, Donington Park (10 laps, 19.57 miles)

1 A. Bedford *(Honda)*, 10m 56.9s, 85.79mph
2 R. Appleyard *(Honda)*; 3 K. Beckett *(LCR Bartol)*; 4 D. Lemon *(Honda)*; 5 A. Patterson *(Honda)*; 6 S. Lawton *(Honda)*; 7 R. Orme *(EMC)*; 8 P. Corrigan *(Honda)*; 9 C. Palmer *(MBA)*; 10 D. Collinson *(Honda)*.
Fastest lap: A. Bedford *(Honda)*, 1m 20.8s, 87.19mph (record)

Round 5 10 July, Knockhill (12 laps, 15.46m)

1 D. Lemon *(Honda)*, 12m 41.9s 73.09mph
2 K. Beckett *(Bartol LCR)*; 3 S. Lawton *(Honda)*; 4 C. Palmer *(MBA)*; 5 P. Corrigan *(Honda)*; 6 D. Collinson *(Honda)*; 7 A. Cooper *(MBA)*; 8 K. Donaldson *(Waddon)*; 9 A. Eccles *(Yamaha)*; 10 C. Coghlan *(Honda)*.
Fastest lap: A. Bedford *(Honda)*, 1m 18s, 76.07mph

Round 6 17 July, Snetterton (8 laps, 15.336m)

1 A. Bedford *(Honda)*, 10m 24.9s, 88.34mph
2 D. Lemon *(Honda)*; 3 R. Orme *(EMC)*; 4 D. Fabian *(MBA)*; 5 K. Mawdsley *(Honda)*; 6 S. Lawton *(Honda)*; 7 M. Carkeek *(Scitsu)*; 8 S. Edwards *(Rotax)*; 9 G. Buckle *(MBA)*; 10 C. Palmer *(MBA)*.
Fastest lap: A. Bedford *(Honda)*, 1m 15.2s, 91.77mph

Round 7 31 July, Cadwell Park (18 laps, 15.283m)

1 A. Patterson *(Honda)*, 14m 38.8s, 62.64mph
2 A. Bedford *(Honda)*; 3 R. Orme *(EMC)*; 4 K. Beckett *(Bartol LCR)*; 5 G. Dickinson *(MBA)*; 6 R. Blow *(Honda)*; 7 S. Lawton (Honda); 8 G. Buckle *(MBA)*; 9 D. Lemon *(Honda)*; 10 A. Cooper *(MBA)*.
Fastest lap: A. Patterson *(Honda)*, 47.5s, 64.35mph

Round 8 3 September, Mallory Park (12 laps, 16.44 miles)

1 A. Bedford *(Honda)*, 11m 11.7s, 88.11mph
2 R. Orme *(EMC)*; 3 K. Beckett *(Bartol)*; 4 A. Patterson *(Honda)*; 5 G. Buckle *(MBA)*; 6 S. Lawton *(Honda)*; 7 D. Lemon *(Honda)*; 8 G. Dickinson *(MBA)*; 9 R. Blow *(Honda)*; 10 A. Cooper *(MBA)*.
Fastest lap: A. Bedford *(Honda)*; 55.1s, 89.5mph

Round 9 10 September, Scarborough (10 laps, 24.1 miles)

1 R. Orme *(EMC)*, 20m 05.1s, 72.10mph
2 S. Lawton *(Honda)*; 3 L. McMaster *(Honda)*; 4 A. Cooper *(MBA)*; 5 R. Blow *(Honda)*; 6 D. Lemon *(Honda)*; 7 R. Lennon *(Honda)*; 8 B. Robertson *(Honda)*; 9 J. Cresswell *(Honda)*; 10 R. Lee *(Honda)*.
Fastest lap: A. Bedford *(Honda)*, 1m 56.8s, 74.39mph

Round 10 2 October, Cadwell Park (8 laps, 17.39 miles)

1 A. Bedford *(Honda)*, 13m 37.9s, 76.55mph
2 R. Orme *(Rotax)*; 3 A. Patterson *(Honda)*; 4 R. Appleyard *(Honda)*; 5 G. Buckle *(MBA)*; 6 K. Beckett *(Bartol)*; 7 D. Lemon *(Honda)*; 8 M. Carkeek *(Honda)*; 9 S. Lawton *(Honda)*; 10 R. Blow, *(Honda)*.
Fastest lap: A. Bedford *(Honda)*, 1m 40.5s, 77.87mph (record)

Round 11 22 October, Brands Hatch (14 laps, 16.85 miles)

1 A. Bedford *(Honda)*, 12m 21.4s, 81.82mph
2 D. Lemon *(Honda)*; 3 A. Caughey *(Honda)*; 4 L. McMaster *(Honda)*; 5 P. McCallen *(Honda)*; 6 M. Carkeek *(Honda)*; 7 S. Lawton *(Honda)*; 8 G. Buckle *(MBA)*; 9 S. Edwards *(Rotax)*; 10 M. Harrison *(Honda)*.
Fastest lap: A. Bedford *(Honda)*, 52.2s, 83.00mph (record)

Final Championship Positions (11 rounds, best nine scores count)

1 A. Bedford, 129 points
2 D. Lemon, 72; =3 S. Lawton, 63 (69), R. Orme, 63; 5 K. Beckett, 57; 6 A. Patterson, 39; 7 D. Collinson, 34; 8 M. Carkeek, 27; 9 G. Buckle, 26; 10 R. Appleyard, 24.

BRITISH OPEN SIDECAR

The World Champions Steve Webster and Tony Hewitt were in a class of their own with their LCR Krauser. Even lethargic push starts which left them towards the tail end of the field presented no problem and they ran out easy winners of the first four rounds.

In the final meeting at Brands in late October, their tactics went awry. From another slow start they pulled through to challenge the leader, Fowlers duo Barry Brindley and Grahame Rose, but just as they looked to be making their decisive move for the lead the race was red flagged due to a crash. At the time Brindley, with another Krauser powered outfit, was in front and so took the race. In fairness to Brindley and Rose, they were out in a class of their own, admittedly chasing the tail of Webster, but well clear of the rest.

The most closely contested place in the championship was for third, with Dennis Bingham and Gary Irlam on the Padgett-powered LCR just edging Irish aces Lowry Burton and Pat Cushnahan by five points for the position. It was Burton, with Geoff Rushbrook and Geoff Leitch, who was involved in a frightening crash at Brands, causing the stoppage which gave Brindley his win over Webster.

The sad fact is that while the open class of the sport is by no means lacking in support and can boast the World Champions, the racing has a long way to go to match that of the more closely fought F2 class.

Round 1 3 April, Donington Park (12 laps, 23.48 miles)

1 S. Webster/T. Hewitt *(Krauser)*, 15m 28.3s, 91.07mph
2 B. Brindley/G. Rose *(Krauser)*; 3 S. Abbott/S. Smith *(Yamaha)*; 4 D. Molyneux/A. Langton *(Yamaha)*; 5 M. Burcombe/C. Hardman *(Yamaha)*; 6 G. Thomas/K. Morgan *(Yamaha)*; 7 G. Hardwick/S. Parker *(LCR);* 8 D. Bingham/G. Irlan *(Padgett)*; 9 P. Atkinson/G. Simmons *(Yamaha)*; 10 D. Rumble/G. Keep *(Yamaha)*.
Fastest lap: S. Webster/T. Hewitt *(Krauser)*, 1m 15.60s, 93.19mph (record)

Round 2 21 May, Carnaby (16 laps, 19.2 miles)

1 S. Webster/T. Hewitt *(Krauser)*, 14m 52.8s, 78.06mph
2 D. Bingham/G. Irlam *(Padgett)*; 3 L. Burton/P. Cushnahan *(Yamaha)*; 4 C. Greatrex/G. Scott *(Yamaha)*; 5 D. Molyneux/A. Langton *(Yamaha)*; 6 K. Howles/S. Pointer *(Yamaha)*; 7 S. Hall/S. Buck *(Yamaha)*; 8. G. Shand/J. Shedden *(Special)*; 9 A. Westhead/B. Thear *(Yamaha)*; 10 S. Pullen/T. Darby *(Yamaha)*.
Fastest lap: S. Webster/T. Hewitt *(Krauser)*, 53.5s, 81.24mph

Round 3 10 July, Knockhill (12 laps, 15.46 miles)

1 S. Webster/T. Hewitt *(Krauser)*, 14m 33.3s, 79.7mph
2 B. Brindley/G. Rose *(Krauser)*; 3 D. Brown/B. Nelson *(Yamaha)*; 4 L. Burton/P. Cushnahan *(Yamaha)*; 5 T. Baker/J. Cochrane *(Yamaha)*; 6 D. Rumble/G. Keep *(Yamaha)*; 7 S. Pullen/T. Darby *(Yamaha)*; 8 D. Shand/T. Darby *(Suzuki);* 9 D. Bingham/G. Irlam *(Padgett)*; 10 D. Low/J. Low *(Suzuki)*.
Fastest lap: S. Webster/T. Hewitt *(Krauser)*, 56.3s, 82.42mph

Round 4 17 July, Snetterton (12 laps, 23.004m)

1 S. Webster/T. Hewitt *(Krauser)*, 14m 19s, 96.4mph
2 B. Brindley/G. Rose *(Krauser)*; 3 Y. Kumagaya/B. Barlow *(Yamaha)*; 4 L. Burton/J. Tailford *(Yamaha)*; 5 G. Rushbrook/G. Leitch *(Yamaha)*; 6 M. Boddice/E. Yarker *(Yamaha)*; 7 D. Bingham/G. Irlam *(Padgett)*; 8 C. Stirrat/S. Prior *(Yamaha)*; 9 C. Greatrex/G. Scott *(Yamaha)*; 10 A. Westhead/B. Thear *(Yamaha)*.
Fastest lap: S. Webster/T. Hewitt *(Krauser)*, 1m 8.2s, 101.91mph

Round 5 2 October, Cadwell Park (10 laps, 21.74 miles)

1 S. Webster/T. Hewitt *(Krauser)*, 16m 14.3s, 80.32mph
2 B. Brindley/G. Rose *(Krauser)*; 3 D. Bingham/G. Irlam *(Yamaha)*; 4 M. Smith/G. Hollis *(Yamaha)*; 5 G. Thomas/K. Morgan *(Yamaha)*; 6 P. Atkinson/G. Simmons *(Yamaha)*; 7 G. Shand/P. Gravel *(Suzuki)*; 8 S. Hall/S. Buck *(Yamaha)*; 9 R. Bellas/G. Knight *(Yamaha)*; 10 D. Rumble Jnr/G. Keep *(Yamaha)*.
Fastest lap: S. Webster/T. Hewitt *(Krauser)*, 1m 33.4s, 83.79mph (record).

Round 6 23 October, Brands Hatch (11 laps, 13.2 miles)

1 B. Brindley/P. Coombes *(Krauser)*, 9m 18.4s, 85.35mph
2 S. Webster/T. Hewitt *(Krauser)*; 3 K. Howles/S. Pointer *(Yamaha)*; 4 C. Stirrat/S. Prior *(Yamaha)*; 5 J. Drew/B. Houghton *(Yamaha)*; 6 G. Thomas/K. Morgan *(Yamaha)*; 7 M. Reddington/R. Parker *(Yamaha)*; 8 B. Ford-Dunn/A. Pirie *(Yamaha)*; 9 D. Rumble Jnr/G. Keep *(Yamaha)*; 10 R. Lawrence/A. Rawlings *(Yamaha)*.
Fastest lap: S. Webster/T. Hewitt *(Krauser)*, 48.7s, 88.97mph.

Final Championship Positions

1 S. Webster/T. Hewitt, 87 points
2 B. Brindley/G. Rose, 63; 3 D. Bingham/G. Irlam 31; 4 L. Burton/P. Cushnahan 26; 5 G. Thomas/G. Keep 16; 6 K. Howles/S. Pointer 15; 7 D. Molyneux/A. Langton 14; 8 C. Stirrat/S. Prior 11; =9 D. Brown/B. Nelson, Y. Kumagaya/B. Barlow, C. Greatrex/G. Scott, S. Abbott/S. Smith, all 10.

BRITISH FORMULA TWO SIDECAR CHAMPIONSHIP

Gary Pinchin

The pro F2 sidecar lobby has always argued that close racing is the keynote of the class and this year's British Championship underlined their case. All season long there was never more than a handful of points separating the leading three crews and the series went to the final race at Scarborough with any one of them capable of winning the title.

Retford's Andrew Witherington and John Jackson looked likely favourites going to the hilltop seaside venue at Scarborough, holding a handy five point lead over rivals Mick Hamblin and Bob Smith, with Eddie Wright and Andy Wilson one point further behind. Witherington had already taken the victor's spoils three times to Hamblin's single win at

Mallory Park in June, but Wright had also hit three wins. Motorcycle and car dealer Wright would have been more likely to have retained the title he won in '86, but for a huge accident at Mallory the week prior to the final race. He had seen his series lead disappear after Witherington won the race, followed home by the Shelbourne Yamaha of Hamblin.

So it all came down to Scarborough, and Hamblin won the race to take the series, while Wright's second place pulled him back to equal runner-up in the final reckoning, with Witherington who was down in fifth at Scarborough.

Round 1 4 April, Donington Park (10 laps, 19.57 miles)

1 A. Witherington/J. Jackson *(Yamaha)*, 14m 20.83s, 81.84mph
2 M. Hamblin/R. Smith *(Yamaha)*; 3 J. Holden/D. Burgess *(Yamaha)*; 4 J. Heys/C. Hefti *(Yamaha)*; 5 E. Wright/A. Wilson *(Yamaha)*; 6 R. Hanks/T. Hanks *(Yamaha)*; 7 B. Crook/J. Hornby *(Yamaha)*; 8 N. Burgess/S. Hanson *(Armstrong)*; 9 S. Judkins/N. Moore *(Yamaha)*; 10 S. Noble/M. Parker *(Yamaha)*.
Fastest lap: A. Witherington/J. Jackson *(Yamaha)*, 1m 23.73s, 84.14mph

Round 2 2 May, Brands Hatch (14 laps, 16.8 miles)

1 A. Witherington/J. Jackson *(Yamaha)*, 12m 54.3s, 78.34mph
2 M. Hamblin/R. Smith *(Yamaha)*; 3 E. Wright/I. Marchant *(Yamaha)*; 4 K. Galtress/N. Shelton *(Yamaha)*; 5 B. Ford-Dunn/A. Pirie *(Yamaha)*; 6 J. Heys/C. Hefti *(Yamaha)*; 7 A. Williams/M. Sheppard *(Yamaha)*; 8 D. Saville/A. Peach *(Yamaha)*; 9 D. Brindley/N. Roche *(Yamaha)*; 10 A. Delmont/W. Brammer *(Yamaha)*.
Fastest lap: A. Witherington/J. Jackson *(Yamaha)* & M. Hamblin/R. Smith *(Yamaha)*, 53.8s, 80.54mph (record)

Round 3 12 June, Mallory Park (12 laps, 16.44 miles)

1 M. Hamblin/B. Smith *(Yamaha)*, 11m 27.2s, 86.12mph
2 A. Witherington/J. Jackson *(Yamaha)*; 3 K. Galtress/N. Shelton *(Yamaha)*; 4 J. Heys/C. Hefti *(Yamaha)*; 5 M. Whittington/I. Caulton *(Yamaha)*; 6 B. Ford-Dunn/A. Pirie *(Yamaha)*; 7 D. Saville/D. Hall *(Yamaha)*; 8 E. Wright/I. Marchant *(Yamaha)*; 9 J. Brindley/C. Jones *(Yamaha)*; 10 D. Brindley/N. Roche *(Yamaha)*.
Fastest lap: M. Hamblin/B. Smith *(Yamaha)*, 55.9s, 88.22mph

Round 4 19 June, Donington Park (10 laps, 19.57 miles)

1 B. Ford-Dunn/A. Pirie *(Yamaha)*, 13m 59.2s, 83.95mph
2 E. Wright/A. Wilson *(Yamaha)*; 3 M. Hamblin/R. Smith *(Yamaha)*; 4 J. Heys/C. Hefti *(Yamaha)*; 5 D. Brindley/N. Roche *(Yamaha)*; 6 J. Brindley/C. Jones *(Yamaha)*; 7 J. Thompson/P. Burton *(Yamaha)*; 8 I. Ward/N. Fenwick *(Yamaha)*; 9 D. Saville/D. Hall *(Yamaha)*; 10 A. Witherington/J. Jackson *(Yamaha)*.
Fastest lap: E. Wright/A Wilson *(Yamaha)*, 1m 22.5s, 85.39mph

Round 5 26 June, Cadwell Park (8 laps, 17.39 miles)

1 E. Wright/A. Wilson *(Yamaha)*, 13m 21.4s, 78.12mph
2 A. Witherington/J. Jackson *(Yamaha)*; 3 K. Galtress/N. Shelton *(Yamaha)*; 4 B. Ford-

Dunn/A. Pirie *(Yamaha)*; 5 J. Heys/C. Hefti *(Yamaha)*; 6 M. Hamblin/B. Smith *(Yamaha)*; 7 D. Saville/S. Christie *(Yamaha)*; 8 J. Noble/M. Parker *(Yamaha)*; 9 A. Delmont/W. Brammer *(Yamaha)*; 10 D. Brindley/N. Roche *(Yamaha)*.
Fastest lap: E. Wright/A. Wilson *(Yamaha)*, 1m 43.7s, 75.47mph (record)

Round 6 24 July, Mallory Park (12 laps, 16.44 miles)

1 E. Wright/A. Wilson *(Yamaha)*, 9m 31.3s, 86.32mph
2 A. Witherington/J. Jackson *(Yamaha)*; 3 M. Hamblin/R. Smith *(Yamaha)*; 4 J. Brindley/C. Jones *(Yamaha)*; 5 J. Heys/C. Hefti *(Yamaha)*; 6 K. Galtress/N. Shelton *(Yamaha)*; 7 A. Williams/M. Sheppard *(Yamaha)*; 8 J. Coates/M. Williams *(Yamaha)*; 9 J. Thompson/P. Burton *(Yamaha)*; 10 D. Saville/D. Hall *(Yamaha)*.
Fastest lap: A. Witherington/J. Jackson *(Yamaha)* and M. Hamblin/R. Smith *(Yamaha)*, 56s, 88.07mph

Round 7 31 July, Cadwell Park (18 laps, 15.282 miles)

1 E. Wright/A. Wilson *(Yamaha)*, 14m 54.6s, 61.50mph
2 K. Galtress/M. Shelton *(Yamaha)*; 3 J. Brindley/C. Jones *(Yamaha)*; 4 J. Heys/C. Hefti *(Yamaha)*; 5 M. Hamblin/B. Smith *(Yamaha)*; 6 M. Whittington/G. Gibson *(Yamaha)*; 7 D. Brindley/N. Roche *(Yamaha)*; 8 J. Coates/M. Williams *(Yamaha)*; 9 M. Haith/D. Haith *(Yamaha)*; 10 N. Burgess/N. Kay *(Yamaha)*.
Fastest lap: E. Wright/A. Wilson *(Yamaha)*, 48.4s, 63.15mph

Round 8 3 September, Mallory Park, (12 laps, 16.44 miles)

1 A. Witherington/J. Jackson *(Yamaha)*, 11m 21.4s, 86.85mph
2 M. Hamblin/B. Smith *(Yamaha)*; 3 J. Brindley/C. Jones *(Yamaha)*; 4 M. Whittington/I. Caulton *(Yamaha)*; 5 J. Coates/M. Williams *(Yamaha)*; 6 D. Saville/P. Kirkham *(Yamaha)*; 7 R. Dixon/P. Appleby *(Yamaha)*; 8 D. Brindley/N. Roche *(Yamaha)*; 9 B. Hutchinson/S. Birkett *(Yamaha)*; 10 S. Noble/M. Parker *(Yamaha)*.
Fastest lap: M. Hamblin/B. Smith *(Yamaha)*, 55.5s, 88.86mph

Round 9 10 September, Scarborough (12 laps, 28.92 miles)

1 M. Hamblin/B. Smith *(Yamaha)*
2 E. Wright/A. Wilson *(Yamaha)*; 3 J. Coates/M. Williams *(Yamaha)*; 4 D. Saville/D. Hall *(Yamaha)*; 5 A. Witherington/J. Jackson *(Yamaha)*; 6 N. Burgess/N. Kay *(Yamaha)*.

Final Championship Positions

1 M. Hamblin 97
=2 A. Witherington, E. Wright 88; 4 K. Galtress 44; 5 J. Heys 43; 6 J. Brindley 35; 7 B. Ford-Dunn 34; 8 D. Saville 27; =9 M. Whittington, J. Coates 19

ACU/MCA STAR CHAMPIONSHIP

Alan Jeffrey successfully switched from the 500 class to win the 250 Star series by nine points from last year's champion Steve Patrickson. Patrickson was looking to repeat his title double of '87 when he lifted the Star and British titles and going into Donington it looked possible he would repeat it having already wrapped up the British crown again. However, he failed to finish which gave the title to Jeffrey who also failed to add to his score after crashing out of the race.

The 1300 class went to 25-year-old Steve Spray. He had the title sewn up by the penultimate round at Cadwell but went on to score his third win of the series in the final at Donington after a great scrap with Aussie Paul Lewis who was on Luke Taylor's Ron Grant-prepped Suzuki. Spray, riding a privately entered RG500 Suzuki, amassed more than double the points of his closest rival, Mark Linscott who did not contest the full series.

In his first full season of racing John Reynolds took the 350 class in similar fashion to Spray's 1300 victory. Ex-motocrosser Reynolds only won one race but finished every round bar one and with 89 points was 42 clear of runner up Steve Williams, four-time race winner in the year.

The 125 class went to Steve Lawton by five points from Alex Bedford, another rider who did not do all the Star rounds. While Bedford won four races, Lawton didn't take one overall win but scored consistently, with five of his six results in the top three on his Honda.

Last year's Manx GP Newcomers winner Colin Gable won the Production championship. He wrapped it up at round seven at Cadwell. He borrowed a Suzuki in the previous round at Carnaby to stay in the hunt after pranging his Honda in practice and still took second in that round. He finished 26 points ahead of second place Ian Cobby who sneaked the runner-up spot from Mike Hodges by winning the last round at Donington.

Veteran Mick Boddice was the best of the Sidecars. He had help from two passengers, Eddie Yarker and Chas Birks but was a winner with both. Boddice scored three wins in the first four races and then cruised to the title.

Robert Fisher and Trevor Crowe clinched second place overall from Roy Lawrence and Alan Rawlings.

Results

125cc

Round 1 1 April, Brands Hatch (10 laps, 12.036 miles)

1 A. Bedford *(Honda)*, 9m 12.2s, 78.46mph
2 G. Buckle *(MBA)*; 3 D. Collinson *(Honda)*; 4 M. Carkeek *(Scitsu)*; 5 A. Cooper *(MBA)*; 6 D. Lemon *(Honda)*; 7 P. Baldock *(Honda)*; 8 M. Taylor *(Honda)*; 9 D. Moffat *(MBA)*; 10 P. Corrigan *(Honda)*.
Fastest lap: A. Bedford *(Honda)*, 53.4s, 81.14mph

Round 2 17 April, Thruxton (5 laps, 11.48 miles)

1 A. Bedford *(Honda)*, 7m 54.1s, 89.45mph
2 D. Collinson *(Honda)*; 3 G. Buckle *(MBA)*; 4 S. Lawton *(Honda)*; 5 P. Baldock *(Honda)*; 6 P. Corrigan *(Honda)*; 7 R. Blow *(Honda)*; 8 A. Cooper *(MBA)*; 9 J. Leigh *(Honda)*; 10 M. Garside *(Waddon)*.
Fastest lap: A. Bedford *(Honda)*, 1m 32.1s, 92.09mph

Round 3 1 May, Snetterton (7 laps, 13.3 miles)

1 P. Corrigan *(Honda)*, 10m 13.1s, 78.79mph
2 R. Blow *(Honda)*; 3. S. Lawton *(Honda)*; 4 P. Baldock *(Honda)*; 5 A. Cooper *(MBA)*; 6 P. Streets *(Honda)*; 7 G. Buckle *(MBA)*; 8 A. Bedford *(Honda)*; 9 R. Lee *(Honda)*; 10 M. Harrison *(Honda)*.
Fastest lap: M. Carkeek *(Scitsu)*, 1m 22.0s, 84.12mph

Round 4 15 May, Mallory Park (10 laps, 13.7 miles)

1 A. Bedford *(Honda)*, 9m 54.7s, 82.93mph
2 M. Carkeek *(Scitsu)*; 3 S. Lawton *(Honda)*; 4 A. Caughey *(Honda)*; 5 A. Cooper *(MBA)*; 6 P. Baldcock *(Honda)*; 7 P. Luther *(Honda)*; 8 P. Corrigan *(Honda)*; 9 G. Buckle *(MBA)*; 10 T. Flinton *(MBA)*.
Fastest lap: M. Carkeek *(Scitsu)*, 58.0s, 85.03mph

Round 5 3 July, Scarborough (8 laps, 19.28 miles)

1 A. Bedford *(Honda)*, 16m 13.6s, 76.5mph
2 R. Blow *(Honda)*; 3 S. Lawton *(Honda)*; 4 T. Flinton *(MBA)*; 5 A. Cooper *(MBA)*; 6 M. Carkeek *(Scitsu)*; 7 P. Corrigan *(Honda)*; 8 R. Lennon *(Honda)*; 9 D. Tinsley *(Yamaha)*; 10 I. Lodge *(Wicks)*.
Fastest lap: A. Bedford *(Honda)*, 1m 59s, 73.02mph

Round 6 14 August, Carnaby (12 laps, 13.2 miles)

1 G. Buckle *(MBA)*, 12m 19.7s, 70.66mph
2 S. Lawton *(Honda)*; 3 P. Corrigan *(Honda)*; 4 A. Cooper *(MBA)*; 5 M. Carkeek *(Yamaha)*; 6 G. Dickinson *(MBA)*; 7 R. Blow *(Honda)*; 8 M. Harrison *(Honda)*; 9 P. Baldcock *(Honda)*; 10 D. Flather *(Wicks)*.
Fastest lap: P. Corrigan *(Honda)*, 59.9s, 72.72mph

Round 7 28 August, Cadwell Park (8 laps, 17.39 miles)

1 A. Patterson *(Honda)*, 14m 15.4s, 73.19mph
2 S. Lawton *(Honda)*; 3 G. Dickinson *(MBA)*; 4 G. Buckle *(MBA)*; 5 R. Blow *(Honda)*; 6 D. Flather *(Wicks)*; 7 A. Machin *(Honda)*; 8. P. Baldock *(Honda)*; 9 S. Harrison *(Honda)*; 10 D. Brown *(MBA)*.

Fastest lap: A. Patterson *(Honda)*, 1m 44.4s, 74.96mph

Round 8 30 October, Donington Park (8 laps, 15.66 miles)

1 P. Appleyard *(Honda)*, 11m 05.2s, 84.74mph

2 D. Lemon *(Honda)*; 3 M. Carkeek *(Scitsu)*; 4 R. Murphy *(Honda)*; 5 S. Lawton *(Honda)*; 6 G. Buckle *(MBA)*; 7 A. Cooper *(MBA)*; 8 M. Harrison *(Honda)*; 9 P. Corrigan *(Honda)*; 10 R. Lorimer *(Honda)*.

Final Championship Positions

1 S. Lawton 68 points; 2 A. Bedford 63; 3 G. Buckle 56; 4 R. Blow 42; 5 M. Carkeek 41; 6 P. Corrigan 40; 7 A. Cooper 39; 8 P. Baldock 28; 9 D. Collinson 22; 10 D. Lemon 17.

250cc

Round 1 1 April, Brands Hatch (10 laps, 12.036 miles)

1 G. Cowan *(Yamaha)*, 8m 14.6s, 83.23mph
2 S. Patrickson *(Hejira)*; 3 R. Orme *(Yamaha)*; 4 E. Laycock *(EMC)*; 5 M. Barker *(Honda)*; 6 A. Godber *(Yamaha)*; 7 D. Butler *(Yamaha)*; 8 A. Jeffrey *(Yamaha)*; 9 G. Noel *(Exactweld)*; 10 I. Newton *(Honda)*.
Fastest lap: S. Patrickson *(Hejira)*, 49.7s, 87.18mph

Round 2 17 April, Thruxton (6 laps, 14.14 miles)

1 S. Patrickson *(Hejira)*, 9m 00.6s, 94.14mph
2 A. Jeffrey *(Yamaha)*; 3 C. Fogarty *(Honda)*; 4 M. Nelson *(Yamaha)*; 5 M. Westmorland *(Yamaha)*; 6 D. Redgate *(Yamaha)*; 7 S. Sawford *(Yamaha)*; 8 G. Lee *(Yamaha)*; 9 D. Butler *(Yamaha)*; 10= I. Jones *(Yamaha)*; A. Buckingham *(Armstrong)*.
Fastest lap: S. Patrickson *(Hejira)*, 1m 26.8s, 97.17mph

Round 3 1 May, Snetterton (7 laps, 13.3 miles)

1 A. Jeffrey *(Yamaha)*, 8m 54.5s, 90.38mph
2 C. Fogarty *(Honda)*; 3 A. Godber *(Yamaha)*; 4 N. Bosworth *(Aprilia)*; 5 G. Ramsey *(Yamaha)*; 6 S. Sawford *(Yamaha)*; 7 M. Barker *(Honda)*; 8 T. Hutton *(Yamaha)*; 9 M. Westmorland *(Honda)*; 10 A. Buckingham *(Armstrong)*.
Fastest lap: N. Bosworth *(Aprilia)*, 1m 13.2s, 94.27mph

Round 4 15 May, Mallory Park (10 laps, 13.7 miles)

1 A. Jeffrey *(Yamaha)*, 11m 06.2s, 88.83mph
2 P. Hubbard *(Yamaha)*; 3 M. Nelson *(Yamaha)*; 4 G. Ramsey *(Yamaha)*; 5 A. Godber *(Yamaha)*; 6 M. Barker *(Honda)*; 7 S. Sawford *(Yamaha)*; 8 P. Grubb *(Yamaha)*; 9 T. Hutton *(Yamaha)*; 10 D. Butler *(Yamaha)*.
Fastest lap: G. Ramsey *(Yamaha)*, 53.9s, 91.5mph

Round 5 3 July, Scarborough (8 laps, 19.28 miles)

1 M. Westmorland *(Honda)*, 15m 8.7s, 76.5mph
2 M. Barker *(Honda)*; 3 A. Jeffrey *(Yamaha)*; 4 D. Hirst *(Yamaha)*; A. Sproston *(Yamaha)*; 6 S. Smith *(Yamaha)*; 7 P. Wakefield *(Rotax)*; 8 G. Lee *(Yamaha)*; 9 N. Barker *(Yamaha)*; 10 S. Smith *(Yamaha)*.
Fastest lap: S. Patrickson *(Rotax)*, 1m 50.8s, 78.42mph

Round 6 14 August, Carnaby (12 laps, 13.2 miles)

1 S. Patrickson *(Rotax)*, 11m 20.0s, 76.87mph
2 K. Mitchell *(Yamaha)*; 3 I. Newton *(Honda)*; 4 C. Martin *(Aprilia)*; 5 A. Garner *(Yamaha)*; 6 A. Jeffrey *(Yamaha)*; 7. M. Barker *(Honda)*; 8 T. Hutton *(Yamaha)*; 9 S. Sawford *(Yamaha)*; 10 M. Nelson *(Yamaha)*.
Fastest lap: S. Patrickson *(Rotax)* and K. Mitchell *(Yamaha)*, 55.4s, 78.63mph

Round 7 28 August, Cadwell Park (8 laps, 17.39 miles)

1 S. Patrickson *(Rotax)*, 13m 15.5s, 78.70mph
2 R. Orme *(Rotax)*; 3 M. Barker *(Honda)*; 4 A. Jeffrey *(Yamaha)*; 5 A. Muggleton *(Yamaha)*; 6 T. Couzens *(Rotax)*; 7 G. Ramsey *(Yamaha)*; 8 M. Nelson *(Yamaha)*; 9 T. Hutton *(Yamaha)*; 10 I. Taylor *(Yamaha)*.
Fastest lap: S. Patrickson *(Rotax)*, 1m 37s, 80.68mph

Round 8 30 October, Donington Park (8 laps, 15.66 miles)

1 R. Orme *(Rotax)*, 10 m 38.1s, 88.34mph
2 A. Machin *(Rotax)*; 3 T. Couzens *(Rotax)*; 4 A. Muggleton *(Yamaha)*; 5 T. Clow *(Rotax)*; 6 M. Henrys *(Yamaha)*; 7 T. Hutton *(Yamaha)*; 8 M. Nelson *(Yamaha)*; 9 P. Knight *(Yamaha)*; 10 B. Stanley *(Yamaha)*

Final Championship Positions
1 A. Jeffrey 68 points; 2 S. Patrickson 57; 3 M. Barker 41; 4 R. Orme 37; 5 M. Nelson 25; 6 M. Westmorland 23; 7 C. Fogarty 22; 8 A. Godber 21; 9 G. Ramsay 18; 10= S. Sawford, G. Cowan, T. Hutton and T. Couzens 15.

350cc

Round 1 1 April, Brands Hatch (10 laps, 12.036 miles)

1 S. Williams *(Yamaha)*, 8m 47.4s, 82.15mph
2 M. Whiting *(Yamaha)*; 3 S. Hislop *(Yamaha)*; 4 J. Reynolds *(Yamaha)*; 5 S. Moss *(Yamaha)*; S. Coker *(Exactweld)*; 7 S. Ruth *(Hejira)*; 8. D. Higgins *(Yamaha)*; 9. T. Sanders *(Yamaha)*; 10 B. Stanley *(Yamaha)*.
Fastest lap: S. Williams *(Yamaha)*, 51.1s, 84.7mph

Round 2 17 April, Thruxton (6 laps, 14.14 miles)

1 S. Williams *(Yamaha)*, 8m 43.8s, 97.15mph
2 S. Hislop *(Yamaha)*; 3 J. Reynolds *(Yamaha)*; 4 D. Higgins *(Yamaha)*; 5 T. Sanders *(Yamaha)*; 6 I. Jones *(Yamaha)*; 7 M. Nelson *(Yamaha)*; 8 S. Bevington *(Yamaha)*; 9 B. Evans *(Yamaha)*; 10 S. Moss *(Yamaha)*.
Fastest lap: S. Williams *(Yamaha)*, 1m 25.2s, 99.55mph

Round 3 1 May, Snetterton (7 laps, 13.3 miles)

1 S. Hislop *(Yamaha)*, 9m 6.4s, 88.41mph
2 J. Reynolds *(Yamaha)*; 3 I. Redley *(Yamaha)*; 4 B. Stanley *(Yamaha)*; 5 M. Nelson

(Yamaha); 6 K. Fawsitt *(Yamaha)*; 7 S. Ruth *(Hejira)*; 8 R. Aldis *(Yamaha)*; 9 D. Irons *(Yamaha)*; 10 P. Armes *(Yamaha)*.
Fastest lap: I. Redley *(Yamaha)*, 1m 15.6s, 91.28mph

Round 4 15 May, Mallory Park (12 laps, 16.44 miles)

1 S. Williams *(Yamaha)*, 10m 56.3s, 90.17mph
2 S. Hislop *(Yamaha)*; 3 J. Reynolds *(Yamaha)*; 4 M. Nelson *(Yamaha)*; 5 D. Higgins *(Yamaha)*; 6 I. Jones *(Yamaha)*; 7 B. Stanley *(Yamaha)*; 8 T. Sanders; 9 G. Lee *(Yamaha)*; 10 M. Llewellyn *(Yamaha)*.
Fastest lap: S. Williams *(Yamaha)*, 52.9s, 93.23mph

Round 5 2 July, Scarborough (8 laps, 19.28 miles)

1 T. Sanders *(Yamaha)*, 17m 04.3s, 67.86mph
2 I. Harrison *(Yamaha)*; 3 B. Parrish *(Yamaha)*; 4 Stephen Smith *(Yamaha)*; 5 Stuart Smith *(Yamaha)*; 6 S. Ruth *(Yamaha)*; 7 A. Bailey *(Yamaha)*; only seven finishers.
Fastest lap: T. Sanders *(Yamaha)*, 2m 5.9s, 69.01mph

Round 6 14 August, Carnaby (12 laps, 13.2 miles)

1 J. Reynolds *(Yamaha)*, 11m 33.5s, 75.37mph
2 I. Dugdale *(Yamaha)*; 3 A. Lewis *(Yamaha)*; 4 T. Sanders *(Yamaha)*; 5. A. Atkinson *(Yamaha)*; 6. G. Mitchell *(Yamaha)*; 7 M. Nelson *(Yamaha)*; 8 I. Harrison *(Yamaha)*; 9 N. Grant *(Yamaha)*. Only nine finishers.
Fastest lap: J. Reynolds *(Yamaha)* and A. Lewis *(Yamaha)*, 57s, 76.42mph

Round 7 28 August, Cadwell Park (8 laps, 17.39 miles)

1 T. Sanders *(Yamaha)*, 13m 27.30s, 77.55mph
2 J. Reynolds *(Yamaha)*; 3 M. Llewellyn *(Yamaha)*; 4 M. Brown *(Yamaha)*; 5 I. Burnett *(Yamaha)*; 6 M. Nelson *(Yamaha)*; 7 R. Peers-Jones *(Yamaha)*; 8 A. Atkinson *(Yamaha)*; 9 B. Wilcox *(Yamaha)*; 10 S. Ruth *(Yamaha)*.
Fastest lap: T. Sanders *(Yamaha)*, 1m 37.9s, 79.94mph

Round 8 30 October, Donington Park (8 laps, 15.66 miles)

1 S. Williams *(Yamaha)*, 10m 35.6s, 88.68mph
2 J. Reynolds *(Yamaha)*; 3 A. Lewis *(Yamaha)*; 4 T. Sanders *(Yamaha)*; 5 M. Perry *(Yamaha)*; 6 S. Bevington *(Yamaha)*; 7 M. Heath *(Yamaha)*; 8 S. Munday *(Yamaha)*; 9 M. Crompton *(Yamaha)*; 10 R. Murdock *(Yamaha)*

Final Championship Positions
1 J. Reynolds 89 points; 2 S. Williams 60; 3 T. Sanders 57; 4. S. Hislop 49; 5 M. Nelson 27; 6 A. Lewis 20; 7 D. Higgins 17; 8 M. Harrison 15; 9 S. Ruth 14; 10 B. Stanley 13.

1300cc

Round 1 1 April, Brands Hatch (10 laps, 12.036 miles)

1 M. Farmer *(750 Suzuki)*, 8m 31.5s, 84.71mph

2 T. Bourne *(1100 Suzuki)*; 3 M. Linscott *(750 Suzuki)*; 4 S. Buckmaster *(588 Norton)*; 5 S. Spray *(500 Suzuki)*; 6 S. Manley *(500 Suzuki)*; 7 E. Laycock *(500 Honda)*; 8 D. Burford *(1100 Suzuki)*; 9 H. Selby *(750 Yamaha)*; 10 D. Crampton *(750 Suzuki)*.
Fastest lap: M. Linscott *(750 Suzuki)*, 49.8s, 87.0mph

Round 2 17 April, Thruxton (6 laps, 14.14 miles)

1. M. Farmer *(1100 Suzuki)*, 8m 33.3s, 99.14mph
2 S. Spray *(500 Suzuki)*; 3 M. Linscott *(1100 Suzuki)*; 4 S. Williams *(750 Yamaha)*; 5 T. Bourne *(1100 Suzuki)*; 6 L. Burgan *(750 Suzuki)*; 7. R. Bennett *(1100 Suzuki)*; 8 K. Mawdsley *(750 Suzuki)*; 9 R. Hurst *(1000 Kawasaki)*; 10 D. Crampton *(750 Suzuki)*.
Fastest lap: M. Linscott *(1100 Suzuki)*, 1m 22.8s, 102.43mph

Round 3 1 May, Snetterton (7 laps, 13.3 miles)

1 K. Irons *(750 Honda)*, 7m 15.3s, 95.12mph
2 B. Morrison *(750 Honda)*; 3 S. Buckmaster *(588 Norton)*; 4 R. Bennett *(1100 Suzuki)*; 5 T. Bourne *(1100 Suzuki)*; 6 S. Spray *(500 Suzuki)*; 7 H. Selby *(1100 Suzuki)*; 8 S. Kibble *(500 Suzuki)*; 9 M. Seward *(750 Yamaha)*; 10 M. Lomas *(500 Suzuki)*.
Fastest lap: K. Irons *(750 Honda)*, 1m 11.3s, 96.79mph

Round 4 15 May, Mallory Park (12 laps, 16.44 miles)

1 S. Spray *(500 Suzuki)*, 10m 54.4s, 90.44mph
2 S. Buckmaster *(588 Norton)*; 3 S. Henshaw *(500 Suzuki)*; 4 M. Linscott *(1100 Suzuki)*; 5 R. Bennett *(1100 Suzuki)*; 6 S. Williams *(750 Yamaha)*; 7 T. Bourne *(1100 Suzuki)*; 8 D. Crampton *(750 Suzuki)*; 9 M. Phillips *(500 Suzuki)*; 10 M. Plato *(750 Suzuki)*.
Fastest lap: S. Spray *(500 Suzuki)*, 53.8s, 91.67mph

Round 5 2 July, Scarborough (8 laps, 19.28 miles)

1 S. Spray *(500 Suzuki)*, 15m 46.9s, 73.41mph
2 S. Henshaw *(750 Honda)*; 3 R. Crossley *(1100 Suzuki)*; 4 C. Corner *(600 Honda)*; 5 D. Ashton *(1100 Suzuki)*; 6 A. McDonald *(1100 Suzuki)*; 7 G. Thrush *(600 Honda)*; 8 M. Hodges *(750 Suzuki)*; 9 M. Searle *(1000 Yamaha)*; 10 M. Linscott *(750 Honda)*.
Fastest lap: S. Spray *(500 Suzuki)*, 1m 55.1s, 75.49mph

Round 6 14 August, Carnaby (12 laps, 13.2 miles)

1 A. McGladdery *(588 Norton)*, 11m 23.7s, 76.45mph
2 C. Corner *(750 Honda)*; 3 R. Bennett *(1100 Suzuki)*; 4 D. Crampton *(750 Suzuki)*; 5 R. Crossley (1100 Suzuki); 6 T. Bourne *(1100 Suzuki)*; 7 G. Baldcock *(750 Yamaha)*; 8 S. Waller *(750 Suzuki)*; 9 M. Searle *(750 Yamaha)*; 10 L. Carter *(750 Suzuki)*.
Record lap: S. Spray *(500 Suzuki)*, 54.9s, 79.34mph

Round 7 28 August, Cadwell Park (8 laps, 17.39 miles)

1 T. Nation *(588 Norton)*, 12m 56.7s, 80.61mph
2 S. Spray *(500 Suzuki)*; 3 S. Chambers *(750 Honda)*; 4 A. McGladdery *(750 Honda)*; 5 D. Crampton *(750 Suzuki)*; 6 S. Henshaw *(750 Honda)*; 7 M. Linscott *(750 Honda)*; 8 C. Corner *(750 Honda)*; 9 D. Ireland *(750 Honda)*; 10 S. Waller *(750 Suzuki)*.
Fastest lap: S. Spray *(500 Suzuki)*, 1m 35.5s, 81.95mph

Round 8 30 October, Donington Park (8 laps, 15.66 miles)

1 S. Spray *(500 Suzuki)*, 10m 06.2s, 92.98mph
2 P. Lewis *(1100 Suzuki)*; 3 S. Williams *(750 Bimota)*; 4 D Crampton *(750 Suzuki)*; 5 T. Bourne *(750 Honda)*; 6 J. Higgins *(750 Suzuki)*; 7 T. Poole *(750 Suzuki)*; 8 G. Baldock *(750 Yamaha)*; 9 C. Breeze *(750 Yamaha)*; 10 D. Redgate *(750 Suzuki)*.

Final Championship Positions
1 S. Spray 80 points; 2 T. Bourne 39; M. Linscott 33; 4 S. Buckmaster and M. Farmer 30; 6 R. Bennett 28; 7 S. Henshaw and D. Crampton 27; 9 S. Williams 23; 10 R. Crossley 16.

750cc Production

Round 1 1 April, Brands Hatch (10 laps, 12.036 miles)

1 M. Curtis *(Suzuki)*, 8m 57.9s, 80.55mph
2 R. Stringer *(Suzuki)*; 3 I. Simpson *(Suzuki)*; 4 M. Hodges *(Suzuki)*; 5 P. Walden *(Suzuki)*; 6 C. Gable *(Honda)*; 7 M. Linscott *(Suzuki)*; 8 A. McDonald *(Suzuki)*; 9 H. Mason *(Suzuki)*; 10 B. Doyle *(Suzuki)*.
Fastest lap: R. Stringer *(Suzuki)*, 52.5s, 82.53mph

Round 2 17 April, Thruxton (6 laps, 14.14 miles)

1 P. Warden *(Suzuki)*, 9m 01.6s, 93.96mph
2 I. Cobby *(Suzuki)*; 3 M. Hodges *(Suzuki)*; 4 M. Linscott *(Suzuki)*; 5 N. Allison *(Suzuki)*; 6 R. Smith *(Suzuki)*; 7 P. Booler *(Suzuki)*; 8 J. Trigger *(Suzuki)*; 9 B. Watts *(Suzuki)*; only 9 finishers.
Fastest lap: C. Gable *(Honda)*, 1m 28.6s, 95.73mph

Round 3 1 May, Snetterton (7 laps, 13.3 miles)

1 B. Morrison *(Honda)*, 8m 49.6s, 91.21mph
2 C. Gable *(Honda)*; 3 J. Gainey *(Honda)*; 4 I. Cobby *(Suzuki)*; 5 I. Duffus *(Honda)*; 6 P. Warden *(Suzuki)*; 7 M. Curtis *(Suzuki)*; 8 H. Selby *(Suzuki)*; 9 M. Linscott *(Suzuki)*; 10 J. Roach *(Suzuki)*.
Fastest lap: B. Morrison *(Honda)*, 1m 13.8s, 93.51mph

Round 4 15 May, Mallory Park (12 laps, 16.44 miles)

1 J. Gainey *(Honda)*, 11m 08.9s, 88.47mph
2 C. Gable *(Honda)*; 3 S. Hislop *(Honda)*; 4 I. Cobby *(Suzuki)*; 5 M. Hodges *(Suzuki)*; 6 M. Linscott *(Suzuki)*; 7 J. Brown *(Honda)*; 8 P. Warden *(Suzuki)*; 9 S. Wright *(Suzuki)*; 10 J. Lofthouse *(Suzuki)*.
Fastest lap: J. Gainey *(Honda)*, 54.9s, 89.83mph

Round 5 3 July, Scarborough (8 laps, 19.28 miles)

1 C. Gable *(Honda)*, 15m 20.6s, 75.51mph
2 M. Hodges *(Suzuki)*; 3 S. Vanes *(Yamaha)*; 4 R. Rose *(Suzuki)*; 5 M. Linscott

(Honda); 6 L. Carter *(Suzuki)*; 7 I. Cobby *(Suzuki)*; 8 R. Wright *(Suzuki)*; 9 D. Holmes *(Yamaha)*; only nine finishers.
Fastest lap: C. Gable *(Honda)*, 1m 53.2s, 76.76mph

Round 6 14 August, Carnaby (12 laps, 13.2m)

1 L. Carter *(Suzuki)*, 11m 51.5s, 73.46mph
2 C. Gable *(Suzuki)*; 3 I. Cobby *(Suzuki)*; 4 S. Wright *(Suzuki)*; 5 M. Curtis *(Suzuki)*; 6 M. Hodges *(Suzuki)*; 7 R. Smith *(Suzuki)*; 8 D. Holmes *(Yamaha)*. Only eight finishers.
Fastest lap: L. Carter *(Suzuki)*, 58.1s, 74.97mph

Round 7 28 August, Cadwell Park (8 laps, 17.39 miles)

1 C. Gable *(Honda)*, 13m 49.3s, 75.49mph
2 M. Hodges *(Suzuki)*; 3 I. Cobby *(Suzuki)*; 4 L. Carter *(Suzuki)*; 5 J. Gainey *(Honda)*; 6 S. Wright *(Suzuki)*; 7 R. Rose *(Suzuki)*; 8 R. Smith *(Suzuki)*; 9 A. Ball *(Suzuki)*; 10 D. Holmes *(Yamaha)*.
Fastest lap: J. Gainey *(Honda)*, 1m 41.1s, 77.41mph

Round 8 30 October, Donington Park (8 laps, 15.66 miles)

1 I. Cobby *(Suzuki)*, 11m 05.5s, 87.32mph
2 C. Gable *(Honda)*; 3 J. Gainey *(Honda)*; 4 N. Nottingham *(Suzuki)*; 5 S. Wright *(Suzuki)*; 6 M. White *(Suzuki)*; 7 R. Smith *(Suzuki)*; 8 R. Steele *(Suzuki)*; 9 A. Ball *(Suzuki)*; 10 R. Gordon *(Suzuki)*.

Final Championship Positions
1 C. Gable 93 points; 2 I. Cobby 77; 3 M. Hodges 53; 4 J. Gainey 41; 5 P. Warden 29; 6 L. Carter 28; 7 M. Linscott and M. Curtis 25; 9 S. Wright 21; 10 R. Smith 16.

Sidecar

Round 1 1 April, Brands Hatch (10 laps, 12.036 miles)

1 G. Thomas/P. Chappell *(Yamaha)*, 8m 59.3s, 80.34mph
2 J. Drew/B. Houghton *(Windle)*; 3 R. Fisher/T. Crone *(Suzuki)*; 4 R. Lawrence/T. McGahan *(Yamaha)*; 5 A. Westhead/B. Thear *(Yamaha)*; 6 S. Hall/S. Buck *(Yamaha)*; 7 M. Reddington/P. Gravel *(Yamaha)*; 8 G. Thomas/K. Morgan *(Yamaha)*; 9 S. Fuller/D. Roalf *(Windle)*; 10 M. Bingham/P. Hutchinson *(Yamaha)*.
Fastest lap: G. Thomas/P. Chappell *(Yamaha)* & M. Reddington/P. Gravel *(Yamaha)*, 52.2s, 83.00mph

Round 2 17 April, Thruxton (6 laps, 14.14 miles)

1 M. Boddice/E. Yarker *(Yamaha)*, 8m 48.9s, 96.22mph
2 R. Lawrence/S. Parker *(Yamaha)*; 3 B. Gray/R. Holden *(Yamaha)*; 4 M. Burcombe/C. Gibbard *(Yamaha)*; 5 R. Fisher/T. Crowe *(Suzuki)*; 6 D. Rumble/G. Keep *(Yamaha)*; 7 M. Searle/T. Hopkinson *(RCL)*; 8 G. Thomas/K. Morgan *(Yamaha)*; 9 C. Stirrat/S. Prior *(LCR)*; 10 S. Hall/S. Buck *(Yamaha)*.
Fastest lap: M. Boddice/E. Yarker *(Yamaha)*, 1m 26.1s, 98.51mph

Round 3 1 May, Snetterton (7 laps, 13.3 miles)

1 M. Boddice/E. Yarker *(Yamaha)*, 8m 52.7s, 90.68mph
2 G. Thomas/K. Morgan *(Windle)*; 3 R. Fisher/T. Crone *(Suzuki)*; 4 B. Gray/R. Holden *(Yamaha)*; 5 M. Thompson/I. Stapleton *(Yamaha)*; 6 S. Hall/S. Buck *(Yamaha)*; 7 A. Westhead/B. Thear *(Yamaha)*; 8 M. Reddington/P. Gravel *(Yamaha)*; 9 L. Hurst/G. Hurst *(Yamaha)*; 10 E. Cornes/G. Wellington *(Yamaha)*.
Fastest lap: M. Boddice/E. Yarker *(Yamaha)*, 1m 13.7s, 93.63mph

Round 4 15 May, Mallory Park (12 laps, 16.44 miles)

1 M. Boddice/C. Birks *(Yamaha)*, 11m 00.8s, 89.56mph
2 R. Lawrence/G. Mapletoft *(Yamaha)*; 3 M. Searle/T. Hopkinson *(Yamaha)*; 4 D. Hallam/S. Parker *(Yamaha)*; 5 G. Rushbrook/G. Leitch *(Ireson)*; 6 K. Howles/S. Pointer *(Yamaha)*; 7 S. Hall/S. Buck *(Ireson Yamaha)*; 8 D. Hurrell/R. Hawkins *(Yamaha)*; 9 M. Bembridge/T. Wilde *(Yamaha)*; 10 P. Croft/N. Harding *(Yamaha)*.
Fastest lap: M. Searle/T. Hopkinson *(Yamaha)*, 53.2s, 92.70mph

Round 5 14 August, Carnaby (12 laps, 13.2 miles)

1 E. Wright/A. Wilson *(Yamaha)*, 11m 26.5s, 76.14mph
2 D. Bingham/G. Irlam *(Yamaha)*; 3 G. Rushbrook/G. Leitch *(Yamaha)*; 4 R. Fisher/T. Crowe *(Yamaha)*; 5 M. Boddice/E. Yarker *(Yamaha)*; 6 R. Lawrence/A. Rawlings *(Yamaha)*; 7 D. Hurrell/R. Hawkins *(Yamaha)*; 8 V. Butler/R. Bidwell *(Yamaha)*; 9 W. Scarth/L. Scarth *(Yamaha)*;10 R. Bellas/G. Knight *(Suzuki)*.
Fastest lap: E. Wright/A. Wilson *(Yamaha)*, 56.1s, 77.65mph

Round 6 14 August, Carnaby (12 laps, 13.2 miles)

1 G. Rushbrook/G. Leitch *(Yamaha)*, 11m 34.0s, 75.31mph
2 D. Bingham/G. Irlam *(Yamaha)*; 3 R. Lawrence/A. Rawlings *(Yamaha)*; 4 M. Boddice/E. Yarker *(Yamaha)*; 5 G. Bell/J. Tailford *(Yamaha)*; 6 R. Fisher/T. Crowe *(Yamaha)*; 7 G. Shand/J. Shedden *(Yamaha)*; 8 R. Bellas/G. Knight *(Suzuki)*; 9 D. Hurrell/R. Hawkins *(Yamaha)*; 10 M. Searle/T. Hopkinson *(Yamaha)*.
Fastest lap: G. Rushbrook/G. Leitch *(Yamaha)*, 56.4s, 77.23mph

Round 7 28 August, Cadwell Park (8 laps, 17.39 miles)

1 E. Wright/A. Wilson *(Yamaha)*, 13m 41.4s, 76.22mph
2 R. Fisher/T. Crone *(Suzuki)*; 3 R. Bellas/G. Knight *(Suzuki)*; 4. N. Smith/C. Hollis *(Yamaha)*; 5 G. Bell/J. Tailford *(Yamaha)*; 6. M. Boddice/E. Yarker *(Yamaha)*; 7. R. Lawrence/A. Rawlings *(Yamaha)*; 8 M. Smith/K. Webster *(Yamaha)*; 9 L. Pallister/I. Mariner *(Yamaha)*; 10 V. Jefford/P. Hill *(Suzuki)*.
Fastest lap: E. Wright/A. Wilson *(Yamaha)*, 1m 40.4s, 77.95mph

Round 8 30 October, Donington Park (8 laps, 15.66 miles)

1 K. Howles/S. Pointer *(Yamaha)* 10m 37.2s, 88.46mph
2 D. Bingham/G. Irlam *(Yamaha)*; 3 M. Smith/K. Webster *(Yamaha)*; 4 M. Reddington/R. Parker *(Yamaha)*; 5 E. Wright/A. Wilson *(Yamaha)*; 6 R. Fisher/T.

Crowe *(Yamaha)* 7 S. Hall/T. Martin *(Yamaha)* 8 M. Thompson/I. Stapleton *(Yamaha)*; 9 R. Lawrence/A. Rawlings *(Yamaha)*; 10 J. Drew/B. Houghton *(Yamaha)*.

Final Championship Positions
1 M. Boddice/E. Yarker/C. Birks 64 points; 2 R. Fisher/T. Crowe 56; 3 R. Lawrence/A. Rawlings 53; 4 E. Wright/A. Wilson and D. Bingham/G. Irlam 36; 6 G. Rushbrook/G. Leitch 31; 7 K. Howles/S. Pointer 20; 8 S. Hall/S. Buck 19; 9 B. Gray/R. Holden 16; G. Thomas/P. Chappell 16.

HONDA CBR CHALLENGE

Gary Pinchin

The destiny of the championship in the second and final year of the Honda CBR Challenge was in doubt right until the final race at Brands Hatch. It was another super season of close-fought racing in this one-make contest with seven different riders winning races in the nine-round championship.

Only defending champion Geoff Johnson and Ian Simpson managed to win more than once, but the title fell to the quiet, unassuming Eric McFarlane. He won the penultimate race at Cadwell to go into Brands with a six-point advantage over nearest rival Simpson and clinched the title with a well-judged second-place ride behind Gary Weston in a tense final.

Simpson, with his Scotspeed-entered, Metzeler-shod bike, actually led the first half of the race before Weston swept by into a healthy lead, but behind it was all-out war with McFarlane and Simpson involved in a five-man race for second place. Experienced McFarlane, on his Avon-shod, Moto Services Ltd CBR, kept his head and second place, while young Simpson, perhaps feeling the pressure, faded to fifth behind Brian Nicholson and Chris Brenneck.

Johnson lucked-out this year, crashing at Knockhill with Ian Waine, which effectively put both of them out of contention for the title. Other race winners included Morrison, Iain Duffus and Charlie Corner.

Results

Round 1 3 April, Donington Park (10 laps, 19.57 miles)

1 G. Johnson, 13m 32.94s, 86.66mph
2 B. Morrison; 3 I. Simpson; 4 M. Edwards; 5 I. Waine; 6 A. Cummings; 7 E. McFarlane; 8 G. Allott; 9 S. Hislop; 10 G. Thrush.
Fastest lap: G. Johnson, 1m 19.15s, 89.01mph (record)

Round 2 21 May, Carnaby (12 laps, 14.4 miles)

1 I. Simpson 11m 33.5s, 75.37mph
2 E. McFarlane; 3 G. Johnson; 4 B. Morrison; 5 M. Edwards; 6 A. Cummings; 7 G. Weston; 8 C. Corner; 9 J. Moodie; 10 G. Thrush.
Fastest lap: B. Morrison 56.7s, 76.19mph

Round 3 9 July, Knockhill (12 laps, 15.46m)

1 I. Duffus, 12m 0.8s, 77.25mph
2 B. Morrison; 3 E. McFarlane; 4 I. Simpson; 5 S. Hislop; 6 J. Reynolds; 7 B. Nicholson; 8 D. Ashton; 9 M. Edwards; 10 J. Brown.
Fastest lap: S. Hislop, 59s, 78.65mph

Round 4 17 July, Snetterton (10 laps, 19.17m)

1 I. Simpson, 12m 25.1s, 92.62mph
2 E. McFarlane; 3 J. Reynolds; 4 A. Batson; 5 D. Ashton; 6 I. Duffus; 7 S. Hislop; 8 S. Ives; 9 B. Nicholson; 10 W. Coulter.
Fastest lap: A. Batson, 1m 13.5s, 93.89mph

Round 5 20 August, Thruxton (8 laps, 18.848m)

1 C. Corner, 12m 18.60, 91.87mph
2 G. Weston; 3 A. Cummings; 4 J. Reynolds; 5 D. Ashton; 6 S. Ives; 7 G. Johnson; 8 J. Moodie; 9 B. Morrison; 10 P. Armes.
Fastest lap: S. Ives, 1m 27.90, 96.49mph

Round 6 3 September, Mallory Park (12 laps, 16.44 miles)

1 B. Morrison, 10m 59.7s, 89.71mph
2 E. McFarlane; 3 J. Reynolds; 4 I. Scott; 5 B. Nicholson; 6 D. Ashton; 7 I. Simpson; 8 G. Johnson; 9 C. Brenneck; 10 G. Weston.
Fastest lap: E. McFarlane, 54.1s, 91.16mph

Round 7 25 September, Donington Park (8 laps, 20.00 miles)

1 G. Johnson, 14m 29.73s, 82.78mph
2 E. McFarlane; 3 W. Coulter; 4 B. Nicholson; 5 I. Simpson; 6 B. Morrison; 7 M. Edwards; 8 A. Batson; 9 G. Weston; 10 F. Finch.
Fastest lap: B. Morrison, 1m 46.78s, 84.28mph

Round 8 1 October, Cadwell Park (8 laps, 17.39 miles)

1 E. McFarlane, 13m 29s, 77.39mph
2 I. Simpson; 3 B. Morrison; 4 C. Corner; 5 G. Weston; 6 B. Nicholson; 7 G. Johson; 8 H. Selby; 9 W. Coulter; 10 D. Ashton.
Fastest lap: E. McFarlane, 1m 39.6s, 78.57mph

Round 9 22 October, Brands Hatch (14 laps, 16.85 miles)

1 G. Weston, 12m 13.1s, 82.74mph
2 E. McFarlane; 3 B. Nicholson; 4 C. Brenneck; 5 I. Simpson; 6 B. Morrison; 7 W. Coulter; 8 C. Corner; 9 J. Moodie; 10 A. Buckingham.
Fastest lap: G. Weston, 51.1s, 84.79mph

Final Championship Positions

1 E. McFarlane, 129 points

2 I. Simpson, 117; 3 B. Morrison, 111; 4 G. Johnson, 81; 5 G. Weston, 74; 6 B. Nicholson, 65; 7 A. Cummings, 54; 8 C. Corner, 53; 9 J. Reynolds, 52; 10 D. Ashton, 46.

BATTLE OF THE TWINS

Gary Pinchin

The Battle of the Twins was re-born in the UK for 1988 largely thanks to the efforts of twins enthusiast Gordon Anderson. He pooled together numerous sponsors, including Dunlop Tyres who put their name to the championship, and came up with an eight-race campaign which featured full grids and good racing.

The series was largely a Ducati benefit with Wayne Mitchell winning the title on a Steve Wynne-prepared 750 by eleven points from Mark Ward's 600 example. Mitchell took three wins to Ward's one. Another Wynne-entered machine finished third; the impressive looking Bimota 750 Ducati of journalist Mark Forsyth, who only joined the series after three rounds had been run. Dave Brown, winner of the opening round at Cadwell Park was fourth overall with the Tedal Racing 600 Ducati.

Roger Marshall took a pair of wins on the Quantel Cosworth in the two races he contested, enough for seventh in the point standings. The only other non-Ducati race winner was Peter Warden. He actually led the standings after winning the third round at Donington with Chris Clarke's Guzzi, but sadly lost his life while racing a Suzuki production bike at a Cadwell club race.

Results

Round 1 13 March, Cadwell Park (15 laps, 12.7 miles)

1 D. Brown *(600 Ducati)*, 13m 46.6s, 55.46mph
2 J. Hesselwood *(750 Ducati)*; 3 P. Warden *(950 Moto Guzzi)*; 4 R. Price *(750 BSA)*; 5 R. Cutts *(750 Norton)*; 6 P. Klatkiewicz *(750 Ducati)*; 7 D. Railton *(884 Ducati)*; 8 N. McIntosh *(750 Norton)*; 9 G. Baines *(864 Ducati)*; 10 A. Evans *(600 Ducati)*.
Fastest lap: D. Brown *(600 Ducati)*, 53.9s, 56.7mph.

Round 2 17 April, Thruxton (6 laps, 14.14 miles)

1 R. Marshall *(820 Cosworth)* 8m 51.10s, 95.82mph
2 W. Mitchell *(750 Ducati)*; 3 P. Warden *(950 Moto Guzzi)*; 4 M. Ward *(600 Ducati)*; 5 M. Brookes *(750 Ducati)*; 6 D. Brown *(750 Ducati)*; 7 B. Swallow *(885 Ducati)*; 8 D. Railton *(884 Ducati)*; 9 T. Knight *(750 Ducati)*; 10 N. McIntosh *(750 Norton)*.
Fastest lap: R. Marshall *(820 Cosworth)*, 1m 25.7s, 98.97mph.

Round 3 2 May, Donington Park (8 laps, 15.7 miles)

1 P. Warden *(920 Moto Guzzi)*, 12m 17.0s, 76.47mph
2 M. Ward *(600 Ducati)*; 3 J. Heselwood *(750 Ducati)*; 4 D. Railton *(884 Ducati)*; 5 G. Baines *(883 Ducati)*; 6 T. Knight *(750 Ducati)*; 7 P. Klatkiewicz *(750 Ducati)*; 8 S. Roberts *(750 Ducati)*; 9 R. Armstrong *(948 Moto Guzzi)*; 10 C. Carey *(750 Ducati)*.
Fastest lap: M. Ward *(600 Ducati)*, 1m 29.8s, 78.45mph.

Round 4 25 June, Aberdare Park (14 laps, 10.5 miles)

1 W. Mitchell *(750 Ducati)*, 10m 41s, 58.97mph
2 M. Forsyth *(750 Bimota)*; 3 B. Doyle *(750 Ducati)*; 4 A. Bennallick *(750 Triumph)*; 5 M. Dowkes *(500 Weslake)*; 6 J. Heselwood *(750 Ducati)*; 7 D. Gallagher *(750 Ducati)*; 8 P. Klatkiewicz *(750 Ducati)*; 9 R. Tremlin *(750 Ducati)*; 10 G. Baines *(883 Ducati)*.
Fastest lap: W. Mitchell *(750 Ducati)*, 44.75s, 58.97mph.

Round 5 3 July, Scarborough (8 laps, 19.28 miles)

1 M. Ward *(600 Ducati)*, 15m 34.5s, 74.38mph
2 D. Brown *(750 Ducati)*; 3 J. Heselwood *(750 Ducati)*; 4 D. Gallagher *(750 Ducati)*; 5 M. Brookes *(750 Ducati)*; 6 B. Doyle *(750 Ducati)*; 7 G. Baines *(883 Ducati)*; 8 T. Rutter *(750 Ducati)*; 9 R. Armstrong *(950 Moto Guzzi)*; 10 J. Raybold *(600 Ducati)*.
Fastest lap: M. Ward *(600 Ducati)* 1m 55.1s, 75.49mph.

Round 6 14 August, Knockhill (15 laps, 19.32m)

1 W. Mitchell *(750 Ducati)*, 15m 48.45s, 73.39mph; 2 N. Jeffries *(750 Ducati)*; 3 M. Forsyth *(750 Bimota)*; 4 D. Brown *(600 Ducati)*; 5 D. Gallagher *(750 Ducati)*; 6 B. Doyle *(750 Ducati)*; 7 C. Carey *(750 Ducati)*; 8 P. Klatkiewicz *(750 Ducati)*; 9 I. Hamilton *(1000 Egli Vincent)*; 10 G. Baines *(883 Ducati)*.
Fastest lap: W. Mitchell *(750 Ducati)*, 1m 1.22s, 75.08mph

Round 7 29 August, Darley Moor (10 laps, 15.0m)

W. Mitchell *(750 Ducati)*, 10m 59s, 81.94mph; 2 M. Ward *(600 Ducati)*; 3 M. Forsyth *(750 Bimota)*; 4 C. Carey *(750 Ducati)*; 5 J. Summerfield *(600 Ducati)*; 6 P. Klatkiewicz *(750 Ducati)*; 7 R. Tremlin *(750 Ducati)*; 8 M. Lyon *(600 Ducati)*; 9 G. Baines *(883 Ducati)*; 10 T. Rutter *(750 Ducati)*.
Fastest lap: W. Mitchell *(750 Ducati)*, 1m 4s, 84.37mph

Round 8 25 September, Snetterton (8 laps, 15.2m)

1 R. Marshall *(820 Cosworth)*, 9m 51.4s, 93.35mph; 2 I. Cobby *(920 Moto Guzzi)*; 3 M. Forsyth *(750 Bimota)*; 4 T. Knight *(750 Ducati)*; 5 W. Mitchell *(750 Ducati)*; 6 M. Ward *(600 Ducati)*; 7 M. Brookes *(750 Ducati)*; 8 T. Rutter *(750 Ducati)*; 9 C. Carey *(750 Ducati)*; 10 M. Lyon *(750 Ducati)*.
Fastest lap: R. Marshall *(820 Cosworth)*, 1m 12.2s, 95.58mph.

Final Championship Positions

1 W. Mitchell *(750 Ducati)*, 63 points; 2 M. Ward *(600 Ducati)*, 52; 3 M. Forsyth *(750 Bimota)*, 42; 4 D. Brown *(600/750 Ducati)*, 40; 5 J. Heselwood *(750 Ducati)*, 37; 6 P. Warden *(950 Moto Guzzi)*, 35; 7 R. Marshall *(820 Cosworth)*, 30; 8=B. Doyle *(750 Ducati)* and P. Klatkiewicz *(750 Ducati)*, both 20; 10 M. Brookes *(750 Ducati)*.

CLASSIC BIKE MAGAZINE CHAMPIONSHIP

Jim Reynolds

Classic racing confirmed its depth of talent both young and mature in the results of the *Classic Bike* magazine Championship. Fought out over eight rounds at National meetings, it confirmed the great talent of 500cc title winner Dave Pither. This 34-year-old builder's merchant foreman from Moreton-in-the-Marsh, Gloucestershire, remains the rider anyone has to beat to prove they have arrived.

A few men did finish ahead of Pither during the year. Yorkshireman Mike Dowkes got to the flag first at Mallory Park and on the twisting parkland path of Aberdare in South Wales, proving that a Weslake twin can be made to go fast and far enough to win; Lancashire lad John Cronshaw rode his remarkable BSA Gold Star to win at Brands Hatch and Snetterton; Bob Newby showed the sheer speed of the late Syd Mularney's four-valve Manx Norton at Donington. But super-consistent Dave Pither, on a single-cylinder G50 Seeley owned by butcher Mick Iaberer, never finished lower than fourth in any round, won more races than anyone with victories at Thruxton, Scarborough and Cadwell Park, and took the crown for the second time.

David Dearden dominated the contest for the 350 title, riding in seven rounds and winning six on banker David Bailey's sleek red Italian Aermacchi. It was a deserved win for the man who finished runner-up for the two previous years, but there is strong young talent emerging in the 350 class that will leave Dearden no time to relax in the future. Michael Attrill, riding in his first full National season and travelling across from the Isle of Wight for each race, slipped past Dearden in the Mallory Park race, and suprised paddock pundits by staying there. Second in the title race, Michael is planning a full-season campaign for 1989. Third at the end of the season was veteran Ted Edwards, proving that a Ducati can challenge the established Aermacchi dominance; but close behind Ted in the final count was another youngster in his first National season – John Barton.

With Suzuki and Yamaha two-strokes proving their speed in recent years, few thought they could be beaten in 1988. But 21-year-old bike mechanic Martin Studer, another rider in his first full National season, finished second in the first round on his single-cylinder Greeves 'Silverstone' and gathered enough points through sheer tenacious riding to take the title at his first attempt. Outpaced by the Japanese twins, the Greeves was prepared superbly by Martin and his father and proved 100 percent reliable. Second overall was Dave Kershaw, returning to National racing wth a Yamaha TD1C, while ex-moto-crosser Dave Rumbold had a solid season on a TR250 Suzuki to finish third.

Results

500cc: 1 Dave Pither *(Taberer Seeley)* 91 points (best of seven of eight results); 2 John Cronshaw *(Unity BSA)* 76; 3 Mike Dowkes *(Titchmarsh Weslake)* 71.

350cc: 1 David Dearden *(Aermacchi)* 102; 2 Michael Attrill *(Aermacchi)* 67; 3 Ted Edwards *(Ducati)* 48.

250cc: 1 Martin Studer *(EWS Greeves)* 82; 2 Dave Kershaw *(Yamaha)* 64; 3 Dave Rumbold *(Evans Suzuki)* 51.

Period One (Pre 1964): 1 Trevor Beharrell *(1960, 350 AJS)* 37; 2 Ian Austin *(1956, 350 BSA)* and Grant Sellares *(1954, 350 Norton)* 14 each.

Classic Bike Magazine/Norman Hyde Championship

The howling exhaust note of three-cylinder Triumphs dominated the races and results of the 'Classic Bike' Magazine/Norman Hyde Championship. Catering for non-Japanese classics of the 60s and 70s, the title race in 1988 saw five possible winners in the list before the final round at Donington Park in October.

Regular Triumph Trident competitor Tony Osborne finally took the Hyde cup on his 750cc Norman Miles-entered replica of the old works racers. It was a reward for consistent riding and sheer guts, because Tony broke a thumb in a fall at Carnaby in August and struggled to ride at Cadwell Park two weeks later. But the eight points for his gritty fourth place made all the difference, and he finally beat Dave Pither on the Thompsons' 830cc Miles-framed Trident by just six points!

Pither was the late-season hot number, after Yamaha works rider Geoff Johnson surprised many by winning at Scarborough on sponsor Hyde's own road demonstrator, with a racing engine fitted for the occasion. A major threat after two second places, Johnson missed the last round when a fall in a non-Championship meeting left him with a broken pelvis. His place on the Hyde bike was taken by Londoner Chris Thomas, who impressed with a close second to the on-form Pither despite never having ridden a Trident until the day before. But the consistent scoring of Tony Osborne in the early rounds made the difference and he took the title without winning one round of the seven in the series.

Nottingham's Tony Price looked a likely winner on his stark, simple and remarkably speedy twin-cylinder BSA-Norton. Tony won at Snetterton and Carnaby, but a broken arm from a Cadwell round fall left him unfit for the final race and he finished equal third with Trevor Osborne.

Championship results:
1 Tony Osborne *(750 Miles Engineering Triumph)* 50 points; 2 Dave Pither *(830 Thompson Triumph)* 44; 3= Trevor Osborne *(750 Rolacam BSA-3)* and Tony Price *(750 BSA-Norton)* 42 each; 5 Asa Moyce *(750 Miles Engineering Triumph)* 27; 6 Geoff Baines *(863 Wings Couriers Ducati)* 19.

IRISH RACING

Ivan Davidson and Gary Pinchin

Ulster Grand Prix, 30 July Dundrod

With Joey Dunlop making a disastrous tyre decision in the World TTF1 race (see main World Championship TTF1 review section for full details), the local hero was left to salvage lost pride by winning the second of the two 350cc races with his Honda RS250.

In a similar vein to the North West 200 250/350 race earlier in the season, the race was a thriller with Dunlop clinching his 34th Dundrod victory by a machine's breadth on the line from Woolsey Coulter. Welshman Steve Williams took third, only half a second adrift, with Eddie Laycock fourth.

It was a good meeting for Dubliner Laycock. He finished second to Reid in the first 350 race, but riding Joe Millar's 500 Honda was in unstoppable form in the Senior, winning by 17 seconds from Dunlop. Laycock's fastest lap was an incredible 121.39 mph on the undulating road course.

Senior (9 laps, 66 miles)
1 E. Laycock *(500 Honda)*, 120.14mph
2 J. Dunlop *(750 Honda)*; 3 S. Hislop *(750 Honda)*; 4 S. Cull *(500 Honda)*; 5 N. Jeffries *(750 Honda)*; 6 D. Leach *(500 Suzuki)*; 7 S. McClements *(750 Suzuki)*; 8 A. McGladdery *(750 Suzuki)*; 9 R. Dunlop *(750 Honda)*; 10 D. Griffith *(750 Honda)*.
Fastest lap: E. Laycock *(500 Honda)*; 3m 39.5s, 121.39s (record)

Superstock (6 laps, 45 miles)
1 N. Jeffries *(Honda)*, 101.66mph
2 D. Griffith *(Honda)*; 3 A. McGladdery *(Suzuki)*; 4 G. Lingham *(Kawasaki)*; 5 S. Hislop *(Honda)*; 6 A. Moyce *(Kawasaki)*; 7 R. Dunlop *(Honda)*; 8 S. Johnson *(Suzuki)*; 9 P. Hogg *(Suzuki)*; 10 E. Galbraith *(Suzuki)*.
Fastest lap: S. Hislop *(Honda)*; 4m 13.1s, 105.27mph

1st 350 (9 laps, 66 miles)
1 B. Reid *(350 Yamaha)*, 109.09mph
2 E. Laycock *(250 EMC)*; 3 W. Coulter *(250 Honda)*; 4 J. Dunlop *(250 Honda)*; 5 I. Newton *(250 Rotax)*; 6 P. McCallen *(250 Honda)*; 7 C. Martin *(250 Aprilia)*; 8 L. McMaster *(350 Yamaha)* 9 T. Head *(350 Yamaha)*; 10 A. Irwin *(250 Yamaha)*.
Fastest lap: E. Laycock *(250 EMC)*, 3m 59.0s, 111.48mph

2nd 350 (9 laps, 66 miles)
1 J. Dunlop *(250 Honda)*, 112.31mph
2 W. Coulter *(250 Honda)*; 3 S. Williams *(350 Yamaha)*; 4 E. Laycock *(250 EMC)*; 5 B. Reid *(250 EMC)*; 6 P. McCallen *(250 Honda)*; 7 S. Cull *(250 Honda)*; 8 I. Newton *(250 Rotax)*; 9 C. Dowd *(350 Yamaha)*; 10 A. Irwin *(250 Yamaha)*;
Fastest lap: J. Dunlop *(250 Honda)*, 3m 53.3s, 114.21mph
For Formula One race details see world TTF1 championship review

The North West 200, 21 May, Portstewart
Bangor's Steve Cull was in superb form at the North West 200, winning a hat-trick of races on the high-speed 8.9-mile Portstewart-Coleraine-Portrush road course.

First, with the Francis Neill Racing Honda 500, he took the opening Superbike race – a relatively easy victory over Dublin's Eddie Laycock on a similar Millar Honda. Then, riding Neill's 250 Honda, he won a closely fought 250/350 scrap which had the local experts calling it the best race ever seen in Ireland. Cull had to win a five-bike battle for the lead to take the chequered flag. Carl Fogarty, Woolsey Coulter, Alan Irwin, Cull and Laycock swapped positions throughout until Cull made a decisive move at the Juniper Hill chicane on the final lap.

The treble came in the North West 200 race itself, with Cull just pipping Joey Dunlop on the line. This was after Cull had slipped off the 500 Honda at York Hairpin on the last lap. He had lost a twelve-second lead over Dunlop but remounted quickly and passed the 750 Honda within sight of the flag to up his day's winnings to over £5,000.

Gary Cowan, who had overshot the new chicane in the first 250/350 race and dropped downfield, sped to an easy win in the 'Junior' North West 200. Joey Dunlop scored his only win of the day in the Production 750 and Kenny Irons took the 1300 Production honours riding a Yamaha.

North West 200 (6 laps, 53.4 miles)
1 S. Cull *(500 Honda)*, 27m 33.5s, 116.26mph; 2 J. Dunlop *(750 Honda)*; 3 K. Irons *(750 Honda)*; 4 R. Marshall *(750 Suzuki)*; 5 S. Henshaw *(500 Suzuki)*; 6 B. Woodland *(1000 Yamaha)*; 7 T. Nation *(750 Suzuki)*; 8 J. Lofthouse *(750 Suzuki)*; 9 B. Gladwin *(750 Yamaha)*; 10 D. Hill *(750 Suzuki)*.
Fastest lap: S. Cull *(500 Honda)*, 4m 33.2s, 117.28mph

250/350 (6 laps, 53.4 miles)
1 S. Cull *(250 Honda)*, 29m 31.2s, 108.54mph; 2 C. Fogarty *(250 Honda)*; 3 A. Irwin *(250 Yamaha)*; 4 W. Coulter *(250 Honda)*; 5 E. Laycock *(350 Yamaha)*; 6 I. Newton *(250 Rotax)*; 7 G. Cowan *(250 Yamaha)*; 8 F. Morrison *(250 Yamaha)*; 9 R. Dunlop *(350 Yamaha)*; 10 D. Johnston *(350 Yamaha)*.
Fastest lap: S. Cull *(250 Honda)*, 4m 53.2s, 109.28mph

Junior North West 200 (6 laps, 53.4 miles)
1 G. Cowan *(250 Yamaha)*, 29m 15.3s, 109.52mph; 2 W. Coulter *(250 Honda)*; 3 J. Dunlop *(250 Honda)*; 4 I. Newton *(250 Honda)*; 5 A. Irwin *(250 Yamaha)*; 6 S. Cull *(250 Honda)*; 7 B. Reid *(250 EMC)*; 8 M. Carter *(350 Yamaha)*; 9 E. Roberts *(250 Kimoco)*; 10 S. Hazlett *(350 Yamaha)*.
Fastest lap: G. Cowan *(250 Yamaha)*; 4m 50.7s, 110.22mph

Superbike (6 laps, 53.4 miles)
1 S. Cull *(500 Honda)*, 27m 28.5s, 116.62mph; 2 E. Laycock *(500 Honda)*; 3 A. McGladdery *(750 Suzuki)*; 4 S. Hislop *(750 Honda)*; 5 C. Fogarty *(750 Honda)*; 6 M. Farmer *(1100 Suzuki)*; 7 S. McClements *(750 Suzuki)*; 8 S. Henshaw *(500 Suzuki)*; 9 B. Woodland *(1000 Yamaha)*; 10 N. Jeffries *(750 Honda)*.
Fastest lap: S. Cull *(500 Honda)*, 4m 33.2s, 117.28mph

750 Production (6 laps, 53.4 miles)
1 J. Dunlop *(Honda)*, 29m 22.4s, 109.08mph; 2 R. Rose *(Suzuki)*; 3 I. Newton *(Suzuki)*; 4 S. Berwick *(Suzuki)*; 5 W. Coulter *(Honda)*; 6 D. Chatterton *(Suzuki)*; 7 G. Rondelli *(Suzuki)*; 8 I. Gibson *(Kawasaki)*; 9 M. Carter *(Suzuki)*.
only nine finishers
Fastest lap: S. Hislop *(Honda)*, 4m 47.6s, 111.4mph

1300 Production (6 laps, 53.4 miles)
1 K. Irons *(Yamaha)*; 28m 59.8s, 110.50mph; 2 T. Nation *(Suzuki)*; 3. J. Lofthouse *(Suzuki)*; 4 S. Allen *(Yamaha)*; 5 R. Marshall *(Suzuki)*; 6 A. McGladdery *(Suzuki)*; 7 M. Farmer *(Suzuki)*; 8 N. Jeffries *(Honda)*; 9 B. Woodland *(Yamaha)*; 10 D. Hill *(Kawasaki)*.
Fastest lap: T. Nation *(Suzuki)*, 4m 46.2s, 111.95mph

MAJOR IRISH MEETINGS

Cookstown 100, 23 April

Two race wins and three new lap records was the splendid performance from Tandragee sensation Phillip McCallen at the Cookstown 100, the opening road race of the 1988 Irish road racing season.

In the best race of the day former World F2 champion Brian Reid looked a safe bet in the 350 after opening a gap with a new lap record on the penultimate lap. But then his Yamaha lost its edge and McCallen, with a new lap record, caught and passed the leader in the closing stages.

McCallen took the 250 race from slow starting Reid but just missed out on the finish line of the 125 race to Robert Dunlop despite another record-breaking last lap.

125cc (6 laps, 42 miles)
1 R. Dunlop *(Honda)*; 2 P. McCallen *(Honda)*; 3 L. McMaster *(Honda)*; 4 R. White *(Honda)*; 5 C. Hanna *(MBA)*; 6 J. Leigh *(Honda)*.

200cc (6 laps, 42 miles)
1 F. McConnell *(Yamaha)*; 2 R. Smyth *(Yamaha)*; 3 D. Jamison *(Yamaha)*; 4 J. Sands *(Yamaha)*; 5 N. Lindsay *(Yamasaki)*; 6 G. Jamison *(Yamaha)*.

250cc (6 laps, 42 miles)
1 P. McCallen *(Honda)*; 2 B. Reid *(EMC)*; 3 N. Hudson *(Honda)*; 4 S. Cull *(Honda)*; 5 D. Young *(ECM)*; 6 J. Guy *(Honda)*.

350cc (6 laps, 42 miles)
1 P. McCallen *(Yamaha)*; 2 N. Hudson *(Yamaha)*; 3 B. Reid *(Yamaha)*; 4 M. Carter *(Yamaha)*; 5 J. Byrne *(Yamaha)*; 6 J. Rea *(Yamaha)*.

351–1000cc (5 laps, 35 miles)
1 S. Cull *(500 Honda)*; 2 N. Hudson *(351 Yamaha)*; 3 P. Cranston *(750 Honda)*; 4 S. McClements *(998 Suzuki)* 5 R. Hazleton *(374 Yamaha)*; 6 R. Dunlop *(750 Honda)*.

Classic (6 laps, 42 miles)
1 M. Elwood *(750 Triumph)*; 2 B. Swallow *(500 Velocette)*; 3 D. Storey *(500 Seeley BSA)*; 4 G. Barron *(750 Rickman)*; 5 S. Kavanagh *(750 Ducati)*; 6 D. Shimmin *(350 Norton)*.

Tandragee 100, 7 May
Brian Reid and Philip McCallen were the stars of the Tandragee 100 road races scoring two wins apiece. McCallen once more took the 125 and 250 races, again with record-breaking efficiency, while Reid captured the feature Tandragee 100 in a race of attrition which saw most of the fancied runners fall by the wayside and took the 350 race after disposing of early leader Johnny Rea.

Rea had his moment of glory in the 1000cc, though, the Anderton Suzuki rider inheriting the lead from the luckless Steve Cull who had hit gearbox problems with the Neill Honda.

125cc (7 laps, 35 miles)
1 P. McCallen *(Honda)*; 2 L. McMaster *(Honda)*; 3 A. Caughey *(Honda)*; 4 C. Hanna *(MBA)*; 5 J. Leigh *(Honda)*; 6 G. Stevenson *(Honda)*.

200cc (7 laps, 35 miles)
1 T. Ritchie *(Yamaha)*; 2 F. McConnell *(Yamaha)*; 3 D. Lowry *(Honda)*; 4 J. Rogers *(Yamaha)*; 5 R. Nesbitt *(Yamaha)*; 6 N. Lindsay *(Yamasaki)*.

250cc (7 laps, 35 miles)
1 P. McCallen *(Honda)*; 2 N. Hudson *(Honda)*; 3 S. Cull *(Honda)*; 4 M. Barr *(Rotax)*; 5 J. Guy *(Honda)*; 6 G. Higginson *(Honda)*.

350cc (7 laps, 35 miles)
1 B. Reid *(Yamaha)*; 2 J. Rea *(Yamaha)*; 3 P. McCallen *(Yamaha)*; 4 M. Carter *(Yamaha)*; 5 L. McMaster *(Yamaha)*; 6 D. Johnston *(Yamaha)*.

351–1000cc (7 laps, 35 miles)
1 J. Rea *(500 Suzuki)*; 2 S. McClements *(998 Suzuki)*; 3 M. Swann *(500 Suzuki)*; 4 M. O'Neill *(500 Suzuki)*; 5 P. Cranston *(750 Honda)*; 6 J. Elliott *(750 Suzuki)*.

Tandragee 100 (7 laps, 35 miles)
1 B. Reid *(350 Yamaha)*; 2 P. McCallen *(250 Honda)*; 3 N. Hudson *(250 Honda)*; 4 M. Swann *(500 Suzuki)*; 5 L. McMaster *(350 Yamaha)*; 6 P. Cranston *(750 Honda)*.

Classic (7 laps, 35 miles)
1 S. McClements *(500 Norton)*; 2 B. Swallow *(500 Velocette)* 3 G. Barron *(750 Rickman)*; 4 S. Walls *(686 Triton)*; 5 S. Kavanagh *(750 Ducati)*; 6 G. Millar *(350 Aermacchi)*.

Leinster 200, 15 May
The Leinster 200 at Mondello Park was Southern Ireland's most important short circuit meeting of the season, hosting a round of the MCN/EBC Superstock championship (see

Superstock section for details of the race).

Alan Irwin beat the mainland invaders in both of the 1000cc races, the International being a closely fought battle involving four riders, often abreast under braking for the corners. Irwin's lap record of 74.09mph ultimately gave him the edge although he had to survive a wild last-lap slide to hang on for the win. Gary Cowan also posted two wins, the 250 and 350 national races, but crashed out of the 250/350 International whilst hassling eventual winner Woolsey Coulter in the early running.

1000cc International (15 laps, 18.6 miles)
1 A. Irwin *(500 Honda)*; 2 M. Farmer *(750 Suzuki)*; 3 J. Whitham *(750 Suzuki)*; 4 D. Dixon *(500 Suzuki)*; 5 K. Irons *(750 Honda)*; 6 P. Mellor *(750 Suzuki)*.

1000cc (10 laps, 12.4 miles)
1 A. Irwin *(500 Honda)*; 2 P. Mellor *(750 Suzuki)*; 3 R. Hurst *(750 Kawasaki)*; 4 J. Whitham *(750 Suzuki)*; 5 D. Dunlop *(500 Suzuki)*; 6 T. Nation *(750 Suzuki)*.

Junior International (15 laps, 18.6 miles)
1 W. Coulter *(250 Honda)*; 2 J. Guy *(350 Yamaha)*; 3 F. Morrison *(250 Yamaha)*; 4 A. Patterson *(250 ECM)*; 5 J. Byrne *(350 Yamaha)*; 6 M. Swann *(350 Yamaha)*.

350cc (10 laps, 12.4 miles)
1 G. Cowan *(Yamaha)*; 2 J. Guy *(Yamaha)*; 3 M. Swann *(Yamaha)*; 4 D. Young *(Yamaha)*; 5 M. Carter *(Yamaha)*; 6 A. McCauley *(Yamaha)*.

250cc (10 laps, 12.4 miles)
1 G. Cowan *(Yamaha)*; 2 W. Coulter *(Honda)*; 3 J. Guy *(Honda)*; 4 A. Patterson *(ECM)*; 5 R. Beers *(Yamaha)*; 6 D. Young *(ECM)*.

125cc (10 laps, 12.4 miles)
1 A. Patterson *(Honda)*; 2 C. Turlte *(Honda)*; 3 R. Lorimer *(Honda)*; 4 M. Topping *(Honda)*; 5 J. Leigh *(Honda)*; 6 K. Beckett *(Bartol)*.
Superstock results in MCN/EBC Superstock review section

Killinchy 150, 17/18 June

Joey Dunlop had to wait until the feature race of the day, the Kevin Martin Memorial, to score his first win. Still, he did it in style on the 7.4 mile Dundrod course at the Killinchy 150 meeting, all but equalling his own lap record in the process. Earlier he had played a runner-up role in the 1000cc race to Eddie Laycock and to Brian Reid in the combined 250/350 race.

With Phillip McCallen sidelined through injury Alan Caughey rode a superb 125cc race to beat the favourites, Robert Dunlop – on the McCallen Laverty Honda – and Leslie McMaster.

Kevin Martin Memorial (7 laps, 51.8 miles)
1 J. Dunlop *(750 Honda)*; 2 E. Laycock *(500 Honda)*; 3 S. McClements *(998 Suzuki)*; 4 J. Rea *(500 Suzuki)*; 5 D. Leach *(750 Yamaha)*; 6 R. Dunlop *(750 Honda)*;

1000cc (7 laps, 51.8 miles)
1 E. Laycock *(500 Honda)*; 2 J. Dunlop *(750 Honda)*; 3 R. Dunlop *(750 Honda)*; 4 S. McClements *(998 Suzuki)*; 5 D. Leach *(500 Suzuki)*; 6 R. Campbell *(500 Suzuki)*.

250/350cc (7 laps, 51.8 miles)
1 B. Reid *(350 Yamaha)*; 2 J. Dunlop *(250 Honda)*; 3 E. Laycock *(250 EMC)*; 4 N. Hudson *(250 Honda)*; 5 S. Cull *(250 Honda)*; 6 L. McMaster *(350 Yamaha)*.

250cc (5 laps, 37 miles)
1 K. Ferguson *(Yamaha)*; 2 D. Reid *(Yamaha)*; 3 F. McConnell *(Yamaha)*; 4 T. Ritchie *(Yamaha)*; 5 R. Smyth *(Yamaha)*; 6 D. Jamison *(Yamaha)*.

125cc (5 laps, 37 miles)
1 A. Caughey *(Honda)*; 2 R. Dunlop *(Honda)*; 3 L. McMaster *(Honda)*; 4 D. Lemon *(Honda)*; 5 J. Leigh *(Honda)*; 6 R. White *(Honda)*.

Milverton Road Races, 1/2 July
The Milverton Road Races, formerly known as the Skerries, proved that Phillip McCallen had lost none of his speed as he took the 125 and 250 double in his first outing since recovering from injury.

Veteran Sam McClements proved race winning was not the exclusive property of the youthful riders. He scorched to a double, winning the 1000cc race with his big Suzuki and then dominating the Classic event on a 500 Norton, despite the efforts of Mick Poxon on a 750 Trident.

Johnny Rea made amends for his defeat at the hands of McClements in the 1000cc race to win the Grand Final, while Dublin's Marc Carter scored his first ever road race victory in a crash-strewn 350 event.

Grand Final (12 laps, 34.8 miles)
1 J. Rea *(500 Suzuki)*; 2 S. McClements *(998 Suzuki)*; 3 P. McCallen *(250 Honda)*; 4 M. Swann *(500 Suzuki)*; 5 M. Carter *(350 Yamaha)*; 6 M. Farmer *(750 Suzuki)*.

1000cc (12 laps, 34.8 miles)
1 S. McClements *(998 Suzuki)*; 2 J. Rea *(500 Suzuki)*; 3 M. Swann *(500 Suzuki)* S. Cull *(500 Honda)*; 5 L. Quinn *(750 Yamaha)*; 6 C. Dowd *(750 Kawasaki)*.

350cc (12 laps, 34.8 miles)
1 M. Carter *(Yamaha)*; 2 D. Johnston *(Yamaha)*; 3 M. Swann *(Yamaha)*; 4 R. Hazelton *(Yamaha)*; 5 S. Rea *(Yamaha)*; 6 P. Hogan *(Yamaha)*.

250cc (12 laps, 34.8 miles)
1 P. McCallen *(Honda)*; 2 S. Cull *(Honda)*; 3 S. Henry *(Honda)*; 4 F. Morrison *(Yamaha)*; 5 R. Boland *(EMC)*; 6 G. Millar *(Yamaha)*.

125cc/200cc (10 laps, 29 miles)
1 P. McCallen *(Honda)*; 2 A. Caughey *(Honda)*; 3 L. McMaster *(Honda)*; 4 J. Leigh *(Honda)*; 5 T. Ritchie *(Yamaha)*; 6 M. Topping *(Honda)*.

Classic (8 laps, 23.2 miles)
1 S. McClements *(500 Norton)*; 2 M. Poxon *(750 Triumph)*; 3 G. Barron *(750 Rickman)*; 4 F. O'Callaghan *(750 Triumph)*; 5 K. Wilkie *(750 Triton)* 6 T. Reid *(350 Honda)*.

Temple 100, 30 July

Phillip McCallen was in good form at the Temple 100, the oldest road race in the UK. In spite of incessant rain throughout the meeting he again shone, taking the 125 and 350 races, but had to play second fiddle to Banbridge resident Noel Hudson in the 250 class.

English visitor Dave Shields cakewalked the 80cc event from Ireland's top tiddler rider Alan Patterson. In the big class Sam McClements used all his experience to beat Johnny Rea by 10 seconds in the abysmally wet conditions.

1000cc (7 laps, 38.5 miles)
1 S. McClements *(998 Suzuki)*; 2 J. Rea *(500 Suzuki)*; 3 M. Swann *(500 Suzuki)*; 4 D. Gallagher *(750 Ducati)*; 5 S. Rea *(375 Yamaha)*; 6 G. Jamison *(750 Suzuki)*.

350cc (7 laps, 38.5 miles)
1 P. McCallen *(Yamaha)*; 2 N. Hudson *(Yamaha)*; 3 J. Rea *(Yamaha)*; 4 L. McMaster *(Yamaha)*; 5 S. Rea *(Yamaha)* 6 M. Swann *(Yamaha)*.

250cc (7 laps, 38.5 miles)
1 N. Hudson *(Honda)*; 2 P. McCallen *(Honda)*; 3 J. Rea *(Yamaha)*; 4 S. Cull *(Honda)*; 5 D. Young *(ECM)* 6 R. Duncan *(ECM)*.

200cc (5 laps, 27.5 miles)
1 T. Ritchie *(Yamaha)*; 2 F. McConnell *(Yamaha)*; 3 P. Irwin *(Yamaha)*; 4 N. Lindsay *(Yamaha)*; 5 K. Ferguson *(Yamaha)*; 6 G. Ferguson *(Yamaha)*.

125cc (5 laps, 27.5 miles)
1 P. McCallen *(Honda)*; 2 A. Caughey *(Honda)*; 3 J. Knox *(Honda)*; 4 M. Topping *(Honda)*; 5 I. Kirk *(Honda)*; 6 C. Hanna *(Honda)*.

80cc (5 laps, 27.5 miles)
1 D. Shields *(Yamaha)*; 2 A. Patterson *(Huvo)*; 3 S. McClenaghan *(Kawasaki)*; 4 B. Jamison *(KTM)*; 5 G. Fleming *(Yamaha)*; 6 J. Leigh *(KTM)*.

Neil Robinson Memorial, 8 Oct

In just two seasons the Neil Robinson Memorial meeting at Kirkistown has become the major short circuit event in Ireland, hosting a round of the Superstock championship and enticing riders from the mainland to compete in the other classes.

World TTF1 Champion Carl Fogarty lived up to his mantle by taking overall victory in the Neil Robinson races, having won the first and finishing runner-up to Darren Dixon in the second.

Jamie Whitham won the Sunflower trophy race from the Suzuki 500s of Steve Spray and Darren Dixon, but the locals had plenty to cheer with Alan Patterson winning the 125 and first 350, while Woolsey Coulter took the second 350 race.

1st Neil Robinson Memorial (12 laps, 17.95 miles)
1 C. Fogarty *(750 Honda)*; 2 J. Whitham *(750 Suzuki)*; 3 A. Irwin *(500 Suzuki)*; 4 D. Leach *(750 Honda)*; 5 R. McCurdy *(500 Suzuki)*; 6 G. Farlow *(750 Honda)*.

2nd Neil Robinson Memorial (12 laps, 17.95 miles)
1 D. Dixon *(500 Suzuki)*; 2 C. Fogarty *(750 Honda)*; 3 D. Leach *(750 Honda)*; 4 P. Mellor *(750 Suzuki)*; 5 R. McCurdy *(500 Suzuki)*; 6 R. Dunlop *(750 Honda)*.

Overall
1 C. Fogarty; 2 D. Dixon; 3 D. Leach.

Sunflower Trophy (12 laps, 17.95 miles)
1 J. Whitham *(750 Suzuki)*; 2 S. Spray *(500 Suzuki)*; 3 D. Dixon *(500 Suzuki)*; 4 D. Leach *(750 Honda)*; 5 P. Mellor *(750 Suzuki)*; 6 S. Cull *(500 Honda)*.

1st 350 (10 laps, 14.96 miles)
1 A. Patterson *(250 Rotax)*; 2 K. Mitchell *(250 Yamaha)*; 3 R. Orme *(250 Rotax)*; 4 E. Laycock *(250 EMC)*; 5 P. McCallen *(250 Honda)*; 6 S. Hislop *(250 Honda)*.

2nd 350 (10 laps, 14.96 miles)
1 W. Coulter *(250 Honda)*; 2 R. Orme *(250 Rotax)*; 3 P. McCallen *(250 Honda)*; 4 K. Mitchell *(250 Yamaha)*; 5 S. Hislop *(250 Honda)*; 6 E. Laycock *(250 EMC)*.

125cc (10 laps, 14.96 miles)
1 A. Patterson *(Honda)*; 2 P. McCallen *(Honda)*; 3 A. Caughey *(Honda)*; 4 R. Appleyard *(Honda)*; 5 L. McMaster *(Honda)*; 6 D. Lemon *(Honda)*.

1st Sidecar (12 laps, 17.95 miles)
1 B. Brindley/P. Coombes *(Krauser)*; 2 D. Brown/B. Nelson *(Yamaha)*; 3 G. Bell/J. Tailford *(Yamaha)*; 4 D. Molyneux/C. Hardman *(Yamaha)*; 5 D. Bingham/J. Bingham *(Yamaha)*; 6 D. Rumble jnr/G. Keep *(Yamaha)*.

2nd Sidecar (12 laps, 17.95 miles)
1 B. Brindley/P. Coombes *(Krauser)*; 2 D. Brown/B. Nelson *(Yamaha)*; 3 G. Bell/J. Tailford *(Yamaha)*; 4 L. Burton/P. Cushnahan *(Yamaha)*; 5 D. Molyneux/C. Hardman *(Yamaha)*; 6 D. Bingham/J. Bingham *(Yamaha)*.
Superstock results in MCN/EBC Superstock review section

ROAD RACING CHAMPIONSHIPS

Ivan Davidson

On the pure road courses the 'man of the year' was 24-year-old Tandragee sensation Phillip McCallen. He was a joint winner of the Irish 125cc Road Racing series in 1987 with Robert Dunlop, but this year he simply blew everyone aside to take no less than six championships. He won the 125, 250 and 350 classes in both the Ulster and Irish Championships. The Irish series being a combination of the Ulster rounds plus races from Southern Ireland. McCallen won an unprecendented 14 road races during the season and re-wrote the record books wherever he raced on the Laverty backed bikes.

Perhaps the next Joey Dunlop, Philip McCallen dominated both the Ulster and Irish Championships.
(John Savage, Newton Ardes Chronicle)

In the 125 class his nearest rivals, Alan Caughey and Leslie McMaster, fought a bitter battle for the runner-up spot in each championship, with Caughey getting the verdict in both.

Banbridge veteran Noel Hudson took runner-up in the two 350 championships and in the Ulster 250 but Steve Cull on Francis Neill's Honda took second in the Irish 250 with Hudson third.

Trevor Ritchie won the Irish 200cc series for the second time in three years, but Frank McConnell beat him by five points to ace the Ulster 200 series.

Consistent finishing netted Michael Swann the 1000cc Ulster and Irish titles. In the Ulster he beat Johnny Rea by a handsome 19-point margin but clinched the Irish crown after title hopeful, veteran Sam McClements, was a non-starter in the final round when his Suzuki 1000 failed during the sighting lap of the Killalane meeting.

Irish Road Racing Championship

Final Championship Positions

125cc
1 P. McCallen, 137 points; 2 A. Caughey, 103; 3 L. McMaster, 92; 4 C. Hanna, 77; 5 M. Topping, 72; 6 R. Dunlop, 54; 7 J. Leigh, 45; 8 H. Devlin, 36; 9 M. Richardson, 35; 10 R. White, 34.

200cc
1 T. Ritchie, 114 points; 2 K. Ferguson, 105; 3 F. McConnell, 86; 4 P. Irwin, 55; 5 N. Lindsay, 53; 6 M. Curtin, 51; =7 N. Jamison and D. Jamison, 40; 9 R. Smyth, 39; 10 R. Graham, 37.

250cc
1 P. McCallen, 128 points; 2 S. Cull, 110; 3 N. Hudson, 76; 4 S. Henry, 60; 5 B. Reid, 51; 6 G. Millar, ; 7 T. Ritchie, 41; 8 D. Young, 40; 9 F. Morrison, 39; 10 J. Dunlop, 33.

350cc
1 P. McCallen, 92 points; 2 N. Hudson, 76; 3 B. Reid, 75; 4 M. Carter, 70; 5 L. McMaster, 65; 6 J. Rea, 59; 7 J. Byrne, 51; 8 A. McCauley, 45; 9 M. Swann, 41; 10 S. McCleneghan, 39.

350–1000cc
1 M. Swann, 108 points; 2 S. McClements, 92; 3 J. Rea, 74; 4 R. Campbell, 69; 5 M. Elwood, 51; 6 P. Cranston, 41; 7 E. Galbraith, 35; 8 C. O'Neill, 35; 9 G. Jamison, 34; 10 S. Cull, 33.

Ulster Road Racing Championships

Final Championship Positions

125cc
1 P. McCallen, 97 points; 2 A. Caughey, 69; 3 L. McMaster, 62; 4 C. Hanna, 59; 5 R. Dunlop, 54; 6 M. Topping, 48; 7 R. White, 34; 8 J. Leigh, 32; 9 G. Stevenson, 31; 10 M. Richardson, 30.

200cc
1 F. McConnell, 86 points; 2 T. Ritchie, 81; 3 K. Ferguson, 71; 4 N. Lindsay, 53; 5 N. Jamison, 45; 6 D. Jamison, 40; 7 P. Irwin, 35; 8 R. Nesbitt, 31; 9 R. Smyth, 28; 10 G. Jamison, 28.

250cc
1 P. McCallen, 88 points; 2 N. Hudson, 76; 3 S. Cull, 76; 4 B. Reid, 41; 5 T. Ritchie, 41; 6 J. Dunlop, 33; 7 S. Henry, 32; 8 G. Fleming, 32; 9 J. Guy, 30; 10 D. Young, 29.

350cc
1 P. McCallen, 83 points; 2 N. Hudson, 76; 3 B. Reid, 75; 4 L. McMaster, 59; 5 J. Rea, 59; 6 M. Carter, 50; 7 J. Byrne, 31; 8 A. McCauley, 28; 9 R. Duncan, 26; 10 M. Swann, 26.

350–1000cc
1 M. Swann, 76 points; 2 J. Rea, 57; 3 R. Campbell, 53; 4 M. Elwood, 51; 5 S. McClements, 45; 6 P. Cranston, 41; 7 G. Jamison, 34; 8 R. Hazelton, 30; 9 R. Dunlop, 25; 10 C. O'Neill, 25.

SHORT CIRCUIT CHAMPIONSHIPS

Alan Irwin may have lost the Embassy short circuit title to Johnny Rea but he was once again untouchable in the Irish and Ulster 1000cc championships on the short circuits with the McManus Honda.

Eighteen-year-old Alan Patterson was the short circuit 'find of the season'. In addition to the Regal 125 championship, he won both Irish and Ulster 125 and 80cc championships. It was the second season Patterson had dominated the 80cc class.

Phillip McCallen proved his talents weren't just on the pure road courses. He took the Ulster 250 title, albeit on a tie-breaking, better winning record than Johnny Guy after the pair finished equal on 123 points. McCallen also finished fifth in the Irish 250 which was won by Larne's Ray McCombe, riding an ex-Steve Cull Honda, from Redline Yamaha-mounted Fran Morrison with only five points separating them.

David Jamison and Johnny Rea completed respective doubles in the 200 and 350 classes and Dubliner John Byrne was F2 Irish champion after a close-run season with Rea.

Quality of racing helped make up for thin grids in the Sidecar championships. Ards brothers Reggie and Danny Blain took the Irish series from Belfast pair James Killough and Peter O'Neill, but the positions were reversed in the Ulster championship.

IRISH SHORT CIRCUIT CHAMPIONSHIPS

Final Championship Positions

80cc
1 A. Patterson, 120 points; 2 M. McClenaghan, 117; 3 B. Jamison, 88; 4 R. Fleming, 83; 5 R. Murdock, 71; 6 G. Hughes, 58; 7 L. Gibson, 58; 8 N. Jamison, 50; 9 H. Wright, 39; 10 B. Ferguson, 37.

125cc
1 A. Patterson, 127 points; 2 C. Turtle, 96; 3 L. McMaster, 94; 4 P. McCallen, 79; 5 M. Topping, 75; 6 R. Lorimer, 64; 7 S. Harrison, 63; 8 A. Caughey, 58; 9 K. Beckett, 57; 10 R. Murphy, 56.

200cc
1 D. Jamison, 117 points; 2 R. Glasgow, 70; 3 K. Ferguson, 54; 4 J. Clarke, 48; 5 T. Ritchie, 43; 6 N. Robinson, 42; 7 D. Lowry, 42; 8 R. Nesbitt, 34; 9 N. Jamison, 32; 10 E. Johnston, 28.

250cc
1 R. McCombe, 111 points; 2 F. Morrison, 106; 3 J. Guy, 95; 4 D. Young, 94; 5 P. McCallen, 83; 6 G. Cowan, 77; 7 A. Patterson, 73; 8 R. Beers, 66; 9 C. Turtle, 62; 10 G. Fleming, 55.

350cc
1 J. Rea, 120 points; 2 J. Guy, 118; 3 M. Swann, 114; 4 P. Owens, 104; 5 D. Young, 85; 6 C. Dowd, 57; 7 J. Byrne, 55; 8 L. McMaster, 54; 9 A. Swann, 52; 10 B. Boland, 41.

350–1000cc
1 A. Irwin, 154 points; 2 M. Swann, 131; 3 R. McCurdy, 101; 4 G. Farlow, 82; 5 D. Dunlop, 68; 6 J. Rea, 50; 7 J. Elliott, 49; 8. D. Young, 46; 9 E. Galbraith, 40; 10 P. Lynch, 35.

Formula 2
1 J. Byrne, 85 points; 2 J. Rea, 73; 3 G. Farlow, 69; 4 C. Dowd, 57; 5 N. Moore, 52; 6 R. White, 49; =7 J. McWilliams and D. Mills, 44; 9 S. Ferguson, 35; 10 J. McCrory, 30.

Sidecar
1 R. Blain/D. Blain, 135 points; 2 J. Killough/P. O'Neill, 128; 3 M. Murphy/J. Cush, 82; 4 K. Owens/E. Owens, 79; 5 A. Kennedy/J. Clark, 75; 6 E. Blain/H. Condon, 68.

Reggie and Danny Blain en route *to the Irish Sidecar Championship.*
(John Savage, Newton Ardes Chronicle)

ULSTER SHORT CIRCUIT CHAMPIONSHIPS

Final Championship Positions

80cc
1 A. Patterson, 157 points; 2 B. Jamison, 140; 3 M. Clenaghan, 126; 4 R. Fleming, 103; 5 N. Jamison, 82; 6 R. Murdock, 75; 7 L. Gibson, 70; 8 R. Wright, 66; 9 P. Magee, 51; 10 T. Brown, 48.

125cc
1 A. Patterson, 161 points; 2 L. McMaster, 142; 3 A. Caughey, 106; 4 P. McCallen, 103; 5 K. Beckett, 81; 6 P. Lorimer, 76; 7 G. Stevenson, 71; 8 C. Turtle, 70; 9 R. White, 69; 10 D. Lemon, 68.

200cc
1 D. Jamison, 179 points; 2 T. Ritchie, 105; 3 K. Ferguson, 94; 4 R. Glasgow, 91; 5 C. Bell, 87; 6 N. Robinson, 85; 7 J. Clarke, 79; 8 N. Jamison, 55; 9 G. Stevenson, 48; 10 R. Smyth, 41.

250cc
1 P. McCallen, 123 points (2 wins); 2 J. Guy, 123; 3 R. McCombe, 118; 4 D. Young, 112; 5

G. Cowan, 107; 6 R. Beers, 93; 7 O. McArdle, 84; 8 E. McManus, 75; 9 G. Brennan, 71; 10 A. Patterson, 67.

350cc

1 J. Rea, 160 points; 2 J. Guy, 145; 3 A. Swann, 106; 4 L. McMaster, 102; 5 D. Young, 89; 6 P. Owens, 86; 7 M. Swann, 80; 8 C. Dowd, 66; 9 G. Swann, 64; 10 R. White, 47.

350–1000cc

1 A. Irwin, 171 points; 2 M. Swann, 135; 3 J. Rea, 124; 4 G. Farlow, 103; 5 J. Elliott, 99; 6 D. Dunlop, 94; 7 R. McCurdy, 94; 8 D. Young, 62; 9 S. Ferguson, 42; 10 P. Owens, 40.

Sidecars

1 J. Killough/P. O'Neill, 114 points; 2 R. Blain/D. Blain, 112; 3 K. Owens/E. Owens, 74; 4 A. Kennedy/J. Clark, 68; 5 E. Blain/H. Condon, 68; 6 M. Murphy/J. Cush, 67.

REGAL 125cc CHAMPIONSHIP

Eighteen-year-old Alan Patterson from Dundrod ended his Regal 125cc championship-winning year in style by taking a slender victory in the final race of the year at Kirkistown from his nearest rival Leslie McMaster. Riding Alec Waugh's Honda, Patterson won five of the nine races and finished runner-up in three others. His only non-finish was in the very first round at Aghadowey when he fell. Ricky White won the race.

Alan Caughey recorded his best ever championship finish by taking third overall on his Honda.

Final Championship Positions

1 A. Patterson *(Honda)*, 169.5 points; 2 L. McMaster *(Honda)*, 156; 3 A. Caughey *(Honda)*, 137; 4 G. Stevenson *(Honda)*, 109.5; 5. M. Topping *(Honda)*, 106; 6 S. Harrison *(Honda)*, 100; 7 R. Lorimer *(Honda)*, 92.5; 8 P. McCallen *(Honda)*, 91; 9 C. Turtle *(Honda)*, 80.5; 10 J. Clarke *(Honda)*, 75.

Embassy Championship

Larne's Johnny Rea is the new Embassy Champion. He won five races on the trot with the Leslie Anderton RG500 Suzuki to oust Alan Irwin from the top of Irish short circuit racing.

In fairness to McManus Honda rider Irwin, Champion for the past two seasons, he missed two races due to illness. He had won the opening round at Aghadowey but could not match Rea's speed as the season progressed. Rea had clinched the title at the penultimate round, Nutts Corner, which was just as well because his Suzuki failed at Kirkistown at the final meeting and he was forced to ride his 350 Yamaha.

George Farlow on Winton McAdoo's RC30 Honda was a shock winner of the last race, the first win for a four-stroke in the 1988 Embassy series. Irwin, hoping to oust 500 Suzuki rider Michael Swann from second in the points, led early on but his Honda lost power and he slipped downfield.

Final Championship Positions

1 J. Rea *(500 Suzuki)*, 247 points; 2 M. Swann *(500 Suzuki)*, 223; 3 A. Irwin *(500 Honda)*, 207; 4 D. Dunlop *(500 Suzuki)*, 189; 5 O. McArdle *(250 Honda)*, 166; 6 D. Young *(350 Yamaha)*, 164; 7 R. Beers *(250 Yamaha)*, 156; 8 J. Guy *(350 Yamaha)*, 152; 9 G. Farlow *(750 Honda)*, 150; 10 J. Elliott *(750 Suzuki)*, 139.

350cc Joe Lindsay Memorial Series

Wrapping up a great season, Johnny Rea maintained his grip on the 350 class, winning the Joe Lindsay Memorial series for a record fourth time. The 17-round series blends short circuit races and pure road course events.

Johnny Guy, Champion two seasons ago, lost all chance of the title in the penultimate round at Kirkistown when he retired and Rea took second to Leslie McMaster. Davy Woods' protegé McMaster scored three wins in the series and wound up third overall in the standings.

Final Championship Positions

1 J. Rea, 205 points; 2 J. Guy, 162; 3 L. McMaster, 139; 4 M. Swann, 126; 5 A. Swann, 117; 6 D. Young, 114; 7 P. Owens, 113; 8 J. Byrne, 69; 9 C. Dowd, 63; 10 P. McCallen, 61.

200cc Joe Dunlop Series

Final Championship Positions

1 D. Jamison, 137 points; 2 T. Ritchie, 92; 3 N. Robinson, 92; 4 C. Bell, 72; 5 R. Glasgow, 66; 6 J. Clarke, 63; 7 K. Ferguson, 57; 8 G. Stevenson, 48; 9 N. Jamison, 46; 10 R. Smyth, 41.

Southern Ireland Championships

Final Championship Positions

EBC Professional Short Circuit Championships
1 E. Galbraith, 77 points; 2 P. Lynch, 74; 3 F. Morrison, 70.

HL1 Oils Clubman Championships
1 B. Mullane, 59 points; 2 M. Nash, 52; 3 G. Cronin, 49.

Loughshinny MCC Pure Road Race Championship
1 M. Carter, 78 points; 2 S. Kavanagh, 61; =3 B. Boland and J. Byrne, 43.

125–200 Southern Centre Championship
1 H. Devlin, 67 points; 2 G. Hughes, 66; 3 M. Curtin, 58.

THE RIDERS

ABBOTT Steve

Born 16/2/55, Nottingham, Great Britain
Marital status Single
First race 1977
Titles 1984 British sidecar Champion *(Yamaha)*
First Grand Prix 1980 Great Britain, Silverstone, sidecar *(Yamaha)*
World Championship positions
1982 12th sidecar *(Yamaha)*
1983 25th sidecar *(Yamaha)*
1984 7th sidecar *(Yamaha)*
1985 7th equal sidecar *(Yamaha)*
1986 6th sidecar *(Yamaha)*
1987 6th sidecar *(Yamaha)*
1988 10th sidecar *(Yamaha)*
Other successes
1984 Winner sidecar TT *(Yamaha)*

AUINGER August

Born 3/5/55, Lambach, Austria
Marital status Married to Margaret
First race 1974
First Grand Prix 1979 Austria, Salzburgring, 125cc *(Morbidelli)*
First Grand Prix win 1985 West Germany, Hockenheim, 125cc *(MBA)*
Grand Prix victories 5 (125cc)
World Championship positions
1979 12th 125cc *(Morbidelli)*
1980 15th 125cc *(Morbidelli)*
1981 14th 125cc *(Morbidelli)*
1982 6th 125cc *(MBA)*
1983 10th 125cc *(MBA)*
1984 5th 125cc *(MBA)*
1985 3rd 125cc *(MBA)*
1986 4th 125cc *(MBA)*
1987 5th 125cc *(MBA)*
1988 16th 250cc *(Aprilia)*

BALDE Jean-Francois

Born 29/12/59, Hyeres, France
Marital status Single
First race 1968
First Grand Prix 1973 France, Paul Ricard, 500cc *(Kawasaki)*
First Grand Prix win 1981 Argentina, Buenos Aires, 250cc *(Kawasaki)*
Grand Prix victories 5 (2 250cc), (3 350cc)
World Championship positions
1974 41st 500cc *(Kawasaki)*
1975 38th 250cc *(Yamaha)*
1975 26th 350cc *(Yamaha)*
1975 46th 500cc *(Yamaha)*
1976 17th 250cc *(Yamaha)*
1976 18th 350cc *(Yamaha)*
1977 29th 250cc *(Kawasaki)*
1978 13th 250cc *(Kawasaki)*
1979 8th 250cc *(Kawasaki)*
1980 3rd 250cc *(Kawasaki)*
1981 2nd 250cc *(Kawasaki)*
1981 3rd 350cc *(Kawasaki)*
1982 12th 250cc *(Kawasaki)*
1982 3rd 350cc *(Kawasaki)*
1983 8th 250cc *(Yamaha)*
1984 9th 250cc *(Pernod)*
1985 18th 250cc *(Pernod and Yamaha)*
1986 5th 250cc *(Honda)*
1987 18th 250cc *(Rotax)*
1988 29th equal 250cc *(Rotax)*

BALDWIN Mike

Born 15/1/55, Pasadena, California, USA
Marital status Married to Lynsey
First race 1976
Titles 1978 AMA Formula One Champion *(Yamaha)* 1982, 1983, 1984 and 1985 AMA Formula One Champion *(Honda)*
First Grand Prix 1979 Austria, 500cc *(Suzuki)*
World Championship positions
1979 13th 500cc *(Suzuki)*
1985 11th 500cc *(Honda)*
1986 4th 500cc *(Yamaha)*
1987 18th 500cc *(Yamaha)*

Other successes
1978 **1st** Suzuka Eight-Hour Race, Japan *(Yamaha)*
1978 **1st** Canadian round Formula One 750cc *(Yamaha)*
1981 **1st** Suzuka Eight-Hour Race, Japan *(Honda)*
1984 **1st** Suzuka Eight-Hour Race, Japan *(Honda)*
1988 19th 500cc *(Honda)*

BIANCHI Pier Paolo

Born 11/3/52, Rimini, Italy
Marital status Married to Lucia. One son, Claudio
First race 1968
Titles 1972 Italian 50cc Champion *(Minarelli)*. 1973 Italian 50cc Champion *(Minarelli)*. 1974 Italian 50cc Champion *(Minarelli)*. 1975 Italian 125cc Champion *(Morbidelli)*. 1976 Italian 125cc Champion *(Morbidelli)*. 1980 Italian 125cc Champion *(MBA)*
First Grand Prix 1973 Italian, Monza 125cc *(Yamaha)*
First Grand Prix win 1976 Austria, Salzburgring, 125cc *(Morbidelli)*
World Titles 3 (125cc)
Grand Prix victories 27 (two 80cc) (25 125cc)
World Championship positions
1973 22nd 125cc *(Yamaha)*
1974 17th 125cc *(Minarelli)*
1975 2nd 125cc *(Morbidelli)*
1976 **1st** 125cc *(Morbidelli)*
1977 **1st** 125cc *(Morbidelli)*
1978 3rd 125cc *(Minarelli)*
1979 10th 125cc *(Minarelli)*
1980 **1st** 125cc *(MBA)*
1981 3rd 125cc *(MBA)*
1982 4th 125cc *(Sanvenero)*
1983 8th 125cc *(Sanvenero)*
1984 3rd 80cc *(Casal)*
1985 2nd 125cc *(MBA)*
1986 8th 125cc *(MBA)*
1986 8th 80cc *(Seel)*
1987 7th 125cc *(MBA)*
1988 18th equal 125cc *(Garelli)*

BILAND Rolf

Born 1/4/51, Baden, Switzerland
Marital status Single
First race 1970
First Grand Prix 1974 Austria, Salzburgring, sidecar *(Crescent)*
First Grand Prix win 1975 Germany, Hockenheim, sidecar *(Yamaha)*
World Titles 4 (sidecar)
Grand Prix victories 52 (sidecar)
World Championship positions
1974 9th sidecar *(Crescent)*
1975 3rd sidecar *(Yamaha)*
1976 4th sidecar *(Yamaha)*
1977 2nd sidecar *(Yamaha)*
1978 **1st** sidecar *(Yamaha)*
1979 **1st** B2A sidecar *(Yamaha)*
1979 2nd B2B sidecar *(Yamaha)*
1980 2nd sidecar *(Yamaha)*
1981 **1st** sidecar *(Yamaha)*
1982 2nd sidecar *(Yamaha)*

1983 **1st** sidecar *(Yamaha)*
1984 4th sidecar *(Yamaha)*
1985 3rd sidecar *(Yamaha)*
1986 8th sidecar *(Krauser)*
1987 3rd sidecar *(Krauser)*
1988 2nd sidecar *(Krauser)*

BODDICE Mick

Born 22/11/47, Birmingham, England
Marital status Married to Jan. One son, Michael. One daughter, Susan
First race 1964
Titles 1973 British sidecar champion *(Yamaha)*
First Grand Prix 1965 Holland, Assen, sidecar *(Yamaha)*
World Championship positions
1980 23rd sidecar *(Yamaha)*
1981 9th sidecar *(Yamaha)*
1982 15th sidecar *(Yamaha)*
1984 19th equal sidecar *(Yamaha)*
Other successes
1983 Winner Sidecar TT *(Yamaha)*
1984 Winner Sidecar TT *(Yamaha)*
1985 Winner Sidecar TT *(Yamaha)*
1987 Winner Sidecar TT *(Yamaha)*
1988 Winner both Sidecar TT *(Yamaha)*

BRIGAGLIA Domenico

Born 12/6/59, Sassari, Italy
Marital status Single
First race 1979
First Grand Prix 1982 Italian, Misano, 125cc *(MBA)*
First Grand Prix win 1986 Belgium, Spa Francorchamps, 125cc *(MBA)*
Grand Prix victories 1 (125cc)
World Championship positions
1982 16th 125cc *(MBA)*
1984 17th equal, 125cc *(MBA)*
1985 6th 125cc *(MBA)*
1986 3rd 125cc *(MBA)*
1987 4th 125cc *(MBA)*
1988 5th 125cc *(Rotax)*

BURNETT Roger Peter

Born 2/3/60, Brigg, England
Marital status Married to Belinda
First race 1981
Titles 1986 British Champion *(Honda)*
First Grand Prix 1984 Great Britain, Silverstone 500cc *(Suzuki)*
World Championship positions
1985 17th 500cc *(Honda)*
1986 20th 500cc *(Honda)*
1987 11th 500cc *(Honda)*
1988 18th 500cc *(Honda)*
Other successes
1984 3rd European 500cc Championship *(Suzuki)*
1986 **1st** British Motoprix Championship *(Honda)*
1986 **1st** Senior Isle of Man TT *(Honda)*

CADALORA Luca

Born 17/5/63, Modena, Italy
Marital status Single
First race 1981
Titles 1982 Italian Junior Champion 125cc *(Villa)*
First Grand Prix 1984 Italian, Misano
First Grand Prix win 1986 West Germany, Nurburgring, 125cc *(Garelli)*
Grand Prix victories 6 (4 125cc) (2 250cc)
World Titles 1 (125cc)
World Championship positions
1984 8th equal 125cc *(MBA)*
1985 17th equal 125cc *(MBA)*
1986 **1st** 125cc *(Garelli)*
1987 7th 250cc *(Yamaha)*
1988 6th 250cc *(Yamaha)*

CARDUS Carlos

Born 29/9/59, Barcelona, Spain
Marital status Single
First race 1979
Titles 1982 Spanish 250cc Champion *(JJ*

Cobas), 1983 Spanish 250cc Champion *(JJ Cobas)*
First Grand Prix 1983 South Africa, Kyalami, 250cc *(JJ Cobas)*
World Championship positions
1983 28th 250cc *(JJ Cobas)*
1984 25th 250cc *(JJ Cobas)*
1985 12th 250cc *(JJ Cobas)*
1986 12th 250cc *(Honda)*
1987 5th 250cc *(Honda)*
1988 9th 250cc *(Honda)*
Other successes
1983 European 250cc Champion *(JJ Cobas)*
1986 Winner Barcelona 24-Hour Race *(Ducati)*

CARTER Alan

Born 19/8/64, Halifax, England
Marital status Single
First race 1981
First Grand Prix 1983 South Africa, Kyalami, 250cc *(Yamaha)*
First Grand Prix win 1983 France, Le Mans, 250cc *(Yamaha)*
Grand Prix victories 1 (250cc)
World Championship positions
1983 12th 250cc *(Yamaha)*
1984 9th 250cc *(Yamaha)*
1985 7th 250cc *(Honda)*
1986 17th equal 250cc *(Cobas)*

CHILI Pier Francesco

Born 20/6/64, Bologna, Italy
Marital status Single
First race 1982
First Grand Prix 1985 San Marino, Misano, 125cc *(AEB)*
World Championship positions
1986 10th equal 500cc *(Suzuki)*
1987 8th 500cc *(Honda)*
1988 9th 500cc *(Honda)*
Other successes
1985 European 125cc Champion *(AEB)*

CORNU Jacques

Born 15/5/53, Aigle, Switzerland
Marital status Married to Chantal. Two daughters, Eloolie and Justine Maud
First race 1974
Titles 1977 Swiss 500cc Champion *(Yamaha)*. 1978 Swiss 250cc, 350cc and 500cc champion *(Yamaha)*
First Grand Prix 1979 Czechoslovakia, Brno, 250cc *(Yamaha)*
First Grand Prix win
Grand Prix victories 2 (250cc)
World Championship positions
1980 8th 250cc *(Rotax)*
1980 7th 350cc *(Yamaha)*
1981 8th 350cc *(Yamaha)*
1982 17th 250cc *(Yamaha)*
1982 7th 350cc *(Yamaha)*
1983 9th 250cc *(Yamaha)*
1984 6th 250cc *(Yamaha)*
1985 10th 250cc *(Honda* and *Parisienne)*
1986 7th 250cc *(Honda)*
1987 9th 250cc *(Honda)*
1988 3rd 250cc *(Honda)*
Other successes
1982 World Endurance Champion *(Kawasaki)*

CRIVILLE Alex

Born 4/3/70, Barcelona, Spain
Marital status Single
First race 1985
First Grand Prix 1987 Spain, Jerez, 80cc *(Derbi)*
World Championship positions
1987 11th 80cc *(Derbi)*
1988 31st equal 125cc *(Derbi)*
2nd 80cc *(Derbi)*
Other successes
1987 3rd European Championship 80cc *(Derbi)*

DE RADIGUES Didier

Born 27/3/58, Louvain, Belgium
Marital status Single
First race 1977
Titles 1978 Belgian 750cc Champion *(Yamaha)*. 1979 Belgian 750cc Champion *(Yamaha)*. 1980 Belgian 250cc Champion *(Yamaha)*
First Grand Prix 1979 Spain, Jarama, 350cc *(Yamaha)*
First Grand Prix win 1982 Italy, Misano, 350cc *(Chevallier-Yamaha)*
Grand Prix victories 4 (2 250cc), (2 350cc)
World Championship positions
1980 18th 250cc *(Yamaha)*
1981 9th 250cc *(Yamaha)*
1981 17th 350cc *(Yamaha)*
1982 6th 250cc *(Chevallier-Yamaha)*
1982 2nd 350cc *(Chevallier-Yamaha)*
1983 3rd 250cc *(Chevallier-Yamaha)*
1984 9th 500cc *(Chevallier-Honda)*
1985 8th 500cc *(Honda)*
1986 7th 500cc *(Honda)*
1987 12th 500cc *(Cagiva)*
1988 7th 500cc *(Yamaha)*

DORFLINGER Stefan

Born 23/12/48, Nagold, Germany (Swiss citizen)
Marital status Single
First race 1974
First Grand Prix 1973 German, Hockenheim, 50cc *(Kreidler)*
First Grand Prix win 1980 Belgian, Zolder, 50cc *(Kreidler)*
World Titles 4 (2 50cc), (2 80cc)
Grand Prix victories 18 (9 50cc), (9 80cc)
World Championship positions
1973 11th 50cc *(Kreidler)*
1974 9th 50cc *(Kreidler)*
1975 6th 50cc *(Kreidler)*
1976 8th 50cc *(Kreidler)*
1976 9th 125cc *(Morbidelli)*
1977 6th 50cc *(Kreidler)*
1977 9th 125cc *(Morbidelli)*
1978 6th 50cc *(Kreidler)*
1978 13th 125cc *(Morbidelli)*
1979 10th 50cc *(Kreidler)*
1979 10th 125cc *(Morbidelli)*
1980 2nd 50cc *(Kreidler)*
1980 12th 125cc *(Morbidelli)*
1981 3rd 50cc *(Kreidler)*
1981 11th 125cc *(MBA)*
1982 **1st** 50cc *(Kreidler)*
1982 24th 125cc *(MBA)*
1983 **1st** 50cc *(Kreidler)*
1983 23rd 125cc *(MBA)*
1984 **1st** 80cc *(Zundapp)*
1985 **1st** 80cc *(Krauser)*
1986 3rd 80cc *(Krauser)*
1987 4th 80cc *(Krauser)*
1988 3rd 80cc *(Krauser)*
37th equal 125cc *(Honda)*

DUNLOP William Joseph

Born 25/2/52, Ballymoney, Northern Ireland
Marital status Married to Linda. Four children, Julie, Donna, Gary and Robert
First race 1970
First Grand Prix 1985 Great Britain, Silverstone, 250cc *(Honda)*
World Championship positions
1985 28th 250cc *(Honda)*
Other successes
1977 **1st** Jubilee Isle of Man TT *(Yamaha)*
1979 **1st** Ulster Grand Prix 500cc and 1000cc *(Yamaha)*
1980 **1st** Classic Isle of Man TT *(Yamaha)*. Ulster Grand Prix 250cc and Classic *(Yamaha* and *Suzuki)*
1982 TT Formula One World Champion *(Honda)*
1983 TT Formula One World Champion *(Honda)*. **1st** Formula One Isle of Man TT *(Honda)*

1984 TT Formula One World Champion *(Honda)*. **1st** Formula One Isle of Man TT *(Honda)*. Isle of Man TT lap record 118.48mph *(Honda)*
1985 TT Formula One World Champion. **1st** Formula One, Senior and Junior Isle of Man TT *(Honda)*
1986 TT Formula One World Champion *(Honda)*. **1st** Formula One Isle of Man TT *(Honda)*. MBE in New Year's Honours list
1987 2nd TT Formula One World Championship *(Honda)*. **1st** Formula One and Classic Isle of Man TT *(Honda)*
1988 2nd TT Formula One World Championship *(Honda)*. **1st** TT Formula One Classic and Junior races Isle of Man TT *(Honda)*

FERRARI Virginio

Born 19/10/52 Pellegrino Parmense, Italy
Marital status Single
First race 1972
Titles 1978 Italian Senior 500cc Champion *(Suzuki)*. 1978 Italian Senior 750cc Champion *(Yamaha)*
First Grand Prix 1975 Italian, Imola 500cc *(Paton)*
First Grand Prix win 1978 Germany, Nurburgring, 500cc *(Suzuki)*
Grand Prix victories 2 (500cc)
World Championship positions
1976 21st 500cc *(Suzuki)*
1977 12th 500cc *(Suzuki)*
1978 11th 500cc *(Suzuki)*
1979 2nd 500cc *(Suzuki)*
1982 11th 500cc *(Suzuki)*
1984 10th 500cc *(Yamaha)*
Other successes
1987 TT Formula One World Championship *(Yamaha)*

FOGARTY Carl George

Born 1/7/65 Blackburn, England
Marital status Single
First race 1983
Other successes
1985 **1st** 250cc Newcomer Manx Grand Prix, Isle of Man *(Yamaha)*
1988 TT Formula One World Champion

GARDNER Wayne Michael

Born 11/10/59, Wollongong, New South Wales, Australia
Marital status Single
First race 1977
Titles 3rd 1979 Australian 350cc Championship *(Yamaha)*. 1981 Winner Swann Championship *(Yamaha)*. 1984 Winner Swann Championship *(Honda)*. 1985 Winner Swann Championship *(Honda)*
First Grand Prix 1983 Dutch, Assen, 500cc *(Honda)*
First Grand Prix win 1986 Spain, Jarama, 500cc *(Honda)*
World Titles One 1987 500cc *(Honda)*
Grand Prix victories 14 (500cc)
World Championship positions
1984 7th 500cc *(Honda)*
1985 Joint 4th 500cc *(Honda)*
1986 2nd 500cc *(Honda)*
1987 **1st** 500cc *(Honda)*
1988 2nd 500cc *(Honda)*
Other successes
1979 **1st** 750cc Class Castrol Six-Hour Race Australia *(Yamaha)*
1980 **1st** unlimited class Castrol Six-Hour Race Australia *(Yamaha)*
1982 British Streetbike Champion *(Honda)*
1982 **1st** unlimited class Castrol Six-Hour race Australia *(Honda)*
1982 **1st** Suzuka Eight-Hour Race, Japan *(Honda)*

1983 British TT Formula One Champion *(Honda)*
1983 ITV World of Sport Champion *(Honda)*
1984 British TT Formula One Champion *(Honda)*
1984 British 500cc Champion *(Honda)*
1984 MCN Masters Champion *(Honda)*
1984 Australian Swann Series Champion *(Honda)*
1985 ITV World of Sport Champion *(Honda)*
1985 **1st** Suzuka Eight-Hour Race, Japan *(Honda)*
1985 **1st** Selangor Grand Prix *(Honda)*
1986 **1st** Suzuka Eight-Hour Race, Japan *(Honda)*

GARRIGA Juan

Born 29/3/63, Barcelona, Spain
Marital status Single
First race 1980

Titles 1984 Spanish 250cc Champion *(Yamaha)*. 1984 Spanish Endurance Champion *(Ducati)*
First Grand Prix 1984 Spanish, Jarama, 250cc *(Yamaha)*
Grand Prix victories 3 (250cc)
World Championship positions
1985 18th 250cc *(Cobas)*
1986 16th 500cc *(Cagiva)*
1987 11th 250cc *(Yamaha)*
1988 2nd 250cc *(Yamaha)*
Other successes
1984 Winner Barcelona 24-Hour Race *(Ducati)*
1985 Winner Barcelona 24-Hour Race *(Ducati)*

GIANOLA Ezio

Born 13/6/60, Lecco, Italy
Marital status Single
First race 1980
Titles 1981 Italian Junior TT4 Champion, 125cc *(Malanca)*
First Grand Prix 1983 Italian, Monza, 125cc *(MBA)*
First Grand Prix win 1985 France, Le Mans, 125cc *(Garelli)*
Grand Prix victories 4 (125cc)
World Championship positions
1983 18th 125cc *(MBA)*
1984 14th 125cc *(MBA)*
1985 4th 125cc *(Garelli)*
1986 6th 125cc *(MBA)*
1987 6th 125cc *(Honda)*
1988 2nd 125cc *(Honda)*

GRESINI Fausto

Born 23/1/61, Imola, Italy
Marital status Single
First race 1979
Titles 1982 Italian 125cc Champion *(MBA/Garelli)*
First Grand Prix 1982 Italian, Misano 125cc *(MBA)*

First Grand Prix win 1984 Sweden, Anderstorp, 125cc *(Garelli)*
World Titles 2 1985 125cc *(Garelli)*
Grand Prix victories 18 (125cc)
World Championship positions
1985 9th 125cc *(MBA/Garelli)*
1984 3rd 125cc *(MBA/Garelli)*
1985 **1st** 125cc *(Garelli)*
1986 2nd 125cc *(Garelli)*
1987 **1st** 125cc *(Garelli)*
1988 21st 125cc *(Garelli)*

HASLAM Ron

Born 22/6/56, Langley Mill, Notts, England
Marital status Married to Anne. One son, Leon and one daughter, Emma
First race 1971
Titles 1979 TT Formula One British Champion *(Honda)*. 1981 British Streetbike Champion *(Honda)*. 1981 MCN British Superbike Champion *(Honda)*. 1982 TT Formula One British Champion *(Honda)*. 1984 ITV World of Sport Champion *(Honda)*.
First Grand Prix 1977 Great Britain, Silverstone, 500cc *(Honda)*
World Championship positions
1983 8th 500cc *(Honda)*
1984 5th 500cc *(Honda)*
1985 Joint 4th 500cc *(Honda)*
1986 9th 500cc *(Honda)*
1987 4th 500cc *(Honda)*
1988 11th 500cc *(Honda)*
Other successes
1979 TT Formula One World Champion *(Honda)*
1980 TT Formula Three World Champion *(Honda)*
1982 **1st** Isle of Man TT Formula One race *(Honda)*

HERREROS Manuel

Born 20/4/63, Villarrobledo, Spain
Marital status Single
First race 1981
Titles 1982 Spanish Junior 80cc Champion *(Derbi)*
First Grand Prix 1985 Spain, Jarama, 80cc *(Derbi)*
First Grand Prix win 1986 Germany, Nurburgring, 80cc *(Derbi)*
Grand Prix wins 2 (80cc)
World Championship positions
1985 4th 80cc *(Derbi)*
1986 2nd 80cc *(Derbi)*
1987 2nd 80cc *(Derbi)*
1988 4th 80cc *(Derbi)*
15th equal 125cc *(Derbi)*

HERWEH Manfred

Born 14/6/54, Lampertheim, Hessen, West Germany
Marital status Married to Edelgard. One son, Joachim
First race 1976
Titles 1982 German 250cc and 350cc Champion *(Yamaha)*
First Grand Prix 1980 Germany, Nurburgring, 250cc *(Yamaha)*
First Grand Prix win 1982 Germany, Hockenheim, 350cc *(Yamaha)*
Grand Prix victories 6 (5 250cc), (1 350cc)
World Championship positions
1982 26th 250cc *(Yamaha)*
1982 13th 350cc *(Yamaha)*
1983 7th 250cc *(Real Rotax)*
1984 2nd 250cc *(Real Rotax)*
1985 8th 250cc *(Real Rotax)*
1986 19th equal 250cc *(Aprilia)*
1987 15th 250cc *(Honda)*
1988 15th 250cc *(Honda)*

HISLOP Steven

Born 11/1/62, Hawick, Scotland
Marital status single
First race 1983
Other successes
1983 2nd Newcomers Manx Grand Prix 350cc
1987 **1st** Isle of Man TT Formula Two 350cc *(Yamaha)*
1988 **1st** Isle of Man TT Production B race

HUEWEN Keith

Born 23/8/57, Southend, England
Marital status Single
First race 1975
Titles 1979 British Champion *(Yamaha)*
First Grand Prix 1980 Great Britain, Silverstone, 350cc *(Yamaha)*
World Championship positions
1980 18th 350cc *(Yamaha)*
1981 6th 350cc *(Yamaha)*
1981 26th 500cc *(Suzuki)*
1983 15th 500cc *(Suzuki)*
1984 19th 500cc *(Honda)*
Other successes
1983 MCN Champion *(Suzuki)*
1987 British Superstock Champion *(Yamaha)*

IDDON Paul

Born 27/9/57
Marital status Single
First race 1977
First Grand Prix 1985 Great Britain, Silverstone 500cc *(Suzuki)*
Other successes
1986 2nd TT Formula One World Championship *(Suzuki)*
1987 3rd TT Formula One World Championship *(Suzuki)*

IGOA Patrick

Born 8/3/59, Anglet, France
Marital status Single
First race 1979
First Grand Prix 1981 France, Paul Ricard, 250cc *(Yamaha)*
World Championship positions
1987 12th 250cc *(Yamaha)*
1988 14th 500cc *(Yamaha)*
Other successes
1982 Winner Bol d'Or *(Honda)*
1984 Winner World Endurance Championship *(Honda)*
1985 Winner World Endurance Championship *(Honda)*
1986 Winner World Endurance Championship *(Honda)*

JOHNSON Geoffrey

Born 1/9/52, Darlington, Britain
Marital status Married to Christine. Two children, Zoe and Emma
First race 1974
Other successes
1980 Winner Senior Manx Grand Prix *(Yamaha)*
1984 Winner of 1000cc Production TT *(Kawasaki)*
1985 Winner of 1000cc Production TT *(Honda)*
1987 Winner of 750cc Production TT *(Yamaha)*

JONES Derek Martin

Born 28/2/42, London, England
Marital status Married to Carol. One son, Darren
First race 1970
Titles 1978 British Sidecar Champion *(Yamaha)*
First Grand Prix 1977 France, Paul Ricard, sidecar
First Grand Prix win 1980 Great Britain, Silverstone, sidecar

Grand Prix victories 1 (sidecar)
World Championship positions
1980 7th sidecar *(Yamaha)*
1981 4th sidecar *(Yamaha)*
1982 6th sidecar *(Yamaha)*
1983 6th sidecar *(Yamaha)*
1984 5th sidecar *(Yamaha)*
1985 18th sidecar *(Yamaha)*
1986 9th sidecar *(Yamaha)*
1987 8th sidecar *(Yamaha)*
1988 6th sidecar *(Yamaha)*

KNEUBUHLER Bruno

Born 3/12/46, Zurigo, Switzerland
Marital status Married to Romy
First race 1969
First Grand Prix 1972 Germany, Nurburgring, 350cc and 500cc *(Yamaha)*
First Grand Prix win 1972 Spanish, Barcelona, 350cc *(Yamaha)*
Grand Prix victories 5 (1 50cc), (3 125cc), (1 350cc)
World Championship positions
1972 6th 350cc *(Yamaha)*
1972 3rd 500cc *(Yamaha)*
1973 2nd 50cc *(Kreidler)*
1973 9th 250cc *(Yamaha)*
1973 33rd 350cc *(Yamaha/Harley Davidson)*
1973 6th 500cc *(Yamaha)*
1974 2nd 125cc *(Yamaha)*
1974 5th 250cc *(Yamaha)*
1974 12th 350cc *(Yamaha)*
1975 6th 125cc *(Yamaha)*
1975 9th 250cc *(Yamaha)*
1975 20th 350cc *(Yamaha)*
1976 8th 125cc *(Yamaha/MZ)*
1976 7th 350cc *(Yamaha)*
1977 26th 250cc *(Yamaha)*
1978 29th 500cc *(Suzuki)*
1980 4th 125cc *(MBA)*
1981 27th 250cc *(Rotax)*
1982 15th 125cc *(MBA)*
1983 2nd 125cc *(MBA)*
1984 8th equal *(MBA)*
1985 5th 125cc *(MBA)*
1986 6th 125cc *(MBA)*
1988 23rd 500cc *(Honda)*

KOBAYASHI Masaru

Born 26/12/59, Ibaraki, Japan
Marital status Single
First race 1981
Titles 1982 Japanese 250cc Champion *(Yamaha)*. 1984–85 Japanese 250cc Champion *(Honda)*
First Grand Prix 1987 Japan, Suzuka, 250cc *(Honda)*
First Grand Prix win 1987 Japan, Suzuka, 250cc *(Honda)*
Grand Prix victories 1 (250cc)
World Championship positions
1987 14th 250cc *(Honda)*
1988 24th 250cc *(Honda)*

KOCINSKI John

Born 20/3/68, Little Rock, Arkansas, USA
Marital status Single
First race 1981
First Grand Prix 1988 Japan, Suzuka, 250cc *(Yamaha)*
World Championship positions
1988 19th 250cc *(Yamaha)*
Other successes
1985 WERA National Endurance Champion
1987 AMA National 250cc Champion
1988 AMA National 250cc Champion *(Yamaha)*

LAVADO Carlos Alberto Jones

Born 25/5/56, Caracas, Venezuela
Marital status Married to Alicia
First race 1976

First Grand Prix 1978 Venezuela, San Carlos, 250cc *(Yamaha)*
First Grand Prix win 1979 Venezuela, 350cc *(Yamaha)*
World Titles 2 1983 250cc *(Yamaha)*, 1986 250cc *(Yamaha)*
Grand Prix victories 19 (17 250cc and 2 350cc)
World Champion positions
1978 17th 250cc *(Yamaha)*
1979 14th 350cc *(Yamaha)*
1980 6th 250cc *(Yamaha)*
1980 13th 350cc *(Yamaha)*
1981 4th 250cc *(Yamaha)*
1981 5th 350cc *(Yamaha)*
1982 5th 250cc *(Yamaha)*
1982 5th 350cc *(Yamaha)*
1983 **1st** 250cc *(Yamaha)*
1984 3rd 250cc *(Yamaha)*
1985 3rd 250cc *(Yamaha)*
1986 **1st** 250cc *(Yamaha)*
1987 10th 250cc *(Yamaha)*
1988 11th 250cc *(Yamaha)*

LAWSON Eddie

Born 11/3/58, Upland, California, USA
Marital status Single
First race 1965
Titles 1978 USA Western Region 750cc Champion *(Yamaha)*. 1981 and 1982 USA Superbike Champion *(Kawasaki)*
First Grand Prix 1981 Germany, Hockenheim, 250cc *(Kawasaki)*
First Grand Prix win 1984 South Africa, Kyalami, 500cc *(Yamaha)*
World Titles 3, 1984 500cc *(Yamaha)*, 1986 500cc *(Yamaha)*, 1988 500cc *(Yamaha)*
Grand Prix victories 26 (500cc)
World Championship positions
1983 4th 500cc *(Yamaha)*
1984 **1st** 500cc *(Yamaha)*
1985 2nd 500cc *(Yamaha)*
1986 **1st** 500cc *(Yamaha)*
1987 3rd 500cc *(Yamaha)*
1988 **1st** 500cc *(Yamaha)*
Other successes
1980 **1st** Daytona 100 Lightweight *(Kawasaki)*
1981 **1st** Daytona 100 Lightweight *(Kawasaki)*
1986 **1st** Daytona 200 Superbike *(Yamaha)*

LEWIS Paul

Born 3/7/60, Melbourne, Australia
Marital status Married to Lynn
First race 1974
Titles 1979 Australian 125cc Champion *(Morbidelli)*. 1980 Australian 125cc Champion *(Morbidelli)*. 1981 250cc Australian Champion *(Yamaha)*
First Grand Prix 1983 Great Britain, Silverstone, 500cc *(Suzuki)*
World Championship positions
1983 19th equal 500cc *(Suzuki)*
1985 24th equal 500cc *(Suzuki)*
1986 17th equal 500cc *(Suzuki)*
Other successes
1979 250cc Australian Grand Prix winner *(Yamaha)*
1980 125cc Australian Grand Prix winner *(Morbidelli)*
1981 250cc Australian Grand Prix winner *(Yamaha)*
1982 125cc Australian Grand Prix winner *(Morbidelli)*

McCONNACHIE Ian

Born 10/1/65, Blackburn, England
Marital status Single
First race 1981
Titles 1982 British 50cc Production Champion *(Aspes)*. 1984 80cc Champion *(Kreidler)*
First Grand Prix 1983 France, Le Mans, 50cc *(Rudge/Kreidler)*

First Grand Prix win 1986 Great Britain, Silverstone, 80cc *(Krauser)*
Grand Prix victories 1 (80cc)
World Championship positions
1985 6th 80cc *(Krauser)*
1986 6th 80cc *(Krauser)*
1987 5th 80cc *(Krauser)*
1988 28th 125cc *(Cagiva)*
22nd 80cc *(Autisa)*

McELNEA Rob

Born 12/12/59, Scunthorpe, England
Marital status Married to Sharon. One daughter, Janice
First race 1977
First Grand Prix 1983 Great Britain, Silverstone 500cc *(Suzuki)*
World Championship positions
1984 11th 500cc *(Suzuki)*
1985 9th 500cc *(Suzuki)*
1986 5th 500cc *(Yamaha)*
1987 10th 500cc *(Yamaha)*
1988 10th 500cc *(Suzuki)*
Other successes
1980 **1st** Senior Manx Grand Prix, Isle of Man *(Yamaha)*
1983 **1st** Classic TT Isle of Man *(Suzuki)*
1983 **1st** Dutch round Formula One World Championship *(Suzuki)*
1984 **1st** Classic TT Isle of Man *(Suzuki)*
1984 **1st** Senior TT Isle of Man *(Suzuki)*

McGLADDERY David Andrew

Born 16/8/54, Co. Durham, England
Marital status Married to Margaret. Two sons, Danny and Nick
First race 1976
First Grand Prix 1986 Great Britain, 500cc *(Honda)*
Other successes
1979 Winner 250cc Newcomers Manx Grand Prix *(Yamaha)*
1984 5th TT Formula One World Championship *(Suzuki)*
1986 5th TT Formula One World Championship *(Suzuki)*

McLEOD Donnie

Born 16/6/55, Glasgow, Scotland
Marital status Single
First race 1977
Titles 1978 Scottish 250cc Champion *(Yamaha)*, 1983 British Startrack Champion *(Yamaha)*, 1984 British 250cc Champion *(Yamaha)*
First Grand Prix 1982 Great Britain, Silverstone, 250cc and 350cc *(Yamaha)*
World Championship positions
1983 30th 250cc *(Yamaha)*
1984 18th 250cc *(Yamaha)*
1985 14th 250cc *(Armstrong)*
1986 10th 250cc *(Armstrong)*
1987 21st 250cc *(EMC)*
1988 12th 250cc *(EMC)*
23rd equal 500cc *(Honda)*

MACKENZIE Niall Macfarlane

Born 19/7/61, Stirling, Scotland
Marital status Single
First race 1981

Titles 1984 British Circuit Promoters 350cc Champion *(Armstrong)*
1985 British 250cc and Circuit Promoters 350cc Champion *(Armstrong)*
1986 British 250cc Champion *(Armstrong)*
First Grand Prix 1984 British, Silverstone 250cc *(Armstrong)*
World Championship positions
1985 28th 250cc *(Armstrong)*
1986 21st equal 250cc *(Armstrong)*
1986 10th equal 500cc *(Suzuki)*
1987 5th 500cc
1988 6th 500cc *(Honda)*

MAGEE Kevin

Born 16/7/62, Horsham, Victoria, Australia
Marital status Married to Julie. One son, Jake
First race 1981
Titles 1985 Australian TZ 350cc Yamaha Champion
First Grand Prix 1987 Japan, Suzuka 500cc *(Yamaha)*
First Grand Prix win 1988 Spain, Jarama, 500cc *(Yamaha)*
Grand Prix victories 1 (500cc)

World Championship positions
1987 16th equal 500cc *(Yamaha)*
1988 5th 500cc *(Yamaha)*
Other successes
1986 **1st** Australian Castrol Six-Hour race *(Yamaha)*
1987 **1st** Suzuka Two/Four race *(Yamaha)*
1987 **1st** Suzuka Eight-Hour race *(Yamaha)*
1987 **1st** Japanese round TT F1 Championship, Sugo *(Yamaha)*
1988 **1st** Suzuka Eight-hour race *(Yamaha)*

MAMOLA Randy

Born 10/11/59, Santa Clara, California, USA
Marital status Single
First race 1972
Titles 1972 AMA National Mini-Bike Champion *(Yamaha)*
First Grand Prix 1979 Venezuela, San Carlos, 250cc and 350cc *(Yamaha)*
First Grand Prix win 1980 Belgium, Zolder, 500cc *(Suzuki)*
Grand Prix victories 13 500cc
World Championship positions
1979 4th 250cc *(Yamaha)*
1979 8th 500cc *(Suzuki)*
1980 2nd 500cc *(Suzuki)*
1981 2nd 500cc *(Suzuki)*
1982 6th 500cc *(Suzuki)*
1983 3rd 500cc *(Suzuki)*
1984 2nd 500cc *(Honda)*
1985 6th 500cc *(Honda)*
1986 3rd 500cc *(Yamaha)*
1987 2nd 500cc *(Yamaha)*
1988 12th 500cc *(Cagiva)*
Other successes
1986 **1st** Kuala Lumpur Grand Prix *(Yamaha)*
1986 **1st** Malaysian Grand Prix *(Yamaha)*

MANG Anton (Toni)

Born 29/9/49, Inning, West Germany
Marital status Married to Colette
First race 1971
Titles 1978 German 350cc Champion *(Kawasaki)*. 1979 German 250cc and 350cc Champion
First Grand Prix 1974 Austria, Salzburgring, 350cc *(Yamaha)*
First Grand Prix win 1976 Germany, Nurburgring, 350cc *(Yamaha)*
World Titles 5, 1980 250cc, 1981 250cc and 350cc, 1982 350cc, 1987 250cc
Grand Prix victories 42 (1 125cc), (33 250cc), (8 350cc)
World Championship positions
1975 26th 350cc *(Yamaha)*
1976 5th 125cc *(Morbidelli)*
1977 5th 125cc *(Morbidelli)*
1977 25th 500cc *(Suzuki)*
1978 5th 250cc *(Kawasaki)*
1978 16th 350cc *(Kawasaki)*
1979 6th 250cc *(Kawasaki)*
1979 4th 350cc *(Kawasaki)*
1980 **1st** 250cc *(Kawasaki)*
1980 2nd 350cc *(Kawasaki)*
1981 **1st** 250cc *(Kawasaki)*
1981 **1st** 350cc *(Kawasaki)*
1982 2nd 250cc *(Kawasaki)*
1982 **1st** 350cc *(Kawasaki)*
1983 18th 500cc *(Suzuki)*
1984 5th 250cc *(Yamaha)*
1985 2nd 250cc *(Honda)*
1986 4th 250cc *(Honda)*
1987 **1st** 250cc *(Honda)*
1988 8th 250cc *(Honda)*

MARSHALL Roger Alan

Born 5/4/51, Cleethorpes, England
Marital status Married to Jane. Three children, Adam, Nina and Drew
First race 1970
Titles 1975 British Champion *(Yamaha)*. 1977 British Champion *(Yamaha)*. 1982 British Champion, TT Formula One British Champion *(Suzuki)*. 1983 British Champion *(Honda)*. 1985 British Champion, TT Formula One British Champion *(Honda)*. 1987 British 1300cc Champion *(Suzuki)*
First Grand Prix 1979 Great Britain, Silverstone, 500cc *(Yamaha)*
World Championship positions
1984 23rd 500cc *(Honda)*
Other successes
1982 MCN Superbike Champion *(Suzuki)*
1983 3rd TT Formula One World Championship *(Honda)*
1984 2nd TT Formula One World Championship *(Honda)*
1987 5th TT Formula One World Championship *(Suzuki)*

MARTINEZ Jorge

Born 29/8/62, Alcira, Spain
Marital status Single
First race 1978
Titles 1981 Spanish 50cc Champion *(Bultaco)*. 1982 Spanish 50cc Champion *(Bultaco)*. 1983 Spanish 80cc Champion *(Derbi)*. 1984 Spanish 80cc Champion *(Derbi)*. 1985 Spanish 80cc Champion *(Derbi)*
First Grand Prix 1982 Spain, Jarama, 50cc *(Bultaco)*
First Grand Prix win 1984 Holland, Assen, 80cc *(Derbi)*
World Championships 4 (3 80cc) (1 125cc)
Grand Prix victories 30 (21 80cc) (9 125cc)
World Championship positions
1984 4th 80cc *(Derbi)*
1985 2nd 80cc *(Derbi)*
1986 **1st** 80cc *(Derbi)*
1987 **1st** 80cc *(Derbi)*
1988 **1st** 80cc *(Derbi)*
1st 125cc *(Derbi)*

MELLOR Philip

Born 10/11/55, Huddersfield, England
Marital status Married to Christine
First race 1976
Titles 1980–81 British Honda 125cc Champion. 1986 ACU Metzeler Production Machine Champion 1300cc and 750cc *(Suzuki)*. 1987 ACU Metzeler Production Machine Champion 1300cc *(Suzuki)*
First Grand Prix
Other successes
1983 Winner Junior TT *(Yamaha)*
1984 Winner 250cc Production TT *(Yamaha)*
1986 Winner 750cc Production TT *(Suzuki)*

MICHEL Alain

Born 23/2/53, Montelimar, France
Marital status Married to Dominique
First race 1975
Titles 1983 French sidecar champion *(Yamaha)*
First Grand Prix 1976 France, Le Mans, sidecar *(Yamaha)*
First Grand Prix win 1977 France, Paul Ricard, sidecar *(Yamaha)*
Grand Prix victories 12 (sidecar)
World Championship positions
1976 9th sidecar *(Yamaha)*
1977 5th sidecar *(Yamaha)*
1978 2nd sidecar *(Yamaha)*
1979 12th sidecar *(Yamaha)*
1979 4th B2B sidecar *(Yamaha)*
1980 3rd sidecar *(Yamaha)*
1981 2nd sidecar *(Yamaha)*
1982 3rd sidecar *(Yamaha)*
1983 4th sidecar *(Yamaha)*
1984 3rd sidecar *(Yamaha)*
1985 7th equal sidecar *(Yamaha)*
1986 2nd sidecar *(Yamaha)*
1987 4th sidecar *(Yamaha)*
1988 4th sidecar *(Krauser)*

MORRISON Brian William

Born 25/11/60, Kirkcaldy, Scotland
Marital status Married to Jill
First race 1983
Other successes
1984 **1st** Scottish Production Champion
1986 **1st** Junior, Senior & Premier Scottish Champion
1987 **1st** Metzeler Production Champion 1300cc
1988 **1st** TT Production C race
1st British Superbike and Seniorstock championships *(Honda)*

NATION Trevor

Born 10/3/59, West Newton, England
Marital status Married to Mandy
First race 1977
First Grand Prix 1984 Great Britain, Silverstone, 500cc *(Suzuki)*
Other successes
1984 Winner 750cc Production TT *(Honda)*
1986 Winner 1300cc Production TT *(Suzuki)*

PETERSEN Dave

Born 20/3/56, Sinoia, Zimbabwe
Marital status Married to Deirdre
First race 1970
Titles 1971–72 Zimbabwe Champion *(Yamaha)*. 1976–77 Zimbabwe Champion *(Suzuki)*. 1982 South African Open Superbike Champion *(Honda)*. 1982 South African 750cc Superbike Champion *(Ducati)*
First Grand Prix 1984 French, Le Mans, 500cc *(Suzuki)*
World Championship positions
1985 24th equal 500cc *(Honda)*
1986 15th 500cc *(Suzuki)*

Other successes
1977 Winner 750cc class Australian Castrol Six-Hour race *(Suzuki)*
1981 Winner of Australian Castrol Six-Hour race *(Suzuki)*

PONS Alfonso (Sito)

Born 9/11/60, Barcelona, Spain
Marital status Married to Laura
First race 1979
First Grand Prix 1981 France, Paul Ricard, 250cc *(Yamaha)*
First Grand Prix win 1984 Spain, Jarama, 250cc *(Cobas)*
Grand Prix victories 8 (250cc)
World Championships 1 (250cc)
World Championship positions
1981 28th 250cc *(Siro-Kobas)*
1982 15th 250cc *(Cobas/Rotax)*
1983 18th 250cc *(Cobas/Rotax)*
1984 4th 250cc *(Cobas/Rotax)*
1985 12th 500cc *(Suzuki)*
1986 2nd 250cc *(Honda)*
1987 3rd 250cc *(Honda)*
1988 **1st** 250cc *(Honda)*

RAINEY Wayne Wesley

Born 23/10/60, Los Angeles, USA

Marital status Married to Shae
First race 1976
First Grand Prix 1984 South Africa, Kyalami 250cc *(Yamaha)*
First Grand Prix win 1988 Great Britain, Donington, 500cc *(Yamaha)*
Grand Prix victories 1 (500cc)
World Championship positions
1984 8th 250cc *(Yamaha)*
1988 3rd 500cc (Yamaha)
Other successes
1983 **1st** USA Superbike Championship *(Kawasaki)*
1987 **1st** USA Superbike Championship *(Honda)*

REGGIANI Loris

Born 7/10/59, Forli, Italy
Marital status Single
First race 1978
Titles 1981 Italian 125cc Champion *(Minarelli)*. 1982 Italian 500cc Champion *(Suzuki)*
First Grand Prix 1980 Italy, Misano, 125cc *(Minarelli)* and 350cc *(Bimota Yamaha)*
First Grand Prix win 1980 Great Britain, Silverstone, 125cc *(Minarelli)*
Grand Prix victories 4 (3 125cc) (1 250cc)
World Championship positions
1980 6th 125cc *(Minarelli)*
1980 21st 350cc *(Bimota Yamaha)*
1981 2nd 125cc *(Minarelli)*
1981 30th 250cc *(Bimota Yamaha)*
1982 13th 500cc *(Suzuki)*
1984 22nd 250cc *(Kawasaki)*
1985 6th 250cc *(Aprilia)*
1987 6th 250cc *(Aprilia)*
1988 13th 250cc *(Aprilia)*

REID Brian

Born 3/9/56, Banbridge, Northern Ireland
Marital status Single
First race 1976

Titles 1981 350cc Ulster Champion *(Yamaha)*. 1982 250cc, 350cc and 500cc Irish Road Racing Champion *(Yamaha)*. 1982 250cc and 350cc Ulster Champion *(Yamaha)*. 1983 350cc and 500cc Ulster and Irish Road Racing Champion *(Yamaha)*. 1984 250cc, 350cc and 500cc Ulster and 250cc and 350cc Irish Champion *(Yamaha)*
Other successes
1985 TT Formula Two World Champion *(Yamaha)*
1986 TT Formula Two World Champion *(Yamaha)*

RICCI Fausto

Born 13/3/61, Ravenna, Italy
Marital status Single
First race 1980
First Grand Prix 1984 Italy, Misano, 250cc *(Yamaha)*
First Grand Prix win 1984 Italy, Misano, 250cc *(Yamaha)*
Grand Prix victories 1 (250cc)
World Championship positions
1984 16th 250cc *(Yamaha)*
1985 5th 250cc *(Honda)*
1986 8th 250cc *(Honda)*
Other successes
1983 2nd European 250cc Championship *(Yamaha)*
1988 **1st** European 250cc Championship

ROCHE Raymond

Born 21/2/57, Ollioules, France
Marital status Single
First race 1975
Titles 1976 French 250cc Champion *(Yamaha)*
First Grand Prix 1976 France, Le Mans, 250cc *(Yamaha)*
World Championship positions
1978 11th 250cc *(Yamaha)*
1978 22nd 350cc *(Yamaha)*
1980 23rd 500cc *(Suzuki)*
1982 28th 500cc *(Suzuki)*
1983 10th 500cc *(Honda)*
1984 3rd 500cc *(Honda)*
1985 7th 500cc *(Yamaha)*
1986 8th 500cc *(Honda)*
1987 13th 500cc *(Cagiva)*
1988 20th 500cc *(Cagiva)*
Other successes
1981 **1st** World Endurance Championship *(Kawasaki)*
1983 **1st** Bol d'Or 24-Hour Race, France *(Honda)*

ROTH Reinhold

Born 4/3/53, Amtzell, West Germany
Marital status Married to Elfriede. One son, Mathias
First race 1975
Titles 1978 German 250cc Champion *(Yamaha)*. 1982 German 500cc Champion *(Suzuki)*. 1983 German 250cc Champion *(Yamaha)*
First Grand Prix 1979 Italy, Imola, 350cc *(Yamaha)*
First Grand Prix win 1987, France, Le Mans, 250cc *(Honda)*
Grand Prix victories One (250cc)
World Championship positions
1979 28th 350cc *(Yamaha)*
1980 27th 250cc *(Yamaha)*
1982 26th 250cc *(Yamaha)*
1983 17th 250cc *(Yamaha)*
1984 13th 500cc *(Honda)*
1985 9th 250cc *(Rotax)*
1986 16th 250cc *(Honda)*
1987 2nd 250cc *(Honda)*
1988 5th 250cc *(Honda)*
Other successes
1982 European 250cc Champion *(Yamaha)*

RUGGIA Jean Philippe

Born 1/10/65, Toulon, France
Marital status Single
First race 1984
World Championship positions
1987 17th 250cc *(Yamaha)*
1988 7th 250cc *(Yamaha)*
Other successes
1985 **1st** RDLC Gauloises Yamaha Cup (350cc)
1985 **1st** RDLC Yamaha European Cup (350cc)

SARRON Christian

Born 27/3/55, Riom (Puy de Dome), France
Marital status Single
First race 1975
First Grand Prix 1976 Czechoslovakia, Brno, 350cc *(Yamaha)*
First Grand Prix win 1977 Germany, Hockenheim, 250cc *(Yamaha)*
World Titles 1, 1984 250cc *(Yamaha)*
Grand Prix victories 7 (6 250cc), (1 500cc)
World Championship positions
1976 28th 350cc *(Yamaha)*
1977 14th 250cc *(Yamaha)*
1977 7th 350cc *(Yamaha)*
1978 15th 350cc *(Yamaha)*
1978 11th 500cc *(Yamaha)*
1979 11th 500cc *(Yamaha)*
1981 23rd 500cc *(Yamaha)*
1982 10th 250cc *(Yamaha)*
1982 8th 350cc *(Yamaha)*
1983 2nd 250cc *(Yamaha)*
1984 **1st** 250cc *(Yamaha)*
1985 3rd 500cc *(Yamaha)*
1986 6th 500cc *(Yamaha)*
1987 7th 500cc *(Yamaha)*
1988 4th 500cc *(Yamaha)*
Other successes
1977 2nd World Formula 750cc Championship *(Yamaha)*
1978 3rd World Formula 750cc Championship *(Yamaha)*

SARRON Dominique

Born 27/8/59, Clermont Ferrand, France
Marital status Single
First race 1979
First Grand Prix 1985 Spain, Jarama, 250cc *(Honda)*
First Grand Prix win 1986 Great Britain, Silverstone, 250cc *(Honda)*
Grand Prix victories 4 (250cc)
World Championship positions
1985 21st 250cc *(Honda)*
1986 3rd 250cc *(Honda)*
1987 4th 250cc *(Honda)*
1988 4th 250cc *(Honda)*
Other successes
1981 **1st** Bol d'Or 24-Hour Race, France *(Honda)*
1982 **1st** Bol d'Or 24-Hour Race, France *(Honda)*
1984 3rd World Endurance Championship *(Honda)*
1986 **1st** Suzuka Eight-Hour Race, Japan *(Honda)*
1987 **1st** Bol d'Or 24-Hour Race, France *(Honda)*
1988 **1st** Bol d'Or 24-Hour Race, France *(Honda)*

SCHWANTZ Kevin

Born 19/6/64, Paige, Texas, USA

First Grand Prix 1986 Holland, Assen, 500cc *(Suzuki)*
First Grand Prix win 1988 Japan, Suzuka, *(Suzuki)*
Grand Prix victories 1 (500cc)
World Championship positions
1986 22nd equal 500cc *(Suzuki)*
1987 15th equal 500cc *(Suzuki)*
1988 8th 500cc *(Suzuki)*
Other successes
1986 Top points scorer, Transatlantic Trophy *(Suzuki)*
1986 2nd Daytona 200cc Superbike *(Suzuki)*
1987 Top points scorer, Transatlantic Trophy *(Suzuki)*

SHIMIZU Masahiro

Born 22/11/64, Kanagawa, Japan
Marital status Single
First race 1982
Titles 1984 Japanese 125cc Champion *(Honda)* 1987 Japanese 250cc Champion *(Honda)*
First Grand Prix 1987 Japan, Suzuka, 250cc *(Honda)*
World Championship positions
1987 13th 250cc *(Honda)*
1988 10th 250cc *(Honda)*

SPAAN Hans

Born 1/2/54, Assen, Holland
Marital status Single
First race 1975
Titles 1979, 1980, 1982 Dutch 50cc Champion *(Kreidler)*. 1983 Dutch 80cc Champion *(Kreidler)*
First Grand Prix 1980 Yugoslavia, Rijeka, 50cc *(Kreidler)*
World Championship positions
1980 6th 50cc *(Kreidler)*
1982 9th 50cc *(Kreidler)*
1983 4th 50cc *(Kreidler)*
1984 6th 80cc *(Kreidler)*
1985 12th 80cc *(Huvo)*
1986 4th 80cc *(Casal)*
1987 13th 80cc *(Casal)*
1988 3rd 125cc *(Holland)*

STREUER Egbert

Born 1/2/54, Assen, Holland

Marital status Married to Karin. One son
First race 1975
Titles Dutch sidecar champion 1978–1986 *(Yamaha)*
First Grand Prix 1978 Austria, Salzburgring, sidecar *(Yamaha)*
First Grand Prix win 1982 Great Britain, Silverstone, sidecar, *(Yamaha)*
World titles 3 (sidecar)
Grand Prix victories 15 (sidecar)
World Championship positions
1978, 27th sidecar *(Yamaha)*
1980 4th sidecar *(Yamaha)*
1981 8th sidecar *(Yamaha)*
1982 4th sidecar *(Yamaha)*
1983 2nd sidecar *(Yamaha)*
1984 **1st** sidecar *(Yamaha)*
1985 **1st** sidecar *(Yamaha)*
1986 **1st** sidecar *(Yamaha)*
1987 2nd sidecar *(Yamaha)*
1988 3rd sidecar *(Yamaha)*

TAIRA Tadahiko

Born 12/11/56, Fukushima, Japan
Marital status Married
First race 1977
Titles 1979 Japanese Junior 350cc Champion *(Yamaha)*. 1980 Japanese 350cc Champion *(Yamaha)*. 1983/84/85 Japanese 500cc Champion *(Yamaha)*
First Grand Prix 1984 Holland, Assen
First Grand Prix win 1986 San Marino, Misano, 250cc *(Yamaha)*
Grand Prix victories 1 (250cc)
World Championship positions
1984 16th 500cc *(Yamaha)*
1985 21st 500cc *(Yamaha)*
1986 9th 250cc *(Yamaha)*
1987 6th 500cc *(Yamaha)*
1988 15th 500cc *(Yamaha)*
Other successes
1981 **1st** Japanese Grand Prix 250cc *(Yamaha)*

TARDOZZI Davide

Born 30/1/59 Ravenna, Italy
Marital status Single
First race 1979
Titles 1982 Italian Endurance Champion. 1984 Italian Formula One Champion *(Yamaha)*
Other successes
1987 4th TT Formula One World Championship *(Yamaha)*
1988 3rd World Superbike Championship *(Bimota)*

WAIBEL Gerhard

Born 17/12/58, Rohrbrunn, West Germany
Marital status Married to Christa. One son, Andy
First race 1977
Titles 1983 German 80cc Champion *(Seel)*. 1983 German 125cc Champion *(MBA)*
First Grand Prix 1979 Germany, Hockenheim 50cc *(Kreidler)*
First Grand Prix win 1979 Germany, Hockenheim 50cc *(Kreidler)*
Grand Prix victories 4 (1 50cc and 3 80cc)
World Championship positions
1979 4th 50cc *(Kreidler)*
1980 12th 50cc *(Kreidler)*
1981 15th 125cc *(MBA)*
1982 14th 125cc *(MBA)*
1983 12th 125cc *(MBA)*
1984 23rd 125cc *(Real)*
1984 5th 80cc *(Real)*
1985 5th 80cc *(Seel)*
1986 5th 80cc *(Krauser)*
1987 3rd 80cc *(Krauser)*
1988 9th 125cc *(Honda)*

WEBSTER Steve

Born 7/1/60, York, England
Marital status Married to Karen, One daughter, Holly
First race 1979

Titles 1982 British Clubmans Sidecar Champion *(Yamaha)*. 1985 British Sidecar Champion *(Yamaha)*
First Grand Prix 1983 Great Britain, Silverstone, sidecar *(Yamaha)*
First Grand Prix win 1986 Belgium, Spa Francorchamps, sidecar *(Yamaha)*
World Titles 2 (sidecar)
Grand Prix victories 7 (sidecar)
World Championship positions
1983 16th sidecar *(Yamaha)*
1984 8th sidecar *(Yamaha)*
1985 4th sidecar *(Yamaha)*
1986 3rd sidecar *(Yamaha)*
1987 **1st** sidecar *(Krauser)*
1988 **1st** sidecar *(Krauser)*

WHITHAM James Michael

Born 6/9/66, Huddersfield, England
Marital status Single
First race 1983
First Grand Prix 1986 Great Britain, Silverstone, 125cc *(MBA)*
Other successes
1988 British Production Champion *(Suzuki)*

WIMMER Martin

Born 11/10/57, Munich, West Germany
Marital status Married to Michaela. One daughter, Miriam
First race 1978
Titles **1st** 1978 German Yamaha Cup. 1981 German 250cc and 350cc Champion
First Grand Prix 1980 Germany, Nurburgring 250cc and 350cc *(Yamaha)*
First Grand Prix win 1982 Great Britain, Silverstone, 250cc *(Yamaha)*
Grand Prix victories 2 (250cc)
World Championship positions
1980 30th 250cc *(Yamaha)*
1981 8th 250cc *(Yamaha)*
1981 12th 350cc *(Yamaha)*
1982 4th 250cc *(Yamaha)*
1982 16th 350cc *(Yamaha)*
1983 6th 250cc *(Yamaha)*
1984 7th 250cc *(Yamaha)*
1985 4th 250cc *(Yamaha)*
1986 6th 250cc *(Yamaha)*
1987 8th 250cc *(Yamaha)*
1988 14th 500cc *(Yamaha)*
Other successes
1987 **1st** Suzuka Eight-Hour Race, Japan *(Yamaha)*

YATSUSHIRO Shunji

Born 26/8/60, Kaya-Shi, Kagoshima-Ken, Japan
Marital status Single
First race 1981
Titles 1981 Japanese Novice 250cc Champion *(Yamaha)*. 1983 Japanese Formula One Champion *(Kawasaki)*. 1984 Japanese Formula One Champion *(Honda)*
First Grand Prix 1986 Austria, Salzburgring 500cc *(Honda)*
World Championship positions
1986 13th 500cc *(Honda)*
1987 9th 500cc *(Honda)*
1988 13th 500cc *(Honda)*

THE CIRCUITS

ANDERSTORP, Sweden

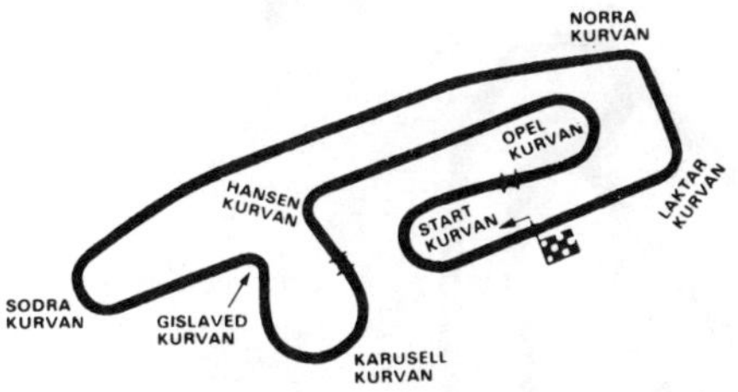

Length 2.505 miles (4.031km)

Contact Address Anderstorp Raceway, Box 180, S-33400 Anderstorp. Tel: 0371 16170. Telex: 70327. Fax: 0371 18296

Location 70 miles (112km) south-east of Gothenburg

Nearest International Airport Gothenburg

Lap records
125cc. Fausto Gresini (I) *Garelli*, 1m43.79s = 86.88mph (139.81kmh) 9/8/87
250cc. Reinhold Roth (D) *Honda*, 1m38.38s = 91.66mph (147.506kmh) 14/8/88
500cc. Eddie Lawson (USA) *Yamaha*, 1m34.43s = 95.49mph (153.67kmh) 14/8/88
Sidecar. Rolf Biland/Kurt Waltisperg (CH) *LCR-Krauser*, 1m38.66s = 91.40mph (147.087kmh) 14/8/88

ASSEN, Holland

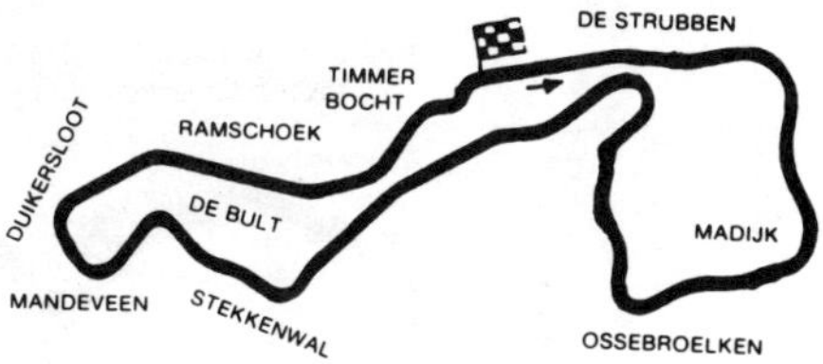

Length 3.81 miles (6.134km)

Contact Address Stichting Circuit van Drenthe, Postbus 150, 9400 AD Assen. Tel: 05920 55000. Telex: 53821 TTASN NL. Fax: 05920 16309

Location 3 miles (5km) south of Assen

Nearest International Airport Amsterdam

Lap records
80cc. Ian McConnachie (GB) *Krauser*, 2m30.79s = 91.00mph (146.445kmh) 28/6/86
125cc. Fausto Gresini (I) *Garelli*, 2m24.02s = 95.28mph (153.329kmh) 27/6/87
250cc. Toni Mang (D) *Honda*, 2m16.0s = 100.89mph (162.37kmh) 25/6/88
500cc. Wayne Gardner (AUS) *Honda*, 2m11.28s = 104.52mph (168.208kmh) 25/6/88
Sidecar. Rolf Biland/Kurt Waltisperg (CH) *LCR-Krauser*, 2m17.35s = 99.90mph (160.775kmh) 28/6/86
TT Formula One. Roger Burnett (GB) *Honda*, 2m18.47s = 99.09mph (159.46kmh) 22/6/88

BRANDS HATCH, Great Britain

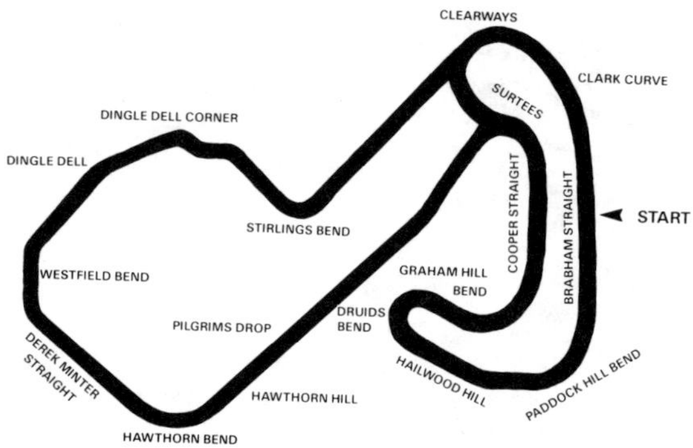

Length Short circuit, 1.2 miles (1.93km) and long circuit, 2.61 miles (4.20km)

Contact Address Brands Hatch Circuit Ltd., Fawkham, Nr Dartford, Kent DA3 8NG. Tel: 0474 872331. Telex: 96172 BRANDS G. Fax: 0474 874766

Location 20 miles (32.18km) south-east of London

Nearest International Airport London Gatwick

Lap records

Short circuit
80cc. Rimmel Swan (NL) *Harmsen,* 57.8s = 74.96mph (120.64kmh) 21/10/84
125cc. Alex Bedford (GB) *Honda,* 53.4s = 81.14mph (130.55kmh) 1/4/88
250cc. Niall Mackenzie (GB) *Armstrong,* 49.1s = 88.24mph (142.00kmh) 20/10/85
350cc. Niall Mackenzie (GB) *Armstrong,* 49.2s = 88.06mph (141.71kmh) 20/10/85
500cc. Kevin Wrettom (GB) *Suzuki,* 23/10/83 and Keith Huewen (GB) *Suzuki,* 48.5s = 89.34mph (143.77kmgh) 23/10/83
1300cc. Roger Marshall (GB) *Suzuki,* 25/10/87 and Doug Polen (USA) *Suzuki,* 48.6s = 89.15mph (143.46kmh) 1/4/88
Sidecar. Steve Webster/Tony Hewitt (GB) *LCR-Yamaha,* 48.3s = 89.70mph (144.35kmh) 21/10/84

Long circuit
125cc. Mark Taylor (GB) *Honda,* 1m50.2s = 84.94mph (136.66kmh) 18/6/88
250cc. David Wilson (GB) *Exactweld,* 1m40.4s = 93.23mph (150.00kmh) 18/6/88
350cc. Steve Coker (GB) *Exactweld* 1m40.3s = 93.32mph (150.15kmh) 19/6/88
500cc. Tony Rodgers (GB) *Tigcraft,* 1m47.7s = 86.91mph (139.83kmh) 19/6/88
1300cc. Jon Higgens (GB) *Suzuki,* 1m38.6s = 94.93mph (152.74kmh) 19/6/88
Sidecar. M. Searle/T. Hopkinson (GB) *RCL,* 1m42.6s = 91.23mph (146.78kmh) 19/6/88

BRNO, Czechoslovakia

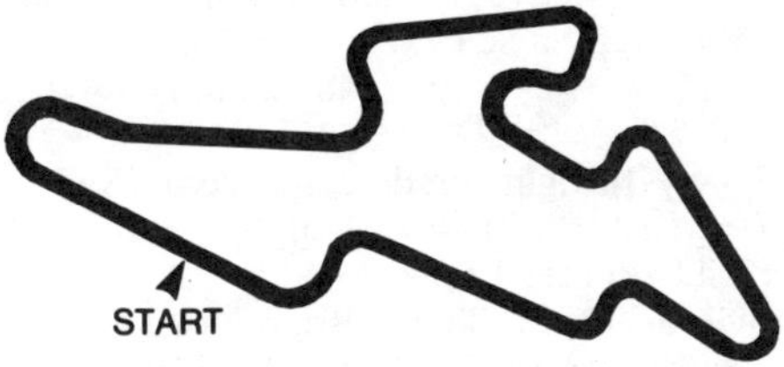

Length 3.35 miles (5.39km)

Contact Address Automotodrom, Automotoklub Brno, Basty 8, CS-657 43 Brno. Tel: 0502 94588. Telex: 63131

Location 100 miles (160 km) north of Vienna, Austria. 120 miles (195km) south-east of Prague

Nearest International Airport Vienna

Lap records

80cc. Gerhard Waibel (D) *Krauser*, 2m24.02s = 83.78mph (134.83kmh) 23/8/87
125cc. Bruno Casanova (I) *Garelli*, 2m18.8s = 87.32mph (140.53kmh) 23/8/87
250cc. Juan Garriga (E) *Yamaha*, 2m09.79s = 92.96mph (149.61kmh) 28/8/88
500cc. Wayne Gardner (AUS) *Honda*, 2m06.24s = 95.58mph (153.82kmh) 28/8/88
Sidecar. Egbert Streuer/Bernard Schnieders (NL) *LCR-Yamaha*, 2m10.47s = 92.48mph (148.83kmh) 28/8/88

CADWELL PARK, Great Britain

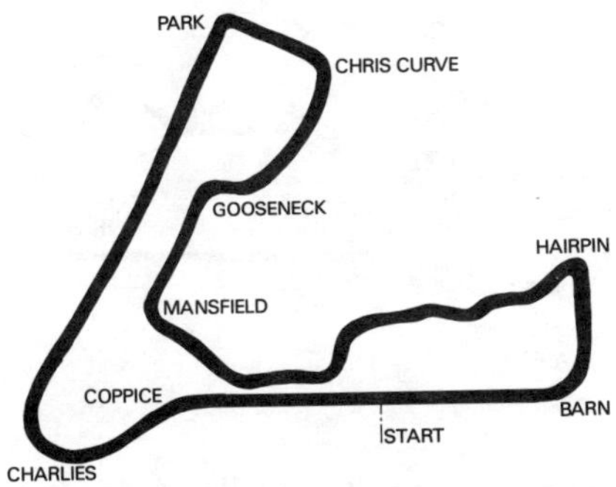

Length 2.17 miles (3.49km)

Contact Address Cadwell Park International Racing Circuit, Cadwell Manor, Louth, Lincolnshire. Tel: 0507 84248. Fax: 0507 84515

Location 5 miles (8km) south of Louth, Lincolnshire

Nearest International Airport Humberside

Lap records

80cc. Doug Flather (GB) *Wicks*, 1m52.3s = 69.69mph (112.13kmh) 31/8/87
125cc. Alex Bedford (GB) *Honda*, 1m40.5s = 77.87mph (125.32kmh) 2/10/88
250cc. Nigel Bosworth (GB) *Aprilia*, 1m35.4s = 82.03mph (132.01kmh) 2/10/88
350cc. Steve Hislop (GB) *Yamaha*, 1m38.7s = 79.29mph (127.58kmh) 31/8/87
Outright & TTF1. Trevor Nation (GB) *Norton*, 1m33.7s = 83.52mph (134.41kmh) 2/10/88
Overall & Sidecars. Steve Webster/Tony Hewitt (GB) *LCR-Krauser*, 1m33.4s = 83.79mph (134.85kmh) 2/10/88

DONINGTON PARK, Great Britain

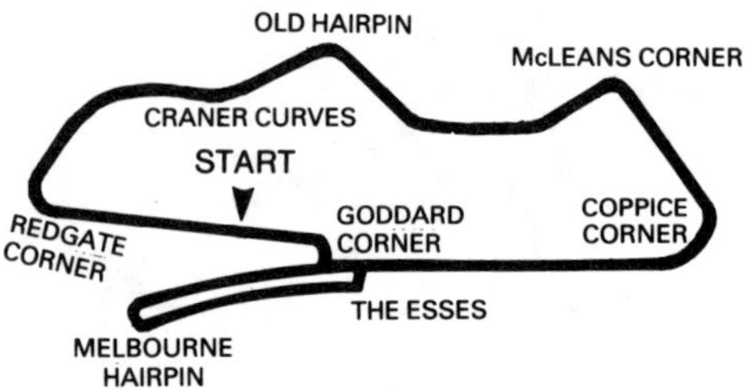

Length Long circuit, 2.5 miles (4.02km) and short circuit, 1.96 miles (3.15km)

Contact Address Donington Park Racing, Castle Donington, Derby DE7 2RP. Tel: 0332 810048. Telex: 377793 DONPAR. Fax: 0332 850422

Location 10 miles (16km) south-east of Derby

Nearest International Airport East Midlands, Castle Donington

Lap records

Long Circuit
80cc. Jorge Martinez (E) *Derbi*, 1m55.44s = 80.04mph (128.78kmh) 2/8/87
125cc. Ezio Gianola (I) *Honda*, 1m45.76s = 85.09mph (136.93kmh) 7/8/88
250cc. Juan Garriga (E) *Yamaha*, 1m38.87s. = 91.02mph (146.47kmh) 7/8/88
500cc. Christian Sarron (F) *Yamaha*, 1m36.21s = 93.54mph (150.53kmh) 7/8/88
Sidecar. Rolf Biland/Kurt Waltisperg (CH) *LCR Krauser*, 1m40.05s = 89.95mph (144.75kmh) 7/8/88
TT Formula One. Trevor Nation (GB) *Norton*, 1m 40.53 = 89.52mph (144.06kmh) 7/8/88

Short Circuit
125cc. Alex Bedford (GB) *Honda*, 1m20.8s = 87.19mph (140.28kmh) 19/6/88
250cc. Steve Patrickson (GB) *Hejira*, 1m16.0s = 92.70mph (149.15kmh) 19/6/88
350cc. Jeff Sayle (AUS) *Yamaha*, 1m16.6s = 91.98mph (148.02 kmh) 29/8/80
500cc/Outright. Freddie Spencer (USA) *Honda*, 1m13.21s = 96.24mph (154.87kmh) 24/4/84
Sidecar. Derek Bayley/Brian Nixon (GB) *Yamaha*, 1m16.2s = 92.47mph (148.81 kmh) 19/6/85

DUNDROD, Northern Ireland

Length 7.40 miles (11.90km)

Contact Address Ulster Centre Promotions Ltd., 60 Donegal Pass, Belfast BT7 1BU, Northern Ireland

Location 10 miles (16km) outside Belfast

Nearest International Airport Belfast

Lap records
250cc. Joey Dunlop (GB) *Honda*, 3m53.3s = 114.21mph (183.79kmh) 17/8/85
350cc. Gary Cowan (GB) *Yamaha*, 3m53.2s = 114.25mph (183.86kmh) 17/8/85
500cc/Outright. Eddie Laycock (IRL) *Honda*, 3m39.46s = 121.39mph (195.35kmh) 30/7/88
Formula One. Norman Brown (GB) *Suzuki*, 3m45.6s = 118.10mph (190.05kmh) 21/8/82
Formula Two. Brian Reid (GB) *Yamaha*, 3m54.0s = 113.86mph (183.23kmh) 7/8/85

GOIANIA, Brazil

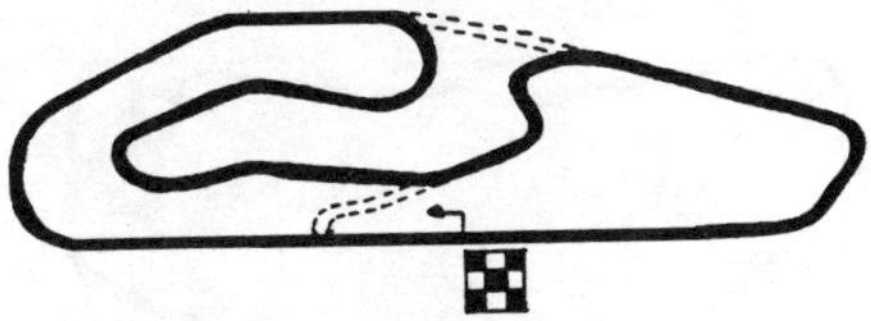

Length 2.38 miles (3.835km)

Contact Address KM6-Estrada de Bela Vista, Goiania. Tel: 0622414122

Location 80kms east of Brasilia

Nearest International Airport Brasilia

Lap records
250cc. Sito Pons (E) *Honda*, 1m31.25s = 93.95mph (151.19kmh) 25/9/87
500cc. Wayne Gardner (Aus) *Honda*, 1m28.79s = 96.62mph (155.49kmh) 25/9/87

HOCKENHEIM, West Germany

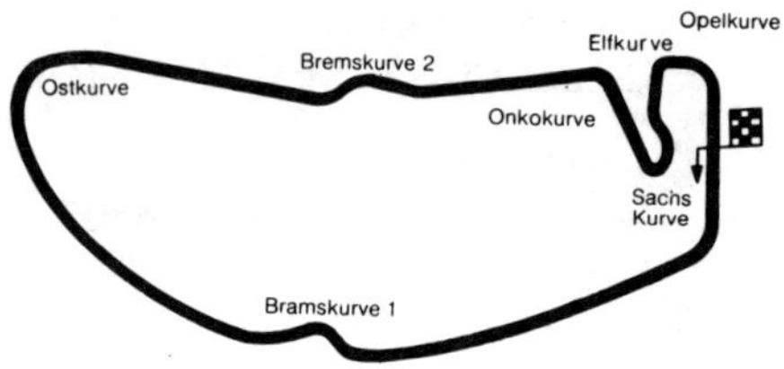

Length 4.21 miles (6.78km)

Contact Address Hockenheim-Ring GmbH, D-6832 Hockenheim. Tel: 6205 7021/7022. Telex: 465984

Location 52 miles (85km) south of Frankfurt

Nearest International Airport Frankfurt

Lap records

80cc. Stefan Dorflinger (CH) *Krauser,* 2m30.72s = 100.75mph (162.14kmh) 29/9/86

125cc. Luca Cadalora (I) *Garelli,* 2m22.14s = 106.83mph (171.93kmh) 29/9/86

250cc. Carlos Lavado (VZ) *Yamaha,* 2m14.06s = 113.21mph (182.18kmh) 17/5/87

500cc. Wayne Gardner (AUS) *Honda,* 2m05.5s = 120.92mph (194.59kmh) 17/5/87

Sidecar. Rolf Biland/Kurt Waltisperg (CH) *LCR-Yamaha,* 2m14.61s = 112.81mph (181.55kmh) 29/9/86

IMOLA, Italy

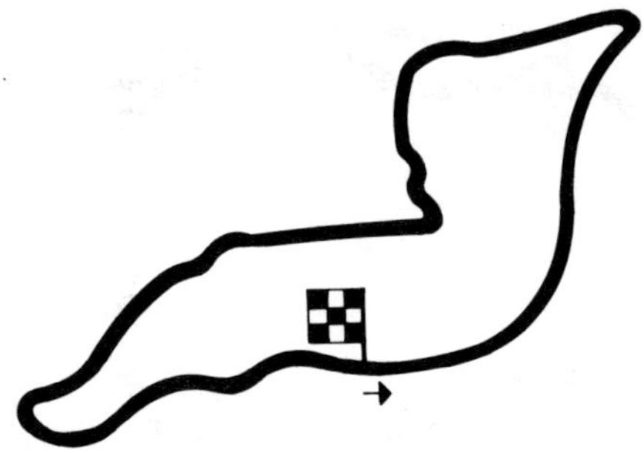

Length 3.13 miles (5.04km)

Contact Address Autodromo Dino Ferrari-Sagis, Viale Dante 32, 1-40125 Bologna. Tel: 0542 31444. Telex: 511393. Fax: 0542 30420

Location 20 miles (32km) south of Bologna

Nearest International Airport Bologna

Lap records

80cc. Jorge Martinez (E) *Derbi,* 2m12.75s = 85.26mph (137.22kmh) 21/5/88

125cc. Jorge Martinez (E) *Derbi,* 2m08.39s = 88.16mph (141.88kmh) 21/5/88

250cc. Dominique Sarron (F) *Honda,* 1m58.69s = 95.36mph (153.47kmh) 21/5/88

500cc. Eddie Lawson (USA) *Yamaha,* 1m54.41s = 98.93mph (159.20kmh) 21/5/88

TT MOUNTAIN CIRCUIT, Isle of Man, Great Britain

Length 37.73 miles (60.72km)

Contact Address The Isle of Man Tourist Board, 13 Victoria Street, Douglas, Isle of Man. Tel: 624 74323. Telex: 627793 MANINF G

Location Isle of Man, 30 miles (48km) off north-west coast of England

Nearest International Airport Ronaldsway (IOM) and Manchester

Lap records
250cc. Joey Dunlop (GB) *Honda*, 19m59.2s = 113.27mph (182.26kmh) 8/6/88
500cc/Outright. Steve Cull (GB) *Honda*, 19m00.6s = 119.08mph (191.63kmh) 10/6/88
TT Formula One. Joey Dunlop (GB) *Honda*, 19m15.4s = 117.56mph (189.19kmh) 6/6/88
TT Formula Two. Steve Hislop (GB) *Yamaha*, 19m57.6s = 113.41mph (182.51kmh) 8/6/88
Sidecar. Jock Taylor/Benga Johansson (GB/S) *Yamaha*, 20m54.2s = 108.29mph (174.28kmh) 8/6/82
Production Class A. Geoff Johnson (GB) *Yamaha*, 19m25.4s = 116.55mph (187.56kmh) 8/6/88
Production Class B. Geoff Johnson (GB) *Yamaha*, 20m02.2s = 112.98mph (181.81kmh) 4/6/88
Production Class C. Steve Hislop (GB) *Honda*, 20m36.6s = 109.83mph (176.74kmh) 3/6/88
Production Class D. Barry Woodland (GB) *Yamaha*, 21m48.6s = 103.79mph (167.02kmh) 3/6/88

JARAMA, Spain

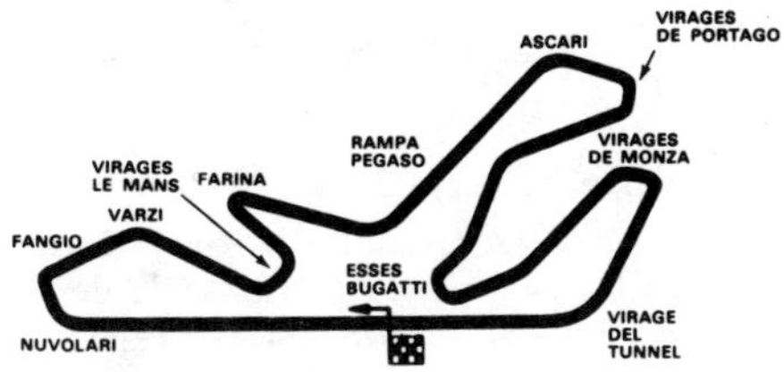

Length 2.058 miles (3.312km)

Contact Address Real Automovil Club de España, Jose Abascal 10, Madrid 3. Tel: 4473200. Telex: 454111 CIJA

Location 17 miles (28km) north of Madrid

Nearest International Airport Madrid

Lap records
80cc. Jorge Martinez (E) *Derbi*, 1m37.52s = 75.97mph (122.25kmh) 13/9/87
125cc. August Auinger (A) *MBA*, 1m33.25s = 79.44mph (127.85kmh) 13/9/87
250cc. S. Pons (E) *Honda*, 1m30.12s = 82.20mph (132.293kmh) 24/4/88
500cc. Wayne Gardner (AUS) *Honda*, 1m27.99s = 84.20mph (135.50kmh) 13/9/87
Sidecar. Rolf Biland/Kurt Waltisperg (CH) *LCR-Yamaha*, 1m34.35s = 78.52mph (126.37kmh) 24/5/81

JEREZ, Spain

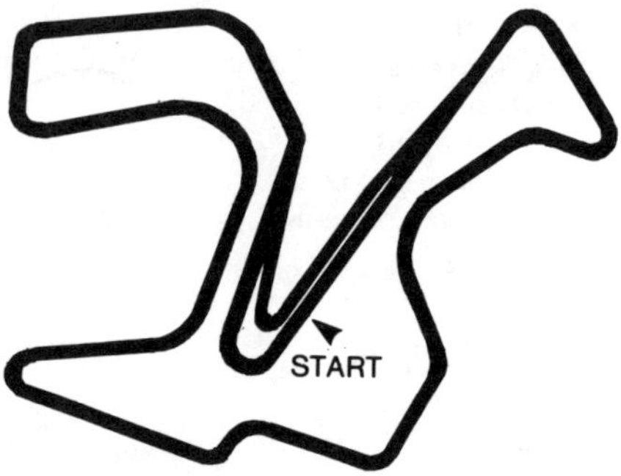

Length 2.62 miles (4.21km)

Contact Address Circuito Permanente de Jerez, Ctra de Arcos, Km 10, Apdo de Correos 1709. Tel: 3456 334166. Telex: 75145 CIRJ

Location 62 miles (100km) south of Seville

Nearest International Airport Seville

Lap records
80cc. Jorge Martinez (E) *Derbi,* 2m02.50s = 77.03mph (123.95kmh) 26/4/87
125cc. Domenico Brigaglia (I) *MBA,* 1m56.92s = 80.52mph (129.58kmh) 26/4/87
250cc. J. Garriga (E) *Yamaha,* 1m51.65s = 84.51mph (136·00kmh) 1/5/88
500cc. Eddie Lawson (USA) *Yamaha,* 1m49.29s = 86.33mph (138.94kmh) 1/5/88
Sidecar. Rolf Biland/Kurt Waltisperg (CH) *LCR-Krauser,* 1m53.58s = 83.07mph (133.693kmh) 26/4/87

LAGUNA SECA, USA

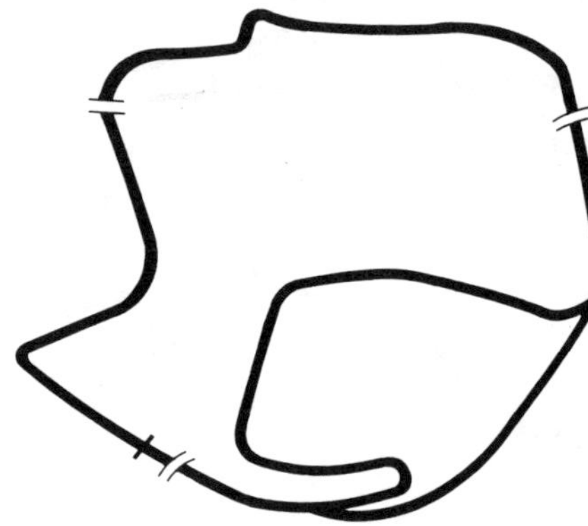

Length 2.18 miles (3.52km)

Contact Address Scramp, PO Box Scramp, Monterey, CA 93940. Tel: 0408 373 1811

Location 10 miles (16km) east of Monterey

Nearest International Airport San Francisco

Lap records
250cc. B. Casanova (I) *Aprilia,* 1m32.32s = 85.63mph (137.80kmh) 10/4/88
500cc. Eddie Lawson (USA) *Yamaha,* 1m29.9s = 87.87mph (141.40kmh) 10/4/88

LE MANS, France

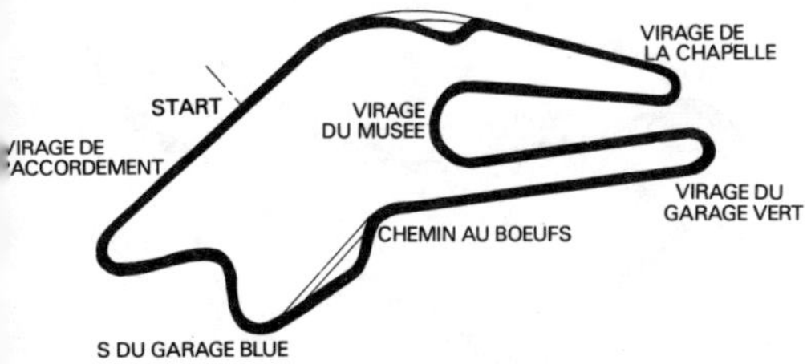

Length 2.63 miles (4.24km)

Contact Address Circuit Bugatti, Cedex 19, F-72040 Le Mans. Tel: 43 725025. Telex: 720637. Fax: 43 726983

Location 124 miles (200km) west of Paris

Nearest International Airport Paris, Orly

Lap records
80cc. Paul Bordes (F) *RB*, 2m16.0s = 76.08mph (122.43kmh) 12/4/87
125cc. Jean-Claude Selini (F) *MBA*, 1m58.43s = 87.39mph (140.64kmh) 12/4/87
250cc. Dominique Sarron (F) *Honda*, 1m48.63s = 95.28mph (153.33kmh) 12/4/87
500cc. Christian Sarron (F) *Yamaha*, 1m47.70s = 96.10mph (154.66kmh) 12/4/87
Sidecar. Alain Michel/Jean-Marc Fresc (F) *LCR-Yamaha*, 1m51.99s = 92.43mph (148.75kmh) 12/4/87

MALLORY PARK, Great Britain

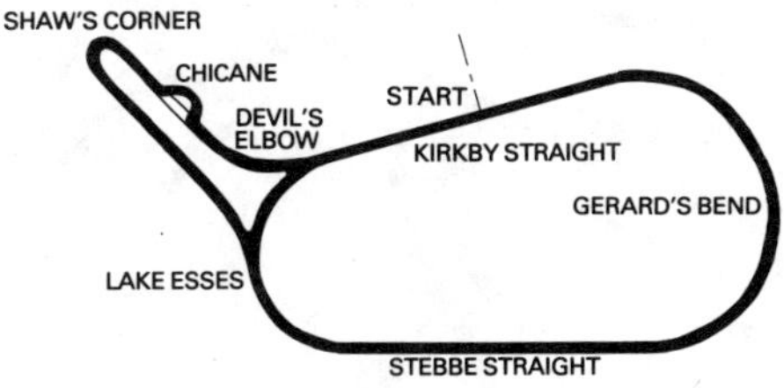

Length 1.37 miles (2.20km)

Contact Address Mallory Park (Motorsport) Ltd., Kirkby, Mallory, Leicester LE9 7QE. Tel: 0455 42931

Location 9 miles south west of Leicester

Nearest International Airport East Midlands

Lap records
125cc. James Witham (GB) *MBA*, 54.90s = 89.83mph (144.56kmh) 27/7/86
250cc. Niall Mackenzie (GB) *Armstrong*, 52.30s = 94.30mph (151.75kmh) 27/7/86
500cc. Roger Marshall (GB) *Honda*, 51.50s = 95.76mph (154.10kmh) 20/4/86
Sidecar. Steve Webster/Tony Hewitt (GB) *LCR-Yamaha*, 51.00s = 96.70mph (155.61kmh) 27/7/86

MISANO, Italy

Length 2.17 miles (3.49km)

Contact Address Autodromo Santamonica, Via del Cano 27, 1-47046 Misano Adriatico. Tel: 0541 615221. Telex: 550596 MONICA

Location 80 miles (128km) south-east of Bologna

Nearest International Airport Bologna

Lap records

80cc. Pier Paolo Bianchi (I) *Seel,* 1m29.65s = 87.03mph (140.05kmh) 23/8/86

125cc. August Auinger (A) *MBA,* 1m24.73s = 92.08mph (148.20kmh) 24/8/86

250cc. Luca Cadalora (I) *Yamaha,* 1m21.82s = 95.91mph (154.34kmh) 30/8/87

500cc. Randy Mamola (USA) *Yamaha,* 1m18.98s = 99.40mph (159.96kmh) 30/8/87

Sidecar. Markus Egloff/Urs Egloff (CH) *LCR-Yamaha,* 1m30.57s = 86.21mph (138.742kmh) 27/3/83

MONZA, Italy

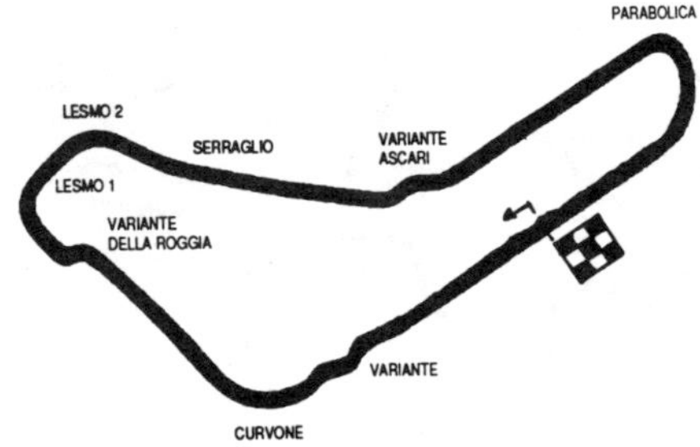

Length 3.604 miles (5·80km)

Contact Address Autodromo Nazionale di Monza, 20052 Monza Parco. Tel: 39329866 Telex: 316434 AMONZA

Location 9 miles (14km) north-east of Milan

Nearest International Airport Milan Linate and Milane Malpensa

Lap records

80cc. Jorge Martinez (E) *Derbi,* 2m09.87s = 99.90mph (160.76kmh) 24/5/87

125cc. Bruno Casanova (I) *Garelli,* 2m03.15s = 105.35mph (169.55kmh) 23/5/87

250cc. Dominque Sarron (F) *Honda,* 1m55.75s = 112.09mph (180.38kmh) 24/5/87

500cc. Wayne Gardner (AUS) *Honda,* 1m49.0s = 119.03mph (191.56kmh) 24/5/87

NURBURGRING, West Germany

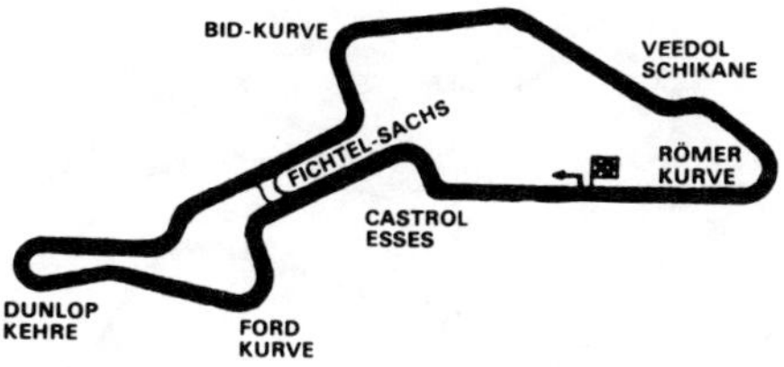

Length 2.81 miles (4.542km)

Contact Address Nurburgring GmbH, D 5489 Nurburg/Eifel. Tel: 02691 2041/2031. Telex: 0863919

Location 70 miles (112km) south-west of Cologne

Nearest International Airport Cologne

Lap records
80cc. Ian McConnachie (GB) *Krauser*, 1m57.01s = 86.83mph (139.74kmh) 25/5/86
125cc. Luca Cadalora (I) *Garelli*, 1m51.73s = 90.94mph (146.35kmh) 25/5/86
250cc. Toni Mang (D) *Honda*, 1m46.90s = 95.05mph (152.96kmh) 25/5/86
500cc. Eddie Lawson (USA) *Yamaha*, 1m43.24s = 98.91mph (158.38kmh) 25/5/86
Sidecar. Rolf Biland/Kurt Waltisperg (CH) *LCR-Krauser*, 1m45.56s = 92.26mph (154.91kmh) 28/5/88

OULTON PARK, Great Britain

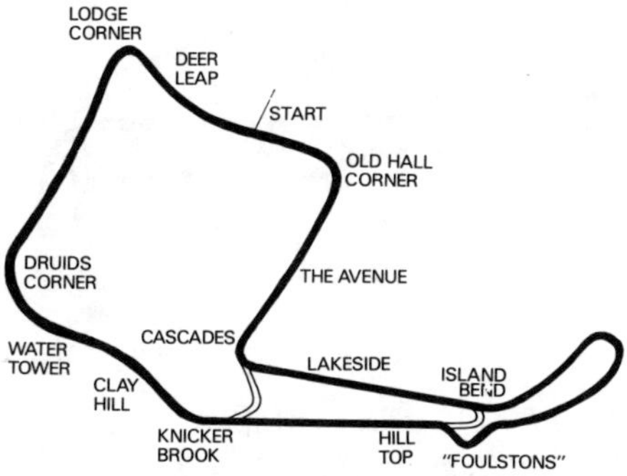

Length 2.77 miles (4.46km)

Contact Address Oulton Park Circuits Ltd., Little Budworth, Taporley, Cheshire CW6 9BW. Tel: 082921 301. Fax: 082921 378

Location 15 miles (24km) east of Chester

Nearest International Airport Manchester

Lap records
250cc. Ian Jones (GB) *Yamaha,* 1m48.9s = 91.53mph (147.29kmh) 4/7/87
350cc. James Hodson (GB) *Yamaha,* 1m48.1s = 92.21mph (148.39kmh) 4/7/87
1300cc. Pete Bennett (GB) *Suzuki,* 1m49.0s = 91.45mph (147.17kmh) 4/7/87
Sidecar. Lindsay and Garry Hurst (GB) *LCR-Yamaha* 1m53.9s = 87.51mph (140.8kmh) 4/7/87

PAUL RICARD, France

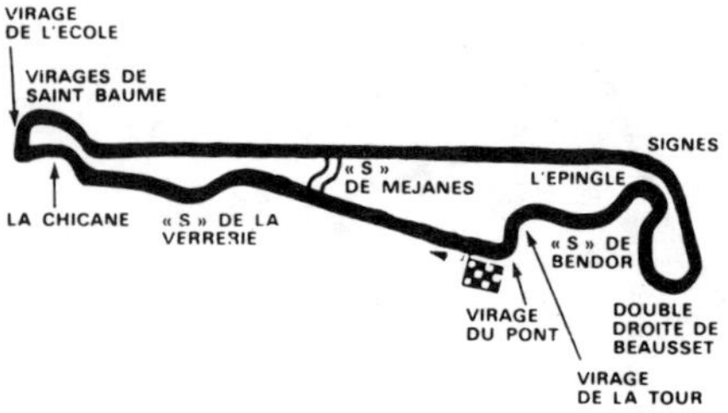

Length 3.610 miles (5.810km)

Contact Address ASA Paul Ricard, Route Nationale 8, F-83330 Le Beausset. Tel: 94 224617/91 547530. Telex: 400988 F

Location 21 miles (35km) east of Marseilles

Nearest International Airport Marseilles

Lap records
125cc. Luca Cadalora (I) *Garelli*, 2m13.35s = 97.46mph (156.54kmh) 20/7/86
250cc. Juan Garriga (E) *Yamaha*, 2m03.37s = 105.35mph (169.53kmh) 24/7/88
500cc. Wayne Gardner (AUS) *Honda*, 1m59.27s = 108.97mph (175.36kmh) 24/7/88
Sidecar. Rolf Biland/Kurt Waltisperg (CH) *LCR-Krauser*, 2m05.23s = 103.78mph (167.01kmh) 24/7/88

PHILLIP ISLAND, Australia

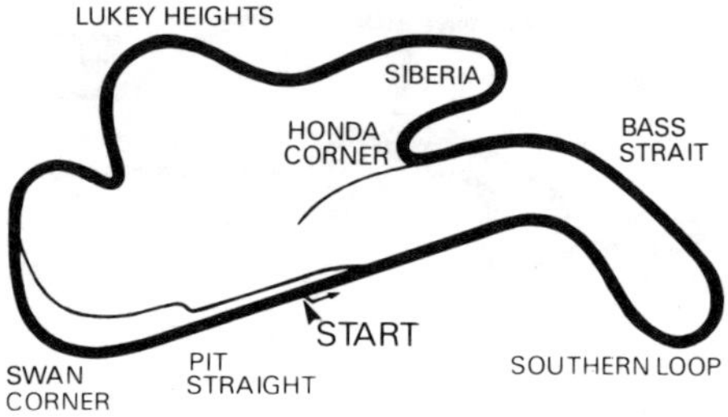

Length 2.76 miles (4.45 km)

Contact Address Level two, 344 St Kilda Road, PO Box 7094, Melbourne 3004. Tel: Office 03 696 2500, Circuit 059 52 1411, Fax: Office 03 696 4500, Circuit 059 52 3160

Location 80 miles (129km) south-east of Melbourne

Nearest International Airport Melbourne

Lap records
None – new circuit

RIJEKA, Yugoslavia

Length 2.59 miles (4.168km)
Contact Address Centre AMS, PO Box 68, 51000 Rijeka. Tel: 051 617777/806584. Tel: 051 424511/424201. Telex: 24512
Location 7 miles (12km) east of Rijeka
Nearest International Airport Trieste (Italy) and Zagreb
Lap records
80cc. Jorge Martinez (E) *Derbi*, 1m40.16s = 93.09mph (149.80kmh) 15/6/86
125cc. C. Catalano (I) *Aprilia*, 1m39.22s = 93.97mph (151.22kmh) 17/7/88
250cc. Juan Garriga (E) *Yamaha*, 1m32.18s = 101.14mph (162.77kmh) 17/7/88
500cc. Christian Sarron (F) *Yamaha*, 1m30.57s = 102.94mph (165.67kmh) 17/7/88
Sidecar. Alain Michel/Michel Burkard (F) *Yamaha*, 1m39.60s = 93.63mph (150.68kmh) 15/6/80

SALZBURGRING, Austria

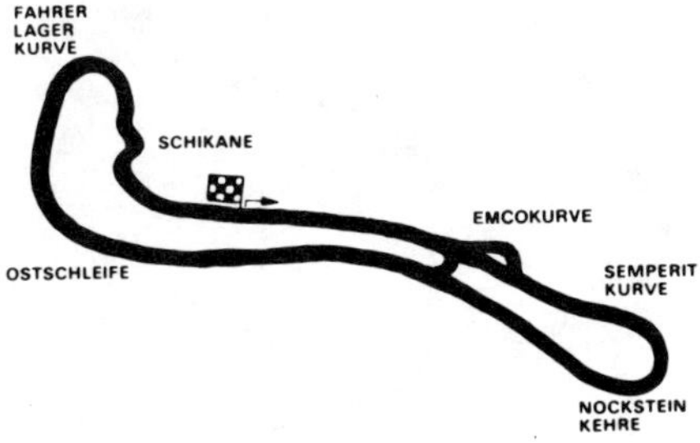

Length 2.63 miles (4.243km)
Contact Address IGMS Salzburgring, Münchner Dundesstrasse 9, A-5020 Salzburg. Tel: 06622 370792. Telex: 633585.
Location 9 miles (15km) east of Salzburg
Nearest International Airport Salzburg
Lap records
80cc. Gerhard Waibel (D) *Krauser*, 1m37.45s = 97.34mph (156.64kmh) 6/6/87
125cc. Fausto Gresini (I) *Garelli*, 1m30.58s = 104.79mph (168.63kmh) 7/6/87
250cc. Jacques Cornu (CH) *Honda*, 1m24.82s = 111.90mph (180.08kmh) 12/6/88
500cc. Didier de Radigues (B) *Yamaha*, 1m20.61s = 117.74mph (189.49kmh) 12/6/88
Sidecar. Rolf Biland/Kurt Waltisperg (CH) *LCR-Krauser*, 1m25.87s = 110.53mph (177.88kmh) 12/6/88

SILVERSTONE, Great Britain

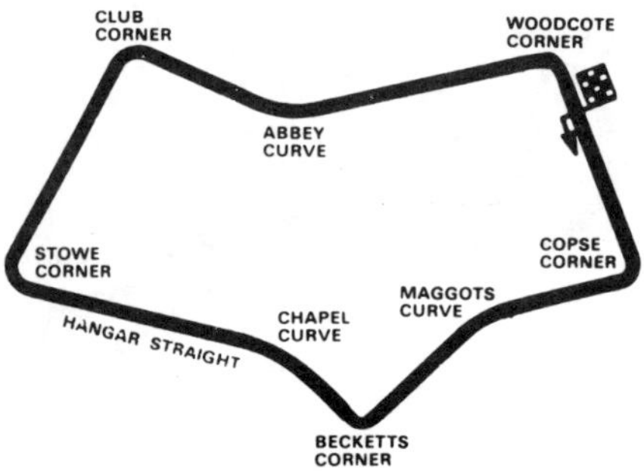

Length Long circuit, 2.932 miles (4.719km) and short circuit, 1.60 miles (2.57km)

Contact Address Silverstone Circuits Ltd., Silverstone, Towcester, Northants NN12 8TN. Tel: 0327 857271. Telex: 311164 SCBRDC

Location 10 miles (16.09km) west of Northampton

Nearest International Airport London Heathrow or Birmingham

Lap records

Long circuit
80cc. Stefan Dorflinger (CH) *Krauser*, 1m43.13s = 102.17mph (164.39kmh) 2/8/86
125cc. Angel Nieto (E) *Garelli*, 1m38.41s = 107.07mph (172.31kmh) 5/8/84
250cc. Christian Sarron (F) *Yamaha*, 1m33.40s = 112.81mph (181.55kmh) 5/8/84
500cc. Kenny Roberts (USA) *Yamaha*, 1m28.20s = 119.47mph (192.27kmh) 31/7/83
Sidecar. Egbert Streuer/Bernard Schnieders (NL) *LCR-Yamaha*, 1m31.64s = 114.98mph (183.75kmh) 2/8/86

Short circuit
250cc. Donnie McLeod (GB) *EMC*, 1m01.4s = 94.28mph (151.72kmh) 17/9/87
1300cc. Gary Noel (GB) *Yamaha*, 1m04.30s = 90.03mph (144.88kmh) 17/9/87

SNETTERTON, Great Britain

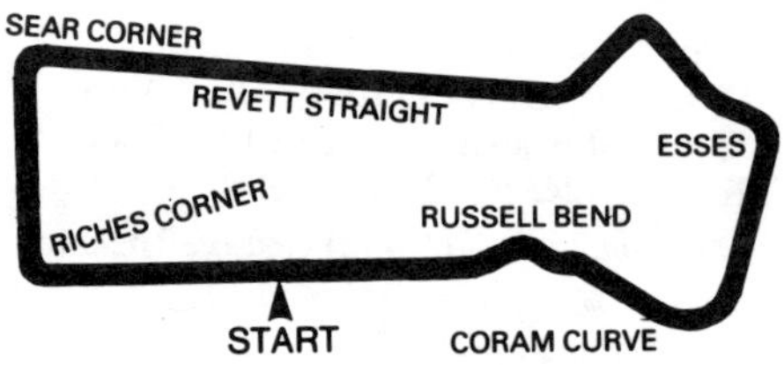

Length 1.91 miles (3.08km)

Contact Address Snetterton Circuit Ltd., Norwich, Norfolk NR16 2JU. Tel: 095387 387/303 Fax: 0953 878220

Location 25 miles (40.23km) south west of Norwich

Nearest International Airport Stansted

Lap records
125cc. Neville Busson (GB) *Honda*, 1m19.7s = 86.58mph (139.33kmh) 9/3/80
250cc. Carl Fogarty (GB) *Yamaha*, 1m09.9s = 98.72mph (158.87kmh) 19/7/86
350cc. Tony Rogers (GB) *Yamaha*, 1m11.8s = 96.11mph (154.66kmh) 5/10/80
Outright/500cc/1300cc. Roger Burnett (GB) *Honda*, 1m08.0s = 101.48mph (163.31kmh) 20/7/86
Sidecar. Derek Bayley/Bryan Nixon (GB) *LCR-Yamaha*, 1m09.9s = 98.72mph (158.87kmh) 14/7/85

SPA-FRANCORCHAMPS, Belgium

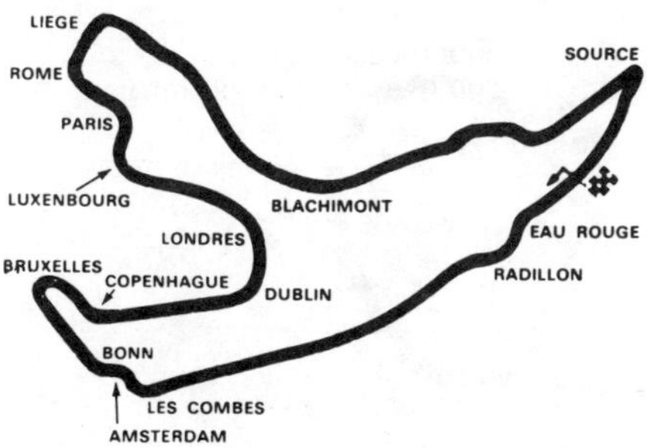

Length 4.33 miles (6.976km)

Contact Address Circuit de Spa-Francorchamps, Route de L'Eau-Rouge 289, B-48 Stavelot. Tel: 87 275138/275258. Telex: 49271 CISPFR

Location 25 miles (40km) south-east of Liege

Nearest International Airports Brussels and Cologne (West Germany)

Lap records

80cc. Stefan Dorflinger (CH) *Zundapp*, 2m58.42s = 87.10mph (140.17kmh) 8/7/84

125cc. A. Auinger (A) *MBA*, 2m45.36s = 93.88mph (151.08kmh) 3/7/88

250cc. Toni Mang (D) *Honda*, 2m32.06s = 102.09mph (165.30kmh) 3/7/88

500cc. Eddie Lawson (USA) *Yamaha*, 2m28.35s = 104.647mph (168.412kmh) 7/7/85

Sidecar. Egbert Streuer/Bernard Schnieders (NL) *LCR-Yamaha*, 2m36.05s = 99.483mph (160.102kmh) 7/7/86

SUZUKA, Japan

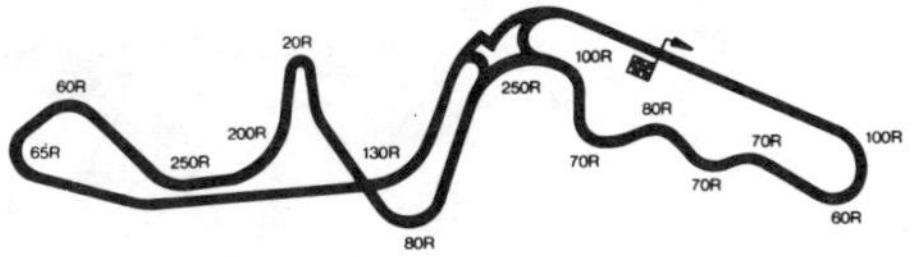

Length 3.69 miles (5.94km)

Contact Address Suzuka Grand Prix Circuit, 7992 Ino-cho, Suzuka-shi, Mie. Tel: 593 781111. Telex: 4947404. Fax: 593 789181

Location 37 miles (60km) from Nagoya

Nearest International Airport Tokyo

Lap records

250cc. Sito Pons (E) *Honda*, 2m19.63s = 93.85mph (151.04kmh) 27/3/88

500cc. Kevin Schwantz (USA) *Suzuki*, 2m15.22s = 96.93mph (155.99kmh) 27/3/88

THRUXTON, Great Britain

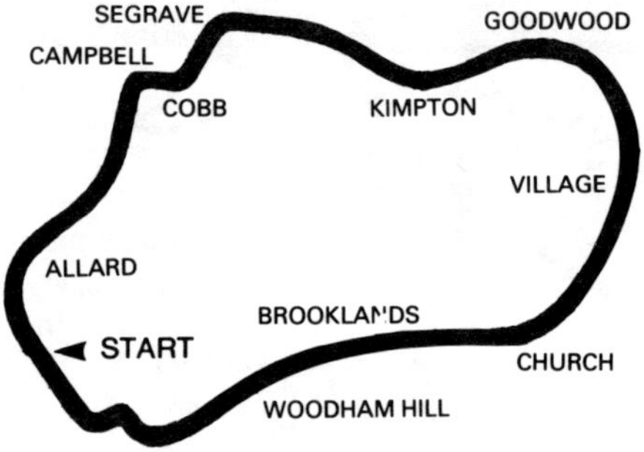

Length 2.35 miles (3.79km)

Contact Address Thruxton (BARC) Ltd, Thruxton Circuit, Andover, Hants
Tel: 026 4772606/4772696. Telex: 47591 BARCPXG

Location 7 miles (11km) west of Andover

Nearest International Airport London Heathrow

Lap records
80cc. Ian McConnachie (GB) *Krauser,* 1m38.9s = 85.75mph (137.99kmh) 13/4/86
125cc. Alex Bedford (GB) *Honda,* 1m30.5s = 93.71mph (150.77kmh) 17/4/88
250cc. Niall Mackenzie (GB) *Armstrong,* 1m24.3s = 100.61mph (161.91kmh) 6/9/86
350cc. Peter Hubbard (GB) *Yamaha,* 1m23.5s = 101.58mph (163.44kmh) 21/8/88
500cc. Roger Burnett (GB) *Honda,* 1m24.0s = 100.97mph (162.46kmh) 6/9/86
Outright Trevor Nation (GB) *Norton,* 1m22.3s = 103.06mph (165.82kmh) 20/8/88
Sidecar. Mick Boddice/Eddie Yarker (GB) *Yamaha,* 1m24.9s = 99.90mph (160.73kmh) 20/8/88

1989 CALENDAR
Arai
3

1989 WORLD CHAMPIONSHIP: 80, 125, 250, 500 AND SIDECAR CLASSES

26 March
Japan *(Suzuka)*
125, 250 and 500 classes

MFJ, Co.,
Honda Land Ltd.,
Akasaka Twin Tower,
Higashi kan, 16F,
2-17-22 Akasaka,
Minato-Ku, J-Tokyo 107.
Tel: (03) 5823221. Telex: 2227048 HONDLA J
Fax: (03) 5823023

9 April
Australia *(Phillip Island)*
125, 250 and 500 classes

The Auto Cycle Council of Australia,
PO Box 132,
Parkholme SA 5043,
Australia.

16 April
USA *(Laguna Seca)*
250, 500 and sidecar classes

Sports Car Racing Association,
Monterey Peninsula,
PO Box Scramp,
Monterey, CA 93490,
USA

30 April
Spain *(Jerez)*
80, 125, 250 and 500 classes

Real Federation Motociclista Española,
General Pardinas 71,
28006 Madrid
Tel: (1) 2625342/2625343
Telex: 47851 RFME E

14 May
Italy *(Misano)*
80, 125, 250 and 500 classes

Federazione Motociclistica Italiana,
70 Viale Tiziano,
1-00196 Roma.
Tel: (6) 3964309 Telex: 620309 FMI I

28 May
West Germany *(Hockenheim)*
80, 125, 250, 500 and sidecar classes

ADAC – Wurttemberg EU,
Sportabteilung AM Neckartor 2,
D-7000 Stuttgart I.
Tel: (0711) 2800135

4 June
Austria *(Salzburgring)*
125, 250, 500 and sidecar classes

ARBO Salzburg,
Munchner-Bundesstrasse 9,
A-5020 Salzburg.
Tel: (0622) 33601 Telex: 633585

11 June
Yugoslavia *(Rijeka)*
80, 250 and 500 classes

Auto-Moto Club Kvarner,
PP 68, YU-51000 Rijeka.
Tel: (051) 617/777 Telex: 24512

24 June
Holland *(Assen)*
80, 125, 250, 500 and sidecar classes

Stichting Circuit van Drenthe,
PO Box 150,
NL-9400 AD Assen.
Tel: (05920) 55000 Telex: 53821

2 July
Belgium *(Spa-Francorchamps)*
125, 250, 500 and sidecar classes

Fédération Motocycliste de Belgique,
550 Chaussée de Louvain,
Bte 7 1030 Bruxelles.
Tel: (2) 7369912/7358751
Telex: 65196 BEMOTO

16 July
France *(Le Mans)*
125, 250, 500 and sidecar classes

ASM de L'AC Ouest,
Cedex 19,
72040 Le Mans.
Tel: (43) 725025 Telex: 720653 ACOUEST

6 August
Great Britain *(Donington Park)*
125, 250, 500 and sidecar classes

Auto-Cycle Union,
Miller House,
Corporation Street,
Rugby, Warwickshire CV21 2DN.
Tel: (0788) 70332 Telex: 311156 ACU G

13 August
Sweden *(Anderstorp)*
125, 250, 500 and sidecar classes

Anderstorp RC,
Box 180,
S-33400 Anderstorp.
Tel: (371) 16170 Telex: 70327

27 August
Czechoslovakia *(Brno)*
80, 125, 250, 500 and sidecar classes

AMS Basty 8,
CS-657, 43 Brno.
Tel: (5) 27674

17 September
Brazil *(Goiania or Rio)*
250 and 500 classes

Confederacao Brasileira de Motociclismo,
Av. Paulista 509-1 and CJ and 104,
Sao Paulo.
Tel: (11) 2842011

1989 TT FORMULA ONE WORLD CHAMPIONSHIP

14 May
Japan *(Sugo)*

MFJ, Sugo Sports Club,
Sugo Murata Cho,
Shibata-Gun,
Miyagi-Pref,
989–14, Japan.

3 June
Great Britain *(Isle of Man)*

Auto-Cycle Union,
Miller House,
Corporation Street,
Rugby, Warwickshire CV21 2DN.
Tel: (0788) 70332 Telex: 311156 ACU G

2 July
Portugal *(Vila Real)*

Clube Automovel de Vila Real,
P-5000 Vila Real.

16 July
Finland *(Kouvala)*

Suomen Moottorilitto RY,
Radiokatu 12,
PO Box 27,
00240 Helsinki.
Tel: (0) 1582251 Telex: 121797 SVUL SF

13 August
Northern Ireland *(Dundrod)*

Ulster Centre Promotions Ltd.,
60 Donegal Pass,
Belfast, BT7 1BU

1989 SUPERBIKE WORLD CHAMPIONSHIP

27 March
Great Britain *(Donington Park)*

Auto-Cycle Union
Miller House,
Corporation Street,
Rugby, Warwickshire CV21 2DN.
Tel: (0788) 70332 Telex: 311156 ACU G

30 April
Hungary *(Hungaroring)*

Magyar Auto es Motosport,
Szovetseg,
Romer Floris U 4/A Pt. 1,
1227 Budapest.
Tel: (1) 152040/158469
Telex: 224218 MAKBP H

14 May
Brazil *(Rio De Janeiro)*

Confederacao Brasileira de Motociclismo,
Av. Paulista 509–1 and CJ and 104,
Sao Paulo.
Tel: (11) 2842011

21 May
Argentina *(Buenos Aires)*

Federation Argentina de Motoclismo,
Campona 5661,
Buenos Aires.
Tel: (1) 5715421 Telex: 22654 CTF AR

4 June
Canada *(Mosport)*

Canadian Motorcycle Association,
Box 448, Station B,
Hamilton, Ontario L8L IJ4.
Tel: (416) 5225705

11 June
USA *(Brainerd)*

American Motorcyclist Association,
PO Box 6114,
Westerville,
Ohio 43081.
Tel: (614) 8912425 Telex: 245392

22 June
Holland *(Assen)*

Stitching Circuit van Drenthe,
PO Box 150,
NL-9400 AD Assen.
Tel: (05920) 55000 Telex: 53821

2 July
Austria *(Oesterreichring)*

Triumph Club Wien,
Cumberlandstr. 31,
A-1140 Wien.
Tel: (222) 892745

30 July
France *(Paul Ricard)*

Moto-Club Paul Ricard,
Route Nationale 8,
F-83330 Le Beausset.
Tel: (94) 224617/225513 &
(91) 547530/547597
Telex: 400988

27 August
Japan *(Sugo)*

MFJ, Sugo Sports Club,
Sugo Murata Cho,
Shibata-Gun,
Miyagi-Pref,
989-14, Japan.

17 September
West Germany *(Hockenheim)*

Badischeer Msc EU, Motodrom,
D-6832 Hockenheim.
Tel: (06205) 7718

24 September
Italy *(Pergusa)*

Federazione Motociclistica Italiana,
70 Viale Tiziano,
1-00196 Roma.
Tel: (6) 3964309 Telex: 620309 FMI I

8 October
Australia *(Oran Park)*

The Auto Cycle Council of Australia,
PO Box 132,
Parkholme SA 5043,
Australia.

15 October
New Zealand *(Manfield)*

New Zealand Auto Cycle Union,
PO Box 968,
Hamilton.
Tel: (71) 393464
Telex: C/O 2273
NZ/21215

1989 FIM COUPE D'ENDURANCE

22/23 April
France *(Le Mans)* 24 hours

ASM de L'AC Ouest,
Cedex 19,
72040 Le Mans.
Tel: (43) 725025 Telex: 720637 ACOUEST

30 July
Japan *(Suzuka)* 8 hours

MFJ, Co.,
Honda Land Ltd.,
Akasaka Twin Tower,
Higashi kan, 16F,
2-17-22 Akasaka,
Minato-Ku, J-Tokyo 107.
Tel: (03) 5823221 Telex: 2227048 Honda J
Fax: (03) 5823023

13/14 August
Belgium *(Spa Francorchamps)* 24 hours

Fédération Motocycliste de Belgique,
550 Chaussée de Louvain,
Bte 7 1030 Bruxelles.
Tel: (2) 7369912/7358751
Telex: 65196 BEMOTO

10/11 September
France *(Paul Ricard)* 24 hours

Moto-Club Paul Ricard,
Route Nationale 8,
F-83330 Le Beausset.
Tel: (94) 224617/225513 and
(91) 547530/547597
Telex: 400988

1989 EUROPEAN CHAMPIONSHIPS

12 March
Portugal *(Sintra)*
125, 500 and sidecar classes

Federacao Portuguesa de Motociclismo,
Av. Duque de Avila 9–5,
1000 Lisboa.
Tel: (1) 525146 Telex: 43447 FISPOR P

19 March
Spain *(Jarama)*
125, 250 and 500 Classes

Real Federation Motociclista Española,
General Pardinas 71,
28006 Madrid.
Tel: (1) 2625343 Telex: 47851 RFME E

2 April
Belgium *(Zolder)*
125, 250 and 500 classes

Fédération Motocycliste de Belgique,
550 Chaussée de Louvain,
Bte 7 1030 Bruxelles.
Tel: (2) 7369912/7358751
Telex: 65196 BEMOTO

9 April
Italy *(Monza)*
125, 250 and 500 classes

Federazione Motociclistica Italiana,
70 Viale Tiziano,
1-00196 Roma.
Tel: (6) 3964309 Telex: 620309 FMI I

7 May
Austria *(Salzburgring)*
125, 250 and 500 classes

ARBO Salzburg,
Munchner-Bundesstrasse 9,
A-5020 Salzburg.
Tel: (0622) 33601 Telex: 633585

21 May
Sweden *(Anderstorp)*
125, 250 and 500 classes
Anderstorp RC,
Box 180,
S-33400 Anderstorp.
Tel: (371) 16170 Telex: 70327

11 June
Czechoslovakia *(Most)*
125, 250, 500 and sidecar classes

AMK. Banske Stavby,
Gottwaldova PS 33,
CS-434 93 Most.
Tel: (035) 79691 Telex: 18421

20 June
Holland *(Assen)*
125, 250, 500 and sidecar classes

Stichting Circuit van Drenthe,
PO Box 150,
NL-9400 AD Assen.
Tel: (05920) 55000 Telex: 53821

9 July
San Marino *(Misano)*
125, 250 and 500 classes

Federazione Sammarinese Motociclistica,
Casella Postale No 30,
Borgo Maggiore, 47031,
Rep Di San Marino.
Tel: (541) 903299/902407
Telex: 505 DIRPOSTE SD

16 July
Yugoslavia *(Rijeka)*
125, 250 and 500 classes

Auto-Moto Club Kvarner,
PP 68, YU-51000 Rijeka.
Tel: (051) 617/777 Telex: 24512

30 July
France *(Paul Ricard)*
125, 250 and sidecar classes

Moto-Club Paul Ricard,
Route Nationale 8,
F-83330 Le Beausset.
Tel: (94) 224617/225513 and
(91) 547530/547597
Telex: 400988

27 August
Great Britain *(Donington Park)*
125, 250, 500 and sidecar classes

Auto-Cycle Union,
Miller House,
Corporation Street,
Rugby, Warwickshire CV21 2DN.
Tel: (0788) 70332 Telex: 311156 ACU G

17 September
West Germany *(Hockenheim)*
125, 250, Superstreet and sidecars

Badischeer MSC EU, Motodrom,
D-6832 Hockenheim.
Tel: (06205) 7718

BRITISH ROAD RACE FIXTURES

March			
4	C	Snetterton Road Races	Bantam Racing Club
5	C	Mallory Park Road Races	EMRA
11	CR	Oulton Park Road Races	Nantwich & DMC
11	C	Five Mile Road Sprint	Jersey MC & LCC
12	N	Cadwell Park Road Races	
12	C	Mallory Park Road Races	Derby Phoenix MCC
18/19	C	Snetterton Road Races	Newmarket MCC
19	C	Mallory Park Road Races	Clubmans Racing Club
24	I	**Brands Hatch Road Races**	
24	C	Darley Moor Road Races	Darley Moor MCRRC Ltd
25	RR	Cadwell Park Road Races	Vincent HRD Owners Club
25/26	C	Snetterton Road Races	Clubmans Racing Club
25/27	R	Santa Pod Drag Races	BDRA
25/27	R	Long Marston Drag Races	NDRA
26/27	C	Pembrey Road Races	Port Talbot MCRC
26	C	Cadwell Park Road Races	Vintage MCC
26/27	I	**World Superbike Championship**	**ACU/Pathfinders & Derby**
27	CR	Oulton Park Road Races	Wirral 100 MC
27	C	Cadwell Park Road Races	Classic RMCC
27	C	Bouley Bay Hillclimb	Jersey MC & LCC
April			
1/2	C	Cadwell Park Road Races	Clubmans Racing Club
2	N	Mallory Park Road Races	Auto 66 Club
2	C	Colerne Road Races	North Glos MCC
8	N	Kirkistown Road Races	
8	C	Cadwell Park Road Races	Retford & DMCC Ltd
8/9	R	North Weald Drag Races	BDRA
9	CR	Mallory Park Road Races	EMRA
15	N	Castle Combe Road Races	Clubmans RC/North Glos MCC
15/16	R	Long Marston Drag Races	NDRA
16	N	Thruxton Road Races	Clubmans/Southampton & DMCC
16	CR	Lydden Road Races	Astra MCC
16	C	Darley Moor Road Races	Darley Moor MCRRC Ltd
22	C	Aintree Road Races	Aintree MCRC
22	C	Cadwell Park Road Races	Bantam Racing Club
22	C	Ouston Road Races	North East MCRC
23	N	Scarborough Road Races	Scarborough Racing Combine
23	C	Mallory Park Road Races	Clubmans Racing Club
29	C	Snetterton Road Races	Newmarket MCC
29	C	Cadwell Park Road Races	Derby Phoenix MCC
29 Apr–1May	R	Santa Pod Drag Races	BDRA

April			
30	N	Snetterton Road Races	
30	C	Mallory Park Road Races	Retford & DMCC Ltd
MAY			
1	N	Brands Hatch Road Races	Kent Racing Combine
1	C	Donington Park Road Races	Clubmans Racing Club
1	C	Les Val Des Terres Hillclimb	Guernsey MC & CC
6	C	Brands Hatch Road Races	Clubmans Racing Club
6/7	N	Carnaby Road Races	Auto 66 Club
6/7	C	Snetterton Road Races	Classic RMCC
7	N	Pembrey Road Races	Aberaman MCC
7	R	York Drag Races	Pennine DRC
14	N	Donington Park Road Races	Pathfinders & Derby MCC
14	C	Three Sisters Road Race	Preston & DMCC
17–20	I	**North West 200 Road Races**	MCUI
20	C	Ouston Road Races	North East MCRC
20/21	C	Snetterton Road Races	Clubmans Racing Club
21	N	Mallory Park Road Races	Retford & DMCC Ltd
27–29	R	Santa Pod Drag Races	BDRA
28	N	Mallory Park Road Races	
28	C	Keevil Road Races	North Glos MCC
28	C	Snetterton Road Races	Vintage MCC
29	C	Pembrey Road Races	Port Talbot MCRC
29	C	Darley Moor Road Races	Darley Moor MCRRC Ltd
29	C	Bouley Bay Hillclimb	Jersey MC & LCC
30	C	Aintree Road Races	Aintree MCRC
May 29–June 9	I	**Isle of Man TT Races**	
		World Formula One	**ACU**
June			
4	C	Pembrey Road Races	Vintage MCC
10	CR	Oulton Park Road Races	Cheshire MCRRC
11	N	Mallory Park Road Races	Retford & DMCC Ltd
17	CR	New Brighton Prom Road Races	Wirral 100 MC
17/18	NR	Long Marston Drag Races	NDRA
17/18	C	Lydden Road Races	Classic RMCC
18	N	Donington Park Road Races	Pathfinders & Derby MCC
18	R	York Drag Races	Pennine DRC
24	N	Aberdare Park Road Races	Aberaman MCC
24	C	Aintree Road Races	Aintree MCRC
24	C	Snetterton Road Races	Bantam Racing Club
24/25	I	**Santa Pod Drag Races**	**BDRA**
24/25	I	**Long Marston Drag Races**	**NDRA**
25	N	Cadwell Park Road Races	Louth & DMCC
25	C	Darley Moor Road Races	Darley Moor MCRRC Ltd

July			
1	C	Oulton Park Road Races	Vintage MCC
1/2	N	Scarborough Road Races	Scarborough Racing Combine
2	C	Mallory Park Road Races	EMRA
3	C	Merthyr Sprint	Merthyr MC
8	C	Brands Hatch Road Races	Clubmans Racing Club
8/9	N	Knockhill Road Races	Knockhil MCRC
8/9	R	Santa Pod Drag Races	BDRA
9	CR	Three Sisters Road Races	Bolton MC/North West Centre
9	C	Pembrey Road Races	Port Talbot MCRC
9	C	Darley Moor Road Races	Darley Moor MCRRC Ltd
15	C	Castle Combe Road Races	North Glos MCC
15	C	Ouston Road Races	North East MCRC
15/16	N	Snetterton Road Races	Snetterton Combine
15/16	R	Long Marston Drag Races	NDRA
15/16	C	Brands Hatch Road Races	Classic RMCC
16	CR	Lydden Road Races	Astra MCC
16	C	Cadwell Park Road Races	Vintage MCC
16	C	Mallory Park Road Races	Derby Phoenix MCC
20	C	Bouley Bay Hillclimb	Jersey MC & LCC
22	C	Aintree Road Races	Aintree MCRC
22	C	Cadwell Park, Road Races	Retford & DMC Ltd
23	N	Mallory Park Road Races	Auto 66 Club
23	C	Pembrey Sprint	Rhondda MC
29	C	Snetterton Road Races	Bantam Racing Club
29	C	Cadwell Park Road Races	Clubmans Racing Club
29/30	N	Cadwell Park Road Races	Clubmans Racing Club
29/30	N	Mallory Park Road Races	Auto 66 Club
29/30	R	TBA Drag Races	BDRA
30	C	Three Sisters Road Races	Vintage MCC
30	C	Mallory Park Road Races	Retford & DMCC Ltd
August			
6	I	**World Championship Road Race Grand Prix**	**ACU**
6	R	York Drag Races	Pennine DRC
9–12	I	**World TT Formula One Road Races (Ireland)**	**MCUI**
12/13	C	Snetterton Road Races	Clubmans Racing Club
13	N	Carnaby Road Races	Auto 66 Club
13	C	Colerne Road Races	North Glos MCC
13	C	Pembrey Road Races	Port Talbot MCRC
13	C	Three Sisters Road Races	Preston & DMCC
19	C	Aintree Road Races	Aintree MCRC
19/20	C	Cadwell Park Road Races	Classic RMCC
20	N	Thruxton Road Races	Clubmans/Southampton & DMCC

August			
20	C	Mallory Park Road Races	EMRA
26	C	Brands Hatch Road Races	Vintage MCC
26/27	I	**European Road Race Championship**	**Pathfinders & Derby MCC**
26/27	N	Pembrey Road Races	Port Talbot MCRC
26/28	R	Santa Pod Drag Races	BDRA
26/28	R	Long Marston Drag Races	NDRA
27	C	Mallory Park Road Races	Clubmans Racing Club
28	N	Cadwell Park Road Races	Louth & DMCC
28	CR	Oulton Park Road Races	Cheshire Centre ACU
28	C	Darley Moor Road Races	Darley Moor MCRRC Ltd
28	C	Les Val Des Terres Hillclimb	Guernsey MC & CC
September			
2/3	I	Mallory Park Road Races	EMRA
2/3	R	Long Marston Drag Races	NDRA
9/10	I	**Scarborough Road Races**	**Scarborough Racing Combine**
9/10	R	North Weald Drag Races	BDRA
10	C	Pembrey Sprint	Rhondda MC
16	C	Snetterton Road Races	Bantam Racing Club
16	C	Aintree Road Races	Aintree MCRC
16	C	Ouston Road Races	North East MCRC
16/17	R	Long Marston Drag Races	NDRA
16/17	C	Cadwell Park Road Races	Vintage MCC
17	N	Brands Hatch Road Races	Kent Racing Combine
17	C	Mallory Park Road Races	Classic RMC
17	C	Darley Moor Road Races	Darley Moor MCRRC Ltd
17	R	York Drag Races	Pennine DRC
23/24	I	**Santa Pod Drag Races**	**BDRA**
23/24	N	Cadwell Park Road Races	Louth & DMCC
23/24	C	Snetterton Road Races	Classic RMCC
24	C	Keevil Road Races	North Glos MCC
24	C	Pembrey Road Races	Port Talbot MCRC
October			
1	I	**World TT Formula One Road Races**	**ACU/Pathfinders & Derby MCC**
7	RR	Thruxton Road Races	Clubmans/Southampton & DMCC
8	N	Snetterton Road Races	Snetterton Combine
8	N/C	Darley Moor Road Races	Darley Moor MCRRC Ltd
8	C	Three Sisters Road Races	Preston & DMCC
8	C	Mallory Park Road Races	Vintage MCC
14	C	Five Mile Road Sprint	Jersey MC & LCC
14/15	I	**Brands Hatch Road Races**	**Kent Racing Combine**
14/15	C	Cadwell Park Road Races	Retford & DMC Ltd

October			
15	NR	Mallory Park Road Races	Auto 66 Club
15	CR	Lydden Road Races	Astra MCC
21	RR	Cadwell Park Road Races	Vincent HRD Owners Club
21/22	N	Carnaby Road Races	Auto 66 Club
21/22	R	Long Marston Drag Races	NDRA
22	C	Cadwell Park Road Races	Vintage MCC
28	C	Silverstone Road Races	Motor Cycling Club
28/29	C	Snetterton Road Races	Clubmans Racing Club
29	C	Mallory Park Road Races	Pegasus MCC
November			
4/5	R	Santa Pod Drag Races	BDRA
December			
26	C	Mallory Park Road Races	Clubmans Racing Club

Key: *I = International, N = National, NR = National Restricted, R = Restricted CR = Centre Restricted, C = Centre.*

IRISH ROAD RACE & SHORT CIRCUIT FIXTURES

March		
27	Kirkistown	Belfast & District MCC
April		
1	Nutts Corner	Mid-Antrim MCC
8	Aghadowey	MCRRCI
15	Cookstown 100 Road Race	Cookstown MCC
22	Kirkistown	Lightweight MCC
29	Aghadowey	Hillsborough MCC
May		
1	Kirkistown	Bandbridge MCC
6	Tandragee 100 Road Race	North Armagh MCC
14	Mondello Park Leinster 200	Leinster MCC
20	International North-West 200	Colerain MCC
June		
17	Killinchey 150 Road Race	Killinchy MCC
24	Aghadowey	MCRRCI
30/1 July	Milverton Road Race (Skerries)	Loughshinny MCC
July		
13	Nutts Corner	Dundrod MCC
22	Nutts Corner	North Armagh MCC
29	Temple 100 Road Race	Temple MCC
August		
5/6	Mondello Park Race of the Year	Fingal MCC
12	Ulster Grand Prix	Ulster Centre Promotions
19	Mid-Antrim 150 Road Race	Mid-Antrim MCC
Sept		
2	Carrowdore 100 Road Race	Belfast & District MCC
9	Killalane Road Race	Loughshinney MCC
16	Aghadowey	MCRRCI
23	Nutts Corner	Mid-Antrim MCC
30	Kirkistown	Killinchy MCC
October		
7	Kirkistown	Belfast & District
14	Kirkistown	Hillsborough MCC

All dates are subject to offical confirmation.

Previous page *Michael Swann hopes to retain next year both the Ulster and Irish Road Race Championships on his 500cc Suzuki.*
(John Savage, Newton Ardes Chronicle)

THE WAY IT WAS
Mick Woollett

Thirty years ago Mick Woollett, who compiles the grand prix statistics for Rothmans, was a sidecar passenger competing in the world championship. Here he takes a look back.

Slap-happy and carefree. That was motocycle racing 30 years ago. Of course for the works riders it was a serious and far more dangerous profession than it is today. But for the bulk of grand prix entries it was a paid holiday. Not very well paid, it's true. Most organisers relied on the riders' enthusiasm to compete – especially our own Isle of Man TT organisers who sowed the seeds of future problems by paying appallingly bad start and prize money.

The majority of riders were completely free agents. They bought a couple of machines early in the year – usually a brace of Nortons or an AJS and a Matchless – for around £1,000 the pair, loaded them into a Ford Transit and set off for the races. Some were sponsored by their local dealers but most were their own masters. They organised starts in the early meetings by post; and if they did not get a reply they would set off regardless and try to arrange a start when they arrived at the meeting. There they would meet organisers from events to be held later in the year. The word would flash round the paddock: 'The man from the German Grand Prix is here. He's signing up entries and is paying good money.' Riders keen to move on to the German would track him down or, if they were well-known, would wait for him to appear.

There was no official starting money scale as there is today and each rider had to haggle to get as much as he could. Organisers obviously wanted big name riders, but they also wanted value for money and would favour competitors able to start in two races above those with only one machine. For this reason the majority doubled up with either 500cc and 350cc machines or 250cc and 125cc. It also led to sidecar competitors, both riders and passengers, taking along 'start money specials' which they rode in the solo classes to help the organiser fill the grid. At that time I was sidecar passenger with Edgar Strub of Switzerland, and he had a very fast 350cc Norton which he occasionally raced.

There were far more international races held in those days – virtually all on genuine road courses or on park circuits. The local motorcycle club would obtain permission to run a race; the roads would be closed for a few hours for practising and on Sunday for the race itself – and everyone had a good time. Safety precautions were minimal. A few straw bales here and there and a rope to keep the crowd from actually standing on the circuit were deemed good enough. One of the first Continental races that I rode in as passenger with former world champion Cyril Smith was at Chimay in Belgium in 1956. We were first away at the start of practice and were soon thundering down the back straight, propelled at some 120mph by an ex-works outside-flywheel Norton engine when Cyril braked, tapped me on the shoulder and pointed ahead. There, without a care in the world, was a Belgian family in their little car, pottering along at 40mph, luckily going the same way as we were. We laughed about it at the time, but supposing they had been coming the other way, round a bend ...

The Austrians used to run their Grand prix on the autobahn just outside Salzburg. In those days the Munich to Vienna stretch ended just beyond Salzburg and somehow the Austrian federation persuaded the local authorities to let them have the last couple of

Mick Woollett partners Cyril Smith to victory at Mettet, Belgium, in 1956.

miles for the race. They laid out a circuit using the two carriageways linked by a hairpin at one end and a tunnel that went under the autobahn at the other, and with a series of bends at a cloverleaf junction in the middle. I actually finished third passengering with Edgar Strub, but we were struck from the results that evening when I was found guilty of kicking a rival passenger during the race – which gives me some sort of claim to fame, I suppose!

Another feature of many races in those days was that competitors and mechanics rode the race machines from the paddock to the centre of the host town for the official weigh-in. It was noisy, great fun and made the local residents very much aware that a race was on and that they should turn out, pay their money and watch the event the following day. Spectators were often a problem. They would crowd forward until they were right on the circuit. At Zaragoza in Spain, where we raced on a park circuit, a policeman, attempting to control the crowd, stepped into the road and was struck and killed by solo competitor Luigi Taveri who later became famous as a Honda factory rider.

The factory riders were very much a group apart. They travelled mainly by car with their machines carried in the factory transporter – in Norton's case a not very imposing

Carefree days – Mick Woollett, in the natty beret, and Cyril Smith relaxing in the Assen paddock.

battleship-grey van. And they stayed in hotels, booking from year to year so that those in the know could find them. For the Belgian Grand Prix Joe Craig and the Norton riders had their headquarters at the Golden Lion in Stavelot village; DKW were at the La Source Hotel alongside the hairpin of the same name, while Gilera were up the road at the Railway Hotel by the level crossing. The 'privateers' camped in the paddock. Cyril Smith had a small van and trailer. We lived in the van and carried the outfit in the trailer. We had a small cooker in the van but that was about all – no table or chairs, no sink or running water – a far, far cry from today's motorhomes.

Because the machines were relatively simple four-strokes they needed little maintenance. With luck, and provided you didn't over-rev it, a Norton engine would do half a season between overhauls. Tyres would last several races and when they became worn you took them along to Dunlop or Avon and got new ones fitted. No baffling choice of mixes or compounds, dry or wet, slick or treads. There was only one compound and tread – all you had to do was to decide the pressure you wanted!

There was little sponsorship apart from dealers who might help a local rider by providing machines at cost price and it was only the plug, oil and petrol companies who put any real money into the sport – notably Lodge, KLG, Castrol, Shell and Esso, who paid top riders good money and who helped everyone by providing their products free of charge.

Competitors all wore plain black or dark-brown leathers and the factory riders, reducing weight to a minimum, used to wear thin, unlined horse-hide, skin-tight suits. The only colour was on the helmets – the good old pudding-basin type which cost £3 for the standard version or £3.50 for the super 'low crown' from Sammy Lewis of Carburton Street off Great Portland Street in London.

The machines carried no advertising at all apart from the maker's name. Travel was complicated by severe customs controls at virtually every frontier – there was no Common Market in those days. Belgium was a particular thorn in the racer's side and used to impose a tax for every day a visiting motor vehicle spent in the country. But not every frontier post imposed the same tax and we soon got to know the little back roads where the *douane* waved you through ... where there's a will there's a way!

Transport was a major problem. The roads were often poor, there was nothing like the motorway network that exists now and the vehicles used were stone-age compared to today's. When I was passengering for Edgar Strub he decided to compete in races in Sweden and Finland. This meant a round trip of some 3,000 miles from his Swiss base. Edgar came up with the cost-saving solution of transporting his BMW outfit with spares, tools and camping gear in a standard VW Beetle! He took all but the driver's seat out, shoe-horned the BMW, less front wheel, into the space alongside the driver, put the spares, tools, camping gear, riding kit and front wheel in the space left, the sidecar on the roof – and set off! I travelled out from England in a small Ford van and we competed in a couple of memorable races, one on a street circuit, including tramlines, around the Olympic Stadium in Helsinki.

I remember that the race organisers installed us in a huge concrete garage and that I slept under the stairs on a pile of workers' overalls. We were good enough to finish third in the race, too – it wasn't that we were no-hopers. It was just the way it was in the 1950s – great fun.

RECORDS

WORLD SOLO CHAMPIONS 1949–88

	50cc/80cc	125cc	250cc	350cc	500cc	Sidecar 500cc
1949	—	N. Pagani	B. Ruffo	F. Frith	L. Graham	E. Oliver/D. Jenkinson
1950	—	B. Ruffo	D. Ambrosini	B. Foster	U. Masetti	E. Oliver/L. Dobelli
1951	—	C. Ubbiali	B. Ruffo	G. Duke	G. Duke	E. Oliver/L. Dobelli
1952	—	C. Sandford	E. Lorenzetti	G. Duke	U. Masetti	C. Smith/R. Clements
1953	—	W. Haas	W. Haas	F. Anderson	G. Duke	E. Oliver/S. Dibben
1954	—	R. Hollaus	W. Haas	F. Anderson	G. Duke	W. Noll/F. Cron
1955	—	C. Ubbiali	H. Müller	W. Lomas	G. Duke	W. Faust/K. Remmert
1956	—	C. Ubbiali	C. Ubbiali	W. Lomas	J. Surtees	W. Noll/F. Cron
1957	—	T. Provini	C. Sandford	K. Campbell	L. Liberati	F. Hillebrand/M. Grunwald
1958	—	C. Ubbiali	T. Provini	J. Surtees	J. Surtees	W. Schneider/H. Strauss
1959	—	C. Ubbiali	C. Ubbiali	J. Surtees	J. Surtees	W. Schneider/H. Strauss
1960	—	C. Ubbiali	C. Ubbiali	J. Surtees	J. Surtees	H. Fath/A. Wohlgemuth
1961	—	T. Phillis	M. Hailwood	G. Hocking	G. Hocking	M. Deubel/E. Horner
1962	E. Degner	L. Taveri	J. Redman	J. Redman	M. Hailwood	M. Deubel/E. Horner
1963	H. Anderson	H. Anderson	J. Redman	J. Redman	M. Hailwood	M. Deubel/E. Horner
1964	H. Anderson	L. Taveri	P. Read	J. Redman	M. Hailwood	M. Deubel/E. Horner
1965	R. Bryans	H. Anderson	P. Read	J. Redman	M. Hailwood	F. Scheidegger/J. Robinson
1966	H. G. Anscheidt	L. Taveri	M. Hailwood	M. Hailwood	G. Agostini	F. Scheidegger/J. Robinson
1967	H. G. Anscheidt	B. Ivy	M. Hailwood	M. Hailwood	G. Agostini	K. Enders/R. Engelhardt
1968	H. G. Anscheidt	P. Read	P. Read	G. Agostini	G. Agostini	H. Fath/W. Kalauch
1969	A. Nieto	D. Simmonds	K. Carruthers	G. Agostini	G. Agostini	K. Enders/R. Engelhardt
1970	A. Nieto	D. Braun	R. Gould	G. Agostini	G. Agostini	K. Enders/W. Kalauch
1971	J. De Vries	A. Nieto	P. Read	G. Agostini	G. Agostini	H. Owesle/P. Rutterford
1972	A. Nieto	A. Nieto	J. Saarinen	G. Agostini	G. Agostini	K. Enders/R. Engelhardt
1973	J. De Vries	K. Andersson	D. Braun	G. Agostini	P. Read	K. Enders/R. Engelhardt
1974	H. van Kessel	K. Andersson	W. Villa	G. Agostini	P. Read	K. Enders/R. Engelhardt
1975	A. Nieto	P. Pileri	W. Villa	J. Cecotto	G. Agostini	R. Steinhausen/J. Huber
1976	A. Nieto	P. Bianchi	W. Villa	W. Villa	B. Sheene	R. Steinhausen/J. Huber
1977	A. Nieto	P. Bianchi	M. Lega	T. Katayama	B. Sheene	G. O'Dell/C. Holland, K. Arthur
1978	R. Tormo	E. Lazzarini	K. Ballington	K. Ballington	K. Roberts	R. Biland/K. Williams
1979	E. Lazzarini	A. Nieto	K. Ballington	K. Ballington	K. Roberts	R. Biland/K. Waltisperg
1980	E. Lazzarini	P. Bianchi	A. Mang	J. Ekerold	K. Roberts	J. Taylor/B. Johansson
1981	R. Tormo	A. Nieto	A. Mang	A. Mang	M. Lucchinelli	R. Biland/K. Waltisperg
1982	S. Dorflinger	A. Nieto	J. L. Tournadre	A. Mang	F. Uncini	W. Schwärzel/A. Huber
1983	S. Dorflinger	A. Nieto	C. Lavado	—	F. Spencer	R. Biland/K. Waltisperg
1984	S. Dorflinger	A. Nieto	C. Sarron	—	E. Lawson	E. Streuer/B. Schnieders
1985	S. Dorflinger	F. Gresini	F. Spencer	—	F. Spencer	E. Streuer/B. Schnieders
1986	J. Martinez	L. Cadalora	C. Lavado	—	E. Lawson	E. Streuer/B. Schnieders
1987	J. Martinez	F. Gresini	A. Mang	—	W. Gardner	S. Webster/T. Hewitt
1988	J. Martinez	J. Martinez	S. Pons	—	E. Lawson	S. Webster/T. Hewitt, G. Simmons

Note: In 1984 the capacity limit for the 50cc class was enlarged to 80cc

WORLD MANUFACTURERS CHAMPIONSHIPS 1949–88

	50cc/80cc	125cc	250cc	350cc	500cc	Sidecar 500cc
1949	—	Mondial	Moto-Guzzi	Velocette	AJS	Norton
1950	—	Mondial	Benelli	Velocette	Norton	Norton
1951	—	Mondial	Moto-Guzzi	Norton	Norton	Norton
1952	—	MV Agusta	Moto-Guzzi	Norton	Norton	Norton
1953	—	MV Agusta	NSU	Moto-Guzzi	Gilera	Norton
1954			No award			
1955	—	MV Agusta	MV Agusta	Moto-Guzzi	Gilera	BMW
1956	—	MV Agusta	MV Agusta	Moto-Guzzi	MV Agusta	BMW
1957	—	Mondial	Mondial	Gilera	Gilera	BMW
1958	—	MV Agusta	MV Agusta	MV Agusta	MV Agusta	BMW
1959	—	MV Agusta	MV Agusta	MV Agusta	MV Agusta	BMW
1960	—	MV Agusta	MV Agusta	MV Agusta	MV Agusta	BMW
1961	—	Honda	Honda	MV Agusta	MV Agusta	BMW
1962	Suzuki	Honda	Honda	Honda	MV Agusta	BMW
1963	Suzuki	Suzuki	Honda	Honda	MV Agusta	BMW
1964	Suzuki	Honda	Yamaha	Honda	MV Agusta	BMW
1965	Honda	Suzuki	Yamaha	Honda	MV Agusta	BMW
1966	Honda	Honda	Honda	Honda	Honda	BMW
1967	Suzuki	Yamaha	Honda	Honda	MV Agusta	BMW
1968	Suzuki	Yamaha	Yamaha	MV Agusta	MV Agusta	BMW
1969	Derbi	Kawasaki	Benelli	MV Agusta	MV Agusta	BMW
1970	Derbi	Suzuki	Yamaha	MV Agusta	MV Agusta	BMW
1971	Kreidler	Derbi	Yamaha	MV Agusta	MV Agusta	BMW
1972	Kreidler	Derbi	Yamaha	MV Agusta	MV Agusta	BMW
1973	Kreidler	Yamaha	Yamaha	Yamaha	MV Agusta	BMW
1974	Kreidler	Yamaha	Yamaha	Yamaha	Yamaha	Busch
1975	Kreidler	Morbidelli	Harley Davidson	Yamaha	Yamaha	Busch-Konig
1976	Bultaco	Morbidelli	—	Yamaha	Suzuki	—
1977	Bultaco	Morbidelli	Yamaha	Yamaha	Suzuki	Yamaha
1978	Bultaco	—	Kawasaki	Kawasaki	Suzuki	Yamaha
1979	Kreidler	Minarelli	Kawasaki	Kawasaki	Suzuki	Yamaha
1980	Kreidler Van Veen	Minarelli	Kawasaki	Bimota/Yamaha	Suzuki	Yamaha
1981	Bultaco	Minarelli	Kawasaki	Kawasaki	Suzuki	Yamaha
1982	—	Garelli	Yamaha	Kawasaki	Suzuki	LCR Yamaha
1983	Garelli	MBA	Yamaha	—	Honda	LCR Yamaha
1984	Zündapp	Garelli	Yamaha	—	Honda	LCR Yamaha
1985	Krauser	MBA	Honda	—	Honda	Yamaha
1986	Derbi	Garelli	Honda	—	Yamaha	LCR Yamaha
1987	Derbi	Garelli	Honda	—	Yamaha	LCR Krauser
1988	Derbi	Derbi	Honda	—	Yamaha	LCR Krauser

Note: In 1984 the capacity limit for the 50cc class was enlarged to 80cc

WORLD SOLO CHAMPIONSHIPS 1949–88

	50cc	80cc	125cc	250cc	350cc	500cc	Total
Agostini, Giacomo *(I)*	—	—	—	—	7	8	15
Nieto, Angel *(E)*	6	—	7	—	—	—	13
Hailwood, Mike *(GB)*	—	—	—	3	2	4	9
Ubbiali, Carlo *(I)*	—	—	6	3	—	—	9
Read, Phil *(GB)*	—	—	1	4	—	2	7
Surtees, John *(GB)*	—	—	—	—	3	4	7
Duke, Geoff *(GB)*	—	—	—	—	2	4	6
Redman, Jim *(SR)*	—	—	—	2	4	—	6
Mang, Toni *(D)*	—	—	—	3	2	—	5
Anderson, Hugh *(NZ)*	2	—	2	—	—	—	4
Ballington, Kork *(SA)*	—	—	—	2	2	—	4
Dorflinger, Stefan *(CH)*	2	2	—	—	—	—	4
Martinez, Jorge *(E)*	—	3	1	—	—	—	4
Villa, Walter *(I)*	—	—	—	3	1	—	4
Anscheidt, Hans Georg *(D)*	3	—	—	—	—	—	3
Bianchi, Pier Paolo *(I)*	—	—	3	—	—	—	3
Haas, Werner *(D)*	—	—	1	2	—	—	3
Lawson, Eddie *(USA)*	—	—	—	—	—	3	3
Lazzarini, Eugenio *(I)*	2	—	1	—	—	—	3
Roberts, Kenny *(USA)*	—	—	—	—	—	3	3
Ruffo, Bruno *(I)*	—	—	1	2	—	—	3
Spencer, Freddie *(USA)*	—	—	—	1	—	2	3
Taveri, Luigi *(CH)*	—	—	3	—	—	—	3
Anderson, Fergus *(GB)*	—	—	—	—	2	—	2
Andersson, Kent *(S)*	—	—	2	—	—	—	2
Braun, Dieter *(D)*	—	—	1	1	—	—	2
De Vries, Jan *(NL)*	2	—	—	—	—	—	2
Gresini, Fausto *(I)*	—	—	2	—	—	—	2
Hocking, Gary *(SR)*	—	—	—	—	1	1	2
Lavado, Carlos *(YV)*	—	—	—	2	—	—	2
Lomas, Bill *(GB)*	—	—	—	—	2	—	2
Masetti, Umberto *(I)*	—	—	—	—	—	2	2
Provini, Tarquinio *(I)*	—	—	1	1	—	—	2
Sandford, Cecil *(GB)*	—	—	1	1	—	—	2
Sheene, Barry *(GB)*	—	—	—	—	—	2	2
Tormo, Ricardo *(E)*	2	—	—	—	—	—	2
Ambrosini, Dario *(I)*	—	—	—	1	—	—	1
Bryans, Ralph *(IRL)*	1	—	—	—	—	—	1
Cadalora, Luca *(I)*	—	—	1	—	—	—	1
Campbell, Keith *(AUS)*	—	—	—	—	1	—	1
Carruthers, Kel *(AUS)*	—	—	—	1	—	—	1
Cecotto, Johnny *(YV)*	—	—	—	—	1	—	1

Degner, Ernst *(D)*	1	—	—	—	—	—	1
Ekerold, Jon *(SA)*	—	—	—	—	1	—	1
Foster, Bob *(GB)*	—	—	—	—	1	—	1
Frith, Freddie *(GB)*	—	—	—	—	1	—	1
Gardner, Wayne *(AUS)*	—	—	—	—	—	1	1
Gould, Rodney *(GB)*	—	—	—	1	—	—	1
Graham, Leslie *(GB)*	—	—	—	—	—	1	1
Hollaus, Rupert *(A)*	—	—	1	—	—	—	1
Ivy, Bill *(GB)*	—	—	1	—	—	—	1
Katayama, Takazumi *(J)*	—	—	—	—	1	—	1
Lega, Mario *(I)*	—	—	—	1	—	—	1
Liberati, Libero *(I)*	—	—	—	—	—	1	1
Lorenzetti, Enrico *(I)*	—	—	—	1	—	—	1
Lucchinelli, Marco *(I)*	—	—	—	—	—	1	1
Muller, Hermann Paul *(D)*	—	—	—	1	—	—	1
Pagani, Nello *(I)*	—	—	1	—	—	—	1
Phillis, Tom *(AUS)*	—	—	1	—	—	—	1
Pileri, Paolo *(I)*	—	—	1	—	—	—	1
Pons, Sito *(E)*	—	—	—	1	—	—	1
Saarinen, Jarno *(SF)*	—	—	—	1	—	—	1
Sarron, Christian *(F)*	—	—	—	1	—	—	1
Simmonds, Dave *(GB)*	—	—	1	—	—	—	1
Tournadre, Jean Louis *(F)*	—	—	—	1	—	—	1
Uncini, Franco *(I)*	—	—	—	—	—	1	1
Van Kessel, Henk *(NL)*	1	—	—	—	—	—	1

WORLD SOLO CHAMPIONSHIPS CLASS BY CLASS 1949–88

50cc	**Total**
Nieto, Angel *(E)* (Derbi 3, Kreidler 1, Bultaco 2)	6
Anscheidt, Hans *(D)* (Suzuki)	3
Anderson, Hugh *(NZ)* (Suzuki)	2
De Vries, Jan *(NL)* (Kreidler)	2
Dorflinger, Stefan *(CH)* (Kreidler 1, Krauser Kreidler 1)	2
Lazzarini, Eugenio *(I)* (Kreidler 1, Iprem Kreidler 1)	2
Tormo, Ricardo *(E)* (Bultaco)	2
Bryans, Ralph *(IRL)* (Honda)	1
Degner, Ernst *(D)* (Suzuki)	1
Van Kessel, Henk *(NL)* (Kreidler)	1

80cc	**Total**
Martinez, Jorge *(E)* (Derbi 3)	3
Dorflinger, Stefan *(CH)* (Zundapp 1, Krauser 1)	2

125cc	**Total**
Nieto, Angel *(E)* (Derbi 2, Minarelli 2, Garelli 3)	7
Ubbiali, Carlo *(I)* (Mondial 1, MV Agusta 5)	6
Bianchi, Pier Paolo *(I)* (Morbidelli 2, MBA 1)	3
Taveri, Luigi *(CH)* (Honda)	3
Anderson, Hugh *(NZ)* (Suzuki)	2
Andersson, Kent *(S)* (Yamaha)	2

125cc (*continued*)	
Gresini, Fausto *(I)* (Garelli)	2
Braun, Dieter *(D)* (Suzuki)	1
Cadalora, Luca *(I)* (Garelli)	1
Haas, Werner *(D)* (NSU)	1
Hollaus, Rupert *(A)* (NSU)	1
Ivy, Bill *(GB)* (Yamaha)	1
Lazzarini, Eugenio *(I)* (MBA)	1
Martinez, Jorge *(E)* (Derbi)	1
Pagani, Nello *(I)* (Mondial)	1
Phillis, Tom *(AUS)* (Honda)	1
Pileri, Paolo *(I)* (Morbidelli)	1
Provini, Tarquinio *(I)* (Mondial)	1
Read, Phil *(GB)* (Yamaha)	1
Ruffo, Bruno *(I)* (Mondial)	1
Sandford, Cecil *(GB)* (MV Agusta)	1
Simmonds, Dave *(GB)* (Kawasaki)	1

250cc	**Total**
Read, Phil *(GB)* (Yamaha)	4
Hailwood, Mike *(GB)* (Honda)	3
Mang, Anton *(D)* (Kawasaki)	3
Ubbiali, Carlo *(I)* (MV Agusta)	3
Villa, Walter *(I)* (Harley Davidson)	3
Ballington, Kork *(SA)* (Kawasaki)	2
Haas, Werner *(D)* (NSU)	2
Lavado, Carlos *(YV)* (Yamaha)	2
Redman, Jim *(SR)* (Honda)	2
Ruffo, Bruno *(I)* (Guzzi)	2
Ambrosini, Dario *(I)* (Benelli)	1
Braun, Dieter *(D)* (Yamaha)	1
Carruthers, Kel *(AUS)* (Benelli)	1
Gould, Rodney *(GB)* (Yamaha)	1
Lavado, Carlos *(YV)* (Yamaha)	1
Lega, Mario *(I)* (Morbidelli)	1
Lorenzetti, Enrico *(I)* (Guzzi)	1
Muller, Hermann Paul *(D)* (NSU)	1
Pons, Sito *(E)* (Honda)	1
Provini, Tarquinio *(I)* (MV Agusta)	1

250cc (*continued*)	
Saarinen, Jarno *(SF)* (Yamaha)	1
Sandford, Cecil *(GB)* (Mondial)	1
Sarron, Christian *(F)* (Yamaha)	1
Tournadre, Jean Louis *(F)* (Yamaha)	1
Spencer, Freddie *(USA)* (Honda)	1

350cc	**Total**
Agostini, Giacomo *(I)* (MV Agusta 6, Yamaha 1)	7
Redman, Jim *(SR)* (Honda)	4
Surtees, John *(GB)* (MV Agusta)	3
Anderson, Fergus *(GB)* (Guzzi)	2
Ballington, Kork *(SA)* (Kawasaki)	2
Duke, Geoff *(GB)* (Norton)	2
Hailwood, Mike *(GB)* (Honda)	2
Lomas, Bill *(GB)* (Guzzi)	2
Mang, Anton *(D)* (Kawasaki)	2
Campbell, Keith *(AUS)* (Guzzi)	1
Cecotto, Johnny *(YV)* (Yamaha)	1
Ekerold, Jon *(SA)* (Bimota Yamaha)	1
Foster, Bob *(GB)* (Velocette)	1
Frith, Freddie *(GB)* (Velocette)	1
Hocking, Gary *(SR)* (MV Agusta)	1
Katayama, Takazumi *(J)* (Yamaha)	1
Villa, Walter *(I)* (Harley Davidson)	1

500cc	**Total**
Agostini, Giacomi *(I)* (MV Agusta 7, Yamaha 1)	8
Duke, Geoff *(GB)* (Gilera 3, Norton 1)	4
Hailwood, Mike *(GB)* (MV Agusta)	4
Surtees, John *(GB)* (MV Agusta)	4
Lawson, Eddie *(USA)* (Yamaha)	3
Roberts, Kenny *(USA)* (Yamaha)	3

500cc (*continued*)

Masetti, Umberto *(I)* (Gilera)	2
Read, Phil *(GB)* (MV Agusta)	2
Sheene, Barry *(GB)* (Suzuki)	2
Spencer, Freddie *(USA)* (Honda)	2
Gardner, Wayne *(AUS)* (Honda)	1
Graham, Leslie *(GB)* (AJS)	1
Hocking, Gary *(SR)* (MV Agusta)	1
Liberati, Libero *(I)* (Gilera)	1
Lucchinelli, Marco *(I)* (Suzuki)	1
Uncini, Franco *(I)* (Suzuki)	1

WORLD SIDECAR CHAMPIONSHIPS 1949–88

	Total
Enders, Klaus *(D)* (BMW 5, Busch Enders 1)	6
Biland, Rolf *(CH)* (Yamaha 3, LCR Yamaha 1)	4
Deubel, Max *(D)* (BMW)	4
Oliver, Eric *(GB)* (Norton)	4
Streuer, Egbert *(NL)* (LCR Yamaha)	3
Fath, Helmut *(D)* (BMW 1, URS Fath 1)	2
Noll, Wilhelm *(D)* (BMW)	2
Scheidegger, Fritz *(CH)* (BMW)	2
Schneider, Walter *(D)* (BMW)	2
Steinhausen, Rolf *(D)* (Busch Konig)	2
Streuer, Egbert *(NL)* (LCR Yamaha)	2
Webster, Steve *(GB)* (Krauser)	2
Faust, Willy *(D)* (BMW)	1
Hillebrand, Fritz *(D)* (BMW)	1
Holzer, Bruno *(CH)* (Yamaha)	1
O'Dell, George *(GB)* (Yamaha)	1
Oswesle, Horst *(D)* (Munch URS)	1
Schwarzel, Werner *(D)* (Seymaz Yamaha)	1
Smith, Cyril *(GB)* (Norton)	1
Taylor, Jock *(GB)* (Yamaha)	1

WORLD SIDECAR MANUFACTURERS CHAMPIONSHIPS 1949–88

		Total
BMW	*(D)*	18
Yamaha	*(J)*	6
Norton	*(GB)*	5
LCR Yamaha	*(CH)*	4
Busch Konig	*(D)*	2
LCR Krauser	*(CH)*	2
Busch Enders	*(D)*	1
Munch URS	*(D)*	1
Seymaz Yamaha	*(CH)*	1
URS Fath	*(D)*	1

GRAND PRIX WINNERS (SOLO) 1949–88

	50cc	80cc	125cc	250cc	350cc	500cc	Total
Agostini, Giacomo *(I)*	—	—	—	—	54	68	122
Nieto, Angel *(E)*	27	1	62	—	—	—	90
Hailwood, Mike *(GB)*	—	—	2	21	16	37	76
Read, Phil *(GB)*	—	—	10	27	4	11	52
Redman, Jim *(SR)*	—	—	4	18	21	2	45
Mang, Toni *(D)*	—	—	1	33	8	—	42
Ubbiali, Carlo *(I)*	—	—	26	13	—	—	39
Surtees, John *(GB)*	—	—	—	1	15	22	38

Duke, Geoff *(GB)*	—	—	—	—	11	22	33
Ballington, Kork *(SA)*	—	—	—	17	14	—	31
Martinez, Jorge *(E)*	—	24	6	—	—	—	30
Taveri, Luigi *(CH)*	6	—	22	2	—	—	30
Bianchi, Pier Paolo *(I)*	—	3	24	—	—	—	27
Lazzarini, Eugenio *(I)*	18	—	9	—	—	—	27
Spencer, Freddie *(USA)*	—	—	—	7	—	20	27
Lawson, Eddie *(USA)*	—	—	—	—	—	26	26
Anderson, Hugh *(NZ)*	8	—	17	—	—	—	25
Roberts, Kenny *(USA)*	—	—	—	2	—	22	24
Villa, Walter *(I)*	—	—	—	20	4	—	24
Sheene, Barry *(GB)*	1	—	3	—	—	19	23
Ivy, Bill *(GB)*	—	—	14	7	—	—	21
Provini, Tarquinio *(I)*	—	—	6	14	—	—	20
Hocking, Gary *(SR)*	—	—	—	5	6	8	19
Lavado, Carlos *(YV)*	—	—	—	17	2	—	19
Tormo, Ricardo *(E)*	15	—	4	—	—	—	19
Andersson, Kent *(S)*	—	—	14	4	—	—	18
Gresini, Fausto *(I)*	—	—	18	—	—	—	18
Dorflinger, Stefan *(CH)*	9	8	—	—	—	—	17
Degner, Ernst *(DDR)*	7	—	8	—	—	—	15
Saarinen, Jarno *(SF)*	—	—	—	8	5	2	15
Anscheidt, Hans Georg *(D)*	14	—	—	—	—	—	14
Braun, Dieter *(D)*	—	—	6	7	1	—	14
Cecotto, Johnny *(YV)*	—	—	—	2	9	3	14
De Vries, Jan *(NL)*	14	—	—	—	—	—	14
Gardner, Wayne *(AUS)*	—	—	—	—	—	14	14
Mamola, Randy *(USA)*	—	—	—	—	—	13	13
Anderson, Fergus *(GB)*	—	—	—	3	7	2	12
Haas, Werner *(D)*	—	—	4	7	—	—	11
Katayama, Takazumi *(J)*	—	—	—	3	7	1	11
Simmonds, Dave *(GB)*	—	—	10	—	—	1	11
Bryans, Ralph *(IRL)*	7	—	—	2	1	—	10
Gould, Rodney *(GB)*	—	—	—	10	—	—	10
Hansford, Gregg *(AUS)*	—	—	—	4	6	—	10
Lomas, Bill *(GB)*	—	—	—	1	7	1	9
Graham, Leslie *(GB)*	—	—	1	—	2	5	8
Lansivuori, Teuvo *(SF)*	—	—	—	2	5	1	8
Pileri, Paolo *(I)*	—	—	7	1	—	—	8
Pons, Sito *(E)*	—	—	—	8	—	—	8
Armstrong, Reg *(IRL)*	—	—	—	2	1	4	7
Carruthers, Kel *(AUS)*	—	—	—	7	—	—	7
Ekerold, Jon *(SA)*	—	—	—	1	6	—	7
Lorenzetti, Enrico *(I)*	—	—	—	5	2	—	7

Mortimer, Charles *(GB)*	—	—	3	2	1	1	7
Sarron, Christian *(F)*	—	—	—	6	—	1	7
Uncini, Franco *(I)*	—	—	—	2	—	5	7
Van Kessell, Henk *(NL)*	7	—	—	—	—	—	7
Amm, Ray *(SR)*	—	—	—	—	4	2	6
Bertin, Guy *(F)*	—	—	6	—	—	—	6
Cadalora, Luca *(I)*	—	—	4	2	—	—	6
Herweh, Manfred *(D)*	—	—	—	5	1	—	6
Liberati, Libero *(I)*	—	—	—	—	2	4	6
Lucchinelli, Marco *(I)*	—	—	—	—	—	6	6
Masetti, Umberto *(I)*	—	—	—	—	—	6	6
Pasolini, Renzo *(I)*	—	—	—	6	—	—	6
Phillis, Tom *(AUS)*	—	—	4	2	—	—	6
Toersen, Aalt *(NL)*	6	—	—	—	—	—	6
Ambrosini, Dario *(I)*	—	—	—	5	—	—	5
Auinger, August *(A)*	—	—	5	—	—	—	5
Balde, Jean Francois *(F)*	—	—	—	—	5	—	5
Frith, Freddie *(GB)*	—	—	—	—	5	—	5
Hartle, John *(GB)*	—	—	—	1	1	3	5
Hartog, Wil *(NL)*	—	—	—	—	—	5	5
Hollaus, Rupert *(A)*	—	—	4	1	—	—	5
Kavanagh, Ken *(AUS)*	—	—	—	—	4	1	5
Kneubuhler, Bruno *(CH)*	1	—	3	—	1	—	5
McIntyre, Bob *(GB)*	—	—	—	2	2	1	5
Sandford, Cecil *(GB)*	—	3	2	—	—	—	5
De Radigues, Didier *(B)*	—	—	—	2	2	—	4
Dodds, John *(AUS)*	—	—	1	2	1	—	4
Drapal, Janos *(H)*	—	—	—	1	3	—	4
Gianola, Ezio *(I)*	—	—	4	—	—	—	4
Herrero, Santiago *(E)*	—	—	—	4	—	—	4
Jansson, Borje *(S)*	—	—	3	1	—	—	4
Katayama, Hoshimi *(J)*	3	—	1	—	—	—	4
Lodewijkx, Paul *(NL)*	4	—	—	—	—	—	4
Pagani, Nello *(I)*	—	—	2	—	—	2	4
Parlotti, Gilberto *(I)*	—	—	4	—	—	—	4
Reggiani, Loris *(I)*	—	—	3	1	—	—	4
Rittberger, Herbert *(D)*	4	—	—	—	—	—	4
Ruffo, Bruno *(I)*	—	—	1	3	—	—	4
Sarron, Dominique *(F)*	—	—	—	4	—	—	4
Smith, Barry *(AUS)*	3	1	—	—	—	—	4
Stastny, Frantisek *(CS)*	—	—	—	—	3	1	4
Takahashi, Kumimitsu *(J)*	—	—	3	1	—	—	4
Waibel, Gerhard *(G)*	1	3	—	—	—	—	4
Buscherini, Otello *(I)*	—	—	2	—	1	—	3
Campbell, Keith *(AUS)*	—	—	—	—	3	—	3

Cann, Maurice *(GB)*	—	—	—	3	—	—	3
Duff, Mike *(CDN)*	—	—	1	2	—	—	3
Fernandez, Patrick *(F)*	—	—	—	1	2	—	3
Findlay, Jack *(AUS)*	—	—	—	—	—	3	3
Foster, Bob *(GB)*	—	—	—	—	3	—	3
Garriga, Juan *(E)*	—	—	—	3	—	—	3
Grant, Mick *(GB)*	—	—	—	2	—	1	3
Grassetti, Silvio *(I)*	—	—	—	2	1	—	3
Hennen, Pat *(USA)*	—	—	—	—	—	3	3
Kanaya, Hideo *(J)*	—	—	—	1	1	1	3
Leoni, Gianni *(I)*	—	—	3	—	—	—	3
Mendogni, Emilio *(I)*	—	—	2	1	—	—	3
Milani, Alfredo *(I)*	—	—	—	—	—	3	3
Pagani, Alberto *(I)*	—	—	—	—	—	3	3
Perris, Frank *(GB)*	—	—	3	—	—	—	3
Robbs, Tommy *(IRL)*	—	—	1	1	1	—	3
Rossi, Graziano *(I)*	—	—	—	3	—	—	3
Rougerie, Michel *(F)*	—	—	—	2	1	—	3
Timmer, Theo *(NL)*	3	—	—	—	—	—	3
Van Zeebroeck, Julien *(B)*	3	—	—	—	—	—	3
Williams, Charlie *(GB)*	—	—	—	2	1	—	3
Wimmer, Martin *(D)*	—	—	—	3	—	—	3
Bergamonti, Angelo *(I)*	—	—	—	—	1	1	2
Bonero, Gianfranco *(I)*	—	—	—	1	—	1	2
Canellas, Salvador *(E)*	1	—	1	—	—	—	2
Cornu, Jacques *(CH)*	—	—	—	2	—	—	2
Dale, Dickie *(GB)*	—	—	—	—	1	1	2
Doran, Bill *(GB)*	—	—	—	—	1	1	2
Ferrari, Virginio *(I)*	—	—	—	—	—	2	2
Gandossi, Alberto *(I)*	—	—	2	—	—	—	2
Graham, Stuart *(GB)*	1	—	1	—	—	—	2
Herreros, Manuel *(E)*	—	2	—	—	—	—	2
Herron, Tom *(IRL)*	—	—	—	1	—	1	2
Huberts, Jan *(NL)*	2	—	—	—	—	—	2
Itoh, Mitsuo *(J)*	2	—	—	—	—	—	2
Kassner, Helmut *(D)*	—	—	—	1	1	—	2
McCandless, Cromie *(IRL)*	—	—	1	—	—	1	2
Middelburg, Jack *(NL)*	—	—	—	—	—	2	2
Monneret, Pierre *(F)*	—	—	—	—	1	1	2
Palazzese, Ivan *(YV)*	—	—	2	—	—	—	2
Rutter, Tony *(GB)*	—	—	—	—	2	—	2
Saul, Eric *(F)*	—	—	—	1	1	—	2
Schwantz, Kevin *(USA)*	—	—	—	—	—	2	2
Shepherd, Alan *(GB)*	—	—	—	1	—	1	2
Vitali, Maurizio *(I)*	—	—	2	—	—	—	2

Wheeler, Arthur *(GB)*	—	—	—	2	—	—	2
Wood, Tommy *(GB)*	—	—	—	1	1	—	2
Agostini, Duilio *(I)*	—	—	—	—	1	—	1
Ahearn, Jack *(AUS)*	—	—	—	—	—	1	1
Aureal, Jean *(F)*	—	—	1	—	—	—	1
Barrington, Manliff *(IRL)*	—	—	—	1	—	—	1
Bell, Artie *(IRL)*	—	—	—	—	1	—	1
Bolle, Jacques *(F)*	—	—	—	1	—	—	1
Brett, Jack *(GB)*	—	—	—	—	—	1	1
Brigaglia, Domenico *(I)*	—	—	1	—	—	—	1
Bruins, Jan *(NL)*	1	—	—	—	—	—	1
Caldarella, Benedicto *(RA)*	—	—	—	—	—	1	1
Carpenter, Phil *(GB)*	—	—	—	—	—	1	1
Carter, Alan *(GB)*	—	—	—	1	—	—	1
Casoli, Paolo *(I)*	—	1	—	—	—	—	1
Celso, Santos Adu *(BR)*	—	—	—	—	1	—	1
Chevallier, Oliver *(F)*	—	—	—	—	1	—	1
Coleman, Rod *(NZ)*	—	—	—	—	1	—	1
Colnago, Giuseppe *(I)*	—	—	—	—	—	1	1
Conforti, Pierluigi *(I)*	—	—	1	—	—	—	1
Copeta, Angelo *(I)*	—	—	1	—	—	—	1
Creith, Dick *(IRL)*	—	—	—	—	—	1	1
Czihak, Edmund *(D)*	—	—	—	—	—	1	1
Daniell, Harold *(GB)*	—	—	—	—	—	1	1
Emmerich, Ingo *(D)*	1	—	—	—	—	—	1
Felgenheier, Rudi *(D)*	—	—	—	1	—	—	1
Ferri, Romolo *(I)*	—	—	1	—	—	—	1
Filice, Jim *(USA)*	—	—	—	1	—	—	1
Freymond, Roland *(CH)*	—	—	—	1	—	—	1
Frutschi, Michel *(CH)*	—	—	—	—	—	1	1
Fugner, Horst *(DDR)*	—	—	—	1	—	—	1
Graf, Ulrich *(CH)*	1	—	—	—	—	—	1
Grau, Benjamin *(E)*	—	—	1	—	—	—	1
Guilleux, Herve *(F)*	—	—	—	1	—	—	1
Gustavsson, Leif *(S)*	—	—	1	—	—	—	1
Hasegawa, Hiroshi *(J)*	—	—	—	1	—	—	1
Kafka, Gerd *(A)*	—	1	—	—	—	—	1
Ireland, Dennis *(NZ)*	—	—	—	—	—	1	1
Ito, Fumio *(J)*	—	—	—	1	—	—	1
Jefferies, Tony *(GB)*	—	—	—	—	1	—	1
Kissling, Jorge *(RA)*	—	—	—	—	—	1	1
Kobayshi, Masaru *(T)*	—	—	—	1	—	—	1
Korhonen, Pentti *(SF)*	—	—	—	—	1	—	1
Lega, Mario *(I)*	—	—	—	1	—	—	1
Leoni, Guido *(I)*	—	—	1	—	—	—	1

Magee, Kevin *(USA)*	—	—	—	—	—	1	1
Marsowszky, Guyla *(CH)*	—	—	—	1	—	—	1
McConnachie, Ian *(GB)*	—	1	—	—	—	—	1
McCullough, Ray *(IRL)*	—	—	—	1	—	—	1
Minter, Derek *(GB)*	—	—	—	1	—	—	1
Molloy, Ginger *(NZ)*	—	—	—	1	—	—	1
Morishita, Isao *(J)*	1	—	—	—	—	—	1
Mudford, Ken *(NZ)*	—	—	—	—	1	—	1
Muller, Hermann Paul *(D)*	—	—	—	1	—	—	1
Nash, Godfrey *(GB)*	—	—	—	—	—	1	1
Newbold, John *(GB)*	—	—	—	—	—	1	1
Newcombe, Kim *(NZ)*	—	—	—	—	—	1	1
North, Alan *(SA)*	—	—	—	—	1	—	1
Palomo, Victor *(E)*	—	—	—	—	1	—	1
Rainey, Wayne *(USA)*	—	—	—	—	—	1	1
Reitmaier, Fritz *(D)*	—	—	1	—	—	—	1
Ricci, Fausto *(I)*	—	—	—	1	—	—	1
Roth, Reinhold *(D)*	—	—	—	1	—	—	1
Sala, Guido *(I)*	—	—	1	—	—	—	1
Schneider, Bertie *(A)*	—	—	1	—	—	—	1
Schurgers, Jos *(NL)*	—	—	1	—	—	—	1
Selini, Jean Claude *(F)*	—	—	1	—	—	—	1
Spaggiari, Bruno *(I)*	—	—	1	—	—	—	1
Stollinger, Edi *(A)*	—	—	—	1	—	—	1
Tadahiko, Taira *(J)*	—	—	—	1	—	—	1
Tanaka, Teisuke *(J)*	—	—	1	—	—	—	1
Thurow, Gerhard *(D)*	1	—	—	—	—	—	1
Tournadre, Jean Louis *(F)*	—	—	—	1	—	—	1
Van Dongen, Cees *(NL)*	—	—	1	—	—	—	1
Van Dulmen, Boet *(NL)*	—	—	—	—	—	1	1
Venturi, Remo *(I)*	—	—	—	—	—	1	1
Williams, John *(GB)*	—	—	—	—	—	1	1
Williams, Peter *(GB)*	—	—	—	—	1	—	1

GRAND PRIX WINNERS 1949–87

Argentina

	50cc	80cc	125cc	250cc	350cc	500cc	Sidecar
1961 Buenos Aires	—	—	T. Phillis *(Honda)*	T. Phillis *(Honda)*	—	J. Kissling *(Matchless)*	—
1962 Buenos Aires	H. Anderson *(Suzuki)*	—	H. Anderson *(Suzuki)*	A. Wheeler *(Guzzi)*	—	B. Caldarella *(Matchless)*	—
1963 Buenos Aires	H. Anderson *(Suzuki)*	—	J. Redman *(Honda)*	T. Provini *(Morini)*	—	M. Hailwood *(MV Agusta)*	—
1981 Buenos Aires	—	—	A. Nieto *(Minarelli)*	J. F. Baldé *(Kawasaki)*	J. Ekerold *(Bimota)*	—	—

	50cc	80cc	125cc	250cc	350cc	500cc	Sidecar
1982 Buenos Aires	—	—	A. Nieto *(Garelli)*	—	C. Lavado *(Yamaha)*	K. Roberts *(Yamaha)*	—
1987 Buenos Aires	—	—	—	S. Pons *(Honda)*	—	E. Lawson *(Yamaha)*	—

Austria

	50cc	80cc	125cc	250cc	350cc	500cc	Sidecar
1971 Salzburgring	J. De Vries *(Kreidler)*	—	A. Nieto *(Derbi)*	S. Grassetti *(MZ)*	G. Agostini *(MV Agusta)*	G. Agostini *(MV Agusta)*	A. Butscher–J. Huber *(BMW)*
1972 Salzburgring	—	—	A. Nieto *(Derbi)*	B. Jansson *(Derbi)*	G. Agostini *(MV Agusta)*	G. Agostini *(MV Agusta)*	K. Enders–R. Engelhardt *(BMW)*
1973 Salzburgring	—	—	K. Andersson *(Yamaha)*	J. Saarinen *(Yamaha)*	J. Drapal *(Yamaha)*	J. Saarinen *(Yamaha)*	K. Enders–R. Engelhardt *(BMW)*
1974 Salzburgring	—	—	K. Andersson *(Yamaha)*	—	G. Agostini *(Yamaha)*	G. Agostini *(Yamaha)*	S. Schauzu–W. Kalauch *(BMW)*
1975 Salzburgring	—	—	P. Pileri *(Morbidelli)*	—	H. Kanaya *(Yamaha)*	H. Kanaya *(Yamaha)*	R. Steinhausen–J. Huber *(Busch König)*
1976 Salzburgring	—	—	P. Bianchi *(Morbidelli)*	—	J. Cecotto *(Yamaha)*	B. Sheene *(Suzuki)*	R. Steinhausen–J. Huber *(Busch König)*
1977 Salzburgring	—	—	E. Lazzarini *(Morbidelli)*	—	—	J. Findlay *(Suzuki)*	R. Biland–K. Williams *(Yamaha)*
1978 Salzburgring	—	—	E. Lazzarini *(MBA)*	—	K. Ballington *(Kawasaki)*	K. Roberts *(Yamaha)*	R. Biland–K. Williams *(Yamaha)*
1979 Salzburgring	—	—	A. Nieto *(Minarelli)*	—	K. Ballington *(Kawasaki)*	K. Roberts *(Yamaha)*	G. Brodin–B. Gällros (B2a) *(Yamaha)* R. Biland–K. Waltisperg (B2b) *(Yamaha)*
1981 Salzburgring	—	—	A. Nieto *(Minarelli)*	—	P. Fernandez *(Bimota)*	R. Mamola *(Suzuki)*	J. Taylor–B. Johansson *(Yamaha)*
1982 Salzburgring	—	—	A. Nieto *(Garelli)*	—	E. Saul *(Chevallier)*	F. Uncini *(Suzuki)*	R. Biland–K. Waltisperg *(LCR-Yamaha)*
1983 Salzburgring	—	—	A. Nieto *(Garelli)*	M. Herweh *(Real Rotax)*	—	K. Roberts *(Yamaha)*	R. Biland–K. Waltisperg *(LCR-Yamaha)*
1984 Salzburgring	—	S. Dorflinger *(Zundapp)*	—	C. Sarron *(Yamaha)*	—	E. Lawson *(Yamaha)*	E. Streuer–B. Schnieders *(LCR-Yamaha)*
1985 Salzburgring	—	—	F. Gresini *(Garelli)*	F. Spencer *(Honda)*	—	F. Spencer *(Honda)*	R. Biland–K. Waltisperg *(LCR-Yamaha)*
1986 Salzburgring	—	J. Martinez *(Derbi)*	L. Cadalora *(Garelli)*	C. Lavado *(Yamaha)*	—	E. Lawson *(Yamaha)*	E. Streuer–B. Schnieders *(LCR-Yamaha)*
1987 Salzburgring	—	J. Martinez *(Derbi)*	F. Gresini *(Garelli)*	A. Mang *(Honda)*	—	W. Gardner *(Honda)*	R. Biland-K. Waltisperg *(LCR-Krauser)*

Belgium

	50cc	80cc	125cc	250cc	350cc	500cc	Sidecar
1949 Spa	—	—	—	—	F. Frith *(Velocette)*	B. Doran *(AJS)*	E. Oliver–D. Jenkinson *(Norton)*
1950 Spa	—	—	—	—	B. Foster *(Velocette)*	U. Masetti *(Gilera)*	E. Oliver–L. Dobelli *(Norton)*
1951 Spa	—	—	—	—	G. Duke *(Norton)*	G. Duke *(Norton)*	E. Oliver–L. Dobelli *(Norton)*
1952 Spa	—	—	—	—	G. Duke *(Norton)*	U. Masetti *(Gilera)*	E. Oliver–S. Price *(Norton)*
1953 Spa	—	—	—	—	F. Anderson *(Guzzi)*	Alf. Milani *(Gilera)*	E. Oliver–S. Dibben *(Norton)*
1954 Spa	—	—	—	—	K. Kavanagh *(Guzzi)*	G. Duke *(Gilera)*	E. Oliver–L. Nutt *(Norton)*
1955 Spa	—	—	—	—	B. Lomas *(Guzzi)*	G. Colnago *(Gilera)*	W. Noll–F. Cron *(BMW)*
1956 Spa	—	—	C. Ubbiali *(MV Agusta)*	C. Ubbiali *(MV Agusta)*	J. Surtees *(MV Agusta)*	J. Surtees *(MV Agusta)*	W. Noll–F. Cron *(BMW)*
1957 Spa	—	—	T. Provini *(Mondial)*	J. Hartle *(MV Agusta)*	K. Campbell *(Guzzi)*	L. Liberati *(Gilera)*	W. Schneider–H. Strauss *(BMW)*
1958 Spa	—	—	A. Gandossi *(Ducati)*	—	J. Surtees *(MV Agusta)*	J. Surtees *(MV Agusta)*	W. Schneider –H. Strauss *(BMW)*
1959 Spa	—	—	C. Ubbiali *(MV Agusta)*	—	—	J. Surtees *(MV Agusta)*	W. Schneider–H. Strauss *(BMW)*
1960 Spa	—	—	E. Degner *(MZ)*	C. Ubbiali *(MV Agusta)*	—	J. Surtees *(MV Agusta)*	H. Fath–A. Wohlgemuth *(BMW)*
1961 Spa	—	—	L. Taveri *(Honda)*	J. Redman *(Honda)*	—	G. Hocking *(MV Agusta)*	F. Scheidegger–H. Burckardt *(BMW)*
1962 Spa	E. Degner *(Suzuki)*	—	L. Taveri *(Honda)*	B. McIntyre *(Honda)*	—	M. Hailwood *(MV Agusta)*	F. Camathias–H. Winter *(BMW)*
1963 Spa	I. Morishita *(Suzuki)*	—	B. Schneider *(Suzuki)*	F. Ito *(Yamaha)*	—	M. Hailwood *(MV Agusta)*	F. Scheidegger–J. Robinson *(BMW)*
1964 Spa	R. Bryans *(Honda)*	—	—	M. Duff *(Yamaha)*	—	M. Hailwood *(MV Agusta)*	M. Deubel–E. Hörner *(BMW)*
1965 Spa	E. Degner *(Suzuki)*	—	—	J. Redman *(Honda)*	—	M. Hailwood *(MV Agusta)*	F. Scheidegger–J. Robinson *(BMW)*
1966 Spa	—	—	—	M. Hailwood *(Honda)*	—	G. Agostini *(MV Agusta)*	F. Scheidegger–J. Robinson *(BMW)*
1967 Spa	H. Anscheidt *(Suzuki)*	—	—	B. Ivy *(Yamaha)*	—	G. Agostini *(MV Agusta)*	K. Enders–R. Engelhardt *(BMW)*
1968 Spa	H. Anscheidt *(Suzuki)*	—	—	P. Read *(Yamaha)*	—	G. Agostini *(MV Agusta)*	G. Auerbacher–H. Hahn *(BMW)*
1969 Spa	Barry Smith *(Derbi)*	—	D. Simmonds *(Kawasaki)*	S. Herrero *(Ossa)*	—	G. Agostini *(MV Agusta)*	H. Fath–W. Kalauch *(URS)*
1970 Spa	A. Toersen *(Jamathi)*	—	A. Nieto *(Derbi)*	R. Gould *(Yamaha)*	—	G. Agostini *(MV Agusta)*	A. Butscher–J. Huber *(BMW)*

	50cc	80cc	125cc	250cc	350cc	500cc	Sidecar
1971 Spa	J. De Vries *(Kreidler)*	—	B. Sheene *(Suzuki)*	S. Grassetti *(MZ)*	—	G. Agostini *(MV Agusta)*	S. Schauzu–W. Kalauch *(BMW)*
1972 Spa	A. Nieto *(Derbi)*	—	A. Nieto *(Derbi)*	J. Saarinen *(Yamaha)*	—	G. Agostini *(MV Agusta)*	K. Enders–R. Engelhardt *(BMW)*
1973 Spa	J. De Vries *(Kreidler)*	—	J. Schurgers *(Bridgestone)*	T. Länsivuori *(Yamaha)*	—	G. Agostini *(MV Agusta)*	K. Enders–R. Engelhardt *(BMW)*
1974 Spa	G. Thurow *(Kreidler)*	—	A. Nieto *(Derbi)*	K. Andersson *(Yamaha)*	—	P. Read *(MV Agusta)*	R. Steinhausen–J. Huber *(König)*
1975 Spa	J. Van Zeebroeck *(Kreidler)*	—	P. Pileri *(Morbidelli)*	J. Cecotto *(Yamaha)*	—	P. Read *(MV Agusta)*	R. Steinhausen–J. Huber *(Busch König)*
1976 Spa	H. Rittberger *(Kreidler)*	—	A. Nieto *(Bultaco)*	W. Villa *(Harley D.)*	—	J. Williams *(Suzuki)*	R. Steinhausen–J. Huber *(Busch König)*
1977 Spa	E. Lazzarini *(Kreidler)*	—	P. Bianchi *(Morbidelli)*	W. Villa *(Harley D.)*	—	B. Sheene *(Suzuki)*	W. Schwärzel–A. Huber *(ARO Fath)*
1978 Spa	R. Tormo *(Bultaco)*	—	P. Bianchi *(Minarelli)*	P. Pileri *(Morbidelli)*	—	W. Hartog *(Suzuki)*	B. Holzer–K. Meierhans *(Yamaha)*
1979 Spa	H. Van Kessel *(Kreidler)*	—	B. Smith *(MBA)*	E. Stöllinger *(Kawasaki)*	—	D. Ireland *(Suzuki)*	R. Steinhausen–K. Arthur (B2a) *(Yamaha)*
1980 Zolder	S. Dörflinger *(Kreidler)*	—	A. Nieto *(Minarelli)*	A. Mang *(Kawasaki)*	—	R. Mamola *(Suzuki)*	J. Taylor–B. Johansson *(Yamaha)*
1981 Spa	R. Tormo *(Bultaco)*	—	—	A. Mang *(Kawasaki)*	—	M. Lucchinelli *(Suzuki)*	R. Biland–K. Waltisperg *(Yamaha)*
1982 Spa	—	—	R. Tormo *(Sanvenero)*	A. Mang *(Kawasaski)*	—	F. Spencer *(Honda)*	R. Biland–K. Waltisperg *(LCR-Yamaha)*
1983 Spa	—	—	E. Lazzarini *(Garelli)*	D. De Radigues *(Chevallier)*	—	K. Roberts *(Yamaha)*	R. Biland–K. Waltisperg *(LCR-Yamaha)*
1984 Spa	—	S. Dörflinger *(Zundapp)*	—	M. Herweh *(Real)*	—	F. Spencer *(Honda)*	A. Michel–J. M. Fresc *(LCR-Yamaha)*
1985 Spa	—	—	F. Gresini *(Garelli)*	F. Spencer *(Honda)*	—	F. Spencer *(Honda)*	E. Streuer–B. Schnieders *(LCR-Yamaha)*
1986 Spa	—	—	D. Brigaglia *(MBA)*	S. Pons *(Honda)*	—	R. Mamola *(Yamaha)*	S. Webster–T. Hewitt *(LCR-Yamaha)*

Brazil

	50cc	80cc	125cc	250cc	350cc	500cc	Sidecar
1987 Goiania	—	—	—	D. Sarron *(Honda)*	—	W. Gardner *(Honda)*	—

Canada

	50cc	80cc	125cc	250cc	350cc	500cc	Sidecar
1967 Mosport	—	—	B. Ivy *(Yamaha)*	M. Hailwood *(Honda)*	—	M. Hailwood *(Honda)*	—

Czechoslovakia

	50cc	80cc	125cc	250cc	350cc	500cc	Sidecar
1965 Brno	— —	— —	F. Perris *(Suzuki)*	P. Read *(Yamaha)*	J. Redman *(Honda)*	M. Hailwood *(MV Agusta)*	—
1966 Brno	—	—	L. Taveri *(Honda)*	M. Hailwood *(Honda)*	M. Hailwood *(Honda)*	M. Hailwood *(Honda)*	—
1967 Brno	—	—	B. Ivy *(Yamaha)*	P. Read *(Yamaha)*	M. Hailwood *(Honda)*	M. Hailwood *(Honda)*	—
1968 Brno	—	—	P. Read *(Yamaha)*	P. Read *(Yamaha)*	G. Agostini *(MV Agusta)*	G. Agostini *(MV Agusta)*	—
1969 Brno	P. Lodewijkx *(Jamathi)*	—	D. Simmonds *(Kawasaki)*	R. Pasolini *(Benelli)*	G. Agostini *(MV Agusta)*	G. Agostini *(MV Agusta)*	—
1970 Brno	A. Toersen *(Jamathi)*	—	G. Parlotti *(Morbidelli)*	K. Carruthers *(Yamaha)*	G. Agostini *(MV Agusta)*	—	K. Enders–W. Kalauch *(BMW)*
1971 Brno	B. Sheene *(Kreidler)*	—	A. Nieto *(Derbi)*	J. Drapal *(Yamaha)*	J. Saarinen *(Yamaha)*	—	S. Schauzu–W. Kalauch *(BMW)*
1972 Brno	—	—	B. Jansson *(Maico)*	J. Saarinen *(Yamaha)*	J. Saarinen *(Yamaha)*	G. Agostini *(MV Agusta)*	K. Enders–R. Engelhardt *(BMW)*
1973 Brno	—	—	O. Buscherini *(Malanca)*	D. Braun *(Yamaha)*	T. Länsivuori *(Yamaha)*	G. Agostini *(MV Agusta)*	K. Enders–R. Engelhardt *(BMW)*
1974 Brno	H. Van Kessel *(Kreidler)*	—	K. Andersson *(Yamaha)*	W. Villa *(Harley D.)*	—	P. Read *(MV Agusta)*	W. Schwärzel–K. Kleis *(König)*
1975 Brno	—	—	L. Gustavsson *(Yamaha)*	M. Rougerie *(Harley D.)*	O. Buscherini *(Yamaha)*	P. Read *(MV Agusta)*	W. Schwärzel–A. Huber *(König)*
1976 Brno	—	—	—	W. Villa *(Harley D.)*	W. Villa *(Harley D.)*	J. Newbold *(Suzuki)*	H. Schmid–J. P. Matile *(Yamaha)*
1977 Brno	—	—	—	F. Uncini *(Harley D.)*	J. Cecotto *(Yamaha)*	J. Cecotto *(Yamaha)*	R. Steinhausen–J. Huber *(Busch Yamaha)*
1978 Brno	R. Tormo *(Bultaco)*	—	—	K. Ballington *(Kawasaki)*	K. Ballington *(Kawasaki)*	—	A. Michel–S. Collins *(Seymaz)*
1979 Brno	—	—	G. Bertin *(Motobecane)*	K. Ballington *(Kawasaki)*	K. Ballington *(Kawasaki)*	—	R. Biland–K. Waltisperg (B2a) *(Yamaha)*
1980 Brno	—	—	G. Bertin *(Motobecane)*	A. Mang *(Kawasaki)*	A. Mang *(Kawasaki)*	—	R. Biland–K. Waltisperg *(Yamaha)*
1981 Brno	T. Timmer *(Bultaco)*	—	—	A. Mang *(Kawasaki)*	A. Mang *(Kawasaki)*	—	R. Biland–K. Waltisperg *(Yamaha)*
1982 Brno	—	—	E. Lazzarini *(Garelli)*	C. Lavado *(Yamaha)*	D. De Radigues *(Chevallier)*	—	A. Michel–F. Burkard *(Seymaz-Yamaha)*
1987 Brno	—	F. Dorflinger *(Krauser)*	F. Gresini *(Garelli)*	A. Mang *(Honda)*	—	W. Gardner *(Honda)*	R. Biland-K. Waltisperg *(LCR-Krauser)*

East Germany

	50cc	80cc	125cc	250cc	350cc	500cc	Sidecar
1961 Sachsenring	—	—	E. Degner *(MZ)*	M. Hailwood *(Honda)*	G. Hocking *(MV Agusta)*	G. Hocking *(MV Agusta)*	—

	50cc	80cc	125cc	250cc	350cc	500cc	Sidecar
1962 Sachsenring	J. Huberts *(Kreidler)*	—	L. Taveri *(Honda)*	J. Redman *(Honda)*	J. Redman *(Honda)*	M. Hailwood *(MV Agusta)*	—
1963 Sachsenring	—	—	H. Anderson *(Suzuki)*	M. Hailwood *(MZ)*	M. Hailwood *(MV Agusta)*	M. Hailwood *(MV Agusta)*	—
1964 Sachsenring	—	—	H. Anderson *(Suzuki)*	P. Read *(Yamaha)*	J. Redman *(Honda)*	M. Hailwood *(MV Agusta)*	—
1965 Sachsenring	—	—	F. Perris *(Suzuki)*	J. Redman *(Honda)*	J. Redman *(Honda)*	M. Hailwood *(MV Agusta)*	—
1966 Sachsenring	—	—	L. Taveri *(Honda)*	M. Hailwood *(Honda)*	G. Agostini *(MV Agusta)*	F. Stastny *(Jawa)*	—
1967 Sachsenring	—	—	B. Ivy *(Yamaha)*	P. Read *(Yamaha)*	M. Hailwood *(Honda)*	G. Agostini *(MV Agusta)*	—
1968 Sachsenring	—	—	P. Read *(Yamaha)*	B. Ivy *(Yamaha)*	G. Agostini *(MV Agusta)*	G. Agostini *(MV Agusta)*	—
1969 Sachsenring	A. Nieto *(Derbi)*	—	D. Simmonds *(Kawasaki)*	R. Pasolini *(Benelli)*	G. Agostini *(MV Agusta)*	G. Agostini *(MV Agusta)*	—
1970 Sachsenring	A. Toersen *(Jamathi)*	—	A. Nieto *(Derbi)*	R. Gould *(Yamaha)*	G. Agostini *(MV Agusta)*	G. Agostini *(MV Agusta)*	—
1971 Sachsenring	A. Nieto *(Derbi)*	—	A. Nieto *(Derbi)*	D. Braun *(Yamaha)*	G. Agostini *(MV Agusta)*	G. Agostini *(MV Agusta)*	—
1972 Sachsenring	T. Timmer *(Jamathi)*	—	B. Jansson *(Maico)*	J. Saarinen *(Yamaha)*	P. Read *(MV Agusta)*	G. Agostini *(MV Agusta)*	—

Finland

	50cc	80cc	125cc	250cc	350cc	500cc	Sidecar
1962 Tampere	L. Taveri *(Honda)*	—	J. Redman *(Honda)*	—	T. Robb *(Honda)*	A. Shepherd *(Matchless)*	—
1963 Tampere	H. G. Anscheidt *(Kreidler)*	—	H. Anderson *(Suzuki)*	—	M. Hailwood *(MV Agusta)*	M. Hailwood *(MV Agusta)*	—
1964 Imatra	H. Anderson *(Suzuki)*	—	L. Taveri *(Honda)*	—	J. Redman *(Honda)*	J. Ahearn *(Norton)*	—
1965 Imatra	—	—	H. Anderson *(Suzuki)*	M. Duff *(Yamaha)*	G. Agostini *(MV Agusta)*	G. Agostini *(MV Agusta)*	—
1966 Imatra	—	—	P. Read *(Yamaha)*	M. Hailwood *(Honda)*	M. Hailwood *(Honda)*	G. Agostini *(MV Agusta)*	—
1967 Imatra	—	—	S. Graham *(Suzuki)*	M. Hailwood *(Honda)*	—	G. Agostini *(MV Agusta)*	K. Enders–R. Engelhardt *(BMW)*
1968 Imatra	—	—	P. Read *(Yamaha)*	P. Read *(Yamaha)*	—	G. Agostini *(MV Agusta)*	H. Fath–W. Kalauch *(URS)*
1969 Imatra	—	—	D. Simmonds *(Kawasaki)*	K. Andersson *(Yamaha)*	G. Agostini *(MV Agusta)*	G. Agostini *(MV Agusta)*	K. Enders–R. Engelhardt *(BMW)*
1970 Imatra	—	—	D. Simmonds *(Kawasaki)*	R. Gould *(Yamaha)*	G. Agostini *(MV Agusta)*	G. Agostini *(MV Agusta)*	K. Enders–W. Kalauch *(BMW)*

	50cc	80cc	125cc	250cc	350cc	500cc	Sidecar
1971 Imatra	—	—	B. Sheene *(Suzuki)*	R. Gould *(Yamaha)*	G. Agostini *(MV Agusta)*	G. Agostini *(MV Agusta)*	H. Owesle–P. Rutterford *(Münch URS)*
1972 Imatra	—	—	K. Andersson *(Yamaha)*	J. Saarinen *(Yamaha)*	G. Agostini *(MV Agusta)*	G. Agostini *(MV Agusta)*	C. Vincent–M. Casey *(Münch URS)*
1973 Imatra	—	—	O. Buscherini *(Malanca)*	T. Länsivuori *(Yamaha)*	G. Agostini *(MV Agusta)*	G. Agostini *(MV Agusta)*	K. Rahko–K. Laatikainen *(Honda)*
1974 Imatra	J. Van Zeebroeck *(Kreidler)*	—	—	W. Villa *(Harley D.)*	J. Dodds *(Yamaha)*	P. Read *(MV Agusta)*	—
1975 Imatra	A. Nieto *(Kreidler)*	—	—	M. Rougerie *(Harley D.)*	J. Cecotto *(Yamaha)*	G. Agostini *(Yamaha)*	—
1976 Imatra	J. Van Zeebroeck *(Kreidler)*	—	P. Bianchi *(Morbidelli)*	W. Villa *(Harley D.)*	W. Villa *(Harley D.)*	P. Hennen *(Suzuki)*	—
1977 Imatra	—	—	P. Bianchi *(Morbidelli)*	W. Villa *(Harley D.)*	T. Katayama *(Yamaha)*	J. Cecotto *(Yamaha)*	—
1978 Imatra	—	—	A. Nieto *(Minarelli)*	K. Ballington *(Kawasaki)*	K. Ballington *(Kawasaki)*	W. Hartog *(Suzuki)*	—
1979 Imatra	—	—	R. Tormo *(Bultaco)*	K. Ballington *(Kawasaki)*	G. Hansford *(Kawasaki)*	B. Van Dulmen *(Suzuki)*	—
1980 Imatra	—	—	A. Nieto *(Minarelli)*	K. Ballington *(Kawasaki)*	—	W. Hartog *(Suzuki)*	J. Taylor–B. Johansson *(Yamaha)*
1981 Imatra	—	—	A. Nieto *(Minarelli)*	A. Mang *(Kawasaki)*	—	M. Lucchinelli *(Suzuki)*	R. Biland–K. Waltisperg *(Yamaha)*
1982 Imatra	—	—	I. Palazzese *(MBA)*	C. Sarron *(Yamaha)*	A. Mang *(Kawasaki)*	—	R. Biland–K. Waltisperg *(LCR-Yamaha)*

France

	50cc	80cc	125cc	250cc	350cc	500cc	Sidecar
1951 Albi	—	—	—	B. Ruffo *(Guzzi)*	G. Duke *(Norton)*	Alf. Milani *(Gilera)*	E. Oliver–L. Dobelli *(Norton)*
1953 Rouen	—	—	—	—	F. Anderson *(Guzzi)*	G. Duke *(Gilera)*	E. Oliver–S. Dibben *(Norton)*
1954 Reims	—	—	—	W. Haas *(NSU)*	P. Monneret *(AJS)*	P. Monneret *(Gilera)*	—
1955 Reims	—	—	C. Ubbiali *(MV Agusta)*	—	D. Agostini *(Guzzi)*	G. Duke *(Gilera)*	—
1959 Cl. Ferrand	—	—	—	—	J. Surtees *(MV Agusta)*	J. Surtees *(MV Agusta)*	F. Scheidegger–H. Burckardt *(BMW)*
1960 Cl. Ferrand	—	—	—	—	G. Hocking *(MV Agusta)*	J. Surtees *(MV Agusta)*	H. Fath–A. Wohlgemuth *(BMW)*
1961 Cl. Ferrand	—	—	T. Phillis *(Honda)*	T. Phillis *(Honda)*	—	G. Hocking *(MV Agusta)*	F. Scheidegger–H. Burckardt *(BMW)*
1962 Cl. Ferrand	J. Huberts *(Kreidler)*	—	K. Takahashi *(Honda)*	J. Redman *(Honda)*	—	—	M. Deubel–E. Horner *(BMW)*

	50cc	80cc	125cc	250cc	350cc	500cc	Sidecar
1963 Cl. Ferrand	H. G. Anscheidt *(Kreidler)*	—	H. Anderson *(Suzuki)*	—	—	—	—
1964 Cl. Ferrand	H. Anderson *(Suzuki)*	—	L. Taveri *(Honda)*	P. Read *(Yamaha)*	—	—	F. Scheidegger–J. Robinson *(BMW)*
1965 Rouen	R. Bryans *(Honda)*	—	H. Anderson *(Suzuki)*	P. Read *(Yamaha)*	—	—	F. Camathias–F. Ducret *(BMW)*
1966 Cl. Ferrand	—	—	—	M. Hailwood *(Honda)*	M. Hailwood *(Honda)*	—	F. Scheidegger–J. Robinson *(BMW)*
1967 Cl. Ferrand	H. Katayama *(Suzuki)*	—	B. Ivy *(Yamatha)*	B. Ivy *(Yamaha)*	—	—	K. Enders–R. Engelhardt *(BMW)*
1969 Le Mans	A. Toersen *(Kreidler)*	—	J. Aureal *(Yamaha)*	S. Herrero *(Ossa)*	—	G. Agostini *(MV Agusta)*	H. Fath–W. Kalauch *(URS)*
1970 Le Mans	A. Nieto *(Derbi)*	—	D. Braun *(Suzuki)*	R. Gould *(Yamaha)*	—	G. Agostini *(MV Agusta)*	K. Enders–W. Kalauch *(BMW)*
1972 Cl. Ferrand	—		G. Parlotti *(Morbidelli)*	P. Read *(Yamaha)*	J. Saarinen *(Yamaha)*	G. Agostini *(MV Agusta)*	H. Luthringshauser– J. Cusnick *(BMW)*
1973 Paul Ricard	—	—	K. Andersson *(Yamaha)*	J. Saarinen *(Yamaha)*	G. Agostini *(MV Agusta)*	J. Saarinen *(Yamaha)*	K. Enders–R. Engelhardt *(BMW)*
1974 Cl. Ferrand	H. Van Kessel *(Kreidler)*	—	K. Andersson *(Yamaha)*	—	G. Agostini *(Yamaha)*	P. Read *(MV Agusta)*	S. Schauzu–W. Kalauch *(BMW)*
1975 Paul Ricard	—	—	K. Andersson *(Yamaha)*	J. Cecotto *(Yamaha)*	J. Cecotto *(Yamaha)*	G. Agostini *(Yamaha)*	H. Schmid–J. P. Matile *(König)*
1976 Le Mans	H. Rittberger *(Kreidler)*	—	—	W. Villa *(Harley D.)*	W. Villa *(Harley D.)*	B. Sheene *(Suzuki)*	R. Biland–K. Williams *(Seymaz)*
1977 Paul Ricard	—	—	P. Bianchi *(Morbidelli)*	J. Ekerold *(Yamaha)*	T. Katayama *(Yamaha)*	B. Sheene *(Suzuki)*	A. Michel–G. Lecorre *(Yamaha)*
1978 Nogaro	—	—	P. Bianchi *(Minarelli)*	G. Hansford *(Kawasaki)*	G. Hansford *(Kawasaki)*	K. Roberts *(Yamaha)*	R. Biland–K. Williams *(Yamaha)*
1979 Le Mans	E. Lazzarini *(Kreidler)*	—	G. Bertin *(Motobecane)*	K. Ballington *(Kawasaki)*	P. Fernandez *(Yamaha)*	B. Sheene *(Suzuki)*	R. Biland–K. Waltisperg (B2b) *(LCR-Yamaha)*
1980 Paul Ricard	—	—	A. Nieto *(Minarelli)*	K. Ballington *(Kawasaki)*	J. Ekerold *(Bimota)*	K. Roberts *(Yamaha)*	R. Biland–K. Waltisperg *(Yamaha)*
1981 Paul Ricard	—	—	A. Nieto *(Minarelli)*	A. Mang *(Kawasaki)*	—	M. Lucchinelli *(Suzuki)*	R. Biland–K. Waltisperg *(Yamaha)*
1982 Nogaro	—	—	J. C. Selini *(MBA)*	J. Tournadre *(Yamaha)*	J. F. Baldé *(Kawasaki)*	M. Frutschi *(Sanvenero)*	—
1983 Le Mans	S. Döflinger *(Kreidler)*	—	R. Tormo *(MBA)*	A. Carter *(Yamaha)*	—	F. Spencer *(Honda)*	R. Biland–K. Waltisperg *(LCR-Yamaha)*
1984 Paul Ricard	—	—	A. Nieto *(Garelli)*	T. Mang *(Yamaha)*	—	F. Spencer *(Honda)*	R. Biland–K. Waltisperg *(LCR-Yamaha)*
1985 Le Mans	—	A. Nieto *(Derbi)*	E. Gianola *(Garelli)*	F. Spencer *(Honda)*	—	F. Spencer *(Honda)*	E. Streuer–B. Schnieders *(LCR-Yamaha)*
1986 Paul Ricard	—	—	L. Cadalora *(Garelli)*	C. Lavado *(Yamaha)*	—	E. Lawson *(Yamaha)*	E. Streuer–B. Schnieders *(LCR-Yamaha)*
1987 Le Mans	—	—	F. Gresini *(Garelli)*	R. Roth *(Honda)*	—	R. Mamola *(Yamaha)*	R. Biland–K. Waltisperg *(LCR-Krauser)*

Great Britain

Isle of Man courses: *Mountain; **Clypse; ***Both courses used

	50cc	80cc	125cc	250cc	350cc	500cc	Sidecar
1949 IOM*	—	—	—	M. Barrington *(Guzzi)*	F. Frith *(Velocette)*	H. Daniell *(Norton)*	—
1950 IOM*	—	—	—	D. Ambrosini *(Benelli)*	A. Bell *(Norton)*	G. Duke *(Norton)*	—
1951 IOM*	—	—	C. McCandless *(Mondial)*	T. Wood *(Guzzi)*	G. Duke *(Norton)*	G. Duke *(Norton)*	—
1952 IOM*	—	—	C. Sandford *(MV Agusta)*	F. Anderson *(Guzzi)*	G. Duke *(Norton)*	R. Armstrong *(Norton)*	—
1953 IOM*	—	—	L. Graham *(MV Agusta)*	F. Anderson *(Guzzi)*	R. Amm *(Norton)*	R. Amm *(Norton)*	—
1954 IOM***	—	—	R. Hollaus *(NSU)*	W. Haas *(NSU)*	R. Coleman *(Norton)*	R. Amm *(Norton)*	E. Oliver–L. Nutt *(Norton)*
1955 IOM***	—	—	C. Ubbiali *(MV Agusta)*	B. Lomas *(MV Agusta)*	B. Lomas *(Guzzi)*	G. Duke *(Gilera)*	W. Schneider–H. Strauss *(BMW)*
1956 IOM***	—	—	C. Ubbiali *(MV Agusta)*	C. Ubbiali *(MV Agusta)*	K. Kavanagh *(Guzzi)*	J. Surtees *(MV Agusta)*	F. Hillebrand–M. Grünwald *(BMW)*
1957 IOM***	—	—	T. Provini *(Mondial)*	C. Sandford *(Mondial)*	B. McIntyre *(Gilera)*	B. McIntyre *(Gilera)*	F. Hillebrand–M. Grünwald *(BMW)*
1958 IOM***	—	—	C. Ubbiali *(MV Agusta)*	T. Provini *(MV Agusta)*	J. Surtees *(MV Agusta)*	J. Surtees *(MV Agusta)*	W. Schneider–H. Strauss *(BMW)*
1959 IOM***	—	—	T. Provini *(MV Agusta)*	T. Provini *(MV Agusta)*	J. Surtees *(MV Agusta)*	J. Surtees *(MV Agusta)*	W. Schneider–H. Strauss *(BMW)*
1960 IOM*	—	—	C. Ubbiali *(MV Agusta)*	G. Hocking *(MV Agusta)*	J. Hartle *(MV Agusta)*	J. Surtees *(MV Agusta)*	H. Fath–A. Wohlgemuth *(BMW)*
1961 IOM*	—	—	M. Hailwood *(Honda)*	M. Hailwood *(Honda)*	P. Read *(Norton)*	M. Hailwood *(Norton)*	M. Deubel–E. Hörner *(BMW)*
1962 IOM*	E. Degner *(Suzuki)*	—	L. Taveri *(Honda)*	D. Minter *(Honda)*	M. Hailwood *(MV Agusta)*	G. Hocking *(MV Agusta)*	C. Vincent–E. Bliss *(BSA)*
1963 IOM*	M. Itoh *(Suzuki)*	—	H. Anderson *(Suzuki)*	J. Redman *(Honda)*	J. Redman *(Honda)*	M. Hailwood *(MV Agusta)*	F. Camathias–A. Herzig *(FCS)*
1964 IOM*	H. Anderson *(Suzuki)*	—	L. Taveri *(Honda)*	J. Redman *(Honda)*	J. Redman *(Honda)*	M. Hailwood *(MV Agusta)*	M. Deubel–E. Hörner *(BMW)*
1965 IOM*	L. Taveri *(Honda)*	—	P. Read *(Yamaha)*	J. Redman *(Honda)*	J. Redman *(Honda)*	M. Hailwood *(MV Agusta)*	M. Deubel–E. Hörner *(BMW)*
1966 IOM*	R. Bryans *(Honda)*	—	B. Ivy *(Yamaha)*	M. Hailwood *(Honda)*	G. Agostini *(MV Agusta)*	M. Hailwood *(Honda)*	F. Scheidegger–J. Robinson *(BMW)*
1967 IOM*	S. Graham *(Suzuki)*	—	P. Read *(Yamaha)*	M. Hailwood *(Honda)*	M. Hailwood *(Honda)*	M. Hailwood *(Honda)*	S. Schauzu–H. Schneider *(BMW)*
1968 IOM*	Barry Smith *(Derbi)*	—	P. Read *(Yamaha)*	B. Ivy *(Yamaha)*	G. Agostini *(MV Agusta)*	G. Agostini *(MV Agusta)*	S. Schauzu–H. Schneider *(BMW)*
1969 IOM*	—	—	D. Simmonds *(Kawasaki)*	K. Carruthers *(Benelli)*	G. Agostini *(MV Agusta)*	G. Agostini *(MV Agusta)*	K. Enders–R. Engelhardt *(BMW)*
1970 IOM*	—	—	D. Braun *(Suzuki)*	K. Carruthers *(Yamaha)*	G. Agostini *(MV Agusta)*	G. Agostini *(MV Agusta)*	K. Enders–W. Kalauch *(BMW)*

	50cc	80cc	125cc	250cc	350cc	500cc	Sidecar
1971 IOM*	—	—	C. Mortimer *(Yamaha)*	P. Read *(Yamaha)*	T. Jefferies *(Yamsel)*	G. Agostini *(MV Agusta)*	S. Schauzu–W. Kalauch *(BMW)*
1972 IOM*	—	—	C. Mortimer *(Yamaha)*	P. Read *(Yamaha)*	G. Agostini *(MV Agusta)*	G. Agostini *(MV Agusta)*	S. Schauzu–W. Kalauch *(BMW)*
1973 IOM*	—	—	T. Robb *(Yamaha)*	C. Williams *(Yamaha)*	T. Rutter *(Yamaha)*	J. Findlay *(Suzuki)*	K. Enders–R. Engelhardt *(BMW)*
1974 IOM*	—	—	—	C. Williams *(Yamaha)*	T. Rutter *(Yamaha)*	P. Carpenter *(Yamaha)*	H. Luthringshauser– H. Hahn *(BMW)*
1975 IOM*	—	—	—	C. Mortimer *(Yamaha)*	C. Williams *(Yamaha)*	M. Grant *(Kawasaki)*	R. Steinhausen–J. Huber *(Busch König)*
1976 IOM*	—	—	—	T. Herron *(Yamaha)*	C. Mortimer *(Yamaha)*	T. Herron *(Yamaha)*	R. Steinhausen–J. Huber *(Busch König)*
1977 Silverstone	—	—	P. L. Conforti *(Morbidelli)*	K. Ballington *(Yamaha)*	K. Ballington *(Yamaha)*	P. Hennen *(Suzuki)*	W. Schwärzel–A. Huber *(ARO Fath)*
1978 Silverstone	—	—	A. Nieto *(Minarelli)*	A. Mang *(Kawasaki)*	K. Ballington *(Kawasaki)*	K. Roberts *(Yamaha)*	A. Michel–S. Collins *(Seymaz-Yamaha)*
1979 Silverstone	—	—	A. Nieto *(Minarelli)*	K. Ballington *(Kawasaki)*	K. Ballington *(Kawasaki)*	K. Roberts *(Yamaha)*	R. Biland–K. Waltisperg (B2a) *(Yamaha)* A. Michel–M. Burkard (B2b) *(Seymaz-Yamaha)*
1980 Silverstone	—	—	L. Reggiani *(Minarelli)*	K. Ballington *(Kawasaki)*	A. Mang *(Kawasaki)*	R. Mamola *(Suzuki)*	D. Jones–B. Ayres *(Yamaha)*
1981 Silverstone	—	—	A. Nieto *(Minarelli)*	A. Mang *(Kawasaki)*	A. Mang *(Kawasaki)*	J. Middelburg *(Suzuki)*	R. Biland–K. Waltisperg *(Yamaha)*
1982 Silverstone	—	—	A. Nieto *(Garelli)*	M. Wimmer *(Yamaha)*	J. F. Baldé *(Kawasaki)*	F. Uncini *(Suzuki)*	E. Streuer–B. Schnieders *(LCR-Yamaha)*
1983 Silverstone	—	—	A. Nieto *(Garelli)*	J. Bolle *(Pernod)*	—	K. Roberts *(Yamaha)*	E. Streuer–B. Schnieders *(LCR-Yamaha)*
1984 Silverstone	—	—	A. Nieto *(Garelli)*	C. Sarron *(Yamaha)*	—	R. Mamola *(Honda)*	E. Streuer–B. Schnieders *(LCR-Yamaha)*
1985 Silverstone	—	—	A. Auinger *(Monnet)*	A. Mang *(Honda)*	—	F. Spencer *(Honda)*	—
1986 Silverstone	—	I. McConnachie *(Krauser)*	A. Auinger *(MBA)*	D. Sarron *(Honda)*	—	W. Gardner *(Honda)*	E. Streuer–B. Schnieders *(LCR-Yamaha)*
1987 Donington	—	J. Martinez *(Derbi)*	F. Gresini *(Garelli)*	A. Mang *(Honda)*	—	E. Lawson *(Yamaha)*	S. Webster–T. Hewitt *(LCR-Krauser)*

Holland

	50cc	80cc	125cc	250cc	350cc	500cc	Sidecar
1949 Assen	—	—	N. Pagani *(Mondial)*	—	F. Frith *(Velocette)*	N. Pagani *(Gilera)*	—
1950 Assen	—	—	B. Ruffo *(Mondial)*	—	B. Foster *(Velocette)*	U. Masetti *(Gilera)*	—
1951 Assen	—	—	Gianni Leoni *(Mondial)*	—	B. Doran *(AJS)*	G. Duke *(Norton)*	—

	50cc	80cc	125cc	250cc	350cc	500cc	Sidecar
1952 Assen	—	—	C. Sandford *(MV Agusta)*	E. Lorenzetti *(Guzzi)*	G. Duke *(Norton)*	U. Masetti *(Gilera)*	—
1953 Assen	—	—	W. Haas *(NSU)*	W. Haas *(NSU)*	E. Lorenzetti *(Guzzi)*	G. Duke *(Gilera)*	—
1954 Assen	—	—	R. Hollaus *(NSU)*	W. Haas *(NSU)*	F. Anderson *(Guzzi)*	G. Duke *(Gilera)*	—
1955 Assen	—	—	C. Ubbiali *(MV Agusta)*	L. Taveri *(MV Agusta)*	K. Kavanagh *(Guzzi)*	G. Duke *(Gilera)*	W. Faust–K. Remmert *(BMW)*
1956 Assen	—	—	C. Ubbiali *(MV Agusta)*	C. Ubbiali *(MV Agusta)*	B. Lomas *(Guzzi)*	J. Surtees *(MV Agusta)*	F. Hillebrand–M. Grünwald *(BMW)*
1957 Assen	—	—	T. Provini *(Mondial)*	T. Provini *(Mondial)*	K. Campbell *(Guzzi)*	J. Surtees *(MV Agusta)*	F. Hillebrand–M. Grünwald *(BMW)*
1958 Assen	—	—	C. Ubbiali *(MV Agusta)*	T. Provini *(MV Agusta)*	J. Surtees *(MV Agusta)*	J. Surtees *(MV Agusta)*	F. Camathias–H. Cecco *(BMW)*
1959 Assen	—	—	C. Ubbiali *(MV Agusta)*	T. Provini *(MV Agusta)*	—	J. Surtees *(MV Agusta)*	F. Camathias–H. Cecco *(BMW)*
1960 Assen	—	—	C. Ubbiali *(MV Agusta)*	C. Ubbiali *(MV Agusta)*	J. Surtees *(MV Agusta)*	R. Venturi *(MV Agusta)*	P. Harris–R. Campbell *(BMW)*
1961 Assen	—	—	T. Phillis *(Honda)*	M. Hailwood *(Honda)*	G. Hocking *(MV Agusta)*	G. Hocking *(MV Agusta)*	M. Deubel–E. Hörner *(BMW)*
1962 Assen	E. Degner *(Suzuki)*	—	L. Taveri *(Honda)*	J. Redman *(Honda)*	J. Redman *(Honda)*	M. Hailwood *(MV Agusta)*	F. Scheidegger–J. Robinson *(BMW)*
1963 Assen	E. Degner *(Suzuki)*	—	H. Anderson *(Suzuki)*	J. Redman *(Honda)*	J. Redman *(Honda)*	J. Hartle *(Gilera)*	M. Deubel–E. Hörner *(BMW)*
1964 Assen	R. Bryans *(Honda)*		J. Redman *(Honda)*	J. Redman *(Honda)*	J. Redman *(Honda)*	M. Hailwood *(MV Agusta)*	C. Seeley–R. Campbell *(FCS)*
1965 Assen	R. Bryans *(Honda)*	—	M. Duff *(Yamaha)*	P. Read *(Yamaha)*	J. Redman *(Honda)*	M. Hailwood *(MV Agusta)*	F. Scheidegger–J. Robinson *(BMW)*
1966 Assen	L. Taveri *(Honda)*	—	B. Ivy *(Yamaha)*	M. Hailwood *(Honda)*	M. Hailwood *(Honda)*	J. Redman *(Honda)*	F. Scheidegger–J. Robinson *(BMW)*
1967 Assen	H. Katayama *(Suzuki)*	—	P. Read *(Yamaha)*	M. Hailwood *(Honda)*	M. Hailwood *(Honda)*	M. Hailwood *(Honda)*	K. Enders–R. Engelhardt *(BMW)*
1968 Assen	P. Lodewijkx *(Jamathi)*	—	P. Read *(Yamaha)*	B. Ivy *(Yamaha)*	G. Agostini *(MV Agusta)*	G. Agostini *(MV Agusta)*	J. Attenberger–J. Schillinger *(BMW)*
1969 Assen	Barry Smith *(Derbi)*	—	D. Simmonds *(Kawasaki)*	R. Pasolini *(Benelli)*	G. Agostini *(MV Agusta)*	G. Agostini *(MV Agusta)*	H. Fath–W. Kalauch *(URS)*
1970 Assen	A. Nieto *(Derbi)*	—	D. Braun *(Suzuki)*	R. Gould *(Yamaha)*	G. Agostini *(MV Agusta)*	G. Agostini *(MV Agusta)*	G. Auerbacher–H. Hahn *(BMW)*
1971 Assen	A. Nieto *(Derbi)*	—	A. Nieto *(Derbi)*	P. Read *(Yamaha)*	G. Agostini *(MV Agusta)*	G. Agostini *(MV Agusta)*	H. Owesle–J. Kremer *(Münch URS)*
1972 Assen	A. Nieto *(Derbi)*	—	A. Nieto *(Derbi)*	R. Gould *(Yamaha)*	G. Agostini *(MV Agusta)*	G. Agostini *(MV Agusta)*	K. Enders–R. Engelhardt *(BMW)*
1973 Assen	B. Kneubühler *(Kreidler)*	—	E. Lazzarini *(Piovaticci)*	D. Braun *(Yamaha)*	G. Agostini *(MV Agusta)*	P. Read *(MV Agusta)*	K. Enders–R. Engelhardt *(BMW)*
1974 Assen	H. Rittberger *(Kreidler)*	—	B. Kneubühler *(Yamaha)*	W. Villa *(Harley D.)*	G. Agostini *(Yamaha)*	G. Agostini *(Yamaha)*	K. Enders–R. Engelhardt *(Busch Enders)*

	50cc	80cc	125cc	250cc	350cc	500cc	Sidecar
1975 Assen	A. Nieto *(Kreidler)*	—	P. Pileri *(Morbidelli)*	W. Villa *(Harley D.)*	D. Braun *(Yamaha)*	B. Sheene *(Suzuki)*	W. Schwärzel–A. Huber *(König)*
1976 Assen	A. Nieto *(Bultaco)*	—	P. Bianchi *(Morbidelli)*	W. Villa *(Harley D.)*	G. Agostini *(MV Agusta)*	B. Sheene *(Suzuki)*	H. Schmid–J. P. Matile *(Yamaha)*
1977 Assen	A. Nieto *(Bultaco)*	—	A. Nieto *(Bultaco)*	M. Grant *(Kawasaki)*	K. Ballington *(Yamaha)*	W. Hartog *(Suzuki)*	R. Biland–K. Williams *(Yamaha)*
1978 Assen	E. Lazzarini *(Kreidler)*	—	E. Lazzarini *(MBA)*	K. Roberts *(Yamaha)*	K. Ballington *(Kawasaki)*	J. Cecotto *(Yamaha)*	W. Schwärzel–A. Huber *(ARO Fath)*
1979 Assen	E. Lazzarini *(Kreidler)*	—	A. Nieto *(Minarelli)*	G. Rossi *(Morbidelli)*	G. Hansford *(Kawasaki)*	V. Ferrari *(Suzuki)*	R. Biland–K. Waltisperg (B2a) *(Yamaha)*
1980 Assen	R. Tormo *(Kreidler)*	—	A. Nieto *(Minarelli)*	C. Lavado *(Yamaha)*	J. Ekerold *(Bimota)*	J. Middelburg *(Yamaha)*	J. Taylor–B. Johansson *(Yamaha)*
1981 Assen	R. Tormo *(Bultaco)*	—	A. Nieto *(Minarelli)*	A. Mang *(Kawasaki)*	A. Mang *(Kawasaki)*	M. Lucchinelli *(Suzuki)*	A. Michel–M. Burkard *(Seymaz-Yamaha)*
1982 Assen	S. Dörflinger *(Kreidler)*	—	A. Nieto *(Garelli)*	A. Mang *(Kawasaki)*	J. F. Baldé *(Kawasaki)*	F. Uncini *(Suzuki)*	R. Biland–K. Waltisperg *(LCR-Yamaha)*
1983 Assen	E. Lazzarini *(Garelli)*	—	A. Nieto *(Garelli)*	C. Lavado *(Yamaha)*	—	K. Roberts *(Yamaha)*	R. Biland–K. Waltisperg *(LCR-Yamaha)*
1984 Assen	—	J. Martinez *(Derbi)*	A. Nieto *(Garelli)*	C. Lavado *(Yamaha)*	—	R. Mamola *(Honda)*	R. Biland–K. Waltisperg *(LCR-Yamaha)*
1985 Assen	—	G. Kafka *(Seel)*	P. P. Bianchi *(MBA)*	F. Spencer *(Honda)*	—	R. Mamola *(Honda)*	R. Biland–K. Waltisperg *(LCR-Yamaha)*
1986 Assen	—	J. Martinez *(Derbi)*	L. Cadalora *(Garelli)*	C. Lavado *(Yamaha)*	—	W. Gardner *(Honda)*	A. Michel–J. M. Fresc *(LCR-Yamaha)*
1987 Assen	—	J. Martinez *(Derbi)*	F. Gresini *(Garelli)*	A. Mang *(Honda)*	—	E. Lawson *(Yamaha)*	E. Streuer–B. Schnieders *(LCR-Yamaha)*

Italy

	50cc	80cc	125cc	250cc	350cc	500cc	Sidecar
1949 Monza	—	—	Gianni Leoni *(Mondial)*	D. Ambrosini *(Benelli)*	—	N. Pagani *(Gilera)*	E. Frigerio–E. Ricotti *(Gilera)*
1950 Monza	—	—	Gianni Leoni *(Mondial)*	D. Ambrosini *(Benelli)*	G. Duke *(Norton)*	G. Duke *(Norton)*	E. Oliver–L. Dobelli *(Norton)*
1951 Monza	—	—	C. Ubbiali *(Mondial)*	E. Lorenzetti *(Guzzi)*	G. Duke *(Norton)*	Alf. Milani *(Gilera)*	Alb. Milani–G. Pizzocri *(Gilera)*
1952 Monza	—	—	E. Mendogni *(Morini)*	E. Lorenzetti *(Guzzi)*	R. Amm *(Norton)*	L. Graham *(MV Agusta)*	E. Merlo–D. Magri *(Gilera)*
1953 Monza	—	—	W. Haas *(NSU)*	E. Lorenzetti *(Guzzi)*	E. Lorenzetti *(Guzzi)*	G. Duke *(Gilera)*	E. Oliver–S. Dibben *(Norton)*
1954 Monza	—	—	G. Sala *(MV Agusta)*	A. Wheeler *(Guzzi)*	F. Anderson *(Guzzi)*	G. Duke *(Gilera)*	W. Noll–F. Cron *(BMW)*
1955 Monza	—	—	C. Ubbiali *(MV Agusta)*	C. Ubbiali *(MV Agusta)*	D. Dale *(Guzzi)*	U. Masetti *(MV Agusta)*	W. Noll–F. Cron *(BMW)*
1956 Monza	—	—	C. Ubbiali *(MV Agusta)*	C. Ubbiali *(MV Agusta)*	L. Liberati *(Gilera)*	G. Duke *(Gilera)*	Alb. Milani–R. Milani *(Gilera)*

	50cc	80cc	125cc	250cc	350cc	500cc	Sidecar
1957 Monza	—	—	C. Ubbiali *(MV Agusta)*	T. Provini *(Mondial)*	B. McIntyre *(Gilera)*	L. Liberati *(Gilera)*	Alb. Milani–R. Milani *(Gilera)*
1958 Monza	—	—	B. Spaggiari *(Ducati)*	E. Mendogni *(Morini)*	J. Surtees *(MV Agusta)*	J. Surtees *(MV Agusta)*	—
1959 Monza	—	—	E. Degner *(MZ)*	C. Ubbiali *(MV Agusta)*	J. Surtees *(MV Agusta)*	J. Surtees *(MV Agusta)*	—
1960 Monza	—	—	C. Ubbiali *(MV Agusta)*	C. Ubbiali *(MV Agusta)*	G. Hocking *(MV Agusta)*	J. Surtees *(MV Agusta)*	—
1961 Monza	—	—	E. Degner *(MZ)*	J. Redman *(Honda)*	G. Hocking *(MV Agusta)*	M. Hailwood *(MV Agusta)*	—
1962 Monza	H.Anscheidt *(Kreidler)*	—	T. Tanaka *(Honda)*	J. Redman *(Honda)*	J. Redman *(Honda)*	M. Hailwood *(MV Agusta)*	—
1963 Monza	—	—	L. Taveri *(Honda)*	T. Provini *(Morini)*	J. Redman *(Honda)*	M. Hailwood *(MV Agusta)*	—
1964 Monza	—	—	L. Taveri *(Honda)*	P. Read *(Yamaha)*	J. Redman *(Honda)*	M. Hailwood *(MV Agusta)*	—
1965 Monza	—	—	H. Anderson *(Suzuki)*	T. Provini *(Benelli)*	G. Agostini *(MV Agusta)*	M. Hailwood *(MV Agusta)*	F. Scheidegger–J. Robinson *(BMW)*
1966 Monza	H. Anscheidt *(Suzuki)*	—	L. Taveri *(Honda)*	M. Hailwood *(Honda)*	G. Agostini *(MV Agusta)*	G. Agostini *(MV Agusta)*	—
1967 Monza	—	—	B. Ivy *(Yamaha)*	P. Read *(Yamaha)*	R. Bryans *(Honda)*	G. Agostini *(MV Agusta)*	G. Auerbacher–B. Nelson *(BMW)*
1968 Monza	—	—	B. Ivy *(Yamaha)*	P. Read *(Yamaha)*	G. Agostini *(MV Agusta)*	G. Agostini *(MV Agusta)*	—
1969 Imola	P. Lodewijkx *(Jamathi)*	—	D. Simmonds *(Kawasaki)*	P. Read *(Yamaha)*	P. Read *(Yamaha)*	A. Pagani *(Linto)*	—
1970 Monza	J. De Vries *(Kreidler)*	—	A. Nieto *(Derbi)*	R. Gould *(Yamaha)*	G. Agostini *(MV Agusta)*	G. Agostini *(MV Agusta)*	—
1971 Monza	J. De Vries *(Kreidler)*	—	G. Parlotti *(Morbidelli)*	G. Marsows-zky *(Yamaha)*	J. Saarinen *(Yamaha)*	A. Pagani *(MV Agusta)*	—
1972 Imola	J. De Vries *(Kreidler)*	—	A. Nieto *(Derbi)*	R. Pasolini *(Aermacchi)*	G. Agostini *(MV Agusta)*	G. Agostini *(MV Agusta)*	—
1973 Monza	J. De Vries *(Kreidler)*	—	K. Andersson *(Yamaha)*	—	G. Agostini *(MV Agusta)*	—	—
1974 Imola	H. Van Kessel *(Kreidler)*	—	A. Nieto *(Derbi)*	W. Villa *(Harley D.)*	G. Agostini *(Yamaha)*	G. F. Bonera *(MV Agusta)*	K. Enders–R. Engelhardt *(Busch Enders)*
1975 Imola	A. Nieto *(Kreidler)*	—	P. Pileri *(Morbidelli)*	W. Villa *(Harley D.)*	J. Cecotto *(Yamaha)*	G. Agostini *(Yamaha)*	—
1976 Mugello	A. Nieto *(Bultaco)*	—	P. Bianchi *(Morbidelli)*	W. Villa *(Harley D.)*	J. Cecotto *(Yamaha)*	B. Sheene *(Suzuki)*	—
1977 Imola	E. Lazzarini *(Kreidler)*	—	P. Bianchi *(Morbidelli)*	F. Uncini *(Harley D.)*	A. North *(Yamaha)*	B. Sheene *(Suzuki)*	—
1978 Mugello	R. Tormo *(Bultaco)*	—	E. Lazzarini *(MBA)*	K. Ballington *(Kawasaki)*	K. Ballington *(Kawasaki)*	K. Roberts *(Yamaha)*	R. Biland–K. Williams *(Yamaha)*
1979 Imola	E. Lazzarini *(Kreidler)*	—	A. Nieto *(Minarelli)*	K. Ballington *(Kawasaki)*	G. Hansford *(Kawasaki)*	K. Roberts *(Yamaha)*	—

	50cc	80cc	125cc	250cc	350cc	500cc	Sidecar
1980 Misano	E. Lazzarini *(Iprem)*	—	P. Bianchi *(MBA)*	A. Mang *(Kawasaki)*	J. Cecotto *(Bimota)*	K. Roberts *(Yamaha)*	—
1981 Monza	R. Tormo *(Bultaco)*	—	G. Bertin *(Sanvenero)*	E. Saul *(Chevallier)*	J. Ekerold *(Bimota)*	K. Roberts *(Yamaha)*	—
1982 Misano	S. Dörflinger *(Kreidler)*	—	A. Nieto *(Garelli)*	A. Mang *(Kawasaki)*	D. De Radigues *(Chevallier)*	F. Uncini *(Suzuki)*	—
1983 Monza	E. Lazzarini *(Garelli)*	—	A. Nieto *(Garelli)*	C. Lavado *(Yamaha)*	—	F. Spencer *(Honda)*	—
1984 Misano	—	P. Bianchi *(Casal)*	A. Nieto *(Garelli)*	F. Ricci *(Honda)*	—	F. Spencer *(Honda)*	—
1985 Mugello	—	J. Martinez *(Derbi)*	P. P. Bianchi *(MBA)*	F. Spencer *(Honda)*	—	F. Spencer *(Honda)*	—
1986 Monza	—	S. Dorflinger *(Krauser)*	F. Gresini *(Garelli)*	T. Mang *(Honda)*	—	E. Lawson *(Yamaha)*	—
1987 Monza	—	J. Martinez *(Derbi)*	F. Gresini *(Garelli)*	A. Mang *(Honda)*	—	W. Gardner *(Honda)*	—

Japan

	50cc	80cc	125cc	250cc	350cc	500cc	Sidecar
1963 Suzuka	L. Taveri *(Honda)*	—	F. Perris *(Suzuki)*	J. Redman *(Honda)*	—	—	—
1964 Suzuka	—	—	E. Degner *(Suzuki)*	J. Redman *(Honda)*	J. Redman *(Honda)*	—	—
1965 Suzuka	L. Taveri *(Honda)*	—	H. Anderson *(Suzuki)*	M. Hailwood *(Honda)*	M. Hailwood *(MV Agusta)*	—	—
1966 Fuji	H. Katayama *(Suzuki)*	—	B. Ivy *(Yamaha)*	H. Hasegawa *(Yamaha)*	P. Read *(Yamaha)*	—	—
1967 Fuji	M. Itoh *(Suzuki)*	—	B. Ivy *(Yamaha)*	R. Bryans *(Honda)*	M. Hailwood *(Honda)*	—	—
1987 Suzuka	—	—	—	M. Kobayashi *(Honda)*	—	R. Mamola *(Yamaha)*	—

Portugal

	50cc	80cc	125cc	250cc	350cc	500cc	Sidecar
1987 Jarama	—	J. Martinez *(Derbi)*	P. Casoli *(MBA)*	A. Mang *(Honda)*	—	E. Lawson *(Yamaha)*	—

San Marino

	50cc	80cc	125cc	250cc	350cc	500cc	Sidecar
1981 Imola	R. Tormo *(Bultaco)*	—	L. Reggiani *(Minarelli)*	A. Mang *(Kawasaki)*	—	M. Lucchinelli *(Suzuki)*	—
1982 Mugello	E. Lazzarini *(Garelli)*	—	—	A. Mang *(Kawasaki)*	—	F. Spencer *(Honda)*	A. Michel–M. Burkard *(Seymaz-Yamaha)*
1983 Imola	R. Tormo *(Garelli)*	—	M. Vitali *(MBA)*	—	—	K. Roberts *(Yamaha)*	R. Biland–K. Waltisperg *(LCR-Yamaha)*
1984 Mugello	—	G. Waibel *(Real)*	M. Vitali *(MBA)*	M. Herweh *(Real)*	—	R. Mamola *(Honda)*	—
1985 Misano	—	J. Martinez *(Derbi)*	F. Gresini *(Garelli)*	C. Lavado *(Yamaha)*	—	E. Lawson *(Yamaha)*	—
1986 Misano	—	P. Bianchi *(Seel)*	A. Auinger *(MBA)*	T. Taira *(Yamaha)*	—	E. Lawson *(Yamaha)*	—
1987 Misano	—	M. Herreros *(Derbi)*	F. Gresini *(Garelli)*	L. Reggiani *(Aprilia)*	—	R. Mamola *(Yamaha)*	—

Spain

	50cc	80cc	125cc	250cc	350cc	500cc	Sidecar
1951 Montjuich	—	—	Guido Leoni *(Mondial)*	—	T. Wood *(Guzzi)*	U. Masetti *(Gilera)*	E. Oliver–L. Dobelli *(Norton)*
1952 Montjuich	—	—	E. Mendogni *(Morini)*	—	—	L. Graham *(MV Agusta)*	E. Oliver–L. Dobelli *(Norton)*
1953 Montjuich	—	—	A. Copeta *(MV Agusta)*	E. Lorenzetti *(Guzzi)*	—	F. Anderson *(Guzzi)*	—
1954 Montjuich	—	—	T. Provini *(Mondial)*	—	F. Anderson *(Guzzi)*	D. Dale *(MV Agusta)*	—
1955 Montjuich	—	—	L. Taveri *(MV Agusta)*	—	—	R. Armstrong *(Gilera)*	W. Faust–K. Remmert *(BMW)*
1961 Montjuich	—	—	T. Phillis *(Honda)*	G. Hocking *(MV Agusta)*	—	—	H. Fath–A. Wolgemuth *(BMW)*
1962 Montjuich	H. Anscheidt *(Kreidler)*	—	K. Takahashi *(Honda)*	J. Redman *(Honda)*	—	—	M. Deubel–E. Hörner *(BMW)*
1963 Montjuich	H. Anscheidt *(Kreidler)*	—	L. Taveri *(Honda)*	T. Provini *(Morini)*	—	—	M. Deubel–E. Hörner *(BMW)*
1964 Montjuich	H. Anscheidt *(Kreidler)*	—	L. Taveri *(Honda)*	T. Provini *(Benelli)*	—	—	F. Camathias–R. Föll *(Gilera)*
1965 Montjuich	H. Anderson *(Suzuki)*	—	H. Anderson *(Suzuki)*	P. Read *(Yamaha)*	—	—	M. Deubel–E. Hörner *(BMW)*
1966 Montjuich	L. Taveri *(Honda)*	—	B. Ivy *(Yamaha)*	M. Hailwood *(Honda)*	—	—	—
1967 Montjuich	H. Anscheidt *(Suzuki)*	—	B. Ivy *(Yamaha)*	P. Read *(Yamaha)*	—	—	G. Auerbacher–E. Dein *(BMW)*
1968 Montjuich	H. Anscheidt *(Suzuki)*	—	S. Canellas *(Bultaco)*	P. Read *(Yamaha)*	—	G. Agostini *(MV Agusta)*	—

	50cc	80cc	125cc	250cc	350cc	500cc	Sidecar
1969 Jarama	A. Toersen *(Kreidler)*	—	C. Van Dongen *(Suzuki)*	S. Herrero *(Ossa)*	G. Agostini *(MV Agusta)*	G. Agostini *(MV Agusta)*	—
1970 Montjuich	S. Canellas *(Derbi)*	—	A. Nieto *(Derbi)*	K. Andersson *(Yamaha)*	A. Bergamonti *(MV Agusta)*	A. Bergamonti *(MV Agusta)*	—
1971 Jarama	J. De Vries *(Kreidler)*	—	A. Nieto *(Derbi)*	J. Saarinen *(Yamaha)*	T. Länsivuori *(Yamaha)*	D. Simmonds *(Kawasaki)*	—
1972 Montjuich	A. Nieto *(Derbi)*	—	K. Andersson *(Yamaha)*	R. Pasolini *(Aermacchi)*	B. Kneubühler *(Yamaha)*	C. Mortimer *(Yamaha)*	—
1973 Jarama	J. De Vries *(Kreidler)*	—	C. Mortimer *(Yamaha)*	J. Dodds *(Yamaha)*	A. Celso San-tos *(Yamaha)*	P. Read *(MV Agusta)*	—
1974 Montjuich	H. Van Kessel *(Kreidler)*	—	B. Grau *(Derbi)*	J. Dodds *(Yamaha)*	V. Palomo *(Yamaha)*	—	—
1975 Jarama	A. Nieto *(Kreidler)*	—	P. Pileri *(Morbidelli)*	W. Villa *(Harley D.)*	G. Agostini *(Yamaha)*	—	—
1976 Montjuich	A. Nieto *(Bultaco)*	—	P. Bianchi *(Morbidelli)*	G. F. Bonera *(Harley D.)*	K. Ballington *(Yamaha)*	—	—
1977 Jarama	A. Nieto *(Bultaco)*	—	P. Bianchi *(Morbidelli)*	T. Katayama *(Yamaha)*	M. Rougerie *(Yamaha)*	—	—
1978 Montjuich	E. Lazzarini *(Kreidler)*	—	E. Lazzarini *(MBA)*	G. Hansford *(Kawasaki)*	—	P. Hennen *(Suzuki)*	—
1979 Jarama	E. Lazzarini *(Kreidler)*	—	A. Nieto *(Minarelli)*	K. Ballington *(Kawasaki)*	K. Ballington *(Kawasaki)*	K. Roberts *(Yamaha)*	—
1980 Jarama	E. Lazzarini *(Iprem)*	—	P. Bianchi *(MBA)*	K. Ballington *(Kawasaki)*	—	K. Roberts *(Yamaha)*	—
1981 Jarama	R. Tormo *(Bultaco)*	—	A. Nieto *(Minarelli)*	A. Mang *(Kawasaki)*	—	—	R. Biland–K. Waltisperg *(Yamaha)*
1982 Jarama	S. Dörflinger *(Kreidler)*	—	A. Nieto *(Garelli)*	C. Lavado *(Yamaha)*	—	K. Roberts *(Yamaha)*	—
1983 Jarama	E. Lazzarini *(Garelli)*	—	A. Nieto *(Garelli)*	H. Guilleux *(Kawasaki)*	—	F. Spencer *(Honda)*	—
1984 Jarama	—	P. P. Bianchi *(Casal)*	A. Nieto *(Garelli)*	A. Pons *(Kobas)*	—	E. Lawson *(Yamaha)*	—
1985 Jarama	—	J. Martinez *(Derbi)*	P. P. Bianchi *(MBA)*	C. Lavado *(Yamaha)*	—	F. Spencer *(Honda)*	—
1986 Jarama	—	J. Martinez *(Derbi)*	F. Gresini *(MBA)*	C. Lavado *(Yamaha)*	—	W. Gardner *(Honda)*	—
1987 Jerez	—	J. Martinez *(Derbi)*	F. Gresini *(Garelli)*	M. Wimmer *(Yamaha)*	—	W. Gardner *(Honda)*	S. Webster–T. Hewitt *(LCR-Krauser)*

South Africa

	50cc	80cc	125cc	250cc	350cc	500cc	Sidecar
1983 Kyalami	—	—	—	J. F. Balde *(Chevallier)*	—	F. Spencer *(Honda)*	—
1984 Kyalami	—	—	—	P. Fernandez *(Yamaha)*	—	E. Lawson *(Yamaha)*	—
1985 Kyalami	—	—	—	F. Spencer *(Honda)*	—	E. Lawson *(Yamaha)*	—

Sweden

	50cc	80cc	125cc	250cc	350cc	500cc	Sidecar
1958 Hedemora	—	—	A. Gandossi *(Ducati)*	H. Fügner *(MZ)*	G. Duke *(Norton)*	G. Duke *(Norton)*	—
1959 Kristianstadt	—	—	T. Provini *(MV Agusta)*	G. Hocking *(MZ)*	J. Surtees *(MV Agusta)*	—	—
1961 Kristianstadt	—	—	L. Taveri *(Honda)*	M. Hailwood *(Honda)*	F. Stastny *(Jawa)*	G. Hocking *(MV Agusta)*	—
1971 Anderstorp	A. Nieto *(Derbi)*	—	B. Sheene *(Suzuki)*	R. Gould *(Yamaha)*	G. Agostini *(MV Agusta)*	G. Agostini *(MV Agusta)*	—
1972 Anderstorp	J. De Vries *(Kreidler)*	—	A. Nieto *(Derbi)*	R. Gould *(Yamaha)*	G. Agostini *(MV Agusta)*	G. Agostini *(MV Agusta)*	—
1973 Anderstorp	J. De Vries *(Kreidler)*	—	B. Jansson *(Maico)*	D. Braun *(Yamaha)*	T. Länsivuori *(Yamaha)*	P. Read *(MV Agusta)*	—
1974 Anderstorp	H. Van Kessel *(Kreidler)*	—	K. Andersson *(Yamaha)*	T. Katayama *(Yamaha)*	T. Länsivuori *(Yamaha)*	T. Länsivuori *(Yamaha)*	—
1975 Anderstorp	E. Lazzarini *(Piovaticci)*	—	P. Pileri *(Morbidelli)*	W. Villa *(Harley D.)*	—	B. Sheene *(Suzuki)*	—
1976 Anderstorp	A. Nieto *(Bultaco)*	—	P. Bianchi *(Morbidelli)*	T. Katayama *(Yamaha)*	—	B. Sheene *(Suzuki)*	—
1977 Anderstorp	R. Tormo *(Bultaco)*	—	A. Nieto *(Bultaco)*	M. Grant *(Kawasaki)*	T. Katayama *(Yamaha)*	B. Sheene *(Suzuki)*	—
1978 Karlskoga	—	—	P. Bianchi *(Minarelli)*	G. Hansford *(Kawasaki)*	G. Hansford *(Kawasaki)*	B. Sheene *(Suzuki)*	—
1979 Karlskoga	—	—	P. Bianchi *(Minarelli)*	G. Rossi *(Morbidelli)*	—	B. Sheene *(Suzuki)*	J. Taylor–B. Johansson (B2a) *(Yamaha)*
1981 Anderstorp	—	—	R. Tormo *(Sanvenero)*	A. Mang *(Kawasaki)*	—	B. Sheene *(Yamaha)*	R. Biland–K. Waltisperg *(Yamaha)*
1982 Anderstorp	—	—	I. Palazzese *(MBA)*	R. Freymond *(MBA)*	—	T. Katayama *(Honda)*	R. Biland–K. Waltisperg *(LCR-Yamaha)*
1983 Anderstorp	—	—	B. Kneubühler *(MBA)*	C. Sarron *(Yamaha)*	—	F. Spencer *(Honda)*	R. Biland–K. Waltisperg *(LCR-Yamaha)*
1984 Anderstorp	—	—	F. Gresini *(Garelli)*	M. Herweh *(Real)*	—	E. Lawson *(Yamaha)*	R. Biland–K. Waltisperg *(LCR-Yamaha)*
1985 Anderstorp	—	—	A. Auinger *(Monnet)*	T. Mang *(Honda)*	—	F. Spencer *(Honda)*	E. Streuer–B. Schnieders *(LCR-Yamaha)*

	50cc	80cc	125cc	250cc	350cc	500cc	Sidecar
1986 Anderstorp	—	—	F. Gresini *(Garelli)*	C. Lavado *(Yamaha)*	—	E. Lawson *(Yamaha)*	A. Michel–J. Fresc *(LCR-Yamaha)*
1987 Anderstorp	—	—	F. Gresini *(Garelli)*	A. Mang *(Honda)*	—	W. Gardner *(Honda)*	R. Biland–K. Waltisperg *(LCR-Krauser)*

Ulster

	50cc	80cc	125cc	250cc	350cc	500cc	Sidecar
1949 Clady	—	—	—	M. Cann *(Guzzi)*	F. Frith *(Velocette)*	L. Graham *(AJS)*	—
1950 Clady	—	—	C. Ubbiali *(Mondial)*	M. Cann *(Guzzi)*	B. Foster *(Velocette)*	G. Duke *(Norton)*	—
1951 Clady	—	—	(1)	B. Ruffo *(Guzzi)*	G. Duke *(Norton)*	G. Duke *(Norton)*	—
1952 Clady	—	—	C. Sandford *(MV Agusta)*	M. Cann *(Guzzi)*	K. Kavanagh *(Norton)*	C. McCand-less *(Gilera)*	—
1953 Dundrod	—	—	W. Haas *(NSU)*	R. Armstrong *(NSU)*	K. Mudford *(Norton)*	K. Kavanagh *(Norton)*	C. Smith–R. Clements *(Norton)*
1954 Dundrod	—	—	R. Hollaus *(NSU)*	W. Haas *(NSU)*	R. Amm *(Norton)*	(2)	E. Oliver–L. Nutt *(Norton)*
1955 Dundrod	—	—	—	J. Surtees *(NSU)*	B. Lomas *(Guzzi)*	B. Lomas *(Guzzi)*	—
1956 Dundrod	—	—	C. Ubbiali *(MV Agusta)*	L. Taveri *(MV Agusta)*	B. Lomas *(Guzzi)*	J. Hartle *(Norton)*	W. Noll–F. Cron *(BMW)*
1957 Dundrod	—	—	L. Taveri *(MV Agusta)*	C. Sandford *(Mondial)*	K. Campbell *(Guzzi)*	L. Liberati *(Gilera)*	—
1958 Dundrod	—	—	C. Ubbiali *(MV Agusta)*	T. Provini *(MV Agusta)*	J. Surtees *(MV Agusta)*	J. Surtees *(MV Agusta)*	—
1959 Dundrod	—	—	M. Hailwood *(Ducati)*	G. Hocking *(MZ)*	J. Surtees *(MV Agusta)*	J. Surtees *(MV Agusta)*	—
1960 Dundrod	—	—	C. Ubbiali *(MV Agusta)*	C. Ubbiali *(MV Agusta)*	J. Surtees *(MV Agusta)*	J. Hartle *(Norton)*	—
1961 Dundrod	—	—	K. Takahashi *(Honda)*	B. McIntyre *(Honda)*	G. Hocking *(MV Agusta)*	G. Hocking *(MV Agusta)*	—
1962 Dundrod	—	—	L. Taveri *(Honda)*	T. Robb *(Honda)*	J. Redman *(Honda)*	M. Hailwood *(MV Agusta)*	—
1963 Dundrod	—	—	H. Anderson *(Suzuki)*	J. Redman *(Honda)*	J. Redman *(Honda)*	M. Hailwood *(MV Agusta)*	—
1964 Dundrod	—	—	H. Anderson *(Suzuki)*	P. Read *(Yamaha)*	J. Redman *(Honda)*	P. Read *(Norton)*	—
1965 Dundrod	—	—	E. Degner *(Suzuki)*	P. Read *(Yamaha)*	F. Stastny *(Jawa)*	D. Creith *(Norton)*	—
1966 Dundrod	—	—	L. Taveri *(Honda)*	G. Molloy *(Bultaco)*	M. Hailwood *(Honda)*	M. Hailwood *(Honda)*	—

1967 Dundrod	—	—	B. Ivy *(Yamaha)*	M. Hailwood *(Honda)*	G. Agostini *(MV Agusta)*	M. Hailwood *(Honda)*	—
1968 Dundrod	—	—	B. Ivy *(Yamaha)*	B. Ivy *(Yamaha)*	G. Agostini *(MV Agusta)*	G. Agostini *(MV Agusta)*	—
1969 Dundrod	A. Nieto *(Derbi)*	—	—	K. Carruthers *(Benelli)*	G. Agostini *(MV Agusta)*	G. Agostini *(MV Agusta)*	K. Enders–R. Engelhardt *(BMW)*
1970 Dundrod	A. Nieto *(Derbi)*	—	—	K. Carruthers *(Yamaha)*	G. Agostini *(MV Agusta)*	G. Agostini *(MV Agusta)*	K. Enders–R. Engelhardt *(BMW)*
1971 Dundrod	—	—	—	R. McCullough *(Yamsel)*	P. Williams *(MZ)*	J. Findlay *(Suzuki)*	H. Owesle–P. Rutterford *(Münch URS)*

Switzerland

	50cc	80cc	125cc	250cc	350cc	500cc	Sidecar
1949 Berne	—	—	N. Pagani *(Mondial)*	B. Ruffo *(Guzzi)*	F. Frith *(Velocette)*	L. Graham *(AJS)*	E. Oliver–D. Jenkinson *(Norton)*
1950 Geneva	—	—	—	D. Ambrosini *(Benelli)*	L. Graham *(AJS)*	L. Graham *(AJS)*	E. Oliver–L. Dobelli *(Norton)*
1951 Berne	—	—	—	D. Ambrosini *(Benelli)*	L. Graham *(Velocette)*	F. Anderson *(Guzzi)*	E. Frigerio–E. Ricotti *(Gilera)*
1952 Berne	—	—	—	F. Anderson *(Guzzi)*	G. Duke *(Norton)*	J. Brett *(AJS)*	Alb. Milani–G. Pizzocri *(Gilera)*
1953 Berne	—	—	—	R. Armstrong *(NSU)*	F. Anderson *(Guzzi)*	G. Duke *(Gilera)*	E. Oliver–S. Dibben *(Norton)*
1954 Berne	—	—	—	R. Hollaus *(NSU)*	F. Anderson *(Guzzi)*	G. Duke *(Gilera)*	W. Noll–F. Cron *(BMW)*
1979 Paul Ricard	—	—	—	—	—	—	R. Biland–K. Waltisperg (B2a) *(LCR-Yamaha)*

United States

	50cc	80cc	125cc	250cc	350cc	500cc	Sidecar
1964 Daytona	H. Anderson *(Suzuki)*	—	H. Anderson *(Suzuki)*	A. Shepherd *(MZ)*	—	M. Hailwood *(MV Agusta)*	—
1965 Daytona	E. Degner *(Suzuki)*	—	H. Anderson *(Suzuki)*	P. Read *(Yamaha)*	—	M. Hailwood *(MV Agusta)*	—

Venezuela

	50cc	80cc	125cc	250cc	350cc	500cc	Sidecar
1977 S. Carlos	—	—	A. Nieto *(Bultaco)*	W. Villa *(Harley D.)*	J. Cecotto *(Yamaha)*	B. Sheene *(Suzuki)*	—
1978 S. Carlos	—	—	P. Bianchi *(Minarelli)*	K. Roberts *(Yamaha)*	T. Katayama *(Yamaha)*	B. Sheene *(Suzuki)*	—
1979 S. Carlos	—	—	A. Nieto *(Minarelli)*	W. Villa *(Yamaha)*	C. Lavado *(Yamaha)*	B. Sheene *(Suzuki)*	—

West Germany

	50cc	80cc	125cc	250cc	350cc	500cc	Sidecar
1952 Solitude	—	—	W. Haas *(NSU)*	R. Felgen-heier *(DKW)*	R. Armstrong *(Norton)*	R. Armstrong *(Norton)*	C. Smith–R. Clements *(Norton)*
1953 Schotten	—	—	C. Ubbiali *(MV Agusta)*	W. Haas *(NSU)*	—	—	—
1954 Solitude	—	—	R. Hollaus *(NSU)*	W. Haas *(NSU)*	R. Amm *(Norton)*	G. Duke *(Gilera)*	W. Noll–F. Cron *(BMW)*
1955 Nürburgring	—	—	C. Ubbiali *(MV Agusta)*	H. P. Müller *(NSU)*	B. Lomas *(Guzzi)*	G. Duke *(Gilera)*	W. Faust–K. Remmert *(BMW)*
1956 Solitude	—	—	R. Ferri *(Gilera)*	C. Ubbiali *(MV Agusta)*	B. Lomas *(Guzzi)*	R. Armstrong *(Gilera)*	W. Noll–F. Cron *(BMW)*
1957 Hockenheim	—	—	C. Ubbiali *(MV Agusta)*	C. Ubbiali *(MV Agusta)*	L. Liberati *(Gilera)*	L. Liberati *(Gilera)*	F. Hillebrand–M. Grünwald *(BMW)*
1958 Nürburgring	—	—	C. Ubbiali *(MV Agusta)*	T. Provini *(MV Agusta)*	J. Surtees *(MV Agusta)*	J. Surtees *(MV Agusta)*	W. Schneider–H. Strauss *(BMW)*
1959 Hockenheim	—	—	C. Ubbiali *(MV Agusta)*	C. Ubbiali *(MV Agusta)*	J. Surtees *(MV Agusta)*	J. Surtees *(MV Agusta)*	F. Camathias–H. Cecco *(BMW)*
1960 Solitude	—	—	—	G. Hocking *(MV Agusta)*	—	J. Surtees *(MV Agusta)*	H. Fath–A. Wohlgemuth *(BMW)*
1961 Hockenheim	—	—	E. Degner *(MZ)*	K. Takahashi *(Honda)*	F. Stastny *(Jawa)*	G. Hocking *(MV Agusta)*	M. Deubel–E. Hörner *(BMW)*
1962 Solitude	E. Degner *(Suzuki)*	—	L. Taveri *(Honda)*	J. Redman *(Honda)*	—	—	M. Deubel–E. Hörner *(BMW)*
1963 Hockenheim	H. Anderson *(Suzuki)*	—	E. Degner *(Suzuki)*	T. Provini *(Morini)*	J. Redman *(Honda)*	—	F. Camathias–A. Herzig *(FCS)*
1964 Solitude	R. Bryans *(Honda)*	—	J. Redman *(Honda)*	P. Read *(Yamaha)*	J. Redman *(Honda)*	M. Hailwood *(MV Agusta)*	F. Scheidegger–J. Robinson *(BMW)*
1965 Nürburg-Sud	R. Bryans *(Honda)*	—	H. Anderson *(Suzuki)*	P. Read *(Yamaha)*	G. Agostini *(MV Agusta)*	M. Hailwood *(MV Agusta)*	F. Scheidegger–J. Robinson *(BMW)*
1966 Hockenheim	H. Anscheidt *(Suzuki)*	—	L. Taveri *(Honda)*	M. Hailwood *(Honda)*	M. Hailwood *(Honda)*	J. Redman *(Honda)*	F. Scheidegger–J. Robinson *(BMW)*
1967 Hockenheim	H. Anscheidt *(Suzuki)*	—	H. Katayama *(Suzuki)*	R. Bryans *(Honda)*	M. Hailwood *(Honda)*	G. Agostini *(MV Agusta)*	K. Enders–R. Engelhardt *(BMW)*
1968 Nürburg-Sud	H. Anscheidt *(Suzuki)*	—	P. Read *(Yamaha)*	B. Ivy *(Yamaha)*	G. Agostini *(MV Agusta)*	G. Agostini *(MV Agusta)*	H. Fath–W. Kalauch *(URS)*
1969 Hockenheim	A. Toersen *(Kreidler)*	—	D. Simmonds *(Kawasaki)*	K. Andersson *(Yamaha)*	G. Agostini *(MV Agusta)*	G. Agostini *(MV Agusta)*	K. Enders–R. Engelhardt *(BMW)*
1970 Nürburgring	A. Nieto *(Derbi)*	—	J. Dodds *(Aermacchi)*	K. Carruthers *(Yamaha)*	G. Agostini *(MV Agusta)*	G. Agostini *(MV Agusta)*	G. Auerbacher–H. Hahn *(BMW)*
1971 Hockenheim	J. De Vries *(Kreidler)*	—	D. Simmonds *(Kawasaki)*	P. Read *(Yamaha)*	G. Agostini *(MV Agusta)*	G. Agostini *(MV Agusta)*	G. Auerbacher–H. Hahn *(BMW)*
1972 Nürburgring	J. De Vries *(Kreidler)*	—	G. Parlotti *(Morbidelli)*	H. Kanaya *(Yamaha)*	J. Saarinen *(Yamaha)*	G. Agostini *(MV Agusta)*	S. Schauzu–W. Kalauch *(BMW)*
1973 Hockenheim	T. Timmer *(Jamathi)*	—	K. Andersson *(Yamaha)*	J. Saarinen *(Yamaha)*	T. Länsivuori *(Yamaha)*	P. Read *(MV Agusta)*	K. Enders–R. Engelhardt *(BMW)*

	50cc	80cc	125cc	250cc	350cc	500cc	Sidecar
1974 Nürburgring	I. Emmerich *(Kreidler)*	—	F. Reitmaier *(Maico)*	H. Kassner *(Yamaha)*	H. Kassner *(Yamaha)*	E. Czihak *(Yamaha)*	W. Schwärzel–K. Kleis *(König)*
1975 Hockenheim	A. Nieto *(Kreidler)*	—	P. Pileri *(Morbidelli)*	W. Villa *(Harley D.)*	J. Cecotto *(Yamaha)*	G. Agostini *(Yamaha)*	R. Biland–F. Freiburghaus *(Seymaz-Yamaha)*
1976 Nürburgring	A. Nieto *(Bultaco)*	—	A. Mang *(Morbidelli)*	W. Villa *(Harley D.)*	W. Villa *(Harley D.)*	G. Agostini *(MV Agusta)*	W. Schwärzel–A. Huber *(König)*
1977 Hockenheim	H. Rittberger *(Kreidler)*	—	P. Bianchi *(Morbidelli)*	C. Sarron *(Yamaha)*	T. Katayama *(Yamaha)*	B. Sheene *(Suzuki)*	R. Biland–K. Waltisperg *(Yamaha)*
1978 Nürburgring	R. Tormo *(Bultaco)*	—	A. Nieto *(Minarelli)*	K. Ballington *(Kawasaki)*	T. Katayama *(Yamaha)*	V. Ferrari *(Suzuki)*	W. Schwärzel–A. Huber *(ARO Fath)*
1979 Hockenheim	G. Waibel *(Kreidler)*	—	A. Nieto *(Minarelli)*	K. Ballington *(Kawasaki)*	J. Ekerold *(Yamaha)*	W. Hartog *(Suzuki)*	R. Steinhausen–K. Arthur (B2a) *(KSA Yamaha)*
1980 Nürburgring	S. Dörflinger *(Kreidler)*	—	G. Bertin *(Motobecane)*	K. Ballington *(Kawasaki)*	J. Ekerold *(Bimota)*	M. Lucchinelli *(Suzuki)*	J. Taylor–B. Johansson *(Yamaha)*
1981 Hockenheim	S. Dörflinger *(Kreidler)*	—	A. Nieto *(Minarelli)*	A. Mang *(Kawasaki)*	A. Mang *(Kawasaki)*	K. Roberts *(Yamaha)*	A. Michel–M. Burkard *(Seymaz-Yamaha)*
1982 Hockenheim	E. Lazzarini *(Garelli)*	—	—	A. Mang *(Kawasaki)*	M. Herweh *(Yamaha)*	R. Mamola *(Suzuki)*	R. Biland–K. Waltisperg *(LCR-Yamaha)*
1983 Hockenheim	S. Dörflinger *(Krauser Kr.)*	—	A. Nieto *(Garelli)*	C. Lavado *(Yamaha)*	—	K. Roberts *(Yamaha)*	E. Streuer–B. Schnieders *(LCR-Yamaha)*
1984 Nürburgring	S. Dörflinger *(Zundapp)*	—	A. Nieto *(Garelli)*	C. Sarron *(Yamaha)*	—	F. Spencer *(Honda)*	E. Streuer–B. Schnieders *(LCR-Yamaha)*
1985 Hockenheim	S. Dörflinger *(Krauser)*	—	A. Auinger *(Monnet)*	A. Wimmer *(Yamaha)*	—	C. Sarron *(Yamaha)*	W. Schwarzel–F. Buck *(LCR-Yamaha)*
1986 Nürburgring	M. Herreros *(Derbi)*	—	L. Cadalora *(Garelli)*	C. Lavado *(Yamaha)*	—	E. Lawson *(Yamaha)*	E. Streuer–B. Schnieders *(LCR-Yamaha)*
1987 Hockenheim	—	G. Waibel *(Krauser)*	F. Gresini *(Garelli)*	A. Mang *(Honda)*	—	E. Lawson *(Yamaha)*	S. Webster–T. Hewitt *LCR-Kauser)*

Yugoslavia

	50cc	80cc	125cc	250cc	350cc	500cc	Sidecar
1969 Opatija	P. Lodewijkx *(Jamathi)*	—	D. Braun *(Suzuki)*	K. Carruthers *(Benelli)*	S. Grassetti *(Jawa)*	G. Nash *(Norton)*	—
1970 Opatija	A. Nieto *(Derbi)*	—	D. Braun *(Suzuki)*	S. Herrero *(Ossa)*	G. Agostini *(MV Agusta)*	G. Agostini *(MV Agusta)*	—
1972 Opatija	J. Bruins *(Kreidler)*	—	K. Andersson *(Yamaha)*	R. Pasolini *(Aermacchi)*	J. Drapal *(Yamaha)*	A. Pagani *(MV Agusta)*	—
1973 Opatija	J. De Vries *(Kreidler)*	—	K. Andersson *(Yamaha)*	D. Braun *(Yamaha)*	J. Drapal *(Yamaha)*	K. Newcombe *(König)*	—
1974 Opatija	H. Van Kessel *(Kreidler)*	—	K. Andersson *(Yamaha)*	C. Mortimer *(Yamaha)*	G. Agostini *(Yamaha)*	—	—
1975 Opatija	A. Nieto *(Kreidler)*	—	D. Braun *(Morbidelli)*	D. Braun *(Yamaha)*	P. Korhonen *(Yamaha)*	—	—

	50cc	80cc	125cc	250cc	350cc	500cc	Sidecar
1976 Opatija	U. Graf *(Kreidler)*	—	P. Bianchi *(Morbidelli)*	D. Braun *(Yamaha)*	O. Chevallier *(Yamaha)*	—	—
1977 Opatija	A. Nieto *(Bultaco)*	—	P. Bianchi *(Morbidelli)*	M. Lega *(Morbidelli)*	T. Katayama *(Yamaha)*	—	—
1978 Rijeka	R. Tormo *(Bultaco)*	—	A. Nieto *(Minarelli)*	G. Hansford *(Kawasaki)*	G. Hansford *(Kawasaki)*	—	—
1979 Rijeka	E. Lazzarini *(Kreidler)*	—	A. Nieto *(Minarelli)*	G. Rossi *(Morbidelli)*	K. Ballington *(Kawasaki)*	K. Roberts *(Yamaha)*	—
1980 Rijeka	R. Tormo *(Kreidler)*	—	G. Bertin *(Motobecane)*	A. Mang *(Kawasaki)*	—	—	R. Biland–K. Waltisperg *(Yamaha)*
1981 Rijeka	R. Tormo *(Bultaco)*	—	L. Reggiani *(Minarelli)*	—	A. Mang *(Kawasaki)*	R. Mamola *(Suzuki)*	—
1982 Rijeka	E. Lazzarini *(Garelli)*	—	E. Lazzarini *(Garelli)*	D. De Radigues *(Chevallier)*	—	F. Uncini *(Suzuki)*	—
1983 Rijeka	S. Dörflinger *(Krauser Kr.)*	—	B. Kneubühler *(MBA)*	C. Lavado *(Yamaha)*	—	F. Spencer *(Honda)*	—
1984 Rijeka	—	S. Dörflinger *(Zundapp)*	—	M. Herweh *(Real)*	—	F. Spencer *(Honda)*	—
1985 Rijeka	—	S. Dörflinger *(Krauner)*	—	F. Spencer *(Honda)*	—	E. Lawson *(Yamaha)*	—
1986 Rijeka	—	J. Martinez *(Derbi)*	—	S. Pons *(Honda)*	—	E. Lawson *(Yamaha)*	—
1987 Rijeka	—	J. Martinez *(Derbi)*	—	C. Lavado *(Yamaha)*	—	W. Gardner *(Honda)*	—

King of the tiddlers – Angel Nieto piloting the 50cc Derbi to yet another victory in the 1969 French Grand Prix.

Grand Prix Winners Merit Table 1949–88

50cc

Total		Total
1:	**Nieto, Angel** *(E)*	**27**
	**Derbi* (13) ***Kreidler* (6) ****Bultaco* (8)	
	1969* – DDR, IRL	
	1970* – D, F, YU, NL, IRL	
	1971* – NL, DDR, S	
	1972* – NL, B, E	
	1975** – E, D, I, NL, SF, YU	
	1976*** – I, NL, S, D, E	
	1977*** – E, YU, NL	
2:	**Lazzarini, Eugenio** *(I)*	**18**
	**Piovaticci* (1) ***Kreidler* (9) ****Iprem Kreidler* (2) *****Garelli* (6)	
	1975* – S	
	1977** – I, B	
	1978** – E, NL	
	1979** – I, E, YU, NL, F	
	1980*** – I, E	
	1982**** – YU, RSM, D	
	1983**** – I, E, NL	
3:	**Tormo, Ricardo** *(E)*	**15**
	**Bultaco* (12) ***Kreidler* (2) ****Garelli* (1)	
	1977* – S	
	1978* – I, B, D, CS, YU	
	1980** – YU, NL	
	1981* – I, E, YU, NL, B, RSM	
	1983*** – RSM	
4:	**Anscheidt, Hans Georg** *(D)*	**14**
	**Kreidler* (6) ***Suzuki* (8)	
	1962* – E, I	
	1963* – E, F, SF	
	1964* – E	
	1966** – D, I	
	1967** – E, D, B	
	1968** – D, E, B	
	De Vries, Jan *(NL)*	**14**
	Kreidler	
	1970 – I	
	1971 – A, D, B, I, E	
	1972 – D, I, S	
	1973 – I, YU, B, S, E	
6:	**Dorflinger, Stefan** *(CH)*	**9**
	**Kreidler* (6) ***Krauser Kreidler* (3)	
	1980* – B, D	
	1981* – D	
	1982* – E, I, NL	
	1983** – F, D, YU	
7:	**Anderson, Hugh** *(NZ)*	**8**
	Suzuki	
	1962 – RA	
	1963 – D, RA	
	1964 – USA, F, TT, SF	
	1965 – E	
8:	**Bryans, Ralph** *(IRL)*	**7**
	Honda	
	1964 – NL, B, D	
	1965 – D, F, NL	
	1966 – TT	
	Degner, Ernst *(D)*	**7**
	Suzuki	
	1962 – TT, NL, B, D	
	1963 – NL	
	1965 – USA, B	
	Van Kessel, Henk *(NL)*	**7**
	**Kreidler* (6) **X16 *Kreidler* (1)	
	1974* – F, I, S, CS, YU, E	
	1979** – B	
11:	**Taveri, Luigi** *(CH)*	**6**
	Honda	
	1962 – SF	
	1963 – J	
	1965 – TT, J	
	1966 – E, NL	
	Toersen, Aalt *(NL)*	**6**
	**Kreidler* (3) ***Jamathi* (3)	
	1969* – D, F, E	
	1970** – B, DDR, CS	
13:	**Lodewijkx, Paul** *(NL)*	**4**
	Jamathi	
	1968 – NL	
	1969 – CS, I, YU	
	Rittberger, Herbert *(D)*	**4**
	Kreidler	
	1974 – NL	
	1976 – F,B	
	1977 – D	
15:	**Katayama, Hoshimi** *(J)*	**3**
	Suzuki	
	1966 – J	
	1967 – F, NL	
	Smith, Barry *(AUS)*	**3**
	Derbi	
	1968 – TT	
	1969 – NL, B	
	Timmer, Theo *(NL)*	**3**
	**Jamathi* (2) ***Bultaco* (1)	
	1972* – DDR	
	1973* – D	
	1981** – CS	
	Van Zeebroeck, Julien *(B)*	**3**
	Kreidler	
	1974 – SF	
	1975 – B	
	1976 – SF	

19: **Huberts, Jan** *(NL)* **2**
Kreidler
1962 – F, DDR

Itoh, Mitsuo *(J)* **2**
Suzuki
1963 – TT
1967 – J

21: **Bruins, Jan** *(NL)* **1**
Kreidler
1972 – YU

Canellas, Salvator *(E)* **1**
Derbi
1970 – E

Emmerich, Ingo *(D)* **1**
Kreidler
1974 – D

Graf, Ulrich *(CH)* **1**
Kreidler
1976 – YU

Graham, Stuart *(GB)* **1**
Suzuki
1967 – TT

Kneubühler, Bruno *(CH)* **1**
Kreidler
1973 – NL

Morishita, Isao *(J)* **1**
Suzuki
1963 – B

Sheene, Barry *(GB)* **1**
Kreidler
1971 – CS

Thurow, Gerhard *(D)* **1**
Kreidler
1974 – B

Waibel, Gerhard *(D)* **1**
Kreidler
1979 – D

80cc — Total

1: **Martinez, Jorge** *(E)* **21**
Derbi
1984 – NL
1985 – E, I, RSM
1986 – E, A, YU, NL
1987 – E, I, A, YU, NL, GB, P
1988 – P, I, D, NL, YU, CZ

2: **Dorflinger, Stefan** *(CH)* **9**
**Zundapp* (4) ***Krauser* (4)
1984* – A, D, YU, B
1985** – D, YU
1986** – I
1987** – CZ
1988** – E

3: **Bianchi, Pier Paolo** *(I)* **3**
**Casal* (2) ***Seel* (1)
1984* – I, E
1986** – RSM

Waibel, Gerhard *(D)* **3**
**Real* (1) ***Krauser* (1)
1984* – RSM
1986** – D(h)
1987** – D

4: **Herreros, Manuel** *(E)* **1**
Derbi
1986 – D

Kafka, Gerd *(A)* **1**
Seel
1985 – NL

McConnachie, Ian *(GB)* **1**
Krauser
1986 – GB

Nieto, Angel *(E)* **1**
Derbi
1985 – F

125cc — Total

1: **Nieto, Angel** *(E)* **62**
**Derbi* (16) ***Bultaco* (4) ****Minarelli* (24) *****Garelli* (18)
1970* – B, DDR, I, E
1971* – A, NL, DDR, CS, E
1972* – A, I, NL, B, S
1974* – I, B
1976** – B
1977** – YV, NL, S
1978*** – SF, GB, D, YU
1979*** – YV, A, D, I, E, YU, NL, GB
1980*** – F, NL, B, SF
1981*** – RA, A, D, F, E, NL, GB, SF
1982**** – RA, A, E, I, NL, GB
1983**** – I, D, E, A, NL, GB
1984**** – I, E, D, F, NL, GB

2: **Ubbiali Carlo** *(I)* **26**
**Mondial* (2) ** *MV Agusta* (24)
1950* – IRL
1951* – I
1953** – D
1955** – F, TT, D, NL, I
1956** – TT, NL, B, IRL, I
1957** – D, I
1958** – TT, NL, D, IRL
1959** – D, NL, B
1960** – TT, NL, IRL, I

3: **Bianchi, Pier Paolo** **24**
**Morbidelli* (14) ***Minarelli* (5) ****MBA* (5)
1976* – A, I, YU, NL, S, SF, E
1977* – D, I, E, F, YU, B, SF
1978** – YV, F, B, S
1979** – S
1980*** – I, E
1985*** – E, I, NL

4: **Taveri, Luigi** *(CH)* **22**
**MV Agusta* (2) ** *Honda* (20)
1955* – E
1957* – IRL
1961** – B, S
1962** – TT, NL, B, D, IRL, DDR
1963** – E, I
1964** – E, F, TT, SF, I
1966** – D, DDR, CS, IRL, I

5: **Gresini, Fausto** *(I)* **18**
Garelli
1984 – S
1985 – A, B, GB
1986 – E, I, S, D(h)
1987 – E, D, I, A, NL, F, GB, SF, CS, RSM

6: **Anderson, Hugh** *(NZ)* **17**
Suzuki
1962 – RA
1963 – F, TT, NL, IRL, DDR, SF
1964 – USA, DDR, IRL
1965 – USA, D, E, F, SF, I, J

7: **Andersson, Kent** *(S)* **14**
Yamaha
1972 – YU, SF, E
1973 – F, A, D, I, YU
1974 – F, A, S, CS, YU
1975 – F

Ivy, Bill *(GB)* **14**
Yamaha
1966 – E, NL, TT, J
1967 – E, F, DDR, CS, IRL, I, CDN, J
1968 – IRL, I

9: **Read, Phil** *(GB)* **10**
Yamaha
1965 – TT
1966 – SF
1967 – TT, NL
1968 – D, TT, NL, DDR, CS, SF

Simmonds, Dave *(GB)* **10**
Kawasaki
1969 – D, TT, NL, B, DDR, CS, SF, I
1970 – SF
1971 – D

11: **Lazzarini, Eugenio** *(I)* **9**
**Piovaticci* (1) ***Morbidelli* (1) ****MBA* (4) *****Garelli* (3)
1973* – NL
1977** – A
1978*** – E, A, I, NL
1982**** – YU, CS
1983**** – B

12: **Martinez, Jorge** *(E)* **9**
Derbi
1988E, E, I, A, NL, B, YU, F, S, CZ

13: **Degner, Ernst** *(DDR/D)* **8**
**MZ* (5) ***Suzuki* (3)
1959* – I
1960* – B
1961* – D, DDR, I
1963** – D
1964** – J
1965** – IRL

14: **Pileri, Paolo** *(I)* **7**
Morbidelli
1975 – E, A, D, I, NL, B, S

15: **Bertin, Guy** *(F)* **6**
**Motobecane* (5) ***Sanvenero* (1)
1979* – CS, F
1980* – YU, CS, D
1981** – I

Braun, Dieter *(D)* **6**
**Suzuki* (5) ***Morbidelli* (1)
1969* – YU
1970* – F, YU, TT, NL
1975** – YU

Provini, Tarquinio *(I)* **6**
**Mondial* (4) ***MV Agusta* (2)
1954* – E
1957* – TT, NL, B
1959** – TT, S

18: **Auinger, August** *(A)* **5**
MBA
1985 – D, GB, S
1986 – GB, RSM

19: **Cadalora, Luca** *(I)* **4**
Garelli
1986 – D, A, NL, F

Gianola, Ezio *(I)* **4**
**Garelli* (2) ** *Honda* (2)
1985* – F
1987* – F
1988** – D, GB

Haas, Werner *(D)* **4**
NSU
1952 – D
1953 – NL, IRL, I

Hollaus, Rubert *(A)*
NSU
1954 – TT, IRL, NL, D

Parlotti, Gilberto *(I)* **4**
Morbidelli
1970 – CS
1971 – I
1972 – D, F

Phillis, Tom *(AUS)* **4**
Honda
1961 – E, F, NL, RA

Redman, Jim *(SR)* **4**
Honda
1962 – SF
1963 – RA
1964 – NL, D

Tormo, Ricardo *(E)* **4**
**Bultaco* (1) ***Sanvenero* (2) ****MBA* (1)
1979* – SF
1981** – S
1982** – B
1983*** – F

27: **Jansson, Börje** *(S)* **3**
Maico
1972 – DDR, CS
1973 – S

Kneubühler, Bruno *(CH)* **3**
**Yamaha* (1) ***MBA* (2)
1974* – NL
1983** – YU, S

Leoni, Gianni *(I)* **3**
Mondial
1949 – I
1950 – I
1951 – NL

Mortimer, Charles *(GB)* **3**
Yamaha
1971 – TT
1972 – TT
1973 – E

Perris, Frank *(GB)* **3**
Suzuki
1963 – J
1965 – DDR, CS

Reggiani, Loris *(I)* **3**
Minarelli
1980 – GB
1981 – YU, RSM

Sandford, Cecil *(GB)* **3**
MV Agusta
1952 – TT, NL, IRL

Sheene, Barry *(GB)* **3**
Suzuki
1971 – B, S, SF

Takahashi, Kunimitsu *(J)* **3**
Honda
1961 – IRL
1962 – E, F

36: **Buscherini, Otello** *(I)* **2**
Malanca
1973 – CS, SF

Gandossi, Alberto *(I)* **2**
Ducati
1958 – B, S

Hailwood, Mike *(GB)* **2**
**Ducati* (1) ***Honda* (1)
1959* – IRL
1961** – TT

Mendogni, Emilio *(I)* **2**
Morini
1952 – I, E

Pagani, Nello *(I)* **2**
Mondial
1949 – CH, NL

Palazzese, Ivan *(YV)* **2**
MBA
1982 – S, SF

Vitali, Maurizio *(I)* **2**
MBA
1983 – RSM
1984 – RSM

43: **Aureal, Jean** *(F)* **1**
Yamaha
1969 – F

Brigaglia, Domenico *(I)* **1**
MBA
1986 – B

Canellas, Salvador *(E)* **1**
Bultaco
1968 – E

Casoli, Paolo *(I)* **1**
MBA
1987 – P

Conforti, Pier Luigi *(I)* **1**
Morbidelli
1977 – GB

Copeta, Angelo *(I)* **1**
MV Agusta
1953 – E

Dodds, John *(AUS)* **1**
Aermacchi
1970 – D

Duff, Mike *(CDN)* **1**
Yamaha
1965 – NL

Ferri, Romolo *(I)* **1**
Gilera
1956 – D

Graham, Leslie *(GB)* **1**
MV Agusta
1953 – TT

Graham, Stuart *(GB)* **1**
Suzuki
1967 – SF

Grau, Benjamin *(E)* **1**
Derbi
1974 – E

Gustavsson, Leif *(S)* **1**
Yamaha
1975 – CS

Katayama, Hoshimi *(J)* **1**
Honda
1967 – D

Leoni, Guido *(I)* **1**
Mondial
1951 – E

Mang, Toni *(D)* **1**
Morbidelli
1976 – D

McCandless, Cromie *(IRL)* **1**
Mondial
1951 – TT

Reitmaier, Fritz *(D)* **1**
Maico
1974 – D

Robb, Tommy *(IRL)* **1**
Danfay Yamaha
1973 – TT

Ruffo, Bruno *(I)* **1**
Mondial
1950 – NL

Sala, Guido *(I)* **1**
MV Agusta
1954 – I

Schneider, Bertie *(A)* **1**
Suzuki
1963, B

Schurgers, Jos *(NL)* **1**
Bridgestone
1973 – B

Selini, Jean Claude *(F)* **1**
MBA
1982 – F

Smith, Barry *(AUS)* **1**
MBA
1979 – B

Spaggiari, Bruno *(I)* **1**
Ducati
1958 – I

Tanaka, Teisuke *(J)* **1**
Honda
1962 – I

Van Dongen, Cees *(NL)* **1**
Suzuki
1969 – E

250cc **Total**

1: **Mang, Toni** **33**
**Kawasaki* (20) ***Honda* (12) ****Yamaha* (1)
1978* – GB
1980* – I, YU, B, CS
1981* – D, F, E, NL, B, RSM, GB, SF, S, CS
1982* – I, NL, B, RSM, D
1984*** – F
1985** – GB, S
1986** – I
1987** – D, I, A, NL, GB, S, CS, P
1988** – J

2: **Read, Phil** *(GB)* **27**
Yamaha
1964 – F, D, DDR, IRL, I
1965 – USA, D, E, F, NL, CS, IRL
1967 – E, DDR, CS, I
1968 – E, B, CS, SF, I
1969 – I
1971 – D, TT, NL
1972 – F, TT

3: **Hailwood, Mike** *(GB)* **21**
**Honda* (20) ***MZ* (1)
1961* – TT, NL, DDR, S
1963** – DDR
1965* – J
1966* – E, D, F, NL, B, DDR, CS, SF, TT, I
1967* – TT, NL, SF, IRL, CDN

4: **Villa, Walter** *(I)* **20**
**Harley Davidson* (19) ***Yamaha* (1)
1974* – I, NL, SF, CS
1975* – E, D, I, NL, S
1976* – F, I, NL, B, SF, CS, D
1977* – YV, B, SF
1979** – YV

5: **Redman, Jim** *(SR)* **18**
Honda
1961 – B, I
1962 – E, F, NL, D, DDR, I
1963 – TT, NL, IRL, J
1964 – TT, NL, I
1965 – TT, B, DDR

6: **Ballington, Kork** *(SA)* **17**
**Yamaha* (1) ***Kawasaki* (16)
1977* – GB
1978** – I, SF, D, CS
1979** – D, I, E, SF, GB, CS, F
1980** – E, F, SF, GB, D

Lavado, Carlos *(YV)* **17**
Yamaha
1980 – NL
1982 – E, CS
1983 – I, D, YU, NL
1984 – NL
1985 – E, RSM
1986 – E, D, A, NL, F, S
1987 – YU

8: **Provini, Tarquinio** *(I)* **14**
**Mondial* (2) ***MV Agusta* (6) ****Morini* (4) *****Benelli* (2)
1957* – NL, I
1958** – TT, NL, D, IRL
1959** – TT, NL
1963*** – E, D, I, RA
1964**** – E
1965**** – I

9: **Ubbiali, Carlo** *(I)* **13**
MV Agusta
1955 – I
1956 – TT, NL, B, D, I
1957 – D
1959 – D, I
1960 – NL, B, IRL, I

10: **Gould, Rodney** *(GB)* **10**
Yamaha
1970 – F, NL, B, DDR, SF, I
1971 – S, SF
1972 – NL, S

11: **Pons, Sito** *(E)* **8**
*Cobas** (1) ***Honda* (2)
1984* – E
1986** – YU, B
1987** – RA
1988** – E, B, YU, S

Saarinen, Jarno *(SF)* **8**
Yamaha
1971 – E
1972 – B, DDR, CS, SF
1973 – F, A, D

13: **Braun, Dieter** *(D)* **7**
Yamaha
1971 – DDR
1973 – YU, NL, S, CS
1975 – YU
1976 – YU

Carruthers, Kel *(AUS)* **7**
**Benelli* (3) ***Yamaha* (4)
1969* – TT, IRL, YU
1970** – D, TT, CS, IRL

Haas, Werner *(D)* **7**
NSU
1953 – NL, D
1954 – F, TT, IRL, NL, D

Ivy, Bill *(GB)* **7**
Yamaha
1967 – F, B
1968 – D, TT, NL, DDR, IRL

Spencer, Freddie *(USA)* **7**
Honda
1985 – SA, I, A, YU, NL, B, F

18: **Pasolini Renzo** *(I)* **6**
**Benelli* (3) ***Aermacchi* (3)
1969* – NL, DDR, CS
1972** – I, YU, E

Sarron, Christian *(F)* **6**
Yamaha
1977 – D
1982 – SF
1983 – S
1984 – A, G, GB

20: **Ambrosini, Dario** *(I)* **5**
Benelli
1949 – I
1950 – TT, CH, I
1951 – CH

Herweh, Manfred *(D)* **5**
Real Rotax
1983 – A
1984 – YU, B, S, RSM

Hocking, Gary *(SR)* **5**
**MZ* (2) ***MV Agusta* (3)
1959* – S, IRL
1960** – TT, D
1961** – E

Lorenzetti, Enrico *(I)* **5**
Moto Guzzi
1951 – I
1952 – NL, I
1953 – I, E

24: **Andersson, Kent** *(S)* **4**
Yamaha
1969 – D, SF
1970 – E
1974 – B

Hansford, Greg *(AUS)* **4**
Kawasaki
1978 – E, F, S, YU

Herrero, Santiago *(E)* **4**
Ossa
1969 – E, F, B
1970 – YU

Sarron, Dominique *(F)* **4**
Honda
1986 – GB
1987 – BR
1988 – I, BR

28: **Anderson, Fergus** *(GB)* **3**
Moto Guzzi
1952 – CH, TT
1953 – TT

Cann, Maurice *(GB)* **3**
Moto Guzzi
1949 – IRL
1950 – IRL
1952 – IRL

Garriga, Juan *(E)* **3**
Yamaha
1988 – P, NL, CZ

Katayama, Takazumi *(J)* **3**
Yamaha
1974 – S
1976 – S
1977 – E

Rossi, Graziano *(I)* **3**
Morbidelli
1979 – YU, NL, S

Ruffo, Bruno *(I)* **3**
Moto Guzzi
1949 – CH
1951 – F, IRL

Wimmer, Martin *(D)* **3**
Yamaha
1982 – GB
1985 – D
1987 – E

35: **Armstrong, Reg** *(IRL)* **2**
NSU
1953 – IRL, CH

Baldè, Jean Francois *(F)* **2**
**Kawasaki* (1) ***Chevallier Yamaha* (1)
1981* – RA
1983** – SA

Bryans, Ralph *(IRL)* **2**
Honda
1967 – D, J

Cadalora, Luca *(I)* **2**
Yamaha
1988 – D, GB

Cecotto, Johnny *(YV)* **2**
Yamaha
1975 – F, B

Cornu, Jacques *(CH)* **2**
Honda
1988 – A, F

De Radigues, Didier *(B)* **2**
Chevallier Yamaha
1982 – YU
1983 – B

Dodds, John *(AUS)* **2**
Yamaha
1973 – E
1974 – E

Duff, Mike *(CDN)* **2**
Yamaha
1964 – B
1965 – SF

Grant, Mick *(GB)* **2**
Kawasaki
1977 – NL, S

Grassetti, Silvio *(I)* **2**
MZ
1971 – A, B

Länsivuori, Tepi *(SF)* **2**
Yamaha
1973 – B, SF

McIntyre, Bob *(GB)* **2**
Honda
1961 – IRL
1962 – B

Mortimer, Charles *(GB)* **2**
**Yamaha* (1) ***Danfay Yamaha* (1)
1974* – YU
1975** – TT

Phillis, Tom (AUS) **2**
Honda
1961 – F, RA

Roberts, Kenny *(USA)* **2**
Yamaha
1978 – YV, NL

Rougerie, Michel *(F)* **2**
Harley Davidson
1974 – SF, CS

Sandford, Cecil *(GB)* **2**
Mondial
1957 – TT, IRL

Taveri, Luigi *(CH)* **2**
MV Agusta
1955 – NL
1956 – IRL

Uncini, Franco *(I)* **2**
Harley Davidson
1977 – I, CS

Wheeler, Arthur *(GB)* **2**
Moto Guzzi
1954 – I
1962 – RA

Williams, Charlie *(GB)* **2**
**Johnson Yamaha* (1) ***Dugdale Yamaha* (1)
1973* – TT
1974** – TT

57: **Barrington, Manliff** *(IRL)* **1**
Moto Guzzi
1949 – TT

Bolle, Jacques *(F)* **1**
Pernod
1983 – GB

Bonera, Gianfranco *(I)* **1**
Harley Davidson
1976 – E

Carter, Alan *(GB)* **1**
Yamaha
1983 – F

Drapal, Janos *(H)* **1**
Yamaha
1971 – CS

Ekerold, Jon *(SA)* **1**
Yamaha
1977 – F

Felgenheier, Rudi *(D)* **1**
DKW
1952 – D

Fernandez, Patrick *(F)* **1**
Yamaha
1984 – SA

Filice, Jim *(USA)* **1**
Honda
1988 – USA

Freymond, Roland *(CH)* **1**
MBA
1982 – S

Fügner, Horst *(DDR)* **1**
MZ
1958 – S

Guilleux, Hervè *(F)* **1**
Kawasaki
1983 – E

Hartle, John *(GB)* **1**
MV Agusta
1957 – B

Hasegawa, Hiroshi *(J)* **1**
Yamaha
1966 – J

Herron, Tom *(IRL)* **1**
Yamaha
1976 – TT

Hollaus, Rupert *(A)* **1**
NSU
1954 – CH

Ito, Fumio *(J)* **1**
Yamaha
1963 – B

Jansson, Börje *(S)* **1**
Derbi
1972 – A

Kanaya, Hideo *(J)* **1**
Yamaha
1972 – D

Kassner, Helmut *(D)* **1**
Yamaha
1974 – D

Kobayashi, Masaru *(J)* **1**
Honda
1987 – J

Lega, Mario *(I)* **1**
Morbidelli
1977 – YU

Lomas, Bill *(GB)* **1**
MV Agusta
1955 – TT

Marsowszky, Guyla *(CH)* **1**
Yamaha
1971 – I

McCullough, Ray *(IRL)* **1**
Yamsel
1971 – IRL

Mendogni, Emilio *(I)* **1**
Morini
1958 – I

Minter, Derek *(GB)* **1**
Honda
1962 – TT

Molloy, Ginger *(NZ)* **1**
Bultaco
1966 – IRL

Müller, Hermann Paul *(D)* **1**
NSU
1955 – D

Pileri, Paolo *(I)* **1**
Morbidelli
1978 – B

Reggiani, Loris *(I)* **1**
Aprilla
1987 – RSM

Ricci, Fausto *(I)* **1**
Yamaha
1984 – I

Robb, Tommy *(IRL)* **1**
Honda
1962 – IRL

Roth, Reinhold *(D)* **1**
Honda
1987 – F

Saul, Eric *(F)* **1**
Chevallier Yamaha
1981 – I

Shepherd, Alan *(GB)* **1**
MZ
1964 – USA

Stöllinger, Edi *(A)* **1**
Kawasaki
1979 – B

Surtees, John *(GB)* **1**
NSU
1955 – IRL

Takahashi, Kunimitsu *(J)* **1**
Honda
1961 – D

Taira, Tadahiko *(J)* **1**
Yamaha
1986 – RSM

Tournadre, Jean Louis *(F)* **1**
Yamaha
1982 – F

Wood, Tommy *(GB)* **1**
Moto Guzzi
1951 – TT

350cc — Total

1: **Agostini, Giacomo** *(I)* **54**
**MV Agusta* (48) ***Yamaha* (6)
1965* – D, SF, I
1966* – DDR, TT, I
1967* – IRL
1968* – D, TT, NL, DDR, CS, IRL, I
1969* – E, D, TT, NL, DDR, CS, SF, IRL
1970* – D, YU, TT, NL, DDR, CS, SF, IRL, I
1971* – A, D, NL, DDR, S, SF
1972* – A, I, TT, NL, S, SF
1973* – F, I, NL, SF
1974** – F, A, I, NL, YU
1975** – E
1976* – NL

2: **Redman, Jim** *(SR)* **21**
Honda
1962 – NL, IRL, DDR, I
1963 – D, TT, NL, IRL, I
1964 – TT, NL, D, DDR, IRL, SF, I, J
1965 – TT, NL, DDR, CS

3: **Hailwood, Mike** *(GB)* **16**
**MV Agusta* (4) ***Honda* (12)
1962* – TT
1963* – DDR, SF
1965* – J
1966** – D, F, NL, CS, SF, IRL
1967** – D, TT, NL, DDR, CS, J

4: **Surtees, John** *(GB)* **15**
MV Agusta
1956 – B
1958 – TT, NL, B, D, IRL, I
1959 – F, TT, D, S, IRL, I
1960 – NL, IRL

5: **Ballington, Kork** *(SA)* **14**
**Yamaha* (3) ***Kawasaki* (11)
1976* – E
1977* – NL, GB
1978** – A, I, NL, SF, GB, CS
1979** – A, E, YU, GB, CS

6: **Duke, Geoff** *(GB)* **11**
Norton
1950 – I
1951 – TT, B, F, IRL, I
1952 – CH, TT, NL, B
1958 – S

7: **Cecotto, Johnny** *(YV)* **9**
**Yamaha* (8) ***Bimota Yamaha* (1)
1975* – F, D, I, SF
1976* – A, I
1977* – YV, CS
1980** – I

8: **Mang, Anton** *(D)* **8**
Kawasaki
1980 – GB, CS
1981 – D, YU, NL, GB, CS
1982 – SF

9: **Anderson, Fergus** *(GB)* **7**
Moto Guzzi
1953 – B, F, CH
1954 – NL, CH, I, E

Katayama, Takazumi *(J)* **7**
Yamaha
1977 – D, F, YU, S, SF
1978 – YV, D

Lomas, Bill *(GB)*
Moto Guzzi
1955 – TT, D, B, IRL
1956 – NL, D, IRL

12: **Ekerold, Jon** *(SA)* **6**
**Yamaha* (1) ***Bimota Yamaha* (5)
1979* – D
1980** – F, NL, D
1981** – RA, I

Hansford, Gregg *(AUS)* **6**
Kawasaki
1978 – F, S, YU
1979 – I, NL, SF

Hocking, Gary *(SR)* **6**
MV Agusta
1960 – F, I
1961 – NL, DDR, IRL, I

15: **Frith, Freddie** *(GB)* **5**
Velocette
1949 – TT, CH, NL, B, IRL

Länsivuori, Tepi *(SF)* **5**
Yamaha
1971 – E
1973 – D, CS, S
1974 – S

Saarinen, Jarno *(SF)* **5**
Yamaha
1971 – CS, I
1972 – D, F, CS

18: **Amm, Ray** *(SR)* **4**
Norton
1952 – I
1953 – TT
1954 – IRL, D

Kavanagh, Ken *(AUS)* **4**
**Norton* (1) ***Moto Guzzi* (3)
1952* – IRL
1954** – B
1955** – NL
1956** – TT

Read, Phil *(GB)* **4**
**Norton* (1) ***Yamaha* (2) ****MV Agusta* (1)
1961* – TT
1966** – J
1969** – I
1972*** – DDR

Villa, Walter *(I)* **4**
Harley Davidson
1976 – F, SF, CS, D

22: **Baldè, Jean Francois** *(F)* **3**
Kawasaki
1982 – F, NL, GB

Campbell, Keith *(AUS)* **3**
Moto Guzzi
1957 – NL, B, IRL

Drapal, Janos *(H)* **3**
Yamaha
1972 – YU
1973 – A, YU

Foster, Bob *(GB)* **3**
Velocette
1950 – B, NL, IRL

Stastny, Frantisek *(CS)* **3**
Jawa
1961 – D, S
1965 – IRL

27: **De Radigues, Didier** *(B)* **2**
Chevallier Yamaha
1982 – I, CS

Fernandez, Patrick *(F)* **2**
**Yamaha* (1) ***Bimota Yamaha* (1)
1979* – F
1981** – A

Graham, Leslie (GB) **2**
**AJS* (1) ***Velocette* (1)
1950* – CH
1951** – CH

Lavado, Carlos *(YV)* **2**
Yamaha
1979 – YV
1982 – RA

Liberati, Libero *(I)* **2**
Gilera
1956 – I
1957 – D

Lorenzetti, Enrico *(I)* **2**
Moto Guzzi
1953 – NL, I

McIntyre, Bob *(GB)* **2**
Gilera
1957 – TT, I

Rutter, Tony *(GB)* **2**
Yamaha
1973 – TT; 1974 – TT

35: **Agostini, Duilio** *(I)* **1**
Moto Guzzi
1955 – F

Armstrong, Reg *(IRL)* **1**
Norton
1952 – D

Bell, Artie *(IRL)* **1**
Norton
1950 – TT

Bergamonti, Angelo *(I)* **1**
MV Agusta
1970 – E

Braun, Dieter *(D)* **1**
Yamaha
1975 – NL

Bryans, Ralph *(IRL)* **1**
Honda
1967 – I

Buscherini, Otello *(I)* **1**
Yamaha
1975 – CS

Celso, Santos Adu *(BR)* **1**
Yamaha
1973 – E

Chevallier, Olivier *(F)* **1**
Yamaha
1976 – YU

Coleman, Rod *(NZ)* **1**
AJS
1954 – TT

Dale, Dickie *(GB)* **1**
Moto Guzzi
1955 – I

Dodds, John *(AUS)* **1**
Yamaha
1974 – SF

Doran, Bill *(GB)* **1**
AJS
1951 – NL

Grassetti, Silvio *(I)* **1**
Jawa
1969 – YU

Hartle, John *(GB)* **1**
MV Agusta
1960 – TT

Herweh, Manfred *(D)* **1**
Yamaha
1982 – D

Jefferies, Tony *(GB)* **1**
Yamsel
1971 – TT

Kanaya, Hideo *(J)* **1**
Yamaha
1975 – A

Kassner, Helmut *(D)* **1**
Yamaha
1974 – D

Kneubühler, Bruno *(CH)* **1**
Yamaha
1972 – E

Korhonen, Pentti *(SF)* **1**
Yamaha
1975 – YU

Monneret, Pierre *(F)* **1**
AJS
1954 – F

Mortimer, Charles *(GB)* **1**
Dugdale Yamaha
1976 – TT

Mudford, Ken *(NZ)* **1**
Norton
1953 – IRL

North, Alan *(SA)* **1**
Yamaha
1977 – I

Palomo, Victor *(E)* **1**
Yamaha
1974 – E

Robb, Tommy *(IRL)* **1**
Honda
1962 – SF

Rougerie, Michel *(F)* **1**
Yamaha
1977 – E

Saul, Eric *(F)* **1**
Chevallier Yamaha
1982 – A

Williams, Charlie *(GB)* **1**
Dugdale Yamaha
1975 – TT

Williams, Peter *(GB)* **1**
MZ
1971 – IRL

Wood, Tommy *(GB)* **1**
Moto Guzzi
1951 – E

500cc **Total**

1: **Agostini, Giacomo** *(I)* **68**
**MV Agusta* (62) ***Yamaha* (6)
1965* – SF
1966* – B, SF, I
1967* – D, B, DDR, SF, I
1968* – D, E, TT, NL, B, DDR, CS, SF, IRL, I
1969* – E, D, F, TT, NL, B, DDR, CS, SF, IRL
1970* – D, F, YU, NL, B, DDR, SF, IRL, I
1971* – A, D, TT, NL, B, DDR, CS, S, SF
1972* – D, F, A, I, TT, NL, B, DDR, CS, S, SF
1973* – B, CS, SF

1974** – A, NL
1975** – F, D, I, SF
1976* – D

2: **Hailwood, Mike** *(GB)* **37**
*Norton (1) **MV Agusta (28) ***Honda (8)
1961 – TT*, I**
1962** – NL, B, IRL, DDR, I
1963** – TT, B, IRL, DDR, SF, I, RA
1964** – USA, TT, NL, B, D, DDR, I
1965** – USA, D, TT, NL, B, DDR, CS, I
1966*** – CS, IRL, TT
1967*** – TT, NL, CS, IRL, CDN

3: **Lawson, Eddie** *(USA)* **26**
Yamaha
1984 – SA, E, A, S
1985 – SA, YU, RSM
1986 – I, D, A, YU, F, S, RSM
1987 – D, NL, GB, P, RA
1988 – USA, P, I, A, F, S, BR

4: **Duke, Geoff** *(GB)* **22**
*Norton (8) **Gilera 14
1950* – TT, IRL, I
1951* – TT, B, NL, IRL
1953** – NL, F, CH, I
1954** – B, NL, D, CH, I
1955** – F, TT, D, NL
1956** – I
1958* – S

Roberts, Kenny *(USA)* **22**
Yamaha
1978 – A, F, I, GB
1979 – A, I, E, YU, GB
1980 – I, E, F
1981 – D, I
1982 – RA, E
1983 – D, A, NL, B, GB, RSM

Surtees, John (GB) **22**
MV Agusta
1956 – TT, NL, B
1957 – NL
1958 – TT, NL, B, D, IRL, I
1959 – F, TT, D, NL, B, IRL, I
1960 – F, TT, B, D, I

7: **Spencer, Freddie** *(USA)* **20**
Honda
1982 – B, RSM
1983 – SA, F, I, E, YU, S
1984 – I, D, F, YU, B
1985 – E, I, A, B, F, GB, S

8: **Sheene, Barry** *(GB)* **19**
*Suzuki (18) **Yamaha (1)
1975* – NL, S
1976* – F, A, I, NL, S
1977* – YV, D, I, F, B, S
1978* – YV, S
1979* – YV, S, F
1981** – S

9: **Gardner, Wayne** *(AUS)* **14**
Honda
1986 – E, NL, GB
1987 – E, I, A, YU, S, CS, B
1988 – NL, B, YU, CZ

10: **Mamola, Randy** *(USA)* **13**
*Suzuki (5) **Honda (4) ***Yamaha (1)
1980* – B, GB
1981* – A, YU
1982* – D
1984** – NL, GB, RSM
1985** – NL
1986*** – B
1987** – J, F, RSM

11: **Read, Phil** *(GB)* **11**
*Norton (1) **MV Agusta (10)
1964* – IRL
1973** – D, NL, S, E
1974** – F, B, SF, CS
1975** – B, CS

12: **Hocking, Gary** *(SR)* **8**
MV Agusta
1961 – D, F, NL, B, DDR, IRL, S
1962 – TT

13: **Lucchinelli, Marco** *(I)* **6**
Suzuki
1980 – D
1981 – F, NL, B, RSM, SF

Masetti, Umberto *(I)* **6**
*Gilera (5) **MV Agusta (1)
1950* – B, NL
1951* – E
1952* – NL, B
1955** – I

15: **Graham, Leslie** *(GB)* **5**
*AJS (3) **MV Agusta (2)
1949* – CH, IRL
1950* – CH
1952** – I,E

Hartog, Wil *(NL)* **5**
Suzuki
1977 – NL
1978 – B, SF
1979 – D
1980 – SF

Uncini, Franco *(I)* **5**
Suzuki
1982 – A, I, NL, YU, GB

18: **Armstrong, Reg** *(IRL)* **4**
**Norton* (2) ***Gilera* (2)
1952* – TT, D
1955** – E
1956** – D

Liberati, Libero *(I)* **4**
Gilera
1957 – D, B, IRL, I

20: **Cecotto, Johnny** *(YV)* **3**
Yamaha
1977 – SF, CS
1978 – NL

Findlay, Jack *(AUS)* **3**
Suzuki
1971 – IRL
1973 – TT
1977 – A

Hartle, John *(GB)* **3**
**Norton* (2) ***Gilera* (1)
1956* – IRL
1960* – IRL
1963** – NL

Hennen, Pat *(USA)* **3**
Suzuki
1976 – SF
1977 – GB
1978 – E

Milani, Afredo *(I)* **3**
Gilera
1951 – F, I
1953 – B

Pagani, Alberto *(I)* **3**
**Linto* (1) ***MV Agusta* (2)
1969* – I; 1971** – I
1972** – YU

26: **Amm, Ray** *(SR)* **2**
Norton
1953 – TT; 1954 – TT

Anderson, Fergus *(GB)* **2**
Moto Guzzi
1951 – CH
1953 – E

Ferrari, Virginio *(I)* **2**
Suzuki
1978 – D
1979 – NL

Middelburg, Jack *(NL)* **2**
**Yamaha* (1) ***Suzuki* (1)
1980* – NL
1981** – GB

Pagani, Nello *(I)* **2**
Gilera
1949 – NL, I

Redman, Jim *(SR)* **2**
Honda
1966 – D, NL

Saarinen, Jarno *(SF)* **2**
Yamaha
1973 – F, A

Schwantz, Kevin *(USA)* **2**
Suzuki
1988 – J, D

34: **Ahearn, Jack** *(AUS)* **1**
Norton
1964 – SF

Bergamonti, Angelo *(I)* **1**
MV Agusta
1970 – E

Bonera, Gianfranco *(I)* **1**
MV Agusta
1974 – I

Brett, Jack *(GB)* **1**
AJS
1952 – CH

Caldarella, Benedicto *(RA)* **1**
Matchless
1962 – RA

Carpenter, Phil *(GB)* **1**
Yamaha
1974 – TT

Colnago, Giuseppe *(I)* **1**
Gilera
1955 – B

Creith, Dick *(IRL)* **1**
Norton
1965 – IRL

Czihak, Edmond *(D)* **1**
Yamaha
1974 – D

Dale, Dickie *GB)* **1**
MV Agusta
1954 – E

Daniell, Harold *(GB)* **1**
Norton
1949 – TT

Doran, Bill *(GB)* **1**
AJS
1949 – B

Frutschi, Michel *(CH)* **1**
Sanvenero
1982 – F

Grant, Mick *(GB)* **1**
Kawasaki
1975 – TT

Herron, Tom *(IRL)* **1**
Yamaha
1976 – TT

Ireland, Dennis *(NZ)* **1**
Suzuki
1979 – B

Kanaya, Hideo *(J)* **1**
Yamaha
1975 – A

Katayama, Takazumi *(J)* **1**
Honda
1982 – S

Kavanagh, Ken *(AUS)* **1**
Norton
1953 – IRL

Kissling, Jorge *(RA)* **1**
Matchless
1961 – RA

Länsivuori, Tepi *(SF)* **1**
Yamaha
1974 – S

Lomas, Bill *(GB)* **1**
Moto Guzzi
1955 – IRL

Magee, Kevin *(USA)* **1**
Yamaha
1988 – E

McCandless, Cromie *(IRL)* **1**
Gilera
1952 – IRL

McIntyre, Bob *(GB)* **1**
Gilera
1957 – TT

Monneret, Pierre *(F)* **1**
Gilera
1954 – F

Mortimer, Charles *(GB)* **1**
Yamaha
1972 – E

Nash, Godfrey *(GB)* **1**
Norton
1969 – YU

Newbold, John *(GB)* **1**
Suzuki
1976 – CS

Newcombe, Kim *(NZ)* **1**
König
1973 – YU

Rainey, Wayne *(USA)* **1**
Yamaha
1988 – GB

Sarron, Christian *(F)* **1**
Yamaha
1985 – D

Shepherd, Alan *(GB)* **1**
Matchless
1962 – SF

Simmonds, Dave *(GB)* **1**
Kawasaki
1971 – E

Stastny, Frantisek *(CS)* **1**
Jawa
1966 – DDR

Van Dulmen, Boet *(NL)* **1**
Suzuki
1979 – SF

Venturi, Remo (I) **1**
MV Agusta
1960 – NL

Williams, John *(GB)* **1**
Suzuki
1976 – B

SIDECAR

1: **Biland, Rolf** *(CH)* **52**
Freiburghaus, Freddy *(CH)*
Williams, Kenny *(GB)*
Waltisperg Kurt *(CH)*
**Yamaha* (19)
***Seymaz Yamaha* (2)
****LCR Yamaha* (21)
*****LCR Krauser* (10)
1976** – D
1976** – F
1977* – A, D, NL
1978* – A, F, I
1979–B2a* – NL, GB, CS
1979–B2b*** – A, CH, Eifelpokal, F
1980* – F, YU, CS
1981* – F, E, B, GB, SF, S, CS
1982*** – A, NL, B, S, SF, D
1983*** – F, A, NL, B, S, RSM
1984*** – F, NL, S
1985*** – A, NL
1987**** – A, F, S, CS
1988**** – P, D, A, NL, B, F

2: **Enders, Klaus** *(D)* **27**
Engelhardt, Rolf *(D)* Kalauch, Wolfgang *(D)*
**BMW* (25) ***Busch Enders* (2)

1967* – D, F, NL, B, SF
1969* – D, IT, SF, IRL
1970* – F, TT, CS, SF, IRL
1972* – A, NL, B, CS
1973* – F, A, D, TT, NL, B, CS
1974** – I, NL

3: **Oliver, Eric** *(GB)* **17**
Jenkinson, Denis *(GB)*; Dobelli, Lorenzo *(I)*; Bliss, Eric *(GB)*; Dibben, Stanley *(GB)*; Nutt, Les *(GB)*
Norton
1949 – CH, B
1950 – B, CH, I
1951 – E, B, F
1952 – E, B
1953 – CH, B, I, F
1954 – TT, IRL, B

4: **Scheidegger, Fritz** *(CH)* **16**
Burkhardt, Hans *(D)* Robinson, John *(GB)*
BMW
1959 – F
1961 – B, F
1962 – NL
1963 – B
1964 – F, D
1965 – D, NL, B, I
1966 – D, F, NL, B, TT

5: **Streuer, Egbert** *(NL)* **15**
Schnieders, Bernard *(NL)*
LCR Yamaha
1982 – GB
1983 – D, GB
1984 – A, D, GB
1985 – B, F, S
1986 – D, A, F, GB, D(h)
1987 – NL

6: **Deubel, Max** *(D)* **12**
Hörner, Emil *(D)*
BMW
1961 – TT, NL, D
1962 – E, D, F
1963 – E, NL
1964 – TT, B
1965 – E, TT

Michel, Alain *(F)* **12**
Lecorre, Gerard *(F)*; Collins, Stu *(GB)*; Burkhard, Michael *(D)*; Fresc Jean-Marc *(F)*
**Yamaha* (1) ***Seymaz Yamaha* (6) ****LCR Yamaha* (5)
1977* – F
1978** – GB, CS
1979–B2b** – GB, Assen
1981** – D, NL
1982*** – CS, RSM
1984*** – B
1986*** – NL, S

8: **Fath, Helmut** *(D)* **11**
Wohlgemuth, Alfred *(D)* Kalauch, Wolfgang *(D)*
**BMW* (5) ***URS Fath* (6)
1960* – B, TT, D, F
1961* – E
1968** – D, SF, Württemberg
1969** – F, NL, B

9: **Schwarzel, Werner** *(D)* **10**
Huber, Andreas *(D)*, Kleis Karl *(D)* Buck, Fritz *(D)*
**König* (5) ***ARO Fath* (4) ****LCR Yamaha* (1)
1974* – D, CS
1975* – NL, CS
1976* – D
1977** – B, GB
1978** – NL, D
1985*** – D

Steinhausen, Rolf *(D)* **10**
Huber, Joseph *(D)*; Kalauch, Wolfgang *(D)*; Arthur, Kenny *(GB)*
**König* (1) ***Busch König* (6) ****KSA Yamaha* (2) *****Busch Yamaha* (1)
1974* – B
1975** – A, TT, B
1976** – A, TT, B
1977**** – CS
1979–B2a*** – D, B

11: **Schauzu, Siegfried** *(D)* **9**
Schneider, Horst *(D)*; Kalauch, Wolfgang *(D)*
BMW
1967 – TT
1968 – TT
1971 – TT, B, CS
1972 – D, TT
1974 – F, A

12: **Camathias, Florian** *(CH)* **8**
Cecco, Hilmar *(D)*; Winter, Harry *(GB)*; Herzig, Alfred *(CH)*; Foll, Roland *(D)*; Ducret, Franz *(CH)*
BMW* (5) ***FCS MBW* (2)**Gilera* (1)
1958* – NL
1959* – NL, D

1962* – B
1963** – TT, D
1964*** – E
1965* – F

Noll, Wilhelm *(D)* **8**
Cron, Fritz *(D)*
BMW
1954 – D, CH, I
1955 – B, CH
1956 – IRL, B, D

14: **Schneider, Walter** *(D)* **7**
Strauss, Hans *(D)*
BMW
1955 – TT
1957 – B
1958 – B, TT, D
1959 – B, TT

Webster, Steve *(GB)* **7**
Hewitt, Tony *(GB)*; Simmons, Gavin (GB)
**LCR Yamaha **LCR Krauser*
1986* – B
1987** – E, D, GB
1988** – GB, S, CZ

16: **Auerbacher, Georg** *(D)* **6**
Dein, Eduard *(D)*; Nelson, Billie *(GB)*; Hahn, Hermann *(D)*
BMW
1967 – E, I
1968 – B
1970 – D, NL
1971 – D

Taylor, Jock *(GB)* **6**
Johansson, Benga *(S)*
Yamaha
1979–B2a – S
1980 – NL, B, SF, D
1981, A

18: **Hillebrand, Fritz** *(D)* **5**
Grünwald, Manfred *(D)*
BMW
1956 – TT, NL
1957 – TT, NL, D

19: **Milani, Albino** *(I)* **4**
Pizzocri, Giuseppe *(I)*; Milani, Rossano *(I)*
Gilera
1951 – I
1952 – CH
1956 – I
1957 – I

20: **Faust, Willy** *(D)* **3**
Remmert, Karl *(D)*
BMW
1955, E, NL, D

Owesle, Horst *(D)* **3**
Kremer, Julius *(D)*; Rutterford, Peter *(GB)*
Münch URS
1971 – NL, SF, IRL

Schmid, Hermann *(CH)* **3**
Matile, Jean Petit *(CH)*
* *König* (1) ** *Yamaha* (2)
1975* – F
1976** – NL, CS

23: **Butscher, Arsenius** *(D)* **2**
Huber, Josef *(D)*
BMW
1970 – B; 1971 – A

Frigerio, Ercole *(I)* **2**
Ricotti, Edoardo *(I)*
Gilera
1949 – I
1951 – CH

Luthringshauser, Heinz *(D)* **2**
Cusnik, Jurgen *(D)*; Hahn, Hermann *(D)*
BMW
1972 – F
1974 – TT

Smith, Cyril *(GB)* **2**
Clements, Bob *(GB)*
Norton
1952 – D; 1953 – IRL

Vincent, Chris *(GB)* **2**
Bliss, Eric *(GB)*; Casey, Mike *(GB)*
**BSA* (1) ***Münch URS* (1)
1962* – TT
1972** – SF

28: **Attenberger, Johann** *(D)* **1**
Schillinger, Josef *(D)*
BMW
1968 – NL

Brodin, Göte *(S)* **1**
Gallros, Billy *(S)*
Yamaha
1979–B2a – A

Harris, Peter *(GB)* **1**
Campbell, Ray *(GB)*
BMW
1960 – NL

Holzer, Bruno *(CH)* 1
Meierhans, Karl *(CH)*
Yamaha
1978 – B

Jones, Derek *(GB)* 1
Ayres, Bryan *(GB)*
Yamaha
1980 – GB

Merlo, Ernesto *(I)* 1
Magri, Edoardo *(I)*
(Gilera)
1952 – I

Rahko, Kalvevi *(SF)* 1
Laatikainen, Kari *(SF)*
Honda
1973 – SF

Seeley, Colin *(GB)* 1
Campbell, Ray *(GB)*
FCS BMW
1964 – NL

World Champions Willi Noll and Fritz Cron race over the cobbles at Monza in 1954.

Other Championship Records

FIM Coupe d'Endurance

1975 (Five rounds)
1=*33 points* Genoud, A. *(CH)* Kawasaki
Godier, G. *(F)* Kawasaki
3=*31 points* Huguet, C. *(F)* Japauto
Ruiz, R. *(F)* Japauto

1976 (Five rounds)
1 *45 points* Chemarin, J. C. *(F)* Honda
2 *42 points* Leon, C. *(F)* Honda
3 *35 points* Huguet, C. *(F)* Honda

1977 (Six rounds)
1=*49 points* Chemarin, J. C. *(F)* Honda
Leon, C. *(F)* Honda
3=*47 points* Williams, C. *(GB)* Honda
Woods, S. *(GB)* Honda

1978 (Six rounds)
1=*72 points* Chemarin, J. C. *(F)* Honda
Leon, C. *(F)* Honda
3 *61 points* Williams, C. *(GB)* Honda

1979 (Six rounds)
1=*49 points* Chemarin, J. C. *(F)* Honda
Leon, C. *(F)* Honda
3 *42 points* Huguet, C. *(F)* Kawasaki

World Endurance Championship

1980 (Seven rounds)
1=*58 points* Fontan, M. *(F)* Honda
Moineau, H. *(F)* Honda
3 *49 points* Huguet, C. *(F)* Kawasaki

1981 (Eight rounds)
1=*81 points* Lafond, J. *(F)* Kawasaki
Roche, R. *(F)* Kawasaki
3 *76 points* Huguet, C. *(F)* Kawasaki

1982 (Eight rounds)
1=*60 points* Chemarin, J. C. *(F)* Kawasaki
Cornu, J. *(CH)* Kawasaki
3=*45 points* Guilleux, H. *(F)* Kawasaki
Lafond, J. *(F)* Kawasaki

1983 (Five rounds)
1=*89 points* Hubin, R. *(B)* Suzuki
Moineau, H. *(F)* Suzuki
3=*84 points* Igoa, P. *(F)* Kawasaki
Lafond, P. *(F)* Kawasaki

1984 (Six rounds)
1=*70 points* Coudray, G. *(F)* Honda
Igoa, P. *(F)* Honda
3=*46 points* Bertin, G. *(F)* Honda
Sarron, D. *(F)* Honda

1985 (Six rounds)
1=*96 points* Coudray, G. *(F)* Honda
Igoa, P. *(F)* Honda
3 *76 points* Oudin, J. P. *(F)* Suzuki

1986 (Six rounds)
1 *105 points* Igoa, P. *(F)* Honda
2 *90 points* Vieira, A. *(F)* Honda
3 *75 points* Coudray, G. *(F)* Honda

1987 (eight rounds)
1=*120 points* Moineau, H. *(F)* Suzuki
Le Bihan, B. *(F)* Suzuki
3 *83 points* Van Vaerenbergh, J. *(B)* Kawas

TT Formula One World Championship

1977 (One round)
1 *15 points* Read, P. *(GB)* Honda
2 *12 points* Nicholls, R. *(GB)* Ducati
3 *10 points* Richards, I. *(GB)* Honda

1978 (One round)
1 *15 points* Hailwood, M. *(GB)* Ducati
2 *12 points* Williams, J. *(GB)* Honda
3 *10 points* Richards, I. *(GB)* Honda

1979 (Two rounds)
1 *25 points* Haslam, R. *(GB)* Honda
2 *23 points* George, A. *(GB)* Honda
3 *18 points* Crosby, G. *(NZ)* Kawasaki

1980 (Two rounds)
1 *27 points* Crosby, G. *(NZ)* Suzuki
2 *25 points* Grant, M. *(GB)* Honda
3 *12 points* Dunlop, J. *(IRL)* Suzuki

1981 (Two rounds)
1 *27 points* Crosby, G. *(NZ)* Suzuki
2 *27 points* Haslam, R. *(GB)* Honda
3 *16 points* Dunlop, J. *(IRL)* Honda

1982 (Three rounds)
1 *36 points* Dunlop, J. *(IRL)* Honda
2 *30 points* Haslam, R. *(GB)* Honda
3 *26 points* Hiscock, D. *(NZ)* Suzuki

1983 (Three rounds)
1 *42 points* Dunlop, J. *(IRL)* Honda
2 *35 points* McElnea, R. *(GB)* Suzuki
3 *26 points* Marshall, R. *(GB)* Honda

1984 (Five rounds)
1 *66 points* Dunlop, J. *(IRL)* Honda
2 *54 points* Marshall, R. *(GB)* Honda
3 *36 points* Rutter, T. *(GB)* Ducati

1985 (Six rounds)
1 *90 points* Dunlop, J. *(IRL)* Honda
2 *40 points* Grant, M. *(GB)* Suzuki
3 *32 points* McGregor, G. *(AUS)* Suzuki

1986 (Eight rounds)
1 *93 points* Dunlop, J. *(IRL)* Honda
2 *61 points* Iddon, P. *(GB)* Suzuki
3 *58 points* Andersson, A. *(S)* Suzuki

1987 (Seven rounds)
1 *49 points* Ferrari, V. *(I)* Bimota-Yamaha
2 *46 points* Dunlop, J. *(GB)* Honda
3 *43 points* Iddon, P. *(GB)* Suzuki

TT Formula Two World Championship

1977 (One round)
1 *15 points* Jackson, A. *(GB)* Honda
2 *12 points* Tuxworth, N. *(GB)* Honda
3 *10 points* Casement, D. *(GB)* Honda

1978 (One round)
1 *15 points* Jackson, A. *(GB)* Honda
2 *12 points* Mason, D. *(GB)* Honda
3 *10 points* Tuxworth, N. *(GB)* Honda

1979 (Two rounds)
1 *30 points* Jackson, A. *(GB)* Honda
2 *22 points* Bowler, R. *(GB)* Honda
3 *14 points* Ward, S. *(GB)* Benelli

1980 (Two rounds)
1 *30 points* Williams, C. *(GB)* Yamaha
2 *22 points* Lucas, M. *(GB)* Honda
3 *14 points* Odlin, P. *(GB)* Honda

1981 (Two rounds)
1 *27 points* Rutter, T. *(GB)* Ducati
2 *22 points* Odlin, P. *(GB)* Yamaha
3 *15 points* Mellor, P. *(GB)* Yamaha

1982 (Three rounds)
1 *45 points* Rutter, T. *(GB)* Ducati
2 *16 points* Nagal, R. *(D)* Ducati
3= *16 points* Fogarty, G. *(GB)* Ducati
Odlin, P. *(GB)* Yamaha

1983 (Three rounds)
2 *39 points* Rutter, T. *(GB)* Ducati
3 *35 points* Mellor, P. *(GB)* Yamaha
3 *22 points* McGregor, G. *(AUS)* Ducati

1984 (Four rounds)
1 *43 points* Rutter, T. *(GB)* Ducati
2 *28 points* Nation, T. *(GB)* Ducati
3 *25 points* Reid, B. *(IRL)* Yamaha

1985 (Four rounds)
1 *45 points* Reid, B. *(IRL)* Yamaha
2 *37 points* Rutter, T. *(GB)* Ducati
3 *24 points* Weeden, J. *(GB)* Yamaha

1986 (Three rounds)
1 *32 points* Reid, B *(IRL)* Yamaha
2 *26 points* Laycock, E. *(IRL)* Yamaha
3 *18 points* McGregor, G. *(AUS)* Ducati

TT Formula Three World Championship

1977 (One round)
1 *15 points* Kidson, J. *(GB)* Honda
2 *12 points* Loan, D. *(GB)* Suzuki
3 *10 points* Peters, B. *(GB)* Suzuki

1978 (One round)
1 *15 points* Smith, W. *(GB)* Honda
2 *12 points* Mortimer, D. *(GB)* Yamaha
3 *10 points* Stephens, J. *(GB)* Honda

1979 (Two rounds)
1 *30 points* Smith, B. *(AUS)* Yamaha
2 *20 points* Hunter, R. *(GB)* Honda
3 *12 points* Smith, W. *(GB)* Honda

1980 (Two rounds)
1 *25 points* Haslam, R. *(GB)* Honda
2 *20 points* Griffiths, C. *(GB)* Aermacchi
3 *18 points* Casement, D. *(GB)* Yamaha

1981 (Two rounds)
1 *30 points* Smith, B. *(Aus)* Yamaha
2 *22 points* Casement, D. *(GB)* Yamaha
3 *17 points* Raybon, D. *(GB)* Yamaha

FIM Formula 750

1973 (Seven rounds)
1 *51 points* Sheene, B. *(GB)* Suzuki
2 *47 points* Dodds, J. *(Aus)* Yamaha
3 *45 points* Findlay, J. *(Aus)* Suzuki

1974 (Three rounds)
1 *27 points* Dodds, J. *(Aus)* Yamaha
2 *22 points* Pons, P. *(F)* Yamaha
3 *16 points* Findlay, J. *(Aus)* Suzuki

1975 (Nine rounds)
1 *46 points* Findlay, J. *(Aus)* Yamaha
2 *45 points* Sheene, B. *(GB)* Suzuki
3 *42 points* Pons, P. *(F)* Yamaha

1976 (Nine rounds)
1 *61 points* Palomo, V. *(E)* Yamaha
2 *59 points* Nixon, G. *(USA)* Kawasaki
3 *47 points* Newbold, J. *(GB)* Suzuki

750 World Championship
1977 (Eleven rounds)
1 *131 points* Baker, S. *(USA)* Yamaha
2 *55 points* Sarron, C. *(F)* Yamaha
3 *45 points* Agostini, G. *(I)* Yamaha

1978 (Ten rounds)
1 *97 points* Cecotto, J. *(YV)* Yamaha
2 *92 points* Roberts, K. *(USA)* Yamaha
3 *55 points* Sarron, C. *(F)* Yamaha

1979 (Ten rounds)
1 *154 points* Pons, P. *(F)* Yamaha
2 *132 points* Frutschi, M. *(CH)* Yamaha
3 *126 points* Cecotto, J. *(YV)* Yamaha

European Championships

1981
50cc (Three rounds)
1 *42 points* Ascareggi, G. *(I)* Minarelli
2 *34 points* Merz, U. *(D)* Kreidler
3 *25 points* Kunz, R. *(D)* Kreidler

125cc (Five rounds)
1 *51 points* Aldrovandi, P. L. *(I)* MBA
2 *42 points* Galbit, M. *(F)* MBA
3 *37 points* Selini, J. C. *(F)* Morbidelli

250cc (Four rounds)
1 *33 points* Hauf, H. *(D)* Yamaha
2 *21 points* Simeon, M. *(B)* Yamaha
3 *20 points* Obinger, M. *(A)* Yamaha

500cc (Three rounds)
1 *42 points* Becheroni, L. *(I)* Suzuki
2 *24 points* Ghiselli, L. *(I)* Suzuki
3 *15 points* Roth, R. *(D)* Suzuki

Sidecar (Three rounds)
1 *30 points* Barker, J./Brushwood, J. *(GB)* Yamaha
2 *20 points* Bingham, D./Bingham, J. *(GB)* Yamaha
3 *20 points* Jelonek, K./Wagner, G. *(D)* Yamaha

1982
50cc (Five rounds)
1 *38 points* Matulja, Z. *(YU)* Tomos
2 *35 points* De Lorenzi, M. *(I)* Minarelli
3 *31 points* Singer, G. *(D)* Kreidler

125cc (Six rounds)
1 *73 points* Carracchi, S. *(I)* MBA
2 *44 points* Piccirillo, L. *(I)* MBA
3 *37 points* Gresini, F. *(I)* MBA

250cc (Seven rounds)
1 *73 points* Roth, R. *(D)* Yamaha
2 *47 points* Rapicault, T. *(F)* Yamaha
3 *39 points* Gouin, A. *(F)* Yamaha

500cc (Five rounds)
1 *41 points* Biliotti, F. *(I)* Suzuki
2 *32 points* Dean, D. *(GB)* Suzuki
3 *30 points* Roth, R. *(G)* Suzuki

Sidecar (Four rounds)
1 *47 points* Barton, M./Cutmore, N. *(GB)* Yamaha
2 *45 points* Abbott, S./Smith, S. *(GB)* Yamaha
3 *30 points* Wrathall, F./Spendlove, P. *(GB)* Yamaha

1983

80cc (Six rounds)
1 *75 points* Abold, H. *(D)* Zundapp
2 *46 points* Fargeri, M. *(I)* Zundapp/Kreidler
3 *25 points* Randall, P. *(GB)* Kawasaki

125cc (Nine rounds)
1 *62 points* Hupperich, W. *(D)* MBA
2 *60 points* Gianola, E. *(I)* MBA
3 *53 points* Cadalora, L. *(I)* MBA

250cc (Nine rounds)
1 *65 points* Cardus, C. *(E)* Kobas/Siroko
2 *53 points* Mertens, S. *(B)* Yamaha
3 *49 points* Ricci, F. *(I)* Yamaha

500cc (Eight rounds)
1 *54 points* Skold, P. *(S)* Suzuki
2 *44 points* Klein, K. *(D)* Suzuki
3 *42 points* Ghiselli, L. *(I)* Suzuki

Sidecar (Six rounds)
1 *50 points* Cousins, K./Hookham, P. *(GB)* Yamaha
2 *48 points* Bayley, D./Nixon, B. *(GB)*Yamaha
3 *42 points* Egloff, M./Egloff, U. *(CH)* Yamaha

1984

80cc (Six rounds)
1 *54 points* Bay, R. *(D)* Casal
2 *31 points* Rossbach, B. *(D)* Casal
3 *30 points* Gschwander, M. *(D)* Casal
Kafka, G. *(A)* Sachs

125cc (Eight rounds)
1 *53 points* Peschke, N. *(D)* MBA
2 *49 points* Hautaniemi, J. *(SF)* MBA
3 *43 points* Meozzi, F. *(I)* MBA

250cc (Eleven rounds)
1 *67 points* Noel, G. *(GB)* Exactweld
2 *66 points* Pagano, P. *(F)* Yamaha
3 *62 points* Guilemet, J. C. *(F)* Yamaha

500cc (Nine rounds)
1 *77 points* Hyvarinen, H. *(SF)* Suzuki
2 *52 points* Lingham, G. (GB) Suzuki
3 *50 points* Burnett, R. *(GB)* Suzuki

Sidecar (Eight rounds)
1 *88 points* Christinat, H. R. *(CH)*/ Fahrni, M. *(CH)*Yamaha
2 *85 points* Progin, R. *(CH)*/ Hunziker, Y. *(CH)* Yamaha
3 *53 points* Casagrande, L. *(CH)*/ Nydegger, R. *(CH)* Yamaha

1985

80cc (Eight rounds)
1 *56 points* Schirhofer, G. *(D)* Krauser
2 *53 points* Van Dongen, J. *(NL)* Huvo
3 *43 points* Koberstein, R. *(D)* Seel

125cc (Six rounds)
1 *82 points* Chili, P. F. *(I)* AEB
2 *51 points* Olsson, H. *(S)* Starol
3 *45 points* Casoli, P. *(I)* MBA

250cc (Ten rounds)
1 *58 points* Matteoni, M. *(I)* Honda
2 *57 points* Brasini, A. *(I)* Yamaha
3 *44 points* Bonhuil, B. *(F)* Yamaha

500cc (Ten rounds)
1 *86 points* Gentile, M. *(CH)* Yamaha
2 *84 points* Iddon, P. *(GB)* Suzuki
3 *75 points* Bogano, V. *(I)* Suzuki

Sidecar (Six rounds)
1 *64 points* Wrathall, F. *(GB)*/
Chapman, K. *(NZ)*/
Spendlove, P. *(GB)* Yamaha
2 *52 points* Bingham, D. *(GB)*/
Bingham, J. *(GB)* Yamaha
3 *35 points* Brindley, B. *(GB)*/
Jones, C. *(GB)* Yamaha

1986

80cc (Five rounds)
1 *54 points* Casanova, B. *(I)* Unimoto
2 *30 points* Bordes, P. *(F)* Seel
3=*24 points* Fischer, J. *(A)* Casal
Zeelenberg, W. *(NL)* Casal

125cc (Six rounds)
1 *61 points* Macciotta, C. *(I)* MBA
2 *51 points* Bordes, P. *(F)* MBA
3 *points* Leitner, M. *(A)* MBA

250cc (Seven rounds)
1 *56 points* Linder, H. *(A)* Rotax
2 *45 points* Ruggia, J. *(F)* Yamaha
3 *34 points* Luzi, U. *(CH)* Yamaha

500cc (Seven rounds)
1 *52 points (two wins)* Messere, M. *(I)* Honda
2 *52 points (one win)* Valesi, A. *(I)* Honda
3 *48 points* Buckmaster, S. *(GB)* Honda

Sidecar (Five rounds)
1 *46 points* Scherer, B. *(D)*
Gess, W. *(D)* Yamaha
2 *45 points* Kumagaya, Y. *(J)*
Makiuchi, K. *(J)* Yamaha
3 *26 points* Nigrowsky, I. *(F)*
Meunier, F. *(F)* Yamaha
Thomas, G. *(GB)*
White, G. *(GB)* Yamaha

1987

80cc (six rounds)
1 *72 points* Miralles, J. *(E)* Derbi
2 *70 points* Juhasz, K. *(H)* Krauser
3 *62 points* Criville, A. *(E)* Derbi

125cc (six rounds)
1 *57 points* Stadler, A. *(D)* MBA
2 *56 points* Catalano, C. *(I)* MBA
3 *38 points* Selini, J. *(F)* MBA

250cc (eight rounds)
1 *57 points* Cardelus, C. *(E)* Covas
2 *47 points* Bradl, H. *(D)* Honda
3 *35 points* Schmid, J. *(D)* Yamaha

500cc (five rounds)
1 *52 points* Fischer, M. *(D)* Honda
2 *42 points* Papa, M. *(I)* Honda
3 *41 points* Amatriain, D. *(E)* Honda

Sidecar (four rounds)
1 *38 points* Millet, J.
Debroux, C. *(F)* Yamaha
2 *35 points* Stolzle, F.
Stolzle, H. *(D)* Yamaha
3 *30 points* Bingham, D.
Bingham, J. *(GB)* Yamaha

BRITISH CHAMPIONSHIPS

Year	Class	Winner	Machine
1958	125cc	Hailwood, M.	*Paton*
	250cc	Hailwood, M.	*NSU*
	350cc	Hailwood, M.	*Norton*
	500cc	Godfrey, T.	*Norton*
	Sidecar	Harris, P.	*Norton*
1959	125cc	Hailwood, M.	*Ducati*
	250cc	Hailwood, M.	*Mondial*
	350cc	Hailwood, M.	*Norton*
	500cc	Hailwood, M.	*Norton*
	Sidecar	Harris, P.	*MBW*
1960	125cc	Hailwood, M.	*Ducati*
	250cc	Hailwood, M.	*Ducati*
	350cc	Hailwood, M.	*AJS*
	500cc	Hailwood, M.	*Norton*
	Sidecar	Boddice, B.	*Norton*
1961	125cc	Shorey, D.	*Bultaco*
	250cc	Hailwood, M.	*Honda*
	350cc	Read, P.	*Norton*
	500cc	Hailwood, M.	*Norton/ MV Agusta*
	Sidecar	Vincent, C.	*BSA*
1962	125cc	Shorey, D.	*Bultaco*
	250cc	Shorey, D.	*Bultaco*
	350cc	Minter, D.	*Petty N'ton*
	500cc	Minter, D.	*Petty N'ton*
	Sidecar	Boddice, B.	*Norton*
1963	125cc	Simmonds, D.	*Tohatsu*
	250cc	Phillips, T.	*Greeves*
	350cc	Read, P.	*Gilera*
	500cc	Read, P.	*Gilera*
	Sidecar	Vincent, C.	*BSA*
1964	125cc	Ivy, B.	*Yamaha*
	250cc	Minter, D.	*Cotton*
	350cc	Cooper, J.	*Norton*
	500cc	Minter, D.	*Norton*
	Sidecar	Vincent, C.	*BMW*
1965	50cc	Ashton, G. F.	*Honda*
	125cc	Ivy, B.	*Yamaha*
	250cc	Simmonds, D.	*Honda*
	350cc	Minter, D.	*Norton*
	500cc	Ivy, B.	*Matchless*
	Sidecar	Vincent, C.	*BMW*
1966	125cc	Scivyer, R.	*Honda*
	250cc	Inchley, P.	*Villiers*
	350cc	Cooper, J.	*Norton*
	500cc	Cooper, J.	*Norton*
	Sidecar	Greenwood	*BSA*
1967	125cc	Carney, M.	*Bultaco*
	250cc	Chatterton, D.	*Yamaha*
	350cc	Croxford, D.	*AJS*
	500cc	Chandler, R.	*Matchless*
	Sidecar	Greenwood, O.	*BSA*
1968	125cc	Curry, J.	*Honda*
	250cc	Cooper, J.	*Yamaha*
	350cc	Barnett, A.	*AJS*
	500cc	Croxford, D.	*Seeley*
	Sidecar	Brown, P.	*BSA*
1969	50cc	Ashton, G. F.	*Garelli*
	125cc	Mortimer, C.	*Villa*
	250cc	Browning, D.	*Yamaha*
	350cc	Mahoney, P.	*Yamaha*
	500cc	Croxford, D.	*Seeley*
	Sidecar	Vincent, C.	*BSA*
1970	50cc	Whiteway, F.	*Suzuki*
	125cc	Sheene, B.	*Suzuki*
	250cc	Machin, S.	*Yamaha*
	350cc	Chatterton, D.	*Yamaha*
	500cc	Williams, P.	*Matchless*
	Sidecar	Vincent, C.	*BSA*
1971	125cc	Sheene, B.	*Suzuki*
	250cc	Machin, S.	*Yamaha*
	350cc	Rutter, T.	*Yamaha*
	500cc	May, P.	*Norton*
	750cc	Tait, P.	*Triumph*
	Sidecar	Vincent, C.	*BSA*
1972	125cc	Machin, S.	*Yamaha*
	250cc	Machin, S.	*Yamaha*
	350cc	Grant, M.	*Yamaha*
	500cc	Harvey, J.	*Yamaha*
	750cc	Potter, D.	*Gus Kuhn Norton*
	Sidecar	Hanks, N.	*BSA*
1973	125cc	Hockley, A.	*Yamaha*
	250cc	Rutter, T.	*Yamaha*
	Solo	Croxford, D.	*Norton*
	Sidecar	Boret, G./ Boret, N.	*König*

Year	Class	Winner	Machine
1974	125cc	Saltwell, D.	*Yamaha*
	250cc	Hockley, A.	*Yamaha*
	Solo	Woods, S.	*Yamaha*
	Sidecar	Hobson, M./	*Windle*
		Russel, K.	*Yamaha*
1975	125cc	Shirtliffe, G.	
	250cc	Chatterton, D.	*Yamaha*
	Solo	Marshall, R.	*Yamaha*
	Sidecar	Hobson, M./	*Windle*
		Birch, H./	Yamaha
		Russel, K.	
1976	50cc	Thompson, S.	*Kreidler*
	125cc	Horton, C.	*Yamaha*
	250cc	Waring, G.	*Yamaha*
	Solo	Parrish, S.	*Yamaha*
	Sidecar	Greasley, D./	*Yamaha*
		Holland, C.	
1977	125cc	Carr, L.	*Morbidelli*
	250cc	Padgett, C.	*Yamaha*
	Solo	Marshall, R.	*Yamaha*
	Sidecar	Hodgkins, B./	*Yamaha*
		Parkins, J.	
1978	125cc	Murray, B.	*Honda*
	250cc	Huxley, D.	*Yamaha*
	Solo	Manship, S.	*Yamaha*
	Sidecar	Jones, D.	*Yamaha*
1979	Solo	Huewen, K.	*Yamaha*
	Sidecar	Greasley, D./	*Busch-*
		Parkins, J.	*Yamaha*
1980	125cc	Higgins, M.	*Morbidelli*
	250cc	Rogers, T.	*Yamaha*
	350cc	Stewart, A.	*Yamaha*
	500cc	Henderson, P.	*Suzuki*
	Solo	Manship, S.	*Yamaha/*
			Suzuki
	TT F1	Grant, M.	*Honda*
	Sidecar	Taylor, J./	*Yamaha*
		Johansson, B.	

Year	Class	Winner	Machine
1981	125cc	Mellor, P.	*Honda*
	250cc	Wild, P.	*Yamaha*
	350cc	Wright, S.	*Yamaha*
	500cc	Dean, D.	*Yamaha*
	Solo	Smith, Bob	*Suzuki*
	TT F1	Crosby, G.	*Suzuki*
	Sidecar	Taylor, J./	*Yamaha*
		Johannsson, B.	
1982	50cc	Patrickson, S.	*Kreidler*
	125cc	Swann, R.	*MBA*
	250cc	Tinker, P.	*Yamaha*
	350cc	Tinker, P.	*Yamaha*
	500cc	Salle, M.	*Suzuki*
	1000cc	Buckmaster, S.	*Yamaha*
	TT F1	Marshall, R.	*Suzuki*
	Sidecar	Ford-Dunn, B./	*Yamaha*
		Pirie, G.	
1983	250cc	Robinson, N.	*Yamaha*
	Solo	Marshall, R.	*Honda*
	TT F1	Gardner, W.	*Honda*
	TT F2	McGregor, G.	*Ducati*
	Sidecar	Ford-Dunn, B./	*Yamaha*
		Pirie, G.	
1984	80cc	Lodge, J.	*Suzuki*
	125cc	Appleyard, R.	*MBA*
	250cc	McLeod, D.	*Yamaha*
	500cc	Gardner, W.	*Honda*
	TT F1	Gardner, W.	*Honda*
	TT F2	Mellor, P.	*Yamaha*
	Sidecar	Abbott, S./	*Yamaha*
		Smith, S.	
1985	250cc	Mackenzie, N.	*Armstrong*
	500cc	Marshall, R.	*Honda*
	TT F1	Marshall R.	*Honda*
	TT F2	Barry, D.	*Yamaha*
	Sidecar	Webster, S./	*Yamaha*
		Hewitt, T.	
1986	250cc	Mackenzie, N.	*Armstrong*
	1300cc	Burnett, R.	*Honda*
	TT F1	Phillips, M.	*Suzuki*
	TT F2	Swann, R.	*Kawasaki*
	Sidecar	Webster, S./	*Yamaha*
		Hewitt, T.	
1987	125cc	Milton, R.	*MBA*
	250cc	Cowan, G.	*Honda*
	1300cc	Marshall, R.	*Suzuki*
	Sidecar	Webster, S./	*Krauser*
		Hewitt, T.	

John Surtees aviates Ballaugh Bridge, riding the works MV Agusta, in the 1957 Junior TT.

Stanley Woods leads eventual winner Tim Hunt in the 1933 French Grand Prix at Dieppe.

TOURIST TROPHY RACES IN THE ISLE OF MAN

Short Course

Year	Winner/Machine	Laps	Mph
1907	C. R. Collier *Matchless Single Cyl.*	10	38.22
1907	H. R. Fowler *Norton Twin. Cyl.*	10	36.22
1908	J. Marshall *Triumph Single Cyl.*	10	40.40
1908	H. Reed *Dot Twin Cyl.*	10	38.50
1909	H. A. Collier *Matchless*	10	49.01
1910	C. R. Collier *Matchless*	10	50.63

Mountain and Clypse Courses

Races marked with an asterisk were run on the Clypse Course.

Lightweight 125cc Class

1951	W. C. McCandless *Mondial*	2	74.85
1952	C. C. Sandford *MV*	2	75.54
1953	R. L. Graham *MV*	3	77.79
1954*	R. Hollaus *NSU*	10	69.57
1955*	C. Ubbiali *MV*	9	69.67
1956*	C. Ubbiali *MV*	9	69.13
1957*	T. Provini *Mondial*	10	73.69
1958*	C. Ubbiali *MV*	10	72.86
1959*	T. Provini *MV*	10	74.06
1960	C. Ubbiali *MV*	3	85.60
1961	S. M. B. Hailwood *Honda*	3	88.23
1962	L. Taveri *Honda*	3	89.88
1963	H. R. Anderson *Suzuki*	3	89.27
1964	L. Taveri *Honda*	3	92.14
1965	P. W. Read *Yamaha*	3	94.28
1966	W. Ivy *Yamaha*	3	97.66
1967	P. W. Read *Yamaha*	3	97.48
1968	P. W. Read *Yamaha*	3	99.12
1969	D. A. Simmonds *Kawasaki*	3	91.08
1970	D. Braun *Suzuki*	3	89.27
1971	C. Mortimer *Yamaha*	3	83.96
1972	C. Mortimer *Yamaha*	3	87.49
1973	T. H. Robb *Yamaha*	3	88.90
1974	C. Horton *Yamaha*	2	88.44

Lightweight 250cc Class

1922	G. S. Davison *Levis*	5	49.89
1923	J. A. Porter *New Gerrard*	6	51.93
1924	E. Twemlow *New Imperial*	6	55.44
1925	E. Twemlow *New Imperial*	6	57.74
1926	C. W. Johnson *Cotton*	7	60.20
1927	W. L. Handley *Rex-Acme*	7	63.30
1928	F. Longman *OK Supreme*	7	62.90
1929	S. A. Crabtree *Excelsior*	7	63.87
1930	J. Guthrie *AJS*	7	64.71
1931	G. W. Walker *Rudge*	7	68.98
1932	L. H. Davenport *New Imperial*	7	70.48
1933	S. Gleave *Excelsior*	7	71.59
1934	J. H. Simpson *Rudge*	7	70.81
1935	S. Woods *Moto Guzzi*	7	71.56
1936	A. R. Foster *New Imperial*	7	74.28
1937	O. Tenni *Moto Guzzi*	7	74.72
1938	E. Kludge *DKW*	7	78.48
1939	E. A. Mellors *Benelli*	7	74.25
1947	M. Barrington *Moto Guzzi*	7	73.22
1948	M. Cann *Moto Guzzi*	7	75.18
1949	M. Barrington *Moto Guzzi*	7	77.96
1950	D. Ambrosini *Benelli*	7	78.08
1951	T. L. Wood *Moto Guzzi*	4	81.39
1952	F. Anderson *Moto Guzzi*	4	83.82
1953	F. Anderson *Moto Guzzi*	4	84.73
1954	W. Haas *NSU*	3	90.88
1955*	W. A. Lomas *MV*	9	71.37
1956*	C. Ubbiali *MV*	9	67.05
1957*	C. C. Sandford *Mondial*	10	75.80
1958*	T. Provini *MV*	10	76.89
1959*	T. Provini *MV*	10	77.77
1960	G. Hocking *MV*	5	93.64
1961	S. M. B. Hailwood *Honda*	5	98.38
1962	D. W. Minter *Honda*	6	96.68
1963	J. Redman *Honda*	6	94.85
1964	J. Redman *Honda*	6	97.45
1965	J. Redman *Honda*	6	97.19
1966	S. M. B. Hailwood *Honda*	6	101.79
1967	S. M. B. Hailwood *Honda*	6	103.07
1968	W. D. Ivy *Yamaha*	6	99.58
1969	K. Carruthers *Benelli*	6	95.95
1970	K. Carruthers *Yamaha*	6	96.13
1971	P. Read *Yamaha*	4	98.02
1972	P. Read *Yamaha*	4	99.68
1973	C. Williams *Yamaha*	4	100.05
1974	C. Williams *Yamaha*	4	94.16
1975	C. Mortimer *Yamaha*	4	99.03
1976	T. Herron *Yamaha*	4	103.55

Junior 250cc

1977	C. Williams *Yamaha*	3	99.62
1978	C. Mortimer *Yamaha*	6	100.70
1979	C. Williams *Yamaha*	6	105.13

1980	C. Williams *Yamaha*	4	102.22
1981	S. Tonkin *Armstrong CCM*	6	106.21
1982	C. Law *Waddon Ehrlich*	6	105.32
1983	C. Law *EMC*	6	108.09
1984	G. McGregor *EMC*	6	109.57
1985	J. Dunlop *Honda*	6	109.91
1986	S. Cull *Honda*	6	109.62
1987	E. Laycock *EMC*	6	108.52

Junior 350cc

1911	P. J. Evans *Humber*	4	41.45
1912	W. H. Bashall *Douglas*	4	39.65
1913	H. Mason *NUT*	6	43.75
1914	E. Williams *AJS*	5	45.58
1920	C. Williams *AJS*	5	40.74
1921	E. Williams *AJS*	5	52.11
1922	T. M. Sheard *AJS*	5	54.75
1923	S. Woods *Cotton*	6	55.73
1924	E. Twemlow *New Imperial*	6	55.67
1925	W. L. Handley *Rex-Acme*	6	65.02
1926	A. Bennett *Velocette*	7	66.70
1927	F. W. Dixon *HRD*	7	67.19
1928	A. Bennett *Velocette*	7	68.65
1929	F. G. Hicks *Velocette*	7	69.71
1930	H. G. Tyrell Smith *Rudge Whitworth*	7	71.08
1931	P. Hunt *Norton*	7	73.94
1932	S. Woods *Norton*	7	77.16
1933	S. Woods *Norton*	7	78.08
1934	J. Guthrie *Norton*	7	79.16
1935	J. Guthrie *Norton*	7	79.14
1936	F. L. Frith *Norton*	7	80.14
1937	J. Guthrie *Norton*	7	84.43
1938	S. Woods *Velocette*	7	84.08
1939	S. Woods *Velocette*	7	83.19
1947	A. R. Foster *Velocette*	7	80.31
1948	F. L. Frith *Velocette*	7	81.45
1949	F. L. Frith *Velocette*	7	83.15
1950	A. J. Bell *Norton*	7	86.33
1951	G. E. Duke *Norton*	7	89.90
1952	G. E. Duke *Norton*	7	90.29
1953	W. R. Amm *Norton*	7	90.52
1954	R. W. Coleman *AJS*	5	91.51
1955	W. A. Lomas *Moto Guzzi*	7	92.33
1956	T. K. Kavanagh *Moto Guzzi*	7	89.29
1957	R. McIntyre *Gilera*	7	94.99
1958	J. Surtees *MV*	7	93.97
1959	J. Surtees *MV*	7	95.38
1960	J. Hartle *MV*	6	96.70
1961	P. W. Read *Norton*	6	95.10
1962	S. M. B. Hailwood *MV*	6	99.59
1963	J. Redman *Honda*	6	94.91
1964	J. Redman *Honda*	6	98.50
1965	J. Redman *Honda*	6	100.72
1966	G. Agostini *MV*	6	100.87
1967	S. M. B. Hailwood *Honda*	6	104.68
1968	G. Agostini *MV*	6	104.78
1969	G. Agostini *MV*	6	101.81
1970	G. Agostini *MV*	6	101.77
1971	A. Jefferies *Yamsel*	5	89.98
1972	G. Agostini *MV*	5	102.03
1973	A. T. Rutter *Yamaha*	5	101.99
1974	A. T. Rutter *Yamaha*	5	104.44
1975	C. Williams *Yamaha*	5	104.38
1976	C. Mortimer *Yamaha*	5	106.78
1982	A. T. Rutter *Yamaha*	6	108.58
1983	P. Mellor *Spondon Yamaha*	6	107.44

Senior 500cc

1911	O. C. Godfrey *Indian*	5	47.63
1912	F. A. Applebee *Scott*	5	48.69
1913	H. O. Wood *Scott*	7	48.27
1914	C. G. Pullin *Rudge*	6	49.49
1920	T. C. de la Hay *Sunbeam*	6	51.48
1921	H. R. Davies *AJS*	6	54.49
1922	A. Bennett *Sunbeam*	6	58.31
1923	T. M. Sheard *Douglas*	6	55.55
1924	A. Bennett *Norton*	6	61.64
1925	H. R. Davies *HRD*	6	66.13
1926	S. Woods *Norton*	7	67.54
1927	A. Bennett *Norton*	7	68.41
1928	C. J. P. Dodson *Sunbeam*	7	62.98
1929	C. J. P. Dodson *Sunbeam*	7	72.05
1930	W. L. Handley *Rudge Whitworth*	7	74.24
1931	P. Hunt *Norton*	7	77.90
1932	S. Woods *Norton*	7	79.83
1933	S. Woods *Norton*	7	81.04
1934	J. Guthrie *Norton*	7	78.01
1935	S. Woods *Moto Guzzi*	7	84.68
1936	J. Guthrie *Norton*	7	85.80
1937	F. L. Frith *Norton*	7	88.21
1938	H. L. Daniell *Norton*	7	89.11
1939	G. Meier *BMW*	7	89.38
1947	H. L. Daniell *Norton*	7	82.81
1948	A. J. Bell *Norton*	7	84.97
1949	H. L. Daniell *Norton*	7	86.93
1950	G. E. Duke *Norton*	7	92.27
1951	G. E. Duke *Norton*	7	93.83

1952	H. R. Armstrong *Norton*	7	92.97
1953	W. R. Amm *Norton*	7	93.85
1954	W. R. Amm *Norton*	4	88.12
1955	G. E. Duke *Gilera*	7	97.93
1956	J. Surtees *MV*	7	96.57
1957	R. McIntyre *Gilera*	8	98.99
1958	J. Surtees *MV*	7	98.63
1959	J. Surtees *MV*	7	87.94
1960	J. Surtees *MV*	6	102.44
1961	S. M. B. Hailwood *Norton*	6	100.60
1962	G. Hocking *MV*	6	103.51
1963	S. M. B. Hailwood *MV*	6	104.64
1964	S. M. B. Hailwood *MV*	6	100.95
1965	S. M. B. Hailwood *MV*	6	91.69
1966	S. M. B. Hailwood *Honda*	6	103.11
1967	S. M. B. Hailwood *Honda*	6	105.62
1968	G. Agostini *MV*	6	101.63
1969	G. Agostini *MV*	6	104.75
1970	G. Agostini *MV*	6	101.52
1971	G. Agostini *MV*	6	102.59
1972	G. Agostini *MV*	6	104.02
1973	J. Findlay *Suzuki*	6	101.55
1974	P. Carpenter *Yamaha*	6	96.99
1975	M. Grant *Kawasaki*	6	100.27
1976	T. Herron *Yamaha*	6	105.15
1977	P. Read *Suzuki*	5	106.97
1978	T. Herron *Suzuki*	6	111.74
1979	S. M. B. Hailwood *Suzuki*	6	111.75
1980	G. Crosby *Suzuki*	6	109.65
1981	M. Grant *Suzuki*	6	106.14
1982	N. Brown *Suzuki*	6	110.98
1984	R. McElnea *Suzuki*	6	115.66

Ultra Lightweight

1924	J. A. Porter *New Gerrard*	3	51.20
1925	W. L. Handley *Rex-Acme*	4	53.45

Sidecar 500cc

1923	F. W. Dixon *Douglas*	3	53.15
1924	G. H. Tucker *Norton*	4	51.31
1925	L. Parker *Douglas*	4	55.22
1954*	E. S. Oliver *Norton*	10	68.87
1955*	W. Schneider *BMW*	9	70.01
1956*	F. Hillebrand *BMW*	9	70.03
1957*	F. Hillebrand *BMW*	10	71.89
1958*	W. Schneider *BMW*	10	73.01
1959*	W. Schneider *BMW*	10	72.69
1960	H. Fath *BMW*	3	84.10
1961	M. Deubel *BMW*	3	87.65
1962	C. Vincent *BSA*	3	83.57
1963	F. Camathias *BMW*	3	88.38
1964	M. Deubel *BMW*	3	89.12
1965	M. Deubel *BMW*	3	90.57
1966	R. Scheidegger *BMW*	3	90.76
1967	S. Schauzu *BMW*	3	90.96
1968	S. Schauzu *BMW*	3	91.09
1969	K. Enders *BMW*	3	92.48
1970	K. Enders *BMW*	3	92.93
1971	S. Schauzu *BMW*	3	86.21
1972	S. Schauzu *BMW*	3	91.85
1973	K. Enders *BMW*	3	91.85
1974	H. Luthringshauser *BMW*	3	92.27
1975	R. Steinhausen *Konig*	3	95.94
1976	R. Steinhausen *Konig*	3	95.94
1977	R. Steinhausen *Konig*	3	96.42

Sidecar 750cc

1968	T. Vinicombe *BSA*	3	85.85
1969	S. Schauzu *BMW*	3	89.83
1970	S. Schauzu *BMW*	3	90.20
1971	G. Auerbacher *BMW*	3	86.86
1972	S. Schauzu *BMW*	3	90.97
1973	K. Enders *BMW*	3	93.01
1974	S. Schauzu *BMW*	3	96.59

Sidecar 1000cc

1975	S. Schauzu/W. Kalauch *BMW*	3	97.55
1976	M. Hobson/M. Burns *Yamaha*	3	97.77
1977	G. O'Dell/K. Arthur *Yamaha*	4	100.03
1977	M. Hobson/S. Collins *Yamaha*	4	99.74
1978	J. Taylor/K. Arthur *Yamaha*	4	101.22
1979	T. Ireson/C. Pollington *Yamaha*	6	102.14
1980	J. Taylor/B. Johansson *Yamaha*	6	103.55
1981	J. Taylor/B. Johansson *Yamaha*	6	107.02
1982	R. Hanks/V. Biggs *Yamaha*	6	101.70
1983	N. Edwards/B. Marris *Yamaha*	6	103.64
1984	S. Abbott/S. Smith *Yamaha*	6	104.01
1985	M. Boddice/C. Birks *Yamaha*	6	104.74

1986	L. Burton/P. Cushanhan *Yamaha*	3	104.53
1986	N. Rollason/D. Williams *Phoenix*	3	103.81
1987	M. Boddice/D. Williams *Yamaha*	3	104.76
1987	L. Burton/P. Cushanhan *Yamaha*	3	105.53

50cc

1962	E. Degner *Suzuki*	3	75.12
1963	M. Itoh *Suzuki*	3	78.81
1964	H. R. Anderson *Suzuki*	3	80.64
1965	L. Taveri *Honda*	3	79.66
1966	R. Bryans *Honda*	3	85.66
1967	S. Graham *Suzuki*	3	82.89
1968	B. Smith *Derbi*	3	72.90

Production Machines

1967	W. A. Smith *250 Bultaco*	3	88.63
1967	N. Kelly *500 Velocette*	3	89.89
1967	J. Hartle *750 Triumph*	3	97.10
1968	T. E. Burgess *250 Ossa*	3	87.21
1968	R. Knight *500 Triumph*	3	90.09
1968	R. Pickrell *750 Dunstall*	3	98.13
1969	A. M. Rogers *250 Ducati*	3	83.79
1969	W. G. Penny *500 Honda*	3	88.18
1969	M. Uphill *750 Triumph*	3	99.99
1970	C. Mortimer *250 Ducati*	5	84.87
1970	R. Whiteway *500 Suzuki*	5	89.94
1970	M. Uphill *750 Triumph*	5	97.71
1971	B. Smith *250 Honda*	4	84.14
1971	J. Williams *500 Honda*	4	91.04
1971	R. Pickrell *750 Triumph*	4	100.07
1972	J. Williams *250 Honda*	4	85.32
1972	S. Woods *500 Suzuki*	4	92.20
1972	R. Pickrell *750 Triumph*	4	100.00
1973	C. Williams *250 Yamaha*	4	81.76
1973	W. A. Smith *500 Honda*	4	88.10
1973	A. Jefferies *750 Triumph*	4	95.62
1974	M. Sharpe *247 Yamaha*	4	86.95
1974	K. Martin *492 Kawasaki*	4	93.85
1974	M. Grant *741 Triumph*	4	99.72
1975	D. Croxford/A. George *748 Triumph*	10	99.60
1976	B. Simpson/C. Mortimer *250 Yamaha*	10	87.00
1984	P. Mellor *250 Yamaha*	3	92.58
1984	T. Nation *750 Honda*	3	102.24
1984	G. Johnson *900 Kawasaki*	3	105.28
1985	M. Oxley *250 Suzuki*	3	94.84
1985	M. Grant *750 Suzuki*	3	104.36
1985	G. Johnson *998 Honda*	3	105.12
1986	B. Woodland *400 Suzuki*	3	99.82
1986	G. Padgett *400 Suzuki*	3	102.98
1986	P. Mellor *749 Suzuki*	3	109.23
1986	T. Nation *1100 Suzuki*	3	111.99
1987	B. Woodland *400 Yamaha*	3	102.98
1987	G. Johnson *750 Yamaha*	3	109.98

Formula 750cc

1971	A. Jefferies *Triumph*	3	102.85
1972	R. Pickrell *Triumph*	5	104.23
1973	P. Williams *Norton*	5	105.47
1974	C. Mortimer *Yamaha*	6	100.52

Classic 1000cc

1975	J. Williams *Yamaha*	6	105.33
1976	J. Williams *Suzuki*	6	108.18
1977	M. Grant *Kawasaki*	6	110.76
1978	M. Grant *Kawasaki*	6	112.40
1979	A. George *Honda*	6	113.08
1980	J. Dunlop *Yamaha*	6	112.72
1981	G. Crosby *Suzuki*	6	113.58
1982	D. Ireland *Suzuki*	6	109.21

TT Formula I

1977	P. Read *Honda*	4	97.02
1978	S. M. B. Hailwood *Ducati*	6	108.51
1979	A. George *Honda*	6	110.57
1980	M. Grant *Honda*	6	105.29
1981	G. Crosby *Suzuki*	6	111.81
1982	R. Haslam *Honda*	6	113.33
1983	J. Dunlop *Honda*	6	114.03
1984	J. Dunlop *Honda*	6	111.68
1985	J. Dunlop *Honda*	6	113.95
1986	J. Dunlop *Honda*	4	112.96
1987	J. Dunlop *Honda*	6	115.03

TT Formula II

1977	A. Jackson *Honda*	4	99.36
1978	A. Jackson *Honda*	4	99.35
1979	A. Jackson *Honda*	4	101.55
1980	C. Williams *Yamaha*	4	96.24
1981	A. Rutter *Ducati*	4	101.91
1982	A. Rutter *Ducati*	4	108.05
1983	A. Rutter *Ducati*	4	108.20
1984	G. McGregor *Yamaha*	4	108.78
1985	A. Rutter *Ducati*	6	107.79
1986	B. Reid *Yamaha*	6	109.72
1987	S. Hislop *Yamaha*	6	110.40

TT Formula III

1977	J. Kidson *Honda*	4	93.28
1978	W. Smith *Honda*	4	94.47
1979	B. Smith *Yamaha*	4	97.82
1980	B. Smith *Yamaha*	4	91.98
1981	B. Smith *Yamaha*	4	99.66
1982	G. Padgett *Yamaha*	4	96.17

Jubilee Race

1977	J. Dunlop *Yamaha*	4	108.86

Senior Classic

1983	R. McElnea *Suzuki*	6	114.81

Premier Classic

1984	R. McElnea *Suzuki*	6	116.12

Historic TT

1984	S. Cull *350 Aermacchi*	3	94.26
1984	D. Roper *500 Matchless*	3	96.11

Senior 1000cc

1985	J. Dunlop *750 Honda*	6	113.69
1986	R. Burnett *500 Honda*	6	113.98
1987	J. Dunlop *500 Honda*	4	99.85

Dickie Dale riding the most exotic racing machine ever produced – the V-8 Moto Guzzi.